Secret Wars and Secret Policies
in the Americas, 1842–1929

Secret Wars and Secret Policies in the Americas, 1842–1929

Friedrich E. Schuler

UNIVERSITY OF NEW MEXICO PRESS

ALBUQUERQUE

15   14   13   12   11   10   1   2   3   4   5   6

Library of Congress Cataloging-in-Publication Data

Schuler, Friedrich Engelbert, 1960–

  Secret wars and secret policies in the Americas, 1842–1929 / Friedrich E. Schuler.

    p. cm.

  Includes bibliographical references and index.

  ISBN 978-0-8263-4489-2 (cloth : alk. paper)

  1. Latin America—Foreign relations—19th century. 2. Latin America—Foreign relations—20th century. 3. Latin America—Foreign relations—Europe. 4. Europe—Foreign relations—Latin America. 5. Latin America—Foreign relations—Japan. 6. Japan—Foreign relations—Latin America. I. Title.

  F1415.S28 2010

  327.8052090'34—dc22

                            2010035385

Design and Composition: Melissa Tandysh

Text composed in Garamond Premier Pro 11/14

Dedicated to all German Americans, Japanese Americans, Italian Americans, Spanish Americans, and Mexican Americans who fought for liberal democracy against all ideologies.

As never before this time has been made for the intelligence services. In particular this is true as we look at Great Britain and the U.S. The construction of the British World Empire and immigrant and racial questions in North America are, in a certain way, a tempting challenge to try out the art of intelligence. In the future the secret power of intelligence services will be far greater than in the past and the present.

—Former German Intelligence Chief Oberst W. Nicolai, 1923

Contents

Acknowledgments

This book concludes a scholarly marathon of eight years. During those years barely a handful of people believed in this topic and supported me unwaveringly. The small but very exquisite group consisted of Louis R. Sadler and Frederick M. Nunn. I am deeply grateful to them. Michael Geyer knew I would finish, eventually. Quietly hopeful remained Bill Beezley and Friedrich Katz.

Vital encouragement came from my outstanding editors at the University of New Mexico Press. First David Holtby and thereafter his successor, Clark Whitehorn, provided critical understanding and real support. Elisabeth A. Graves's editing skill made all the difference. I could not have written this without their commitment.

Other important sympathizers were Prof. Dr. Reinhard Liehr, Prof. Dr. Holger Meding, Prof. Dr. Ragnhild Fiebig von Hase, and Prof. Dr. Knud Krakau. An immeasurable thank-you goes to the German Mexican historian Dr. Nagel.

Many students contributed to this oeuvre. The most important were Dan Barton, Seonaid Valiant, John Gentry, Martin Patail, Jorge Espinoza, and Tucker Johnson. Steven Andes became a friend and esteemed fellow researcher with much potential for his own academic future. I owe an apology to Wilfred Engelke. I appreciated the discussions with Amy Kiddle. Kathy Meltzer's direction was soulful and a blessing. Stresso Grave's consultancy provided inspiration without splitting hairs. A thank-you goes to Ann Bender.

As important were those who refused to consider that the events in this book actually took place and that the well-being of the United States could ever truly be threatened by European and Asian powers. Their resistance formed a motivating glass ceiling, and the accompanying social-political rejection was a constant thorn in my side, transforming itself into determination to make my case and a reminder not just to have a good argument but to find the "smoking guns." I found many, and they will be presented in this book.

In the initial research years primary and secondary sources for this book arrived only because of Cyril Oberlander, a librarian extraordinaire. Every historian ought to have the luck of such a "professor's librarian." His successor, Sherry Buchanan, continued the excellence he had established at Portland State University's Interlibrary Loan Office.

In Washington, D.C., at the National Archives, Mark Holland helped. A final deep appreciation goes to Mr. Taylor. His death is a loss to our national research community.

In Germany a special word of appreciation needs to go to Frau Meier at the Freiburg Military Archive. In addition I sincerely thank Frau Sabine Schafferdt and the superb staff of the Political Archive at the German Foreign Ministry, first in Bonn and now in Berlin. Everything was always accessible. In the Bundesarchiv, Berlin-Lichterfelde, Herr Goettlicher and Frau Hoffman helped. In Munich Frau Marline Schwarzenau made the Junkers files easily accessible. The archive at the Deutsche Museum remains one of Germany's most under-rated collections.

The section of this book examining Spanish relations with Latin America became possible only because of Señora Pilar Casado in the archive of the Spanish Foreign Ministry, Mr. Zimmerli in the King's Archive, and Don Daniel in the Archivo General de la Administración. In addition, I deeply appreciate the help and discussions with Prof. Dr. Manuel Ros Agudo. He is a major Spanish scholar.

In Great Britain, I did not have to talk to anybody. Still, in Kew Garden's Public Record Office I appreciated the soulless computer that gave me any document I wanted without hesitation. This experience remains surreal.

The wonderful editing of Melissa Schuler elevated this book's initial stages. For many years she was a most loyal companion to a historian. She tolerated piles of paper and endless excitement over new archives, far more than the average U.S. woman would put up with.

A special thanks goes to my colleagues at Portland State University (PSU) for their eight years of patience during the long production *durée* of this tome. Dean Marvin Kaiser understood that historians deserve to be left alone, which made all the difference. I hope that the result of this work returns to PSU enough value for the trust and creative space so many colleagues and administrators provided over the years. Jeff Brown and Diane Gould did much quiet work without which trips abroad would have remained impossible. PSU professor David Horrowitz's originality inspired me, and I appreciate the friendly exchanges with Prof. Ken Ruoff.

The two quiet heroes of eight years, however, remain Sally Hudson and Karen Tosi of the PSU Challenge/Link program. Like Italian mentors from the Middle Ages, they provided eight years of extra work and friendship, so I could earn extra research funds for the next archival trip. It takes money, lots of money, not just friendship to do this historical work. Similarly Prof. Linda Walton was a constant, wonderful ally on my research path. Her warm encouragement, as one of the best chairs of the PSU History Department, will be forever appreciated.

The conclusion of this work was fueled and inspired by a muse. A word of advice. When a muse shows up, she actually makes all the difference. Just like in the movies. Engage with her.

For twenty-nine years the brisk wind of U.S. freedom has blown into my face. It ennobled the good foundation the Germans have laid. This American journey is still alive.

Introduction

⸺⸺⸺⸺⸺⸺⸺⸺⸺⸺⸺⸺⸺⸺⸺⸺⸺⸺⸺⸺⸺⸺⸺⸺⸺⸺⸺⸺⸺⸺

German navy leaders faced a deeply troubling decision. Under what circumstance should the Berlin government allow agents in San Francisco to commit sabotage against Allied ships? When should they spread anthrax viruses among horses and mules waiting in New York's harbor, ready to be shipped to Allied battlefields in Europe?

It was fall 1935, Hitler's third year in power. Several months before the Nazi government had revealed that it was building an army for world conquest. Now, in Berlin, leaders of the naval supply and intelligence service discussed whether, during the next world war, agents working undercover in U.S. cities should again be allowed to poison, dynamite, or incite racial violence. These actions would weaken the Allied ability to fight for democracy. Should the acts of World War I be repeated?

On October 31, 1935, one navy planner wrote to a colleague, pleading emphatically to revise proposed printed instructions for future German agents operating in the United States. He urged caution. Planners should not commit to paper that German soldiers might also work as saboteurs. After all, they were individuals of a seemingly civilized country, where Bach and Beethoven had created pure beauty for the world. True, if a war required them to explode a bomb in the middle of San Francisco harbor, they would do it. They would also dynamite innocent dock workers in New Orleans, if that promised to keep Allied military supplies from being loaded on a ship. But this fact should not be admitted on paper.

At a second office in the German Foreign Ministry, diplomats worked on a related issue, not knowing that navy planners were updating secret warfare instructions across town. In a court battle now more than a decade long, the Foreign

Ministry's Mr. Schmidhuber was defending the German government against claims by U.S. and Canadian factory owners who demanded damages for explosions that occurred during World War I government-ordered sabotage. For years, the best Foreign Ministry lawyers had tried to disprove that the German government had ordered sabotage against U.S. and British factories. Schmidhuber insisted that whoever had caused explosions that wreaked havoc in ammunition plants or whoever had operated an anthrax laboratory in New Jersey in 1915 had acted on his own initiative. Categorically German diplomats denied any responsibility as they looked U.S. lawyers and diplomats straight in the eye. Indeed, in the 1930s, U.S. lawyers never succeeded at producing a single piece of original paper tying German officials to a precise order of sabotage. Years of legal sophistry had debated apart claims until the most flagrant violation of U.S. territory by Germans between 1914 and 1918, twenty years before Hitler, appeared doubtful.

These lawyers did what many historians of German–American and Japanese–U.S. relations, on both sides of the Atlantic and Pacific, continue to do today. Excellent rhetoric and brilliant writing exploit the fact that orders were given verbally and most paper trails have been destroyed. They continue to obfuscate historical proof that German and Japanese soldiers could be a danger to the Americas and operate on U.S. soil.

According to Schmidhuber and his legal team, Germans in the United States during World War I spread only propaganda. But never did they distribute anthrax among horses or sabotage U.S. and Canadian factories.

Unknown to today's apologists the leaders of the German Navy Ministry did make sabotage plans among themselves and allowed for the preparation of such activities during World War II. As the Berlin admirals accommodated themselves to serve Fascism and joined Hitler's war of world conquest, they hesitated nevertheless to commit secret warfare instructions in manuals.

An unknown navy leader of section AII clarified that sabotage would be allowed, if necessary. But planners should be smart and omit it from agent handbooks. Leaders wanted to preserve the cultural smokescreen of German high culture and wonderful castles, which could be used again on the international scene during the next war. The idealized images of high culture would again manipulate the perceptions of naive U.S. citizens and protect most German Americans from asking deeper questions about ethnic longing and national loyalty. The navy planner explained:

To begin with it is suggested . . . to strike the words: ". . . if appropriate also through sabotage"; still today, 15 years after the peace treaty with the

United States, the U.S. sabotage claims have not been cleared up, as the case of von Rintelen teaches us. Looking back it should be stated that the acts of sabotage in the U.S. during the period of neutrality have created far more damage than benefit. Afterwards every German official office has denied to have issued the order to sabotage. On page 14 to 16 [of the manual] it has been pointed out correctly how important general public mood will be in a neutral country for the future flow of supplies. Thus, should an unfortunate coincidence reveal that committing sabotage is listed in an official job manual, unforeseeable damage could be the result.[1]

It took until 2008 to find this first written admission by high-level German bureaucrats in a German archive. German World War I policy had included a wide variety of secret warfare attacks inside the United States. They had not been the acts of just a few patriotic German Americans, drunken with too much love for Emperor Wilhelm II. A small number had worked as Berlin's handmaidens.

This book identifies and analyzes the roots of the mind-set that made possible the sabotage orders, previously described. The fascist fight against democracy and the United States did not start in 1933. Rather, events once Hitler came to power were a continuation of practices and the culmination of processes that had developed since before 1900. It is important to identify and analyze the complex foundations of authoritarian foreign policy that the German Third Reich, Italy's Mussolini, the Japanese emperor, and Franco's Spain rested on. These leaders were not the inventors of secret warfare against the Western Hemisphere. They just brought it to new extremes. This book shines a first bright light on these men and women and their secret practices before 1930. It compares them across nations and continents.

Their victim was not only the United States but also the naive worldview and rich immigrant cultures of German Americans, Japanese Americans, Italian Americans, Spanish Americans, and Latin Americans. Most of them had nothing to do with the imperial activities explained in the following pages. Hopefully their great-grandchildren may learn how antidemocratic governments in Berlin, Tokyo, Rome, Madrid, Mexico City, and Buenos Aires used the lives of their immigrant ancestors to weaken the United States in its fight for democracy. There is historically justified reason for appropriate vigilance. Sentimental ethnic confusion inside the United States will always remain a challenge.

*Imperial Powers
Turn Ethnic People
into a Security Threat
(1860–1914)*

1 Before European and Japanese Governments Manipulated Immigrants in the Americas

---

Before the 1870s, Germans left their small states in the millions and emigrated to the Americas.[1] Their reasons were obvious. Even though the French Revolution and the Napoleonic wars had destroyed the old Europe, aristocrats and reinstated royalty refused to build a modern state legitimized by citizens and popular votes. Aristocrats doubled their efforts to fight ideals proclaimed by U.S. and French revolutionaries. If possible, German elites would preserve monarchic government and enforce a rigidly divided, hierarchical society.

Also the French and British lessons of industrialization were rejected by German princes. One attractive alternative to such sociopolitical pressure was the emigration of peasants. Their Atlantic crossing would be organized through commercial companies, licensed by the government. But once their ships had spit out the third-class travelers onto the docks of New York, these companies and governments would lose sight of their ethnic cargo. These impoverished Germans traveled west, but there was no prince or king who wanted to hold onto them. Only family members left behind in Europe tried to stay in touch with the help of mostly unpredictable mail services, assuming that people could read and write. Often it was good-bye forever.

In Brazil the first German immigrants arrived in 1824. From the very beginning they settled in one region, founding the settlement of Sao Leopoldo in the province Rio Grande do Sul. Already in 1826 the Hanseatic merchant Gildemeister advocated the fantastic idea of a New Germany in South America. In the decades thereafter it remained nothing more than a thrilling political aphrodisiac among merchants in Hamburg and Bremen.

Six thousand immigrants followed over the next decades, establishing a close-knit distinct ethnic community. It was not, however, a German colony.

Ironically it was the Brazilian emperor who wanted to instrumentalize the Germans. Dom Pedro I insisted on their presence in southern Brazil. German immigrants were expected to build a new agricultural way of life in southern Brazil. The emperor saw them as an ethnic settlement belt that fortified Brazil's border region against territorial designs by the rivaling republics of Spanish America. Before 1850 only the Portuguese American elite instrumentalized the ethnic residents of Sao Leopoldo.

In reality German emigrants in North and South America sidestepped such Latin American elite expectations and pursued a deeply personal but also confusing metamorphosis toward Americanization. Some simply refused to assimilate. The emotional and psychological consequences of emigration were not yet exploited by governments in Germany.

Inside the expanding United States, German emigrants developed hundreds of thousands of individual answers to the question of what it meant to be a peasant from Lower Saxony half your life and to finish the other half as a farmer in Minnesota. They worked the prairie that until only recently had belonged to the Lakota. In Latin America many quickly idealized their ethnic German cultural origin, afraid to mix with Afro-Brazilians, Brazilian Native Americans, or natives in Spanish American republics. On the other hand, a few enjoyed mixing more than German culture in Europe would have allowed. Then in 1850, Brazilian immigration law changed. The monarchy stopped gifting land. Germans were expected to purchase it.

In Prussia, other significant changes took place, as far as emigration was concerned. Nationalistic aristocrats debated whether their country had an obligation to protect emigrants. Some argued that the king of Prussia should intervene in South America in case of crisis. Prince Adalbert proposed the construction of a Prussian navy that could operate overseas. But his proposal was rejected.

Prussian elites increasingly demanded to redirect the flow of migrants from the Americas to Eastern Europe. As Prussia strengthened vis-à-vis Russia and Austria, leading politicians desired to redirect emigrants into conquered Polish territory. Now these Germans wanted to build a military settler belt to stop Russian expansion.

By the end of the 1850s the policy debate showed success. On November 3,

1859, the Prussian minister of interior, Heydt, prohibited state grants for new settlement concessions in Brazil. Emigration to Brazil could continue only as individual, private journeys. In spite of the restriction, twenty-eight thousand Germans crossed the Atlantic in the following year. As before, they came only to have a better life—but not to build a New Germany in South America.

In Europe, Prussia, France, and Austria already practiced secret warfare through the manipulation of ethnic groups. Napoleon III in 1859 incited ethnic minorities in Austria-Hungary to put pressure on Emperor Joseph.[2] Once Wilhelm von Bismarck became Prussian chancellor, he too used ethnic issues and people to subvert the political stability of European monarchies. The U.S. historian Donald Mc Kale shows how in 1866, Prussian military leaders incited Hungarians and Slavs living inside Austria-Hungary to shake Austria's political stability through ethnic revolt. The German army high command deployed the same tactic against Russia along its border regions.[3]

In Poland, Bismarck went further. There he deployed settlements to claim Polish territory on behalf of Prussia. He financed a Prussian Settlement Commission that relocated ethnic Germans into occupied Polish territory. Bismarck countered Polish groups nurturing their own ethnic settlement belt.[4]

But when it came to the Americas, Bismarck took a strong stance against using the ethnic card in North and South America. There the lives of ethnic Germans in the Americas were to remain untouched by German manipulations. Bismarck made a wise tactical choice. But it was not a principled moral stance that protected Germans in Minnesota or Rio Grande do Sul from being pulled into secret ethnic warfare plans.

Bismarck remained adamant and prevented the creation of an overseas fleet. Navy enthusiasts won only a compromise. The German navy was allowed to establish overseas stations for German ships abroad. They would allow ships to resupply and offer a moderate form of protection during the next round of imperial war. Indeed, the first overseas stations for the small existing navy were opened in the Mediterranean, East Asia, and the West Indies.[5] The West Indies station functioned in 1867, two years before the April Revolution of Venezuela. Bismarck's personal political standing was strong enough to prevent the creation of a larger overseas fleet.[6] ·

As before, the recasting of how German settlers in South America were seen did not come from German imperialism but from the consequences of French–German enmity. It resulted from how Brazilian elites saw the French–German wars in Europe.

After the 1870s the French–German conflict colored Brazilian elite perceptions against ethnic Germans. In 1870, Dom Pedro II sided with Napoleon III. Right away Brazil's press fell into line. Journalists in the largest cities published critical ideas about German social and cultural practices in South America. No longer were German immigrants appreciated for helping Brazil against Argentine and Paraguayan land claims or how they modernized the monarchy's agriculture.

German naval warfare intensified the debate about potential German activities in Latin America. In 1869, Hans Eduard Knorr was twenty-nine years old and commandeered the Prussian SMS *Meteor*. His orders were to sail to the West Indies and to show the Prussian flag near French, British, and Spanish navy ships. The frigate came to show a German presence in the Venezuelan Civil War.[7]

By the time the SMS *Meteor* reached the Caribbean islands, France and Germany were at war, and Captain Knorr took it upon himself to do more than show the flag. In the name of Emperor Wilhelm I he waged war wherever he sighted a French ship.

First Knorr attempted to damage the flow of French supplies by waging cruiser warfare. He attempted to exploit U.S. disgust against Napoleon III, whose soldiers had been stationed across El Paso only the previous year. On August 13, 1870, Knorr met Captain Irving, the commander of the USS *Intake*. Knorr asked him to make available his resources and to make it easier to assemble an ad hoc Prussian auxiliary cruiser fleet. The German wanted to telegraph Berlin for approval using the U.S. Key West Naval Station. But in Washington, D.C., German Ambassador von Gerolt rejected Knorr's request, fearing violation of U.S. neutrality law.[8] Thereafter Knorr pursued his very own singular cruiser war.

On November 9, 1870, in front of the Spanish Port of Havana, Knorr discharged a broadside into the French *aviso Bouvet*. The *Bouvet* responded in kind and damaged the *Meteor* badly. As Knorr's fortunes turned, his men steered the wounded ship into Havana's port, triggering a miniature French naval blockade. Then Napoleon III was defeated in Europe, and the French captain ended the blockade. Even though Knorr was saved by luck, he was received in Germany as a hero. He was promoted to admiral of the newly merged Prussian and north German merchant marine.

This French–German naval exchange off Havana was more than a curious historical footnote. It represents the opening salvo of a fifty-year-long German–French clash on many levels. Naval insiders now saw German ships in a more complex strategic light.

Knorr's experience encouraged a growing number of German planners to include Latin American and North American coastlines in their soon-to-be-drawn-up naval contingency plans. Knorr himself employed his status to move newly installed emperor Wilhelm II toward favoring the construction of a German overseas fleet.

The German 1871 victory suggested that they permanently target French colonial commerce and its maritime connections with the West Indies. As Germany still had no fleet, navy planners circumvented the refusal of politicians by building auxiliary cruisers.

The private German shipping agencies German Lloyd and the Hamburg America Line also accommodated the government's wishes for the design and outfitting of express steamers. When France, Austria-Hungary, Japan, and the United States joined this trend by 1890, an increasing number of private ships were built as if, one day, they would serve as warships in an imperial war fought far from home.[9] The U.S.–Spanish war proved the underappreciated power of auxiliary ships in the Caribbean. The ethnic loyalty of private shipowners was enlisted to help, an imperial power far away from Europe.[10]

The French navy counted four hundred warships at that time. It was logical to attack and sink them wherever and however Germany could. Ethnic merchant ships could perform a considerable war function supported by supply stations. The context for the activities of ethnic merchants, therefore, changed. Such fear was based on fact, not cultural prejudice.

Also, other powers showed few qualms in using the same strategy. In 1877, Russia began to consider the use of merchant ships as auxiliary cruisers. Eventually, the tsar took the next step and built a state-owned merchant marine that could serve him in times of peace and war. Boundaries between trade ships, warships, and state-licensed pirate ships were blurred.

Contrary to popular belief, Japan and Latin America had experienced selective contact since the 1500s.[11] After 1845, along the Peruvian coast, a handful of Japanese traders lived a self-determined life. They earned a living as labor organizers for Chinese coolies and transported them across the Pacific to Callao, Peru.

In 1866, the Japanese crown gave Japanese commoners the legal right to leave their homeland. A tiny number of men took advantage of the opportunity. First, Japanese peasants left Japan in 1869, trying a life as settlers in California on the Wakamatsu Tea and Silk Farm Colony. The colony leaders experimented with imported mulberry trees, silk cocoons, tea plants, and bamboo roots. But the experiment failed.

The 1870 U.S. Census registered fifty-five Japanese. Ten years later, the number had doubled to 148.[12] These men lived private lives in a mixed ethnic context in the Americas and were not manipulated by the Japanese government.[13]

In 1877, nineteen-year-old sailor Manzo Nagano arrived in British Columbia and refused to sail home. Instead, he remained in the British colony and, for more than a decade, lived as the only individual Japanese on record in this northern part of the American continent. He made a living salmon fishing and longshoring. None of these independent lives were connected to international relations.

The imperial court in Tokyo, at that time, continued to brush aside all arguments in favor of a greater-Pacific design and insisted on a focus on gaining power in Korea on the Asian mainland. In 1874, Japanese gunboats were dispatched to Korean coastal waters. Six warships, in the ensuing Kangwah incident, forced the Korean emperor to agree to extraterritorial Japanese rights in Korea. This event marked the beginning of a century-long confrontation among Japan, China, and Russia over eastern Asia.

Unlike in Germany or Great Britain, there existed neither large numbers of Japanese merchants who traded globally nor a powerful Japanese navy that could help in the creation of a global Japanese imperial presence. In Tokyo, the emperor and his aristocratic clans remained content with building a great Pacific power. This meant confronting imperial Korea, China, and Russia. Aristocratic clans and bureaucratic advisers, however, did notice and study the lessons of European colonialism.

A few thinkers begged to differ and advocated a wider expansion across the Pacific. In 1876, Enemoto Takeaki suggested that Japan buy from imperial Spain the islands of the Marianas, Carolines, and Palau. A second idea was the creation of outposts for trade on newly acquired islands. A third one was to use islands to house convicts. Their prison labor would build bases and supply stations for a future navy and trading companies. In these visions, Japanese Pacific expansion was an effort to find space for those who should be "cleansed" from Japanese society. The creation of foreign markets for domestic industrial production and the establishment of outposts for the navy remained secondary.

These were precious years, when immigrants and immigrant communities pursued their own paths, inventing myriad ideas of what it meant to be ethnic in the Americas. All of them had come for personal reasons, not to serve as pawns in the international power plays of any colonial empire. Certainly, they were no security threat.

Before 1880, ethnic immigrants in the Americas defined their identity to a surprising degree without the involvement of the government of their country of origin. The imperial monarchies of Spain and Portugal were becoming too weak and the rising imperial monarchies of Germany, Japan, and Russia were not yet strong enough to reach across the oceans and define the lives and identities of ethnic communities.

Foreign elites invited Japan to expand farther than the Asian mainland into the western Pacific. In 1881, Hawaiian royalty invited a Japanese presence onto their islands to counter U.S. groups that wanted to annex the Hawaiian islands. The royal dynasty even proposed a Hawaiian–Japanese alliance based on marriage between Princess Kaiulan and the Japanese crown prince. Such a union was to create the base for a Japanese–Hawaiian Empire spanning from the middle of the Pacific to the Asian mainland. Together, Hawaii and Japan would reject Western annexation and its humiliating tools of unequal treaties and extraterritoriality.[14]

The Japanese court rejected it. Emigration had to remain limited to contract labor. Temporary emigration remained under state control. As long as laborers had to return to Japan, foreign governments could not argue that their presence was part of a hidden aggressive design to acquire colonies.

In the words of the U.S. historian Alan Takeo Moriyama, an ideal and unique form of government-sponsored emigration emerged: "an orderly closely regulated system with protection, even interference from both governments involved. . . . [T]his form not only protected the emigrants but also maintained in international circles Japan's image as a modern nation."[15] It took until the early 1880s for the Japanese cabinet to link itself with ethnic movements toward the Americas. In this decade it warmed up to the idea of organizing Japanese citizens going abroad, but still only for a limited time.

Domestic social issues still drove this policy change, not desires for national territorial expansion. Nevertheless politicians assigned a new national purpose to the emigration of individuals. First, sending abroad single men as contract laborers offered a social safety valve, as well as the earnings of foreign currency incomes. Perhaps it would also alleviate domestic economic depression and relieve pressure coming from population growth.

The first military function of ethnic settlement emerged in one region. In Japan's north, members of the samurai group colonized the northern islands of Hokkaido. Nationalists, in this move northward, were organized into a first settlement belt. Their presence was seen as a physical bulwark against southward imperial Russian expansion.

In 1885, the administrative chief of the Tokyo police, Yoko Tosaku, revived the idea to send Japanese convicts southward. Japanese prisoners could establish core settlements on Palau, Mindanao, the Carolines, and the Marshall Islands. Later these first settlements could develop into future trading outposts and navy refueling stations.[16]

In sum, the thinking about using ethnic settlements among Japanese political and bureaucratic elites was undergoing a major shift. Emigration now not only solved private hardship but also promised to be beneficial to the growing navy, traders, and domestic social policy makers. Japanese emigrants could no longer simply leave their country as workers. Japanese government policy increasingly tried its best to make their presence abroad serve the nation at home.

Lower-ranking Japanese politicians were the first to go one step further. They suggested that the presence of emigrants gave special rights to Japan. For example, in 1884, Suzuki Tsunenori took things into his own hands and acted as if he had political authority outside Japan. His government sent him to the Marshall Island Lae only to investigate the murder of a Japanese sailor. But once he arrived he went further and claimed the island for the emperor. Raising the Japanese flag on Lae, from Tokyo's elite vantage point, endangered Japan's official policy priorities of treaty revision and the removal of discriminating tariff rules.[17] Not surprisingly, after Suzuki returned to Japan, the foreign minister sent him to Lae for a second time. This time his instruction was to pull down the flag, return to Tokyo, and resign from the foreign service.

The public face of Japan's foreign policy had been preserved. Treaty revision and economic tariffs were more important than the acquisition of a small island. But superficial appearances hid a more complex reality.

Officially, Tokyo's cabinet had distanced itself from Suzuki's annexation. Privately, however, the foreign minister rewarded Suzuki by giving him a ship for the sole purpose of continuing his explorations of the southern Pacific. No further instructions were needed. Suzuki sailed back to the southern Pacific and lived as imperial explorer and travel writer, intensifying his advocacy of island annexation by the national government. Japanese navy leaders particularly appreciated his reports from the Southern Sea identifying first targets for future acquisitions. According to the German historian Wieland Wagner, the same texts would fuel expansionist "southern fever" in the 1920s.[18]

In the second half of the 1880s, the torch of expansion into the Pacific passed from individuals to traders, companies, and private organizations. Some of them were partially funded by the government, stopping short of political annexation. In 1885, the idea of a South Sea Society that would colonize the southern region of the mid-Pacific reemerged. In 1886, after imperial Spanish bureaucrats asked Tokyo for closer economic relations, Foreign Minister Inoue dispatched the Japanese consul of Hong Kong to explore the Spanish colonial business in the Philippines. He returned with reports of positive opportunities and the availability of land for peasants from the Kyushu region.[19]

In 1890, Taguchi Ukichi, Japan's Adam Smith, encouraged politicians to occupy Pacific islands that were not yet controlled by Europeans through trade companies.[20] The U.S. historian John J. Stephan reminds us that "a number of intellectuals, influenced by Social Darwinism and impressed by the European colonization of the Americas, Australia and Siberia played on paper with how Japan could expand overseas through emigration."[21] These men interconnected emigration, trade, and imperial expansion.

In the end, Taguchi Ukichi moved from journalistic advocacy to action. The compensation funds for aging samurai financed the trading company Nanto Shokai from May 1890 on. This company dispatched schooners with goods to the area between Guam, Palau, and Ponape to build Japanese trade outposts. Now the presence of ethnic Japanese trade was to make permanent territorial acquisitions. Emigration was no longer just about temporary relief from domestic population pressure or the earning of national income through remittances. By 1880 ethnic Japanese emigration and the associated trade were two tools of imperial expansion in the Pacific. Japan had begun to rival Great Britain, Germany, France, and the United States.[22]

Should Japanese imperialism expand only on the Asian Pacific side, or should it continue along the Pacific coasts of the Americas? And should ethnic Japanese settlers be used again to take over land? In 1889, as imperial Spain looked increasingly unable to hold on to the Philippines, Fukumoto Nichinan and Suganuma Teifu conducted a Japanese intelligence mission into the Spanish colony. Afterward they advocated annexation and the placement of emigrants to assure Japanese conquest.[23] In 1891, Oishi Masami went further and advocated crossing the Pacific. In 1893, Setzu Nagasawa pointed at the islands of Hawaii as a springboard for peaceful expansion.[24]

But also foreign governments encouraged the contracting of Japanese laborers beyond Hawaii, to the United States, Australia, and Mexico. By then six hundred Japanese workers worked in the mines of French New Caledonia. After 1892, employers in Peru, India, Hong Kong, New Caledonia, Canada, and Brazil requested Japanese contract labor.[25]

Suddenly Tokyo's royal court reversed its stance and discouraged southern expansion. The zeal of independent expansionists was curbed, and the Asian mainland was reasserted as the priority expansion target. In May 1891 Enemoto Takeaki, a leading advocate of expansion through emigration, found his zeal curtailed as he was put in charge of an office inside the ministry.

Takeaki bucked the attempt to constrain him as a government official. He created an emigration office inside his ministry. His office insisted that emigration had to be aggressively useful to the nation while still prohibiting open territorial annexation. The U.S. historian Todd A. Henry explains this evolving type of overseas expansion:

> In contrast to passive, North American–bound *dekasegi* emigration and aggressive colonial expansion aimed at the Asian continent, Enomoto Takeaki favored emigrant-led colonization, an assertive, yet peaceful method of overseas expansion. In the case of his 1890's project to Mexico, this involved the acquisition of an "informal colony" on which to relocate Japanese settlers who would provide Japan with raw materials in exchange for its manufactured goods.[26]

Takeaki prepared the ground for a more acquisitive Japanese presence in the Americas. He began by sending scouts to investigate living conditions and locations in the Philippines, Malaysia, New Hebrides, and Fiji. From there he ventured further to allow Japanese exploration of Latin America's "coastal territory."[27] In 1891, for 175 days, he accompanied four government surveyors to Mexico.[28] The men reported that Mexico offered positive living conditions. Soon thereafter, Mexico became an accepted location for future Japanese settlements.

Closer to Japan, Takeaki acted openly aggressive. In 1891, he annexed the island of Iwo Jima for the empire. In early 1892, he sent two navy ships to Manila, the Philippines. While the crews investigated settlement conditions, they also gathered intelligence about Spanish colonial fortifications.[29]

Then, abruptly, in 1892, Takeaki's service as foreign minister was terminated. Still, during his years in office he had demonstrated that emigration and territorial aggression could be two sides of one Japanese policy.

Even though the aggressive expansionist Enemoto Takeaki was out of office, the new government continued to fuse individual emigration with national interest. In 1894, Foreign Minister Munmitsus sent a secret mission to Australia to examine settlement locations and potential markets. The mission report encouraged trade expansion. In the same year workers were sent to Fiji to build a Japanese city far away from Japan.[30] Two years later trade with the Philippines was strengthened with the opening of a consulate. The presence of Japanese trade and ethnic settlers created dominance at a time when imperial Japan did not yet possess a navy strong enough to conquer Spanish colonial land through force.

Even Enemoto Takeaki reemerged in a semiofficial role. In February 1893, he founded the semiofficial immigration society Shokumin Kyokia. He explained its task: "Emigration is urgent and must truly be a national policy of Japan. . . . This society is not satisfied with desk arguments only, it plans to carry the policy out by considering ways and means."[31]

The era when Japanese emigrants were merely poor individuals trying to eke out a living abroad was coming to a close. The action of Tokyo's leaders destroyed the innocence of Japanese individuals living abroad. Takeaki sponsored a new, second expedition to Mexico. For 133 days its team investigated the southern states of Guerrero, Oaxaca, and Chiapas.[32]

Mexican president Porfirio Díaz provided unexpected help, inviting emigrants to live in a settlement belt in a contested region with Guatemala. In 1894 the Japanese imperial diet officially declared Mexico as an approved emigrant destination. A first Japanese settlement was to open in the southwestern region of Soconusco, Mexico.

Finally, a third expedition brought the agricultural specialist Bunzo Hashiguchi to Mexico. His investigations included the strategic Tehuantepec Railroad.[33] Obviously these semiofficial explorations were never just curious adventurism but, in fact, the careful planning of ethnic settlements with special consideration to key strategic locations and access to navy and railroad connections. During times of peace this was only skillful development planning. In times of war, in an instant, such planning offered real strategic advantages.

A watershed in Japanese government behavior took place in 1894. The geographical focus of Japanese emigration changed after the Japanese navy defeated the larger Chinese imperial fleet.[34] Overnight China's defeat allowed Japanese expansion into Taiwan, the Liaotung Peninsula of southern Manchuria, and the Pescadores Islands. The Chinese monarchy was humiliated through forced payments of significant indemnities and the imposition of an unequal commercial treaty.

For the first time, the Japanese monarchy controlled land in mainland Asia, making it possible to join in the similar colonial imperialism by British, Russian, French, German, and U.S. rivals. Once again, the potential settlement of areas in the southern Pacific and Mexico was less interesting. Future activities and the priority of Japan's army, navy, and Foreign Ministry became absorbed with Asia.

Emigration to other continents received less government attention and was handed to private companies operating under a new 1894 emigration law. Now the government only set the parameters for these emigration companies and, in times of national crisis, reserved for itself the right to intervene.[35] From now on southward and cross-Pacific expansion was limited to the goals of emigration, trade, and indirect colonial acquisition.

Japanese emigration into North and South America became a business venture, which shuttled individuals across the Pacific with hardly any consideration for their personal welfare. Thirty emigration companies operated in Tokyo, Osaka, Yokohama, and Sendai cities.[36] The first Japanese expansionary fever toward the western Pacific had receded.

Nevertheless, on the eastern realm of the Pacific, Japanese naval observers and Japanese military representatives stationed on Taiwan, closer to the Philippines, took a first step toward seeking permanent contact with anti-imperialist revolutionaries. Spanish queen regent Maria Christina's position in the Philippines was undermined by Japanese soldiers. In Tokyo, between 1896 and 1898, low-level Japanese diplomats and intelligence agents of the army eagerly advocated in favor of support for anti-Spanish rebels. Japanese diplomats were in favor of expanding their activities from protecting trade and ethnic settlements to maintaining contact with revolutionaries.

Now, in 1896, it became feasible to think that in the not-too-distant future, this huge Spanish island archipelago could be divided among imperial competitors including Japan.[37] Already a few individuals took matters into their own hands.

First, Japanese nationalists Suganuma Teifu, Fukumoto Nichinan, Takatsu Goro, and Sugino Sotaro visited the islands to learn about the evolving situation. Second, the Japanese consul in Manila interacted with Andres Bonifacio of the Katipunan rebel group. Tagawa Moritaro, according to Saniel the oldest Japanese living in the Philippines, functioned as volunteer interpreter. Also the Japanese navy ship *Kongo* stopped in Manila in 1896, and Moritaro again worked as translator when officers talked with rebels.[38]

Japanese interest was reciprocated. Soon thereafter Filipinos requested military support from Tokyo. One month before revolutionary fighting began in the Philippines, Bonifacio turned to Tagawa Moritaro, asking him to purchase Murata guns. In order to support the rebels with money, a civilian front organization was to be set up. Pretending to work for profit, this outfit would, in reality, earn money to buy arms for revolutionaries.

Now also, Japanese intelligence observed Philippine revolutionary activity. The Japanese General Staff in Taiwan processed incoming intelligence.[39]

From Tokyo, the Imperial Household Agency sent Fukuba Itsuto to investigate the Spanish. More importantly, he performed his intelligence work in the archipelago while serving as president of the Japanese Citizen Association.[40] To say it differently, by 1897 diplomats, spies, and ethnic community coexisted in this geographic theater.

Philippine rebels, between 1896 and 1898, continued to do their utmost to secure official support from Tokyo. By 1897, Consul Sakamoto introduced a new reason for potential Japanese expansion in the Pacific, urging Tokyo to give in to rebel overtures. He favored support because, he thought, both sides shared a racial Philippine Japanese background against imperial Spain.

The chief of the general staff of the Taiwan military, Major General Tatsumi Naobumi, agreed and considered sending a military detachment to occupy Manila, at the same time as U.S. admiral Dewey was blockading the bay. In Tokyo's military offices, cooler heads prevailed. Japan's military leadership instructed the general in Taiwan: "The control of the South Sea is an idea [to be achieved] in Japan's national policy but today is an inopportune time. You must positively not meddle in war. While you maintain neutrality you must continue protecting the lives and property of the Japanese in Manila."[41]

The 1898 defeat of the Spanish fleet only intensified their efforts. The rebels wanted support from Tokyo, not just from some individuals and diplomats stationed in the local community. Saniel followed the story based on rebel biographies.

In August 1898, rebels requested to buy 600,000 yen worth of weapons from Tokyo. Jose Alejandrino, Faustino Lichauco, and Mariano Ponce negotiated in Tokyo.[42] A Tokyo military department offered secret training to Filipino rebels. And yet the imperial government never backed the rebel movement in a decisive way.

To really appreciate the extent to which Japanese elites felt comfortable manipulating the longings of ethnic people, we need to close with a quick look at the official Japanese–Spanish relationship at that time. Japanese sympathy was not as clear-cut pro-Filipino as diplomats made rebels believe. The archives reveal that imperial Japan also assisted imperial Spain against the rebels. When the Spanish legation requested police surveillance of the Filipinos meeting in the Japanese capital, the government happily provided the requested support.[43] The Ministry of Interior observed Filipino rebels in Tokyo, and the Ministry of Finance inspected ships to stop possible weapons exports.

Eventually, Filipino rebels learned painfully about the manipulative extent of Japanese elite decision makers "sympathy." On August 31, 1898, Teodoro Sandiko had hand-carried a copy of a declaration of independence to the Japanese consul. But elites in Tokyo looked the other way and refused to recognize it.[44]

In the end, in Paris, France, the imperial powers negotiated a diplomatic settlement about the Philippines' future. In December 1898, the entire archipelago went to the United States. Right away, imperial Japan acquiesced to the conference's decision, and remaining support for the rebels stopped.

Still, the Filipino revolution proved that by 1896 members of the Japanese army and navy had encouraged national liberation movements against other colonial powers in Asia. Japanese help could mean at least limited arms supplies and selective diplomatic encouragement but also the manipulation of themes of Asian racial brotherhood. Even worse, all these violations of sovereignty had been managed using the cover of ethnic Japanese communities.

2   Becoming Useful

The First Japanese and German Experiments with Ethnic Manipulations in the West

E thnic emigrants and their outlook on life did not change after 1880. However, waves of imperial rivalries changed the global political context of their presence abroad.

Policy makers in Berlin and Tokyo looked at ethnic communities in a new way. As Germany and Japan considered expansion, imperial rivalry suggested that they also consider using ethnic communities in the Americas as pawns in anticipation of potential acquisition moves. At first in Berlin there was merely debate over whether and how potential acquisitions could be brought about. An opportunity for territorial acquisition was not quite there yet.

In 1884, Bismarck reversed his categorical opposition to German colonialism overseas. In November 1884, he hosted in the German capital an international conference to lay the ground rules for the future of colonialism in Africa. Some German politicians looked already further, to Asia and the weak Spanish colony of the Philippines.

The British historian Sebastian Balfour proves that already in 1885, only a few months after the conference in Berlin and four years before the Spanish defeat in 1889 in Cuba, "Germany above all had cast acquisitive eyes at Spanish possessions."[1] Bismarck even allowed a brief contest over ownership of the island of Yap in the Carolines archipelago. For true change, however, German imperialists had to wait until Bismarck left the German chancellery.

In 1888, Wilhelm II ascended to the German throne. Soon he clashed with Bismarck. The new emperor wanted to acquire colonies not just where Bismarck desired them, in Eastern Europe and Africa, but also in Asia and Latin America. Germany should be a world colonial power. As the months progressed the German emperor increasingly asserted himself and sided with the political faction pushing for a large German navy with global reach. Only such a fleet would guarantee a global German Empire.

By early 1890 the young emperor and the old chancellor could no longer work together constructively. On March 30, 1890, Bismarck resigned and was replaced by Leo von Caprivi as new German chancellor.[2]

Chancellor Caprivi, together with Prussian minister of trade Freiherr von Berlepsch, Marshall von Bieberstein, and Prussian minister of finance Miquel, immediately introduced a more differentiated stance as far as emigration and empire were concerned. In their view settlements in Latin America and Asia could at least offer an attractive alternative to the saturated German domestic market, even if German settlers would not yet be used as Trojan horses of imperialism. Furthermore, sending German exports to ethnic settlements abroad promised an effective way to circumvent growing tariff walls around the preferred U.S. market. For these men the German government should definitely reconnect with emigrants and, thereafter, maintain a permanent bond at the very least for the sake of the German economy.

Right away important government ministries and Hanseatic trade houses demanded an even stronger policy reorientation. The government should also lift its 1850s prohibition of company-organized emigration to Brazil. Against them argued diplomats from the Foreign Ministry, the Ministry of Interior, and associated Prussian ministries. A bureaucratic tug-of-war over emigration unfolded between supporters of overseas emigration and groups keen to affirm the exclusive emigration focus toward Eastern Europe. Wilhelm II favored the first group.

Wilhelm II proved himself to be politically erratic, untrustworthy, and dangerously irrational. Suddenly in November 1897, he ordered the seizure of the Chinese Kiachow region. Apparently, the order was based on his whim, given against the objections of German economic, military, and diplomatic circles. Decision making in this German Empire promised to be confused. Now that Bismarck was not centering policy, the emperor, the armed forces, diplomats, and even merchants might act for their particular interest but try to argue that it was the policy of an entire people.

Even worse, Wilhelm II rapidly resorted to secret treaties. For example, he guaranteed the tsar control over the Chinese city of Port Arthur. One year later, the German monarchy established its own formal, ninety-nine-year lease on the Shantung Peninsula.[3] Against the background of these examples in Asia, who could rule out that one day something similar might occur in a failing Latin American republic or monarchy? Wilhelm II deserved to be treated with suspicion. German colonial policy stopped coming from a clear, rational decision-making process according to familiar imperial rules and, therefore, became dangerous.

In 1894, the head of the North German Lloyd Company, Adolph Woermann, had decided to travel to South America to further the interests of his global shipping business. He wanted to identify growing passenger routes. This partisan of emigration to Brazil returned to Germany in November 1895 with the news that southern Brazil was an ideal territory that could offer Wilhelm II's monarchy an overflow territory for its increasing population pressures.

The details Woermann provided reassured skeptical Germans that a distinct colony could thrive in Brazil. In particular it required support to maintain their German language and culture. He emphatically advocated a change in emigration policy, plus state subsidies for shipping companies traveling to the Americas. Of course his shipping company would be a major benefactor of the renewed flow of emigrants to Brazil.

Next merchant Woermann joined navy enthusiasts and pushed for additional permanent German naval stations in Latin America. In the end, the emperor's imperial adventurism, Woermann's Hanseatic business drive, and rivaling bureaucratic policy priorities mustered enough joint pressure to bring about a reevaluation of the official prohibition of company-organized emigration to Brazil. The 1850 Heydtsche Reskript prohibition was about to be weakened.

The Brazil of the 1890s was very different from that of the 1850s. In November 1889 the Brazilian monarchy collapsed. Financial insiders of imperial politics understood that Dom Pedro had stumbled as much over the weak financing of his nation as over political questions. One voice encouraged scheming imperialists that the collapse had been "un crise tant politique que financiere."[4] Weak financing of a Portuguese American nation could become an Achilles heel, triggering a further disintegration of Brazil that could be manipulated for European imperial acquisitions with great ease.

Then the new, temporary Brazilian transition government called for renewed immigration from Germany. General Fonseca abolished the Brazilian monarchy and signed a provisional government decree on June 28, 1890, in favor of a more active immigration policy. Now that slavery had been prohibited, Brazilian politicians needed Europeans to work as plantation wage laborers, and they wanted European workers to staff a yet-to-be-created new industry. For that purpose the weak republic issued land concessions for 31 million hectares, to house 1.4 million people! It also offered funds for European shipping agencies able to carry large numbers of immigrants to Brazil. In 1891, a first republican constitution affirmed unrestrained, continued enthusiasm for immigration.

In 1896, Brazilian decision making about emigration moved from the central government to regional capitals. European imperialists understood that this could translate into a weakening of Brazil's ability to resist future separatist fantasies. Thus the country became the priority target to explore what a distinct ethnic group of Germans could accomplish politically. This was normal thinking for the period, and protagonists could not imagine that World War I would soon wipe such paradigms away.

Local German voices from Brazil nurtured fantasies about an exclusive ethnic enclave. The new German diplomat, stationed in Petropolis, reported that Germans had developed a strong position in the states of Santa Catharina and Para. He insisted that they dominated the social and political processes of their states. For example, the city of Joinville "was almost entirely in German hands."

Wilhelm II and other Germans wanted to see it as a possibility for domination. Wilhelm requested "as soon as possible a report about the arrangements of immigration and other means for the strengthening of Germandom."[5] Publicly, he continued to act the more restrained monarch.

Wilhelm's blessing was sufficient to allow a new German government commission to constitute itself in 1896. It studied the resumption of government-supported emigration to Brazil. The surviving protocol of one of its session from April 4, 1896, offers a rare, authentic look at the thoughts and positions of the different factions.

Secretary of State von Buelow and Admiral Tirpitz emerged as strong and skilled supporters of the resumption of state-endorsed emigration. Unlike Japanese elite politicians in the 1880s, these German leaders wanted a deliberate social-political strategy attached to state-sponsored emigration to Brazil. Still, they had to make concessions.

Showing respect for Germans favoring the continued exclusivity of colonization of the stolen Polish areas, they agreed to limit emigration to Brazil to five hundred to one thousand emigrants per year. In case of national crisis they agreed that emigration to Brazil should stop altogether.

On the other hand, settlements in Brazil should be equipped with an institutional network that challenged assimilation. Operating a German church and a school was expected to reinforce cultural core assumptions and social identity-building rituals. They would maintain sufficient foundations for later political plans. Ethnic distinctiveness would be preserved until diplomatic or economic treaties, even a small marine landing, could force open imperial political boundaries into existence.

State Minister von Buelow confirmed a German position that wanted to see the glass half full: "We have great interests in southern Brazil, if we can bring about such a settlement of modest proportions. With the necessary reservations then we would assure us a future without endangering our interests at home. Also his Majesty and the German chancellor are in favor of granting the concession."[6] Next, Director Reichardt of the Foreign Ministry stated that supporters might soon build political hopes on local infrastructure projects in Brazil that seemed to move toward project initiation:

> His Majesty had expressed general sympathy for the endeavor, plus reinforced his interest by committing this company to the projected figures. Recently he has inquired about the matter. In essence the society is nothing else than a further development of the old Hamburg Colonization Club. A refusal of the concession would mean not only the ruin of this colonization company, but also future German interests. In Hamburg a railroad enterprise for Southern Brazil was in the planning phase, and, in Southern Germany, Count Furstenberg and other magnates had raised a capital of RM 15,000,000 in order to support railroads and other enterprises in southern Brazil. These efforts undertaken by strong capital interests were very encouraging in order to counter English influence and in order to further interest circles in Germany.

Another participant revealed details about deeper German motivations in Brazil. Brazilian leaders had been presented with demands for an informal colony: "We wanted to have a terrain where German peasants were already settled and the climate would help German workers. For this purpose the provinces of Santa Catharina, Rio Grande do Sul and Paraná appeared suitable. At that time the general Postmaster of Brazil had come [to Germany] in order to negotiate." It is critical to realize that already Germans had demanded extraterritorial rights from the Brazilians. Extraterritoriality was the essence of an informal colony. Here is a summary of past demands:

> The [Brazilian] General Postmaster stated that he personally was . . . quite open to the matter but he could not give the right [to Germany] to have its own legal system [*Gerichtsbarkeit*] and colonial security system. This

was the reason why negotiations failed previously. Today such a guarantee still has not been offered. The Brazilians are half wild and the Germans are threatened with losses.

Now, in 1896, pro-imperial factions wanted to ask for guarantees for the independence of evolving German communities for a second time. This also included the use of a potential German fleet to conduct gunboat diplomacy if only to prevent mismanagement by the Brazilians. State Minister von Buelow interrupted and agreed that

> it was "... necessary to assure guarantees for the Germans in Brazil." However, the best guarantee would remain first a strong navy and, second, that the German element in Brazil would live as compact as possible. Then the Brazilian government would not dare to move too close to the Germans. Already during the last civil war, they [Germans] had formed their own regiments and brigades, it is in our interest not to stop the movement of Germans.

Buelow knew that the Brazilian central government was weak. Therefore his advocacy of a strong ethnic German block in the state of Santa Catharina was justified publicly merely as a defensive measure against indigenous people. The German element was "to face the indigenous people as compact as possible."

The German navy included southern Brazil in its contingency planning. In 1897, plans outlined the mobilization of a small naval force to threaten gunboat diplomacy against the Brazilian nation or a smaller Brazilian state. Such action was not as farfetched as it might sound. Already in 1871, on the first leg of its world cruise, the German *Nymph* put in at Rio de Janeiro to support a German merchant and to protest the Brazilian government's behavior toward a local German consul. The plan in 1897 went further and considered a temporary occupation of parts of southern Brazil. What Brazilian navy could confront such a group of German ships? Would U.S., British, or French boats seriously have traveled to the area to repel a small German group of ships at the Brazil coastline? It is highly doubtful.

One month later the government commission agreed to find a compromise solution that placated supporters of emigration to the Polish territories. The resumption of emigration to Brazil was opened only in principle and would depend on case-by-case approval. On June 4, 1896, the Royal State Ministry adopted

1. As German government members reengaged with Brazilian German communities in 1897 they hoped that they could connect with independent regional immigrant economies and cultures (Ibero Amerikanisches Institut, Stiftung Preussischer Kulturbesitz, Bildarchiv, Berlin).

the commission's suggestion and signed a decree on July 30. From 1897 on, the German chancellor had the right to grant new concessions in Brazil, tied to the approval of the national council.[7]

As soon as company emigration was allowed again the Hansa colonization company invested 1,500,000 RM in 1896. This amount included payments to the Brazilian government and territorial rights over 650,000 hectares of jungle in Santa Catharina. In the future this land could be divided into twenty thousand lots, with 25 hectares for each farmer and 1.5 family members. To say it differently, in theory fifty thousand German settlers could try not to assimilate on preplanned agricultural plots in southern Brazil. The initial projection for first-year emigration to cross the Atlantic was one thousand individuals. In the years thereafter the number was expected to increase. In the end this process would have an altogether unexpected end, brought about by average German people. However, German aristocratic and business elites proceeded to keep the door open for a future opportunity to acquire parts of Brazil. That commoners might not play along never occurred to them.

Von Buelow moved up in the German government in 1897 and became the German secretary of foreign affairs. Whereas Wilhelm II was impulsive in exploiting opportunities, von Buelow was highly intelligent and had his impulses under control. He preferred to wait until realistic opportunities offered themselves for exploitation. He had worked as secretary at the 1884 Africa conference in Berlin. There he witnessed firsthand how imperial powers could add and subtract continents and peoples, disregarding entirely the fates of individuals.

One lesson he observed was that, under the right circumstances, British politicians would be willing to engage in secret temporary alliances with Germany. The exploitation of such opportunities could translate into territorial gain for German imperialism anywhere in the world.

Case in point were secret negotiations between Great Britain and Germany in the very same year of 1897. Germans talked about Brazil while the wrecking and future division of Portugal's colonies were preplanned in much greater detail. Namibia and Angola were separated from Brazil only by a short moderate ocean passage. Until today these British–German agreements about Portuguese Africa remain out of most history books, and therefore a key case of the dangerous secret opportunistic policy that German leaders were willing to engage in, in 1897, continues to be unmentioned.

The Portuguese colonial empire was expected to collapse in the very near future. Experts of its financial health had learned that Portugal, if it wanted to remain a colonial power, needed drastic financial reform of its national budget. Otherwise immediate bankruptcy would endanger the government in Lisbon. This meant that Portugal and its colonies would fall under international receivership. Until today historians of this period miss the significance of the Portuguese case as inspiration of what could happen in Portuguese America. Buelow's world political knowledge was excellent, and he understood the analogy between Portugal and Brazil. As Great Britain and Germany proceeded to divide Portugal's African colonies, the national security context of ethnic settlement in Brazil was obvious.

In 1898, while the future of Spanish possessions in Asia and the Caribbean was decided by the new force of modern naval power, the future of Portuguese colonies was supposed to be changed using loan guarantees. First the British alone were using finance diplomacy to force concessions from the Portuguese. From May to June 1898, while the U.S. navy fought the Spanish, Portugal's diplomat

2. Under the right international political circumstances, Reich Chancellor Bernhard von Buelow would have attempted to impose German imperialism over Brazil. They failed to materialize during his tenure (Library of Congress, Washington, D.C.).

Soveral negotiated with British diplomat Chamberlain. The talks failed to establish a loan agreement that would bail out Portugal. Great Britain, Portugal's traditional political protector but also manipulator, was not willing to offer an easy way out. Portuguese leaders were not receiving relief, and Portuguese colonies might be up for redistribution earlier than assumed.[8] And what repercussions would a collapse of Portugal have for Brazil?

In 1898, most of Spain's colonial territory was taken away. The ensuing imperial distribution demonstrated that Germany would insist on and gain at least minor territory, even as part of a diplomatic settlement.

This process, unfolding between 1898 and 1910, offered select ethnic communities located across the globe as a less perfect but workable base for a new role. Now that imperial planners had to make the move from grandiose royal expansion toward creating pragmatic support organizations for twentieth-century navies, the needs of modern naval technology urged the use of ethnic communities as a minor war support organization.

More precisely, dramatic geopolitical shifts during 1898 were creating a new understanding of national security. The esteemed U.S. historian Akira Iriye defines the paradigm shift:

> What characterized the decades after the 1880s was a new conception of national security. Colonies overseas, naval-based spheres of influence and particularistic concessions began to play vital roles in a country's defense system. They, as well as rapid industrialization and armament at home, were indexes of power, their retention and extension were considered to contribute to the security and strengthening of the mother country. It was no accident that during this period foreign policy was strongly determined by, if not identical with, military policy.[9]

New possibilities for how global naval battles could be fought forced honor-bound aristocrats to conceive of imperial rivalries in a new way. First, the conversion of navies from wind to steam power made the construction of larger battleships possible. More importantly, coal-producing steam power allowed for the first time naval battles at any location in the world, relatively unimpeded by weather conditions. Naval battles could be fought wherever admirals chose.

There remained only one, critical limitation; coal-fueled navies required coaling stations across the world. Without dependable refueling capacities, imperial navies could neither engage their rivals nor defend their colonies. Suddenly, in the 1880s only empires with colonies enjoyed an unquestioned right to maintain a coaling station. Imperial Great Britain and France, owning colonies stretching from Europe to Asia, were simply lucky. In contrast, Germany and Japan lacked colonies at the right geopolitical locations to be helpful to their navies. They still had to acquire them or become dependent on the conditional tolerance of imperial rivals. What if a sympathetic ethnic community was located just off major naval shipping lanes?

Then there were colonial empires that had colonies for refueling but lacked access to modern naval technology. Planners in Madrid and Lisbon might fix their budgets, but they wondered how they could create a convincing global military presence as their agricultural empires failed to provide the funds to pay for modern naval technology. Also naval planners in Berlin, Moscow, and Tokyo found their national territory poorly positioned as they projected their desires for more global power into the twentieth century.

These global naval environment changes were a simple fact, unalterable by monarchic family connections, religious convictions, or secret European diplomacy. Technological breakthroughs of the nineteenth century were giving birth to a new aristocracy of technocrats whose demands required attention. Imperialists who discounted the new demands of technology could be swiftly pushed out of continents, literally within months.

On the very same day that the Spanish–American War ended, on August 31, 1898, the British diplomat Balfour informed the Portuguese diplomat Soveral about the possibility of a loan for Portugal's southern African colonies. Most importantly, it included British openness to enter into a German–English agreement about the future of Portuguese colonies, in case Portugal would collapse. A joint British–German loan extended to a bankrupt Portugal would end its financial sovereignty in Africa. In this joint imperial move the power of finance would be the tool to open backdoors, in Africa.

Then a smaller German naval contingent could join the British navy if it would be necessary to enforce loan payments through gunboat diplomacy off Portuguese Africa's coast. During those years the exploration of limited British–German joint naval cooperation progressed. No document suggests that a joint British–German action in Latin America in the future was undesirable or, even, should be ruled out.

German secretary Buelow ordered diplomat Tattenbach to search for additional information to gain a deeper understanding of opportunities for German influences over the Portuguese colonies. The Germans also evaluated the weakness of Belgium and British competition.[10]

Then German policy shifted, as the Lisbon government proved to be not yet as weak as the one in Madrid. This time the direct approach of advancing German–English power in Africa shifted from financial to commercial imperialism.

A lesser third option was investment in a multinational charter company. As immediate land acquisition and indirect control through loans had failed, Count Tattenbach suggested owning shares of Portuguese charter companies.[11]

In August 1885, talks had explored the fusion of the Mozambique and Zambezi companies. German investment in these charter companies would guarantee a continued German presence until this financial influence over a charter company could be turned into political influence over the entire colony. In Africa German politicians contented themselves with a holding pattern. The fact that they acted with restraint did not mean that they had given up long-term imperialist interests in that region. They assumed the same stance in Latin America.

Even popular voices pointed the way. For example, the writer and politician Paul Rohrbach, when asked what to do about Brazil, pointed to the example of Portugal, which never had become a formal colony of Great Britain. Through the Treaty of Methuen this Iberian nation, nevertheless, had been made an informal colony of Great Britain. Germans should impose a German social group onto a southern Brazilian region or state that was economically active and productive. Yes, such emigrants could be citizens of a new Brazil, but their economic relations should follow the example of the British–Portuguese relationship or that of white colonists in South Africa.[12]

Between 1889 and 1893 the All-German-Society demanded to do what was necessary for the creation of a sister country of the German Reich in Brazil, even against the resistance of Brazilian Germans themselves and U.S. voices. The German historian Brunn minimizes these words as the "mumblings in the fever of Fleet propaganda" and takes them as an indication of the insatiable hunger and lack of reality of German expansionists' agitation.[13] Altogether, he states, these voices remained a minority, proving that there were many others who opposed these ideas as fantastic. This interpretation falls too short.

In Berlin Wilhelm II exploited the poor showing of German naval forces in the Philippines to initiate an unprecedented twentieth-century fleet construction program. Already in April 1898, Admiral Tirpitz, now state secretary of the navy, had told German audiences that the U.S.–German rivalry in the Pacific would have ended more in German favor if imperial Germany could have deployed a larger modern fleet. A German fleet needed to be built now, shifting the balance of power among the world's navies and allowing German admirals to engage their British and U.S. colleagues during the next imperial competition. Admiral Tirpitz submitted his first fleet bill financing new battleships and global colonial outreach.[14]

While the building of the fleet remained to be accomplished and aggressive naval policy would be unrealistic for years to come, in other regions German policy makers continued to place select "stepping-stones" in anticipation of sudden future opportunities for acquisition. Elite government members knew that these stepping-stones could be used at a later time. And if these early foundations for future German imperialism were not built, then there would be none to unify in one concentrated effort to translate their singular physical presence into highly interconnected, exclusive political control at a later, more opportune time.

In the minds of German elites and promoters of German emigration, the future of this Portuguese American space in Brazil did not yet have to be defined

"Der Segen des alten Germanen"
Aufgeführt von Schulkinder des Deutschen
Schulverein Catharinenstrasse in Joinville, Brasilien
zum Schulfest am 27 Juni 1909.

3. Brazilian German intellectual elites resisted assimilation and had continued the performance of German folklore inside Brazil to create and to protect so-called language islands (Ibero Amerikanisches Institut, Stiftung Preussischer Kulturbesitz, Bildarchiv, Berlin).

further. Instead it sufficed to view Brazil as an increasingly overripe plum on a Portuguese American tree that would fall naturally into the hands of those German elites and commoners willing to take the time to wait. Later, after such conquest, the various German factions would have to fight over whether a German Brazilian region would be dominated by the goals of middle-class merchants, an ethnic emigrant folk culture, or the upper-class greed of aristocratic imperialists. In 1896, under "an imagined tree of history," it was enough to strengthen one's stance in expectation of the ripe Brazilian plum falling one day into "the German apron," ready for the catch.

In the words of German historian Brunn, "The lifting of the 1850 Heydtsche Rescript, and the starting fleet propaganda . . . contributed to the idea" that South America was becoming an economic realm and a future area to project popular longings "that one could conquer here through peaceful means—the means of a targeted German emigration into—a new part of the earth."[15]

In the following years writings about Brazil and South America continued to be published in greater numbers. A peaceful and economic conquest was still mentioned in 1902 and 1905 at a Colonial Congress of German emigration to South America.

From the autumn of 1899 until the summer of 1901, Count Hatzfeldt worked with Lord Lansdowne to see how far a special German–British relationship could go.[16] But relations between Germany and Great Britain became more difficult again. From the summer of 1901 on, German–British negotiations became more and more tedious.

It took until December 1901 to break the will of the Dutch colonialists in South Africa. Then King Edward wrote to the British ambassador in Berlin, Sir Frankel, in a letter to the Germans that he hoped that Germany and England would continue to cooperate on all points. But it would be difficult to define this cooperation in a formal agreement. Such a treaty would undoubtedly encounter serious opposition and difficulties in the British Parliament's lower house.

In the meantime the German Foreign Ministry wanted to assure that German immigrants to Brazil would not assimilate into Brazilian society. On April 1, 1902, a German Central Office for Immigration was founded, officially by the German Colonial Club. In reality it was financed by the Foreign Ministry. In order to hide the nature of this direct government tool the office presented itself as the project of a passionate civic group. Thus opponents of German emigration to Brazil had greater difficulty accusing it as imperial immigration tool, which it was. It existed only because Buelow's Foreign Ministry financed it with 35,000 RM.

Its director had worked previously as the general counsel of Porto Alegre.[17] From the first day of its existence the office steered German emigrants to southern Brazil. Interestingly German historian Brunn does admit that "inside the inner circle of the government, when admitted openly, they hoped for a peaceful penetration of Brazil with the help of a populist basis."[18]

All the German diplomats were waiting for was the still expected failure of the Brazilian republic. As long as it was impossible to occupy the region militarily, German ethnic settlers were supposed to act as a social class, thoroughly imprinting this region with German ethnicity, social practices, and business.[19] All of them were anti-Brazilian and anti-Portuguese.

4. German railroad construction in Paraná and Santa Catarina, Brazil, around 1900 (Ibero Amerikanisches Institut, Stiftung Preussischer Kulturbesitz, Bildarchiv, Berlin).

Suddenly, north of Brazil, a limited experiment exploring the first joint British–German cooperation in Latin America offered itself. On January 2, 1902, the British undersecretary responsible for South America inquired of the German chargé d'affaires, Herman Baron von Eckardstein, whether a joint British–German naval action against Venezuela might not be of interest.

During these months Emperor Wilhelm II did not wish to mount any drastic action against the Venezuelan president, Castro, because his brother was visiting the United States. Thus the Germans did not react until July 1902. By August, the British also wanted to invite the United States. In the end, by November 12, Buelow reported that Edward VII and the British government were prepared to undertake a limited joint action against Castro.[20]

On December 9, the German cruiser *Vineta* and the gunboat *Panther* captured the Venezuelan vessels *General Crespo* and *Totumo*. The British dispatched a squadron to capture Venezuelan ships. In the end four Venezuelan ships were immobilized by joint British–German action.

Some diplomatic insiders hoped that joint naval undertaking would help the growth of deeper cordial relations between London and Berlin. Here the potential of limited Anglo-German cooperation in select Latin American regions was defended.

Suddenly, because of British frustration about German behavior during its fight against the Dutch in South Africa, King Edward VII wanted to end the explorations of British–German cooperation. Also Chancellor Buelow feared that the British Balfour government might even fall over the Venezuela explorations. In the words of Canadian historian Holger Herwig, "The new prime minister Arthur James Balfour struggled loyally alone to adhere to the policy of corporation with Germany off Venezuela."[21] Buelow had grander things in mind. He was not eager to gamble with German world politics on a small Venezuelan side warfare field. Now, in February 1903, the Venezuelan–German/British struggle was settled. Herwig identifies the event as a watershed. The British government in London was realizing that it stood in serious danger of alienating the United States: "Cabinet and parliament were of one mind that the British possessions in North and South America depend[ed] for their continued existence much more upon the United States benevolence than upon Germany."[22] Thus ended this attempt by Buelow and Wilhelm II to increase the foundation of future German imperialism in Brazil. But their general political outlook would continue until the 1930s.

This particular chapter in the imperial game in Latin America through German emigration failed not because of the British or the U.S. navy or the Brazilians. It failed because average German people simply refused to emigrate to Brazil. Common and poor people did not perform the role that German elites had assigned them in their strategy. Between 1904 and 1914 only 1 percent of German emigrants, about four hundred people per year, chose Brazil as their destination. Correctly the German historian Brunn states, "There could not have been a higher contradiction between 'high national task and reality.'"[23]

North Africa next gained higher priority for German elites. German chancellor Buelow turned his attention away from Brazil in 1903. He and Wilhelm II refocused on confronting France. French possessions in northern Africa and Asia Minor, in particular Morocco, appeared as more realistic immediate targets.

But scholars should not throw out the baby with the bath water. The refusal of common German emigrants to relocate to Brazil did not mean that aristocrats gave up their schemes for some form of colony in Brazil. Also Buelow and Wilhelm II's shift of attention to northern Africa did not end it. The expanding German economic influence in cherished Brazil would resurface in 1913. And in 1918, Count Luxburg would admit that elites were still waiting to take advantage of a Brazilian collapse and create a German colony on the cheap.

On the public imperial political world stage, Latin America was no longer the most obvious backdrop for German activities. But behind the scenes aggressive,

5. Unsurfaced coastal road near São Sebastião, Brazil. Still in 1930, the head of German Brazilian propaganda insisted that this was virgin territory where reality did not apply. On the back of the picture he exclaimed: "Here the world seems to be just created and the feeling of space is limitless" (Ibero Amerikanisches Institut, Stiftung Preussischer Kulturbesitz, Bildarchiv, Berlin).

lesser options continued to be played out successfully. The German kaiser might act foolish, but, in particular, German naval officials had laid the bureaucratic foundations that future elites could build on.

German secretary of navy and admiral Tirpitz continued building his bureaucratic foundations in preparation of a global German navy, trying to disregard but also exploit the ups and downs of formal and informal imperialism. He had to build the global communication, supply, and intelligence connections that would serve a German navy in any future imperial expansion, including when it was time to refocus on Latin America.

Already on March 11, 1895, German diplomats had discussed whether Germany needed coal refueling stations and naval bases. The Foreign Ministry wanted to ask first the navy command for input.[24] They replied that they needed to acquire refueling stations.

Two years later, after Admiral Tirpitz had replaced Admiral Knorr as head of the navy, it was decided to build a fleet that eventually could contest British world naval might. It should also be strong enough to take on the French navy.[25] The strategy was to destroy the British in one large battle in the North Atlantic. Still, the German navy should also have the ability, to a limited degree, to operate globally.

On April 24, 1898, a second high-level meeting discussed the creation of a chain of global maritime bases. Two of the islands identified for possible acquisition or purchase were the Danish Caribbean islands of St. John and the Dutch West Indies. For Admiral Knorr German control over St. John promised that Germans could even think about an eventual conflict with the United States.[26] Any German navy of global reach should have a reliable base near the Panama Canal.

On July 1, 1898, the evolution of the U.S.–Spanish war made discussions about future bases only more pressing.[27] At least, German naval planners suggested, private businessmen should start acquiring coaling stations. The existing navy was not yet strong enough to take territory at gunpoint. In January 1899, German entrepreneurs tried to buy Danish St. John with the knowledge of naval leaders.[28] But buying naval bases proved difficult.

Admiral Tirpitz, in a parallel effort, configured a global strategy that would go hand in hand with German interests in the Pacific and American regions, especially in case of war. In October 1899, this also meant considering the strategic value of the future Panama Canal.

The same year Germany experienced one modest gain. In October, Germany and the United States agreed to share access to the critical Samoan deepwater port of Pago Pago, a secure place close to the major shipping lanes approaching South America. The British were compensated with the Solomon Islands.[29] Canadian historian Holger Herwig points out that the German presence in Samoa was also a first attempt to project force into future shipping lanes leading to the future Panama Canal.[30]

There existed a faction in the navy that thought that Germany did have a sphere of influence in Latin America. They imagined a variety of ways to establish German power in South America. Tirpitz believed that Germany could use participation in an international canal consortium to become an appreciated member of a future great power alliance in South America. Until then, private investment could prepare the ground for physical territorial acquisitions later. A third option considered was eventually building a common German–South American front against the United States. A second sphere of influence supporter was Admiral Otto von Diederichs. For him German interests were specifically tied to Colombia and Guatemala. He thought that Germans could also acquire Dutch Guyana.

Historian Holger Herwig explains:

> It became imperative for planners in Berlin to plant the German flag somewhere in the Caribbean basin. Such a base could serve as an anchor in the projected German cable network, could provide a coaling station for both merchant and naval vessels and could serve as a center from which to harass the eastern terminus of the [Panama] canal, when completed in case of war. For a matrix of reasons, ranging from national prestige to maritime strategy, Berlin became interested in the western American hemisphere in general and in Venezuela in the western American hemisphere in particular, wooing to its geographical location.[31]

If German admirals were correct, in the not-too-distant future, they could reject the Monroe Doctrine and, as part of a European alliance, split South America in half. One would be given to Europeans, and a second sphere would belong to the United States. German ownership of bases close to the Caribbean, then, served more than refueling needs. The German presence would also attempt to block U.S. expansion toward South America.[32]

Tirpitz's preparations included the collection of all available statistical data about German financial investment across the globe. The results were published in June 1900.

In the same month the Reichstag passed the second Navy bill. If the money would be spent as envisioned, Germany would double the size of its fleet. Then Germany could project power into the world's oceans with 38 battleships, 20 armored ships, and 38 light cruisers. The military potential of this naval growth strategy was explained by a navy spokesman: "If we wish to promote the powerful overseas policy and to secure worthwhile colonies we must be prepared first and foremost for a clash with England and America."[33]

6. The Brazilian Bank for Germany, ready to serve customers and investors (Ibero Amerikanisches Institut, Stiftung Preussischer Kulturbesitz, Bildarchiv, Berlin).

Now German planners considered three possible scenarios for naval battles along the U.S. coast. First, the German navy might attack and conquer an island in the Caribbean. Second, German naval forces might attack the U.S. mainland, and third, the German navy might draw a U.S. fleet into one, decisive battle.[34] This included calculating how many ships it would take to fight a U.S. fleet in the Caribbean.

In 1902, Prince Heinrich was scheduled to sail on a goodwill mission to the United States. People close to him informed the German ambassador to the U.S. that the prince planned to tell President Roosevelt that Germany would continue to insist on a South American sphere of influence. In the end, Prince Heinrich was persuaded to keep this claim to himself, for the time being. It had taken a major intervention by Foreign Ministry diplomats to assure princely discretion.

Still in the same year a second private German consortium approached the Mexican government, according to the Mexican historian Friedrich Katz, asking to purchase Mexico's Baja California Peninsula. When asked why, the Germans told Mexican negotiators that its protected waters were close to the United States and the Panama Canal and it was an "excellent place for naval operations."[35]

The German ambassador in Washington did his best to educate the sphere of influence supporters that German territorial acquisitions in the Western Hemisphere were out of the question because of the tough convictions of President Roosevelt. Then Chancellor von Buelow chimed in and discouraged the sphere of influence faction. In other words, members of the German royal house shared the South American power dreams of rising admirals. Not mentioning them in public did not mean that they had been abandoned.

Even though on the highest political level German interests in Latin America could not be admitted, and the official interest remained Africa and southeastern Europe, German naval war planners could not lose interest in ethnic communities in foreign and American ports. To the contrary, German naval leaders

7. When German prince Heinrich visited the United States in 1904 he planned to tell President Roosevelt that he believed in a German sphere of influence in Latin America. Wiser German diplomats convinced him to repress this heartfelt conviction until more opportune circumstances (Library of Congress, Washington, D.C.).

increasingly pushed the naval military motives into the forefront of debates about German emigrants in North and South America. In the absence of German colonies, ethnic Germans and their resources had to be relied upon in order to make limited auxiliary cruiser warfare against French and British interests possible along North and South American coasts.

In the coming years, whatever increases of state funds the German government could devote to overseas fleet building, once built these ships would operate still without the protection of a German colony in the Americas. Among themselves, German mid-level naval planners were angry that past efforts to acquire a colony in the Western Hemisphere had failed.

Toward the kaiser, however, navy officials pretended to be loyal soldiers and developed the second-best option: the navy had to develop a network of hidden anchor places along the American coast and in the Pacific, where a secret supply service would provide the ships with ammunition and food supplies.[36] Lacking well-stocked colonial harbors, German warships would have to refuel in calm, protected natural bays along the American coasts. Security needs also required locations far away from telegraph stations that might give away a German cruiser's sudden presence.

The solution was obvious. Berlin leaders expected that some ethnic German merchants in North and South American harbors would be willing to provide clandestine support for such warships, even though their country of residence wanted to remain neutral in the conflict. This was the way ethnic German merchants in the Americas, their companies, and their business connections were quietly slipping into German war plans.

German auxiliary naval warfare preparations began with a systematic inspection of the American coastlines. Using smaller ships, German naval intelligence traveled along coastlines to lay the military geographic groundwork for future naval warfare.

Admiral Raeder explored isolated coastal places in the Americas hoping to find uninhabited sheltered locations that offered secrecy. In May 1903, SMS *Gazelle* appeared in Newport. SMS *Falke* traveled through the West Indies and explored Central America. In 1904, Emperor Wilhelm II ordered the exploration and mapping of Canada's west coast. In 1905 and 1906, SMS *Panther* inspected the west coasts of Canada and the United States. In 1907, the Atlantic east coast and Canadian harbors were scouted. On occasion such intelligence work included sending troops onto foreign land. It might also mean endorsing a German individual as consul who could look at a geographic region with military questions in mind.[37]

On November 9, 1907, discussions proceeded to settle an observer at one bridgehead of the Mexican Tehuantepec Railroad. A Mr. Krietzler wanted to buy land close to the railroad. A German diplomat proposed that Krietzler could also serve as German vice-consul of Tehuantepec. The rising importance of the route across the isthmus made it desirable to have a permanent representative stationed there for observation. Previously merchants had proven unreliable. Mr. Krietzler was willing to observe the terminals, including looking for possible future Japanese ethnic settlements and the construction of fortifications. This required knowledge "not only about being a well-trained Prussian administrator but also the experiences that Krietzler brought from his trips through Latin America."[38]

Farther north German officers toured the ports of British Montreal, Quebec, and Halifax hoping to gather relevant military geographic data. By 1908, anchorages and meeting places had been identified for resupply missions to serve auxiliary cruisers along the U.S. west coast.[39]

Explorations yielded mixed results. The German admiralty rated locations along the North American west coast as poor. The U.S. and Canadian east coasts received better ratings. The western Pacific coast offered good locations and greater secrecy. In Latin America, the West Indies and South American Atlantic coasts yielded even a few undiscovered places. The South American west coast received only fair ratings. Still, Admiral Raeder pushed ahead, emphasizing the importance of developing this global network before imperial war broke out; "decades of work during times of peace had identified hidden refueling places for cruisers and tested them repeatedly."[40] By 1910, basic German military-geographic evaluation of all American coasts for future naval warfare against the British, French, or the United States had been completed.

Next Tirpitz established supply connections between preselected places and American harbors. By 1911, the Germans imposed a grid over the map and divided it into the districts of North America, the West Indies, Brazil, and La Plata, as well as west coast and southwest America.

Each zone was assigned an individual who worked as naval supply manager. He would build and supervise the regional naval military organization. This meant identifying German merchants in his area and exploring whether some of them would be willing to use their resources and cover as merchants to also secretly supply the naval network. Admiral Raeder believed that their business connections provided sufficient cover to purchase additional coal and supplies on the open market. These men also had to preselect work crews for loading and unloading ship supplies. Their business would also do the accounting for the

German imperial navy. Once they agreed to perform secret work, their obligations were put in writing; little was left to chance. Some German businessmen far from Germany were becoming an undercover supply service and, if necessary, intelligence officers of the navy.

As promised, they negotiated the required supplies and maintained, in select American ports, a minimum supply of coal or petroleum products. Plus they maintained ships that could deliver them to the prearranged secret meeting places. Similar agreements covered the shipment of ammunition.

In the words of Admiral Raeder: "Thus the supply work of the German trade world in favor of the navy, once war broke out, was legally ascertained. Besides, the sense of nationalism of German merchants certainly created the expectation that this could be expected anyway, as long as we did not expect things that were in violation of neutrality law."[41] This statement is misleading. From the very beginning of war, perhaps still during peace, the ethnic German merchants were expected to do more than supply ships. Being a member of the supply network could also mean working as a naval spy. Section leaders in American ports were to report hostile shipping activity to a preselected German intelligence liaison. District heads in Buenos Aires, Rio, São Paulo, and Acapulco were responsible for the collection, evaluation, processing, and forwarding of all relevant data for the conduct of the war in their district.[42] They, in turn, sent the data via oceanic cables to Berlin.

This district head also enlisted German captains, merchants, and sailors, who, while smoking a cigarette on deck, gathered naval information and, on occasion, befriended the harbor master.

Emperor Wilhelm II and the German navy were still not satisfied with these efforts. A final task was to "disturb the supply of foodstuff, raw petroleum, and raw materials" of the enemy. After 1909, Great Britain had to import two-thirds of its annual food supply. Stockpiles in England could feed people only for four to eight weeks. The flow of food from Latin America into British harbors was a worthwhile target to interrupt. Raeder stated, "In every war where England is the opponent of the German Empire, priority is given to the damage of English trade, and the English ship traffic to Great Britain and its colonies."[43]

Select ethnic Germans were also expected to fight, as soldiers, quietly in American ports and disrupt British commerce supplying the British home front.

By 1910, British merchant lanes in South America were an important German target. British traffic to the West Indian Islands was a fourth target. In sum German ethnic communities were beginning to play an important role in economic warfare as a naval military support organization.[44]

In order to keep cover the majority of ethnic Germans in American ports were not included in or informed about these warfare preparations. Not surprisingly, after World War I and World War II they most vehemently protested against British and U.S. accusations that they had been part of a secret military organization controlled by Berlin military leaders. And yet small but critical sectors of the German ethnic community had been militarized before World War I to serve as secret warriors. From Admiral Raeder's point of view it was a natural development: "It was therefore a national duty to employ, if possible, the force that was resting with a strong merchant marine in the fight against the stronger might."[45] This service was successfully built. After World War I one of its leaders wrote an evaluation of the operations during the war.[46] His extensive study showed that the service was functioning so well that it could not only supply ships but also transmit military orders from the United States to Germany's Far Eastern squadron. In addition to organizing food and fuel it also operated a newspaper-monitoring service extracting open source material for intelligence. From 1914 on the naval supply organization also operated one office that contributed to the organization of revolutionary uprisings in British territories. The San Francisco office helped secret German campaigns against India and Canada.

District leaders closely shadowed British naval intelligence. They discovered a Marconi transmitter station in Vancouver and a pro-British Japanese service operating wireless transmitters in Southern California already in 1914. One report claimed that the Japanese operated mobile signal stations out of cars.[47]

Finally, in 1912, the general staff of the German navy agreed to coordinate better with the German army during the next war, linking the supply base and naval intelligence network, if necessary, to operations on the European battlefield.[48]

Within ten years the German–British naval race had turned select ethnic German communities, private companies, and individuals into spies and economic warfare organizations. The warfare needs of Berlin had redefined ethnic work, community, and individuals. After 1910, it all depended on an order from Berlin.

At the same time, in Tokyo, a tiny number of Japanese army professionals pondered whether ethnic groups in Europe could do more for Japan than earn profit for companies and increase trade. The Japanese army decided to manipulate ethnic and socialist groups living in Russia to subvert the defensive capacity of its imperial rival. Even though this campaign used ethnic groups other than Japanese emigrants, the events demonstrate that, if necessary, select Japanese elites had begun to use ethnic manipulations for the purposes of warfare beyond Asia. The army crossed a most important threshold. Ethnic Japanese emigrants, around the Pacific, of course, had no idea that their army was expanding the use of ethnic subversion.

In 1900 in Europe, a large number of ethnic groups lived as subjects of imperial Russia. It should not be surprising that Polish and Finnish ethnic separatists, just like Filipinos before them, had approached Japanese military attaché Akashi Motojiro in Europe asking whether Japan would support their separatist struggle to break free from Russia.

First, Polish revolutionaries promised the Japanese attaché that they would manipulate Polish soldiers serving in the Russian army through propaganda. This would weaken Russian morale and combat effectiveness.[49] Second, the Finnish ethnic nationalist Konni Zilliacus talked to the Japanese army officer.[50] Right away Attaché Akashi recognized the potential damage that ethnic separatists could inflict during the next Russian–Japanese war. Four years after the collapse of Spanish control over the Philippines, the military attaché advised his general staff in Tokyo that an uprising of foreign ethnic and socialist separatists at Russia's European border could noticeably weaken the morale and effectiveness of Russian troops in Asia. Such subversion might pressure Russian diplomats to enter into peace negotiations early.

A second attaché, Major Tanaka Giichi, echoed this evaluation and promised his superiors "that the movement of revolutionaries and minority nationalities could create shock waves throughout the Tsarist regime."[51] Japanese support for Polish and Finnish separatists might also divert Russian military force, stationed along the Far Eastern border, to European border areas. Then Russian strength along the border with imperial China would weaken, allowing greater freedom of action to Japan. The U.S. historian Ian Nish cautions that this was not yet Japanese support for Polish and Finnish independence but only a temporary tactic to deploy during war.[52]

In 1903, the Japanese military leadership decided that the time for open hostilities against Russia had come. Russia's growing strength and the completion of the Trans-Siberian Railroad demanded action, before Japan would no longer have a chance to defeat a Russian military already superior on paper. In October, Vice Chief of Staff General Kodama ordered the use of every conceivable tool that promised success, including

> assistance to the Russian revolutionary party, confusion of Russian intelligence by purchasing a news gathering organization, purchase of Russian agents and their use; promotion of discord on the Black Sea, support for

independence of states on the Baltic Sea coast; disruption of the transport of arms to Siberia; close relations with the British and German governments, improvement of European public opinion towards Japan.[53]

Preparations began months before war would be initiated. Later, after the war, when the secret subversions were discovered, such silent preparations during peace increased fears and suspicions among military planners in the United States and other imperial capitals. They were proof that one should always be on guard about Japanese elite intentions. The Japanese army had added ethnic disintegration and support for socialist revolutionaries to its war tool inventories outside the Japanese mainland.

Disintegration work commenced; in August 1903, Akashi requested a first budget from Tokyo headquarters asking to fund separatist propaganda in the amount of 100,000 yen. Tokyo's military agreed but specified that the money must be distributed among a variety of organizations. Funding was to go to ethnic separatists but also to ideological foes of the tsar, in particular socialist revolutionaries.[54]

A Finnish cover carried separatist money into Russia. There separatists were told that private U.S. sympathizers had donated the funds, eager to finance only protests of Russian masses, but not the use of bombs by terrorists. As requested, the money was divided among ethnic Ukrainians, Georgians, Belorussians, and socialists.

Polish socialist leaders undertook a much longer trip to Tokyo to ask for increased funding to sustain a Polish military uprising inside Russia.[55]

In December 1903, ongoing Japanese–Russian negotiations over spheres of influence in Korea and China were allowed to collapse. Emperor Mejii chaired a special cabinet council that ordered the move from aggressive diplomacy to open war by February 1904.[56] The next Russian–Japanese imperial war was on its way.

As war was imminent Attaché Akashi Motojiro moved to Stockholm, the capital of neutral Sweden. He assumed a newly created position, exclusively dedicated to the management of ethnic subversion. His colleague in London helped him. First they focused on organizing anti-Russian groups into a more united political front. Next Akashi, using Finnish socialists as go-between, tried to fuse the campaigns of ethnic nationalists and socialists. They cofinanced a conference in Paris for October 1904 and a second one in April 1905 in Geneva. Hopefully, the meetings would produce closer cooperation between ethnic and ideological subversives and create more painful headaches for Russia's monarchy. This delicate subversion was financed by 1,000,000 yen.[57] Japanese military intelligence had put Russian socialists on their payroll.

In July 1904, Japan's General Staff attempted the destruction of the Trans-Siberian Railway and incited ethnic Poles, serving in the Russian imperial army, to surrender.

In January 1905, Russia's catastrophic loss of Port Arthur created an unprecedented national crisis among the average Russian populace. During Bloody Sunday on January 22, tsarist police repressed anti-monarchic demonstrations and, more importantly, further politicized the Russian people, increasing a reservoir of discontent available for Japanese exploitation.

Few realized that Japan's subversive war effort was needed to create a breakthrough at the diplomatic table. After an extremely bloody battle at Mukden, Tokyo had to admit more than seventy thousand casualties. Japan could not politically sustain such a high casualty rate. It was time to probe for peace negotiations, hastened by ethnic secret warfare. In March 1905, Japanese generals ordered to get parts of Russia to revolt if the tsar refused to enter into diplomatic negotiations. Military Attaché Akashi Motojiro received another 1,000,000 yen to lay the groundwork for potential regional revolutions inside Russia.[58] He received help from select Japanese diplomats in Europe.

In the end such preparations proved unnecessary. The tsar agreed to negotiate a settlement with Japan. Right away Japanese subversion in Europe quietly stopped. In September 1905, Attaché Akashi closed his office in Sweden and returned to Tokyo. To this day his activities remain out of history books.[59] Japanese subversion had spread from Asia to Europe. If Japan would clash with the United States one day, why shouldn't Japanese generals also deploy the weapon of ethnic subversion in the U.S. sphere of influence? U.S. military planners had to come to terms with this likelihood, based on the cases presented so far.

Until then Japan innovated further on the use of ethnic Japanese settlers. In Korea, Tokyo's bureaucrats used Japanese emigrants to establish a physical Japanese presence in a territory where Japan did not enjoy sovereignty. Japanese policy makers deployed ethnic emigrants for the first time as an ethnic vanguard. They functioned as advance troops, currently disguised as settlers, until a final conquest could occur at a more opportune time. Unassuming Japanese emigrants were becoming part of a strategy of imperial conquest in Asia.

The strategy was simple. In 1904, the imperial government officially designated Korea as an area for Japanese acquisition. On May 1, 1904, the cabinet agreed to back official emigration to the area and to send emigrants, not as contract laborers but as agricultural colonists.[60] Japanese colonists established a physical presence on the ground without the use of warfare. Once established, these colonies would be difficult to remove through political means or diplomacy.

This emigration was driven neither by domestic problems nor by the profit motive. Its key motive was deceptive, territorial conquest while avoiding open aggression. Korea became a laboratory for this indirect conquest practice.

This is not just an interpretation of historical events. In 1906, Goto Shimpei, one of its architects, confirmed that policy makers acted with deliberation:

> On the surface our suzerain position in Korea today would appear to have been the product of victory in both war and diplomacy. In reality, however, this outcome was neither so sudden nor simply achieved. Our acquisition of suzerain status was based upon the past immigration of our people to Korea, giving us superior claim over other powers and creating a reality that could not be challenged with words or arguments.[61]

This indirect aggression through settlement was not a onetime occurrence. In 1905, after the Japanese army gained limited power in Manchuria, northern China, army planners deployed ethnic emigrants for a second time. As before, they founded ethnic communities. Later they could exercise political and social influence when Japanese soldiers would be obliged to withdraw in 1907. As in Korea, some Japanese leaders opposed such an idea, and dissent was voiced among the highest government levels. But this opposition was not strong enough to stop it.

In Manchuria army planners faced different conditions than in Korea. The Ssup'ingkai Protocol demanded that the Japanese army evacuate Manchurian territory completely by April 1907. Ethnic immigrants in this area could not simply be present to settle down and to live as agricultural colonists protected by Japanese forces.

These ethnic colonies had to be organized for dual use. In times without open war they had to represent Japanese influence in a constructive, peaceful way. In times of open conflict these established settlements were expected to supply Japanese soldiers who would fight in that area. In Manchuria, ethnic Japanese emigrants were military colonists. The Japanese leadership, with some notable dissenters, was determined to "leave as a parting gift to the people of Manchuria a Trojan Horse."[62] Goto Shimpei, after colonizing Taiwan and penetrating Korea with settlers, now injected into Manchuria *bunsoteki bubi*—military preparedness in civilian dress. Since the goal was not to achieve a quick occupation, small steps were enough to extract value while waiting for war in a contested territory.

This tactic consisted of short-term projects, always keeping in mind their usefulness for future aggression. First, Japanese-led capitalist development exercised by the colonists became a core daily activity. Japanese investment would finance development, inserting Japanese companies into centuries-old Chinese frontier culture. Development meant operating meatpacking plants, growing livestock herds, promoting horse breeding, and creating tree nurseries. In times of peace these activities created employment for ethnic settlers. At the same time they grew military supplies in a frontier zone. Once war became possible the same livestock herds would provide the necessary meat to feed the invading Japanese divisions. Meatpacking plants would process the army's provisions. Horses would serve as draft animals and help cavalry as they charged the Russian enemies. Tree nurseries provided wood for cooking and military construction projects.

Trade was the second step. A trade cooperative called the Manchurian Trade Cooperative was created. Its priority was marketing and logistical support for the introduction of Japanese products into Manchuria. But it also challenged the prominence of Russian goods that had penetrated the markets previously.

Third, Japanese investment financed small local health centers and larger, regional hospitals where they took care of the health care needs of colonists. Of course they could also serve Chinese people. These demonstrated that development under Japanese leadership was beneficial to non-Japanese ethnic groups. It was a splendid campaign to court Manchurian hearts and minds away from the inconsiderate Russians.

Fourth, Japanese financial tools were introduced in a dual-use fashion. Previously the conversion of Japanese military scrip into silver yen, exclusively provided by the Yokohama Specie Bank, had helped the expansion of Japanese culture and commerce outside sovereign territory.[63] In Manchuria no national Chinese central bank ready to enforce a government monopoly of currency existed. Neither did the Chinese manage the punishing ups and downs of an economy without a controlled money supply. An expanded use of one Japanese currency quietly created a reliable, constructive economic climate and practice. It also meant pushing aside Russian currency.

Yoshihisa Tak Matsusaka argues that at the core of this policy stood two aspects: a patient long-term view and a way of seeing what was possible to accomplish at a given time. Using ethnic military settlers was an ingenious way of practicing the "art of the possible," until open violence made sense.

There can be no doubt that by 1905 in Asia and Europe, Japanese leaders were instrumentalizing the presence of ethnic settlers, the pain of oppressed foreign ethnic groups, and the utopias of socialists for the purposes of weakening, even destroying, enemy governments. The techniques served conquest. The question remained whether and when these techniques would be exported and applied in North or South America. Later, we will see that the lessons and techniques developed for Asia and Europe would also be partially introduced into North and South America. Japanese arms suppliers would appear first in 1909 during a Chilean–Peruvian confrontation. The Mexican Revolution would provide the context for a first offer to experiment with yen currency and foreign debt. The final step, the use of ethnic groups in intelligence and the encouragement of localized subversion, would emerge in Peru at the end of 1918. In other words, the events described on the previous pages were the laboratories of related Japanese activities in the Americas beginning during World War I. Of course, Japanese Americans and emigrants to Latin America did not know this.

For the time being ethnic Japanese life in Latin America was not about conquest. Already from 1900 on, emigrants wanting to work in the Americas took advantage of the expansion of Japanese foreign trade across the Pacific. Their personal hopes were made possible by unprecedented, reliable steamship service between Japan and San Francisco. Also Latin American entrepreneurs were increasingly interested in experimenting with Japanese contract labor. A small number of plantation and mine owners in Mexico, Peru, and Brazil employed a still very limited number of Japanese laborers, with little consideration of imperial great power manipulations.

In Mexico, in 1903, Thomas Mora, the nephew of Minister of Finance Jose Limantour, founded the Compania Japonesa Mexicana de Comercio y Colonizacion. This company joined its Tokyo partner, Imin Kaisha, to transport workers to Mexico. One year later, five hundred Japanese workers were shipped to the Boleo copper mines in Baja California, Mexico. But workers quickly realized how terrible working conditions were there and considered alternatives. Fifty workers ran away and disappeared into the horizon's vastness. The remaining 450 returned to Japan.[64] Contract labor in Mexico remained a difficult, often painful existence.

In Peru, future president Augusto B. Leguia, then only a manager of a sugar company, asked the Morioka Emigration Company to bring laborers to his Andean plantation. The first 790 workers arrived in 1898 to work on sugar and cotton plantations. In 1903, they were joined by an additional one thousand emigrants for the expanding rubber plantations.[65]

Bolivia was at least visited by Japanese labor export investigators. After conducting an in-depth study of potential settlement areas in northern Bolivia, they certified also a lasting future for Japanese workers in this American country. In Chilean mines, in 1903, 120 immigrants worked in the most inhumane working conditions. Brazil was still too far away and, therefore, transport costs remained too high to initiate labor exports without government subsidies.

Finally, gathering clouds of renewed Japanese–Russian war in China added a new incentive to deepen Japanese–Latin American trade. Yusaburo Yamagata, from 1903 on, managed a fishery off Ancon, Peru, and organized shipments of coal from the Andean region to Japan. The demand for coal increased as the Japanese–Russian imperial rivalry was heating up again.

First Japanese–Chilean commercial treaty negotiations were pondered. A few Japanese importers wanted to increase the flow of Chilean nitrates to Japan. Since Japanese nitrate deposits were small, the huge holding of Chilean nitrate was of particular military importance. Unlike Brazilian coffee and Peruvian coal, Chilean nitrates could be used for fertilizing Japanese fields and colonies but also to make bombs to kill Russians.[66]

In January 1905, Chile's Admiral Jorge Montt had traveled to Japan. There, navy officials impressed him with visits of naval bases at Yokosaka, Kure, and Sasebo.[67] For the first time, a Latin American navy representative sought closer ties with the Japanese navy.

In the end emigration remained the most important link. Until the Japanese–Russian war the story of Japanese emigration to North and South America remained exclusively a business story. The emigration-for-profit enterprise took advantage of Latin American labor shortages. It shared with imperialism only the utter disregard for the welfare of individuals.

The previous pages demonstrated the evolving differentiation of Japanese experiments with ethnic politics before the Battle of Tsushima. Previously, Japanese ethnic politics had meant ocean exploration, a tool for the relief of domestic social pressure, limited contract labor in Hawaii, a search for economic markets in Australia, sympathy for revolutionaries in the Philippines, colonial occupation in Taiwan, and exploitative work for contract laborers in Latin America.

Then two political events outside Latin America expanded this labor export business into an international political issue. First, as Hawaii became part of the United States, in April 1900, U.S. law prohibited contract labor on the islands. Suddenly, Japanese emigration companies faced the loss of their best labor export market.

Quickly individual emigrants and companies adjusted. People grasped that they could travel farther across the ocean, not only as contract laborers but, even better, as free workers. Suddenly Hawaii was no longer a final destination but only a harbor where Japanese transferred to a second steamship that carried them on to job markets in Canada, Mexico, and, of course, the United States. Now U.S. company managers, too, enjoyed taking advantage of noncontract ethnic workers who worked for a pittance.

In this changing business environment, the smuggling of Japanese workers from Mexico and Canada across the U.S. border expanded into a cottage industry, with offices and even short-term lodging facilities.

From 1900 on this process was no longer the limited government-controlled system that the Japanese government had imagined in the 1890s. After May 1899, former competitors consolidated efforts. Competition over the remaining emigration destinations intensified. At least the imperial government tried to address the worst dislocation and introduced a monthly graded quota system. Calls for a stronger central administration of emigration increased in Tokyo. But private business leaders lobbied in favor of self-regulated emigration business. Over the next few years, the number of professional emigration companies declined from thirty to eighteen.[68]

The end of the war against Russia triggered a new economic depression in Japan. Soldiers returned from Russia to civilian life, only to find unemployment or not enough land to farm. Once again emigration offered itself as an obvious alternative, and the flow of people to the Americas intensified. Private emigration companies intensified their for-profit shipping of individuals to Mexico. Five thousand three hundred twenty-one Japanese applied for passports to travel to Mexico in 1906, the largest number ever.[69]

Regional xenophobic and racist voices did, nevertheless, decry real changes in the pattern of Japanese immigration. A U.S. commission reported the arrival of ten thousand immigrants between 1906 and 1907. These were not just alarmist words but a correct description of a new unregulated migration movement. Regularly Japanese emigrants, once they disembarked in Guaymas, Mexico, or after a short time working on a contracted job in Mexico, took their lives into their own hands and ran away into the United States.[70] After 1905, the movement of Japanese immigrants across the Pacific into Mexico unfolded differently than Japanese government planners had intended when they privatized emigration in the 1890s. Now it was a most serious political issue that impacted the highest level of Japanese–U.S. political relations. The U.S. navy leadership was not as alarmed as Californian politicians.

Popular opposition, particularly among "white" workers, against the growing number of free Japanese who competed for jobs in Australia, the United States, and Canada became another issue. These white individuals were deeply steeped in a tradition of anti-Chinese stereotypes and racism. After 1900 the increasing arrivals of Japanese reinforced such popular stereotypes and reinvigorated principled opposition against Asian immigrants among labor union members. Racist labor organizations in particular demanded the creation of laws to make life difficult for Japanese. Ideally, Japanese people should be kept out of the United States. In no time, this corrosive combination of popular anti-Asian racism and targeted labor union activism succeeded in turning these hostile feelings into local anti-Japanese laws.

In Canada, in 1897, Canadian workers had pushed to end unlimited Japanese immigration. The Japanese consul was able to block this first legal attack. Even though he won against this first anti-Japanese attack, he advised the Tokyo government to enact a voluntary ban on emigration, hoping to limit future outbursts of anti-Japanese anger. His actions, however, did not stop anti-Japanese activism. Labor unions and racist groups passed the so-called Natal acts, which used local laws to oppose national laws and international British–Japanese agreements.[71] A curious coalition emerged, composed of the Japanese consul, national-level Canadian administrators, and British diplomats, together trying to find ways to oppose the racist activities of a growing number of local Canadians living along the west coast.

Also in the United States, after 1890, the anti-Chinese movement of the 1850s shifted its focus to the Japanese. In 1902, the Chinese Exclusion Act was renewed. Here, too, populists and labor groups appreciated anti-Japanese xenophobia as a powerful unifying issue. In particular, the Hearst paper publications contributed their share of ethnic hatred. Anti-Japanese activism was an accepted major feature of California politics.[72]

Closer to Japan, in the area of Queensland, Australia, the government introduced for the first time an immigration ceiling. In government circles, discussions shifted from "the human right of colored people to freely enter Australia to the method by which to restrict Asian immigration in the most humane way possible." By 1901, political parties across the entire spectrum agreed to a "White Australia" policy. In 1902 a settler's law codified limits further.[73]

The final factor affecting Japanese emigrants was the 1906 Japanese victory over the Russians. Technological as well as political strategic implications supercharged the interplay of imperialism, emigration, and suspicions over secret government machinations.

The 1905 defeat of the Russian naval forces during the battle of Tsushima further clarified what it meant to operate a modern navy. Tsushima was the first major naval battle conducted by steamships. All the way from the European Baltics, the Russian command dispatched thirty-eight ships to fight the Japanese fleet in the Pacific. These ships traveled from the Baltic Sea around Africa, passing India, until they entered into the Pacific Ocean. Throughout the trip the lack of coal refueling remained a major obstacle and impaired the Russians' progress. Once the two navies met, only three Russian ships escaped the ensuing disaster into the Port of Vladivostok.

Japanese admiral Togo and his modern ships had pounded the Russians into the bed of the ocean. He won because his ships traveled faster than the Russians'. Equally important, his modern heavy canons shot farther than those of the tsar. Speed and firing distance plus accuracy had proven critical. The Russian defeat promoted the Japanese fleet to the strongest and best-supplied naval force in the Pacific.[74]

The world's key naval analysts studied the Battle of Tsushima and applied its lessons. The British Empire was rich enough to provide Admiral Fisher with the money to put into construction a new class of battleships, its prototype represented by the newly built battleship MS *Dreadnought*. She was the first major battleship that ran entirely on steam turbines and made the world's other battleships obsolete.

German admiral Tirpitz tried to match the British move and refocused the German naval construction program. However, the smaller German Empire, in the long run, could not generate enough state funds to compete easily with the British. Also in the United States, President Roosevelt made the expansion and modernization of the U.S. fleet his pet project. Tsushima ushered in a new round of more sophisticated naval constructions.

The Japanese government's reaction to this changing context was slow and contradictory. Actions focused on removing the emigration conflict, which created the most public political burden for the contemporary U.S.–Japanese relationship. In April 1907, Japan's imperial diet allocated 4,000 yen to finance research about redirecting immigration to Brazil.[75] Tokyo wanted to await the outcome of that research before Brazil would be licensed as a destination.

3 Mexico Discovers Japan as a Potential Strategic Wedge against the United States

In Mexico, Porfirio Díaz's administration also examined the strategic implications of the Japanese naval victory. Initially, the immigration issue remained in the background.

In 1906, Mexico did not have a navy that could engage credibly with any Japanese fleet that might appear in the near future along its Pacific coast. President Díaz understood that Mexicans had to accept the fact that the Japanese navy and the United States were now the remaining dominant rivals in the Pacific. Mexicans had to relate in this new context.

Immediately there existed very real theoretical strategy concerns. One was the strategic function of the Isthmus of Tehuantepec Railroad, scheduled to open in 1907. As the Panama Canal remained under construction for years to come, this Mexican railroad promised a real strategic advantage for any empire needing to move troops from the Caribbean to the Pacific Ocean and back.

The U.S. military was aware of this option since the initial survey had been realized by a U.S. engineer from New Orleans who also was an army major.[1] Would this commercial Mexican rail line play a military function in a U.S.–Japanese war?

Some made the suggestion to internationalize the Tehuantepec Railroad from its inauguration on. But most Mexicans' nationalist pride rejected such a violation of sovereignty. In the end, Porfirio Díaz's administration only built fortifications at the railroad heads.[2]

Mexican elites were inspired by Japan's victory and naval potential. Some hoped for the very real possibility of defeating the U.S. navy and changing the politics of the entire Western Hemisphere. The German ambassador reported that some government members and average Mexicans were thinking, from the bottom of their hearts, that the United States deserved a defeat by Japan.[3] Educated urban Mexicans fantasized most strongly that Mexican–Japanese cooperation against the United States could expand Mexico's political power in international affairs vis-à-vis the United States.

In Tokyo, Mexican diplomats were in an even greater fever. The historian Friedrich Katz cites the Mexican ambassador in Tokyo confiding to his German counterpart that "there would be an armed conflict between the United States and Japan. Mexico could only gain from such a war as some benefits would surely emerge for Mexico. My ideal would be the break up of the United States as a result of such a war in which south and west would break away from the northern states. Then Mexico would be able to breathe."[4]

In the end more sober Mexican voices won the day. Keener officials rejected playing with fire and thought that Japan's victory at Tsushima implied deeper danger for Mexico. Undersecretary of Foreign Affairs Mr. Alagara proposed that Mexico should remain neutral in a U.S.–Japanese war. Three months later Foreign Secretary Mariscal admitted that Mexico would not be able to prevent a Japanese force from gaining a foothold in western Mexican ports. In that case he considered it possible that U.S. forces might insist on taking over Mexico's defense. Perhaps the United States would insist on leasing Magdalena Bay a second time.

Then there were explorations of U.S.–Japanese war scenarios. In case of a defeat of the U.S. navy, Mexico could matter as a potential battleground between Japanese and U.S. land forces. A U.S. land army might choose to invade Mexico to deter or answer a Japanese landing. In case of a U.S. invasion, should Mexico ask about support from other Latin American republics? Indirectly Tsushima might force a test case of the often invoked solidarity of American peoples.[5]

Military specialists put forward a more intelligent hypothesis. One Mexican observer thought that as long as the construction of the Panama Canal was not finished, the United States could not start a war against Japan. But he, too, played with the thought that it would be smart for Japan to launch any war against the United States before the Panama Canal's completion.

In 1905, the Japanese had demonstrated an outstanding ability to select the right moment to trigger another imperial war against Russia. Two years later German observers expected that Japan's generals would do the same in a Japanese–U.S. war. And they predicted that it should include the use of irregular forces and tactics.

While Mexican diplomats indulged in regional theoretical fantasies about the new strategic importance of their country, Germans pondered global specifics. What if Japan could gain a permanent Mexican bridgehead and project force northward. One military planner wrote, "It is not completely out of the question that Japan might intend to make a landing in Mexico after repelling the American fleet, to use it as a base of operations for an attack on California."[6] How would this affect the global imperial rivalry?

In 1907, German staff discussed the role "that might be played by Mexico in the event of a Japanese–American conflict as a possible base of operations." The German military attaché in Mexico informed his superiors in Berlin "that Japan still wants to have the option, in the event of war with the United States, to form a large contingent from its reservists in Mexico."[7] The historian Friedrich Katz discovered that German diplomats disguised themselves as tourists and took spy trips along the Mexican coast, trying to see for themselves where Japanese immigrants were settling in Mexico. Professional German observers emphasized that talk about Japanese war preparations was sensationalist and unfounded.

A U.S.–Japanese war on Mexican soil was considered to be most unlikely. Rather, the Panama Canal might be a more likely location for a clash.[8]

A different question was if and how much the Díaz administration might be willing to cooperate with Japanese forces. The German ambassador thought it possible that Japan would be willing to enter into a defensive or offensive alliance in exchange for the right to land on Mexican territory. But any presence of Japanese soldiers on Mexican soil might also bring about a nationalist backlash and trigger a collapse of the weakening Díaz administration.[9]

A German observer estimated that the Japanese General Staff in any war plan was certainly considering the option of an alliance with Mexico.[10] Before a landing, Japanese scouts would explore Mexico's west coast. If a Japanese fleet could depart from an unknown Japanese port, unnoticed by U.S. observers, it would be strong enough to land in Mexico even against Mexican objection.

A final victorious scenario imagined a prior Japanese conquest of the Philippines and Hawaii. After gaining naval supremacy in the Pacific, Japan might try to blockade ports of the western United States and force Washington into signing a peace agreement. During such negotiations a Japanese landing in Mexico might exert further pressure against the United States, but it would not invade U.S. territory. But the German diplomat, too, emphasized that it was unlikely that Japan, even "in the drunkenness of a major naval victory," would allow itself to follow such a daring adventure. The 80,000,000 U.S. citizens, among them 15,000,000 strong men, could not be defeated by a mere 100,000 Japanese soldiers.

What if a Japanese invasion tried to break away parts of the United States, for example, California? But even then the presence of a mere ten thousand Japanese emigrants and reservists would not be enough to function as the core of an invasion army against the United States. Japan would have to land a larger army in Mexico first to join emigrant reservists.

German consensus settled on an attack on the Panama Canal region as more likely than one on California. Conquering the Panama Canal would bring a major strategic advantage. If the Japanese were able to occupy the canal zone, then they could dominate the Pacific.[11]

As far as the timing of a potential attack was concerned, Germans identified the completion of the Panama Canal as a watershed. The U.S. army would do its utmost to keep the canal from the Japanese. To achieve this goal they would not hesitate to send land forces through Mexico or Central America to Panama. In contrast, the Japanese would try to land in Central America farther away from the canal to establish a beachhead.

Finally such evaluations trickled up to the elite level between the German emperor and leading U.S. politicians. The German ambassador in Washington mentioned to President Roosevelt rumors about possible Japanese designs in Mexico.[12] In Berlin, Emperor Wilhelm II repeated unsubstantiated allegations to the U.S. ambassador. The sun was setting as far as the innocence of the ethnic settlers in Mexico was concerned.

Mexicans were inspired by learning about Chilean progress in Japanese–Chilean negotiations. Already in January 1905, Chile's Admiral Jorge Montt had traveled to Japan. There, navy officials impressed him with visits of imperial naval bases at Yokosaka, Kure, and Sasebo. For the first time, a South American navy representative sought closer ties with the Japanese navy. Thereafter diplomatic contacts deepened. And on August 3, 1907, the Chilean government signed a treaty of friendship, commerce, and transportation with Japan. The Mexican newspaper *Tiempo* celebrated the event as proof of Chilean independence in international affairs. The treaty demonstrated elegance and firmness at a time when the United States began to take measures against Japan. The Mexican journalist expressed hope that "Japan in Latin America was becoming a bulwark against the outrageousness of the Monroe Doctrine which European Powers had failed to address or were not willing to do so." Some Mexican journalists wanted Japan to play the role of counterweight to the United States. One Mexican voice explained, "Japanese might could play the same role on the Latin American continent that Great Britain had played in Europe. Japan might create alliances between two or three powers and then they will clean up the humiliating guardianship which since some time ago the United States was exercising vis-à-vis the American continent."

From that perspective "Asian danger would reveal itself as a protection which might enable nations to develop without foreign interference." Elites close to Mexico City establishment newspaper the *Mexican Herald* turned excitedly against such argument. Ideas of Japan as an alliance partner were described as wild, undignified, and chimerical.[13]

Reality proved stranger than speculation. As later pages will show, at least one Chilean naval attaché was willing to admit that, indeed, Chile had reached a verbal agreement with Japan, defining Chilean–Japanese cooperation in case of a Japanese–U.S. war.

Then the Isthmus of the Tehuantepec Railroad was opened. On January 26, 1907, the Mexican city of Coatzacoalcos received the highest political Mexican honor. President Porfirio Díaz himself arrived with his entourage to inaugurate the railroad. He was accompanied by Minister of Finance José Limantour and Minister of Communication Fernandez. After opening triumphal arches Díaz and his friends boarded the steamer *Louis Luckenbach*. Then Díaz climbed into a crane and used it to unload the first symbolic crate of freight, transferring it to a railroad car to travel south to Salina Cruz.[14]

Also present were a few Japanese trade ships, awaiting the opening of this railroad connection. Some carried passengers who were dressed in something resembling a uniform. Right away ignorant, paranoid popular rumor suggested that their presence might be a Japanese plot, the delivery of a core of Japanese army members close to the U.S. border in preparation of a war.[15] But when everything was said and done no Japanese navy fleet appeared on the horizon. Thus U.S.–Japanese interaction quickly refocused on emigration and trade.

Three policy approaches dominated. First, Japanese policy toward the United States—as elite policy priority—was reasserted, ranking above policy toward Latin America. Japanese diplomats doubled efforts to remove the conflict originating from uncontrolled immigration. The xenophobia on the regional U.S. political level was to be alleviated to protect positive relations on the elite U.S.–Japanese level.

Already on May 14, 1905, local Californian organizations had moved from mere political agitation to the creation of a political anti-immigration organization: the founding of the Japanese Exclusion League. Its battle cry called to keep Japanese emigrants out of California.[16] Legal harassment, commercial boycotts, and newspaper campaigns against ethnic Japanese immigrants intensified. By the end of 1905, California's members of Congress carried the ethnic hatred from the West Coast into the halls of U.S. Congress.

Immediately after the departure of the U.S. Great White Fleet from Tokyo harbor, U.S. secretary of state Elihu Root approached Japan's ambassador to Washington, Takahira Kogoro. Both men negotiated a framework that put in writing the first formal "understanding" of where the boundary of the emerging Japanese–U.S. rivalry should be located.

In the first week of February 1908, the Japanese vice minister of foreign affairs told the German diplomat Mum that the reduction of immigration to Mexico was a courtesy to the United States. Officially stated reasons were that Mexico had provided comparatively low wages and an unsuitable climate.[17] By April 1908, Mexican diplomat Pacheco confirmed that Count Hayashi had agreed to stop Japanese emigration to Mexico in its entirety. However, if Mexico would need agricultural workers in the future, a reversal of the stop would be possible. Until then U.S. wishes would prevail.[18]

These agreements did create immediate change at the U.S.–Mexican border. In 1908, the U.S. immigration authority confirmed that the number of ethnic Japanese crossing into the United States had decreased significantly.[19]

On the political level, too, Japan and the U.S. government reached an understanding about the division of power in the Pacific. The resulting Root–Takahira Agreement of 1908 recognized a sphere of influence in the Pacific for both powers. Japan received support for the annexation of Korea and gained the status of a "special position" in Manchuria. The United States received recognition for its Open Door Policy in China but also assurances for the integrity and independence of China. The political powder keg of immigration also began to be defused. The smuggling of Japanese and Koreans into the United States was prohibited even when the emigrants' visas allowed them to work in Hawaii, Mexico, or Canada.

In April 1907, Japan's imperial diet allocated 4,000 yen to finance research about opening immigration to Brazil.[20] The government would await its outcome before a government license was issued to Brazil as an official destination.

The throttling and redirection of immigration did not affect the evolution of Japanese–Mexican trade relations. In October 1907, the Japanese ambassador returned to Japan for a vacation but also to work forcefully for an expansion of bilateral trade relations. In particular a permanent first shipping connection was to be established between Japan and the port of Salina Cruz, the head station of the strategic Tehuantepec Railroad.[21]

In 1909–10, a Japanese investment group in Osaka explored fishing operations along Mexico's west coast and conducted a coastal marine survey. Then a fishery contract was signed in 1911.[22] Military experts knew that a marine survey also carried information of military value about coastal geography.[23]

In Canada, the status of Japanese immigration also worsened. Initially Japanese and Canadian elites had expected that the signing of the 1906 British–Japanese Treaty of Commerce and Navigation would intensify and improve Japanese–Canadian relations. But Consul Kishiro Morikawa reported that popular opposition and xenophobia toward Japanese emigrants on the west coast only increased. Even worse, California labor organizations were reaching out to Canadian sympathizers. An occasional riot broke out.

The head of Japan's Bureau of Commerce, Count Ishii, agreed to explore informal agreements leading to a face-saving solution. In the end, in 1908, Canadian leaders agreed to the Lemieux–Ishii Agreement limiting Japanese immigration to Canada.[24] Japan's Foreign Minister Hayashi acquiesced to a policy of least resistance, giving entrance only to four hundred immigrants per year.

Now even plantation owners started their own lobbying campaign to convince Brazil's central government to subsidize a new Japan–Brazil shipping connection.[25] Still, they could not agree on the best route. One faction preferred to transport coffee beans and emigrants around South America. Their opponents preferred to go east, around Africa, including a stop in South Africa.[26] Suddenly, the momentum for Japanese immigration to Brazil stopped. In May 1906, Fukashi Sugimura, the strongest advocate of closer ties, died of a cerebral hemorrhage in Petrópolis. Overnight Brazil had lost its most skilled and influential advocate for Japanese immigration.

Redirecting emigration to South America was the other side of throttling Japanese emigration to Canada, the United States, and Mexico. A detailed study of the situation inside Mexico began. In October 1907, Mr. Yada, the second secretary of the Mexico City legation, was ordered to travel through all Mexican states and to assess the working conditions of emigrants.

He identified only two workplaces, in Chiapas and in one mine in Sonora, where laborers characterized their situation as content. Emigrants complained about bad food, insufficient pay, and harsh treatment. In particular U.S. employers seemed to treat Japanese emigrants poorly.

The diplomat Minoji Arakawa warned Tokyo that the many problems caused by emigration needed to be addressed in the immediate future, otherwise even Mexican leaders might object to a continuation of unregulated movement of emigrants.[27]

The issue of Japanese emigration to Mexico even generated discussion in Japanese newspapers. On November 20, 1907, the Japanese newspaper *Nishi Nishi Shinbun* cited a Japanese diplomat who blamed Mexico for its conditions. Because Mexico only had an upper class and a lower class, Mexico's politicians seemed uninterested in attracting a Japanese higher class wanting to stay in the country permanently and to contribute to the formation of a middle class.[28]

In April 1907, Japan's diet allocated 4,000 yen to finance research about immigration to Brazil. Once finished, the study of Brazil reported excellent prospects. Conditions in Brazil, in comparison to Australia, Canada, the United States, and Mexico, seemed ideal.[29] First, there existed no labor union activism against Japanese immigration. Second, growing emigration promised to create greater demand for the import of Japanese products. Third, the ambassador assured that massive, unobstructed immigration to South America would not cause friction in international politics.[30]

Already in 1905, Fukashi Sugimura, Tokyo's diplomat, had explored how Japanese labor emigration to Portuguese America could be made profitable. Previously, he had worked as director of the Foreign Ministry's Bureau of Commerce.[31]

First, Fukashi Sugimura lobbied Brazilian national and regional bureaucrats to support immigration from Japan. Second, in May 1905 he toured potential settlement areas in southern Brazil. He looked at port facilities, hotels, railroad transportation, and other state-supported colony projects. After his return he proposed a fare subsidy to finance a shipping connection between Brazil and Japan. Third, he suggested the opening of a Japanese consulate in Brazil's south to shape Japanese ethnic life as well as trade with Brazil.

As emigrants settled in southern Brazil, the diplomat predicted, demand for Japanese goods would go up. In the end regular Japanese–Brazilian trade would become sustainable.[32] His report arrived at Tokyo's Foreign Ministry on June 30, 1905. Thereafter he prepared to travel to Argentina to explore possible settlement sites in 1906.

Interestingly, Brazilian politicians traveled to the United States to examine for themselves any justifiable basis for anti-Japanese hatred in California and Texas. The emigrants they met made positive impressions. After their return, the Brazilian government appropriated 500 *contos* as an initial subsidy to a new navigation company connecting Japan with Brazil.[33]

In 1907, the new Japanese ambassador to Brazil, Sadatsuchi Uchida, resumed lobbying in favor of emigration expansion.[34] In the end his work showed success. Foreign Minister Hayashi accepted the recommendations of Ambassador Uchida, and on February 25, 1908, the Tokyo government allowed the Imperial

Emigration Company to send the first emigrants.[35] Brazil was beginning to turn from a country without Japanese immigration into its most important Latin American destination for immigrants in North and South America.

Leaders in Latin American states adopted new attitudes toward Japan. In the minds of Mexican and Central American policy makers, Japan was becoming a country whose politicians and soldiers could be courted to function, possibly, as a counterweight against the United States. Whereas before Latin American leaders appreciated France, Great Britain, and Germany as possible counterweights, now imperial Japan emerged as a power that could confront the United States.

Japan's rise encouraged, in particular, Mexican fantasies about a future, large U.S.–Japanese naval battle. Individuals close to the Mexican Díaz administration nourished an anxious hope that, somehow, Mexico could find a new, discrete ally in Japan to reduce the influence of the United States in Latin America.

Fortunately for U.S. leaders, Japanese naval and military leaders, for several years to come, established priorities based on their true strengths and remained focused on the Asian side of the Pacific. Also for Japanese business elites, emigration to Latin America, after the Russian–Japanese war, remained a normal business without hidden designs. It remained an economic expansion in which the presence of ethnic Japanese was expected to play a prominent role. Japanese trade expansion into South America would have taken place with or without the help of ethnic laborers and colonists. With growing anti-Japanese pressure in Australia, Canada, and the United States, Latin American countries along the Pacific west coast became more attractive.

*The Secret Warfare
That Established the Benchmark
for Future Allied War Fears
(1910–18)*

4   The Mexican Revolution

The First Complex Japanese Policy in Latin America beyond Diplomacy

E xpansion of Japanese trade finally came to include arms deliveries. For the first time, the Mitsui Company selected a permanent representative for Mexico. After years of activities by individual entrepreneurs and smaller companies, Mitsui, one of the large zaibatsus, a horizontally integrated multinational business, sold to the Díaz government. Military hardware sales were its business.

And Mexico was not the only Latin American country where Japanese arms manufacturers emerged, eager to compete against European suppliers. In 1908, the Bolivian military considered Japanese weapons in addition to establishing diplomatic relations with this rising power in anticipation of a possible U.S.–Japanese clash.[1]

In 1909, Chilean relations with Peru had deteriorated rapidly to the level of war breaking out. Peru's military forces expected backing from the United States. The Hungarian historian Ferenc Fischer discovered a German diplomatic report stating that the Japanese ambassador offered the Chilean armed forces military hardware, in anticipation of a Chilean–Peruvian war. Unnamed Japanese arms manufacturers, most likely including Mitsui, promised the delivery of all necessary equipment within thirty days. Never before had Japanese armament suppliers been involved so closely in a major inter-American military conflict.

A few Latin American voices registered the arrival of Japanese arms merchants and ties with Latin America governments as a concern. The Guatemalan president thought that Japanese diplomats in Central America were acting in inexplicable ways. He feared that Mexico might enter into a secret treaty with Japan. He too circulated rumors that Japan wanted to obtain a land base inside

Mexico. Rumors about Japanese government settlers wanting to disrupt the construction of the Panama Canal were rampant.[2]

Of course, Latin American general publics remained unaware of the increasingly complex Japanese–Latin American relations. What they saw was Japan's participation at Mexico's 100th Anniversary of Independence Celebration in 1910.[3]

In 1910, the Japanese Empire dispatched to Mexico's anniversary celebration not just a token delegation crossing the Pacific on a regular civilian ship. Instead, it dispatched the navy vessel *Iumora*. A small delegation of the *Iumora*, led by Japanese admiral Moriyama, disembarked in Manzanillo, Acapulco, and began a long trek toward Mexico City. Once in Mexico City days of celebration of the deepening Mexican–Japanese friendship began. Mexican secretary of war General Manuel González Cosio hosted a banquet at a Chapultepec café.

After the toasts of the Mexican officers, Admiral Moriyama spoke words that tried to identify the aspects that Japan and Mexico were sharing in 1910. He mentioned the braveness of soldiers, the location of both capitals in a valley at the foot of a snow-covered volcano, and that Mexican and Japanese flags of war were both composed of red, white, and green segments. In Japan, a large green band was added to a unit flag once it distinguished itself in battle. The admiral exclaimed,

> Let us drink to the progress and prosperity of both nations because some day, in the not very distant time, Mexican and Japanese armies will be seen crowned with glory, united and, I want you to know, that if at any time the Mexican people should become involved in an international conflict, Japan will feel honored to endeavor to give full support, especially if some neighboring countries should be concerned.[4]

In 1910, a mid-level Japanese naval representative painted the scenario of a future U.S.–Mexican war and held out the potential of Japanese military assistance. His words symbolized how fast and how much Japanese–Latin American relations had changed since the Japanese victory over Russia in 1905.

But it was Mexican officials who advocated further deepening of the Mexican–Japanese bond. In the capital President Díaz went to great lengths to treat Japanese diplomats, navy officers, and big-business representatives as equals to European and U.S. diplomats. When the topic of a possible U.S.–Japanese war came up Díaz promised a Japanese diplomat neutrality. In Tokyo, the Mexican ambassador used darker words. A U.S.–Japanese war, it was hoped, would distract or even weaken Washington and, therefore, offer Mexico "more breathing space."[5] Tokyo's elites deflected discussing the issue whenever the idea of a war was raised.

8. A newly discovered picture of a Japanese navy delegation posing for a souvenir photo in Mexico City (Library of Congress, Washington, D.C.).

Still, Japan and President Díaz, in the words of U.S. historian William Schell, enjoyed their strategic flirtation. The Mexican president had become confident enough to pursue a complex policy, consisting of cultural, diplomatic, naval, and economic ties. Díaz hoped to move toward a "Mexican symbiosis with the Orient," and Mexico would become a supplier of raw materials and oil for industrialization, shipped by the Japanese rather than the American merchant marine.[6] The president, determinedly, presented Japanese–Mexican ties as an alternative to those with the United States. Months thereafter, Díaz's son was talked about as a likely candidate for ambassador to Tokyo.

Reactions to the words from both sides caused enough attention and worry in diplomatic circles that in March 1911, in Tokyo, Count Komura emerged to address the issue informally. The elite politician assured the German diplomat Montgelas that rumors about a possible Japanese–Mexican alliance against the United States were baseless. Correctly the German ambassador wrote to the

German chancellor in Berlin that Japan's political elite remained opposed to a Mexico–Japan alliance.

Mexican diplomats saw the situation differently. For them the "diplomatic glass" was half full, not half empty. Mexican diplomat Pacheco, posted in Tokyo, affirmed that in the last years a spontaneous rapprochement between Japan and Mexico had taken place. Furthermore, he insisted that Mexico and Japan were tied to each other by identical racial roots. This transpacific social tie had blossomed after the Japanese victory over the Russians. Both shared an undesirability for U.S. citizens. Finally, the establishment of a direct Mexican–Japanese shipping connection was bringing the two countries closer economically. Only the idea of an offensive or defensive alliance remained unaddressed.

Mexican diplomats enjoyed thinking about Mexican–Japanese ties in starkly symbolic anti-U.S. terms. One expressed nationalist pleasure by mentioning that Wilhelm II was currently asserting an independent stance in Mexico, asserting a German interest during the emerging revolution. He understood this as a clear rejection of the United States, the Monroe Doctrine, and any U.S. sense of entitlement to act as custodian of the entire world.[7]

President Díaz and his diplomats did not experience the fruition of their strategic flirtation. In 1911, Mexican politicians and peasants with a domestic outlook began sustained regional revolutions that made it impossible to predict future Mexican foreign policy. It became increasingly uncertain to say who defined foreign policy in Mexico and who was Mexico's authentic voice in foreign affairs.

Interestingly, even though Mexico plummeted deeper and deeper into revolution Japanese–Mexican ties never severed. To the contrary, most major revolutionaries who gained temporary control of Mexico explored, in some fashion, the revival of the strategic flirtation with Japan.

After Díaz's fall, Interim President Francisco de la Barra maintained business relations with a Japanese syndicate eager to operate in Mexico. Thereafter, President Madero continued the contact.[8] His brother Eduardo could be seen in a photo preparing for a state visit to Japan that never took place.[9] Then the counterrevolutionary General Huerta established himself long enough as Mexican dictator so that he could devote time to a substantive revival of ties.

Huerta was a masterful manipulator and always saw ties with Japan as a channel that would help him militarily against the Constitutionalist revolutionaries who were determined to drive him out of office. He began negotiations about Japanese arms deliveries in the first half of 1913. Talks concluded on June 2, 1913, when his Mexican army and Mitsui signed an initial agreement for the purchase of fifty thousand rifles. A second purchase negotiation for twenty-five thousand carbines was concluded on July 21, 1913. In August, Huerta bought seventy-five hundred artillery shells.[10] In other words, in 1913, Japan's Mitsui moved next to French, German, and U.S. arms suppliers, conquering a growing share of the Mexican arms market.

Mitsui was represented by T. Onodera. When he did not broker weapons deals he worked as correspondent for the Tokyo newspaper *Asahi Shinbun*. Also he played a leading role inside the ethnic Japanese community of Mexico, serving as head of the Japanese residential organization Sociedad Japonesa de Mexico. Onodera could act in these three capacities without the professional restrictions of a diplomat but still with key access to revolutionary factions and government ministers living in Mexico City and Tokyo.[11]

Mitsui took a second step and offered the sale of machinery that could produce weapons. In August 1913, Mitsui representatives explored a joint venture with Huerta. By then the U.S. government had imposed an arms embargo against him, and his need for a nationally based arms manufacturer was painfully obvious.[12] National arms manufacture would strengthen Huerta's stance against the gathering revolutionary opposition, which supplied itself freely from abroad. The U.S. administration was aware of Huerta's talks with Japan but did not want to intervene at that point. Weapons talks never stopped. In October 1913, General Manuel M. Velazquez sailed to Japan to receive the Mitsui weapons.[13]

In June 1913, Huerta turned the arrival of newly appointed Japanese Ambassador Adachi into a spectacle. The ambassador had traveled on the battleship *Izumo* and was accompanied by a vice admiral who followed the ambassador to the capital. Huerta used the admiral's presence to launch a week-long cross-Pacific celebration, an honor that he did not extend to French or German boats and their captains. At the Mexico City train station Mexican children waving Japanese flags welcomed both men.[14] Huerta's demonstrative courting of Japan was rewarded with positive results.

Ambassador Adachi was inspired by the exuberant welcome and the expressions of friendship. Not surprisingly, he advised Tokyo to develop two policies toward the Americas. The first and most important one would remain the U.S.–Japanese relationship. But a second one should focus on Japanese–Mexican relations. Adachi lectured his superiors that Japan was a country "behind in the expansionist race in Latin America, Japan should follow the same policies that the other Western Powers had taken."[15] The ideal occasion to take this important step was the Mexican Revolution, and Huerta's economic, political, and military needs were vehicles that could bring about Japan's entry into the imperial contest over Latin America. But all Huerta knew was what Japanese politicians might be interested in.

On July 19, *El Diario* reported that longtime Japanese residents had approached the Huerta administration to obtain new land for settlement. Rumors had it that the entire state of Morelos was under consideration for lease to Japan for colonization. Of course, this would have been a cruel, cynical offer as the entire state of Morelos was in the midst of Emiliano Zapata and his villagers' revolutionary fight for life. Huerta would have tossed immigrants in the midst of a deadly war zone.

The Japanese historian Kunimoto declares these approaches to be empty gestures without serious intent behind them.[16] Still, Gilberto Ramirez cites German Ambassador Kardoff as reporting similar, alleged Japanese explorations to Berlin on July 27, 1913. A third source reports that Huerta's foreign minister Moheno discussed plans with interested Japanese partners that other diplomats classified as "insane."[17]

Next Huerta tried to kill two birds with one stone. He removed Félix Díaz, his rival and Porfirio Díaz's nephew, by appointing him ambassador to Japan. This appointment, however, was also an attempt to deepen the Mexican–Japanese bond. And in Japan the gesture was understood.

In mid-July 1913, Mexico's secretary of foreign relations sent a telegram to Luis G. Pardos in Mexico's Tokyo legation asking him to communicate the appointment of General Félix Díaz as next Mexican ambassador to Japan. The diplomat did as told. He walked to the Japanese Foreign Ministry and asked for Díaz's official accreditation. He was told that, first, the emperor himself would have to be consulted. The Foreign Ministry asked for patience. It would take a few days to receive the emperor's answer. More importantly, the Mexican diplomat was given the impression that it would be best for Félix Díaz to await further notice while still being on the American continent.

Three days later, the Japanese vice minister of foreign affairs called the Mexican diplomat and informed him that the Japanese emperor would be absent the entire summer. Besides, his health was very delicate, and therefore nobody could say when the emperor would return. Ideally General Díaz should postpone his departure until the emperor was well again. After his return to Tokyo he could be expected to welcome Díaz personally.

On the American side of the Pacific, the Mexican Foreign Ministry and General Díaz realized that these reasons were merely a pretext, to avoid a more embarrassing situation. Japan's elite politicians were not yet willing to engage publicly in the close ties Mexico's bureaucrats, arms dealers, and diplomats had become accustomed to.

General Díaz did not give up easily. He continued his journey up the U.S. coast and asked his diplomat in Tokyo to visit the Japanese Foreign Ministry a second time and to insist on his immediate accreditation.

The second time the ministry promised a more concrete answer in the near future. Still it asked that Díaz's trip across the Pacific should be postponed. If Díaz were to come to Japan he would be welcomed only as an individual but not as a diplomatic representative. An official recognition would depend entirely on the emperor, and he could not be contacted right now.

Félix Díaz had left Mexico and entered the United States at San Diego, California. From there he continued to Los Angeles. There he learned that Mexican diplomats in Tokyo were continuing to work on his behalf. Thus Díaz traveled on to Portland, Oregon, from where a third telegram petitioning accreditation was sent. General Díaz arrived in Seattle on August 9, 1913, and stayed for two days. Newspapers wrote that he was approaching Vancouver, B.C., to take a boat to Japan.

In public speculations circulated as to why Díaz was being sent to Japan. Journalists argued that he was sent away because he was a political rival to General Huerta. Or perhaps he was to travel to Japan to arrange a treaty that would offer Japan previously unknown privileges in the sectors of trade and economy. Díaz himself offered a third version. He told Canadian reporters that his visit represented a Mexican thank-you mission reciprocating Japan's 1910 visit to the Mexican independence celebration.

The Japanese business community in the United States and Japanese American leaders were enthusiastic about Díaz's prospects and did their utmost to contribute to his future success in Tokyo. In Seattle, he was received by the Japanese consul and a small delegation of Japanese and Japanese Americans. The next day he met with a former Japanese minister of finance, Dr. Juichi Soyeda, and honorary member and secretary of the Tokyo Chamber of Commerce Tadao Kamiya. A private reception of Japanese Americans or Japanese businessmen took place on August 10.

The following morning, Díaz took the boat to Vancouver, hoping to catch the *Empress of Russia* to his final destination in Japan. Within the next forty-eight hours, however, everything changed. On August 12, Díaz received a firm final rejection from Japan.[18]

From Tokyo the secretary of the Mexican legation reacted with outrage. He demanded that Japan should suffer consequences for making Mexico look weak in public. But he also communicated how much Japanese society, bureaucrats, and businessmen had been open to deepening ties with Huerta. He explained to Díaz in a letter:

> While the government would not have recognized you, officially the public in general would have received you as the most favorite ambassador and a most elaborate reception had been planned, wherein all classes of society were to take part. I am certain that the House of Mitsui, the Rothschilds of Japan, and Mr. Asano, President of Tokyo Kishan Kaisha S.S. Co. had prepared festivals and banquets for you, as well as [would] have been done by several societies and merchants of this part in Tokyo. If you should come out when parliament opens you might have brought about the downfall of the present government.[19]

This exaggerated description indicates how much Japanese mid-level sectors and select groups remained interested in Mexico, in 1913, even though the Mexican government was rapidly falling out of favor with the U.S. Wilson administration. Japanese companies selling weapons, trade, and shipping saw no problem doing business with Huerta.

From Tokyo, a German diplomat offered additional details. On July 28, he remarked that journalists were beginning to appreciate Mexico as a racial brethren. Stormy Mexican contestations of friendship were accepted with pleasure and satisfaction also because U.S.–Mexican differences seemed to intensify.

Tokyo's public embarrassment about the General Félix Díaz accreditation seemed strong. On August 18, the *Japan Times* wrote that diplomatic negotiation between the two countries had been postponed. Previously, papers close to the Bureaucratic Party had asked the Japanese people to prepare themselves for Díaz's visit and offered him and his group a heartfelt reception. Now three newspapers, representing factions opposed to the Yamamoto government, used the Díaz event to criticize it. His rejection was interpreted as a sign of inability and a hesitation of Japanese diplomacy.

The Osaka paper *Asahi* explained that an alliance between Japan and Mexico could come about by knowing about each other, trusting each other, and sharing interests. The Japanese did not yet know Mexico enough, and Díaz's visit would have helped in this regard. Once again, the papers invoked that Japan and Mexico shared the same ancestors and, therefore, they remained connected: "The love between Japan and Mexico was older than the hostile attitude between Mexico and the United States." One article suggested that a Japanese individual might have traveled by boat to Mexico before Europeans arrived in 1521. Journalists could not understand why Japanese leaders did not express more interest in Mexico: "They thought that Japan's expansion was possible and no opportunity should be wasted." For them Japan was a mighty country and powerful. It should no longer engage in such timid diplomacy vis-à-vis the United States. Such aggressive, expansionist Japanese factions put forward vivid scenarios. Japan, in theory, could conquer the Philippines and the Hawaiian islands, even land troops in Mexico. Some stated that it might be possible to defeat the U.S. navy since Japanese ships were superior over the U.S. fleet.

But others argued that after a successful landing of Japanese troops, the U.S. government would never tolerate the presence of Japanese in either Mexico, Hawaii, or the Philippine Islands. More importantly, the United States was perceived as strong enough to build a new second fleet in order to fight a second naval battle with Japan. In contrast, Japan's larger industry was expected to refuse to make available similarly large resources to launch a second war. As long as this assessment was correct Japanese diplomats were certain that the government "took the matches out of the hands of the chauvinists, asking the Mexican government to postpone the dispatch of General Díaz for an undetermined time."[20]

Change next originated from the political activism of the Japanese ambassadors in Mexico and Brazil. Even though at the Tokyo elite level, interest in Latin America did not figure prominently, Japanese ambassadors working on the continent acted as ardent salesmen in favor of intensifying Japanese–Latin American connections. In Brazil, from 1905 on, Ambassador Shugijama was the force that laid down the groundwork that made Brazil the largest recipient of Japanese immigrants after 1908.

In 1913, Ambassador Mineichiro Adachi in Mexico insisted on an activist role. He wanted more than just a show of Japan's flag in Mexico's ports. Just like imperial Great Britain, Germany, Austria-Hungary, the Papacy, France, Spain, and the United States, he wanted Japan to take sides in the revolution. The rejection of Félix Díaz, in retrospect, was only an irritation in the evolving Japanese–Mexican relationship.

Mineichiro Adachi urged Tokyo's leaders to assume a distinctly different political stance toward Latin America and to pursue it independently from the Japanese–U.S. relationship. On the one hand, the turbulence of Mexican revolutions required diplomats to proceed with political flexibility and wisdom. On the other hand, the intensifying ups and downs after President Madero's murder also created opportunities to develop a Japanese Mexican policy that was no longer dominated by the needs of the U.S.–Japanese relationship.

Japanese diplomats moved in this direction, apparently in disregard of official guidelines from Tokyo. Even though the Foreign Ministry continued to prohibit its diplomats from granting political asylum to Latin American politicians—and therefore keep Japan from being caught up in Latin America revolutions—interestingly already in 1912, Japan's ambassador had provided temporary shelter to the surviving family members of the murdered President Francisco Madero.[21]

Now, Adachi argued in favor of a more assertive naval presence off Mexico's coast. Tokyo's navy should dispatch imperial warships to assure the physical safety of ethnic Japanese in Mexico. Such a decision would only follow what the navies of Great Britain, Germany, and the United States were doing.[22] More ships off Mexico would get other foreign powers used to the idea that a Japanese naval presence in the American Pacific was a normal, acceptable practice. Why should Japanese naval missions be limited to the western Pacific only?

Tokyo's Foreign Office conferred first with its ambassador to Washington. Since he did not object, Tokyo's bureaucrats followed Adachi's suggestion, and the navy dispatched more warships to Mexican harbors. Soon came the battleship *Izumo*, the flagship of its second squadron, which had fought and defeated the Russian navy during the Russian–Japanese war. Its commander was not an average captain but Vice Admiral Denzo Mori.

After *Izumo*'s arrival Denzo Mori eagerly accepted an invitation from Victoriano Huerta, assembled a visiting delegation, and traveled for days across rugged mountain ranges until he and his men arrived in Mexico City. There, the Japanese visitors enjoyed a high-level reception that lasted five days.

Huerta regrouped fast following the diplomatic embarrassment over Félix Díaz's diplomatic accreditation months before. First, in November 1913, Huerta sent a fifty-year-old brigade general to Tokyo as military attaché. He was expected to stay until summer 1914 and function as chief of a six-men-strong weapons purchasing commission. He was politically outspoken and did not hide his enmity against the United States. By then Japanese shipping companies were transporting weapons to Mexico hidden under loads of coal.[23]

Second, Huerta selected former interim president de la Barra to travel to Japan. Once again the official reason was that of a thank-you visit in response to Japan's visit to the hundred-year anniversary.

Tokyo welcomed this Mexican diplomat. His visit became a subtle demonstration of mutual interest, even in times of revolution and strong anti-U.S. policy.

Francisco de la Barra was received in December 1913 with highest honors.[24] A variety of aristocrats, company leaders, and government ministers courted the

Mexican representative, just as Huerta had courted the Japanese ambassador and admiral in the summer of 1913.

It quickly became obvious that the Mexican visit was more than saying thank you for the 1910 Japanese visit to Mexico. De la Barra engaged in extensive political talks. Foreign Minister Makino discussed bilateral relations with de la Barra at least six times. Historian of Mexico William Schell suggests that the talks might have included discussions about the use of Mexico's Magdalena Bay as a refueling location by the Japanese navy. He suggests that the folders in one Mexican archive show that General Huerta went further. The Condumex Archive contains a folder that is labeled in such a way as to suggest that Huerta explored linking Japanese arms supplies with Mexican support for Japanese use of Magdalena Bay. The record has not yet been accessible to scholars.[25]

On December 25, 1913, Francisco de la Barra received a public pro-Mexico celebration in Japan's capital. The zaibatsus Mitsui and Shibusawa eagerly courted the guest of honor. Rather than sending company managers, the Barons Mitsui and Shibusawa personally talked with de la Barra.[26] Both gave him the impression that they were very interested in forging closer economic ties with Mexico.[27]

Talks concluded with Foreign Minister Makino suggesting the duplication of a joint statement proclaiming a bright new future in Japanese–Mexican ties. Suddenly, de la Barra became cautious. At that time a too-public announcement indicating a deepening of Mexican–Japanese bonds might send the wrong signal internationally, in particular to anti-Japanese critics inside the United States. Thus the Mexican delegation leader asked the Japanese foreign minister to refrain from publishing the desired statement of appreciation.

But honors continued. First the Mexican delegation was received by the emperor of Japan. The royal court displayed great skill and elegance, signaling continued but discrete interest in Mexico. Royal displays of respect and honor remained within normal limits. The emperor invited them to a breakfast and organized a royal hunt. There Mr. de la Barra met Tokyo's most important personalities from the world of finance, commerce, and the press as well as representatives of Latin American embassies.

Tokyo's population and press were again more enthusiastic than the elites. Newspaper articles were friendly and demanded a more celebratory treatment. De la Barra was supposed to have been picked up at the train station and housed in the emperor's palace, not a hotel.

Indeed, de la Barra received the public honor of a torch parade on December 26, 1913. At least two speakers addressed him with special tributes and presented him with two swords and a samurai uniform. From there, the parade moved on to the

Mexican legation, where its diplomat showered de la Barra with profuse praise.[28] De la Barra left Tokyo on December 20 to travel through the country, including a trip to the tomb of Emperor Momomaya.[29] At the very end of the visit, de la Barra received the highest medal a former Latin American president had ever received in Tokyo.

After his return to the increasingly beleaguered Mexican capital, de la Barra reported to General Huerta that Japanese companies wanted to deepen economic ties. In addition, he brought with him a shipment of fifteen thousand Mitsui rifles and a promise that a Mexican–Japanese small arms factory could be delivered in the near future.[30]

But Huerta, by then, was under dire straits. Any Japanese help would have to concentrate first on keeping him in office in Chapultepec Castle. Otherwise, a different revolutionary president would assemble and use the Japanese arms manufacture technologies. Japanese support for Huerta had to mean strengthening him against the United States, Brazil, Argentina, and Chile, which wanted his resignation and democratic elections. In late 1913, the Japanese ambassador abandoned his previously cautious moves and became outright pro-Huerta.

Until December 1913, Adachi had helped Huerta with the financing of the Mitsui weapons purchases. And when unemployed Japanese emigrants had been found stranded along the U.S.–Mexican border, he had advocated sending them to Calexico, near the U.S. border, despite ongoing, intense local racism and the provisions of the U.S.–Japanese gentlemen's agreement.[31] When U.S. Marines had landed personnel in Veracruz, Ambassador Adachi had shared with the wife of U.S. embassy staffer O'Shaugnessy that he was intervening diplomatically on behalf of Huerta.[32] Skillfully, he followed the example of Germany, which had allowed British forces to take the lead against the United States, hiding in Great Britain's shadow.

Now, in 1914, Adachi advised his superiors in Tokyo to exploit a possible U.S.–Mexican war. Adachi told Tokyo to manipulate U.S.–Mexican tensions to realize its own policy goals vis-à-vis the United States. Unless he heard otherwise from his superiors he would help Huerta, that is, increase tensions in the U.S.–Mexican relationship.[33] This was unprecedented diplomatic activism by a Japanese ambassador in Latin America.

A third step was financial relief for Huerta. Adachi advised his superiors to purchase Mexican debt, bringing financial relief to Huerta. He claimed that Vice Admiral Denzo Mori, during his visit to Mexico City, had examined some Mexican government accounts and declared them to be satisfactory. Japanese investment in Mexican government debt could lift General Huerta's financial isolation and provide at least temporary financial breathing space for his embattled dictatorship.[34]

The Huerta administration reciprocated such dedicated new Japanese political affection. At a dinner, Mexican foreign minister Lopez Portillo y Rojas implied to diplomats Mexico's desire for Japanese support, though he did not state it directly.[35] Even more important symbolically, Huerta personally asked Japan to take over the administration of Mexican embassies and consulates inside the United States, in case U.S. president Wilson would invade Mexico and a Mexican–U.S. war would break out.

It was a devilish offer, a move that could create all kinds of misunderstandings in the minds of the U.S. public and the Wilson administration. Suddenly, Tokyo's political elites pulled back from engagement. Still, by January 1914, in Washington, D.C., Adachi's activism was becoming a topic of discussion between U.S. secretary of state Lansing and the Japanese ambassador to the United States.[36]

Only then did Tokyo's foreign minister Kato reign in Adachi and assert the U.S.–Japanese relationship as the priority in the Americas. He declined General Huerta's offer to take over Mexican embassies inside the United States.[37] Even Prime Minister Shigenoby Okuma tried to repair the damage his ambassador had created and issued an official statement clarifying Japan's attitude vis-à-vis Mexico. In case of a U.S.–Mexican war, imperial Japan would remain neutral. Also, Adachi should no longer involve himself in the purchase of additional artillery for Huerta. The backdoor of Mitsui's weapons for Mexico was beginning to close.

These Japanese–Mexican discussions and tentative explorations of differentiated ties were communicated to Germany and began to educate the German chancellor about Mexico's ongoing flirtations with as many Japanese leaders and companies as were willing to engage. They raised awareness among leaders in Berlin that the anti-U.S. faction in Mexico might become a conduit for pulling Japan, at best, closer to Germany but, at least, further away from the United States.[38]

While Japan's government tried to reassure the U.S. diplomat of strategic military disinterest, a Japanese commodore secretly conducted Japan's first major military intelligence inspection of Mexico. In February 1914, Admiral Keizaburo Moriyama and his cruiser docked again in Manzanillo, Mexico. Squadron leader Commodore Denzo Mori was again on board. By now he was about thirty-three years old and very well educated. He spoke not only Spanish but also French, English, German, and Italian. Previously, after distinguishing himself in the Russian–Japanese war he had held positions in Germany, France, and Italy.[39]

Denzo Mori started the long horse trip from Manzanillo to Mexico City for a private audience with General Huerta. The Japanese commodore asked for and received permission to inspect the key land route along Mexican railroad lines going north toward the U.S. border. This railroad would function as the central line to move troops toward the U.S. border. If Japanese troops would ever land along the middle Pacific coast and reach Mexico City, this railroad would carry them along the same route that French troops had traveled to El Paso, Texas, in the 1860s.

While in the Mexican capital he shared basic information about the mobilization of Japanese troops. He told his Mexican listeners about an agreement between the Japanese navy and merchant marine that would allow the transport of large amounts of troops, if so ordered. The Japanese merchant marine could be summoned to Japan by shortwave radio.

General Huerta gave Denzo Mori one Mexican commander and two officers to accompany him on his trip through revolutionary Mexico. They received the most generous letters of recommendation by Minister of War Blanquet and were guarded by one regiment of lancers. In March 1914, they reached Guanajuato and toured Jalisco and Colima at key locations. Commodore Denzo made systematic notes about Mexican military barracks, hospitals, public buildings, railway workshops, smelters, and fortifications. This included taking photographs of the conditions of roads, soil, and industrial sites. Denzo preserved this data in a notebook that he carried in his baggage at all times.

From Mexico's lower west coast his train crossed central Mexico toward the strategic ports of Veracruz and Tampico. There too he took countless photographs and discussed the unloading of troops. Then the group turned north.

At San Luis Potosi Denzo Mori studied the capacity of its railroad intersection. He perceived this location as a critical place to reach the U.S. border. Other strategic cities visited were Torreón, Monterey, and Aguascalientes. During this phase of the trip an informer heard him say a second time that these locations could function as "great strategic stations in case of a conflict with the U.S." He added that with good military leadership and suitable preparations, Mexico "had no reason to fear the exaggerated power of the Yankees."

In Torreón Denzo was honored with a banquet where various generals stationed in the Mexican north celebrated him. During the dinner he exclaimed in French to his translator, "The power of the U.S. would fall. When Mexican and Japanese troops advance by way of a lovely town of the Laguna region they would cover themselves with glory and conquer the proud colossus of the North."

The Japanese commodore made a second statement urging an eventual attack on the United States. In Aguascalientes, at a banquet held at General Ruelas's private residence, he said "that it was necessary to overthrow the power of the United States at all cost and that someday there might be a Mexican–Japanese alliance because the United States wants to monopolize the commerce of the world and the U.S. wants to weaken Mexico to use her freely."

Denzo characterized U.S. support for the Constitutionalists during the revolution as a first step to dismember Mexico, which the United States was looking forward to. And "when Mexico would be defenseless then the U.S. would fall upon it like the snake would fall upon the helpless rabbit which it has hypnotized."

By now the Mexican interpreter had no doubt what Denzo was doing in Mexico. Visual confirmation happened one morning:

One morning I went to see Mori at his hotel. . . . I went to his sitting room or study and saw on his table, a map up of the United States and half of the Mexican Republic and on which were various arrows indicating invasions of the United States with explanations with each arrow. . . . When the Commodore came out of his bedroom he hastily covered the map with some papers, but I did not show that I had seen it or that it had attracted my attention.

The map also showed the Hawaiian Islands and signs of occasional updates. U.S. fears about Japanese military skills were justified. It was wrong to brush them aside simply as racism or xenophobia.

From Tokyo newspaper editors and informed observers watched Huerta's decline. At the end of April 1914, a German diplomat reported that the hostilities between the United States and Mexico were finding great interest in Japan. Political insiders still warned against Japan appearing to be in favor of Mexico. And Count Komura had to reassure interested observers that any Mexican hope for or U.S. suspicion of Japanese actions was not justified. He insisted that Japan had no important interest in Mexico and remained focused on China, where it wanted to act in concert with other powers as pursuing a peaceful policy. In case of Mexican–U.S. war Japan would observe unequivocal neutrality.[40]

Tokyo had declined to represent Mexico diplomatically in the United States, claiming to lack sufficient numbers of consulates along the U.S.–Mexican border. German admiral Hintze reported that the Japanese press, in particular the paper *Nishi Nishi*, criticized this stance as meek.[41]

Dictator Huerta did his utmost to hang on to power, even if it meant experimenting with racial clashes along the U.S.–Mexican border. He spent 300,000 pesos to pay bandits inside Texas to attack U.S. citizens and U.S. properties. Small clashes with bandits were supposed to cause an overreaction by the U.S. army. He sent Generals Argumedo and Rojas toward the border with the task of organizing uprisings. General Rincon Gallardo focused on recruiting groups in Zacatecas for this purpose.[42] Japan did know about this strategy three years before the Zimmerman Telegram.

In July 1914, the opening for Japan created by Huerta's counterrevolution was closing. The Constitutionalists and the U.S., Argentine, and Chilean governments proved strong enough to force Huerta's resignation from the presidential office. Huerta survived. He and his family traveled on British and German navy vessels into Spanish exile. World War I was beginning in Europe and the Near East, providing even greater opportunities for Japan to intervene in conflicts along the Latin American Pacific coast.

In Europe German military leaders were about to embark on another limited imperial war against France and Russia, believing that Great Britain would happily remain neutral. Nobody fathomed that it would mushroom into World War I.

5   Four Waves of Secret Warfare

The First Wave: Seven Targets for Secret Commando Raids

The German army and German diplomats, beginning in 1914, pushed ethnic communities further toward becoming a security threat. Previously, the German navy had selected and inducted only a small number of German Americans to provide clandestine assistance during an imperial war, most likely against Great Britain. They would supply warships in violation of international law and support economic warfare fought along North and South American coasts. Germany had created a noteworthy secret fighting force stationed on American continents. Some Germans appreciated exquisite music and expressive paintings but also extensive espionage.

But in 1914, planners also reimagined ethnic communities as active players in secret war campaigns. In these secret campaigns the emotions and longings of immigrants and their descendants inside the Americas would play a critical role. The price was the innocence of ethnic minorities' lives.

In July 1914, in London and Berlin, there remained hope in elite political circles that the current political crisis would remain contained. But in August, the British cabinet did not act as Germans had hoped. The British and their Japanese ally entered the war and joined Russian and French efforts. German hopes for British neutrality had crashed. Limited European war rapidly mushroomed into a global confrontation, pulling in distant colonies and ethnic minorities on every continent. Now, this was an unprecedented clash between imperial powers and their industrial war machines.

This war transformed theoretical explorations of secret warfare from before

1914 into damaging acts. From the very beginning strategies of ethnic subversion and manipulation dovetailed with industrial warfare.

U.S. and Latin American policy makers learned that European powers disregarded their national sovereignty and appealed to minorities to participate in war on the side of their ethnic origin, rather than obey the law in their country of residence or new citizenship. For the first time in the twentieth century secret warfare was acted out inside Canada, the United States, and Latin America.

The lesson was crude but promising. The manipulation of American ethnic minorities done at the right time could provide the final push to collapse an empire or deprive critical resources that were needed on European battlefields. At the very least ethnic subversion could attain painful concessions at the negotiation table. The tactic was not pretty and not the least sophisticated, but, as we will see, it would generate a significant amount of fear and mayhem. After 1919 these experiences provided the benchmark for the 1920s and World War II.

The following can only provide a summary of activities. Like the British, imperial Berlin and Japan instrumentalized ethnic groups in the Americas without asking them, establishing facts that caused suspicion vis-à-vis ethnic groups inside the United States.

By 1913, German navy planners had prepared for limited naval engagements against British or U.S. naval forces along Pacific and Atlantic coastlines. As long as possible they would use neutral and select Latin American harbors as staging grounds for very limited naval supply activity and economic warfare.

Navy planners, thinking in terms of cruisers and sailors, had not foreseen that the first war campaign would not focus on naval issues at all. The first struggle between German and British forces focused on the financing of global war.

German and British planners expected that the United States would remain neutral during war. Thus in August 1914, both governments sent specialists to New York to explore how to obtain raw materials and enlist factories and financial resources within the framework of the laws of neutrality.

On August 10, 1914, Bernhard Dernburg, former German minister of colonial affairs and friend of German banking circles, traveled to Hamburg to meet General Director Albert Ballin. Ballin was a close adviser of Emperor Wilhelm II and the director of Germany's largest international shipping agency, called Hapag Lloyd. Ballin and Dernburg met to prepare a trip by Dernburg to New York for the purpose of raising US$100,000,000 for the empire.[1]

Initially, they imagined that this trip would unfold just as previous business loan negotiations had. The German offer was expected to attract U.S. investors since it was secured by German government treasury notes. Later it was intended to finance a camouflaged raw material–purchasing organization. It would be operated as a New York branch office of a "Central Purchasing Office" headquartered in Berlin.

The New York branch office would be run by Heinrich F. Albert, who would accompany Dernburg to the United States. In public, Albert was to act as a private businessman. Inside his New York office, however, he would manage a sophisticated war material–purchasing operation—everything from negotiations with U.S. businessmen to account management to, finally, the transport of raw materials on the ships of the Hapag Shipping Agency to German factories to make weapons.[2] Albert's office would buy manufactured goods, raw material, and also weapons and supplies. He would also scout the U.S. markets for Midwestern wheat and oils as well as cotton from the U.S. South.

Dernburg and Albert left Hamburg and crossed the Atlantic by boat. Their ship maneuvered without damage through intensifying naval blockade warfare and docked in New York City on August 23, 1914. They immediately opened an office at Broadway No. 41-45, the same building that housed the Hapag Shipping Agency.

As planned, the two men contacted acquaintances in private banking circles. While U.S. neutrality laws prohibited the granting of government loans to nations at war, private banks could provide money and loans to anyone they liked. Legally, it was seen as just business, not as a political act. Dernburg and Albert expected to easily find a private bank willing to be associated with Germany.[3] Their efforts did not differ from similar attempts by French, British, and Russian negotiators trying to find money for their war efforts in the United States.

Previously, British wars had been financed, most often, by the House of Rothschild. This British–Rothschild cooperation had required the creation of branch offices in Europe, Latin America, and Asia but not in the United States. Now, without a Rothschild branch office on Wall Street, the U.S. bankers of the House of Morgan saw an opportunity to fund the British. Moreover, they already maintained a banking branch in London, and majority owner Jack Morgan held pro-British sentiments. In September, his bank financed a $12,000,000 war credit for imperial Russia. One month later it began to procure not just money but also weapons for the tsar.[4]

U.S. private bankers approached this war in a much more partisan fashion than previous wars. Influential bankers disregarded a neutral profit motive and rushed into nationalist partisanship.

Previously, German war efforts had enjoyed the help of the bank of Kuehn, Loeb and Speyer Co. But now that they were asked to fund a British–German clash, pro-British board members vetoed the requests of Dernburg and Albert, still canvassing Manhattan for money for the Prussian army.[5] After several weeks of gentleman-like meetings in luxurious Wall Street bank offices, Dernburg and Albert had to report to Berlin that they could not find one bank willing to float a substantial loan for Germany. The largest Wall Street companies chose Great Britain over Germany. Midsize and smaller companies fell into line and followed their lead, with a few notable exceptions of ethnic German and Irish bankers. Economic warfare in 1914 proved as difficult as battlefield maneuvers.

In Europe and Asia, the German campaigns did not unfold as planned. Violating neutral Belgium, the German general Hellmuth von Moltke failed to win a quick victory against the French. The British entry on the side of the Allies was an unmitigated disaster for Germany. To make matters worse, Japan eagerly exploited the confusion in Europe, executed the terms of its naval alliance with Great Britain, and occupied German possessions along the Chinese coastline. By mid-September 1914, General von Moltke was asked to resign.

The surprises kept coming. The Turks in the Ottoman Empire decided to defy the London government and to annex Egypt, bordering on the Suez Canal. By November 1914, Japanese navy ships hunted German naval forces not only along China's coast but, jointly with the British navy, along the Canadian, U.S., and Mexican Pacific coasts. This complex reality had not been anticipated in prewar German battle plans. Now secret war might quickly put Germany's enemies off-balance. From a military-diplomatic vantage point it made sense to try.

Initially, German secret warfare tried to divert British resources away from European battlefields. One campaign tried to reduce the number of British ships available to protect the British coast. Thus German agents encouraged the tribes of northwestern India to create disturbances against British colonial rule, either through internal upheaval or through an invasion from a neighboring country. If successful, the trouble would force the British Admiralty to move ships from the Atlantic to India and to leave the British coastline exposed. If the British Isles were more vulnerable to German naval attack, perhaps the British would prefer political settlement.

Outside Europe, Germans encouraged religious ethnic tensions to turn from opposition into anti-British violence. First, Islamic tribes were baited to start a pan-Islamic, religious nationalist uprising against British Christians.

Second, the emir of Afghanistan was encouraged to invade India and add pressure from the outside. A German–Turkish expedition traveled to Persia to set events into motion.

In the region that is now Iraq, Germans fanned religious ethnic tensions to separate Great Britain further from Sunnis, Shi'ites, and Kurds. Germans asked Shi'ite leaders in Baghdad to fight against the Christian British. Farther north, a German office was opened in Damascus, which in turn, operated smaller branches in Djidda and Medina, all of them designed to incite ethnic hatred, turning Arabs against British. Indeed, the sheriff of Mecca took over pro-German propaganda work among pilgrims visiting the holy cities of Mecca and Medina.[6] These secret activities were planned and executed out of a joint German–Turkish office in Constantinople.

Another target included British Egypt, Sudan, and the Suez Canal, the most critical transport route between Great Britain and India. On August 25, 1914, Undersecretary Zimmerman called for the "destruction of English reign" in these areas. In October, preparations for a German–Turkish military assault against the Suez Canal began. It was to be fought with at least twenty to thirty thousand soldiers, supported with German material and advisers. This foreign army was to attract local tribes living in the canal's vicinity to join the fighting and create a local nationalist uprising against the vital trade route.

Farther south, German agent Leo Frobenious was sent to Ethiopia. He was to urge the Abyssinian emperor to attack British Sudan. If victorious, the Ethiopians were promised a piece of Sudan as reward.[7]

France and her colonies in North Africa were a second target. Here, the Germans approached the religious brotherhood of the Sanusi, based in Libya. Their uprising was to tie down French colonial troops before they could help on European battlefields. Also, they were asked to attack British Egypt from the west. The German company Mannesman, working out of the German consulate in Tripoli, encouraged North African Arabs and Berbers to revolt against the French. Anti-French groups in Algeria and Tunisia were supplied weapons from the German consulate in Barcelona. French Morocco was targeted from Spanish Morocco. German propaganda targeted ethnic Germans serving in the French Foreign Legion, encouraging desertions.[8] Every uprising would force the French to ship more troops to Africa, thus weakening French troop strengths on European battlefields.

Imperial Russia was Germany's third target. German agents contacted tsarist enemies spanning the continent from Scandinavia to Turkey hoping that they would be open to German backing. Socialist groups were to destabilize

Russia from the inside by exploiting worker discontent in industrial centers. Copenhagen functioned as one operational base for preparations in Stockholm, where eight German agents worked full time on supporting groups scheming inside Russia. In addition, the German military ran ten agents inside Russia as agitators. The uprisings or sabotage they incited might force the Russian monarchy into peace negotiations.

Northern Europe's Stockholm and Copenhagen also served as covert bases targeting Russia's northern border regions. There Guenther Wesendonck fomented secession movements by appealing to ethnic Poles and Finns yearning for independence. On August 6, plans were drawn for insurrections in Finland, enticing Finns with the promise of a Finish state. Ethnic separatists in Latvia, the region of Kurland, and Poland were to sponsor a future, potential independent state. Religious manipulation in this northern part of the world meant that Catholic Poles should act with hostility against Russian Orthodox parishioners.[9]

In southeastern Europe, German agents reinforced the ethnic grievances of Jewish groups persecuted by repeated state-sanctioned Russian pogroms. The German consul in Bucharest promised 50,000 Reichsmarks in gold for an uprising in Bessarabia and, once victorious, the emancipation of its ethnic Jewish people.[10]

Agents of the Austro-Hungarian Empire undertook their own secret warfare. For example, Austrians did disintegration work in Azerbaijan and the Ukraine. And they approached separatist groups in Turkmenistan. Georgian independence movements in particular soon became dependent entirely on German financial support.[11]

Constantinople, today Istanbul, headquartered a special German commission that focused on creating revolutions in the Russian Caucasus, southern Russia, and Persia.[12]

Wherever there was Russian, British, or French interest, Germany tried to create as many disturbances as possible. Whether it was political opposition, social discontent, or sabotage, Germans would do whatever it took to add straws to the "backs of the camels" of rival empires. Hopefully leaders in Moscow, London, and Paris would fear the mayhem, buckle politically, and agree to terms of peace that the Germans wanted. Now we can pay renewed attention to the U.S. setting.

In New York, how could Military Attaché Franz von Papen and Naval Attaché Captain Karl Boy-Ed contribute to the German secret war across the globe? First, von Papen decided to divert enemy troops from reaching the European battlefields where the Allies desperately needed them. He would do his utmost to disrupt the flow of reservists and soldiers from abroad to European battlefields in Belgium.

Great Britain was part of an alliance with Japan. Tokyo might be asked to dispatch Japanese troops to Belgium. The German General Staff wanted to be prepared and, therefore, ordered the agent to disrupt the deployment of troops via Siberia or via Canada.

First, German observers in Japan tried to identify signs of troop mobilizations in Japanese ports. Second, agents in the German consulate in Honolulu were to announce any arrival of Japanese ships with recruits, refueling for a journey to Vancouver, Canada. So far no troop transporter had been discovered. Third, in Peking Admiral Hintze targeted the Trans-Siberian Railroad for destruction. As long as Military Attaché von Papen did not have to deal with Japanese troops on the ground in Canada, he contributed from the United States to Hintze's sabotage preparations against the Siberian railroad. Von Papen's communication facilities on the East Coast proved critical for Hintze's reports about sabotage in Siberia to reach Berlin.[13]

At the same time von Papen prepared a last-resort battle scenario if troops were not transported by railroad through Canada but south by ship through Central America. The alternative to the Canadian railroad route could only be the Panama Canal, which had just opened operations.

In San Francisco von Papen enlisted a Mr. von Petersdorff to head a sabotage team for the Panama Canal. Papen's document is the first proof that Germans were not just dreaming about testing whether the U.S. army would be able to protect the Panama Canal but, in fact, were preparing its destruction in World War I, if that proved advantageous.[14] A German attack was not just big talk or a theoretical exercise for a low-level general in Berlin but actually had been planned and prepared. That it did not take place does not reduce the seriousness of this military preparation. Historians should not belittle the idea of a German attack on the Panama Canal anymore.

Von Papen connected preparations in the Far East and the Panama Canal with destruction in Canada. Forcing British politicians in London to give in to German demands meant attacking its Canadian colony.

While a few German agents were attempting to detect the shipment of Japanese troops from Asia to the railhead of the Canadian railroad in Vancouver, B.C., von Papen traveled in late 1914 to the U.S. West Coast to personally supervise preparations for attacking Canada. Here the German military attaché was using the territory of the United States as a hinterland to stage and manage several global subversion campaigns.

One German sabotage team focused on the Canadian railway network. In the U.S. Pacific Northwest a Lt. von Baerensprung was recruited to lead a group of reservists.[15] His staging ground was Seattle. After the order to deploy he would lead a sabotage team to destroy the large bridges crossing the Fraser River and the Pitt River.

West Coast work also included running cruiser warfare with auxiliary cruisers up and down the Pacific Coast. The headquarters for this activity were secret German offices in San Francisco.[16]

The West Coast was also the location to plan attacks against supplies for the Russians. Ambassador Bernstorff writes in "Deutschland und Amerika" that deliveries out of San Francisco to Russia departing from the U.S. West Coast were targeted by General Consul Franz von Bopp. He was backed by Vice-Consul Eckhard von Schack and an attaché named Wilhelm von Brincken. One documented action tried to buy the services of Louis J. Smith, a previously unknown individual, to strike against shipments to Russia.

For that purpose German consul General von Bopp in San Francisco hired in 1915 U.S. detective Charles C. Crowley and subcontracted sabotage. He was to sink ships carrying weapons to Vladivostok, Russia. In order to smuggle the bombs on the ships he approached the wife of the Russian ambassador. She was asked to accept "dried fruit packages" as gifts from California fruit growers and forward them to the Russian Red Cross. If she accepted them, they would travel on the same boats as the armaments.[17] Once the ships passed the Golden Gate Bridge and reached the open sea they would explode.

It appears that von Papen directed the work against transports leaving Seattle.[18]

After focusing on western Canada, Franz von Papen identified weak spots along the entire length of the Canadian railroad. First German commandos were supposed to gather in U.S. urban areas to start an attack against Canada.[19] The important point is that Papen did not just use a few saboteurs but, rather, systematically recruited German citizens residing in the United States but owing military service to Germany for commando raids.

He put together four small groups of reservists counting between fifty and one hundred men. Men in Seattle, St. Paul/Minnesota, Chicago, and Detroit were selected to cross the border and attack the British colony.[20] The names of team members remain undiscovered until today. But the operation had moved beyond scenarios on paper.

Next, von Papen reported to Berlin the establishment of depots housing weapons and dynamite along the Canadian border. Then he pondered how to save the men's lives if they were discovered by Canadian troops. He proposed that they should wear special insignia on their sleeves so that they could claim protection as combatants under the Geneva Convention. They would operate as irregular undercover teams.

Papen reported the creation of two additional sabotage teams. One targeted an unidentified tunnel in the Rocky Mountains and had begun to march toward the tunnel, but progress was hampered by heavy snowfall. A second team is listed on paper but remains unidentified as far as its composition and its target are concerned.[21]

There cannot be a source more convincing than von Papen's personal summary report to Berlin at the conclusion of his trip to the West Coast. Whereas British intelligence agents remained limited to bits and pieces of individual confessions, von Papen stated in writing that in times of war German military attachés would enlist reservists not just to travel home as draft law required. But they could be assembled secretly and invade Canada from U.S. soil, creating major U.S.–British tensions. Undercover invasions from U.S. soil would spread panic and confusion, hopefully causing Canadian politicians to lose their resolve and stop the shipment of troops from Canada to European battlefields. One scheme planned to land German reservists near the U.S. Great Lakes. Once they crossed into Canada they would terrorize Canadians. A second plan imagined the landing of a mixed party of German and Indian agitators on the west coast of British Columbia. The British records offer only one sentence that confirms this plot.[22]

First a spot was to be established as beachhead on the west coast of Canada. Men and material would gather there and push into Canada. They would be assisted by German warships and German reservists waiting in the United States. Initially German naval attaché Boy-Ed supported the proposal. But after a joint conference the plan was set aside until further notice.

There were other invasion scenarios. One plan proposed the spreading of agitation propaganda and small explosions among a terrified Canadian populace, combined with rumors of invasions.

This could even mean an invitation to the U.S. government to attack Canada. Already in August 1914, the distinguished German general von Moltke considered, according to German historian Fritz Fischer, the idea of offering Canada to the incoming Wilson administration for national expansion. On August 5, 1914, one source reports: "The mood in America is pro-German, reported Moltke, perhaps one could nudge the United States for a naval action against England, for which one might offer Canada as price of victory."[23]

Again German reservists waiting in New York would be used. Dynamite was to be supplied by Felix Sommerfeld, who held, at that time, the concession to import dynamite into the state of Chihuahua for Mexican revolutionary General Villa.

The confession of Agent von der Goltz detailed a proposal by a Mr. Schumacher from Oregon, who had asked for money to carry out raids on towns situated along the coast of the Great Lakes. He proposed to put reservists in motorboats, arm them with machine guns, and help them cross the lakes and shoot into Canadian towns. Agent von der Goltz explained: "This letter was from a man named Schumacher, who lived in Oregon, at Eden Bower Farm. He had written to the embassy suggesting that we secretly outfit motor boats armed with machine guns and using Buffalo, Detroit, Cleveland and Chicago as bases for raids against Canadian cities and towns on the Great Lakes."[24]

However, the German embassy leadership in Washington rejected this proposal, as they feared that Schumacher was a British agent provocateur.[25] Today there is no proof in British archives that the proposal was not genuine.

By December 1914, discussions and explorations about how Canadian territory could be violated on the cheap continued. On December 14, 1914, Department IIIb leader Rudolf Nadolny and Undersecretary Arthur Zimmermann explored the staging of a small border violation that could become a bigger international political conflict.[26]

According to the German historian Reinhard Doerries, Albrecht Wirth "presented Minister Nadolny with a plan to first . . . occupy . . . Western Canada and then Eastern Canada" using mercenaries and ethnic troops.[27] Von Papen in New York should be the one to develop such an idea into a plan.

This was not the only time that Canada was discussed. Another proposal envisioned disgruntled Native American tribes, living in the northwestern United States, as bands invading southern Canadian territory.[28]

One agent's confession illustrates the ideas behind the use of ethnic Germans as border violators:

A penetration into Canada . . . , perhaps, might be realized even though under great difficulties. At first this could be merely a daring strike of a relatively small number of troops, perhaps at 3 or 4 places in the East or Middle West. Immediately thereafter we could open recruiting places

9. Rudolph Nadolny, working for the German army high command during World War I, was intimately involved in designing, selecting, and transmitting to the United States information about subversive warfare opportunities. Not a single word addressed these activities of his career in his memoirs. After World War I he became an esteemed diplomat of the Weimar Republic (Politisches Archiv des Auswaertigen Amts, Berlin).

on Canadian territory while pushing prepositioned supplies across the border. No doubt we should have enormous following, at least enough in order to beat to death with bats all troops that have remained inside Canada. The base for the initial small troops should be in the U.S., the existing sport, gun, veteran and other German clubs.[29]

In late 1914, attack plans targeted Canadian infrastructure. Lieutenant Horn blew up part of the Croix River bridge, near the Maine–Canadian border. In January 1915, von Papen sent Hans Boehm from Maine to scout parts of the border and identify targets. But his sabotage attack failed because the weather was too cold.[30]

Another group would blow up the locks connecting the Great Lakes, railway junctions, and grain elevators. In this case Irish revolutionaries would help

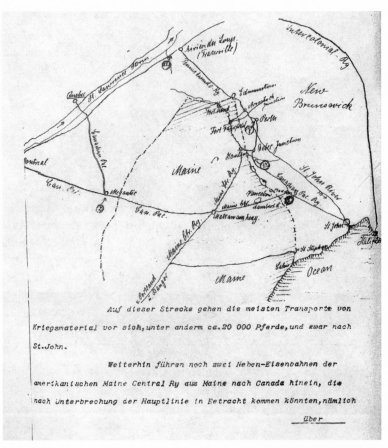

Auf dieser Strecke gehen die meisten Transporte von

Kriegsmaterial vor sich,unter anderm ca.20 000 Pferde,und zwar nach

St.John.

Weiterhin führen noch zwei Neben-Eisenbahnen der

amerikanischen Maine Central Ry aus Maine nach Canada hinein, die

nach Unterbrechung der Hauptlinie in Betracht kommen könnten,nämlich

_____über_____

10. A 1914/1915 hand-drawn map of the Western Canadian Coast Railroad identifying key military infrastructure points that merited sabotage attacks (Captured German Records, T-136, 30, National Archives of the United States, Washington, D.C.).

Germany commit sabotage. The execution of the plan was entrusted to Agent von der Goltz, alias Bridgeman Taylor. He reported to Dr. Kraske, the vice-consul in New York. The German diplomat was also the channel of communication with von Papen.[31]

The most surprising discovery is that in the United States Military Attaché von Papen was also involved in secret warfare planning toward Africa. The German leadership wanted to use German soldiers present in the Americas to launch the attack from South America. German reservists congregating in Chile and Argentina were being prepared to fight the British in Africa.

In 1914, British naval intelligence intercepted a series of German telegrams that instructed their German agents and diplomats in Buenos Aires and Valparaiso, Chile, to buy weaponry and to organize reservist Germans awaiting transport to Europe to the war front.[32]

On November 10, 1914, the Berlin government ordered a confidential agent in Valparaiso to mobilize and to equip twenty-one hundred ethnic German citizens—out of a total of five thousand located in Chile and Argentina—with gear, guns, and ammunition.[33] They would become a military expedition to German southwest Africa to fight British troops. In the following weeks lead agents kept Berlin informed about expedition preparations. But they did not inform individual German reservists, about to be drafted, of what role they would play in the near future.[34]

Neutral Chilean territory became a staging area for acts of war against Great Britain. Clearly this was a violation of Chile's neutrality, and if discovered, it would seriously burden German–Chilean and Chilean–British diplomatic relations.[35]

Already, the German naval supply service was violating Chilean law when it used Chilean ports and two Kosmos steamers to secretly supply a recently arrived German naval squadron. They would fight British warships.[36]

In the small southern Chilean port of Puerto Montt, Berlin planners intended to load the reservists onto a ship, pretending that they would be transported to Europe. Once they had reached open sea, however, the captain would turn east, and the reservists would be told that Africa was the final battlefield deployment.

By November 1914, the Chilean government had discovered the German neutrality violation. In accordance with guidelines for the behavior of neutral countries during international war, it informed Germany that it would allow in the future only a limited amount of supply for German ships. Also, the German consul was asked for assurance that the purpose of future trips was purely commercial.[37] Publicly, German diplomats assured the Chilean government that the violation of Chilean neutrality law had been the act of individual captains, not the dutiful execution of a German order from Berlin.[38]

In Berlin, planners proceeded as if the Chilean concerns did not matter. On November 14, 1914, the naval agent was instructed to "keep it strictly secret that the objective is South West Africa. Dispatch follows. Make every preparation. A commission will be sent out to arrange sailing."[39]

In November, Argentina also emerged in the expedition preparations. On November 20, 1914, Berlin ordered the Buenos Aires branch of the Banco Aleman Transatlantico to handle the financing of the mission. Brauss, Mahn and Co., an ethnically German-owned company, received 1,500,000 RM to buy weapons and ammunition. And 800,000 RM were given to the consulate general to cover additional costs. From Buenos Aires the bank was to wire 1,500,000 RM to Valparaiso to the account of Mr. Westdarp at Folsch & Co.[40]

Even German Ambassador Luxburg, in Buenos Aires, was involved in weapon purchase negotiations. On December 18, 1914, Argentinean military bureaucrats, using Italian intermediaries, offered 30,000 Mauser rifles, 30,000,000 cartridges, 372 Krupp field and mountain guns, and 141,000 shells. This was enough equipment to outfit an entire division. At first it looked as if the weapons would be used to supply Turkish troops, Germany's ally.[41]

In Chile, German agents took care of technical issues. First, on December 5, 1914, troop vaccinations for tropical Africa were discussed. Second, a steamer was to be selected that carried a wireless transmitter on board. Suddenly the Chilean government refused to release a German ship because of continuing suspicions that German assurances were hiding a darker truth.[42]

One day before Christmas Eve, 1914, Berlin officials instructed Luxburg to limit his purchase to two thousand rifles and two million cartridges. This purchase would outfit the German southwest Africa expedition.[43] Thereafter negotiations proceeded, and on February 9, 1915, an Argentine army faction presented a draft contract. Suddenly, the Argentine government let it be known that something sinister was unfolding. It is likely that the British navy leaked the content of the intercepted cables to anti-German groups in the Argentine government.

One day before, in Chile, the German ship SS *York* was finally allowed to take on coal. It would carry the German reservists to Africa.[44]

From then on German agents had greater difficulty organizing Germans in Argentina and Chile for covert activities. First French and British weapons purchasers began to compete for the weapons that Minister Luxburg wanted to buy. Then on February 13, 1915, Argentinean president Dr. de la Plaza confronted his military and prohibited the sale of war material to all countries involved in war. But still in March 1915, Argentine civilian power seemed too weak to force its will on the military. German naval attaché Müller reported to Berlin that he could purchase weapons if the admiralty accepted them in lot size.[45]

Also the British Caribbean was a minor location for creating unrest. There, von Papen again participated as planner of ethnic uprisings. Agent von der Goltz had told von Papen of the uprising potential in Jamaica. Von Papen encouraged von der Goltz to proceed and promised to protect him from potential execution if discovered by giving him the rank of navy captain. Von der Goltz provides details:

> Another plan we considered more carefully, involved an expedition against Jamaica. . . . Jamaica was none too well defended and it seemed fairly probable that with an army of ragamuffins which I could easily recruit in Mexico and Central America, we could make a success of its. Arms were easy to secure. In fact, we had a very well equipped arsenal in New York.[46]

Jamaica remains underresearched for German activities. German consul Otto helped Mexican dictator Huerta book his passage into Spanish exile, and he forwarded secret funds to pay the labor subversion office run by Hans Liebau in the United States. He knew that the Kulenkampf Company collected coal in Jamaica in late 1914 to supply German warships illegally.[47]

The Second Wave: Allied War Production

In New York, in 1914, as the tide turned unexpectedly on the western front against a quick German victory, Jack Morgan and his U.S. bank partners redoubled their efforts to employ their funds and contacts only for the Allies. This meant not only providing money but also starting and managing in New York a purchasing organization for the British. On December 16, in its London branch, Morgan showed British minister of ammunition Lloyd George a draft contract for a proposed purchasing organization, just as the Germans had planned to create in New York. Three weeks of negotiation followed, and on January 15, 1915, the British Army Council and the Admiralty signed Morgan's draft agreement.

Next the House of Morgan recruited Edward Stettinus as head of the New York supply organization. He moved into a Morgan bank building situated close to Wall Street, hired 175 employees, and began to build a private export syndicate for Great Britain. Stettinus, unlike Dernburg and Albert, was backed by generous financing and quickly became the linchpin of British supply operations in the Americas. His first purchase acquired $12,000,000 worth of horses.[48]

Imperial Great Britain had not "just entered the war." It also succeeded at creating a financial and economic supply base in the United States, while Germany failed. As the war dragged on, by early 1915, the world's imperial trade patterns and financial linkages that had existed for decades were changing unpredictably. The Atlantic was becoming a contested war zone, a potential grave for ships trying to bring goods through economic blockades.

German war planners had to admit that the neutral United States and its resources were no longer a source of help but a pipeline that fueled their enemies. The ever growing flow of goods from New York, Baltimore, and New Orleans to Bristol and Manchester had to be attacked. Great Britain, somehow, had to be denied this critical advantage. But how to realize such a policy and respect U.S. sovereignty was a dilemma.

Politically, Germany had to respect U.S. neutrality. Since any U.S. company selling ammunition to Allied purchasing agents could not be attacked openly, German military leaders decided that they could resort to secret warfare to hinder U.S. business ventures that were only dealing with the Allies.

Chief of Staff Erich von Falkenhayn redefined the priority of German secret warfare inside the United States from obtaining loans and ammunition for the German army to destroying as much as possible the economic lifelines that nurtured the British, French, and Russian war effort.[49] Thus German agents explored how U.S. goods could be kept away from Allied war machines in Europe. Whatever helped Germany's enemies became a target for German warfare.

Since Germany could not land its troops on American beaches without a declaration of war, war planners had to find proxy forces that might be willing or could be manipulated into using violence against Allied supplies. Individuals who could be manipulated to act against the British were select members of ethnic groups trying to shake off the yoke of British colonialism. Socialists and anarchists could be enlisted to damage factories where working conditions were abominable. The autonomous struggle for labor rights and social justice lent itself also as a sabotage vehicle in Mexico and Canada.

In early 1915, German planners did not think of secret wars inside the Americas as an effort to topple the U.S. government or to defeat democracy. Of course, they realized that they would burn most of their transatlantic political bridges built in the last decades. German violence against British interests violated all the good faith and goodwill between U.S. and German political elites that had been created by ties of emigration, commerce, and cultural exchanges.

Incredibly, war planners thought that they could disrupt manufacturing inside U.S. factories and not pay a political price. Somehow, they were sure that blowing up warehouses and ships would pressure only the British cabinet in favor of peace negotiations. There was neither discussion nor care that it would turn more members of the U.S. Congress pro-British, that German biological warfare against draft animals inside U.S. East Coast cities would set a most dangerous precedent, or that incitement to anti-Japanese riots in U.S. West Coast cities would tarnish ethnic minorities in California for decades. Berlin did not mind that these activities would change forever the way U.S. governments would perceive ethnic groups as part of its citizenry. The policy makers were delusional to think that after the war the world would continue to function as before 1914. Thus began a deliberate, reckless betrayal of ethnic lives, unfolding in the name of Germany but not in any interest of ethnic German Americans.

Already in fall 1914, Military Attaché von Papen had suggested to Berlin to disrupt U.S. industrial production for Allied clients. On December 10 von Papen submitted proposals to the Ministry of War to enter into contracts with American war ammunition companies so that they could not supply the Allies. Initially he proposed to spend $25,000,000 to tie up U.S. production gradually. German secret warfare department IIIB agreed in the second week in 1915.

On January 15, 1915, Berlin also gave a general order approving the use of sabotage inside the United States. Unexpectedly, on February 3, 1915, the chief of the general staff reported that it was possible to buy the entire U.S. powder production. The American Malvin Rice had provided information to this extent and claimed to be close to President Wilson.

Major Michelis was selected to negotiate, but Malvin Rice refused to become involved himself. However, he was willing to support an absolutely reliable German agent. The German Foreign Ministry suggested Agent Franz von Rintelen, who then worked at the Staff of the Navy. On February 23, von Rintelen was selected for the special mission. Incredibly, the German navy asked the U.S. embassy in Berlin to assure von Rintelen safe-conduct passage across the Atlantic. Following U.S. denial von Rintelen was issued a forged Swiss passport for the Atlantic crossing.

Once in New York von Rintelen was shocked. Rice's tip proved incorrect. To the contrary, DuPont Powder Co. almost exclusively reserved its facilities for production for the Allied powers and had signed already long-term contracts. In the end, von Rintelen had to switch tactics and focus on hindering the supply of Allied powers with ammunition from the United States.[50]

By coincidence, the leaders of the German purchase organization in New York experienced a minor financial success in March 1915. German financial agents

Heinrich Albert and Friedrich Dernburg obtained funds making possible larger industrial secret warfare disruptions.

Just as anglophile bankers had helped the British Empire, a few German American and Irish American bankers, out of personal conviction, began to help Germany. The small bank of G. Amsinck and Co. and its managing director, Adolph von Pavenstedt, and Baron Reginald von Schroeder emerged as key supporters willing to defy the example of the House of Morgan. Chase National Bank vice president Carl J. Schmidlapp also contributed.[51] At the German-American Bank President Albert Tag chipped in, and at the Federal Trust Company in Boston President Joseph Neil, an Irish American, backed the German Empire as long as it damaged Great Britain and promised Ireland's independence. Even the establishment bank of Kuehn und Loeb signed a small token loan of $400,000.

Together this small group of banks advanced $10,000,000, 90 percent less than Dernburg and Albert had hoped for in 1914. Right away, hostile pressure from the House of Morgan cut $3,000,000 of the original amount.[52] The remaining $7,000,000 was not enough money to make a measurable difference in supplying the German war machine in Europe, but it was more than enough money to finance expanded secret warfare inside the Americas.

Work began to disrupt the flow of supplies for a few months. Heinrich Albert's disguised purchasing commission took on an additional unexpected task, to help Albert, Karl Boy-Ed, and Franz von Papen wherever possible.[53] Berlin approved Military Attaché von Papen's economic warfare plans on March 24, 1915.[54] German agents would use fear tactics, labor strikes, and explosives to upset the flow of goods every step of the way.

First, the expansion of private weapon production companies should be discouraged. In 1914, the number of U.S. factories capable of assembling weapons was still relatively small. A Mr. Willemin offered von Papen the disruption of machine gun assembly from Providence, R.I.[55] Germany intended to slow down their expansion by depriving Allied administrator Edward Stettinus and U.S. investors of machines, parts, and raw materials. If their raw materials were not available on the public market, then shells, ammunition, and hardware could not be assembled in the amount generals in London and Moscow needed to avoid peace negotiations.

Raw materials were supposed to be taken off the U.S. market. For example, Dr. Hugo Schweitzer informed about removing bromide from the U.S. market. Industrial dyes were a second prominent target.[56]

Machine parts scarcity was created by buying up available manufactured parts, causing delays of at least months. The work was done through straw men. Second $3,500,000 of Heinrich Albert's money financed the construction of the Bridgeport Projectile Company.[57] Its managers purchased on the open market as many hydraulic presses and acid-proof containers and as much black powder as possible.[58]

Frivolous lawsuits became a second tool to deprive U.S. companies of the use of important patents. For example, manufacturers like Carnegie Steel Company (Pittsburgh), Indian Steel Company (Gary, Indiana), and Tennessee Coal, Iron, and Railroad Company needed machines to produce benzol and other chemicals. Benzol was necessary to manufacture ammunition. At the end of 1915, Carl Recklinghausen filed lawsuits to slow down the manufacture of benzol-producing machines.[59] The German army financed this legal diversion with $25,000 to $30,000, hoping to gain a postponement for two months.

Third, in addition to technology, the Germans targeted the labor pool that manufactured the supplies. If workers could be separated from their machines, production would be interrupted and slowed down. Perhaps it would also become more expensive. The Allied powers were supposed to wait for their orders as long as possible.

The simplest strategy was to remove workers physically from the assembly line. In this case ethnicity offered an enticing appeal. Many German Americans, Hungarian Americans, and Irish Americans could be counted upon to act against producing for Great Britain. First, immigrant workers who still held German and Austrian-Hungarian citizenship were discouraged from working for the war industry by threats of legal consequences published in community newspapers.

Then Germany targeted members of U.S. Congress to pass anti-British laws. Already during the *Lusitania* crisis a Professor Hall wrote resolutions for labor organizations.[60]

By the end of May, Agent von Rintelen joined the effort and communicated a timeline for likely congressional action against President Wilson. In the first week of June, Rintelen used Mrs. von Schmidt-Pauli to hand over a draft program for a worker conference. The labor conference was to pass a petition and then insist on presenting it to President Wilson around June 20. The petition demanded a special congressional session to impose payment of huge indemnities in favor of Germany and Austria-Hungary because "U.S. government behavior was damaging them." In the words of von Rintelen: "This whole action has been dressed up U.S. American without any German campaign and therefore should be rather effective."[61] Naval Attaché Boy-Ed was now financing von Rintelen's work with $500,000.[62]

On June 11, 1915, von Rintelen wired a report to Berlin about the progress of his work. He now employed David Lamar to further this work.[63] The prominent U.S. Labor Peace Council—still advised by former secretary of state William Jennings Bryan and former U.S. Ambassador to Madrid Taylor but also financially supplemented by Agent von Rintelen—asked to see President Wilson to

11. Some U.S. pacifists and labor organizations received funding from the German government during World War I. The secret support aimed at slowing down private manufacturing for the Allied powers and forcing Great Britain to agree to a peace compromise (Library of Congress, Washington, D.C.).

submit a formal protest against the export of weapons to the Allies and to shame him publicly into more pro-German behavior. Rintelen reported that the writing of the protest petition had taken several days. As promised, it accused the Federal Reserve, that is, the government's bank created by order of Congress, of most severe neutrality violations. From then on Congress had fourteen days to call a special session. Von Rintelen was certain that his plan would work out as designed.

The protesters were received only by Secretary of State Lansing. U.S. congressmen Buchanan and Fowler and former senator Monahan visited Lansing on June 22 and handed him the petition.

While Berlin hoped for congressional action, Agent von Rintelen encouraged and contributed financially to an upcoming conference of U.S. labor leaders in Philadelphia. Its resolutions were supposed to reinforce the attempted intimidation of the president.

Woodrow Wilson rejected the petition's demands on July 23, 1915. Thereafter, the members of Congress departed from von Rintelen's timetable but not yet his strategy. According to rules of political civility they wanted to give the president a second opportunity to pass an immediate export prohibition.

Even though a prohibition by Congress had been stopped for the time being, von Rintelen tried to disrupt the financial market. In early July the floating of a massive, private pro–French and British bond of $300,000,000 was expected. Because of von Rintelen's machinations its issuing was postponed. When it would be relaunched became uncertain. Would this postponement create peace negotiations in a way the German monarchy desired? Von Rintelen's campaign had scared away, for the time being, enough private investors.

Von Rintelen worked until July 6, 1915, under the assumption of continued anonymity inside the United States. On that day Naval Attaché Boy-Ed learned that his cover had been blown. Von Rintelen's personal safety was in danger, and he should be called back to Berlin. It was time to cross the Atlantic toward Germany. But even then von Rintelen's departure was only a frustrating interruption for German action. Other genuine German American activists stayed in the United States and received continued German support.

On July 22, Heinrich Albert and Franz von Papen published an announcement in German American papers informing readers that, according to German law, it was illegal for workers holding German citizenship to manufacture weapons for the enemy. Second, they created an office that relocated ammunition workers into civilian jobs. For that purpose, the German military's secret warfare department provided Hans Liebau with money.[64] On August 4, 1915, he opened an office in New York and staffed it with ten employees. The Austrian-Hungarian government also planned to contribute significant money.

A Hungarian consul estimated that, in South Bethlehem, the steel industry employed twenty-one thousand workers. Only seven thousand steelworkers had U.S. citizenship. The rest had kept citizenship papers of Germany, Hungary, and Russia. Ethnically there were also Lithuanians, Slovaks, and Ruthenians, who could be frightened.[65]

Major branch offices were opened in Chicago, Bridgeport, Cleveland, Detroit, Pittsburgh, and Philadelphia. In cities where minor arms production took place, German consuls helped out. First, "Organization Liebau," as it was called, registered as many German Americans and Austrian-Hungarians as possible. Then, it approached these men and urged them to move into work in the civilian sector. German historian Reiling discovered that one office manager visited seventy-five companies in the first thirty days to counsel workers away from their jobs.

In public, the Liebau office offered the appearance of U.S. citizenry activism and committed private funding. Behind the scenes, the German government provided between $14,000 and $27,500. Imperial Austria-Hungary contributed $3,250.[66] Only $11,900 came from unsuspecting U.S. citizen donations. Their political fire provided a wonderful cover for German military intelligence financing of U.S. antiwar movements.

The Liebau project was successful. From August 1915 to March 1916, 5,679 ethnic workers quit the armament industry and were placed elsewhere—3,529 of them were German Americans, and 2,150 were Austrian-Hungarians.[67] One source estimated that the project deprived U.S. arms manufacturers of 12,602 ethnic resident alien workers. Three-fifths of them held German passports, and two-fifths were Austrians or Hungarians. The Liebau office also provided an unknown number of U.S. citizens with help to leave the military sector.

This secret campaign continued until April 1916. After that the work had run its course, and the Germans stopped financial support.

Parallel to disrupting employment patterns Berlin caused and financed strikes to keep workers away from machines. Thus the German army piggybacked onto U.S. workers' social struggle for basic labor rights and higher wages. Of course, successful strikes drove up production costs, making the British defense more expensive.

A few sources survive that prove serious German and Austrian-Hungarian subversion efforts to create as many strikes in the armament sector as possible. Already in the winter of 1914, Naval Attaché Boy-Ed had approached the Irish

12. Captain Boy-Ed shared responsibility for German sabotage on the high seas, contributing to the weakening of weapons deliveries to the Allied powers (Library of Congress, Washington, D.C.).

socialist labor leader James Larkin, asking him to put socialist strikers and labor violence into the service of the German war effort. Irish hatred for Great Britain was enlisted. Larkin's comrades were Irish American workers.[68] Irish American hatred was becoming a German war resource.

Attaché Boy-Ed talked in detail to Larkin about a variety of ideas.[69] He offered Larkin $200,000 if he agreed to join the German payroll.[70] On the U.S. East Coast there were other labor agent provocateurs on the German payroll who remain anonymous until today. German consulates had observed independent socialists and anarchists in the past, hoping to identify movements hostile to German interests. Now in New York, business manager Albert contributed $200,000 to start strikes in New York.[71] Austrian-Hungarian Ambassador Dumba also conducted undercover work in support of labor strikes among Austrian-Hungarians at the Bethlehem Steel Co.[72]

The exploration of socialist and German military cooperation continued in the following months. In the summer of 1915, it was Jim Larkin again, this time pressed for cash, who asked to renew contact with the German attaché. Boy-Ed asked Larkin what it would take to create more strikes. The Irishman projected that between $10,000 and $20,000 might suffice to start a deeper, organized, more systematic U.S. strike movement. The outcome of the contact remains undocumented. After spending time with labor movements in California Larkin traveled to Butte, Montana, where he talked to Agent Kuno Meyer.[73]

How effective was the subversive labor campaign? In November 1915, German Ambassador Bernstorff, sending an update from Washington to Berlin, reported four groups working to increase the number of strikes. Together, they were targeting 110 companies. In ninety-four companies they successfully created strikes that lasted between one and four weeks, causing the desired delay.[74] A second source confirmed that disruptions created through manipulations of ethnic workers and socialists delayed production. Eventually most strikes were settled.

On occasion strikes by longshoremen slowed food and weapon transports that reached Canadian and U.S. ports. In New York, the majority of longshoremen were of German and Irish ethnic origin. German agents planned to spend $1,000,000 to finance a four-week-long strike among longshoremen. In Boston, Bosch manager Otto Heins considered spending $50,000 per week to keep seven thousand men from work.[75]

In a final note, secret German military funding in Boston coincided with secret financing offered by Irish American leaders. Eager to use the war to create an independent Ireland, prominent Irish Americans were offering $1,000,000 for the creation of a major strike. Every participating striker was promised $10.00 per week.[76]

Once Allied weaponry, food, and animals were loaded onto ships they faced the potential of being targeted for German sabotage. In April 1915, on the U.S. East Coast, Lieut. Robert Fay and two Germans arrived. Their task was to disable Allied ammunition ships by destroying their steering mechanism.[77] Agent von Rintelen met with and financed saboteurs Wolpert, Bode, Scheele, and Schimmel.[78]

Setting fires was a second method to make ships unusable. For that purpose Captain Frederick Hinsch hired a subagent. He directed ten to twelve workers to do their deadly work at the naval yards of Baltimore, New York, Norfolk, and Newport.[79] In Baltimore, Consul Mr. Carl A. Luederitz recruited saboteurs from crews of interned ships.[80] Often ships, fully loaded, that made it onto the open sea were destroyed with time-delayed bombs that saboteurs had smuggled on board before they left the harbor. Military Attaché von Papen admitted that one of his jobs had been the organization of placement of bombs onto ships.[81]

Successful sabotage made the movement of goods unpredictable and dangerous. It discouraged shipowners, captains, and crews from signing up. Finally, the expanding destruction also pushed up insurance rates and the costs of transporting munitions.

The Third Wave: Poisoning Relations with Canada and Mexico

Secret wars in the Americas did not remain limited to the destruction of economic targets and ships. The poisoning of political relationships among Great Britain, the United States, Canada, and Mexico was a constant feature. German leaders desired three possible outcomes.

First, any serious political conflict that could be created between Canada and the United States would make it more difficult for U.S. businessmen and investors to manufacture for Canada's colonial motherland, Great Britain. Second, any small uprising or ethnic disturbance along the Canadian–U.S. border or in the Caribbean might motivate U.S. and British policy makers to send troops that otherwise would have been available for European battlefields. Third, the best region to tie down large numbers of U.S. soldiers and resources was the already revolutionary setting along the U.S.–Mexican border.

In sum any secret German activity that pulled the United States into any kind of war on the North American continent would make it difficult, preferably impossible, to join the British war effort. U.S. generals should never be able to deploy U.S. troops to European battlefields. Perhaps ethnic groups inside the United States could exert political pressure on U.S. lawmakers to convince banks and companies to be less friendly to Great Britain's war economy. And U.S. policy remained dependent on an electorate whose votes might demand to keep U.S. troops out of the war. German and Austrian grand manipulations might separate the United States politically from the Allied powers altogether.

None of these actions intended to destroy the United States or defeat democracy itself. And yet, for the first time, in 1915 German military agents experimented with how to use secret political warfare within an open democratic society and in coordination with secret campaigns taking place on the other side of the Pacific and the Atlantic. Since Germany could not send a significant number of guerilla troops to U.S. border zones, war planners had to find proxy groups willing to do the fighting. The work began by identifying ethnic groups and existing conflicts that could be manipulated from a distance.

Mexico was the most promising target. In comparison to Canada and Jamaica, uprising plans in Mexico progressed from plan to action. The beginnings can be traced to February 1915. They continued until 1920!

The second time that German reservists, but not German Americans, are mentioned in surviving sources is January 1915. A war correspondent for the *International News* attached to the General Staff reported that on January 2, General Antonio Diaz Soto y Gama, Zapata's chief adviser and author of his famous Plan de Ayala, told a source about a visit by a German agent called Krumm-Heller who had come to his office that day. He showed German passports and letters of introduction from high German officials. Claiming to speak in the name of the government he warned that U.S. policy consisted of weakening Mexico to the point where it could not resist a U.S. invasion. Previously Krumm-Heller had tried to be received by Pancho Villa but had failed. Now he offered to Zapata's deputy:

> I have at my immediate command 150 trained German officers. Some are in Mexico others in the U.S. General Villa has plenty of good fighters but he lacks men to train them. I offer you my services and the services of these men free of charge, with the understanding that they are to take charge of General Villa's army and train it. Germany has no ulterior motives and she's friendly to Mexico and has money invested in you and this is simply approval for friendship.[82]

When Villa was informed about Krumm-Heller's advance he exploded: "Tell this . . . to the German spy, to go to the devil with his propositions that I'm running my army and need no outside help. Furthermore that Mexico is friendly to the U.S. and the U.S. is friendly to Mexico. Tell them all that I give him is about 20 hours to get out of my country."[83] On the following day Krumm-Heller disappeared, and General Villa left for the border to keep his appointment with U.S. general Scott. Three months later Krumm-Heller resurfaced in Carranza's army at the rank of colonel. Perhaps he even participated at the Battle of Celaya with five other German soldiers in a commanding role.

South of the U.S. border, in 1915, it made no sense to organize German Mexicans to violate the U.S.–Mexican border. Also, economic warfare and industrial sabotage in Mexico made no sense, as Mexico did not manufacture weapons for European battlefields. The one exception was Mexico's oil supply for the British navy.

Indeed, the German navy targeted Mexican oil production in 1915 for sabotage. Preparatory talks took place in Galveston, Texas, on February 22, 1915, and in New Orleans. Two days later plans were finalized. Von Papen had sent Agent von Petersdorff to the Tampico area preparing to sabotage oil storage tanks and pipelines. His last name is identical to the name of the agent who had been in charge of destroying a gate at the Panama Canal, in case Japanese troops were coming through.[84]

Suddenly, on March 11, 1915, the German admiralty ordered the campaign stopped. One possible interpretation of this decision, according to Mexican Revolution historian Friedrich Katz, is that the expected damage would not justify spending the required amount of money.[85]

Already in 1911, the German leadership had enjoyed access to the revolutionary Madero group through Felix Sommerfeld, Madero's intelligence chief for northern Mexico. Following Madero's assassination by General Huerta, Agent Sommerfeld moved on and worked as one of several weapons purchasers for Pancho Villa.[86]

From late 1914 on Sommerfeld relocated to New York to conduct business for Pancho Villa from the Hotel Astor. Around March 1915, the Mississippi Valley Trust Company in St. Louis, Missouri, opened an account for Sommerfeld. At the same time the German embassy opened an account owned by Bernstorff and Albert.[87] The account was used to pay the bills of the Western Cartridge Company, Alton, Illinois, which supplied Villa's army with weapons at the value of $380,000. From April on Sommerfeld also knew about von Rintelen in New York.[88]

In April 1915, Sommerfeld selectively supplied Military Attaché von Papen with key information. One surviving letter betrays detailed Allied arms purchases in the United States. It was information that could change the outcome of a war campaign.[89] Then, a document arrived in Berlin on May 15, 1915. It was unsigned, and the author cannot be inferred. It proposed one plan that would keep the Allied powers from obtaining U.S.-proposed manufactured ammunition. The writer described:

In April or May 1915, American companies were shipping monthly about 100 million infantry cartridges plus a large amount of dynamite and material that is being used for the manufacturing of ammunition. Sommerfeld told the writer about these contracts and suggested that Germany should sign a contract with the arms manufacturers for $20,000,000 (U.S.). Such an order would keep the companies busy for the next six to eight months. He suggested the manufacture of 7 mm Mauser guns and German Mauser 7.9 mm. Later the cartridges could be sold to Mexico and South American states and Spain who were all using the same caliber. Even better the sale would make a small profit because the contracts could be made for cheap prices.

Felix A. Sommerfeld is familiar with Mexican policy for four years now. He was adviser and agent of confidence of President Madero in all diplomatic missions and has held the same position for General Villa. Besides, he was in charge of purchasing ammunition and war material in the U.S. Therefore, he visits all factories and he knows their capacities to produce. Since then Sommerfeld, who is an excellent patriot, has tried very hard to find out what can be done best in order to support Germany.

All contracts with armament companies include a clause, which voids them, in the moment the United States is involved in a conflict. Everybody knows the policy of the United States vis-à-vis Mexico, and one can firmly be convinced that the government [unreadable] however very much in favor of an intervention are also the governments of Texas and Arizona, which are situated directly at the Mexican border. About two months ago, an incident took place at the border of Arizona, which almost would have caused the intervention. Then the chief of the General Staff [of the United States] based on advice of Secretary of War Garrison has been sent to the border by President Wilson in order to negotiate with President Villa. These negotiations unfolded due to the mediation of Felix A. Sommerfeld. At this moment he would be willing, as he has explained to me repeatedly, it would be an easy thing to do to provoke [a U.S.] intervention.

He summarized the advantageous consequences for Germany as following. It would create an embargo of ammunition for the Allied powers and keep the ammunition in the United States to fight the intervention.

On the other hand, Sommerfeld does not know German policy at that point in time, and did not want to act without German consent.

The writer predicted that a similar situation should surely come again:

Felix Sommerfeld talked to me about it and is firmly convinced that a U.S. intervention into Mexico can be brought about. The Allied powers have ordered 400,000 guns from Winchester and Remington factories, of which each have to deliver 200,000. Monthly they have to deliver 15,000 to 18,000 guns beginning in the fall. Besides the Allies ordered 100,000

French military guns from other factories which have not produced war material previously and they are now beginning to manufacture it.

Besides Mr. Sommerfeld who is the originator of these ideas, only I do know about his plan. Both of us refrain from discussing it with the German ambassador on site, because we are of the conviction, that the fewer people know about it the better it is, and besides, that this delicate affair can be decided only at the appropriate department. After familiarizing yourself with this report, I'm asking you to have the decision reach Mr. Sommerfeld through me, either directly or indirectly, either a yes or no. Finally I want to mention, we both Felix Sommerfeld and I have given our German word of honor that we will not talk to any other person about your decision.[90]

The German historian Doerries proposes that financial agent Dernburg was the author who communicated Sommerfeld's idea to Berlin. Most importantly, Admiral Henning von Holtzendorff, Undersecretary Zimmerman, and Gottlieb von Jagow knew about the plan and endorsed it in May 1915.[91] No German reply, however, has been found in the archive documents. Most likely there existed early on introductory thoughts, plans, and attempts to create war along the U.S.–Mexican border.

Another plot was encouraged by von Rintelen. He backed railroad entrepreneur Andrew D. Meloy to help Díaz's General Mondragon to launch an uprising and his ascendance to Mexico's presidency. Russian military attaché to Paris Ignatieff would serve as a cover. These men wanted the help of the Deutsche Bank. It was not a plot by this financial institution.[92]

During this time Villa's Sommerfeld and Stallforth banked together, having access to tremendous information. Until Carranza's selection as the next Mexican president they shared it selectively with von Papen or directly with the military in Berlin. Regardless of success for Mondragon, von Rintelen hoped the plot would trigger renewed profound violence along the border and redirect the Allied flow of armaments to the U.S.–Mexican border, away from the trenches of World War I.

Mexican general Huerta had never been a stooge of any empire. Once he arrived in Spanish exile, in late 1914, he himself began efforts to return to the Mexican presidency. In the United States, exiled cabinet members of the former president, Porfirio Díaz, were making their own plans to return to power through a coup d'etat. Eventually, former foreign minister Enrique Creel convinced the group of exiles to reconnect with Huerta in Barcelona and to support his return as future president of Mexico. The revolutionaries Pascual Orozco and Félix Díaz were selected as heads of regional uprisings.[93]

In early 1915, the offer from Mexican exiles in the United States reached Huerta in Barcelona. Somehow, the German navy learned about the two groups joining forces and explored whether it could jump on the bandwagon. Department IIIb sent an agent to Barcelona to discuss details with Huerta.

The German navy did not care about Huerta "either as human being" or as Mexican politician. What mattered was his potential and will to enact hostile actions against the United States.

First, since U.S. president Wilson had been responsible for forcing Huerta out of his Mexican dictatorship, a reinstalled Huerta was expected to hate the United States and, most likely, act against U.S. interests. Second, German backing in 1915 might help gain Huerta's cooperation when it came to future German access to Mexican oil. Perhaps he would cut off the British and establish German business in Mexico's petroleum sector. Third, once Huerta moved back into Chapultepec Castle, the German navy would ask him to conduct policy in such a way that was helpful to German submarine warfare against British and U.S. ships operating in shipping lanes close to New Orleans and British Honduras.

Huerta's wrath against U.S. leaders also promised that he would be willing to launch an attack from land when the German navy decided to pursue unrestricted naval warfare against transports coming from South America, the Caribbean, or New Orleans. Agent von Rintelen explained the strategy: "It was my intention that Mexico should attack the United States if we definitely proclaimed unrestricted submarine warfare against the United States. We should, in that case, have to reckon with America's entry into the conflict and we wanted to tie our new opponent to her own border."[94] In the best case, Huerta might allow the operation of a German submarine base along Mexico's Pacific or the Gulf of Mexico coastline, dangerously close to the recently opened Panama Canal.

Talks in Spain with Huerta progressed satisfactorily. The German government was willing to spend large amounts of money to allow the purchase of weaponry for Huerta. Probably in expectation of a U.S. arms embargo during the planned uprising, both sides stipulated that "German U-boats were to land weapons along the Mexican coast. Abundant funds were to be provided for the purchase of armaments and Germany would agree to furnish Mexico with moral support. In that event Mexico would take up arms against the United States. And Huerta would have his revenge."[95]

These words were publicized in 1917 in von Rintelen's memoirs. He exaggerated how easy it seemed to jump from finding a common enemy in the United States to establishing an alternative government south of the Rio Grande. Nevertheless, historian Friedrich Katz documents that the German naval intelligence service did deposit a total of $12,000,000 in Cuban and Mexican bank accounts as financial backing for the coup. Barbara Tuchman proves that the Deutsche Bank in Havana, Cuba, opened an account in the name of Huerta for the amount of 800,000 pesos. Another 95,000 pesos were placed in a Mexican account.

Naval contact Carl Heynen, a partner in one of Mexico's largest shipping agencies, also worked with Heinrich Albert in New York. Together with Federico Stallforth and his brother in Chihuahua, the men purchased eight million rounds of ammunition for Huerta in St. Louis. German historian Reiling discovered that von Papen traveled to the U.S.–Mexican border to scout possibilities for German reservists to help Huerta. He also considered depositing funds at Brownsville, El Paso, and San Antonio to finance disturbances along the border.[96]

In the end the plan specified that Huerta was expected to cross from Newman, New Mexico, into Mexico to demand political leadership. A military campaign would unroll as a dual attack. In the north, Pascual Orozco would coordinate uprisings in Mexican border cities. In the south, Félix Díaz was to lead groups of revolutionaries against Mexico City.

Once his uprising concluded successfully and Huerta declared war against the United States, more secret German money was promised. In addition, the German navy would provide naval defenses against auxiliary cruisers and submarines.[97]

Huerta left Barcelona for the United States in March 1915. He arrived in New York City on April 13, 1915. There, he connected with the ongoing preparations.

In June Huerta concluded coup preparations. On June 25, he took a train with San Francisco as its final destination. At a stop in St. Louis he suddenly changed trains and proceeded to Newman, New Mexico, a very short distance from the border. There, Pascual Orozco was expecting Huerta, ready to help him cross into Mexico.

Huerta made it to Newman without problems. However, when he stepped off the train he was welcomed not only by Orozco but also by U.S. Treasury agent Zachary Cobb. Then Secret Service agents arrested the baffled former dictator, and the coup collapsed. Only Pascual Orozco was able to escape back into Mexico on July 2.

Then, on July 24, 1915, in New York, U.S. Secret Service agents stole Heinrich Albert's bag during a subway ride. It contained detailed and extensive financial information about German secret operations inside the United States at that time. From August 15 on, documents found in Albert's bag were published in *New York World* and the *Chicago Tribune*.[98] German naval and military intelligence but also the camouflaged, fledgling German purchasing commission would never again operate without observation by U.S. counterintelligence. By the end of 1915, Dernburg, von Papen, and Boy-Ed had left the United States. A major first chapter in German secret warfare had ended.

Fortunately for the Wilson administration, great economic and political damage, so far, had been kept at bay. Unfortunately for ethnic minority groups inside the United States, the captured bag of Heinrich Albert contained highly disturbing and irrefutable proof that the German government was using a variety of ethnic groups inside the United States to create disturbances and subversions.

German diplomats, Emperor Wilhelm II, and German military intelligence joined these subversions with similar activities in other countries in an effort to change balances of power on battlefields, oceans, and also negotiation tables. No doubt there was German secret warfare in Asia and the Near East as well as in the United States. Splendid isolation in 1914 and 1915 was a fiction.

The Fourth Wave: Six Ethnic Groups inside the United States and the 1916 U.S. Presidential Elections

How could we be so naive as to believe that the United States was spared the manipulation of domestic ethnic groups by imperial powers during World War I? Scholars have analyzed in detail ethnic warfare in Europe, Africa, the Near East, and Asia. The U.S. historians Louis R. Sadler, Charles Harris, and Friedrich Katz have done so for Mexico and the U.S.–Mexican border. But somehow the historical territory inside the United States remains curiously untouched by activities that soiled other continents. The following pages will provide, at least, an introductory look at activities involving the Germans, the Japanese, the Indians, and the Irish. It is an invitation for future scholars to expand the object of study and to dig deeper.

Irish rage against the British was an obvious, well-known fact in European diplomatic circles centuries before World War I. For decades some Irish Americans and Irish revolutionaries had come to appreciate U.S. territory as a safe haven for plotting against Great Britain. In July 1914, Irish revolutionary Roger Casement traveled to the northeastern part of the United States to buy weapons to use in the next round of killing in this old Irish–British enmity.[99] Also he hoped to recruit new Irish American volunteers in Philadelphia. Finally, he looked forward to recruiting in Philadelphia new Irish Americans who would provide secret financial support. German historian Reinhard Doerries convincingly demonstrates that the Irish pursued this path of action independently of any form of German contract.[100]

Elsewhere in the United States, long before the war, descendants of German immigrants had organized themselves in the Deutsch Amerikanische National Allianz or German American National Alliance (DANA). Originally DANA simply functioned as a mutual aid society, just like similar ones nurtured by Chinese, Italian, or Hispanic ethnic groups in the United States. It gained more prominence after 1901 as it featured prominently during the visit of Germany's Crown Prince Heinrich to the United States.[101] Before 1914, the longing by some German Americans to play a true nationwide role could not be realized with DANA. In 1907, the U.S. Congress even provided the German American National Alliance with a distinct charter affirming that it was only a patriotic cultural organization and that it was not involved in international affairs.

DANA first demonstrated select regional importance when brewers increasingly clashed with other domestic U.S. groups eager to impose a prohibition of alcohol on U.S. society. This conflict quickly assumed several cultural-social layers. One of them was a cultural war of "German beer" against "British temperance." German brewers increased funding to DANA as it became a domestic ethnic pressure group working against prohibition.

In the years that followed DANA succeeded at gaining a respectable ability to influence regional elections. In matters of prohibition an endorsement or flagging by DANA could make a difference. In regions with a strong ethnic German presence DANA also delivered votes in campaigns seeking to support the teaching of German in U.S. schools. Still this modest regional strength remained limited to competition in cultural battles, such as those over alcohol and German as a second language.

As temperance movements were identified with British nativism and drinking beer was seen as a core German ethnic activity, this cultural war helped grow DANA. Membership expansion and regional political success also emboldened its head, Charles Hexamer. He hoped that his organization could soon move from regional to national political powerhouse. Hexamer's ego was encouraged in a way that would not be helpful to Germany in the future.

In this context the enemies of all things British inside the United States were also discovered by DANA. Already in 1908 Hexamer and DANA had entered

13. Dr. Charles Hexamer attempted to make a personal political career out of taking ethnic advocacy in the name of German Americans to unprecedented damaging heights (Library of Congress, Washington, D.C.).

into a contract with the Irish Catholic Order of the Ancient Hibernian. The two organizations signed an agreement of cooperation. What this so-called cooperation entailed in detail remains unidentified.

In 1911, two hundred delegates met in Washington, D.C., for the DANA national convention focusing on the welfare of German Americans.[102] By the end of 1913, the organization boasted two million members organized in twelve hundred chapters across the nation. These statistics could easily be misread. It meant only that DANA showed a nationwide presence. When World War I broke out it was not an effective streamlined organization able to execute effectively the political will of a few leaders or a propaganda guideline coming from Berlin. Hexamer acted both as a genuine, driven U.S. ethnic activist and as somebody who wanted to be more powerful.

When World War I broke out, DANA head Hexamer grabbed German needs as an opportunity to exploit a theme that would bring him both recognition from Germany and finally a nationwide elevation of respect among German Americans. If claiming direct support from Berlin helped in the pursuit of power in the United States, he had no qualms about exploring this avenue. It was a poor choice because Hexamer had no experience navigating a global propaganda war in which all sides manipulated ethnic issues.

Only beginning in 1914 did the German army and German diplomats push ethnic communities inside the United States further toward becoming a security threat. Previously, the German navy had selected and inducted a small number of reservists in North and South America to provide clandestine assistance during a war against Great Britain. German Ambassador to the U.S. Count Bernstorff explained in October 1914, "The mood against us in England appears to be so thoroughly embittered that it can't get any worse. German declarations for the Irish, the Poles, the Jews, the Finns etc. could only have a positive effect here."[103] More and more ethnic popular sentiments in the United States were courted during the first months of the war to put pressure on the British to remove themselves from the war and return to neutrality. In this propaganda war the emotions and longings of ethnic groups inside the Americas began to play a significant role. The price was the loss of innocence of ethnic minorities vis-à-vis Germany and Austria-Hungary as well as subsequent accusations.

In fall 1914, making oneself helpful meant suggesting to German military propagandists that the Irish–German cultural dalliance against the British could be expanded inside the United States. Right away, Military Attaché von Papen, Attaché von Igel, and Ambassador von Bernstorff paid attention. Others say that it was Irish revolutionary Casement himself who approached von Papen, asking for money, logistical support, and, most importantly, German diplomatic recognition for a new independent Irish state, once a revolution during World War I could break Ireland out of the British Empire.[104]

On August 9, 1914, following a mass meeting of Irish associations in the United States, von Papen and Casement explored German military support for the Irish independence struggle. Von Papen recognized that German support for Irish nationalism in the United States, regardless of its outcome, could win more Irish American journalists for the German war effort in the immediate weeks to follow. Their sympathy "will influence public opinion inside the U.S. favorably and can mean assistance for Germany." In October 1914, German Ambassador von Bernstorff joined von Papen and recommended to Berlin to intensify Irish–German cooperation.[105] They endorsed Roger Casement's travel to the Foreign Ministry in Berlin for further talks. Albert personally wrote to Germany that thirteen million Irish were "human material" ready to be manipulated.[106]

Before 1914, inside the United States there existed a German press office that conducted traditional press campaigns in favor of Germany, if political need arose.[107] In September 1914, von Papen initiated a change of its operation. The organization's new focus became targeted ethnic hearts and minds press campaigns. Von Papen opened a new press office, financed by the German Foreign Ministry. This Central Office for Foreign Service (Auslandsdienst) received money also from Heinrich Albert in New York. This was no longer just spontaneous letters to the editor by German Americans. It was German government press manipulation of U.S. ethnic public opinion through newspapers or films.

In November 1914, Irish–German cooperation began to nudge Irish nationalists in the United States.[108] And in Berlin, Casement offered to Germany what Polish and Finnish revolutionaries had offered the Japanese Empire: if Germany supported Irish separatists, he and his men would weaken moral fortitude within the British army, subverting Irish recruits. He predicted "a total stop of British recruiting in Ireland, and, in addition, possibly an alienation of Irish recruits already won, to mutinies of Irish troops and even to unrest inside Ireland." In return, Casement wanted the German navy to transport Irish revolutionaries and weapons to the Irish coast. Soon thereafter a major Irish uprising would weaken British bargaining power further in international affairs.[109]

But such extensive demands required time to discuss. In the meantime both sides agreed to start joint ethnic propaganda inside the United States. From then on the flames of Irish nationalism inside the Americas was also fanned by German agitators. This propaganda sought to discredit the British among U.S. newspaper readers in general and Irish and also German ethnic organizations in particular.

For that purpose Germany sent Dr. Kuno Meyer, a renowned expert on Celtic culture, to the United States. His lectures invoked a joint Irish/German past, based on Celtic history. It was no coincidence that he also talked in favor of Irish separatism. Roger Casement, in turn, instructed his fellow activist Joseph Mc Garrity "to get the Irish and Germans in the U.S. absolutely united wherever Kuno Meyers goes."[110] In 1914, propaganda manipulations joined the intense economic warfare described previously.

Documents also reveal German manipulation of Japanese Americans. The German tactic was to create violent conflicts between Anglo-Americans and Japanese Americans. Then, it was hypothesized, the Japanese government would become absorbed with dealing with the crisis of its descendants in the United

States. This would turn the Japanese elite's attention away from exploiting temporary German weakness in China.

Ironically this manipulation campaign was helped by the genuine individualism of Japanese emigrants residing along the U.S.–Mexican border. In the second half of 1914 and early 1915, several emigrants had run away from their Mexican labor contracts and enlisted as mercenaries for Mexican revolutionary factions. From the outside, however, it remained unclear whether their action was an individual decision or a Japanese government–sponsored campaign. Local racist U.S. writers' stereotypes, of course, encouraged the idea of a conspiracy. Today we know that this interpretation was wrong.

In this economically depressed region joining a revolutionary faction meant paid work that was less and less available in Mexican agriculture or mining. The likelihood of survival as a mercenary was great in 1914 and early 1915. Fighting was still mostly sporadic and not yet a senseless slaughter. Japanese individuals earned $3.00–5.00 pay per day.

To make matters more complex Japanese mercenaries could be found on all sides. Even the U.S. army recruited Japanese immigrants as agents. The U.S. historians Louis R. Sadler and Charles Harris discovered that their task consisted of poisoning Pancho Villa.[111] In another extreme case a source mentions a regional recruiter who offered eight hundred laborers as mercenaries for hire to a warlord.[112] Such a large contingent of men willing to fight promised to make a significant difference in a region where armies often did not count more than five hundred men. Even better, some Japanese recruits had been through basic military training and the Russian–Japanese war.

Then there were Chinese Mexicans, who appreciated the revolutionary situation as an opportunity to smuggle opium. Slowly the region of Baja California was slipping out of the hands of the Mexican government. Together with warlord Cantu, Chinese immigrants supplied opium to revolutionaries and U.S. citizens of San Diego. Business was good and encouraged the creation of an autonomous zone bordering on the United States. During 1915, Esteban Cantu forged alliances with Chinese and Chinese Mexican smugglers serving lower California.[113]

In sum, ethnic Japanese and Chinese, along the U.S.–Mexican border, fought and smuggled for pay, not for the Japanese emperor or Carranza's race war dreams.[114] They simply joined Italian, German, and Polish adventurers whose activities also flourished in the border region.

None of the Japanese and Chinese realized that, in Berlin, military propagandists had decided to spread incendiary lies about them among the U.S. West

Coast population. Manipulators developed a campaign casting Japanese living between Baja California and Oregon as the already present vanguard of a later Japanese invasion of the western Pacific. Invisible German propaganda interjected itself into local Oregonian and Californian political struggles, nurturing xenophobia.

The evidence that was found after World War I allows at least an educated guess of the German work. Already on July 27, 1914, Undersecretary Zimmermann wrote to German Ambassador Bernstorff in Washington, D.C., to fan anti-Japanese sentiment inside the United States. A secret German propaganda office hidden somewhere inside the United States should produce incendiary lies. Its camouflaged articles would be offered to U.S. newspapers. In particular Zimmerman suggested that they pay attention to Randolph Hearst's anti-Japanese vitriol and explore whether it could be enhanced for German goals.[115]

A propaganda campaign should warn of a plot to separate territory from the United States. The perpetrators were supposed to be ethnic immigrants and Japanese companies, shipping agencies, and secret agents. Two recent events in Asia were pointed out as an example of what was about to happen to California.

The first event cited was the recent takeover of the German concession in Chinese Shantung. Immediately after World War I started Japanese soldiers had occupied the German concession in a surprise move and kept it separate from China. Propaganda argued if it could happen to Shantung, then it could also happen in California, Oregon, Washington, or Baja California.

German propagandists wanted U.S. citizens to be scared into believing that secret Japanese forces were preparing an attack on the United States. It was Germans who reinforced anti-Japanese racism among Californians, Oregonians, and Washingtonians.

The second example cited was Japanese activity in the Philippines. Propaganda was supposed to argue that Japanese business expansion represented an intermediate step toward later imperialist occupation. There too, Germans declared the presence of ethnic settlers to be an outpost for future physical conquest.

Finally, German propaganda identified alleged preparations inside the United States. One German press release was to argue that Japanese exchange students in the United States were really espionage agents. And the Japanese steamship connection between Nagasaki and San Francisco was declared a pipeline that delivered Japanese agents directly onto U.S. territory. Shipping agencies and students would work with Japanese big business and repeat strategies used against Korea, Manchuria, and China. When the time was opportune, a command to start a war would come from Japan.

14. Newspaper owner George Viereck and his *New Yorker Staats-Zeitung* functioned as a major propaganda conduit for Germany during World War I (Library of Congress, Washington, D.C.).

Incendiary newspaper articles were supposed to encourage these rumors to spread by creating a hostile atmosphere. Headlines such as "We have enough colored Citizens: No Japanese as citizen in America—in California are living 60,000 Japs" were to heighten popular tension and encourage action. The German propagandist Sylvester Viereck admitted that he hired at least one writer to compose racist press dispatches and leaflets. In May 1915, Viereck helped in the distribution of 300,000 copies of a pamphlet along the West Coast. A second leaflet campaign took place in 1916.

In the United States, in July 1915 Undersecretary Zimmerman's proposal was discussed in German diplomatic circles. One of the individuals hired to translate parts of the plan into action turned out to be a swindler. He took German money and never acted on his instructions. Others, however, did their awful work.

German government funding paid for the distribution of an anonymous leaflet in Seattle called "Preparedness for the Pacific Coast." It urged readers to proceed with war preparations and to arm themselves in expectation of a Japanese attack.[116]

The historian Roger Daniels discovered a proposal by the journalist Edward Lyell Fox to the German military attaché to fund the performance of anti-Japanese theater plays. In addition he wanted to hire agent provocateurs. He assured the Germans:

> Any anti-Japanese move would have the support of Mr. Hearst.... [T]here should be a play produced in New York, Chicago, San Francisco, and Los Angeles that will send its audiences out of the theatres, heated to the fever point against the Japanese.... [T]he public mind thus prepared, play the trump card with trouble on the Pacific Coast.... [R]ioting in San Francisco, etc against a few Japanese [would be easy to arrange with hired thugs].[117]

From there it was just a small step to approach California labor leaders and use the existing anti-Japanese and anti-Chinese labor movement to carry violence into areas where ethnic Japanese and Chinese people were living. Fox suggested that "the Asiatic Exclusion League, the anti-Japanese organization of the Pacific Coast, enter the plan. Its president has served a term in jail, he will do anything made worth his while.... [I]t would be an easy matter to use some young and 'innocent' prostitutes to the detriment of the Japanese."[118] For example, a detective agency could be used to hire ethnic Japanese prostitutes and use individual agitation within Anglo society to give a bad name to Japanese female immigrants in general.[119]

Finally, Germans targeted U.S. clergy. Press releases should emphasize that ethnic Japanese refused to be Christians and nurture a sense of religious culture clash. Perhaps pastors could be manipulated toward preaching anti-Japanese hatred.[120]

Racism and xenophobia among U.S. citizens might be encouraged to the point of popular unrest, which, likely enough, could shake Japanese–U.S. relations. And it might weaken the British–Japanese alliance against Germany, so German officials' experiments with a U.S. propaganda campaign to create tension between Japan and the United States continued.

The German embassy in Mexico City was in charge of anti-French ethnic groups in the United States. From the Mexican capital the French will to fight against Germany was supposed to be weakened by turning Syrian Americans against France. The vehicle of propaganda was a publication.

Many Syrians had felt abandoned by the Ottoman Empire since before World War I. German propaganda pretended to speak for them in anticipation of a better postwar scenario. In Mexico, Germans hired Antonio Letayf, a pro-German

Syrian, to propagandize against France. They financed a newspaper to capture the minds and hearts of twenty thousand Syrians in Mexico and eighty thousand Syrians in the United States. Its articles encouraged Syrian readers to seek a bond with Germany in preparation of the postwar world. Upper-class Syrians could not be swayed by this simple press propaganda. Their financial interests helped them to stay closer to France. But lower-class Syrians might be won over by a German pitch.[121]

When World War I began, hopeful, politically extreme activists of the German American National Alliance offered their existing organizational infrastructure—without any mandate of the average German American membership—to the German ambassador and the German military attaché for an entirely new activity. No longer would they focus on domestic cultural and social policy; this leadership wanted to deploy its members as voters to elect individuals willing to conduct international relations not according to the national security vision of the U.S. government but, rather, according to the abstract, theoretical understanding of international law, regardless of the context of 1914. Not by coincidence, it would also help the policy of Emperor Wilhelm II. Never before in the twentieth century had a few leaders of German Americans dared to speak, without authorization from membership or encouragement from Berlin, for millions of U.S. citizens of German ancestry or manipulated for national gain their cultural issues and psychological confusion over the emotional adjustment triggered by immigration.

From 1915 on, in the eyes of imperial planners, German Americans were pondered as one unified ethnic bloc whose actions and votes might bring relief to the conduct of war. This assumption was not without merit that warranted experimentation. There were German American individuals with a long tradition of political activism whose activism inside the United States could, now, be more than domestic political expression or self-directed minority protection.

This policy was realized under pressure of war, trying to bring about favorable diplomatic negotiations in the next few months, not an attempt to topple the political order of the United States. Unlike the German navy, which had spent years building its clandestine intelligence organization, German propaganda and voting manipulation needed to resort to an existing structure outside the control of any German military body. The most promising political and social organization, with an existing national network of communication, was the German American National Alliance.

Under conditions of worldwide warfare such assumed collective behavior would be of even greater service. In the international conflict between Great Britain and Germany its influence could create breathing space for Emperor Wilhelm, his aristocratic elite, and the confused Prussian army at a loss how to end the war with a win. Supporters of this idea on both sides of the Atlantic argued that such a bloc could be created by appealing to ethnic origin and cultural practice, though never because the action of the ethnic bloc was in the interest of German Americans.

Finally, there existed a small number of German Americans who nurtured a utopian ethnic ideal that was commonplace in the early twentieth century. They were certain that descendants of German immigrants had indescribable but real essential bonds with the culture and nation of their ancestors. This quasi-biological tie with Germany, they hypothesized, should weigh still more than the experience as citizens of the United States. If pro-British individuals influenced the White House in favor of British goals, why shouldn't select German Americans lobby the White House on behalf of Emperor Wilhelm II? This was the mind-set within which DANA president Hexamer and a few regional chapter presidents pushed their own agenda for political greatness and pulled the rest of the German Americans into historical disrepute.

President Hexamer tried to prove his helpfulness with fund-raising prowess in addition to propaganda tips. DANA backed its claim of usefulness during a world war with a financial demonstration. A fund-raiser collected $300,000 for German and Austrian organizations.[122]

As the fighting in Europe derailed, the German government could not resort to a proven and effective national propaganda organization built by the German monarchy. Any existing nationwide organization, even a weak one like the DANA, appeared increasingly attractive to use. Even better, ethnic Germans in general had voted against the Democratic Party of the current president, Woodrow Wilson. Perhaps German American voting preferences could one day be instrumentalized in national elections.[123]

After pointing Military Attaché von Papen and his propaganda operation toward German–American–Irish cooperation, and fund-raising for war victims, Hexamer next lent himself and the symbolic power of his office to the creation of a political coalition against any U.S. support for the British. On January 30, 1915, Hexamer suddenly spoke as the founder of an American Independence Conference. The presidency of the organization was accepted by ex-congressman Richard Bartholdt.[124] Right away the group engaged in vigorous legal activism against ammunition exports that favored the Allied powers. Clearly, Hexamer had moved beyond culture wars over alcohol and regional politics. He aspired to exercise influence in national and international political, and indirectly military, matters. Hexamer had begun to spend in this war the political and social capital of the entire DANA and squander the complex appreciation of German American contributions to the United States made before 1914. This was still legal activity. But freedom to be an activist should not be confused with a guarantee against intense political backlash, even harsh personal consequences.

Hexamer knew that he was leading DANA membership astray and into potential trouble. Local chapters of the American Independence Committee were supposed to select individuals as chapter leaders who carried a U.S. last name. Local activism was supposed to appear as a genuine U.S. political expression, not German American partisanship. This way they would appear as credible U.S. voices speaking on behalf of the kaiser, not as German Americans possibly financed by German government organizations.[125] The DANA had thrown its hat in the ring against private U.S. companies wanting to manufacture for Allied forces.

From 1914 until the sinking of the *Lusitania* in May 1915, propaganda guidelines from Berlin focused on demanding fair U.S. behavior in the war. German propaganda was to educate the U.S. public that "Germany did not pursue policy to engage America in some form of war[; one had] to avoid the appearance as if one wanted to interfere in Americas affairs, but at the same time demand fair play."[126] In May, after the sinking of the *Lusitania*, this changed. From then on, it was not just shaping popular opinion among ethnic groups inside the United States. It was an effort funded by a government representative, with knowledge of the German ambassador and military officials, to bring about policy change through the ballot box. Heinrich Albert, the government representative who contributed financially to the violent campaign against Allied weapons, also contributed financing to the ethnic manipulation of votes. In his notes he admitted that "propaganda tried to get in close touch with groups that had a pro German attitude, who could, at the same time, take influence on the public opinion as well as influence the coming vote at the next elections and therefore influence the government. First and foremost this meant German-Americans."[127]

Hexamer and some DANA chapters stood in the midst of these activities in spring 1915. From then on what happened inside the United States was both a genuine antiwar movement and a conspiracy whereby German army money secretly supported local socialist and anarchist labor organizations and ethnic groups protesting against the United States. Innocent U.S. activism had long since left the political arena. And it was no longer just voicing an opinion. Instead, agitation became a personal attack on President Wilson himself.

In a few instances the broadening activities began to tear at the fabric of the complex German American community. In New Orleans, German consul Dr. Paul Roh was invited to join the local chapter of the neutrality society. Correctly, he refused, because as a diplomat he was legally prohibited from doing so.[128] A unique diplomatic opposition figure was the German consul in New York, who complained increasingly and aggressively against war support operations by Military Attaché von Papen. He did not want to violate diplomatic custom.[129]

After the sinking of the *Lusitania*, German propaganda became more aggressive and abandoned the demand for fair play. These partially foreign-backed propaganda campaigns against President Wilson showed results. The White House had to take notice of protest meetings in Chicago, Milwaukee, St. Louis, Wilmington, New Orleans, Los Angeles, and Indianapolis. At several meetings German American and Irish speakers jointly harangued Great Britain and its support by U.S. arms exporters. In 1915, John Devoy, the editor of the *Gaelic-American*, Henry Weissman, and Alphonse G. Koelble jointly attacked President Wilson in their articles.[130] The German American Horace Brand, editor of the newspaper *Staats-Zeitung* in Chicago, also helped by Irish American organizations, took the next step. He petitioned members of Congress to pass laws that would prohibit the export of all contraband with the exception of foodstuffs.

A General Committee of Friends of Peace met at Madison Square Garden in June with former secretary of state William Jennings Bryan as speaker. On July 2, in the Maenner Chor Hall, East 5th Street, the organizers voted to expand and to invite the German American National Alliance, the Austro-Hungarian Society, American women of German descent, Irish American societies, the Truth Society, and the Neutrality League to send delegates to a national antiwar conference to be held around Labor Day.

This occurred on the same day as Secret Agent von Rintelen financed the fake National Labor Peace Council. Two weeks beforehand a delegation had attempted to petition President Wilson. Now they would be trying it again with branches in New York, Massachusetts, Pennsylvania, Delaware, Missouri, and Indiana.[131] By summer 1915, the organization had attracted the membership "of two ex-U.S. presidents, more than a dozen ex-members of the cabinet, and seventeen governors of states" and many other community members.[132]

In Brooklyn, on July 11, 1915, Henry Weissman and ten delegates from the Brooklyn DANA demanded that a national conference of German American societies be held. It was to advocate on behalf of peace. Their plan was to participate in the upcoming DANA national convention in San Francisco and to back the national peace plan conference on Labor Day in Chicago.[133]

As World War I slipped into its second year and pressure on the German monarchy grew, imperial war planners and select community leaders began efforts to act as speakers for all German Americans and their U.S. descendants, with disregard for how this tie to international conflict and increasing U.S.–German confrontation would be interpreted after the war. On August 2, 1915, Hexamer's personal ambitions, the needs of the German government and misplaced belief in an ethnic essence by German Americans came together at the German American National Alliance national convention. It was the first time that German American activists from across the country met during a world war. Five hundred delegates congregated at the West Coast location. President Hexamer personally instructed national representatives about the content of the message they were to take back to their local chapters in U.S. states.

Until recently any documents explicitly linking official German government financing with specific propaganda manipulations of elections through the German American National Alliance have remained undiscovered. In August 2009, in Berlin, a collection of the German Ministry of Interior was found to hide a single surviving summary report, written by Heinrich Albert himself. It is the first proof that the DANA political campaign was partially financed by the German government.

Albert wrote to Berlin:

The pro German American circles are encouraged to engage in a pro German activist politics through the organization of the Red Cross, which the local General Consulate had poorly prepared. Excellence Dernburg leans for this work mainly on the German American National Alliance; its influence is born out of the fact that it represents so many votes in elections, so that all parties have to take it into consideration.[134]

When Charles Hexamer spoke at the national convention he, therefore, did not just express himself. He worked on behalf of Germany.

Hexamer told participants that the DANA was preserving the German community as a separate cultural group that was currently living inside the United States. Germans were not to disappear within the U.S. melting pot but contribute to the United States as a separate ethnic group, a unique civilization inside U.S. society that would make all parts of U.S. society more noble. In the eyes of the DANA and Hexamer, German immigrants were to U.S. society what Greeks had been to Rome. Germans had a superior culture.[135]

The 1915 DANA convention produced the desired support. Participants cheered when they heard that Germany had destroyed Warsaw. The delegates sang "The Star-Spangled Banner" but also Germany's national anthem, "Germany above Everything." During the convention, at the Panama-Pacific Exposition a special German Day was celebrated. During the celebration Hexamer was joined by German consul Franz Bopp, the man who was in charge of West Coast German sabotage and who knew about parallel unfolding ethnic manipulations by Indians inside the United States.[136]

At the end of the convention Hexamer was reelected as president. He left the convention feeling that he had received a mandate to proceed with the forging of a united German–American political bloc. Once forged it could be thrown into international debates in a way that this German American speaker saw fit. He never cared to coordinate with the government in Berlin.

Luck helped U.S. policy makers. Over the summer von Rintelen's secret financing of labor groups, the German effort to put General Huerta back on the Mexican presidential chair, and Mr. Albert's role as paymaster for a wide variety of anti-Allied activities were revealed. In particular the theft of Albert's bag in summer 1915 had provided disturbing hard evidence that expressions of ethnic German American voices were not just individual legal expressions of convictions but, sometimes, aggressive German government–subsidized war propaganda.

Regardless, in September 1915, propaganda work using ethnic Germans continued. President Hexamer interjected himself and used the authority of his office to influence once again the flow of war funding. Hexamer telegraphed an appeal to the DANA branches: "I call upon every true American to write to every financial institution in which he has deposited money, protesting against the use of his money for the proposed Anglo-French loan." In addition he advised every depositor in a bank to withdraw all the money he does not actually need and invest it in U.S. securities, state and municipal bonds, and first-class public utility and industrial bonds.[137]

This was a veiled skilled attack on U.S. investment financing military manufacturing. Rather than asking investors to make money available to the U.S. government, which then could chose to extend benevolent neutrality to the Allied powers, Hexamer tried to divert investment to state and municipal bonds beyond the control of the U.S. executive. Technically, this was not illegal, but it was nevertheless a brilliant move pressuring international financial markets.

In regional DANA chapter branches alliance leaders and members did not follow the call uniformly. But Hexamer's call did find selective followings. Still in 2004, the Rensselaer County Historical Society proudly reported that in 1915, the local German American National Alliance branch and its nine hundred members boycotted banks that sold pro-Allied bonds.[138]

Manipulation of the U.S. Congress also was tried a second time. Congressman Richard Barthold from Missouri sponsored a bill that prohibited the export of all war material. His presentation used the scare tactic of arguing that the German and Austrian kinship of twenty-five million Americans "who cast at least five million votes" would be part of the political process. He collected two million signatures, backed by German government–paid German-language newspapers and ethnic German pastors favoring a weapons embargo. It was an impressive showing against U.S. companies producing for the Allies and democracy.

Then there was T. L. Marsalis, a real estate operator, who lobbied on behalf of the DANA in Washington, D.C. He conferred with Senators Stone, O'Gorman, Gore, and Martine and Congressman Kitchin, the Democratic leader of the House. This was not illegal work, but it was a clear demonstration that the radical faction inside the DANA was zeroing in on exploiting the upcoming U.S. presidential election next.

By late 1915, the personal attacks on President Wilson showed results. As he increasingly identified with the pro-British faction inside the United States, he addressed the issue publicly on December 7, 1915. He stated that there were people "who have poured the poison of disloyalty into the very arteries of our national life, who have sought to bring the authority and good name of this government into contempt, to destroy our industries wherever they thought it effective for their vindictive purpose to strike at them and to debase our politics to uses of foreign intrigues."[139] The presidential elections of 1916 were coming up, and ethnic politics would again play a significant, but different, new role. The U.S. electoral system had not been faced for a long time with the potential manipulation of its electorate under conditions of international war.

First there were unsubstantiated rumors. The *New York Times* talked about creating a secret organization to impact U.S. local, regional, and national elections. Without substantiation, the paper wrote that prominent German Americans had received a mailer stating that "in view of the serious political position of all Americans of German blood arising from the unjust and unfounded statements of President Woodrow Wilson . . . it is our holiest duty to revenge to the utmost our curtailed rights as citizens of this country." The circular contended that it was necessary to form a better organization and closer union to show the "nativists what we can do," since "all mass meetings and protest meetings are useless if we are not in a position to show our strength at the ballot box." The document suggests that this was an initiative that came from inside the activist faction of the German American camp.[140]

By March 1916, the German American National Alliance itself helped to sort fear from fact. On March 7, 1916, A. Godshe, the alliance president's confidential secretary, admitted to the *New York Times* that votes of its members would be organized in such a way that they would attempt to influence the outcome of the U.S. presidential election. Ideally, he stated, "the alliance . . . favors the election of a president who is neither pro-British nor anti-German."[141]

As important was his admission that his organization was helping the German war effort in violation of its 1907 charter prohibition. Nine years after receiving the charter, the DANA fought as a deeply political organization to scare U.S. travelers off the ships of belligerent nations; it worked in favor of declaring an embargo on contraband of war; and it continued to make efforts to prevent the U.S. Federal Reserve banks from subscribing to foreign loans.[142]

Victor Ridder, the brother of the editor of the *Staats-Zeitung*, stated on April 23, 1916, that the German American vote was being organized in a campaign against any presidential candidate not acceptable to German Americans.[143] The start of this effort was being made in April in an effort to see that no congressman or senator was returned to Washington who was not in opposition to President Wilson. Ridder is reported to have said, "It is true that my brother and the *Staats-Zeitung* are using all the influence in their power to see that as large a vote as possible is going to support men for Congress Senators and Representatives who are not in sympathy with President Wilson and who can be depended upon to oppose him to the last."[144] In regard to the voting behavior of German Americans who planned to vote Democratic he admitted that "there will be no attempt to swing the entire German American vote until after both the Democratic and Republican parties select their nominees for President, but we will support that candidate who is satisfactory to German-Americans and fight the other."[145]

Individual German Americans went further. In Milwaukee, Wisconsin, Leo Stern targeted the Republican Party. His "Wisconsin Plan" hoped to put into the White House a pro-German candidate by changing the composition of the delegation of the upcoming national Republican nominating convention:

It is necessary that a portion of the delegations to the Republican National Conventions—a quarter to a third, shall consist of approved distinguished German-Americans. With this end in view an interview with the Chairman for the Republican State Committee is necessary. I personally have done this here, and out of twenty six delegates to the National Convention we have been conceded then—I believe that equal representation should be secured in every other state and if in a majority of the states this number could be secured only such a candidate would be nominated as represents the neutral American situation desired by us.[146]

By March, alliance chapters began their attempt to influence the outcome of the presidential elections. In late March, in New Jersey, a county-level alliance went on record against Wilson and asked all chapters in the state of New Jersey to follow its example in the first week of April.[147] On April 2, 1916, the statewide New Jersey committee followed the recommendation.[148] In Massachusetts, at the end of May, the German American National Alliance at its annual meeting expressed sympathy for the Irish Uprising in Dublin and even expressed support for Irish independence from Great Britain. Professor John A. Walz, from Harvard University, was reelected as its state alliance president.[149]

In Chicago a resolution was issued by the Chicago Stadtverband, the city alliance of the German American National Alliance. The Illinois branch sent out a summons to the local chapters asking that Germans stop voting for a particular party candidate and focus their vote based on what would hurt the British cause the most. In May 1916, it stated in its bulletin:

We must act as if it is well known: the German vote is divided almost equally between the two great parties. It forms in a sense the tongue of the wagon. If the German vote swings to one side the other is lost beyond hope as has been proved in earlier elections.

Now is the time. . . . Therefore you German-Americans away with all party wrangling at this grave hour. The Fatherland above party. Let us German-Americans show that we are worthy of our fathers.

The important question now is: How can this work be successfully accomplished? Should a new organization be founded for this purpose (No we have the National Alliance). Can the German-American vote be controlled (Lists should be made and workers in every district selected).

How shall we inform the national convention of the sentiment among the German Americans (By mass meetings by working on the local party leaders by summoning all German American leagues and alliances to cooperate).[150]

Similar events took place in Iowa, Pennsylvania, and Tacoma, Washington.[151] On May 29, the New Jersey German-American National Alliance selected Hughes as the preferred candidate for nomination at the upcoming Republican convention.

Turning the vote against President Wilson moved next to influencing the upcoming 1916 national conventions. To prepare for this effort the German-American Central Bund of Pennsylvania, the parent of the German American National Alliance, sponsored a national meeting in Chicago on May 30. There, invited representatives of German organizations from across the country would be asked to engage in new voting behavior for German American individuals. Party affiliation or particular policy issues were not supposed to matter anymore. Instead, the candidates should gather to form a strong ethnic bloc, a maneuver that should be repeated during the upcoming conventions. The initial conference in Chicago would give "expression to the united opinion of the American citizens of German descent and birth with reference to certain presidential candidates and in order to give that opinion expression and weight." This conference would form a national German-American Conference Committee in preparation of the conventions. Purposely the impression of an emerging united German American bloc was supposed to be created.[152] It remained to be seen how many party leaders would be willing to follow this call.

On May 30, representatives, mostly from the Midwest and East Coast, did assemble in Chicago in the Kaiserhof Hotel near Jackson Boulevard. German American clubs that could not afford to send a representative were asked to endorse the conference's outcome.[153] Fiery appeals were issued before the conventions:

German ideals can be realized only when we have become a political power and has there ever been a time when there has been more need for us to be united politically than at the present time? Are we not surrounded everywhere by enemies?

... We must above all things tear ourselves away from every day party yoke so that we may be in a position to give our votes in the next election wholly without reference to the past.[154]

Hexamer distributed a memo at his own expense, declaring that "no self-respecting American of German birth or extraction can vote for President Wilson."

On June 10, 1916, the Republican nomination went to Hughes. Radical German American leaders felt that their plan was working. There was no Democratic candidate the DANA felt like endorsing.

Now, at least select German American organizations seemed to follow President Hexamer's propaganda and publicly endorsed Hughes. On June 13, the National Council of the Teutonic Sons of America endorsed him.[155] In Chicago, Louis E. Brandt stated that the Illinois organization was about to mail letters to three million members in the country to support Mr. Hughes.[156]

John B. Mayer, president of the Central Alliance of Pennsylvania, on August 5, 1916, shared that representatives of the religious, singing, sport, and military state branches of the national alliance from forty-two states showed up for the endorsement.[157] The Ohio German Alliance endorsed Hughes and Herrick in October.[158]

But influencing the German American vote was all that the activists with possible German financing could do. They could not control individual German Americans. DANA president Hexamer's dramatic charge against Wilson did not produce easy uniform success. For example, the chapter in Buffalo did not back one candidate but, rather, suggested that each member should vote his conscience. Second, the North American Gymnastic Union, with fifty thousand members, declined to follow invitations.[159] In Ohio, the Canto and Gallion branch defied the state organization. In other states similar events took place.[160]

President Hexamer and the DANA organization's leadership knew during the entire time that they were burning the German American community's reputation as fast as they could. In October Hexamer wrote from Philadelphia:

> Since our National Alliance is not permitted to spend a cent for the election of a federal official without its president and its board of the directors being liable, according to paragraph 83 and 37, I am using for this letter my private business paper. The time has now come when German-Americans must come out openly and fearlessly for Hughes and Fairbanks. If Wilson is elected, our political impotence will be sealed and we shall be made powerless for a long time.[161]

Until election day candidate Hughes continued to look promising for Hexamer. Before, as a stereotype most German Americans could be expected to vote for the Republican Party. And not since Andrew Jackson had a Democratic president been reelected to return to the White House. At the eve of election day, 1916, Hughes appeared to have a solid lead. On November 8, the *New York Times* even declared Hughes the next president of the United States. Could it be that Hexamer's efforts had helped to push Wilson out of the White House? The *New York World* and other papers declared Hughes the winner soon thereafter. The Midwest voted Republican. Even President Wilson prepared himself for a likely defeat.

It would take the arrival of California's vote to reverse Hughes's increasingly likely victory. California gave Wilson thirteen electoral votes.[162] Now, on paper Wilson had won 277 votes, and Hughes only had 254 votes. Still, Hughes held out for fourteen days before he conceded defeat.

U.S. historian S. D. Lovell states, first, that it is "doubtful that a great majority of German-American voters followed the German-American National Alliance's lead." Second, the effect of the "German-American vote for Hughes was very probably counterbalanced by the vote of non German-Americans who disliked conscious hyphenism."[163] Third, the election of 1916 turned on several issues, not one single issue. Not the least, for the first time 25 percent of all forty-eight participating states included women in the voting process.

Nevertheless, the defeat of the radical German American ethnic activist faction within DANA should not be misinterpreted to mean that there was no credible German attempt or serious nationwide effort to use a domestic ethnic group to change the man in the White House in favor of German war policy.[164] The year 1916 showed that the German American camp contained a special, radical ethnic rights faction that could be engaged and used for German goals from the other side of the Atlantic. And in World War I this strategy was tried.

As soon as the U.S. Congress declared war against Germany Hexamer urged all DANA chapters to act as loyal citizens of the United States. Officials close to the British nevertheless filed a lawsuit that investigated the financial links between German-named breweries, among them Pabst and Hamm, and regional chairs of the DANA in St. Paul, Milwaukee, and Indianapolis. The global context of propaganda was now clashing with the anti-prohibition, national policy goals of brewers and the activism of select German Americans.

Nevertheless, in Germany the influential Count Reventlow exclaimed that German Americans had become traitors. Transatlantic expectations about ethnic bonds proved particularly painful and complex.[165]

Indians, just as the Irish, had worked for more than a century to destroy British colonialism. The famous mutiny of 1857 remained prominent in the idealized memory of many Indian elites until World War I.[166] In Germany, Indian expatriates had organized themselves into anti-British clubs. The prominent Indian Nationalist Party opened an office in Berlin, and some of its members were known to German government offices. Probably Wilhelm II's government provided small stipends already before World War I.[167]

One group living in voluntary exile in the United States prepared for a new anti-British plot. Led by a so-called Society for the Advancement of India, it intended to carry sedition and unrest into British India.

Small groups of supporters from within the Indian American community wanted to contribute to such an attack. In particular, U.S. state university colleges as well as labor camps in the northwest where Indians worked as cheap laborers served as recruiting grounds. Selectively Hindu students and workers were recruited to travel back to India, when the time was right, to commit acts of terror or help in the mutiny of British Indian troops. One of the elite financiers of this campaign was the maharaja of Baroda, a rich, influential prince. Middle-class Indians contributed smaller financial donations.[168]

In 1908, Indians on the U.S. East Coast opened a headquarters in New York at 364 West 120th Street.[169] Additional social organizations opened in Chicago, Denver, Seattle, St. John, and New Brunswick.

In 1913 Indian activism was strengthened with the publication of a newspaper in California published by Har Dyal. It attempted a unifying multiethnic approach, trying to appeal to Hindus, Sikhs, and Muslims in India to attack the British jointly as Indians. The propaganda paper's name was *Ghadr*, meaning "mutiny."

Not surprisingly, German military and naval attachés in New York recognized the potential of Indian hatred to hurt the British. Von Papen went further in his support for the Indians than for the Irish or the Japanese. Support for India came to mean not only backing propaganda and the exploration of joint guerilla warfare but immediate military cooperation with Indian revolutionaries living inside the United States.[170] Either way academic institutions and a small number of professors and intellectuals featured prominently in preparations for revolt from U.S. soil.

Unlike in the Irish–German case, where military support came about only slowly, Germans were determined to carry out fast violence and mutiny in India. From the very beginning the German consulate in San Francisco assigned its Leutnant der Landwehr Reserve von Brinken to help with coordinating Indian groups to achieve mutiny.[171] In 1914 and 1915, the diplomatic immunity of the

German consulate in San Francisco, and the secrecy it afforded, was being used to weaken the British armed forces. After Canada and the Panama Canal, India was the third target for German diplomatic employees working in California.

The details of Indian–German cooperation were worked out in New York. Apparently, a clandestine German office in Shanghai also helped.[172] With the help of Carlos Heynen in Mexico, arms were purchased and forwarded to kill British soldiers in Karachi, India.[173] Heynen shipped thirty thousand rifles and twelve million rounds of ammunition into Bengal on the SS *Maverick*.[174] British intelligence frustrated this German-backed preparation for a second uprising.

In February 1916, German military intelligence announced that Dr. Chakravarty would head a new, German military–financed, East Coast office of Indian revolutionaries.[175] The Indian doctor traveled via Mexico to New York with orders from Indian groups in Germany. One order was to expand activities into the British colonies of the Caribbean, many close to Mexico.

The main goal was the recruitment of Indian emigrants willing to travel to India as revolutionary fighters. By May 1916, Indian agents had managed to recruit in Trinidad three dozen individuals willing to fight for Indian independence.[176] Soon thereafter the men demanded weapons.

By July 1916, the recruitment of Trinidad terrorists for India was no longer enough. In Port of Spain, Francis E. M. Hussain was charged with building an organizational foundation for a Hindu ethnic uprising in the Caribbean itself. Indian revolutionaries and their German backers were fantasizing that an uprising in this British colony might establish the first Hindu republic in the Caribbean. Its success and the news of Hindus governing themselves in Trinidad and Tobago were expected to travel through the international press to India and inspire Hindus there to repeat the Caribbean example.[177]

British Guyana was selected as a second location for Hindu uprisings in Latin America. By August 1916, German Ambassador Bernstorff reported to Berlin that Chakravarty and his supporters had organized a group of West Indians in the colony. There too Francis Hussain, a lawyer in Port of Spain, was involved. He was using an unknown Gongoles Party and proclaimed it to be a revolutionary vanguard organization.[178]

It should not surprise that conspirators dreamed that anti-British revolutions in the Caribbean might have a ripple effect north of the Panama Canal. One agent argued that "a strong fighting body of colored people would have ramifications all over Central America, including British Guyana and Guatemala."[179]

Mid-level Indian operators urged Berlin to continue to strive toward open insurrection in the Caribbean: "Arms can be easily smuggled there and if we can get some of the German officers of this country to go there and lead them there is every possibility that we can hold quite a while."[180] Indian revolutionaries and Indian Americans at all times acted independently but appreciative of the flow of German military money. Throughout fall 1916, Indian leaders urged Berlin to send weapons and trainers to the Caribbean. Everybody was enthusiastic about the prospects and waited only for the final German go-ahead.[181] But it did not come.

Then leading Indian revolutionary figures began to consider forbidden alternatives to cooperation with Germany. If the Germans were not willing to rain mayhem on India in 1916, perhaps Japanese elites might be more open to help with less hesitation.

In fall 1916, the new Terauchi administration in Tokyo was visited by Dr. Chakravarty. He explained in greater detail anti-British plots and the desired use of Chinese territory as a staging ground to invade India.[182] Also Indian Nobel Prize winner Rabindranath Tagore visited Prince Okuma and Premier Terauchi to explain ongoing plots. Both men asked for tolerance to use Japanese territory, even though Japan was Great Britain's ally!

According to German sources, these Indian revolutionaries left their meetings with Japanese nobility with the feeling that they were not opposed to Indian plans. They were only displeased that imperial Germany was their backer. Japanese intelligence was also monitoring Indian rebel groups traveling through Japan to the United States. They reported their activities to the leadership, but they did not stop their journey. Moreover, the Japanese government already maintained a basic intelligence network inside India.[183]

Late in 1916, in the United States, Indian revolutionary leaders received unexpected, sobering news from Germany. In Berlin, their plans for the Caribbean still did not receive the same priority as German plots backing ethnic uprisings in Russia, Finland, Poland, and the Near East.

The reason did not address Indian needs. Mostly U.S. presidential elections were still expected to elect a more pro-German candidate. Large-scale German-backed uprisings in Central America and the Caribbean, before November 1916, would only motivate U.S. voters not to vote for the candidate considered more friendly toward Germany. Indian revolutionaries were told that 1916 was not the year of rebellion. German naval intelligence only wanted to launch unrestricted submarine warfare, not yet revolution against Trinidad.

German military conspirators in Berlin did invest heavily in the Indian cause. Still, their work focused on propaganda, establishing a smoother-running reporting and intelligence service, and recruiting future revolutionaries among the

Chinese. Interestingly it involved an ever more complex use of Japanese individuals. Mr. Huelsen from the army's Department IIIb reported that a Japanese individual with the name Hideo Nakao had been sent from Berlin with new instructions for New York's India committee and Mr. Chakravarty.[184] This campaign was supported with 50,000 RM.

Nakao waited in Oslo in the Hotel Angleterre at Karl Johansgate 2 to receive his instructions.[185] First he would sneak through Carranza's Mexico into the United States. Then he would reorganize the propaganda pertaining to India. For that purpose a confidant in Bombay would be installed. He in turn would order messengers to carry news into India's regions. Secret printing centers were established in Baroda and Hyderabad. Pamphlets and books printed there would be forwarded to anti-British princes inside India.

Intelligence traffic outside of India was supposed to be helped by creating an export company that would offer a cover for carrying secret information. This "Far Eastern Agency" would employ ethnic Indians, Japanese, and Chinese who would carry mail out of India and on to Berlin.

In Calcutta the recruitment of Chinese individuals from the Chinese colony explicitly for revolutionary work was to begin. And for the first time attempts were made to enlist Japanese consuls and captains in India if they showed themselves open to help.

The plan also included propaganda work inside Japan. In Tokyo Indian propaganda targeted important social and political leaders. With their help a permanent pro-India sentiment was supposed to be built. Hideo Nakao was to select skilled individuals willing to work for the Germans inside Japan. Agents sent from the New York committee to Japan would help him.

Finally, Hideo Nakao involved himself in renewed attempts to detonate the tracks of the East Siberian Railroad. The Zinc and Leadmine in Tetiuhe was singled out as a target. Nakao was told the engine parts and machinery that needed to be sabotaged.[186] His telegram cover name was Sphinx.[187]

In August 1917, the German army high command still had not backed the Indians in the United States in a way they had expected. Now Indian revolutionaries looked for new supporters with greater determination than before. One German agent warned about Japanese–Indian contacts in Tokyo:

> We were informed confidentially that influential government circles in
> Japan declared that financial help was assured, provided that the moment
> chosen for the movement accorded with Japan's interests as war with

England was expected. Please reply at once as to preliminary disbursements as control of the movement threatens to pass from our hands into those of Japan.[188]

In fall 1917, German agents in charge of cooperating with Indian revolutionaries presented an extensive new plan to Berlin's army leadership. By now Mexico City had become the headquarters for actions against India. The Germans reported from Mexico: "The movement to India was entirely organized. The mutiny of native troops was secured, English power certainly insufficient. They were in touch with movement of South China. Dr. Sun Yat Tsen and Governor Yeunan had 30,000 troops for Central Movement as well as ammunition supply. German refugees were gathering along Turkestan border." The plans had been worked out by Dr. Karl Gebberman, agricultural adviser for the formerly royal German government in New Guinea. His helper was Vincent Kraft, who had once owned a plantation in the Dutch colony of Indonesia. The German high command had sent Kraft to Indonesia to incite revolution before 1917. Kraft's plans were evaluated as excellent, whereas agents in Mexico counseled caution about Gebberman.[189]

It is likely that by late 1917, Japanese agents inside the United States, on their own, communicated with Indian rebels. For example, a U. Iwashi, a law student at Colombia University, New York, identified himself as a member who was part of a still unknown secret service.[190]

At first, contacts in Japan and Japanese banks had mattered only because of German operations. For example, in fall 1917, the Indian nationalist M. N. Roy, after assuming the leadership of anti-British work for the Germans, decided to travel to Japan, courtesy of German intelligence funds. A Mexican diplomatic passport was supposed to protect him diplomatically. After his arrival in Japan, he was to receive help from the Mexican consul in Yokohama and access to the financial services of Japanese banks.[191] Also, the Japanese agent Nakiao traveled from Mexico to Tokyo, this time to purchase arms for Carranza. Once in Tokyo he, too, was expected to get in touch with Mexico's diplomatic representation. Its commercial attaché, Jimenez, and another embassy colleague were expected to join him in the effort.[192] Finally, German agent Vincent Kraft and his assistant, Mr. Martin, planned to travel from Mexico to Tokyo to find out for themselves how much Japanese agencies were willing to help with Hindu conspiracies against Great Britain's colonial India.[193] But by fall 1917, in the realm of anti-British plots, German, Indian, Mexican, and Japanese agents and institutions found themselves increasingly exchanging favors.

By the end of the summer of 1917, Japanese bureaucrats moved from sympathetic tolerance toward other countries' plots to interested but still peripheral involvement. On August 27, agents reported that "Japanese government circles assured financial help." There was one downside to the Japanese encouragement. Japanese leaders wanted Indian revolutionaries to act when it was in the Japanese interest, not when imperial Germany wanted to strike.[194] Even though Tokyo bureaucrats admitted a growing sympathy for Indian plots against the British Empire, for the time being, "under no circumstances would they want to reveal themselves vis a vis Great Britain."[195]

Previously, Japanese police inspectors had reported on Indian revolutionaries plotting against Great Britain on Japanese soil. Select elite members apparently read police reports about anti-British activities. Still, the German records show that mid-level representatives and Indian nationalists were willing to explore "very carefully (Japanese would feel out) a relationship with a (German) military representative, but never a diplomat."[196] Japanese intelligence was no longer just listening to imperial German and Hindu plot ideas. Now they were open to becoming handmaidens.

The discovery of select Spanish individuals and the exploitation of their dislike for anti-U.S. policy make for a final fascinating story. It was far less planned, and Germans almost had to be forced to see this "ethnic resource." It was also the beginning of ever deeper cooperation after 1920.

Before the war German leaders had strongly discounted the importance of Spain. A few businessmen had urged politicians to pay more attention to Madrid. They did so with racist expectations, thinking that Spaniards were "from the hot realm of the Mediterranean" and could easily be patronized.

But it took the outbreak of World War I for German leaders to pay renewed, increasingly serious attention to Madrid. First the goal was a political understanding with King Alfonso XIII. In 1914, when a swift German victory failed to materialize, Wilhelm II, aristocrats, and diplomats expected that solidarity between royals and a shared rivalry against France might easily convince Spanish royalty to join the war on the German side.

As German agents did their best to make up for prewar disregard of Spain a surprising fact emerged. Germans needed Spaniards and Spanish territory far more than Iberian imperialists needed the German monarchy.

After 1914, no political manipulation proved strong enough to pull Spain into the German war camp. Still, German traders and the navy realized how much they needed Spanish business intermediaries and Spanish territory to communicate with Latin America or to menace U.S. interests in the Western Hemisphere. The steadily intensifying economic war over Latin America among Germany, Great Britain, and the United States gave Madrid an importance it had not even enjoyed before 1898. Germans had to learn to endure humbling demonstrations of Spanish independence, idiosyncrasy, and iron political determination.

Spanish elites, too, discovered that history was providing them with unexpected opportunities. Before the war, most members of elite society had not presumed to act as equals with British, German, or French aristocrats. Even Alfonso XIII had remained isolated within European politics. But from 1914 on, the skilled bargaining by the king and government members established Spain as a power with real importance inside Europe and beyond. U.S. analysts, observing these frustrating yet expanding German–Spanish–Latin American triangulations, took note.

In May 1915, the Italians abandoned neutrality and switched to the Allied camp. Overnight, Spain mattered for more than just its anti-British and anti-French policy potential. Now, simple geographic proximity to the last open lines of communication and trade with South America and the Caribbean gave Madrid, Barcelona, Cartagena, and Vigo unprecedented strategic importance.

In Madrid, German Ambassador Ratibor tried to tempt the Spanish cabinet and the king with promises of territorial gains after a German victory. Spaniards were promised parts of territories contingent upon a defeat of France and Portugal. The Germans explained that after a sinking of the British navy, Portuguese territory would be undefended and open for Spanish conquest. Next, they exploited an emotional vulnerability in Spanish hearts caused by British control over Gibraltar. After a German victory in World War I, the German Empire promised Alfonso XIII to negotiate a return of Gibraltar. Finally, the Germans also hinted at likely support for future Spanish war campaigns against French colonies in North Africa.

Alfonso XIII was no royal fool. Rather than extend royal goodwill to Wilhelm II, Alfonso presented Berlin with a very expensive tab for a military industry at a time when Germany faced a most serious financial challenge of its own. Regardless of pro-German feelings, the king asked that Spanish participation in the war be prepared first by giving Spaniards the capacity to defend themselves against France and Italy. Second, Alfonso demanded help to outfit a new, modern Spanish navy. Third, a new, reliable, and independent Spanish military industrial base was to be built, providing Spain with a guaranteed nationally produced supply of arms and ammunition.

Spanish elites not only refused to be swayed by Germans but, from the very beginning of the war, turned German offers into bargaining chips that they cashed in for concessions from Great Britain and France. Spaniards could not avoid the global imperial clash among Germany, Great Britain, France, Russia, and Japan. But having to live through it, Spaniards extracted, repeatedly, advantages that neither the British nor the Germans could refuse. Being desired by all sides afforded Spain benefits that it could never achieve during peace.

Slowly, German diplomats admitted that even though the concept of "a Spanish card" was a helpful metaphor in strategic debates in Berlin, inside Spain, Spanish elites and common Spaniards could not be reduced to "a card"; nor could they be played at the whim of foreigners. An honest appraisal of German political efforts to bring Spain into the German camp was that of complete failure. Spanish political groups were too numerous and too divided to be easily united into one national constructive and cooperative political camp. In meetings, Germans were told what they wanted to hear. But afterward, Spanish leaders exploited the vagaries of the war for their own benefit.

From 1915 on, neutral Spanish ports were the last safe havens in the western Mediterranean where German merchant ships could load coal and water before crossing the Atlantic for Mexico, Central America, the Caribbean, Venezuela, Brazil, Uruguay, and Argentina.[197] First, at a time when airplanes could not reach South America or shoulder any cargo, German Atlantic trade would have been almost impossible without Spanish harbors. Second, the British and French economic blockade in the Atlantic would have been more effective. And third, ethnic German communities in Guatemala, Chile, and Argentina insisted on access to the Spanish railheads in Cádiz and Barcelona. At these terminals, coffee, hides, and grain were repackaged and forwarded to neutral Switzerland, the "back door" of trade into Germany, Hungary, and Austria.

Also, for the German navy, Spain provided critical communication facilities. Neutral shipping agencies, mail services, and wireless signal stations in German embassies and consulates operated as critical relay stations to pass telegrams between Europe and the Americas.

Of course, German captains of submarines and raiders also appreciated occasional Spanish fuel and food. They made it easier to operate far from Germany and to intercept Allied ships traveling from Argentina, Brazil, or Bermuda.

From 1916 on, it mattered less whether King Alfonso XIII could be pulled into the German camp. What mattered most was that Spain, as a territory—its coastlines, Atlantic islands, and ports—had to remain neutral to be used effectively by Germans.

Quickly the Spanish–German relationship added a secret warfare component. Neutral Spain gained rapidly in the esteem of German secret warfare specialists. As in the U.S. setting, German planners were caught unprepared and had to improvise in the first months of the war.

Initially, Spain was seen only as a staging ground for attacks against French and British property. The methods used were the same as in the United States. In 1915, a Professor Doctor Steine from Cameroon alerted the German Foreign Office to the possibility of creating a strike in the Rio Tinto pyrite mines in Spain, a property of the British Rothschild family. Ambassador Ratibor estimated that socialists and anarchists would need 1,000,000 pesetas to finance such paralyzing labor action. The German Ministry of War provided 350,000 RM.

Of course, the German ambassador and his Madrid embassy must not appear to be connected to the subversion. For that purpose a cover company was created called Faehnrich Gesellschaft. However, by the time the plans were prepared, funded, and approved, the British owners had assuaged the Spanish workers and the opportunity for this strike had passed. The seed money for subversion, however, was not returned to Berlin.

Instead, the funds were handed to Naval Attaché Hans von Krohn, who diversified activities. He expanded warfare from labor unrest to the destruction of French and Portuguese manufacturing sites. Added to his target list were also Spanish factories that manufactured grenades for export to England. Superiors in Berlin approved sabotage against industries inside Spanish territory in summer 1915.[198] Explosives that agents were supposed to smuggle inside the factories did not arrive until November or December 1915.

Another initiative was stranger than fiction. A as-yet-unidentified cousin of Alfonso XIII's told Germans that he was dreaming about leading his own personal secret operations financed by them. His secret royal warfare was supposed to expand Spanish influence in Oran, Algeria, and also regain Gibraltar. Additional money was to fund a subversive separatist movement against France. Its agitation and destruction were supposed to create enough French outrage to provoke French forces to retaliate and to cross the Spanish border. In turn, this French invasion was expected to unify rivaling Spanish factions in favor of a Spanish attack against France. Such a small Spanish–French regional war would divert French troops from northern European trenches and push Spain into the German war camp. German military attaché Kalle discussed these ideas with King Alfonso XIII. For the time being, the Spanish monarch limited his cousin's ambitions to subversive press propaganda inside southern France.

Spanish cities also served as neutral, Spanish-speaking meeting places for discussions between German and Mexican agents. In 1915, as soon as deposed Mexican dictator Huerta arrived in his Barcelona exile, German naval agents traveled to Spain to connect with Mexican exiles planning Huerta's return to Mexico City. Large sums of German money were deposited in Havana, hoping to fuel the return of Mexican nationalists who were against the United States out of principle. In May 1916, the German military sent Agent Herman Wupperman to German military attaché Kalle in Spain.[199] First, Wupperman was to assemble components into chemical bombs. These chemical bombs would poison animals shipped to the Allies.[200] Second, he was to cross the border from Spain into Portugal to blow up weapons depots and ammunition factories. Third, after crossing the Spanish Pyrenees into France, he was to dynamite French railroad lines. Fourth, he was to place bombs on ships carrying iron ore transports from Bilbao, Spain, to British ports.[201]

German agents used neutral Spain to open anti-French intelligence networks in Algeria and Tunis. A network of spies was estimated to cost 25,000 pesetas, and the accounting office in Berlin sent a first payment of 20,000 pesetas on August 8, 1916.[202] Another mad suggestion by Prof. Kleine proposed the release of cholera bacillus into rivers along the Spanish–Portuguese border. They would infect Portuguese drinking water farther downstream; planners in Berlin rejected this horrific scenario, fortunately.

Most importantly, the arrival of Agent Wupperman in Spain also meant increasing sabotage and poisonings in Latin America.[203] German military attaché Kalle, contributing to secret activities in Latin America, guided Herman Wupperman in his communications with subagents in Havana.[204] In July 1916, Wupperman, now code named Arnold, was ordered to relocate to Argentina and its existing networks.[205]

At the Río de la Plata, too, agents were planning to poison wheat shipments leaving for the ports of Liverpool and Bristol, Great Britain. In addition, anthrax was to infect Argentine mules before they could be shipped off to the British Indian army in the Near East. Wupperman received live anthrax or glanders cultures via boat couriers. Most likely, he manufactured on-site additional amounts in South America.[206]

By the end of 1916, Germany used neutral Spain in ever more complex ways. All the political promises that Germany had made in 1915 had not materialized. Enough ships of the British fleet had survived the 1916 Battle of Jutland to protect Portuguese and French colonies. Spanish royalty had to continue repressing its imperial designs against its Iberian neighbor and the Mediterranean. By January 1917, the economic dislocations due to World War I were straining Spain's political culture to the breaking point. From then on Spain was more likely to break apart in revolutionary struggles than to be unified and used by any war camp. The economic consequences of the war were eroding the political compromises that had carried Spanish political peace between elite political factions.

Spain's domestic political turmoils never interrupted the work of the German naval intelligence service. On February 5, 1917, the German organization in Spain was restocked with 5,000,000 RM for propaganda work. Then, on February 22, Spanish police officers in Cartagena saw a mysterious man walking close to their city's harbor. After his arrest the man identified himself as Harry Wood, U.S. citizen, who was working for German intelligence. In the water, close to where Wood was arrested, the police saw thirty-one floating buoys. As they lifted them out of the water they found attached to them thirty-one boxes. Once opened onshore they revealed dynamite, guncotton, and gasoline wrapped in waterproof cloth.[207]

Such a major public find of illegal German sabotage material put embarrassing pressure on the Spanish government. It provided evidence to those Spanish political factions eager to move the country into the British camp. It took almost one month to trace the secret operation to the appropriate office in Berlin and to provide the Spanish leadership with a satisfactory explanation.[208] On March 3, King Alfonso XIII was told that the material had been designated for sabotage in South America, not Spain. The crates were merely waiting in shallow waters off Cartagena for a ship ready to pick them up and carry them to South America. Officially the dynamite was needed to sink quarantined German ships in South American ports.[209]

Perhaps this was a truthful explanation. The king pretended to be satisfied. Interestingly, he never asked Germany to stop involving his country in secret action. Rather, he demanded better coordination between German diplomats and army and navy officers.[210]

Spanish banking connections with Latin America gained importance. Berlin diplomats explored whether German bank branches operating out of Madrid could replace the leading role that bank branches in the United States had played, administering the finances of intelligence work in Latin America. In March, a German agent talked with a German businessman to explore whether Germany "for possible needs" could obtain in Buenos Aires a larger credit for South and Central America. Since open wire transfers were not appropriate for obvious reasons, a credit with ethnic German merchants in Buenos Aires was suggested. The idea was to use wool from the warehouses of German merchants in Buenos Aires as collateral for a loan from the German government to fund clandestine war.[211] Also German ethnic businessmen in Mexico began to rely more on Spanish banking services.

Next, between 1917 and 1919, Spanish shipping agencies and their crews became critical to keeping secret communication flowing between German lead agents and cells in Argentina. Germans identified one shipping company that traveled every fourteen or fifteen days from Cádiz to pass through Puerto Rico, Havana, the Panama Canal, Barranquilla, and La Guaira in Venezuela. The British navy could only stop and search these ships but not prevent them from proceeding with secret German mail as long as it remained undiscovered by Allied searches. An analysis of intercepted letters and interrogations of agents showed that "nearly all the enemy agents going to Europe or returning and who have been reported to us, travel on the Spanish steamers. This of course is natural, they find on these ships an assistance and often a complicity."[212] This also meant that Spaniards were willing to smuggle smaller amounts of money in the diplomatic pouch from Germany, through Spain and Havana, to Mexico. The bag would be forwarded to Veracruz and from there on to Mexico City. One of the alleged couriers was a Mr. Weyl, who was connected to the Timmerman family, which operated the smelter Melchior Successor.[213]

An important German mail route started in Buenos Aires in the Wolf Building at Calle Peru 375. The building housed German businesses but also the German consulate. From there recruiters would carry secret mail to bars at the port. There, on March 2, 1917, the recruiter, a Señor Faille, worked out of Al Siberita and the Nelson Bar. He selected prostitutes to carry mail for 100 pesos onto Spanish ships, where first-class stewards were waiting to transport them to Spain.[214] Only the most important German messages were hurried to Europe via wireless transmitter. Another mail distributor was Adolfo Poppi, who forwarded mail on the *Infanta Isabel* to Barcelona. A third recruit was one Manuel Perez Castro.[215]

German intelligence realized that there were enough angry pro-German Spaniards willing to work quietly for Germany. The use of Spanish ships and couriers was not a Spanish government conspiracy but the result of individual pro-German ethnic sympathy directed against the United States and Great Britain.

Mr. Deschamp, the commander of the *Isabel de Bourbon*, was from Catalonia and virulently pro-German. His animosity was fueled by feelings of revenge against the United States after his service in the U.S.–Spanish war. Francisco

Morel served as captain of the *Leo XIII* and helped Germans. Jesus Cira Olana commandeered the *Reina Victoria*, which he used to carry German passengers, propaganda, and mail. German agents in particular preferred travel on Spanish ships over those of the Allied powers, where they could be arrested more easily. Other ships Germans used belonged to the Spanish Transatlantic Co., the Pinillos Co., and Sobrinos de Ezquiaga. Mail to the Italian city Genoa as well as the United States traveled on ships of the Sobrinos Izquierdo.[216]

If hatred of Great Britain and the United States failed to motivate crew members of the Spanish boats, sometimes money did the trick. A Swedish stoker working on the *Infanta Isabel de Borbon* earned extra money by carrying secret correspondence in a double-bottomed parrot cage.[217]

Once the letters had been placed on ships, only the creativity of their carriers kept them from British discovery. In July 1918, the second steward on the *Leon XIII*, whose main job was to take care of provisions and food, placed letters in cans for foodstuffs and in barrels in the steward's room.

Also, select Spanish merchants assisted Germans. A most serious violation of international law occurred in Bogotá when the Spanish legation made available its diplomatic pouch to forward private letters to Germany. In Bogotá, businessman Heinrich Hess instructed his partners in Germany: "A magnificent opportunity has occurred to renew our correspondence through the honorable legation of Spain accredited to this capital who agreed to receive letters for Germany and forward them to their destination through Spanish America to Berlin."[218] Once the mail from Argentina arrived in Spain it was forwarded to false Spanish addresses. From there it made its way to other European destinations.

Agent Arnold left Argentina in early February 1917 for Spain to discuss ongoing sabotage and possibly new instructions.[219] The Spaniard Manuel Barreiro, an honorary Mexican consul in Madrid, in August 1918 left Madrid and took a Spanish ship, allegedly working as a courier between the German embassies in Madrid and Mexico City.[220] Between Mexico and the United States, according to Agent Boehm, the majority of couriers were Spanish women.[221]

In exceptional cases, the goodwill of anti-U.S. Spanish captains could mean German access to a Spanish wireless transmitter. On March 18, 1918, halfway between Las Palmas and Cádiz a German submarine met with the *Infanta Isabel* at 8:45 a.m. Soon, three German officers and fifteen armed sailors climbed on board, heading straight for the telegraph wireless room. For eight consecutive hours the Germans communicated through *Infanta Isabel*'s transmitter with a coastal transmitter in Cádiz.[222]

6 Japan's Navy Exploits the Opportunities World War I Offers

Already in 1914 the war, originally intended to be limited to the European continent, changed the context for Japanese–Latin American relations and Japanese–U.S. relations. The fighting in Europe delighted the leadership of the Japanese navy because the limited war turning into a global German–British struggle offered a universally accepted justification to conduct naval warfare also along the American coasts of the Pacific Ocean. Within months the Japanese navy, as junior partner of the British navy, moved from showing the flag in front of Mexico's coast during revolutionary unrest to refueling in Mexican Pacific ports in order to hunt German warships. It searched for auxiliary cruisers wherever they might hide between the Tierra del Fuego and Alaska.

Great Britain's alliance with Japan, entered into in 1902, was invoked in 1914. On August 23, the London government formally requested that the Japanese navy join its navy in the Pacific and attack German possessions, ships, and secret supply networks. German merchant cruisers were inflicting great damage on British commerce and British security in the Far East. They had to be destroyed.

Germany's naval warfare in the Pacific attempted to slow down the transport of British supplies from New Zealand and Australia to Europe. Cutting Great Britain off from vital Asian supplies could effectively starve British soldiers in Belgium and send their leadership to the diplomatic negotiation table. The German cruiser *Emden*, operating between Singapore and Ceylon during that period, sank over twenty Allied ships. The hunt for the *Emden* showed how difficult and drawn out the fight was. It took forty-eight Japanese and British ships to locate and eliminate this single ship.[1] Then Japan's *Asama* and the cruiser *Hizen* followed the German gunboat *Geier*, in October 1914, all the way from the eastern Pacific to Honolulu, Hawaii. British–Japanese units also hunted the cruiser *Leipzig* as it patrolled up and down the North American west coast, ready to attack ships of the Canadian Pacific Line, which carried goods and ammunition to imperial Russia. Finally, there was the mighty German warship of Admiral Spee. It harassed British shipping routes traveling out of the Río de la Plata into the southern Pacific.

Then, a small British fleet finally located a German squadron resting sixty miles off the Chilean coast. But in November 1914, the Germans inflicted a punishing defeat upon the fleet, sinking two British cruisers. Among themselves British planners admitted that a six-week interruption of trade because of German warships' menacing might force Britain to the negotiation table to accept and to establish German demands for world power. The support of the Japanese navy was crucial for the British to hold the Germans back in the Pacific.

It took until December 1914 for a British task force to defeat Admiral Spee's cruiser group in the Battle of the Falklands. The Japanese ships *Idzumo, Hizen*, and *Asama* joined the search for the remaining German warships. Few people realized that it was the Japanese navy that executed the order "to patrol the West Coast of North America, with the vicinity of San Bartholome Bay as the base of operations." Japan protected the shipping routes used by merchant ships up and down the Pacific coastline.[2]

In April 1915, Californians and the Hearst press became aware of how close the Japanese navy was operating to the U.S., Mexican, and Chilean coasts. That month the cruiser *Asama* ran aground during a storm while refueling in Mexico's Magdalena Bay. The *Asama's* beaching led to the travel of Commander Iwano Chokuei, superintendent of the Yokusuka Naval Shipyard, and Lieutenant Hashiguchi Yasutaka, a chief engineer, to northern Mexico. For more than two weeks 250 Japanese sailors, helped on occasion by neutral U.S. contractors, worked feverishly to free the heavy Japanese warship from the rock off the Mexican coast. Rudolph Hearst and his racist press had a field day, distorting the boat's presence until it became a war scare.

U.S. secretary of the navy Josephus Daniels tried to ignore the popular xenophobia and racism as much as possible, but the accidental presence of the Japanese ship nevertheless rekindled anti-Japanese agitation along the entire west coast.[3] Previous pages showed how German propaganda dovetailed with it.

In this instance, there was no reason to fear the presence of the Japanese navy's ship. In the first six weeks of the war, Japanese navy support for the British stayed within the limits of the agreements of the British–Japanese naval accord. It operated off American Pacific coasts only to join the hunt for enemy ships.

Several miles inland from the beached Japanese ship, the chaos of the Mexican Revolution continued. However, on Mexican territory, the Japanese Foreign Ministry succeeded in protecting Japanese–U.S. relations from alternative, more aggressive policy ideas growing among Japanese naval leaders and businessmen. Japanese diplomacy continued to follow the lead of U.S. policy. In October 1915, Argentina, Brazil, Chile, and the United States grudgingly swallowed the least bitter pill and accepted the Coahuilan revolutionary Venustiano Carranza as the next Mexican president. While this recognition extended only on the de facto level, the Foreign Ministry in Tokyo recognized Carranza as well.

Japan's political elites concentrated their aggressive actions against Chinese regions. Foreign Minister Kato was determined to exploit European weakness and establish an unequivocal Japanese sphere of influence over China. He had to achieve this goal before the Allied powers and imperial Germany could end the war and devote new resources to counter Japanese expansion inside China. Kato synthesized a variety of Japanese policies into the now famous Twenty-one Demands on January 18, 1915. He attempted to exclude other foreign powers from negotiating China's future.[4]

This first Japanese attempt to cash in on the war in the Asian sphere failed. In Tokyo, as the shock over the failure settled, Minister Kato became its first victim. He resigned. The second victim was the Foreign Ministry and its unequivocal supremacy in foreign affairs. The failing China initiative changed the power distribution among rivaling factions. It became possible to execute one imperial policy against that of another policy faction. Policy depended less and less on the final word of the Foreign Ministry and increasingly on the particular interests of political, military, economic, or political factions. As the Foreign Ministry could only object but no longer control, for the first time activities ranging from diplomacy to the funding of secret uprisings by Japanese business conglomerates could be found in the quiver of Japanese policy abroad, including Latin America.

In Micronesia the Japanese Foreign Ministry experienced this fraying of policy control outside Japan. In October 1914, the Japanese cruiser *Asama* participated in the taking of the Marshal and Caroline Islands farther south. Japan's exploitation of this unforeseen opportunity created by World War I occurred without a single Japanese casualty. In Japan the government immediately faced pressure groups, which launched press and political campaigns to keep the formerly German Micronesian islands permanently occupied.[5]

The Navy Ministry and Navy Minister Yashiro counseled for caution and were against a permanent occupation of the islands. But Vice Chief of Staff Admiral Inoue Yoshika and the Naval Affairs Division insisted on a permanent occupation. Regardless of the decision inside Tokyo, in the end, naval squadrons in the South Sea received the order to occupy the German possessions. This step suggested that lower-ranking navy officials, in the fog of a world war, could and would overrule cabinet orders.

The Japanese navy occupied every Micronesian island with the exception of Guam and the British Gilberts. Most importantly, just as the Japanese army deployed settlers to establish a permanent ethnic Japanese presence in Manchuria, the navy now

undertook a vigorous effort throughout the islands to place a permanent Japanese imprint on them. The administrative structures, the education and indoctrination of the indigenous population, the encouragement of Japanese enterprises and the discouragement of involvement by other foreign powers, all reflected the official assumption that Japan was in the islands to stay.[6]

In this part of the Pacific, the Japanese navy felt strong enough to disregard U.S. and British interests and to place ethnic Japanese settlers on South Sea islands. Japanese control backed by the presence of settlers would be difficult to undo later, at the negotiation table. The alliance with the British offered the Japanese navy the opportunity to occupy the German islands and to win a refueling station in the Pacific.

As soon as the navy had established physical control over the islands, ethnic settlers arrived. Government commissions followed and gathered every conceivable fact about the islands' geography and resources. On the other side of the globe in Europe, Japanese diplomats dropped hints that they wanted to hold onto the islands after the war, regardless how the wheel of imperialism would turn.[7]

One key question to answer is whether this Japanese outreach was defensive and limited to the Asian Pacific coast or also took place in the Americas at the same time. We should be discerning when considering the words of Foreign Minister Kato Takaaki. He said that Japan had entered into World War I because of the English–Japanese alliance treaty but also because of "the opportunity to sweep up bases in Eastern waters and to advance the Empire's position in the world."[8] By 1915, military and navy forces showed no qualms about overruling cautionary cabinet politicians and dispatching navy ships, government experts, and ethnic settlers to grab territory when the opportunity offered itself. In this process ethnic settlers played an important role. During times of war, under the right strategic conditions, the Japanese government did not stop the exploitation of ethnic Japanese settlers to advance warlike goals. New sources suggest that in 1915 Central America and the Panama Canal were within view of groups in Tokyo.

There was one feeler whereby the Kato administration tried to explore whether the navy could quietly encourage a coup in Panama. The historical archive of the German embassy in Madrid preserves a set of documents from 1915 that record a cautious attempt by Minister Kato to negotiate a Japanese lease over islands off Panama's Pacific coast.

First there is a letter inviting Antonio Burgos, Panama's diplomatic representative in Spain, to identify political factions in Panama that might be interested in discussing a Japanese lease of the islands of Jicaron and Coibita. Then Burgos was to forward to them a questionnaire that explored possible terms of cooperation. After completion, the questionnaire was supposed to be returned to Kato's office in Tokyo. This initiative was kept at a semiprivate level, well below an official inquiry through regular diplomatic channels. The use of private stationary and absence of government insignia offered Kato deniability if the proposal fell into U.S. hands.

The author proposed, first, the construction of a port facility on the islands to service and supply Japanese ships. Second, the bay at Chiriquí would be fortified, and third, a new railroad would connect the city with the town of Pedregal.

The reward for a Panamanian government willing to enter into a Japanese lease and, therefore, to provoke a diplomatic confrontation with the United States and Great Britain would be considerable but not excessive. Kato's office offered a onetime payment of 2,000,000 pounds sterling and, thereafter, an annual lease payment of 55,000 pounds sterling.[9] Nevertheless, this was enough money to encourage a small coup to create, at least, temporary political change in Panama City—long enough to sign a lease with Japan. Finally, diplomat Burgos was offered a bribe to forward the inquiry to a Panamanian faction willing to sign an agreement. It would establish Japan's first naval base in the Americas.

In the end, the exploration failed. Diplomat Burgos did not behave as expected. The informal feeler and the bribe insulted him. He shared the incident with German diplomats in Madrid, who identified the attempt only as an ideal opportunity to increase U.S.–Japanese tension during World War I.

Within weeks Burgos was recruited as a German propaganda agent. That meant that the German Foreign Ministry provided him with travel funds to take a boat to Washington, D.C. There he was to increase President Wilson's worries about Japanese intentions in the Americas. German records show that Burgos did inform the White House as the Germans had hoped.

Also U.S. records confirm that he traveled to the United States in 1915.[10] The State Department learned about the Japanese offer, but its officials decided not to do anything about it. German hopes of increased friction between Japan and the United States were disappointed. Soon thereafter, Kato became the sacrificial lamb for his failed Twenty-one Demands initiative toward China. Eventually Kato and Burgos disappeared from the historical record.

Still Kato's letter was the third Japanese attempt to lease a base along Latin America's coastline. The Hungarian scholar Ferenc Fischer shows that before World War I, Japan threw its hat into the ring to lease the Galapagos Islands from Ecuador. Next, the U.S. historian William Schell discovered in Mexican archives that the Huerta administration talked with intermediaries about a possible Japanese lease of Magdalena Bay.[11] The feeler in Panama had been attempt number three. The Latin American Pacific realm had become a permanent part of Japanese imperialism for the Japanese navy. Undertakings in Asia and the Americas were increasingly the same.

For the remainder of 1915, the situation remained too unstable for a renewal of Japanese–Mexican military relations. Unlike Germany, Japanese diplomats and commercial companies did not reach out to other revolutionary factions.

The financial underpinning of the new Carranza government was a disaster. Two years earlier, when his revolutionary faction had conquered Mexico City for the first time, he had issued 60,000,000 pesos' worth of paper money. During Huerta's counterrevolution, Carranza issued an additional 43,000,000 pesos for use in the territory he controlled. Later, Huerta and other factions pumped another 600,000,000 pesos into Mexico's revolutionary economy. By the summer of 1915, catastrophic hyperinflation was destroying 90 percent of the Mexican peso's value.[12]

In the fall of 1915, delegates at the Pan-American Conference meeting at Niagara Falls, Canada, floated the idea of strengthening the new Carranza administration with a major dollar loan. But no bank was willing to make a quick move.

By then, Mexico's traditional European financiers France, Germany, and Great Britain were unable to devote money to Carranza. The financing of their world war was far more important than strengthening a shaky Mexican administration.

In February 1916, a U.S. delegation visited Mexico to investigate Carranza's financial situation. Afterward, the financial experts recommended the creation of a U.S. financial commission for Mexico. The commission was supposed to take charge of collection and disbursement of national income until Mexico's defaulted loan obligations were redeemed.[13] The delegation could not have made a more insulting suggestion to Carranza. He rejected it.

Carranza's desperate financial situation made him vulnerable. Private Japanese financiers saw an opportunity. In spring 1916, Toshio Onodera, the president of the Japanese Association in Mexico and Mitsui representative, approached Carranza and offered 50,000,000 yen.

The offer represented the first feeler of informal Japanese financial imperialism in Latin America exploiting revolutionary hardship to establish significant Japanese financial influence in Mexico. The yens promised to constitute the stock of a new central Mexican bank and would afford Carranza the option of establishing true fiscal control over his country. As important was that it offered him unprecedented independence from the financial system that Europeans and U.S. banks had established in the last fifty years. As European investors proved incapable and U.S. investors unwilling to help Mexico, private Japanese banks had decided to extend their activities from processing the remittances of ethnic Japanese to exploring how to prop up Carranza. The U.S. historian Madeleine Chi has described how Japanese experts studied and applied financial aggression to contribute to the conquest of Asian countries.[14] A Mexican central bank based on yen reserves promised to be a major event in the expansion of Japanese imperial groups into Latin American affairs.

What happened after the extension of Onodera's offer remains sketchy. The Japanese donor bank wanted to remain anonymous until its owners felt comfortable enough to identify themselves. President Carranza did not reject the offer outright, and his advisers discussed other parts of the proposal with great enthusiasm. But a Mexican central bank based on yen did not become a reality.

In October 1915, a Japanese businessman, Fukutaro Teresawa, on his own initiative, jumped the gun and offered Tokyo's leadership informal contacts with Venustiano Carranza. Teresawa introduced himself to the Japanese embassy in Mexico City as Carranza's adviser and asked Foreign Minister Kato in Tokyo and the imperial cabinet to pay attention to the unstable revolutionary situation along the U.S.–Mexican border. In case they were interested, Teresawa offered to arrange either secret or public talks with Carranza. Claiming to speak for Mexico's president, Teresawa hinted at Mexican mineral concessions and future access to ports. These promises would become reality once Carranza had consolidated his hold over the Mexican nation and defeated his revolutionary rival Pancho Villa and other, smaller faction leaders.[15]

Tokyo's Foreign Ministry establishment took only notice of Fukutaro Teresawa's feeler. It asked its embassy in Mexico City to provide more personal information about this unknown confidant of Carranza.[16] Also Carranza never mentioned in any document that the man was representing him. Not surprisingly, no further contact took place. Tokyo's Foreign Ministry refused to rush back into active policy in Mexico until Venustiano Carranza had established himself firmly as a viable power holder.

Even though Japanese secret naval policy was frustrated in 1915, the revival of Japanese emigration to Latin America proved easier. In the spring of 1916, in Brazil, the planters of São Paulo rediscovered how much they needed immigrant laborers to sustain their plantation economy. Now that warfare in the Atlantic discouraged the travel of Italian and Spanish temporary laborers, São Paulo planters reestablished friendly immigration laws for Japanese. On May 12 Paulistas not only pretended to overlook racial fears but also restored fare subsidies for Japanese immigrants willing to make the long but safer trip across the Pacific or around southern Africa.

Tokyo's Foreign Ministry welcomed the Brazilian gesture. Bureaucrats realized that in the next years Brazil would be a much safer destination than Mexico, Japan's premier destination for temporary laborers before 1914. Unlike Mexico, Brazil was not in revolutionary turmoil. Even better, it did not share a border with the United States. In other words, anti-Japanese racists in the United States were likely to feel less threatened by Japanese emigration to Brazil than emigration to Mexico's Sonora or Baja California.

Change in world transportation patterns reinforced Brazil's rise as the new emigration destination for Japanese. Naval warfare in the Mediterranean made travel dangerous from Japan to Europe via the faster Suez Canal route. Increasingly, Japanese shipowners tolerated the longer and more expensive route around South Africa's Cape Horn. From there a stop at Buenos Aires and Rio de Janeiro or São Paulo was an acceptable detour before venturing on to Portugal or Spain.

15. Travel from Japan to Brazil across the Pacific as well as around Africa became normal during World War I (Ibero Amerikanisches Institut, Stiftung Preussischer Kulturbesitz, Bildarchiv, Berlin).

Coincidentally, the Japanese–British naval alliance encouraged Japanese private enterprise to expand business with British colonies in Africa. Japan's first official trade commission to Africa in 1916 focused on opportunities in eastern Africa. Increasing African trade required improved legal representation. Thus on August 14, 1916, Tokyo's diplomatic representation in Cape Town, South Africa, was elevated from honorary consulate to consulate. The same consulate was also charged with assisting Japanese emigrants trying to reach Brazilian plantations via South Africa.[17]

In August 1916, the Brazilian government provided a second round of incentives to Japan. It granted exclusive rights to the Compania Antune and its subcontractor, Brazilian Emigration Society, to transport ten thousand contract workers to Brazil. Also, the Iguape Municipal Council proposed to confer upon the Brazilian Colonization Company 14,000 hectares for Japanese immigrant settlers. Aoyagi constructed a second settlement colony called the Registro Colony. Planners hoped to attract an initial three hundred colonist families in

1916. Few contemporaries realized that Japanese emigration to Latin America was changing from temporary contract labor to permanent settlement.

In Tokyo, bureaucrats intensified their involvement in how emigration was organized. Whereas before administrators had mostly focused on licensing shipping agencies for emigration business, now they financed in Brazil a medical clinic for emigrants, a tile factory that manufactured material for housing construction, and an experimental farm.[18] Finally, in December 1916, the government paid the private Osaka Shosen Line as well as the Japan Mail Steamship Co. a much needed government subsidy for their service to Brazil. In addition, the Ministry of Communication designated the route an official mail line. By early 1917, Japanese emigration to Latin America had graduated from simple temporary contract labor, preferably to Mexico, to an increasingly government-managed settlement enterprise focused on Brazil.

Despite these efforts, in 1916, the number of emigrants participating in this renewed Tokyo–Brazil cooperation remained miniscule. That year only four families relocated from Japan to Brazil. From São Paulo, an additional sixteen immigrant families moved to the new settlements. And yet increased government involvement in emigration signaled new, growing government interest in Latin America. The empire expected its emigrants to create and to sustain ethnic colonies, which elite politicians knew they could exploit later as their own exclusive imperial projects once an opportunity offered itself.

In 1916, deeper changes took place in Japanese military planning. The lessons of Europe suggested to planners that future imperial wars would last longer, would be more expensive, and would require much from both nation and ethnic individual. Ethnic Japanese would have to contribute to future war efforts. And warfare of this future type was too complicated to be left to civilians. Japan's naval planners embarked on a radical break with past military traditions, including developing their own armament industry.[19]

First naval thinkers reconceptualized war and drafted plans that would ensure the fastest possible mobilization of money, guns, and horses. Second, army planner Colonel Koiso Kuniaki and Ugaki Kazunari, chief of the army's Military Affairs Section, evaluated Japan's strategic situation in terms of achieving victory in the new sustained global wars. The two men concluded that Japan's existing colonies could not provide the necessary raw materials for such a prolonged war. China's reserves, in contrast, could.

Third, a systematic survey of Japan was conducted, and bureaucrats pondered how the entire people should be involved in the next great war. The solutions they offered for the future required that during the next war all Japanese would be involved.

This included also ethnic Japanese outside Japan's mainland. Planning for national defense now included, at least conceptually in ministry offices, all ethnic Japanese. Of course they were never asked, and elites assumed that they would fall into line, whether in Manchuria or Mexico.

The first noticeable change came in October 1916. General Terauchi assumed leadership of a new cabinet, and Japan's scope of international action became more aggressive. It began the next profound change in the administration and policy of Japanese foreign affairs.

Japanese premier Terauchi's key adviser, Nishihara Kamezo, articulated in October 1916 the new policy opportunities that future emigration to Latin America should offer to elites. Nishihara's policy wish list, dated October 2, 1916, stated that emigration—no longer just to Asia but also to Latin America—could serve global imperial territorial ambitions.

Nishihara suggested to settle annually one-fifth of Japan's excess population in Asia and Latin America. About one hundred thousand peasants and their families should relocate to Mexico, Peru, or Brazil. Their relocation would help General Terauchi's administration in three areas. The presence of ethnic people was turning into a political trump card. First, as before World War I, emigration would lighten population pressures inside the Japanese homeland.

Second, the mere presence of settlers would expand Japanese influence in destination countries. The ethnic commercial tastes of settlers would create demand for imports of Japanese goods into Latin America. The growing number of Japanese light manufactured goods would finally join those of Great Britain, Germany, France, and the United States in the markets of Mexico City, Lima, and São Paulo. For the first time ethnic settlements could serve as bridgeheads for targeted economic penetration of Latin American markets.

Third, Nishihara believed that the Latin American destination of settlers could be used as a bargaining chip vis-à-vis U.S. politicians. A diversion of emigrants from Mexico to Brazil might be used to win concessions from national U.S. politicians who worried about regional racist political movements inside the United States.[20]

Nishihara's document was only a proposal, but it proved that as Japanese laborers became Latin American settlers they unwittingly became Terauchi's spearhead for future imperial expansion. Nishihara's note documents that Premier Terauchi was cognizant that, after 1916, the innocent, personal struggle for survival by emigrants across the Pacific was also an instrument for an imperial push into the Americas.

On the outside critics could not argue that Japan nurtured increased Japanese influence in Latin America. No member of U.S. Congress could argue that an aggressive imperial design was unfolding here. World War I offered Terauchi opportunities that previously would have resulted in an immediate international crisis. The German–British global contest centered around Europe brought Japan a windfall of opportunity in Latin America.

What this imperial push could accomplish or how Japan would use it in the future did not have to be decided in 1916. But the figurines for future power plays—ethnic settlers, companies, bank and military advisers—were being moved onto the playing fields of Latin America.

During early 1916 Mexican efforts to invite Japanese military contributions and involvement in opposition to the U.S. had steadily been repeated. In summer 1916, Mexican negotiators learned that a change of government would take place soon in Tokyo and bring into power new leaders with more willingness to allow arms exports to Mexico. Most likely, direct Japanese–Mexican naval and military contacts would sideline diplomats' objections. A resumption of Japanese–Mexican arms exportation promised to take place sooner rather than later.

The prediction was correct. By late summer Mexican attaché Vargas contracted machinery for a cartridge factory and a gunpowder plant. Jose Carpio, Mexican minister of war and Obregón's chief of staff, personally supervised the shipment of the machinery from Japan to Mexico. Still, it took until November 1916 to find a ship, the *Kotohira Maru*, to transport the machinery, Mexican supervisors, and a small number of Japanese technicians across the Pacific. The ship was scheduled to arrive in Mexico in February 1917.

Carranza's military agents were learning how to use Japanese technology to increase Mexico's domestic arms manufacturing base. These were private armament sales, not yet government sales to Latin American rebels.

Finally in December 1916, Japanese arms sales joined technology exports. In December 1916, Mexican general consul Burns, in New York, placed an illegal order for twenty million rounds of ammunition. As soon as U.S. agents discovered this violation of the U.S. arms embargo and stopped it, a private Japanese supplier jumped in and offered to ship the Carranza administration eight million rounds and, a few weeks later, the remaining twelve million. An additional seventy-five million rounds would be available for later purchase. In the meantime, the *Kotohira Maru* continued to approach the Mexican coast; after stopping in Salina Cruz the ship was redirected to Manzanillo.[21]

16. Villa's artillery in Mexico during the Carranza revolution against Huerta's government. There were never enough weapons. Creating an autonomous supply of weapons was a goal that all Mexican revolutionary factions shared (Library of Congress, Washington, D.C.).

After the ship pulled into the harbor on February 14, 1917, the *New York Times* published an exaggerated story stating that two hundred Japanese technical advisers were also disembarking.[22] The Japanese captain contradicted the report and explained that the arms and the components of the armament factory were a private deal, not a conspiracy. Carranza wanted to use the ammunition to battle Pancho Villa. After unloading, Mexican trucks moved the ammunition and the ammunition plant to Molina del Rey outside Mexico City, accompanied by a small number of Japanese technicians.[23]

The weapons and the machinery were unloaded into a radically changing world political situation. Several weeks before, Germany had declared unrestricted submarine warfare. Also, U.S. president Wilson had broken off diplomatic relations with Germany. Now the world was waiting to see whether he would lead his country to the side of the Allied powers. The changes meant that the Atlantic would be tossed into a most ferocious ocean-wide naval campaign, making it almost certain that reliable arms supplies for Mexico, in the future, would have to come from Japan. Even better, the Pacific was open for Japanese trade with Latin America.

Once the U.S. broke diplomatic relations with Germany and entered the war on the side of the Allied powers, the importance of Mexico also increased for the Japanese. Relocating German offices dealing with anti-British and anti-U.S. operations brought their interests in Japanese weapons, bank accounts, and couriers with them.

The year 1917 brought an intensification of Japanese–South American trade relations. Japanese trade during these months spread from Mexico and Brazil to other Latin American countries. In early February, Japan offered Panama a treaty of commerce. Chile, too, encouraged an expanded Japanese economic presence. Already the mining companies Kuhara, Asano, and Turasawa had sent engineers to Chile to evaluate deposits in Chilean mines. Now more private Japanese capital was ready to invest in raw material export from South America.

The collapse of Russia into revolution confirmed that in the postwar world Japan's economic ties with China, Manchuria, and now perhaps Siberia would be of unprecedented importance. The Chilean diplomat in Tokyo was determined to educate politicians in Santiago, Chile, about emerging business opportunities in Asia.[24]

On October 22, 1917, the Chilean minister in Tokyo urged his superiors in Santiago to pay more attention to Japan's expansion. Competition for loading space during World War I was increasing freight rates to a level where the cost of shipping ore from Pittsburgh, Pennsylvania, to Tokyo was the same as shipping ore from Chile to Japan. Pointing at the recent deepening of Brazilian–Japanese connections, the Chilean diplomat urged Santiago also to subsidize a direct shipping route between Japan and Valparaiso, Chile. This development could turn Valparaiso into a gateway for exports to the markets of Bolivia and Argentina. The Chilean diplomat had begun talks with the Tokyo Kisen Kaisha shipping company, which, in turn, was talking to Japan's minister to Peking about a direct Chilean–Japanese shipping line that would also stop in Shanghai.

The Chilean hoped that Japan's need of agricultural fertilizer might be a business opportunity. Japanese settlers in Korea and Manchuria were expanding their agricultural settlements and with them their need for fertilizers. For example, Japanese mulberry trees in these colonies and in Japan required about one million quintals of fertilizer for cultivation. Also, Chilean fertilizers might help Japanese rice farmers. In 1917, no large-scale, organized export linkage existed. Only missionaries were smuggling small amounts of nitrates into China.

Which product could Chile import in return from imperial Japan? The Chilean diplomat suggested coal. Also promising was Japanese military hardware. Already in 1906, a Chilean admiral had traveled to Kobe and Yokohama to study the Japanese navy and the aftermath of the Battle of Tsushima. Now Chilean generals and admirals should consider purchasing Japanese dreadnoughts, submarines, machine guns, ammunition, and machinery for armament factories. There was no longer a reason to limit arms purchases to British, French, and German supply companies. Japanese arms sales to Chile might also increase appreciation among Chilean army and navy members for Japan as a formidable naval power in the southeastern Pacific.

In the end, the opportunities arising out of the Russian Revolution became the decisive factor that brought the Chilean and Japanese governments closer. Japanese elites planned a military expedition into Siberia, and use of Chilean nitrates gained critical importance. Only Chile could provide on short notice enough saltpeter to manufacture gunpowder for artillery shells. Without Chilean nitrates an invasion of Siberia would be far more complicated to realize. While Japanese bureaucrats remained unenthusiastic about a more formal Japanese–Chilean trade agreement, they became adamant about buying as much Chilean nitrate as possible. By 1919, the year of Japan's participation in an Allied invasion of Siberia, Japanese imports of Chilean nitrates amounted to 80,000 tons or two-thirds of its entire supply![25]

By the end of 1917, trade relations spread from Chile to other South American republics. Bolivia, on February 4, 1918, named Victor Munoz Reyes as representative to Japan. In May, he was asked to travel to the Far East to organize the first Bolivian consular corps in Asia. After World War I, Bolivian business would be conducted through China, India, and Japanese offices in Osaka, Kobe, and Tokyo. Bolivia's London office would no longer be in charge of trade with the Pacific.

Ecuadorian officials went further and negotiated a trade treaty of commerce and navigation. It was signed on August 26, 1918.[26] A few months later, a treaty with Paraguay followed.[27]

On the Atlantic side of South America, Argentina and its port of Buenos Aires gained permanent importance for trade with Japan. In 1910, only one Japanese merchant vessel had stopped in the Río de la Plata port. By 1917, ten ships unloaded there. They brought silk, cotton, and woolen goods and additionally electric cord, insulated rubber wire, bicycle accessories, and Panama hats.[28] Interestingly, U.S.-owned companies operating out of Argentina also appreciated the growing Argentinean–Japanese shipping connection. From Argentina, the American

Express Co. transported seeds and meat-packer Swift shipped bones around the Tierra del Fuego for processing in Japan. From Japan, the American Trading Co. shipped silk and rubber to Buenos Aires. Grace and Co. exported rice.

Farther north, in Brazil, a third round of government-led improvement of the emigration business took place. First, Japanese bureaucrats decided that the companies transporting people to Brazil were financially disreputable. In August 1917, Finance Minister Kazue Shoda urged a merger of the overseas companies. As a consequence, the Kaigai Toyo Emigration Co., Nambei Colonization Co., Japan Colonization Co., and Nitt Colonization Co. were united into the Overseas Development Corporation (Kogyo Kabushiki Kaisa) and capitalized with 10,000,000 yen. Second, systematic recruitment efforts in Japan were instituted, using slides, lecture presentations, and, most importantly, loans for start-up capital. This new Brazilian emigration society was expected to bring five thousand laborers to Brazil.[29]

Finally, in the United States, Japanese immigrants and Japanese Americans further diversified their economic influence, though without imperial government involvement. U.S. Japanese Americans moved into regional business ventures, beyond the narrow confines of settlements or contract labor. Individuals began to reap the rewards of years of systematic planning, a long-term business perspective, and hard work. Japanese immigrants and their children, exceeding seventy thousand persons, were emerging as important crop producers, distributors, and retailers of rice, vegetables, and fruit. Their vertical business model paid off.

This prominence could mean owning shares in the California flower market in San Francisco and other cooperatives. It could mean taking the step from single contract laborer to marrying one of the few Japanese women who were allowed to enter the United States after 1908. But, as before, it could mean continuing life as a single laborer living in lodging houses, traveling through California following the agricultural harvest cycle.[30]

Getting closer economically to Latin America did not mean that Japanese leaders lost sight of imperial priorities. On January 9, 1917, the Terauchi cabinet once again confirmed that China would remain, in the near future, Japan's focus for territorial expansion. Ideally, in the postwar world, all foreign powers should ask its government first before acting in China.[31] It was obvious that Tokyo's politicians needed some form of agreement with the United States that guaranteed special Japanese interests in China. The cabinet was willing to allow U.S. financial capital in China to play a secondary role in economic development, if U.S. leaders would be willing to give political guarantees to Tokyo. No wonder that elite leaders strongly suggested exploration of the German feeler of an alliance with Mexico against the United States in February 1917.

The year 1917 concluded almost the way German undersecretary Zimmerman had suggested in his telegram in February. In December, the new Japanese ambassador to Mexico asked President Carranza to approach German Ambassador von Eckardt and ask him whether the two men could establish a direct channel of communication inside Mexico. One last time, one side remained hesitant. This time superiors in Berlin instructed the German ambassador not to accept the overture. If Japan wanted to talk to Germany, it was supposed to do so through its Japanese diplomats in Europe. In late 1917, in Berlin, nobody wanted a repetition of the public debacle of the Zimmerman Telegram.[32]

As soon as the Russian government collapsed the Japanese army elevated ethnic secret warfare to a new level. In December 1917, six junior officers assumed the disguise of innocuous Japanese language and history students and gathered intelligence on both sides of the Siberian border.[33]

In addition, intelligence officers were sent farther west into Russian territory to identify ethnic tribes that would be open to subverting Russia. Majors General Nakajima Masatake and Sakabe traveled westward to identify ethnic leaders who wanted to head puppet states with Japanese support. Tribal chiefs and their ethnic tribes were expected to serve as bulwarks against a communist Russia and also as Japanese outposts projecting Japanese interests into southern Russia against German and Austrian designs. The U.S. historian James William Morley writes: "A regular stream of intelligence officers began to flow into North China, Mongolia, and through the Amur Basin in Siberia and north Manchuria."[34]

In Korea, boundaries between ethnic Japanese settlers, civilian diplomats, and intelligence officers blurred entirely. A secret Japanese army fund in Korea funded twenty-four individuals. Only six of them were officers. The remaining eighteen were Japanese military officials and civilians. They "were organized into networks, those in each city or area reporting regularly, usually to an officer, who in turn forwarded the information to his commander. Reports of mutual interest from the army's agents as well as from its military attaches were usually passed on to the Ministry of Foreign Affairs or other ministry concerned."[35] Also the Japanese consul in Harbin, Sato Naotake, doubled as a military spy.[36]

Japanese support for and manipulation of ethnic separatism became critical to keeping the vast Far Eastern areas unstable enough so that other European governments could not colonize the areas easily.[37] Tokyo sponsored Cossack leader

Ataman Semenoff, allowing him to organize seventy thousand men in eastern Siberia, a force strong enough to defeat and to deter other expeditionary forces.

Finally in May 1918, the Japanese signed a defense treaty with the Chinese government. In exchange for 80,000,000 yen in loans Japan could perform military intelligence and set up logistical installations in North and northeastern China.[38]

In Tokyo these developments meant establishing stricter priorities over what Japanese expansion in the immediate future should mean. Prime Minister Masatake Terauchi, Army General Staff Chief Yusaku Uehara, Vice Chief Giichi Tanaka, Field Marshal Prince Aritomo, and War Minister Oshima, as well as Foreign Minister Ichiro Motono and his successor, Shimpei Goto, pushed for a large-scale unilateral military expedition to Siberia and North Manchuria. Using the Chinese Eastern Railway and Siberian Railway as avenues of invasion, they advocated even more focus on Japanese expansion on the Asian continent.

Any drastic expansion beyond China into Asia would clash immediately with rival German, British, French, and U.S. designs. Politically this meant that the U.S.–Japanese relationship would have to remain peaceful and amicable. Global Japanese imperial expansion, for the time being, should remain limited to economic expansion and emigration.[39] Therefore Japan made a determined effort to come to some diplomatic understanding with the United States.

Even though the Terauchi government pursued predatory expansion in China and, if possible, soon in Manchuria and Siberia, it projected a kinder, gentler face toward the other side of the Pacific. It came in the form of the former trade specialist Ishii, who was sent to the United States to negotiate an understanding with U.S. secretary of state Lansing. Even though they did not produce what Tokyo's nobility had envisioned, they did come to a weak understanding in November 1917, which allowed the Wilson administration to focus on the prosecution of its first fight in a world war. The Lansing–Ishii agreement created a vague understanding about U.S. and Japanese zones in the Pacific.

And yet in Latin America, the Lansing–Ishii agreement did not apply. In South America, individual German and Japanese agents on the ground established first contacts in 1918, even though their headquarters opposed it. In spring 1918, the Japanese consul to Peru, Saito, ran a network of agents and informers around Lima and Callao.[40] Then in May 1918, the leader of the German intelligence network in Peru, Riedel, told his superior in Santiago de Chile: "I have made the acquaintance of a Japanese, a well placed person." It was Consul Saito. By July 1918, the two men were friends.[41]

After friendship came favors in intelligence work. Saito helped Riedel to place agents and mail on neutral Japanese ships traveling to New York.[42]

Cooperation focused on communication with agents in New York, at the time a dangerous place for German agents. Riedel also used Japanese steamers to send packages from Lima, Peru, to Chile.[43] Saito used Spaniards as mail carriers as well. On one Japanese steamer, an officer worked as courier for German packages.[44] Finally, a Japanese bank helped agents of both countries. In Buenos Aires, accounts of the Japanese Yokohama Specie bank began to also pay German agents.[45] Once the German western offensive failed and Germany collapsed in revolution, Consul Saito asked Tokyo for a deepening of regional Japanese–German cooperation. As World War I was winding down, and Russia and German slowly drifted into revolution, Saito pointed out that Japan would be more powerful in Latin America than a probably defeated Germany.

Even though Berlin would soon no longer be able to pursue an imperial policy toward Latin America, formerly German agents would continue to reside in South America. In the near future, as the German Empire disappeared or at least was severely punished for World War I, ethnic Germans would nevertheless continue to travel and work in Latin America. Apparently Saito suggested that if there was no more Wilhelm II to spy for, perhaps select Germans might be happy to work for the Japanese government, which continued to expand its interest in South America.[46]

German agent Riedel wrote to Berlin, in the midst of a monarchic implosion, about the uncertain future of his spy network in Lima and the new possibility of working for the Tokyo government: "Unfortunately funds are dwindling horribly. The only and most advantageous way out is to accept the Japanese offer. Our system is good, these yellow gentlemen are willing to pay well for it. The only obstacle are that wretched language and authorization on the part of German Navy."[47] No German objection was voiced. Immediately after the November armistice, the government in Tokyo agreed that Consul Saito should take over the German networks, at least in Peru. The weakened financial state of the German naval intelligence system had gifted Tokyo with an ideal, experienced network of agents who, at first sight, would not be suspected to work for Japan. These sources prove that as Germany was collapsing, German intelligence officers were simply rehired as Japanese lead agents at the end of 1918. Thus Japanese imperialism in Latin America was no longer that different from its imperialism in China, only a step behind.

Barely twenty years after Japanese explorers had dreamed about more aggressive Japanese imperialism not only in the South Pacific but also along the western Pacific of South America, it was becoming a reality. One and a half years after

German secretary Zimmerman had suggested German–Japanese cooperation in Mexico, a low-level cooperation moved from occasional favor to institutionalization in Peru. Along the Pacific coast of Chile and Peru, Japanese military and diplomatic officials established secret networks that conducted subversion and gathered intelligence on behalf of imperial Japan.

Japanese imperialism no longer just meant emigration and trade. South of the Panama Canal, Japanese spies were working for Tokyo, just as their brethren did in Siberia, Korea, and Manchuria. If Tokyo's military leaders deemed it necessary, Japanese agents would employ illegal practices in the Americas, just as they were doing in Europe and Asia. Of course, Japanese emigrants and ethnic settlers were not informed about the changing context of their struggle for survival. Japan elites cared little whether or not Japanese intelligence work gave rise to intensifying suspicions about Japanese immigrants. Whereas the U.S.–Japanese relationship remained special, the Latin American–Japanese relationship now encompassed everything from emigration, to trade, to investment, to secret warfare.

7 President Carranza Explores Warfare against the United States

Certainly Not a Victim

Before he became Mexican president in 1915, Carranza had dreamed about fanning ethnic tensions inside the United States until the political fabric of the country ripped apart. His motive was revenge for the nineteenth-century U.S.–Mexican war and the recapture of the lost territory as specified in the 1848 Treaty of Guadalupe Hidalgo.

Between 1908 and 1910, as provisional governor of the northern Mexican state of Coahuila, Carranza had moved from dreaming about territorial revision to exploring select aspects of a potential strategy to achieve it. Ideally, Carranza wished for a second civil war, another violent cataclysm between the North and the South of the United States. He saw potential in the rage felt by many African American individuals under the oppressive Jim Crow system inside the United States. In the long run, he expected to exploit their pain and make it work on behalf of Mexican nationalist interests.

During a racial uprising in the United States, he would supply African American rebels or individuals who were able to divide parts of southern U.S. territory, just as Coahuilan caudillo Santiago Vidaurri had supported the Confederates in 1860. After a victorious ending of a second U.S. civil war, he expected to trade his material support for the return of former Mexican territory to the Mexican nation.

Carranza also considered a second scenario: a form of ethnic class warfare in the southern United States might accomplish a similar outcome, if poor ethnic Mexicans, African Americans, or other Hispanic volunteers could be incited to fight white U.S. citizens. Once again, Carranza planned to back the rebels and, later, negotiate the return of territory, until a greater Mexico was reestablished.

Before World War I, Carranza had cautiously explored these ideas at least once. In 1913, he invited a delegation of African American individuals interested in leaving the United States and starting over as black settlers in Mexican territory. At a meeting in Piedras Negras, according to future Mexican president Adolpho de la Huerta, Carranza remained guarded as he talked to community leaders but nevertheless tried to gauge the potential of ethnic and racial frustration among this group of U.S. citizens.[1]

As a provisional governor of a Mexican state, Carranza could not move further. Later Mexican president Huerta preferred strategic flirtations with European and Asian imperial powers over ethnic warfare along the U.S.–Mexican border. Carranza would have to wait until 1915, when the worsening chaos of the Mexican Revolution, inside an unfolding world war, would bring new opportunities to explore deeper the potential of ethnic warfare.

In early 1915, Carranza, still a revolutionary fighting for national office, resumed his exploration of ethnic warfare along the Mexican–U.S. border. The constantly changing fortunes of the revolution had transformed the border zone into an area where fears and suspicions caused as much apprehension as fighting. The fear that ethnic Mexican ranch hands and refugees from northern Mexico would align along ethnic lines against white Anglos was widespread. Opportunistic individuals took advantage of economic chaos and intensified cattle and horse stealing. News about these activities was increasingly pondered in connection with rumors about revenge encouraged by foreign backers. The previous pages proved that concerns were very justified.[2]

In this context, Venustiano Carranza employed ethnic warfare for the first time. But he used it to destroy not U.S. territory but his revolutionary rival Pancho Villa.

In the Lower Valley of the Rio Grande, on January 24, 1915, the Carranzista soldier Basilio Ramos Jr. approached a recruiter for Pancho Villa to ask him whether he was interested in fighting in an upcoming race war along the U.S.–Mexican border.[3] The designated enemy was white Anglo men older than sixteen years. When U.S. intelligence agents learned about the offer they arrested Ramos and found on him a document calling on sympathizers to start a genocidal war. The paper was purportedly signed on January 6, 1915, in the Texas town of San Diego. It identified February 20, 1915, as the day when the uprising and killing would begin. That day the onslaught would be led by Hispanics demanding the independence of Texas, New Mexico, Arizona, and Colorado. It would be backed by a newly created army called the Liberating Army for Races and Peoples. Its leaders were exclusively of "Latin, the Negro and the Japanese race."[4]

After the capture of key cities the rebels would arrest and execute all male Anglo citizens older than sixteen. The plan contained other interesting racial references. It promised Apaches and other Native American tribes the return of their land. Their former homelands would be unified into an independent republic that, later, would request annexation to Mexico. Thereafter, these border states would help African Americans in the United States to conquer "six states of the American Union, which bordered upon those already mentioned." These states were expected to become an African American republic.[5]

U.S. historians Charles Harris and Louis R. Sadler discovered that Carranza's general Emiliano Nafarrate signed the safe-conduct paper for Carranza's conspirators to travel into U.S. territory.[6] They interpret it as an effort to discredit Carranza's rival Pancho Villa, who was gaining ground in the revolutionary coalition. On February 20, 1915, the day of the scheduled uprising, not a single fight was registered along the U.S.–Mexican border.

Thereafter, a revised version of the plan surfaced. This time an author addressed "the Oppressed Peoples of America," made reference to the original Plan of San Diego, and announced a "social revolution in the U.S. and the formation of the Social Republic of Texas, from which base the revolution would spread to New Mexico, Arizona, California, Colorado, Utah and Nevada."[7] Once again historians Louis R. Sadler and Charles Harris were able to link Carranza, but not Hispanic individuals in the Lower Rio Grande Valley, to this call for race war activities. They found a telegram from April 29, 1915, in which a Huertista reported: "I spoke personally with Carranzista [sic] J. S. Pedrosa who is agitating Negroes and Mexico–Texas favor Venustiano. He offered to pay me well to aid him. . . . He continues agitation has agents various towns."[8] A second telegram stated: "Be tranquil. Keep absolutely secret Carranzistas [sic] agitating with secrecy. Negroes and Texans in their favor."[9] Along the U.S.–Mexican border Carranza was practicing what German forces were doing along the U.S.–Canadian border and in the Near East, Africa, and India. Only Carranza fought for regional Mexican political gains.

Following Huerta's failed attempt to regain the Mexican presidency with the help of the German government in spring 1915, the Mitsui representative in Mexico City, Toshio Onodera, approached Carranza's faction in June 1915 and offered the resumption of weapon deliveries to Mexico. Carranza right away promised to honor the terms of Huerta's old undelivered Mitsui orders. Once he was victorious, he promised to pay 10 percent more than the defeated dictator.[10] If Carranza would trump Pancho Villa and Emiliano Zapata, he would have access to one Japanese arms supplier that was not controlled by the U.S. government.

A few months later Venustiano Carranza was able to convince the governments of Argentina, Brazil, Chile, and the United States to grant him temporary de facto recognition as the next Mexican president at the Niagara Falls Conference. Thereafter the number of viable alternative revolutionary factions in Mexico continued to shrink. The U.S. military kept General Huerta imprisoned after his failed coup attempt. Pascual Orozco was shot in the lonely, beautiful canyons of Big Bend, Texas, in the fall. Quietly, in October, President Wilson allowed Carranza to ship Mexican troops across the U.S. border to reinforce Agua Prieta from a besieging Villista army. Thereafter, Carranza's men, thanks to this unexpected U.S. support, destroyed Villa's army in the ensuing battle. At Agua Prieta Villa was reduced to a guerilla leader without international backing.[11] Carranza began the consolidation of the Mexican presidency against Pancho Villa.

Carranza's use of subversion began by stopping it temporarily. Now that he had de facto won diplomatic recognition, he reassigned one organizer of subversion, General Emiliano Nafarrate, away from the border to Tampico. Without his leadership, the ethnic grievances of Mexican Americans and African Americans stopped expressing themselves through systematic border violence.[12] It also meant holding back foreign manipulation offers that would do Carranza more harm than good in 1915. Of course, these backers had priorities other than his own.

Japanese diplomats had kept a politically low but active profile in Mexico. They reported the weak spots of Mexican revolutionary leaders and tried to comprehend their regional differences but also began a cautious transition from being a junior member of British policy in the early years of the revolution to building a permanent intelligence capacity and developing a distinctly Japanese, all-encompassing policy in Mexico.

Carranza had signaled to Japan his astuteness already in 1914. As General Huerta lost military strength inside Mexico, he had less and less funds available to finance a military purchasing agent in distant Tokyo. And yet, in Tokyo, the Mitsui zaibatsu was happy to take over, for the time being, the financing of Huerta's military purchasing agent. Nevertheless, the question raised itself with whom Mitsui would do business if Huerta were to resign or be assassinated like the previous Mexican presidents. Before an answer to this question could be found Carranza approached Mitsui through an agent and asked for a stop of future weapons deliveries to the almost finished Huerta.[13] The Mitsui company obliged. Then it was time to wait until Carranza wanted its services.

Now that Carranza had at his disposal the bureaucracy of a revolutionary nation and diplomats in Mexican embassies and consulates across the world, they needed to be more than carriers of verbal instructions and official memoranda. Right away, Carranza decided to construct a foreign service that served his revolutionary vision better.

Reorganizing Mexico's foreign service and intelligence in early 1916 meant, first, to purge men loyal to former presidents Díaz, Madero, and General Huerta. Second, Carranza dispatched loyal diplomats abroad to defend his hold over Mexico against other rival, revolutionary factions. Third, he ordered a more systematic use of propaganda outlets. They had to focus on explaining Carranzista, but no longer the old constitutionalist political ideas, and to defend Mexico's sovereignty against plots by private U.S. companies.

The instructions for the organization of his secret service arm attached to the Foreign Ministry was inspired by a German blueprint.[14] By mid-1916, Mexican agents in the United States had been reorganized and communicated through a headquarters in San Francisco. Later it shifted to El Paso. North of the Mexican border, Mexico's foreign service employed individuals who were proud and loyal to Carranza. More precisely they represented a revolutionary Mexico eager to solicit U.S. help and trying to keep the Wilson administration friendly toward Carranza.

In South America, Luis Cabrera reorganized Mexican diplomatic posts. In Buenos Aires, Santiago, and Brazil rebuilding meant "frequent interchange of ideas and the selling of the Mexican revolution to conservative South American elites."[15] But Carranza knew that Cabrera also worked in a security environment dominated by British and German intelligence. As neutral Argentina gained greater importance in the struggle between Germany and Great Britain, Cabrera also learned more about the illegal German activity in South America. In contrast to Mexican agents in the United States, Carranza's diplomats in South America aligned themselves with initiatives that made a particular point of rejecting U.S. policy and Pan-Americanism.

In Buenos Aires, nationalists, socialists, anarchists, and Catholics cheered against Pan-Americanism and advocated a Union of Latin America—an organization that would exclude the United States. Mexican diplomats supported their separatist, Catholic Hispanidad feeling and their hatred toward Protestantism and a society built around economic activity. Astute Carranzistas realized that the spiritual renewal movement among Argentine students and also workers might add a strong nationalist voice to the defense of the still weak Carranza administration.

The Argentine Manuel Ugarte personified this political effort. He was one of South America's most vociferous Hispanistas.[16] Unlike Carranza, Ugarte was not only a fiery nationalist but also a racist. Like many others, he imagined the existence of a Latin American race "whose social environment, customs, inclinations, feelings and likings are identical. From a racial perspective, the republics of Hispanic origin could not be more alike."[17] Previously Ugarte had actively explored what could be done to nurture a Latin America separate from U.S. influence. One political vehicle to create and cement a separate racial and cultural realm would be the "Union of Latin America." The first step toward the union was the establishment of communication channels among Spanish American republics of the continent.

Importantly, Ugarte argued that the Mexican Revolution represented a first embodiment of a popular yearning toward a political Latin American Union. And revolutionary Mexican territory assumed the function of a physical divider between the undesired Anglo-Saxon world and a future ethnic Latin American Union.

Thereafter, Ugarte and Argentine followers organized the first Mexican Committee, which later expanded into an Asociacion Latinoamericano. He also managed to gather enough individual, private funds to publish a propaganda journal called the *Revista Americana*. Finally, Ugarte carried the story of Hispanistic ethnic separation renewal on a tour through South America.

When U.S. naval troops landed in Veracruz in 1914, Ugarte was handed a fresh example of U.S. intervention that could be used in anti-U.S. identity building. Ugarte and his group opposed the U.S. landing even though Argentina's conservative government joined the 1915 conference at Niagara Falls for the purpose of selecting the next de facto president of revolutionary Mexico. By then Ugarte's ideas, supporters, and themes had become attractive enough to bring ten thousand people to the streets of Buenos Aires.[18]

Into this charged political environment Carranza dispatched Isidro Fabela as his new representative. He entered a conservative Argentine establishment that remained hostile to the Mexican Revolution and to any suggestion of a greater popular inclusion in national politics. Isidro Fabela therefore found friendly reception only in Ugarte's Buenos Aires group. He engaged in the usual propaganda toward student groups and used Ugarte's hospitality to propagandize for the constitutionalists. He presented Carranza's Mexico as primary speaker at a Mexican anniversary of the Grito de Dolores celebration. Not surprisingly, Carranza's Foreign Ministry extended an invitation to Ugarte for an all-expenses-paid trip to Mexico. Fabela and Ugarte had become friends.[19]

In Central America, Carranza's representative explored secret activities. On the other side of the Mexican–Guatemalan border, Guatemalan politician Estrada Cabrera schemed to keep Carranza weak or, even better, out of Mexico's National Palace. No doubt, Carranza had reason to fear Cabrera. In 1915, when the conference at Niagara negotiated Huerta's succession, the Guatemalan president had tried to prevent Carranza's selection.[20]

As soon as Carranza had received the de facto presidential recognition, he answered Cabrera's machinations by expelling the Guatemalan diplomat from the Mexican capital. After this diplomatic humiliation he searched for additional ways to weaken the Guatemalan president at home. Carefully Carranza explored the potential of secret activity.

He ordered General Francisco Mujica to contact Guatemalan revolutionaries living in Mexican exile and to evaluate the strengths of their movements. Soon thereafter, Generals Álvaro Obregón and Adolfo de la Huerta provided select exiles not only with limited financial support but also with arms. In addition, Carranza's agents mediated between rival Guatemalan factions, hoping to forge a more unified effective Guatemalan opposition against Cabrera's regime in preparation for a serious coup attempt.[21]

Carranza's retooling of diplomatic service, intelligence, and propaganda work did not stop at organizing speaking tours and revolutionary defense. In particular it meant probing whether World War I could bring political and territorial benefits to Carranza.

The first attempt to explore cooperation in secret warfare with Germany occurred in October 1915. A Carranzista general approached Ambassador Heinrich von Eckardt to explore cooperation in plots against British Honduras and Guatemala. The general wanted German money to cover the wages of a thousand-man invasion force. This year Germany did not accept the offer of cooperation. This was most likely because it had recently been embarrassed by the discovery of its substantial backing for a coup that was supposed to bring Victoriano Huerta back into the Mexican presidency.[22] In 1916, a German-supported Mexican invasion of British Honduras would have brought Germany little advantage and only worsened public opinion inside the United States. And

17. Carranza stayed in close touch with select field commanders throughout the revolution (Library of Congress, Washington, D.C.).

yet the incident showed that Carranza discussed offensive acts with Germans from the first year of his presidency on.

Then in September 1916, on the surface, Carranza and Cabrera entered into a treaty that agreed to stop border violations. But the U.S. historian Juergen Buchenau shows that this promise was not worth the paper it was written on. Cabrera never stopped providing shelter for anti-Carranza forces, and the Mexican leader always remained interested in weakening Guatemala and toppling its president.[23]

Carranza was not the only plotter north of the Panama Canal; other Central American politicians and individuals also prepared coups and insurrections. There was Máximo B. Rosales, who wanted to start a revolution against the current Honduran government. He even found fund-raising support in Cedar Rapids, Iowa.[24] He wanted to start his revolt in January 1917. A second Honduran politician fomenting unrest was Alfred Quiñones.[25]

Then there was Nicaraguan liberal Manuel Sediles. After the Chamorro government had come to power in Managua, Sediles had fled to El Salvadorian exile and worked as a propagandist for Carranza. But Sediles was also connected to General Julian Irias, a follower of the deposed Nicaraguan president Zelaya. Irias lived in U.S. exile. In New Orleans, he occasionally conferred with revolutionaries from El Salvador and Honduras, trying to push national unrest toward regional revolution.

Then Irias approached Carranza's minister of war, Álvaro Obregón. He wanted help with the creation and supply of a secret base inside the country. Once established and secured it would serve as a launching pad for revolution inside Nicaragua.[26] These anti-U.S. Nicaraguan liberals were plotting their own revolutions but realized that Carranza's hostile attitude toward the United States might help them. Sediles and Irias hoped that a successful revolution against Chamorro would be only one important stepping-stone toward the formation of a greater anti-U.S. movement in Central America. Thus, it is not surprising to find out that Irias also stood in contact with the Honduran Rosales.[27]

In El Salvador additional revolutionaries schemed. The Honduran minister in Washington identified a Mr. Cornejo and a Mr. Estupinan as plotters. These men too had been in contact with Irias, Rosales, and also Guatemalans and a Mr. Charles Jones in New Orleans.[28] Enrique Cordoba was another El Salvadorian plotter.[29]

Guatemalans continued to plot against President Cabrera throughout 1916, sometimes with and sometimes without Mexican involvement. At the end of July 1916, former Cabrera agent E. F. Pantin reported a gathering of insurrectionists. Reports indicated that Guatemalan rebel leaders were enlisting soldiers who previously had fought for Carranza. Carranza himself was suspected of assisting the effort.[30]

The Costa Rican administration faced plotting under the leadership of the Tinoco family, who worked with sympathetic private U.S. businesspeople. In this country, the promise of future oil riches mattered more than political ideals.[31] Former Mexican generals Blanquet, Mondragon, and Félix Díaz were alleged to be connected to them. This coup would have unfolded regardless of Carranza or World War I.

German aristocrats were approached by Mexican factions for revolutionary help a second time. A plot was offered that was never realized. But in 1917 it would serve as the model for the notorious Zimmermann Telegram. It was developed partly in Madrid by exiled members of the former Díaz administration and Catholic revolutionaries.

Gonzalo N. Enrile left Mexico in February 1916 for Havana, where he caught a boat to Spain hoping to proceed to Berlin.[32] After arrival in Madrid he introduced himself to German Ambassador Prince von Ratibor and offered a letter of introduction from German military attaché to the U.S. Franz von Papen. Enrile requested a German passport, since President Carranza's diplomat in

Madrid had no interest in supporting a counterrevolutionary.[33] Berlin leaders replied that they preferred to keep Enrile in Madrid. Now was not an opportune time to prepare a counterrevolution in Berlin because of German–U.S. relations. Nevertheless, later, Berlin hoped that Enrile could be useful. Also the German leadership still preferred Villa above other revolutionaries.[34] Enrile thus remained in Madrid in a holding pattern.

Then in April 1916, after Villa's raid on Columbus, New Mexico, German Ambassador von Eckardt advised that a Mexican–U.S. war was imminent. On April 7, von Eckardt expected Carranza to approach him and to ask for German weapons that were stored in the United States. Von Eckardt had the impression that Carranza thought war was unavoidable. His tactic seemed to be to win three months' time in order to purchase enough weapons.[35]

Against these events inside Mexico, German diplomats in Berlin decided to at least listen to Enrile's plans for a revolution and a secret Mexican–German alliance. Gonzalo N. Enrile and his aide, Hubert Islas, were asked to travel to Switzerland in early April. From there the men tried to cross into Germany. But they were arrested, and police found plans in Islas's boots that detailed possibilities for German–Mexican cooperation.[36] By April 10, 1916, the Mexican representatives arrived in Berlin. They stayed at the Centralhotel for six days.

By now German secret warfare Department IIIB was aware of their presence.[37] In Berlin they met with Undersecretary Gottlieb von Jagow, to whom they introduced themselves as representatives of the "Nationalist Party." Enrile claimed to be its vice president and spoke in the name of the old Porfirian national army. The German was stunned when the men proposed an alliance against the United States, codified in a secret German–Mexican treaty.[38] The organization solicited 300,000,000 RM from Germany to reconquer Mexico. In exchange they, too, promised to start a race war spreading from the Gulf of Mexico to the Caribbean. In its final stage it was to include parts of the United States and attempt to break territory out of the United States.[39] Undersecretary Zimmerman learned about this proposal but chose not to enter into talks with this group.

By May, Enrile and Islas were asked to leave Berlin for Zurich.[40] From July on, Enrile lived in Spain. German naval intelligence thought it would be possible to keep alive a small connection with this Díaz faction, just in case, for later.

From Madrid, Enrile continued to lobby for a German-financed coup by Félix Díaz. He added the idea that it would help win Japanese support, which would allow Germany to separate Japan from the Allies.[41] But Germans categorically continued to reject Enrile's suggestions.

This meeting in Berlin was a most important interaction, as it painted the possibilities of some kind of German–Mexican–Japanese cooperation in Mexico against the United States in the mind of Undersecretary Zimmermann. Ironically Zimmerman would use the idea developed by anti-Carranza forces and offer it to Carranza the following year as his Zimmerman Telegram.

In Mexico, Pancho Villa's attack on the U.S. town of Columbus had changed Carranza's strategic priority and international diplomacy. Pancho Villa and 484 irregulars attacked Columbus, New Mexico, on March 10, 1916. Three days later, President Wilson's administration requested permission from Mexico to pursue Villa across the border into Mexican territory. As legal justification, merely a way to save face toward Mexican society in general, the U.S. government suggested invoking a late-nineteenth-century treaty that allowed cross-border pursuit of Native American raiding parties. It was a very liberal interpretation of an old international agreement. President Carranza did not approve the request, but Brigadier General Pershing and seven thousand men of his army crossed the Mexican border on March 15, 1916, anyway. From then until the withdrawal of U.S. troops on February 5, 1917, the unauthorized presence of U.S. troops on Mexican territory created unprecedented tensions and intensified Mexican nationalism against the United States. This was the type of ethnic nationalist conflict that German war planners had hoped to create and to exploit, even though they were not responsible for Pancho Villa's attack on Columbus.[42]

Carranza's diplomatic activism also began to reach out to Germany. Carranza explained to the German ambassador that he saw President Wilson caught between his personal goal to enter history, which could be achieved by entering into the war in Europe, and the alternative project by finance circles on Wall Street, which wanted to establish indirect control over Mexico. That would mean the financiers would softened up Mexico with ongoing revolution and then impose a "Cuban solution." Their ultimate goal was the conquest of the oil wells at Tampico.[43]

Part of the strategy had been negotiations with General Obregón at Atlantic City. They presented Carranza with a protocol that demanded recognition of U.S., French, and British reclamations. When the U.S. negotiators were asked to specify a date for withdrawal from Mexico, it was defined only vaguely: it depended on circumstances at the border. Since Carranza failed to get a more precise commitment, he ended the discussions. He saw Wilson as vacillating between U.S. business interests and a policy the American people would want.[44]

Officially, Carranza had appointed Capman Zubaran as his diplomat.[45] But in May 1916, Carranza also appointed the forty-two-year-old general inspector of military and public schools, Major Arnoldo Krumm-Heller, to travel as his propagandist to Germany.

Previously, Krumm-Heller had worked as Madero's full-time doctor. Later he served as a military doctor for the Carranzistas. Also important was his role as grand master of Mexican freemasons, promising Carranza access to twenty thousand Mexicans. Once World War I began, Major Krumm-Heller added the job of propagandist for Germany. By 1916, he had earned Carranza's trust and, therefore, occasionally performed special work between Carranza and the German legation in Mexico City.

Officially Krumm-Heller went to Germany to learn about military schools and to obtain teaching material. German diplomat von Eckardt reported that Krumm-Heller would work as propagandist, writing propaganda articles in Spanish for later distribution in Mexico and South America. In addition he would inform Carranza about European events. His trip would last one year and was government financed.[46]

However, after Krumm-Heller embarked on a boat to cross the Atlantic, British intelligence arrested him. Still, before he was taken away, he was able to hand a secret letter to Baron Waldemar Uxkuell, who happened to travel on the same boat. Uxkuell was protected by diplomatic immunity and therefore was able to transmit a letter from Carranza to Wilhelm II.[47] Its content remained unknown. One source suggests that the letter was written by Count Bernstorff and addressed to Wilhelm II.

Krumm-Heller's suitcase was opened, and investigators found Carranza's propaganda pamphlets and "a large quantity of business documents in German from German banking and mercantile houses in Mexico and South America." Turns out, Carranza's propagandist was also a courier.

Later the British refused to let him proceed to Scandinavia and Germany. Somehow in September 1916, he reemerged in Bern, Switzerland. He tried to start a propaganda service aimed at South America. Its central message would be that the Allied powers were responsible for starting World War I.[48]

At Carranza's first Mexican independence celebration on September 16, 1916, in Mexico City's National Palace, Carranza selected a subtle method to rebuke President Wilson. He invited the entire diplomatic corps plus all leaders of the Mexican government. Von Eckardt attended in military uniform.

Suddenly, during the dinner, Foreign Minister Aguilar took the German representative by his arm and led him to an open balcony facing the Zócalo.

He saw many thousands of Mexicans. When they saw him they yelled, "Viva Alemania!" Then Carranza offered cigars as dessert, wrapped with a picture of Emperor Wilhelm II.[49]

In Mexico, Carranza in the meantime revived his ethnic warfare activity. According to U.S. historians Harris and Sadler, in 1916 Carranza began to use it to force a withdrawal of the U.S. forces of the Pershing expedition from Mexican territory.

Carranza had kept his ethnic subversive recruiters de la Rosa and Aniceto Pizana on his payroll. In April 1916, de la Rosa resurfaced along the U.S. border. More troubling were rumors of some form of ethnic uprising by Hispanics to start between May 10 and 15, 1916. A Jose M. Morin, using the cover name J. M. Leal, was identified organizing Hispanics and Mexicans south of San Antonio and on the Mexican border. Once he found people willing to participate in a May 10 uprising, he gave them a commission in a new "Army of Liberation."[50] Five days before, on May 5, 1916, Wilson imposed an arms embargo against Carranza and mobilized the National Guard units of Arizona, New Mexico, and Texas. Carranza's activities were bringing the U.S.–Mexican border region to a prewar footing.

Carranza could not assure continued, reliable supply of weapons for his forces. At a time when Germany, Japan, and Great Britain fought naval warfare off Mexico's coast, the nation's most basic equipment needs, the weapons that would make it possible to move from guerilla warfare to direct, open engagement of an external enemy, could not be guaranteed. Arms for Mexico still had to be imported, depending on the whims of foreign kings, parliaments, and companies. Carranza had to address this pivotal issue in the midst of revolutionary upheaval.

Already before Villa's attack on Columbus, Ramon F. Iturbide, former Mexico City police chief, had been asked to travel to Japan to visit armament factories and to study its army.[51] Then in February 1916, a still unidentified Japanese company offered Carranza a US$3,000,000 loan to construct a military hardware factory under his control inside Mexico. His advisers, Luis Cabrera and Zubaran Capmany, reacted with great enthusiasm and urged Carranza to explore the offer. Shortly thereafter, in Tokyo, Mexican envoy Manuel Perez Romero was ordered to revive contacts with Mitsui.[52] Colonel Rafael Vargas and Lieut. Angel Gutierrez boarded a boat to sail to Japan to explore the situation in person.

In addition, Mexico's Naval Attaché Manuel del Frago was asked to explore weapons purchases in Japan. At first both discussions proceeded well. But when it came time to place an order they learned that once again the diplomats of Tokyo's Foreign Ministry were objecting. Under the current Japanese cabinet diplomats remained strong enough to oppose companies and individuals close to the Japanese navy who were willing to sell to Carranza. The majority of Japan's weapons continued to be exported to Russia. Unless Carranza identified other serious suppliers in foreign countries, his army simply would not have the hardware to enter into a serious war with the United States, regardless of the president's ferocious nationalist rhetoric.

Next, Carranza's minister of war, Álvaro Obregón, and Foreign Minister Cándido Aguilar made a new attempt to break the resistance of Japan's diplomats. In Mexico City Obregón asked Chargé d'Affaires Tamikuchi Ohta to ask Japan's Foreign Ministry to accept the dispatch of a secret Mexican emissary to buy arms, ammunition, and gunboats.[53]

Fascinatingly he was not the only Mexican revolutionary to do so. On March 21, 1916, after the battle at Naco, Pancho Villa called a meeting of his officers and decided to send Juan Medina as his emissary to Japan.[54] He was to negotiate assistance from the Japanese emperor. Medina was authorized to cede Magdalena Bay to Japan and also to give the Japanese troops authority to travel through Mexico in the event of war between Japan and the United States. Even though Carranza tried to arrest Medina, he reached Japan on January 5, 1917. In Tokyo he made contact with Díaz's former consul, Señor Enriquez. Enriquez cooperated because he hoped to become minister to Japan in the likely case that Carranza would be toppled by rebels in the future. Later Medina claimed to have met the highest Japanese officials, including Count Okuma, the prime minister. The content of their discussion remained unknown.[55]

In May 1916, the Mexican representative of the German electronic concern AEG reported that Carranza wanted to build an independent Mexican wireless station. He wanted only the finest: a Telefunken or a Paulsen system.[56]

Furthermore, the *jefe revolucionario* wanted to build a Mauser machine gun factory inside Mexico. The German Liebau agency, working in the United States, was approached to design the blueprints for a factory that could manufacture 250 Mauser machine guns daily.[57] Once operational, the factory would provide Carranza with an unprecedented number of high-quality machine guns that could help him destroy Pancho Villa but also deter, and possibly even fight, U.S. forces that crossed the Mexican border.

By spring 1916, Carranza prepared for full-fledged war with the United States. U.S. historians Harris and Sadler discovered that Carranza combined a

18. The submarine *Deutschland* also delivered to Baltimore, Maryland, blueprints for Carranza's desired Telefunken wireless transmitter (Library of Congress, Washington, D.C.).

classic military invasion with an undercover ethnic war. The estimated launching date of the attack was set for June 10, 1916.

Carranza's nephew delivered government funds and organized troops under Colonel Estaban Fierros. Fierros in turn employed subversive Luis de la Rosa. By now familiar, the previously seen rhetoric also resurfaced. For example, there was a liberating "Army of Races and Peoples in America," a supposed military arm of a Revolutionary Congress of San Diego, Texas. Harris and Sadler prove that Carranza and his generals were serious about going ahead.

Right away Carranza attempted to pull Japan into the future conflict. He revived Victoriano Huerta's policy of positioning Japan as a bona fide international diplomatic force to mediate between the United States and Mexico. In 1914, Huerta had limited his request to asking Japan to act as Mexico's diplomatic representative in the case of a Mexican–U.S. war.

Now, in 1916, Carranza wanted to pull Japan in deeper. He asked Tokyo to work as mediator if the Pershing expedition would become a U.S.–Mexican war. It would have entangled Japan in an American war.

Tokyo's Foreign Ministry declined. Its diplomats knew what a significant symbolic liability would be created if Japan were to act as mediator in the Americas during a world war. She would have stepped next to the Pan-American Conference system, the Papacy, and other European imperial powers as influential political player in the Western Hemisphere. Carranza wanted to manipulate Japan's expanding stature in the Pacific into a "Japanese card" against the United States.[58]

Fortunately U.S. informants discovered Carranza's war plans. Carranza was informed that U.S. intelligence had learned of the grand design and was observing his preparations.[59] The Germans had not yet delivered the telegraph system as Carranza had desired. To make matters worse, his order for the Mauser machine gun factory was also prevented by enforcement of U.S. neutrality laws.

Nevertheless, on June 18, President Wilson mobilized the remainder of the 112,000 National Guard soldiers from forty-four states and the District of Columbia. On June 21, at the Battle of Carrizal, Carranza's troops succeeded in defeating two squadrons of Pershing's troops. Suddenly, two days later, on June 23, Carranza stopped the raids and pulled his troops back. If cooler heads had not prevailed, nationalism could have started a Mexican–U.S. war for which the United States was poorly prepared and which the German emperor in Berlin so much desired.

After sustained open warfare proved impossible, Carranza resumed the push to establish an independent military-industrial factory system inside the country. It was a prerequisite to fight any war with the United States. In July Carranza and Obregón disregarded objections by the Japanese Foreign Ministry. Mexican arms purchasers contacted individuals inside Japan's navy, hoping that personal relationships would make it possible to overcome the resistance of Japanese diplomats.[60]

This time it worked. Rear Admiral Keizabro Moriyama, chief of staff of the Japanese navy, took a stance different than the Foreign Ministry. He was the same admiral who had visited Mexico as a crew member of the *Izumo* during the Huerta administration. He appreciated the visitors from the country located south of the United States and tried to impress them with references to the growing might of the Japanese navy in the Pacific. To prove his point to the Mexican soldiers he invited them to tour naval bases and shipyards. The admiral expressed regret that Mexican officers had not contacted the imperial navy earlier. He promised weapons from the Japanese navy, regardless of what diplomats had said before.

Indeed, almost on the spot, on August 26, 1916, Mexican negotiators secured an initial, token amount of rifles, purchasing them through the private Akiyuki

Suzuki company. Thereafter the Japanese gave Mexicans the blueprints for a gunpowder factory. By late summer the news turned even more positive.

In October 1916, Colonel Vargas cabled to Mexico City that he expected a change in government in the very near future that would be more open toward the growing enthusiasm of some navy officials vis-à-vis Mexico. It was an important political watershed and marked the weakening power of the Foreign Ministry.

The Mexican colonel's prediction proved correct. On October 9, 1916, Japanese general Terauchi assumed leadership of a new cabinet. If President Carranza wanted to follow his military leaders' advice and deepen Mexican–Japanese relations, the Terauchi cabinet, for the first time, would listen with true sympathy. Indeed, soon thereafter Japanese weapons were released for shipment as promised. The cargo left on the *Kotohira Maru* for Mexico in later 1916.

By October 1916, Carranza also wanted Germany's help. German minister von Eckardt asked his superiors in Berlin to instruct the Vorwerk Company in Valparaiso, Chile, to sell twenty million 7mm cartridges to Venustiano Carranza's forces.[61]

Thereafter Arnoldo Krumm-Heller, by now in Berlin, explored how cooperation with the German Empire could be useful for Mexico. From Japan, military purchasing commissions were supposed to bring home guns and gunboats. From Berlin, Mexican planners wanted guns, wireless technology, and submarines. Wireless transmitters would give Carranza an improved capacity to communicate outside the control of U.S. and British companies. In fall 1916, *U-53* brought the blueprints and most of the exclusive wireless technological components to the United States. Presumably from there, they would reach Mexico City via diplomatic pouch.

Mexican Revolution historian Friedrich Katz discovered that Carranza contributed $5,000 to a covert German effort to cofinance the construction of a German-operated transmitter at Chapultepec, Mexico City. First, in Germany, construction plans were drawn up by the German army. There, German agents hired a Dutch citizen to purchase the hardware. While Mexican negotiators in Japan prepared the shipment of machine tools on the chartered *Kotohira Maru*, German agents prepared shipments of transmitter components from the United States to a port in the Gulf of Mexico.[62]

In the meantime, in Berlin, Attaché Arnoldo Krumm-Heller continued exploratory talks. In November 1916, he submitted a proposal that invited German military instructors and technology into Carranza's army. And just as Attaché del Frago had asked the Japanese to sell Mexico gunboats, Krumm-Heller asked Germans to sell six submarines.[63]

The purchase of submarines must have been a long-term plan. In late 1916, there existed no Mexican personnel who would have been able to operate a submarine under battle conditions. Still, it is another example of how doggedly Carranza pursued the buildup of national force that would at least increase the risks for imperial powers to operate along Mexico's ports. A small Mexican submarine fleet could have changed the balance of power inside the Gulf of Mexico.[64]

In the same month Mexican foreign minister Aguilar charged further the atmosphere of German–Mexican explorations when he stated to a German partner that Carranza would help German submarines operating in the Gulf of Mexico "to the extent of its powers in certain circumstances." It was a brilliant offer that could be read in many ways, without committing anything in detail. It promised Mexican support for German submarines attacking British ships, not neutral U.S. ships. A short while later in Mexico, German agents informed President Carranza that they had finished preparations to construct a naval supply station for German submarines somewhere along Mexico's coast. In order to move from preparation to construction, only Carranza's signature had to be put on paper. It did not come, yet.[65]

After the war, authors interpreted these efforts as an attempt to establish a Mexican–German military alliance. Certainly, Attaché Arnoldo Krumm-Heller was enthusiastic about the possibility of such a transatlantic bond. But his proposal remained a first draft, a basis for future talks as World War I continued to create unpredictable international power constellations.

In December 1916, parts for Mexico's wireless station were loaded onto a U.S. ship leaving for Mexico.[66] At least in the field of signal intelligence, Carranza and the German military had entered into a symbiotic relationship. German officials knew that once Carranza allowed the option of a transatlantic wireless station in Mexico, they too would benefit from its existence.

In South America, in October 1916, the election of Hipólito Irigoyen in Argentina marked the end of conservative oligarchic politics and the possibility of progressive politics. After the selection of Honorio Pueyrredón as new Argentine foreign minister, Mexican foreign minister Cándido Aguilar tried to establish a special relationship with the politicians of Irigoyen's Radical Party. The goal was to forge supportive Mexican–Argentine linkages, not just among students, socialists, and anarchists but also between two progressive governments in power. Even though Argentina's diplomats, from abroad, warned Irigoyen against breaking away from traditional Pan-Americanist policy, Foreign Minister Aguilar did everything to break Argentina out of the Pan-American camp.

First he invited President Irigoyen to raise the status of his diplomatic representation in Mexico to the level of an embassy. If U.S. importance in Mexico was symbolized through the presence of a U.S. embassy, Argentina should demonstrate the equal importance of Latin American solidarity by raising its legation to the level of embassy as well. Carranza promised to make the Argentine ambassador dean of Mexico City's diplomatic corps, lifting him above the U.S. and European ambassadors.

In Central America, Carranza's diplomatic service performed even more radical Mexican courtship. Between Mexico and Panama's border, political groups favored a Central American Union over a Latin American Union. And if such a political union meant eliminating every U.S. influence from the region after the war, Carranza was for it.

Already in June 1916, the El Salvadorian government had published in the *Diario del Salvador* a defense of Carranza against hostile U.S. policy. To make matters more complex, El Salvador acted in cooperation with the Ecuadorian government. In Washington, the El Salvadorian ambassador took a challenging Ecuadorian diplomatic note and submitted it to the Wilson administration. The impression was created that some of Central and South America could proceed jointly against any future U.S. aggression against Mexico.

In October 1916, El Salvadoran president Melendez suggested to a Mexican diplomat that secret Latin American support agreements should be concluded against future incursions by big powers, the United States in particular. One contemporary observer provided an impression of how aggressively anti-American Carranza's diplomats were in Central America:

The young Carrancista military officers who made up the bulk of Mexico's new diplomatic corps displayed an almost naïve excitement about the possibility of a Central American union. "If two or three countries like . . . Argentina, Chile and Mexico could . . . give moral and material aid to . . . this truly patriotic idea . . . while the U.S. is at war," one of them wrote, "confederation would become possible."[67]

To stoke the ire of Central American public opinion, Carranza financed propagandists to promote Native American ethnicity opposed to a social vision striving toward a U.S. melting pot. Pedro Leon, in September 1916, wrote in favor of "Indo-Espanola." In El Salvador, Mexican agents talked about an ongoing Indo-Latin racial fight: "In order to save itself our race needs to unite with the few people that remain clean of the epidemic created by the dollar."[68] In order to influence

Nicaraguan public opinion against the United States, Carranza's diplomats financed the propaganda agent Manuel Sediles. From his El Salvadoran exile he also portrayed the Mexican Revolution as a keystone for Latin America's future.[69]

Now, the story of Carranza's secret warfare activities became more complex. Increasingly, these regional and sometimes just personal initiatives came to the attention not only of Carranza but also of Germany. German observers in Berlin, Mexico City, and Guatemala were trying to identify local and regional troubles that could be fanned into greater insurrection, until they would trigger an intervention by Great Britain or the United States: "It was the ambition of the German plotters to develop a series of simultaneous revolutions so formidable and threatening as to divert the U.S. government from using all its forces in the prosecution of war against Germany."[70]

Before 1914, German observers had appreciated coups if they brought to power a faction that preferred German financing or ownership of part of a country's economic infrastructure. By itself, Germany was not strong enough to gain complete control over any Central American country.

Now, in 1916, the second year of a world war with no end in sight, the traditional Central American political culture of caudillos and countercoups offered Germany two unprecedented gains. First, a successful coup might bring to power an anti-U.S. faction that would be willing to join Carranza and enter into a political arrangement to eliminate U.S. influence from the region. Second, a successful anti-U.S. coup might provoke the Wilson administration to commit more troops of its already small number of military and naval forces. Thus, it might be possible to tie down troops not only along the U.S.–Mexican border but also along Central America's coastlines and in its jungles. And when the United States entered the war on April 6, 1917, every U.S. soldier and sailor who could be kept from being deployed to Europe in the near future was a gain for Germany.

Besides, if German fanning of rebellions could bring about another U.S. troop deployment in Central America, regional consideration of peaceful cooperative Pan-Americanism would be weakened further. After the war, the Wilson administration would have an even harder time arguing that U.S. involvement was strictly economic and peaceful. Unlike during times of peace, a small, German-encouraged or -sponsored coup could accomplish a lot. During the war agents only had to disturb fragile political and social equilibriums without having to build a better society or establish control over an economic sector.

German planners were not interested in Central American countries, only whether disturbances could generate enough trouble to require the sending of

U.S. forces: "In their development of the plot the German agents traded on the antipathy of Liberal leaders in Cuba to the U.S. and their sympathy with the Carranza government in Mexico; on the traditional suspicion existing between El Salvador and Guatemala, as well as the known antipathy of Carranza and his followers to the Cabrera Government in Guatemala."[71]

The *New York Times* identified German minister Dr. Lehman in Guatemala as one mastermind attempting to unify small uprisings into a greater regional war. He even communicated with Ambassador to Mexico von Eckardt.[72] Outside Central America, the expanding global struggle between Great Britain and Germany pulled Mexican politicians even closer to secret warfare.

8 The War Breaks

All Certainties of Imperialism

The Battle of Jutland and the Collapse of Allied War Financing

Already between May 30 and May 31, 1916, the largest and most technologically advanced battleships in the world had clashed off the Danish coast, expecting to settle in one battle the decades-old German–British naval rivalry. Thirty-seven British battleships fought twenty-one German dreadnoughts. The consequences of the great British–German naval battle of Jutland, in May 1916, brought additional significant indirect change.

On paper, a statistical comparison of the two fleets predicted a British victory. Her Majesty's Royal Navy engaged with an advantage in number of ships, speed, and weight of metal. But the first casualty figures reported 6,907 British and 1,547 German sailors as dead and drowned. However, when the smoke cleared, Jutland proved to be a great battle without a clear winner.

In London and Greenwich, British naval enthusiasts were disappointed that the Battle of Jutland did not provide a repetition of the glorious victory of the Battle of Trafalgar, more than a century earlier. On the plus side the British Empire was left with enough ships to project a credible threat by continuing to blockade the German fleet. As before the battle, it was also able to project a credible naval presence across the world's oceans, despite the fact that the Japanese navy had to assist as a junior partner in the Mediterranean and the Pacific.

German navy enthusiasts in Berlin and Wilhelmshaven were also disappointed that the kaiser's famous fleet had failed to destroy its British archenemy. The clash, in fact, had done so much damage to the German naval fleet that, in contrast to the British, many surviving German surface ships needed to be sent to dry docks for repairs. Unlike the British, until damaged ships were repaired and supplemented with new ships, the German navy no longer had enough ships to be present at the same time in the Pacific Ocean, in the Atlantic off Latin America and the United States, and in Europe.

Until then German merchants in the Americas had never depended on German naval protection for their trade business. But now they knew that, during the immediate postwar period, they could not expect the government in Berlin to back reviving economic expansion with a viable overseas navy.

And yet the German navy, as a threat to Allied merchant marines, continued to be dangerous. Its entire submarine fleet, usually working as a defensive backup for the surface fleet, was still left and could sink ships.

If Germany wanted to use these naval forces, their strategy had to change immediately. How could admirals use the remaining parts of their fleet in new ways while the surface fleet was being repaired and rebuilt?

The emperor and diplomats decided to use the large number of submarines in economic warfare against Allied supply shipments. This meant that submarines, for the first time, would operate as offensive weapons in their own right. No longer would they work as defensive support for surface ships only.

Offensive submarine warfare differed drastically from naval battles between capital ships. Submarines approached merchant ships in stealth, surfaced, and then torpedoed freighters loaded with war supplies. This was insidious economic warfare that aimed to systematically cut off supplies of food, raw materials, weapons, and troop reinforcements. Perhaps submarine warfare could put enough pressure on imperial cabinets to return to the negotiation table and to give Germany a victor's peace.[1]

Some German navy leaders had always wanted to use unrestricted submarine warfare. But Kaiser Wilhelm and his diplomats repeatedly rejected the indiscriminate sinking of merchant ships without any prior warning or inspection of loading papers. Rightfully so, they feared it would drive the United States into the war on the side of the Allies.

In June 1916, Admiral Henning von Holtzendorff renewed his efforts in favor of unrestricted submarine warfare. Also Admiral Mueller wrote in his diary:

Finally I want to remark, that I myself still do believe very much in the possibility of ruthless (*ruecksichtslos*) submarine warfare. The U.S. conflict with Mexico, the growing bitterness of the neutrals against Britain's blockade, an increasing harvest outlook, and not the least success on both [military] fronts, are steps on the staircase which lead to such use of submarines, without that such use [war] represents an uncertain political adventure.[2]

A second aspect of the Jutland story was that submarines were becoming technologically sophisticated enough to cross from Germany to the Americas without having to be refueled midway. Already in 1915, the British navy manufacturer Vickers built a submarine that carried enough fuel to cross the Atlantic.[3] By spring 1916, German technicians had pulled even.

U-53, the first long-range German submarine, was initially used as a submarine freighter carrying critical raw materials through the British blockade into German harbors. *U-53* proved that this was possible when it returned to the German port Bremen on August 23. Four months later it successfully slipped through the blockade a second time.[4] Submarine freighters theoretically might allow Germany to postpone the moment when it would run out of raw materials and agree to end the war.

From 1916 on, the neutral coastlines of North and South America were realistically threatened no longer just by surface battle fleets but by submarines. For the first time, American ports and ships could be attacked without any prior visual warning. Previously, a small number of ethnic Germans had been recruited to help in the supply of the surface fleet. Now, if submarine warfare were carried to the U.S. coast, a small number of ethnic individuals would be helping the more ominous, invisible submarine weapon.

German restraint lasted until fall 1916. Then Admiral Holtzendorff, perhaps without imperial authorization, took the submarine and introduced it as an offensive weapon into the Americas. He sent a smaller combat submarine to accompany the submarine freighter *Bremen*. Its operational orders from September 11, 1916, spelled out that it was to accompany the freighter to the U.S. port New London and then move out to the three-mile limit into international coastal water and conduct restricted submarine warfare.[5]

On October 8, 1916, *U-53* attacked British surface warships patrolling North American coastlines. At 5:35 a.m., the first shot of a German submarine off an American coast was fired across the bow of the U.S. vessel SS *Kansan*. In the following days more neutral ships were stopped and searched. If they carried supplies for the British, they were sunk.

The Germans informed the Wilson administration that *U-53* would operate entirely within the rules of international law.[6] German Ambassador Bernstorff became more optimistic and predicted that Germany, after the U.S.

election, might be able to conduct submarine warfare off the U.S. coast without U.S. interference.[7]

German offensive submarine warfare produced immediate economic warfare repercussions. U.S. marine insurance rates for outgoing freighters skyrocketed by 400 percent. A few East Coast ports withdrew war risk coverage on cargo altogether. Now that shipowners were becoming more hesitant to accept freight, trains loaded with supplies backed up in railway yards at critical U.S. ports. Some shipping line owners reconsidered their business with deliveries to Europe altogether.

Mexican president Carranza's secret warfare gained more relevance because Great Britain and France were losing real strength in 1916. As Allied efforts increasingly depended on reliable and unwavering U.S. backing, any weakening of the United States would be able to impact the war as never before. Already in May 1916, British, French, and Russian financial planners wondered how to pay for foodstuffs, material, and ammunition in 1917. European Allied powers had become surprisingly dependent on private U.S. investors buying bonds, U.S. commercial banks administering their sales, and U.S. manufacturers producing Allied supplies. If private U.S. investors, one day, would refuse to finance the war, neither Wilson nor U.S. Congress guaranteed the use of government funds to keep the Allies afloat. In 1916, financial experts reported that the current way of financing war might end sooner than the Allies expected. European Allied leaders understood the threat. In spring 1916, French minister of finance Alexandre Ribot confessed to the English government "that they themselves could not find in America what would be accepted as payment and that we must take on their commitment there, as well as our own, the Russian's and Italian's.... Allied orders amount to nearly ½ of the sum mentioned, about 1.2 Billion Pounds to be found by the end of September, if all orders were delivered."[8]

By the fall of 1916, a British memorandum detailed the extent of the emerging unprecedented dependency on U.S. partners:

> The Ministry of Munitions procured a large percentage of guns, shells, metals, explosives and machine tools from the U.S.; the Army Department considered that there was no substitute for American supplies of oils and petroleum, nor for that of preserved meat; the Board of Trade stated that for cotton, for foodstuffs, for military necessities and for raw materials for industry the U.S. was an absolutely irreplaceable source of supply; the Board of Agriculture emphasized the dependence of Britain on the U.S.

for grains, and finally the Treasury stated baldly that of the 5,000,000 Pound which the Treasury has to find daily for the prosecution of the war about 2 million has to be found in North America and admits that there was no prospect of any diminution without a radical change in the policies of the Allied War Departments.[9]

It was possible to identify the point in time when the Allies could no longer pay: within twelve months, by fall 1917.

Between January and November 1916, private U.S. investors did not realize how brittle the financial spine of the Allies was becoming. Then, on November 28, 1916, rivalries between U.S. bankers, and possibly, President Wilson's quiet encouragement, caused the publication of a warning in the *Federal Reserve Bulletin*. It discouraged the public from investing into short-term Allied securities.[10]

As these credible data became public knowledge investors and commercial banks switched to caution. Right away, the value of war bonds contracted. Even worse, European exchange rates were stretched by a subsequent run on the British pound, requiring massive governmental support purchases behind the scenes. Even then, support purchases failed to prevent a 1,000,000,000-British-pound contraction of the value of Allied war stocks.

From November on, very creative financial methods and the hurried export of British government gold to the United States kept the Allied purchase efforts afloat, but only barely.[11] By the end of January 1917, the British war effort would require US$83,000,000 to keep going in the next months.

To say it differently, Mexican and German machinations, if successful, could change the course of peace negotiations within months. This was not crazy thinking but, in fact, a fair representation of how the global imperial war had developed.

In December 1916, the German admiralty prepared to lay the groundwork for supplying and operating German submarines along the Mexican coast. Ambassador von Eckardt had to ask Carranza whether he would be willing to tolerate submarine activity off the Mexican coast. When the German navy, allegedly, offered Carranza $6,000,000 in exchange for his approval of a secret base, he did not reply.[12]

Preparations for the first permanent German refueling base in Mexico continued anyway. In November the German Foreign Ministry asked its ambassador to communicate to President Carranza that all preparations had been made and only his approval was standing between Germany and the beginning of submarine operations in the Gulf of Mexico.[13] Anticipating unrestricted submarine warfare in the very near future, Berlin inquired what Carranza wanted in exchange for his approval. The previous year, Mexican revolutionaries in U.S. exile were allegedly offered $5,000,000 in exchange for the future use of Tampico as a base by Germany, if their faction came to power in Mexico.[14]

Harshly, the British warned Mexico against any further exploration of German submarine activities in the gulf through a sharp exchange of diplomatic notes. Mexican foreign secretary Cándido Aguilar skillfully replied that Mexico would remain neutral.

Meanwhile, in Germany, Mexican attaché Arnold Krumm-Heller continued to cheerlead for the start of German submarine warfare in the Gulf of Mexico. He suggested Soto la Marina as a place for submarine operations.[15] From there subs could threaten key British oil fields, New Orleans, and trade ships leaving the mouth of the Mississippi. The obvious targets would be sea-lanes between Great Britain and the United States but also future U.S. troop transports departing from New Orleans to European battlefields.

If it were up to the German naval high command, offensive submarine warfare would start after the U.S. presidential election. President Carranza, however, showed a continuing sense of realism. He simply postponed approval. But he also did not prohibit German preparations.[16]

December 1916 proved disappointing for German leaders. Popular pressure from German Americans failed to elect a more pro-German president into the White House. In Europe the Battle of the Somme also concluded without a decisive winner. Now German leaders grasped the last available straw, an act of desperation, and unleashed unrestricted submarine warfare. Field Marshall Hindenburg expanded approval of submarine warfare from Europe to all oceans of the world, even if this would mean that the United States would enter the war on the Allied side.[17]

Germany had to force Great Britain into a victor's peace by August 1, 1917. Otherwise, Germany, too, would have to accept an outcome that it did not desire. The German navy owned 133 submarines, of which approximately fifty would be available for operations.[18] German leaders assembled on January 9, 1917, at the imperial headquarters in Pless and, joined by the emperor, agreed to start unrestricted submarine warfare.[19] Each submarine was assigned a destruction quota of 600,000 tons of merchant ships.

But the Germans faced a surprise in the Mediterranean. British admirals faced such a shortage in ships and manpower that they enlisted Japanese warships to fight in the Mediterranean! Tokyo's Naval Ministry eagerly complied and dispatched a destroyer division to the Mediterranean to shell Austrian and German submarines. By March 1917, a Japanese flotilla made up of a cruiser and eight destroyers was running between Egypt and Marseille. Rear Admiral Sato Kozo escorted Allied ships along this vital shipping route. He and his men gained significant experience in antisubmarine warfare, conducting 348 escort missions involving some 750 ships and covering over 240,000 nautical miles. It was the first serious exposure of the Japanese navy to Western offensive submarine warfare. Thanks to the German threat, Japanese admirals learned the basics of submarine warfare and carried these lessons to be applied later in the Pacific against the United States in World War II.

9   The Zimmerman Telegram
and Its Aftermath

A Research Update

By 1917, Carranza himself had established reliable permanent channels to the German Foreign Ministry. His original motive had been to establish an independent Mexican military manufacturing sector, not secret warfare.[1] But now all war parties were weaker, and Mexico could exploit the desperate world strategic situation. Against this background, an attempt by Secretary Zimmerman and a few of his supporters to take occasional German–Mexican contacts to a more formal operational level was not that farfetched.

The Zimmerman Telegram was an attempt to probe whether factions inside the new Japanese Terauchi cabinet would be more open to some initial, very modest secret cooperation with Germans in the Americas against the United States. It would have established a German/Japanese war theater in the Pacific.

Today many people are familiar with the text of the Zimmerman Telegram. But three telegrams and one letter need to be added to the historical record because they prove the parallel importance of probing Japan, attempting to break her out of the Allied camp. On February 8, Zimmerman cabled to Mexico: "The president might even now, on his own account, sound out Japan. If the President declines from fear of subsequent revenge you are empowered to offer him a definite alliance after conclusion of peace provided Mexico succeeds in drawing Japan into the alliance."[2] A second time, on February 27, Zimmerman asked Ambassador von Eckardt about Japan and President Carranza: "Has he taken any steps with reference to Japan?"[3] When the British arrested German military attaché von Papen he carried with him a letter from Oberleutnant Freiherr v.

Berchheim of the Foreign Department of the German Main Headquarters. The aristocrat von Berchheim, on March 12, 1917, responded to Papen, commenting on his policy designs and interpretations. He praised:

Many thanks for your letter. You can imagine I'm quite proud of you as regards to Mexico. Furthermore, in my job I have always pointed to it and worked for it. As the affair has now happened, one must extract all one can from it, *and it is beyond doubt that the Japanese now know that we are supporting their progress in Lower California....*

Wonderful to say, they seem to have been impressed over there ... and suddenly, rightly or wrongly, to be afraid of Japan. This will however, soon pass and war will certainly come. God knows, whom it will benefit. This present fighting is terrible. That you should be the one, who is supposed to have been at the bottom of it, would fill me with pride. You see, nothing happens in America that you have not touched or created.[4]

A third telegram confirms the ongoing, historically underappreciated importance of Japan as part of the Zimmerman Telegram. Von Eckardt, on May 2, cabled to Germany that he regretted to inform Zimmerman: "Relations with Japan no closer."[5] Zimmerman had explored whether at least in Latin America the Japanese rivalry with the United States was strong enough to bring about the first regional German–Japanese cooperation, at least between intelligence services.

Since Carranza had developed stable and fruitful linkages to select Japanese factions in 1916 it made sense to ask him to pull them into limited cooperation with Germany. A little more than two years later in 1918, Zimmerman would be out of office. But then his suggestion would be taken seriously in Germany and Tokyo. Japanese and German intelligence forces would enter into regional Latin American cooperation in 1918. From that perspective the Zimmerman Telegram was also the German knock on the Japanese door. An answer would not come until 1918 and, then not surprisingly, on Japanese terms.

Regardless of the failure of the Zimmermann Telegram in 1917, Germans resumed preparations for secret war against the United States. Germany prepared for an intelligence war against the United States launched from Mexican soil. And, as Germans expected to win World War I in the second half of 1917, they prepared demands for naval bases in the Caribbean. From there they would project force toward the Panama Canal and against the United States. Before

FIRST APPEARANCE IN HIS NEW ROLE

AS FREDERICK THE GREAT.

AS NAPOLEON I.

THE ONLY WILHELM IN HIS GREAT IMPERSONATIONS.

AS AN OSTROGOTH

AS A GENTLEMAN

·IN THE GREAT MEXICAN EXTRAVACARRANZA

19. The Zimmerman Telegram was either daring or foolish, depending on the view of national caricaturists (Library of Congress, Washington, D.C.).

forcing such peace agreements onto the Allied powers Germans had to win a war against the United States.

Already on December 12, 1916, the Germans requested that its experts define which naval bases Germany would need to acquire as part of the peace negotiations with France.[6] First secret German agents prepared themselves for a time when their financing from Europe would be cut off. Around February 17, 1917, in Berlin, army administrator von Huelsen asked for money to be transferred from the United States to Mexico. Secret war funding was to be generated by selling stored goods in the United States from the war supply company Deutsche Ozean Reederei, registered in Bremen, Germany. The sale was expected to earn about US$1,900,000 for war against the United States.[7]

On the surface it looked like von Eckardt executed diplomacy from Berlin as ordered. In his memoir he recorded his surprise when embassy secretary von Magnus informed him about the content of the Zimmerman Telegram. The two men hid it in a box in a room in the German legation that was always guarded.[8] In his unpublished memoir he claimed to have thought: "What crazyness! Did they not read my reports? The Mexican cadaver is supposed to declare war on the American giant?" It did not matter. He was asked on February 19 to deliver the note to Carranza. He also admitted that he had received detailed specifics about financial support and weapons that would be extended to Carranza.

Foreign Minister Aguilar preferred to receive him in his private residence on February 20. Von Eckardt told Aguilar "that within shortest time a declaration of war by the U.S. president should be expected." Popular mood could also create the situation, which would push Mexico into such a war. Probably Villa would see the moment as opportune. In case of a Mexican–U.S. war Germany was willing to sign an alliance of neutral conduct of war. Abundant money and weapons support were promised. The minister was also supposed to explore whether Japan could be won for such a scenario.[9]

Von Eckardt expected the Mexican president to act as a "coolly calculating statesman, who would not gamble his own and Mexico's fate out of love for Germany." He moved toward pursuing his own vision of policy, constantly correcting, when possible, what military strategists desired in Berlin. Von Eckardt took over the financing for future German sabotage and secret warfare. And he thought that "Carranza needed first and foremost financial aid and thus I began to push in Berlin in favor of more money without Carranza's knowledge."[10] In Berlin, without Carranza's involvement, planners pondered how to supply future subversive troops inside Mexico with weapons. Members of the secret Department IIIb asked the German high command to approve their use of private Japanese arms merchants.

There was also the challenge of communication. On February 14, 1917, German army planners, in expectation of a 1917 victory, met to discuss German postwar signal intelligence and the re-creation of a worldwide telegraph capacity. Key to its communication strategy was ownership of locations where Allied powers could not cut ocean cables or sabotage transmitters. First, China was selected. Second, Argentina became the anchor of the South American station. Mexico would be the third neutral country to receive and to send German cables.[11] Right away work guided by engineer Mr. Rheute began. Previously he had worked for Telefunken in the U.S. station. Now he simply relocated to Mexico to construct the new Mexican station. A British expert revealed that the Chapultepec station would be the strongest one in Mexico. A second similar setup was expected to transmit out of Saltillo, Nuevo León, but it was still out of commission in March 1917.[12]

In addition, an attack on Mexican oil fields was prepared by Berlin military leaders. Some scenario imagined it as a Villista campaign, eventually strong enough to capture the oil fields of the Tampico district.[13] Also from Berlin the Great General Staff ordered saboteur Hilken from the United States to Mexico in January 1917. Once lead army agents in Mexico would give the final OK, he would set the Tampico oil fields on fire.[14] Sabotage at Tampico was once again "valuable from a military point of view."

Finally, a far western Mexican military diversion was prepared. On February 13, 1917, British consuls reported:

> There are 15 German ships on the West Coast of Mexico who were forced to seek internment in Mexican ports during 1914. Of these ships 11 are at Santa Rosalia, one at Guayamas, one at La Paz, one at Topolabampo and one at Mazatlan. Most of these ships are sailing vessels and some are equipped with motor auxiliary engines.
>
> Mr. Ross has information that it is the intention of the Germans to utilize some of these ships for a raid along the Pacific Coast especially in California. It appears to also be the intention to utilize some of them for the smuggling of arms and ammunition.
>
> Officials of the Bank of Sonora are strongly identified with the plotting in this matter. P. Sandoval who is owner of the bank at Mexicali and his brother A. Sandoval. The International Fisheries Company, the Navarro Pacific Company and the Silvio Romero are all involved in the combination and plot with the Germans in the event of actual war being declared by the U.S. against Germany.[15]

In the end, when it became too dangerous for German captains to engage in raids, von Eckardt helped smuggle dynamite north to the ships so that they could destroy themselves and remain unsuitable for the Allied war effort.[16]

While Germans planned and talked about their military needs, Japanese arms merchants already were quietly serving Carranza's. A boat docked in Salina Cruz on January 5, 1917, and was redirected to Manzanillo. It arrived on February 14, 1917, and unloading, the ship's Japanese captain reassured the press that this cargo was only a private delivery. The ammunition and machinery were not part of a Japanese plot but assigned to help Carranza defeat Pancho Villa. From

Manzanillo, ammunition and the machinery were to be shipped to Molino del Rey accompanied by Japanese technicians.[17] What the captain did not know was that German Ambassador von Eckardt had gone to great lengths to provide expert German workers who could assemble the machine parts and begin manufacturing small arms ammunition.[18]

A J. P. Kafopneck, an Austrian, said to be chief engineer for Obregón, was responsible for unloading munitions. Thus 1,600 tons of ammunition and machinery for the manufacture of 30mm and 7mm small arms ammunition left Manzanillo's dock. In addition there were rapid-firing guns and shells from Kenneth Snyder and Colt. Soon a second ship was expected to bring more ammunition and machinery. It would bring some field pieces and a large consignment of ammunition of various calibers.[19] Suddenly the opportunity for aggressive anti-U.S. diplomacy opened up.

On February 1, 1917, Germany declared unrestricted German submarine warfare, including the U.S. coasts and ships. A few days later U.S. president Wilson tried to punish Germany by breaking diplomatic relations with Berlin. He was at a loss about what to do next.

Then Wilson tried another determined diplomatic initiative. On February 3, he issued a global call to the world's neutral nations to follow the U.S. example and to break off diplomatic relations with Germany.

At the same time, observers in Washington, D.C., admitted that it was uncertain whether Wilson and his Democratic Party would even be able to mobilize, in the months to come, enough votes in Congress in favor of a U.S. declaration of war. It was possible that U.S. lawmakers would deny their president a declaration of war.

Mexican president Carranza was the first Latin American nationalist to exploit Wilson's weak domestic political stance. Seven days after Wilson's initiative, Carranza called for the creation of a distinctly American diplomatic assembly, not in order to break relations with Germany but to mediate between Great Britain and Germany. Carranza was willing to accept the United States as part of this body if Wilson was willing to immediately prohibit the sale of war supplies to European powers. An immediate stop of the export of U.S.-manufactured supplies to Great Britain, France, or Russia would have changed, with greatest likelihood, the course of the war in favor of Germany and Austria-Hungary. Indirectly, Carranza's proposal would have contributed to the likely return of the Allies to the peace negotiation table.[20] Afterward Carranza would have asked

Wilhelm II for a special relationship with Mexico. Carranza's strategy was independent, forceful, and politically very incorrect.[21]

Other Latin American governments did not launch a distinct diplomatic counterproposal a la Carranza. But Argentina, Uruguay, Chile, El Salvador, Honduras, and Guatemala extended formal de jure recognition to the Mexican president. They also rejected Wilson's diplomatic initiative, only with more grace than Carranza. Pro-U.S. Central American administrations inquired whether the U.S. government could provide military protection against possible German retribution, in case Central American governments broke relations or declared war against Germany. U.S. secretary of state Lansing had to admit that the United States lacked the means to protect Central American governments against German attacks in February 1917.[22] Even in Panama, the acting governor and the Panamanian president refused to take a political stance in favor of or against Wilson. At least, they stopped German vessels from leaving Colón and removed German crews from on board. U.S. soldiers were allowed to replace them, making certain that German agents could not direct their ships into the canal and sink them.[23]

Argentina's nationalist president, Hipólito Irigoyen, was more blunt. On February 8, he declared his government "at core" in agreement with Wilson's February note. However, he argued, since German submarines had not yet destroyed any Argentinean property, he saw no reason to break Argentine–German diplomatic relations. Even though Germany's submarine warfare threatened access to Argentinean markets as never before, Irigoyen did not even want to send the equivalent of one diplomatic warning shot by severing diplomatic relations. To the contrary, Irigoyen announced that Argentina's pro-Pan-American foreign policy of the last years was ending.

In *La Epoca*, Irigoyen's party's newspaper, he explained that a new period was beginning. Argentine neutrality could no longer be merely a diplomatic stance but had to be replaced by political activism that Argentine representatives needed to carry to other Spanish American capitals.[24] At a time when President Wilson was not sure whether his own Democratic Party and U.S. citizens, in general, would follow him into war, the first popularly elected Argentine president declared that his country would follow Carranza's stance. Unlike Wilson, Irigoyen had the political support in Argentina's Congress to back his controversial position. As if to demonstrate his strength his party blocked parliamentary procedures that would have made progress on a Pan-American, several-years-old Argentinean–Brazilian–Chilean treaty. It was publicly condemned as pro–United States.

U.S. secretary of state Lansing had to inform Wilson that all gains made by Pan-American initiatives between 1900 and 1915 did not translate into continental solidarity in 1917. Even though German submarine activity threatened Latin America's very livelihood and trade lines, the majority of Spanish American governments refused to back the United States even slightly.[25] The U.S. Wilson administration appeared ethnically rejected, politically isolated, and diplomatically helpless south of the Rio Grande.

Next, Venustiano Carranza emphasized anti-U.S. coalition building in Central America. As U.S. and British outrage over the Zimmerman Telegram exploded in his face, he could not wage open war south of the Mexican–Guatemalan border. He could, however, urge sympathetic Latin American presidents to exploit the confusion created by the war and engage in political block building to destroy Pan-Americanism.

A promising vehicle offered itself, by coincidence, when the Central American Court of Justice, in early 1917, decided a suit favorably against the pro-U.S. Nicaraguan administration. Ironically, this court had been created in 1907 with U.S. backing. As other world leaders awaited the outcome of submarine warfare, Central American judges decided in favor of Mexico's friends Costa Rica and El Salvador. Even though the judges did not suggest a nullification of the controversial U.S.–Nicaraguan Chamorro–Bryan treaty, Carranza's propagandists composed articles for sympathetic Central American newspapers that insisted on an outright condemnation of U.S. policy in Central America.[26]

Right away Carranza tried to deepen the bond with El Salvador's President Melendez. He sent his confidential agent Martinez Alomia to San Salvador. Officially, Alomia was to conduct diplomatic negotiations and purchase arms. But unofficially he explored the building of a Mexican–El Salvadoran alliance against the pro-U.S. administrations of Guatemala and Nicaragua. This effort would be backed by joint anti-U.S. propaganda. As a symbol of his appreciation for El Salvador's friendship, Carranza provided President Melendez with a wireless transmitter and aircraft to train pilots.[27]

In the end, Alomia succeeded at purchasing several million rounds of rifle ammunition for Carranza's army. Another source asserts that Alomia also succeeded at negotiating "a secret understanding with Melendez that contained a defensive alliance against Guatemala."[28] Obviously, in the near future, El Salvador would be Carranza's best ally and principal support base in Central America.

Carranza acted toward Nicaragua and its pro-U.S. Chamorro administration with greater care and yet duplicitous chutzpah. Fortunately for the

Mexican leader, President Chamorro appreciated not only protection through U.S. forces but also private corruption and personal profit. Even though Mexico and Nicaragua remained politically opposed to each other, nevertheless Mexican agent Martinez Alomia traveled to Managua. Chamorro seemed impossible to topple from power in the immediate future. Thus Carranza obtained some goodwill through a bribe. A Mexican agent in New York advanced the Nicaraguan leader a modest sum of money, hoping that cold cash would motivate Chamorro to maintain basic, cordial relations with revolutionary Mexico. It worked. Chamorro sold Carranza several million rounds of rifle ammunition above the world market level—a nice profit for his personal fortunes.[29]

Out of sight, Carranza quietly continued to plot against Chamorro. His contact with anti-Chamorro conspirator Irias stayed alive, even though for the time being, Irias remained afraid to take on the Nicaraguan army, trained and armed by U.S. officers.[30]

In the end, Carranza's attempt at alliance building yielded modest results. El Salvador's president gained the support of the Honduran president in favor of a political agreement that joined both countries into the República de Morazán. Carranza pledged military support in case Guatemala's President Cabrera should attack this federation.[31] Also, Carranza promised to support the expansion of this first, small regional bloc when the time was right.

Remarks by Carranza's diplomats in Central America confirmed a deeper, long-term Mexican strategy. They stated that the chaos of World War I might provide a unique opportunity to connect Central American nations with South American nations in a joint political-military project. As long as U.S. forces had to be committed to Europe and could not be deployed to Latin America, Carranza exploited an opening emerging for alternative political arrangements in the Americas. They would be difficult to undo once peace was reestablished. At least the politics of Pan-Americanism would be proved a thing of the past.

Carranza wanted an Argentine or Chilean diplomatic-military commitment to defend a future, expanding Central American union. Eventually, as Central America and Spanish South America reorganized themselves into two regional but ethnically interconnected blocs, they might be able to replace Pan-Americanism with Latin Americanismo.

Finally, we must not forget to mention German interests in this scheme. Even though Carranza acted as his own man, between 1917 and 1918, German Ambassador to Mexico von Eckardt kept tabs on Carranza's Central American machinations. He assured Berlin that his legation and his Mexico City bank accounts would be ready to finance any Central American revolutionary movement, once Berlin identified a suitable one.

Meanwhile, in South America, other Spanish American countries expressed strong reservations against Wilson's diplomacy. In Asunción, Paraguay's leader agreed that unrestricted German submarine warfare "will be greatly damaging to neutral rights, but what needed to be done was not to follow the U.S. president but to hold a convention of South American countries and to consider the question."[32] Paraguayans were willing to include U.S. representatives if such a conference of American neutrals became a reality. However, a U.S. delegation would receive only one vote; thus it could not stop any momentum in favor of Spanish American block building.

Ecuadorian politicians suggested Uruguay as a meeting place where "Latin Americans should decide upon common measures that would guarantee the rights of continental neutrality and to allay the rigors of the struggle."[33] From Quito's perspective, U.S. participation in this conference was not desired.

Already in 1916, Venezuela had called for a conference of neutrals. Now, on March 7, 1917, the Gómez administration spoke a second time in favor of a rights of neutrals conference.[34] But the Caracas government preferred a national stance over joint contributions to an emerging realm.

The Chilean government refused to follow any foreign-inspired, regional political realignment, be it Pan-American or Spanish American. Politicians in Santiago were particularly suspicious of following Argentine leadership.[35] Regardless, Argentina's diplomats asked Peru on March 24 to back the Argentine mediation initiative.[36]

All that President Wilson and Secretary of State Lansing could do against Irigoyen's new push to create a Spanish America under increasing Argentine influence was "to refer it for further study" to the Pan-American Union. From Mexico City, Carranza reinforced the Argentine president. On April 3, Mexican diplomats joined Ecuadorians calling for an American Congress to mediate between Germany and Great Britain. Carranza also won endorsement from sympathetic factions in Colombia.[37]

Presidents Carranza and Irigoyen found in Argentina's Hispanista Manuel Ugarte a propagandist willing to build a broader popular base for their new policy. Ugarte accepted Mexican foreign minister Aguilar's invitation and visited revolutionary Mexico. Thus began his long trip across the Andes to Valparaiso, Chile. From there his ship took him to Lima, Panama, and Havana until it delivered Ugarte to Veracruz, Mexico. At each stop, Ugarte delivered rousing speeches pleading with the general public to support a Spanish American Union.

In 1914, Ugarte had been only an advocate for closer ties between Spain and Latin America. Suddenly, in 1917, Ugarte directly connected the future of Hispanismo with a victory of Germany. Ugarte insisted that Spanish Americans needed to choose between the Allied powers and Germany. Only a German victory could create the needed powerful counterforce against the United States. Germany would support a Latin America that revolved around culture, ethnicity, and spirituality. In contrast, the Allied powers would allow the United States to establish a protectorate over Latin America "infused with trade and individualism."[38]

Ugarte's move into the German war camp was his own choice. Still, German minister von Eckardt did everything in his power to reinforce Ugarte's enthusiasm in Mexico. Von Eckardt provided housing for him but avoided being seen with him in the Zócalo. At a private dinner, however, he encouraged Ugarte to agitate on.

Argentine military attaché Emil Kienkelin, from Scandinavia, who worked as a German agent and propaganda organizer, proposed German financing for Ugarte to publish a Hispanista magazine targeting exclusive Spanish American audiences. Kienkelin wanted Ugarte to publish in Barcelona, Spain, and ship the finished copies to South America, symbolizing a Spanish–Latin American link. After an assumed German victory Ugarte's publication was supposed to move to Berlin and to propagandize in favor of a Spanish–Latin American Union.[39] Kienkelin suggested a first down payment of $35,000 dollars and, thereafter, $8,000 dollars per month to sustain publication. In Berlin, German superiors approved.

Ugarte remained in Carranza's revolutionary Mexico until June 1917. He appreciated the visit as a unique chance to experience a new Latin American reality where a distinct anti-U.S. nationalism was not just talked about but lived and acted out. Inspired, he returned to Buenos Aires to assume a key leadership role in the growing Argentinean youth movement.[40]

Submarine warfare and the breaking of diplomatic relations had also called into question, indirectly, Allied war financing on a global scale. In the twentieth century there had never been a more uncertain investment and financing climate as February 1917. All that the British could do was keep talking to influential circles in New York and Washington. And while a British financial delegation led by S. Hardman Lever waited in Washington, British gold reserves were spent down further and further, day by day. The bank House of Morgan anxiously waited with the British. Still President Wilson could not make up his mind. Imperial Britain's war debt grew to the unfathomable amount of $345,000,000.[41] The

U.S. historian Kathleen Burk laconically explains that "the point had been reached where Britain no longer had control over her external financial affairs, but was at the mercy of events and the American government."[42]

In other words the U.S. government would have to take over Allied war financing.[43] Otherwise Great Britain, France, and Russia would have had to reorganize the financial structure of their war conduct in most radical, uncertain ways. Even if Great Britain and France survived the merciless choke hold of submarine warfare, they would not be in the position to finance and supply a continuing war against Germany themselves.

Few understand today that in the months to come anything was possible; a new political world could explode onto the world stage, and nobody would know how to operate in its financial and trade ruins. This was a highly dangerous time, and weaker politicians would have been happy to enter into any negotiated peace and have monarchy and imperialism limp into another decade of disingenuous peace. Carranza would have much to expect from Wilhelm II.

Into this abyss, on February 20, 1917, German Ambassador von Eckardt handed Undersecretary Zimmermann's offer of German–Mexican–Japanese alliance in case of a U.S.–Mexican war. Carranza's son-in-law and Mexico's foreign minister, Cándido Aguilar, carried the telegram to Colima, where President Carranza was working.

20. Select members of the German military high command toyed with hypothetical offers of U.S. territory to Mexico, hoping to paralyze U.S. support for the Allies but also to break Japan out of the Allied camp (Library of Congress, Washington, D.C.).

Mexico's president did not react with outright rejection; nor did he embrace the offer. Instead, assuming that the offer was and would remain secret in perpetuity, Carranza, Obregón, Aguilar, and his inner circle began careful deliberations.

A few Mexican bureaucrats were trigger happy. Jose Flores of Mexico's Ministry of Defense fantasized about cooperation between ethnic Germans and Mexicans in the United States, once a U.S.–Mexican war would break out. After returning from an exploratory trip to the United States, he remarked that "Japanese and Mexicans had at their disposal 300,000 fire arms and adequate ammunition. At the moment when war is declared against Germany, we will be able to count on at least two hundred thousand Germans in the U.S. and throughout South America."[44]

In Mexico City, Foreign Minister Aguilar walked to Tokyo's legation, where a Mr. Kinta Arai worked, officially as a low-level employee. The two men discussed a possible Japanese reaction to a U.S.–Mexican war. Newly discovered sources identify Arai as the leader of Japan's intelligence network in the Río de la Plata region in 1918.[45] It is unlikely that he rose from low-level clerk in 1917 in Mexico to Buenos Aires intelligence chief within several months. Foreign Minister Aguilar probably knew that Arai was the liaison to Japan's intelligence organization.

Kinta Arai told Aguilar that Japanese politicians would remain focused on China as their immediate priority. This policy required a positive relationship with the United States, and an assistance treaty against the United States was inopportune at that point in time.

This was critically important information as Carranza assembled close government members and military generals to study the implications of the Zimmermann Telegram. They identified the key issue: Who would provide the military hardware to supply Mexico during a Mexican–U.S. war? Perhaps, in the words of Mexican Revolution historian Friedrich Katz, the Zimmerman Telegram was merely a suicidal German trap.[46] Carranza remained cautious and asked Berlin whether it would be able to back him with arms supplies and ammunition.[47] But before he could learn how sincere the German generals were, the shocking Zimmerman Telegram was leaked to the world's public.

Now it harshly convinced President Wilson that German leaders, at heart, had never had any sincere interest in his mediation. Emperor Wilhelm II and the German military leadership avoided diplomacy open to negotiations. The emperor and the Prussian Junkers remained interested only in an all-or-nothing victor's peace. Wilson's ideas about Germany had been based on self-deception.

The public revelation of Zimmerman's scheme eliminated any chance of serious pursuit of his diplomacy.

Right away, Japanese leaders went into default reaction. In Tokyo, Japan's Deputy Foreign Minister Count Shidehara tried to save Japan's esteem by publicly interjecting himself in Japanese–Latin American relations. He issued a rare, categorical denial that imperial Japan was interested in this German offer. From within the core of Japanese elites it was firmly rejected. As long as China remained exclusive policy priority, there was no need to put in writing a potential Japanese–Mexican–German security relationship in the Western Hemisphere. In 1919, this would be different.

The U.S. cabinet exerted pressure on President Wilson to be more decisive. On February 23, cabinet demands became so strong that Wilson reacted angrily.[48] Three days later, on February 26, he asked Congress to grant him the power to arm merchant ships with defensive weapons. It was a first test to see how strongly U.S. pacifists and neutrality supporters would oppose him. Previously, breaking diplomatic relations with Germany had been supported 78 to 5 votes. But would the Congress support the next step and declare war? The U.S. historian Ernest May characterizes the events of February 26 as Wilson's "last adaptation of policy of patient firmness."[49]

German leaders saw that Wilson still did not want war or armed neutrality. Even though the House passed his resolution 403 to 13, pacifists started a filibuster that kept the resolution from becoming a bill and moving into law. It was an embarrassing humiliation for the U.S. president and showed an encouraging lack of U.S. unity at such a critical time. An intercepted telegram stated that, still at that time, Germany financed U.S. pacifists with $50,000.[50]

Wilson's second term as president started on March 4, 1917. After he secluded himself in the White House, Latin American countries saw a U.S. president whose policy had broken down. For eleven days, from March 7 to 19, the future was uncertain, and submarines chipped away at the Allies' lifelines. French, Russian, British, and Japanese leaders, too, could only wait for the outcome of Wilson's continuing hesitation.

In Mexico City German diplomat von Eckardt took charge and increasingly focused his German policy toward Mexico, even though Germany's leaders did not see the U.S.–Mexican border as a war field of top priority. On March 8, 1917, news reached Mexico that the German war department in Japan had proposed to buy weapons for Carranza on a grander scale. Mid-level German officers promised weapons from the other side of the Pacific. In reality the highest German leaders remained reticent toward this solution.[51]

In Washington, on March 19, 1917, Wilson emerged with newfound strength. Now he believed that a U.S. war entry was the correct step to take. Submarine warfare required them to stand up for the rule of law. He could turn to armed neutrality, but it might divide the already strained U.S. society. He talked to his secretary of state on March 19 and his cabinet on the following day.[52] Wilson wanted the United States to join the Allied powers.

Wilson's cabinet endorsed his planned declaration of war on March 21. On March 22, the president asked Congress to convene on April 2 and discuss his request for a declaration of war. America's interest lay in a peace without victory. This time Wilson's hopes were realized as planned, and the U.S. Congress voted in favor of joining World War I on the side of the Allied powers.[53]

In Mexico Carranza remained less impressed, only certain that he needed to protect his supportive relationship with Germany. In the last week of March 1917, Carranza's foreign minister, Aguilar, stepped down from the office of foreign minister. At a final banquet on March 27, 1917, Minister of War Obregón promised von Eckardt that no break of diplomatic relations with Germany would take place. General Aguilar also confirmed that the eventuality of a blatant break in diplomatic relations remained outside the realm of the possible.[54] Yet on April 3, Mexican diplomats backed Ecuadorian politicians to call an American Congress and mediate between Germany and Great Britain.

It took German field marshal Ludendorff until after the U.S. entry into the war on April 3, 1917, to upgrade the priority of the Mexican–U.S. war theater. On that day he appropriated 30,000,000 RM. The purpose was "to support Mexico against the U.S." This could include payment "to support Mexican leaders and partial financing of weapons and ammunition purchases." And Ludendorff and the Admiralty agreed to provide Carranza with 30 repeat-loading guns and 9,000,000 cartridges, 100 machine guns and 6,000,000 cartridges, and six 7.5-cm mountain guns and 2,000 shots, as well as four 10.5-cm howitzers. A German ship was to be chartered under foreign flag to deliver the goods to Carranza. Minister von Eckardt was to identify a secure Mexican port that could receive this small offer and assure that it would reach Carranza.[55]

Until now the Zimmerman Telegram had remained officially unanswered. Publicly Carranza remained unfazed and waited until April 14 to address the offer. Privately, he had communicated to German Ambassador von Eckardt that the British publication of the Zimmerman Telegram had prevented the creation of a German–Mexican alliance: "A [German–Mexican] alliance had been prevented but it would be necessary at a later point in time. First he wanted to receive from the Mexican Congress the right to receive exclusive powers, then he would answer about ammunition and money."[56] Recognizing Germany's desperate need for continued Mexican neutrality, he reassured Ambassador von Eckardt that Germany would receive what it wanted most. U.S. policy would not drive Mexico into the camp of the Allies: "He wanted to remain neutral under all circumstances. However if Mexico would be pulled into the war one would have to see again."[57]

Carranza did the same when he talked with Ambassador Fletcher. He told the other side his partial, convenient truths. He told Fletcher that he would not sign a treaty with Germany.

More correctly this meant that he would not enter into grand written agreements. However, smaller project-related cooperation with Germany continued. To say it differently, the Zimmerman Telegram only changed popular public perception, but not at all Carranza's interest to explore cooperation among German, Mexican, and Japanese factions. Carranza survived the unsolicited German initiative without serious damage at home or abroad.

Von Eckardt reported signs that convinced him of Carranza's continued positive feelings for Germany. For example, at the April 15 opening of the Mexican Congress all ambassadors assembled in Mexico City's National Palace. As soon as U.S. Ambassador Fletcher appeared, spectators hissed and expressed outrage against the United States. In contrast, the German diplomat von Eckardt was welcomed with shouts of "Viva Alemania" and applause.[58] Later von Eckardt wrote about Carranza to Berlin:

> During the World War I Mexico was for Germany. We will mark it for its benefit in German historiography, not as a secondary factor, but, as I believe, in outstanding importance. On the one hand because of her effect on Latin America and, on the other hand, because her obvious affection for us forced our enemy to keep permanently 200,000–500,000 troops at the border....
>
> ... Also Washington knows that the Emperor's picture decorates Carranza's working room. Carranza follows with attention the movement of the German army. In each victory he sees a strengthening of his policy.[59]

With quiet satisfaction Carranza accepted President Wilson's de jure diplomatic recognition, a legal assurance that he was not about to push the irritating Mexican nationalist out of office. This was a significant victory for Carranza.

But Carranza also understood full well the consequences of leading a country situated next to a world power at war. Now Carranza's capital became the "natural" geographic headquarters for secret anti-U.S. work in the Western Hemisphere. Mexico was best suited as a place from which to stage operations that would weaken the United States, its economy, and its army.

Mid-level German diplomats wanted Carranza protected and strengthened. On May 22, von Eckardt cabled to Berlin that in order to protect Carranza he opted against blowing up the oil wells at Tampico. He explained that he did this in the interest of Mexico—its economic interest and because pro-Allied elements in Mexico would be handed a dangerous tool to force Carranza to break diplomatic relations with Germany:

I send confidential agents to Tampico to watch the oil fields to prevent any damage. I received Mexicans who presented in writing the subsequent declaration: Americans pushed us to set the oil fields on fire; others pressured us to say it: The Germans were the ones who would lay the fire. I gave this memorandum to Carranza. In September 1917 the same Mexican individuals reappeared and U.S. ambassador Fletcher offered 5000 pesetas if they would give this proof to him.[60]

Should Carranza change his political mind von Eckardt also had access to interesting alternative supporters on the ground. For example, there was the German Carl Putsch. U.S. intelligence feared his contacts with Santa Maria Native Americans. One theory was that he might enlist the Native Americans to raid big oil wells. His savings amounted to $75,000 in the Hanover National Bank. For some purpose, he withdrew gold monthly in the sum of $2,500. One day the activities stopped. Details remain to be discovered.[61]

It is doubtful that Carranza realized how fortunate he was having von Eckardt as a German diplomat. For Berlin, Carranza was the most appreciated nationalist in Latin America, but nevertheless, he was an entirely replaceable figure should greater strategic considerations demand it.

In contrast, this German diplomat wanted Carranza and Mexico to emerge alive after any confrontation with the United States. Sabotage of Mexican oil fields had to be avoided "as long as Mexico is not ready for war." Von Eckardt recommended to Emperor Wilhelm II that he send Carranza a congratulatory telegram but hold back the saboteurs.[62]

Protecting Carranza also meant including the president in a German intelligence service, which von Eckardt decided to expand. Von Eckardt recruited

French individuals willing to betray France for money. He either bought documents or, if they were available only for a short while, had them photographed.

Von Eckardt admitted: "Whenever I found it appropriate I informed him steadily about all developments, in particular those in the provinces; whenever revolutionary generals or officers through their wild activities undermined the reputation of the current system of government, which continued to wrestle for its life." Carranza, in return "showed a never changing sense of charity and calm, which carried over to his ministers and generals. Even though his regime had not been consolidated as late as summer 1918 an attitude was nurtured in the belief of Germany's success, which he expressed in a telegram to the Emperor on his birthday in 1918, at a time when I already had disturbing thoughts."[63] Even after November 1918 Carranza insisted, "A people which have achieved such incredible things before us work themselves back to the top, she will come back again."[64]

The resulting intelligence and propaganda net was pre-financed with gold from ethnic German merchants in Mexico City. Von Eckardt praised the leading men of the German ethnic merchant group and their aid. In order to claim ignorance, in case of discovery, First Secretary von Magnus issued IOUs. Enough money accumulated to hire full-time propagandists who spread the propaganda across the entire country.[65]

For Carranza, developing options to fight the United States also meant establishing a more independent national financial base for his struggling revolutionary state. If loans and investment would no longer come predominantly from U.S., British, or French banks, then Carranza might be more able to conduct policy free from Allied pressures. Secret economic policy meant the quest for establishing a central bank that did not depend on dollars, pounds, or francs. But what would be the alternative? It could be the Japanese yen and the German reichsmark.

Our ability to track the evolution of this effort remains limited. Until the writing of a thorough financial history of the Mexican Revolution, we can follow only faint but still instructive trends.[66] The few incidents we have to analyze, once again, involve Germany.

Dealings pertaining to Carranza's fifth secret warfare effort emerge already in 1916, at least one year before Germans tried to entice him with a darker, military alliance. In March 1916, Mr. Tomobaso, Japan's main interlocutor with Tokyo elites, approached the newly elected *jefe revolucionario* in Mexico City, asking him if he would consider a major offer of yen. It could form the base of a revolutionary central bank.

Any revolutionary state would, eventually, require an effective monopoly of currency issue. A Carranza-controlled national bank would mean that Villa and Zapata could not control a national financial institution. Ideally Carranza would be able, after military victory, to allow the reestablishment of a capitalist civilian economy. Before the revolution, French banks had backed Mexico's peso. Afterward a national central bank would take that power away from foreigners. Plus foreign companies could hand out less punishment by colluding with foreign banks.

The Japanese offer proved that key *revolucionarios* were thinking beyond military affairs. Three men who can be identified were Rafael Nieto, Carranza's brother-in-law Zambrano, and Luis Cabrera. In the end all we know is that no Mexican central bank based on yen was created in 1916.

By January 1917, Carranza had achieved relative defeat over Francisco Villa. And the establishment of a national central bank became an important item of discussion at the constitutional convention. The U.S. historian Richard Freeman Smith identifies General Zambrano as a traveler in renewed national bank efforts. In January 1917, he explored a $10,000,000 loan from the Bank of Morgan to stock a national Mexican bank.[67]

In February 1917, the British intercepted a letter from Rafael Nieto to Luis Cabrera offering deeper interpretations of Carranza's intent. The letter reads:

> The Carranza government intends to use the threatened German intrigue in an effort to force financial and other aid from the U.S. government. He also stated that the Carranza government will endeavor to bring about a mutual declaration between that government and that of the U.S. and that if this can be accomplished they will eliminate any question of the German intrigue, asking in return our aid for Carranza in the matter of ammunition, financial assistance etc. Nieto also told him that Carranza must have ammunition promptly if he is to subjugate Villa and the other revolutionary forces. . . .
>
> . . . Also Cabrera, although pro German on the surface, is really strongly inclined to favor the U.S.
>
> . . . Nieto is openly attempting to influence the investment of German private capital in Mexican industrial and other securities, as distinguished from governmental funds.[68]

Carranza's team handled this issue not only as a crisis but also as an opportunity.

In April, the Wilson administration dispatched its new diplomat to Mexico. When U.S. Ambassador Fletcher met Carranza he offered him conditional support that could include financial relief. On April 24, Ambassador Fletcher offered Carranza "any help possible." Carranza answered that "such was not necessary, his attitude would remain strictly neutral."[69] But there was more to the story.

At the same time, in March 1917, A. Iselin and Company, a private U.S. bank, had promised Carranza a $20,000,000 loan. Suddenly the U.S. Treasury intervened and refused to coin any gold for Iselin. It could use only U.S. paper dollars.[70]

U.S. Ambassador Fletcher's March loan offer might have been an attempt to check pro-German circles. Already in 1916, the Iselin Co. had functioned as a clearinghouse for financial transactions involving the German–Mexican merchant bank house Stallforth. Then Stallforth had cleared Mexican money notes belonging to groups close to Félix Díaz. One source hints at support from one Stallforth manager:

Osterheld remained manager of Stallforth and Co. with a working arrangement through Legier, noted as clearing agent in transmitting funds for Stallforth to the Swiss Bank Verein and to the Swiss National Bank, Switzerland. Some of the funds have also been dispersed through Lloyds of London and to the French Bank in Paris.

People have been advised that the Swiss banks transmit funds back and forth to Germany as trades were made. Stallforth furnished funds to several Mexicans to go to Europe with the idea of handling business and that these Mexicans did make appropriate arrangements with London houses for the transaction of business through Mexico.

Further arrangements were to be made for the account of Stallforth and German interests both in Mexico and in New York. Hugo Schmidt, representative of the Deutsche Bank giving up his office at 45 Broadway New York made his headquarters at Stallforth.

Luis Cabrera on his visit to this country according to Barbrick discussed with Schmidt and Stallforth the matter of making gold for the Mexican government. The arrangements for this were as follows: Iselin Co. were to receive certificates of import and exports from Dr. Caturegli, Carranza's financial agent in New York. Upon presentation of such certificates and collection by Iselin they were to buy gold for the account of the Mexican government. In order that this company might be fully protected, two contracts were made, one from the Deutsche Sued Amerikanische Bank in Mexico City through their agent A de

Chapeaurouge, Room 601, 31 Nassau Street. Chapeaurouge held power of attorney from this Mexico City Bank.[71]

It would be an exaggeration to present this cooperation as a German conspiracy on behalf of Carranza. Conservatively interpreted, it is, first, an example of how the pro-German business sector of Mexico was being used by Carranza—and delighted to serve in this function—to circumvent pressures and scarcities created by U.S. banks. Second, it was a simple attempt to continue to do business during war and economic blockades. And third, Carranza understood the importance of precious metal and included its acquisition in his many efforts to steer a policy that the U.S. Wilson administration did not prefer.

German observers understood full well its implications. Already twelve months ago Minister von Eckardt had reported Carranza's struggle to obtain metal coinage.[72] In March 1917, he became blunt and drove home the point toward Berlin. He told superiors that those who were able to give Mexico 300,000,000 pesos would be the ones "who could dominate Mexico."[73] He recommended to Berlin to give the money, if at all possible, "in case our current contemporary political and future trade policy demands intensifying Mexico's independence."[74] Legation diplomat Magnus had added that those who float a loan to Mexico, allowing her to refinance her debt, and those who "supervise its use, dominate Mexico economically and therefore politically."[75] The diplomats in the field pointed at the path to pursue. The government and army in Berlin only had to provide the precious metal coinage.

U.S. trade and financial policy had to be dedicated to creating and assuring the financial base for a victory over Germany and its allies. War financing, or more precisely, economic warfare measures, required a stop of the flow of gold out of the United States. Mexico's physical possession of precious metal, versus printed paper money, promised real strength vis-à-vis the future enemy Germany and Austria-Hungary.

As Wilson waffled toward entry into World War I, Carranza was beginning to feel the financial consequences of new U.S. war priorities. More than ever before gold and silver equaled power. Money was strong enough to change positions in political negotiations.

In May 1917, Agustín Legorreta, a director of the Banco de Mexico, emerged as a second negotiator, talking to the U.S. secretary of the interior about potential financing from U.S. banks. As before, these explorations had no positive results.

In April, the German ambassador offered small amounts of currency, potentially gold, to members of Mexico's Senate and Chamber of Deputies. In case

Mexico's financial and food crisis would convince Carranza to break diplomatic relations with Germany, Ambassador von Eckardt had bought the support of influential generals. They promised to depose Carranza in a coup as soon as Mexico's president gave compromising assurances to the United States or reached an agreement detrimental to Germany. Hard cash and precious metal meant real power.[76]

Carranza continued to articulate his financial needs aggressively. He told Germans what it would take for him to fight the United States. At the end of May 1917, he mentioned the amount of at least 200,000,000 Mexican pesos in case of a war, plus ammunition and the operation of submarines in the Gulf of Mexico.[77] In this tally Carranza tried to kill two birds with one stone. He wanted money for war but also enough to stock his national bank. In the first week of July Carranza made the next attempt, this time differentiating between money for banks and money to conduct war. Then he asked for a 100,000,000-peso loan issued in national gold.[78] The Germans reported,

> The need of money here is very urgent. Washington offers a loan of $50,000,000 (U.S.) and is again pressing for a breach with us. President and foreign minister begs me urgently to make a definite offer, if possible of 100,000,000 Mexican Pesos, with an indication when remittance of a portion of it could arrive.[79]

Then the honest, sobering German answer came. On June 8, 1917, Berlin explained that as long as World War I lasted, it would be impossible to remit funds sufficient to function as a loan for the founding of a Mexican central bank. As far as other financial measures were concerned, the German leadership instructed the ambassador:

> You should hold out prospect for considerable assistance for economic purposes after the conclusion of the war.[80]

German generals and Wilhelm II were still acting as if in the near future they could force a peace settlement onto Great Britain and, now, the United States. Thereafter Carranza's Mexico would receive immediate help. German imperialism toward Mexico would intensify.[81]

The secret warfare department administering preparations to make possible a future German–Mexican alliance against the United States, in June, chose the next best possible avenue after admitting its lack of available cash. Looking into Mexico's future after a still assumed German victory, it predicted intense financial Allied pressure on Carranza and Mexico. Then Germany wanted to stand on Mexico's side against the Allies. Secret warfare department diplomat von Huelsen stated, "Mexico needs to know that we want to and can help her out of this situation."[82]

Carranza did not give up the "finance game." So much so that U.S. Ambassador Fletcher became personally interested in finding U.S. bankers almost on behalf of Carranza. Also Fletcher emphatically reported to his superiors that a major foreign loan was of utmost importance to Carranza's political stability. Carranza wanted 150,000,000 pesos to serve bonds that were coming due.[83] Yet private U.S. banks did not share Ambassador Fletcher's political-economic long-term wisdom.

August 1917 passed without any foreign loans to Carranza. Then in September precious metal exports from the United States were officially prohibited altogether. Even if Berlin leaders had been able and willing to stock a Mexican national bank through German American accounts, now it was illegal. Sending German gold by ship across the Atlantic was even more unlikely.

In fall 1917, the secret finance game became adventurous. German mid-level bureaucrats explored new avenues to transport funds illegally to Mexico from locations other than the United States. Just as blockade runners were considered to bring ammunition and a wireless transmitter, couldn't such ships also bring gold and silver coins as well?

On September 3, 1917, von Eckardt cabled that Carranza still wanted 100,000,000 pesos for immediate use. He told the Germans that the loan that Carranza required as a definite condition of his acceptance was to be applied to the payment of interest on arrears on foreign loans, the establishment of order in Mexico, and the provision of money and material for the army and railways. In addition, Carranza specified that he required German diplomatic support in the settlement of foreign mining and railway concessions and with difficulties over the foreign banks, including the Bank of London and Mexico (there were also other conditions about which information has not been received).

Through General Aguilar, Carranza asked for military instruction officers, officers and men to work the local munitions factory, specialists and plans to complete the local rifle factory so as to bring its daily output up to two hundred rifles, and aviation plans and officers to fight and fly the latest models of German fighting airplanes. On October 3, Cándido Aguilar informed the Germans "that Mexico in principle was in alliance with Germany."[84]

As the third quarter of 1917 ended, diplomat von Eckardt expressed desperation that the leadership in Berlin focused more on the eastern front in Europe than on the border between Mexico and the United States. Von Eckardt pleaded, "I thought that Mexico was so important, also in light of other South American countries looking at Mexican behavior that the war account in Berlin would make available 100 Mill Pesos."[85] In the eyes of German generals the likely defeat of Russia deserved continued priority over the unproven bond with Mexico. Later Germans could turn to Latin America. On September 26, the Foreign Office could offer only "the prospect of weapons, military instructors once a U.S.–Mexican war had been brought about. Money from Argentina was about to come." Other "required material support for President appears technically unrealizable."[86] It remained physically impossible to move 100,000,000 pesos in gold into Mexico.

Carranza continued to ask for money from the Germans. A realistic money offer would have made a huge difference while other agents were negotiating for him with potential U.S. sources.

This was a very manipulative Mexican flirtation, as it required the revolutionary state to do nothing. But German megalomania felt courted by these distant political flirtations. In contrast, U.S. investors were willing to help Carranza if he was willing to make key concessions against the recently passed 1917 Mexican Constitution and its articles pertaining to the ownership of petroleum subsoil rights. This would force him to betray his own political achievements.

Financial dalliances with distant Germans—if they ever delivered the money—were easy in comparison. German gold, if physically located in Mexican vaults before any U.S.–Mexican war, could be used as Carranza saw fit, not as Germany had wished. Experience with U.S. banks, companies, and governments had taught him that they would only have to cross the border to enforce the written terms of any contract. In contrast, Germany would remain very far away, even after a victorious peace treaty.

Carranza remained interested in the possibilities of a German mid-size loan, always holding out the possibility of renewed financial and therefore political staying power. U.S. financial experts knew about Carranza's Achilles heel. In the words of U.S. historian Robert Freeman Smith, they used his "need for gold and corn as a lever for bargaining."[87]

In spring 1917, the German army high command sent a new chief agent. Anton Dilger quickly unfolded a whirlwind of activities with various degrees of soundness. This innovative and megalomaniacal man offered Carranza a new grand scheme that included significant financial promises.

The German Foreign Ministry had given him a long ten-point agenda making Germany the center of reestablishing domestic order and completely reordering Mexico's economic structure. It promised loans to service Mexico's debt, a reorganization of domestic debt, and a complete renegotiation of railroad, petroleum, mining, and banking concessions.[88]

As Carranza learned about the deal he cannot possibly have taken Dilger too seriously. Nevertheless, he encouraged him to proceed. Carranza faced profound food and financial shortages. If Dilger, against reason, were to be successful, Carranza would benefit immediately. If not, he would not be worse off.[89]

President Carranza requested that Dilger propose to the Berlin Great Staff that Germany should advance the Mexican government 50,000,000 pesos, 50 percent of his previous demand. He would raise the other half inside Mexico. A second loan to meet current expenses was also requested. On October 10, Carranza suggested that weapons for Mexico should be purchased in Japan. He wanted immediately one thousand guns, fifteen machine guns, and 4-mm cartridges as a test delivery. German military high command representative Kraft was being sent east to purchase these weapons in Japan.[90]

In return Dilger formulated extreme conditions for German cooperation: German interests should be the central government concern in Mexican foreign policy. Germany would supervise any postbellum commercial engagement contemplated by Carranza. Germany should strictly control the disposal of any funds advanced. Supplies of war material should be bought exclusively from Germany. This proposal left in October. It did not reach Berlin until the second week in December.[91]

This information demands that we see Carranza and his policy after the Zimmerman Telegram in a new light. Carranza explored German cooperation with far greater sincerity and determination than so far assumed. The point man to make the elusive German connection deliver real money and contracts became his trusted confidant Isidro Fabela.

Carranza continued his deeply personal, highly important interest in a connection with Germany. This was not a conspiracy but, rather, the preparation of a Mexican–German deal in anticipation of a potential German win in World War I or at least a peace treaty that could expect the resumption of German imperialism in Latin America. Any abdication of Wilhelm II and the end of German monarchy remained unimaginable in 1917.

In November 1917, Isidro Fabela was in South America. Records prove that Fabela conducted business with the Buenos Aires branch of the Banco Aleman. From there he expected to cross the Atlantic to Spain. The artist Fany Anitua wrote in 1918 that Fabela took the *Infanta Isabel de Borbon* from Buenos Aires to Spain. The ship was stopped in mid-ocean by the British destroyer *Edinburgh Castle*. Confronted by British officers, Fabela refused to show his papers, feverishly invoking diplomatic immunity.

Seconds before, he had handed his most sensitive documents to his confidential agent, Manero. Before the British could search him Manero took Fabela's secret documents and hid them in the cabin of the artist. Fany Anitua wrote that Manero "implored her for the sake of her country to save Fabela." She was asked to hide the incriminating papers of the Banco Aleman of Buenos Aires. She destroyed them before she reached Europe.[92] We do not yet know the content of the documents that Fabela carried toward Germany.

By the end of 1917, army agent Dilger himself returned to Europe, desperate to establish reliable contact with Berlin once again. His October proposal had not yet reached Berlin. He and von Eckardt were losing Carranza's favor.

From Madrid, at the end of December, von Eckardt communicated through Dilger that the German situation in Mexico was extremely shaky, and he urged Berlin to adopt Dilger's proposal before January 15, 1918. Von Eckardt insisted that Carranza had repeatedly declined U.S. economic help and was relying on the so-far-unfulfilled promises of Germany.

Mid-level secret warriors kept Carranza engaged, while Berlin leaders looked elsewhere.

By now German subversion showed results in Russia. Lenin and the Bolsheviks had brought the tsar's empire to its end. Soon, Germany, although emaciated from years of war, could focus exclusively on the western front, including the United States and the U.S.–Mexican border. Carranza was correct to consider a potentially victorious German Empire, if the United States fell away from the Allies because of domestic terrorism and subversion.

German naval agent Jahnke was the man in charge of preparing this eventuality. One German subagent stated, "Those American swine we need to do something so that will keep them so busy that they will not have time to ship troops in support to France."[93]

Recruiting Mexican individuals willing to cross the U.S. border into the United States from the midst of the Mexican Revolution was a technique known to all revolutionary factions. Already in 1916 the revolutionary Luis de la Rosa

21. Jahnke's sabotage at Black Tom Pier in New York was one of Germany's most spectacular disruptions during World War I (Library of Congress, Washington, D.C.).

had recruited individuals in Mexico City and asked them to jump into boxcars provided by Carranza's relative Señor Zambrano. They traveled to the border to attack U.S. soldiers camped at San Ignacio.[94]

Now Jahnke planned the preparation of a great multitude of disturbances inside the United States to coincide with the last, decisive military offensive in France. The mayhem in the United States was supposed to be so profound that troops could not be shipped to France and France would have to agree to a peace treaty.

One plan envisioned German agent Ricardo Schwiertz recruiting Germans and German Mexicans in Sonora and imitating Pancho Villa's attack on Columbus, New Mexico. Schwiertz, who lived a somewhat troubled existence, had already worked in 1914 for the German army in Canada trying to obtain geographic intelligence. Then he was deployed to China, where in 1915 he failed to penetrate the former German colony at Kiachou. After returning to Los Angeles he joined Max Boeder, who made explosives for Consul Franz Bopp's networks inside the United States.[95] Being a troubled individual did not keep

Schwiertz from continuing to offer his services to German military intelligence leaders on both sides of the border.

Sonoran revolutionary Plutarco Calles accepted his services in El Claro, Sonora. He kept his headquarters at Hermosillo, only 20 miles from the U.S. border. Not too far away existed a shabby training camp.[96] Calles employed and trained a motley crew of foreigners, including Germans and local Mexicans, to fight Yaqui Indian uprisings. One German agent specified the presence of eighty-seven men ready to engage in local battles in Sonora.[97] Most likely, for the right amount of money, they would be willing to temporarily cross into the United States and make a local attack. A two-day killing spree along the border, based on the experience of Villa's 1916 attack on Columbus, should be enough to create strong racist outrage on the U.S. East Coast and, most likely, another military response. Ideally a small force of Mexican revolutionaries, instructed by German trainers in Sonora, would suffice to create a regional disturbance that could misfire into a war.[98] A new source found in the German Foreign Ministry archive mentions the envisioned use of nine hundred reservists, to which might be added forty-five thousand Mexican soldiers.[99] Even though this seems farfetched, it was contemplated at the time.

22. Mexican German youth, boy scouts, and adult teachers enjoyed paramilitary presentations with planted bayonet still in 1917 (Ibero Amerikanisches Institut, Stiftung Preussischer Kulturbesitz, Bildarchiv, Berlin).

German naval intelligence head Kurt Jahnke selected Lothar Witzke as lead representative inside the United States to begin preparation. He was to cross into the United States in January 1918 to prepare the subversion for the German military high command. Under the cover name Pablo Wabierski, Witzke readied himself, first, to organize terror campaigns under the leadership of autonomous anarchists of the Industrial Workers of the World. Second, he thought it would be relatively easy to create a mutiny among African Americans soldiers serving along the U.S.–Mexico border. Once again a race war was pulled out of the German hat of secret warfare.[100] Jahnke gave the men two months to prepare the floor for later activities, coinciding with the Spring Offensive in France.[101]

Once we cut through the hyperbole of Agent Altendorf's sensationalist newspaper accounts published after World War I, the truth remains that 99 percent of African American soldiers refused to fall for any German call to rise up against the U.S. army leadership.[102] The U.S. leadership never allowed even early planning to proceed. The men were arrested. The German offensive in France still took place, but without the planned diversion in North America.[103] But help for Carranza continued.

On January 13, 1918, Berlin cabled a twofold answer to Madrid.[104] The first addressed Carranza's military needs. Berlin replied that plans for a rifle factory would be furnished. In addition, the purchase of rifles in Japan had been approved.

The second addressed all other pending issues: financial loans, postbellum shipments of raw materials, the construction of an airplane factory, and the dispatch of aviation instructors. These items had to be discussed in person on location in Berlin. Germany was ready to discuss specifics secretly in person so that their messages could not be intercepted by the British. Von Eckardt was to ask Carranza to send his personal agent with full powers of negotiation to talk about a loan and the sale of Mexican raw materials.[105]

Somebody in Berlin, with influence, was able to secure at last the first respectful tokens of money. First, the Dresdner Bank in Madrid received "earnest money" of 100,000 pesos for immediate expenses. Further details would be forthcoming extending 20,000,000 pesos.

Already in December 1917, when the smaller amount of 125,000 pesos had become available through a German merchant house, von Eckardt had talked with Carranza. The merchant agreed to deposit it in a Mexican bank like several other German Mexican businesses. Its use remains unknown. Von Eckardt was relieved. He replied that 20,000,000 pesos would be enough for the legation to cover Carranza's immediate pressing needs. Nevertheless, Germany should continue to make efforts and put together a 100,000,000-peso loan.[106]

Army agent Dilger was not happy with the answer from Berlin. On January 28, he complained bitterly, saying that the request for a Mexican agent to travel to Berlin was merely a pretext to win more time and to defer action. Instead, German–Mexican negotiations should take place in Spain. Department IIIb accepted the proposal and asked Dilger to receive a new supportive answer from Carranza.[107]

British spies never intercepted a Mexican telegram that answered this request. However, in fall 1918, von Eckardt admitted confidentially in an essay that Carranza had expressly agreed to the German request and dispatched Isidro Fabela as his sole confidential agent to explore the reality of such a far-reaching postwar German–Mexican agreement.

Also in Berlin mid-level diplomats and army members continued to do their best. In the fourth week of February 1918, loan talks between Gesandter von Haniel and a Dr. v. Schwabach agreed to a transfer of 10,000,000 pesetas from Berlin to the German Overseas Bank in Madrid. It was a government-guaranteed three-year loan at an interest rate of 6 percent. The Bleichschroeder Bank in Berlin would hand the transaction to the Banco Aleman and Transatlantico in Madrid. From there the credit would be wired to Mexico.[108]

It was a splendid move. Here was a moderate yet significant gesture from Berlin in the midst of deepest World War I. The German government continued to be interested in the life of the Carranza administration, and it was willing to back it with respectful money. Unlike the Zimmermann Telegram, it asked for nothing in return, certainly not a Mexican–U.S. war. In three years either Germany would be a noteworthy survivor of World War I or its support for Carranza would be worthless.

Suddenly there was a possibility of a U.S.–Mexican war. On January 25, the Mexican ambassador to Washington informed Carranza that the United States intended to occupy Tampico and Veracruz. Carranza's foreign minister told von Eckardt that in case of a U.S. blockade Carranza would kick off war, not negotiations. Carranza asked von Eckardt if he had been authorized to enter into an alliance with Mexico. The ambassador said yes, even though that was a lie.[109]

Also in Europe, the course of war seemed to turn in favor of Germany and its allies. On March 14, Russian Communists grudgingly agreed to the humiliating conditions of the Brest-Litovsk Peace Treaty. Seven days later, now with a relatively quiet eastern front, the German war effort refocused on France's destruction. Indeed, on March 24, Paris was bombed by German canons. It was reasonable to imagine that imperial Germany would remain a key player in any postwar scenario. Soon a German monarchic–dominated continent might confront only Great Britain, the United States, and a very weak Japan.

It made sense for Mexico. Fabela left for Europe for a second time. First, he changed ships in Havana, to leave for Spain in either March or April 1918. One source saw him conversing with Ramon de Satorres and Angela Cortijoboth, who had worked as German agents in Spain.[110] A second one saw him accompanied by Carlos Torres, the third secretary of Mexico's legation in Argentina. Also accompanying him were Octavio Barreda, Mexico's consular general to Barcelona, and Calvo Madariaga, the civilian attaché of the Spanish legation in Mexico.

In Havana Fabela stated to Andino Montes that Mexico was not afraid of the United States and would not depend on U.S. loans. Money could also come from somewhere else. The Mexican chargé d'affaires thought that possible German success in France could lead to a loan for Mexico sooner than expected, probably after the German capture of Paris. Most importantly, he asserted that Carranza would not shy away from declaring war against the United States. But preparations for any Mexican–U.S. war beyond a simple border crossing were undertaken exclusively by Carranza himself.[111]

On April 19, 1918, Fabela took a boat to Buenos Aires. The nights before he was seen with a South American diplomat but also the Spanish minister. At a dinner with twenty Mexicans Fabela invoked ethnic solidarity. In a memorandum von Eckardt detailed and emphasized that he had talked with Carranza about loans. More importantly, he admitted that Fabela had been sent to Spain in order to continue on to Berlin for negotiations.[112]

In the last week of April Fabela arrived in Spain again. He was still awaiting news about the continuation of his journey to Berlin to negotiate a Mexican–German agreement about future cooperation.

Lead Agent Dilger, who had worked so hard to convince military bureaucrats in Berlin of the importance of a loan to Carranza, wanted to work with Fabela during those weeks. But Carranza's confidant refused to have anything to do with him. Fabela continued to wait for an opportunity to start to go to Berlin and to begin negotiations with the Germans.[113]

German Ambassador to Spain Ratibor cabled to Berlin that Fabela hoped for the dispatch of a submarine.[114] Several months later the German ambassador explained,

KAMERADEN

23. President Carranza himself was the political personality in Mexico that was most pro-German even after Germany's defeat in 1919 (Library of Congress, Washington, D.C.).

If we can expect the continuation of the world war then I believe ... it is in the interest, that the current government can hold itself, in office and, if attacked, let Mexico offer long-term resistance. Currently, the necessary funds nor the war material exists. On June 17 and 18, 1917 they had been calculated as 100 million pesos.

... [I]f the Imperial government is willing and able to maintain the current government of the Mexican Republic and its resistance against United States, then the president needs to be informed now, not after the war, that money and war material are available. Three months ago Mr. Fabela has left Mexico with the power to negotiate a loan. If he has arrived, in the meantime is not known here.[115]

Curiously, at the same time, the U.S. administration became more open to helping Carranza with precious metals. For example, in April Obregón discussed the question with Frank Polk of the U.S. State Department. Polk supported selective relaxations of the U.S. precious metal embargo and approved a one-time gold import into Mexico in the amount of 4,300,000 pesos in gold, silver, and currency.[116]

Next, in June, President Wilson gave a special speech to Mexican editors, hoping that it would be received as an overture to Carranza. Also in June U.S. secretary of state Lansing authorized Ambassador Fletcher to tell Carranza that he could look forward to his facilitation of a loan by private U.S. interests.[117] Finally, in August 1918, a new plan surfaced announcing a joint U.S.–Mexican financial commission that would supervise the refinancing of Mexico's entire debt. Still, such a loan would require the settlement of "all major questions of an economic and diplomatic character."[118]

In June, the last German offensive against France failed. Fabela's effort too died a quiet death. In July Fabela was expected to head home with his mistress, Baroness Schenk, on the *Reina Victoria*. Imperial Germany was beginning to collapse as an interesting negotiation partner. If the Germans ever sent a larger amount of money to Madrid, the Mexicans never succeeded at transferring it to Mexican banks.[119]

On August 28, 1918, the German General Staff instructed Dilger to stop all campaigns that would drive Mexico into a war with the United States. If Mexico were to experience a defeat by the United States, future German interests would be severely hurt. Suddenly Dilger died unexpectedly in a Madrid hospital.

Around November 12, Berlin ordered all German agents in Madrid to stop all warfare efforts and to communicate the same to Mexico. One month after the German monarchy collapsed into revolution Carranza sent professional diplomat Ortiz to Berlin. Observers thought that the Mexican embassy in Berlin might hold information about German–Mexican negotiations, which Ortiz had come to retrieve and destroy.[120] So far no known sources can answer the question.

10   Argentina's President Hipólito Irigoyen

Personalist Hispanista Secret Diplomacy

From February 1917 on, Irigoyen's nationalism advocated that Spanish language, culture, and shared historical past should be the common denominator of future political cooperation south of the Rio Grande. And German Ambassador to Argentina Luxburg discovered how much he could encourage anti-U.S. ethnic nationalism among average Argentine people, as well as weaken Latin American presidents' remaining sympathy for a renewed Pan-Americanism after World War I. He became Venustiano Carranza's most effective ally.

Irigoyen's appeals to Hispanidad were not undertaken in a Spanish American spirit. Instead, his nationalist, cultural separatism dovetailed with a secret personal diplomacy that disregarded the interests of common Latin Americans. Both Hipólito Irigoyen and Venustiano Carranza manipulated domestic cultural norms and ethnic factions for their single-minded nationalism. Both men invoked a common Spanish, Catholic-infused culture against the Protestant, trade-oriented, and individualistic United States and Great Britain. What looked like a defense of a utopian Hispanic ethnic community was mostly the brinkmanship of two nationalistic egos that brushed aside long-cherished norms of international law and diplomacy. The call for respect for Argentinean cultural values was really a vehicle to forward Argentine supremacy in South America, as well as Mexican primacy in Central America.

An even deeper look suggests that imperial planners in Tokyo and Berlin quickly recognized the value of Argentine and Mexican nationalism. In 1917, both imperial powers were too weak to dominate Mexican or Argentine domestic politics. But they were strong enough to amplify Argentine and Mexican calls for Latin American solidarity against the United States. Even if calls for Hispanic solidarity never brought about Latin American solidarity, they would force the Allied powers to commit valuable resources to South American propaganda, away from the fight against Prussian militarism.

In the United States, President Wilson and Secretary of State Lansing registered a small silver lining in the Latin American setting when five Spanish American administrations broke diplomatic relations with Germany. On April 7, 1917, Cuba and Panama informed the German minister of the rupture of relations. Brazil followed on April 11, Bolivia broke ties on April 13, and Guatemala told German minister Lehman to leave the country on April 27, 1917. Still, breaking diplomatic relations with Germany did not mean that these governments were to follow the United States into war. Out of the five countries on April 7, 1917, only Cuba and Panama immediately took a second step and declared war.[1] And they were the most dependent on the United States.

President Irigoyen, on May 8, 1917, sent notes to the remaining undecided heads of Spanish American capitals asking them to clarify their positions vis-à-vis participation in a national Latin American Congress. By June, President Irigoyen informed Argentine Congress that some Latin American countries had accepted his invitation to participate in a Latin American conference.

Naturally, Carranza's revolutionary Mexico was one of the supporters.[2] Encouraging news also came from Spain. U.S. diplomats in Europe reported about a Spanish group that was eager to form a Spanish–American cultural union with Argentina. On June 18, the U.S. ambassador in Rome reported that Spain was "earnestly for a Pan Spanish Union" and that Argentina was supporting the idea.[3]

Carranza urged Germany to back the emerging movement. He told Ambassador von Eckardt that Argentinean, Spanish, and French administrations were secretly talking about upgrading their diplomatic representations in Mexico from legations to embassies. It would raise Mexico to the same level as the United States. True to form, Carranza suggested that the Germans should not only copy such a step but spearhead it.[4] This time, German Foreign Office members did not react.

On April 11, 1917, the Brazilian administration felt threatened enough by the alleged machinations of Germans in southern Brazil to mobilize two hundred thousand troops along the border with Argentina. In addition, it declared that it was expecting U.S. weapons and ammunition. This surprising show of determination was to discourage any Argentine desires to exploit the unstable situation in southern Brazil. President Irigoyen and the Argentine army answered by mobilizing their armed forces. Still they could deploy only twenty-five thousand men in the region.[5]

Next, the Brazilian government presented Argentina with a yet unknown ultimatum, backed by U.S. and British encouragement. That day Irigoyen had to back down. German minister Count Luxburg, observing how the president struggled to weather the crisis but also fearing that Germany would lose Argentine neutrality, asked Berlin to appoint him as mediator. Next, he suggested that they dispatch a squadron of German submarines to the region. But Berlin was not able to do so at that time. Luxburg feared that such a lukewarm German reaction was not good enough: "Our attitude toward Brazil has created the impression here that our easy-going good nature can be counted on. This is dangerous in South America where the people under thin veneer are Indians. A submarine squadron with full powers to me might probably still save the situation."[6]

By June 12, the proud Argentine president, never having received any tangible German help, ordered the military to withdraw the twenty-five thousand troops. Only a smaller number of regiments remained at the border with Brazil. This time war had been averted, and "certain calm" was registered. The real reason, however, was the lack of ammunition.[7] Now angry, Irigoyen hurried his nationalist diplomacy, severing Argentina from prior arrangements with the United States and Pan-Americanism.

In early July, Count Luxburg was not yet certain about Irigoyen's deeper political goals. His pro-British foreign minister did his utmost to keep the German from private talks with Irigoyen. Finally, the second week of July, Luxburg made headway.[8]

On July 10, Irigoyen received Luxburg, and the two men initiated a very personal Argentine–German diplomacy that bypassed career diplomats in South America and Argentina's Congress and developed secret proposals for Berlin's consideration.[9] Throughout July and August 1917, President Irigoyen, Secretary of State Pueyrredón, and Minister Luxburg brainstormed about how to neutralize the pressures of pro-British Argentineans and members of congress wanting Argentina to break diplomatic relations with Germany.

Negotiating policy without input from Argentina's legislature allowed for curious proposals. For example, in order to avoid more negative press following future sinkings of Argentine ships, Secretary of State Pueyrredón agreed that the few remaining Argentine ships, should German submarines encounter them, could be sunk without a trace. This way bad news could no longer burden the maintenance of neutrality. The foreign minister had agreed to the torpedoing of his own people!

Such determined pro-neutrality diplomacy earned rewards. The German admiralty, on August 25, agreed to make Argentina the only country in the world to be exempt from unrestricted submarine warfare.[10] Also German–Argentinean diplomatic relations were not interrupted, which meant that German agents could operate in the neutral country against Great Britain and the United States.

Luxburg was optimistic that imperial Germany would still be able to realize two policy goals under the current conditions: Germany would keep access to Argentina's market, and Germany "could reorder Southern Brazil. This could be undertaken by Germans alone or with Argentine help."[11] Here the thinking of German factions from 1900 had resurfaced, expressed by one of Wilhelm II's aristocratic ambassadors. His laconic words also insinuate that others in Berlin did not need much explanation and understood what he was referring to. If Germany were to win World War I, the reorganization of Brazil, providing home to at least one German-controlled ethnic region, remained on the table. It was still assumed that the Brazilian republic could break apart due to civil war.

Irigoyen furthered his own secret regional initiatives. First, he planned to conclude a secret mutual assistance treaty with Chile and Bolivia. These three countries would protect each other against any possible U.S. intervention.[12] In the middle of August Irigoyen added Peru to his plan. It would be a regional South American bloc against the United States.

Second, he confronted Great Britain with the customary demand to return the Malvinas/Falkland Islands to full Argentine control. But Irigoyen's third policy was a sensation. He wanted to link secret regional South American assistance pacts with imperial powers from the other side of the Atlantic and Pacific. One German source revealed that "President Yrigoyen aimed at establishing after the war a rapprochement on the one hand with Spain and Germany and, on the other hand with Japan to which a minister will be sent."[13]

While he put these policies in place, Irigoyen revived his efforts for a planned conference of the American neutrals. All these secret policies challenged the Monroe Doctrine by inviting Japan and Germany to become a major power in postwar Latin America.[14]

Count Luxburg was intrigued by the continuing possibilities for Germany. Three months after the United States had entered into the war and Spanish American countries explored taking separate paths from the United States, Luxburg cabled home that Germany could continue to prepare for postwar imperial policy executed from the terrain of at least one remaining neutral South American country.[15] He promised that even if Argentina were to abandon neutrality, Chile would remain neutral. And he thought a neutral Chile would be good enough to achieve imperial German goals.

Suddenly, in September Irigoyen's secret diplomacy was leaked to the press of the American countries. British and U.S. newspapers printed copies of the intercepted Luxburg telegrams, unmasking the many levels of Irigoyen's and Luxburg's manipulations and adventurous future plans. The shocked Argentine public and members of Argentine Congress exploded in outrage.

On September 12, Buenos Aires police remained passive while anti-German protesters attacked German/Argentine property. Lower parts of the German club were burned. Also Foreign Minister Pueyrredón betrayed the secret understandings between him, his president, and the German diplomat and denied what the leaked telegrams were saying about his complicity.

After weeks of public outcry, on October 5, members of the Argentine Congress demanded a break of diplomatic relations with Germany. The German telegrams were immediately made use of as a political weapon attacking Irigoyen and his Radical Party.[16]

President Hipólito Irigoyen allowed the opposition to rage but once again found an elegant way to duck the issue. He refused to break diplomatic relations with Germany and, instead, made Count Luxburg a scapegoat. The ambassador was declared persona non grata. Even then, Luxburg remained in the country in seclusion until further arrangements could be made. German–Argentine diplomatic relations remained alive.

By coincidence, the U.S. administration published economic warfare measures in the Law of Trading with the Enemy, thus intensifying economic sanctions against those companies that wanted to trade with Germany. A few weeks earlier the export of gold from the United States had been prohibited. Finally, the U.S. War Trade Board was created, and the U.S. government began to evaluate propaganda publications in Latin American countries.

Outside Argentina's boundaries the revelation of Luxburg's imperialistic policy goals did produce more serious consequences. The advocacy of territorial adjustments in the Río de la Plata region, perhaps indirectly through ethnic German settlers, had been shared with the Brazilian government several months before the publication of Luxburg's comments in newspapers. But in Uruguay it came as a surprise and created new damage.

On September 18, Uruguay's foreign minister suggested to U.S. secretary of state Lansing some form of political understanding that offered his country

U.S. protection. Ideally the obligation of U.S. protection would be formulated in vague terms, such as "the protection of common interest during and after the war." Also this could mean offering an exchange of material goods. Perhaps other Latin American countries might want to use a U.S.–Uruguayan understanding as a model for their own link with the United States. From Rio, the U.S. ambassador mentioned with relief that if such a treaty could be concluded, the Spanish American bloc idea in the Southern Hemisphere might collapse: "An understanding with, if we could, a nation of Spanish origin by preventing a Spanish [bloc] and removing justification for Spanish jealousy would have obvious advantage."[17]

In Washington, Secretary of State Lansing also expressed delight and signaled interest. For the time being he wanted more specific details before a commitment could be made. Still, the U.S. State Department would give careful consideration to the hint from Montevideo.[18]

Then Argentina's ethnic block-building effort fizzled further. On October 6, Peru broke its diplomatic relations with Germany, and Uruguay followed the next day. Brazil went further and avowed war against Germany on October 26, 1917, though without a formal declaration.[19]

Irigoyen did not lose his head during this turbulent month and simply stayed the course. First, he decreed October 12 a national Argentine holiday celebrating the Spanish race as Dia de la Raza. Second, he issued a new public invitation for a Spanish American conference of neutral powers. On October 28, 1917, Irigoyen invited Colombia, Guatemala, Honduras, El Salvador, Nicaragua, Costa Rica, Panama, Haiti, and Santo Domingo to send delegates to Buenos Aires in early 1918.

The conference was to attack the recently enacted U.S. economic warfare measures. Irigoyen continued to affirm a distinct, independent Latin American foreign policy. He portrayed himself in a dramatic appeal as a cultural separatist and as protector of the proper ethnic identity of Latin American republics.

Venustiano Carranza, from Mexico, did what he could to back Irigoyen. Carranza approached Ambassador von Eckardt, asking him to improve German propaganda in Colombia. Stronger, more systematic propaganda in this Andean country could create enough pro-German popular feeling to prevent a rupture of diplomatic relations. He suggested that von Eckardt dispatch a German propaganda administrator from Mexico to Colombia to build a pro-German organization there.[20] Quietly, Colombia emerged as a new focal point for manipulations by Argentina, Mexico, and Germany.

Carranza was the only Spanish American leader who committed himself to dispatch a delegation to Irigoyen's Congress of Neutrals. In December 1917, a delegation chaired by Luis Cabrera and Ernesto Hidalgo left for Buenos Aires.[21]

It is doubtful that Carranza knew that Irigoyen's administration, once again, was changing course. Even though the president's policy insisted on the strongest possible political boundaries against the United States, his economic experts were negotiating with Great Britain and France a treaty to purchase Argentinean wheat, oats, and linseed at guaranteed prices. While the president talked tough against the Allied powers, the economic arm of his administration had no qualms selling the Allied camp 2,500,000 tons of grain. The negotiations concluded with a treaty on January 14, 1918. More importantly, the treaty provided Great Britain and France with a credit of 200,000,000 gold pesos.[22] On January 22, the treaty became Argentine law.

Suddenly the Congress of Neutrals in Argentina had to be "postponed." Irigoyen could only receive the Mexican delegation in the Casa Rosada. More embarrassing was that Carranza's diplomats were the only ones who had traveled to South America. The Argentine president honored the Mexican nationalists a second time at a farewell meeting in the first week of February 1918.[23]

In the United States, President Wilson had articulated his Fourteen Points at a session of Congress. On February 11, he insisted that Prussian autocracy was making a long-lasting peace impossible. Now he joined British arguments and insisted that Germany should become a democracy. The German emperor and his aristocrats had to lose their power. On February 26, 1918, the United States and the British government rejected the latest German peace proposal. Germans, too, rejected Allied offers. In March, imperial Germany mounted its next massive offensive drive on the western front. Wilhelm II declared that this offensive would decide the war in favor of Germany.

Mexican delegates to the conference of neutrals never gave up. The delegates visited South American countries where they could expect at least a friendly disposition toward Hispanismo and a future renewed push for a Hispanic bloc. Mexican general Montes was to cross the Andes to lobby in Chile. Ernesto Hidalgo was to target factions in Brazil. Argentine Manuel Ugarte joined their effort and propagandized in Ecuador.[24] On April 16, it was reported that the Mexican government approved visits by Luis Cabrera to South American countries in order to convince policy makers to enter into alliances only with countries of Spanish colonial past.

III

In Expectation of Failure
of the League of Nations
(1919–22)

11

Venustiano Carranza and Japanese Spies Move Next to Ethnic Businessmen and Emigrants in Latin America (1919–22)

J apanese immigrants living in the Americas did not realize how complex Japan's outreach into Latin America had become. While diplomats met in Versailles to ponder the creation of a new world political order, ethnic laborers and settlers in California, Mexico, Peru, and Brazil were unaware that Japanese intelligence agents were establishing themselves in the midst of immigrant communities.

A basic intelligence network was established in preparation of a possible U.S.–Japanese military clash if imperial war were to resume. Now Japan's ethnic communities in the Americas also were assigned a military function that they had not performed before. Policy makers in Tokyo reclassified immigrant communities as a civilian cover. This was not a meticulously planned, great conspiracy, but it was, nevertheless, the exploitation of select individuals and their property for strategic concerns.

Four years of world war had radically changed the global political context of Japanese imperialism. The cataclysm had destroyed the empires of Germany, Russia, and the Ottomans. Politically, Great Britain and France had survived the war intact, but its financial cost left these empires perilously near exhaustion. European weakness had helped the United States to emerge as an unwelcome great power but also as a needed arsenal for the Allied powers. New York was now the world's most important financial city.

But military planners simply prepared for renewed large-scale war. Even though diplomats negotiated terms of peace in Versailles, warfare raged on in Poland, Russia, and the Caucasus. Also fires of revolution burned inside Germany, Austria, and Hungary but also Italy, Argentina, Mexico, and China.

Politicians at Versailles promised a new international order that was utterly untested. The diplomats there had been used to navigating a world of monarchies and a Eurocentric policy of great cabinets. As they tried to rearrange the broken pieces of monarchies, empires, and ethnic groups into a new global system, the world's future remained unpredictable. Hopefully, leaders would buy into Wilson's idealist new world vision.

If his vision were to fail, in a short time, global warfare would resume. From the very beginning, the United States would again play a major role. In this context, Latin America, bordering on the United States, would be even more important than between 1914 and 1918. From the vantage point of 1919, the years ahead would be marked not just by the League of Nations but also by preparations for a war involving the United States in anticipation of the Versailles Treaty's collapse.

In Tokyo relations with countries south of the Rio Grande obviously assumed an unprecedented strategic importance. For that reason Japan pursued two policies. One was a civilian, public one at Versailles. The second one unfolded outside the public eye, close to military affairs in South America.

Latin American merchants in Argentina, Bolivia, Peru, Chile, and Mexico experienced the civilian side of Japan's strategic expansion into Latin America. Already in the summer of 1918, the opening of the Yokohama Specie Bank in Buenos Aires had announced a new era for Japanese trade on this side of the Pacific. A direct Japanese–Argentine banking connection in South America allowed traders, for the first time, to settle trade balances in yen, no longer just British pounds, U.S. dollars, French francs, or German reichsmarks. Also, the bank could directly administer Japanese investment funds into select regional markets.

Just as important was that this channel offered unprecedented privacy for transactions between Tokyo and Buenos Aires. After 1919, U.S., British, French, and German bankers could no longer easily observe the flow of yen into South America. The Yokohama Specie Bank in Buenos Aires symbolized that Japanese companies and industrial trusts were ready to stay and to expand business in South America. Few realized that this secure banking channel could also forward payments to intelligence agents who were beginning to arrive regularly from Japan.

Increasingly Japanese trade penetration began with the dispatch of private experts to study opportunities in regional markets. Their research focused on raw material exports. Japanese engineers had already investigated Chilean mines. After November 1918, Bolivia's mining sector, in particular tin mines, received visitors.

In spite of this interest in precious metals, the export of agricultural products to Japan dominated trade with Latin America. Bolivia offered itself as a promising location for rubber plantations. Peru was inviting to cotton growers. Eventually, explorations resulted in a land sale. Dr. Augusto Durand sold 800,000 acres near Huanaco, Peru, close to the Amazon watershed, to a Japanese syndicate. Tokyo's investors planned to grow sugarcane, coffee, and cocoa. An option for a later purchase of 300,000 acres promised additional land to grow more exports.[1]

Parallel to traders, Japanese mid- and small-size manufacturers recognized Latin America as a potential market for their low-tech manufactured goods. As soon as fighting in Europe stopped, the Tokyo Chamber of Commerce dispatched a trade delegation to the United States, which then extended its trip to Central and South American markets.[2] Soon thereafter, cheap Japanese toiletries and toys arrived and became a more normal sight on market displays. This initial distribution of Japanese goods remained restricted to areas where established Japanese immigrants could reinforce demand for goods from home.[3]

New Japanese banks and trade connections required an improved network of consulates to handle customs. Thus diplomats joined private businessmen. Together they codified this budding Latin American–Japanese trade expansion, in treaties of friendship, amity, and commerce. Before World War I, the Bolivian government in La Paz had administered commerce with Asia through its embassy in London. A reorientation came on February 4, 1918, when the Bolivian government appointed diplomat Victor Munoz Reyes as Extraordinary Representative to Japan. Reyes was ordered to manage consular relations directly from Tokyo and open offices in Osaka, Kobe, and Tokyo. A second Bolivian officer focused on trade with China and India. Now, five years after the 1913 negotiation of a Bolivian–Japanese treaty of commerce and amity, both countries were finally breathing life into the document.[4] Ecuador entered into a similar treaty with Japan on August 26, 1918. Paraguay followed suit on November 17, 1919.[5]

Tokyo also focused on the establishment of reliable and predictable transpacific transportation. Japanese steamers began to regularly service the Pacific coast of Latin America, stopping at Acapulco, Mexico, and Valparaiso, Chile.[6] One Japanese mining investor even held out the possibility of financing and constructing a railroad in the near future. It was the first documented offer of Japanese investment in an Andean railroad venture. This changing context served as a frame for the revival of state-sponsored emigration to South America.

Already in August 1918, the Peruvian manager of the Morioka Emigration Company, Tokyo, had stated publicly that Toyo Kisha Kaisha was considering the establishment of Japanese colonies in northern, central, and southern Peru. Once the Bolivian consul opened an office in Japan, talks about a Japanese–Bolivian treaty of immigration were initiated. Eventually negotiations also included land purchases. On December 14, 1919, the *New York Times* reported the purchase of a stretch of land 90 miles long and 20 miles broad in the vicinity of Tarijo, Bolivia. Thus, a third South American region, after Brazil's coastal region and Peru's Loreto province, opened up as a South American destination for Japanese emigrants.[7] Even Argentina began to be mentioned as a country where Japanese ethnic communities could thrive. In the end, Brazil remained the South American country with the greatest promise. The KKKK company, now owning a monopoly on Japanese immigration, advertised three thousand lots for future immigrants in Brazil.

The Japanese government also intensified its involvement with the flow of laborers. No longer did it leave the administration of emigration to private company management. Bureaucrats in the Japanese Ministry of Interior had become more conscious that emigration was a complex social undertaking and provided funds to design improved orientation programs for prospective emigrants.[8] Planners selected Brazil as an area to test prototype colonies. Emigration was changing from an exportation of temporary laborers to the permanent settlement of colonists in Latin America.

Now, state subsidies financed basic infrastructure and services on sites. Settlers in Brazil were offered modest government loans. This was critical start-up money. Finally, Japan's consular service appointed a vice-consul who was charged with "guiding" the development of these communities.[9] Just as Germans, Italians, and Spaniards had involved their consulates in immigration affairs before World War I, now Japanese consulates systematically maintained ties with emigrants in Latin America. Still, influence did not yet mean control.

Surprisingly, these changes did not translate into quick success. Emigration to South America remained undersubscribed. Even though Brazil was ready to welcome twenty thousand contract laborers, only seven hundred immigrants came in 1921.

In Chile, domestic politics even turned hostile. After 1917, the Russian Revolution emboldened Chilean nativists to speak out against any future Japanese immigration. Over the next years fewer than two hundred immigrants dared to travel to Chile.[10]

24. Now Japanese immigrants were welcomed next to Europeans in Brazil's Immigration Reception Halls (Ibero Amerikanisches Institut, Stiftung Preussischer Kulturbesitz, Bildarchiv, Berlin).

In Argentina, the presence of Japanese immigrants remained limited to cities. Even though the Argentine ambassador to Tokyo championed far-reaching colonial Japanese settlement plans, Japanese life in Argentina blossomed only in Buenos Aires and the smaller cities of Córdoba, Tucumán, Salta, Chaco, and Corrientes. Individual poverty was preventing new arrivals from purchasing land. Independently, parents financed schools, at the least trying to re-create some semblances of a Japanese culture in Argentina.

In Buenos Aires, in October 1917, eighty people gathered at the Hotel Phoenix and founded a Japanese Resident Association (Zai-a-Nihon jukai). Right away racial and ethnic divisions of Japan reproduced themselves. Okinawans founded their own organization, Okinama Kenyin Kai. And regional Japanese prefectures opened small associations in Buenos Aires so that emigrants could congregate according to their regional origin.[11]

Most emigrants could not afford to send for a Japanese wife. Quietly they took Argentine wives. Mixed marriages became more common, challenging strong racial taboos. Initial transplants relocated from Peru to Brazil.[12] Japanese commoners, with the exception of a few individuals, had no idea that their government not only was improving the administration of emigration but worked at establishing the first basic intelligence and arms sale apparatus in South America. Part of this effort consisted of connecting with Latin America's armies and rebels, seeking weapons for a possible war. Since Japan and the United States were now the major powers of the Pacific realm, Japanese planners had to take U.S. neighbors into account, just as U.S. planners were pondering the future of Siberia, Mongolia, and China. As long as there was no agreement to rule out a Japanese–U.S. war, military planners prepared for the possibility of an armed clash. The expansion of Japanese–Latin American military relations quietly created a politically loaded context for the development of ethnic communities.

A new, discretely growing sector was arms sales to Latin American militaries. Latin Americans, still not owning independent armament industries of their own, now considered purchase of Japanese weapons as often as they looked at European arms offers. In Mexico Japanese arms merchants supplying factions had become a routine since 1916. After the November 1918 armistice, deliveries only intensified. On December 26, 1919, a Mr. Maxwell, traveling on the *Seiyo Maru*, a ship owned by the Toyo Kisen Kaisha, arrived in Salina Cruz, Mexico. He observed the unloading of sixty-four cases, marked with New Jersey. Supposedly these boxes contained machine parts. Suddenly, one crate slipped out of the crane's hold, hit the dock, and broke open. Out poured rifles, not machine parts.

In Chile, in November 1919, the Japanese steamer *Ainan Mara* caught fire. The police discovered a boat loaded with charred weapons worth 3,000,000 francs. The Chilean army had not ordered them. An educated guess was that, once again, Mexican purchasers were smuggling arms through Valparaiso to Mexico.[13]

Then, South American militaries followed the path that Mexican revolutionaries had beaten to Tokyo's warehouses full of surplus weapons. In 1919, Chile felt threatened by the policies of the newly installed Peruvian president Leguía. In response, Chile mobilized fifteen thousand men, and Peru answered with a mobilization of twelve thousand. Suddenly, Chileans wanted to buy machine guns from Japan plus outdated Hotchkiss cannons and other older material. Chile placed a long-term order totaling 450 tons of Japanese munitions during this crisis. Straight away, six hundred machine guns were to be shipped to Chile on a Japanese ship. At the same time Peruvian officers rushed to Tokyo trying to obtain their own material in preparation of an increasingly possible Peruvian–Chilean war.[14]

Finally, Brazilians, too, ordered machine guns from the Tokyo Gas Kogyo Kaisha company.[15] After 1919, Japanese arms sales regularly reached both the west and east coasts of South America. How much was the Japanese government involved as the Japanese companies Asano, Mitsui, and Okuro eagerly expanded arms deliveries to the entire Western Hemisphere? Was Tokyo indirectly supporting war and rebels in Latin America? Was supporting war and rebels a hidden policy against the Monroe Doctrine?

In April 1920, the Asano, Mitsui, and Okuro companies solved the issue for Tokyo's bureaucrats. Unlike German, French, and British merchants competing fiercely against each other, the Japanese ended their commercial rivalries. The companies combined their efforts and market shares by founding one new joint venture called Tai Bei Gumi. The Japanese government granted it the monopoly for arms exports. Thus an additional commercial layer had been put between the imperial government and revolutionary factions in South America.[16] It was harder than ever to prove that the Japanese government was behind steering arms supplies into Latin American areas of conflict. It should not surprise that Japanese weapon exports were followed by increased military contacts.

Latin American military planners not only purchased weapons but also studied Japanese military tactics and strategy. Once again following the Mexican example, Chilean and Peruvian soldiers and sailors explored what Tokyo's strategists had to offer. In 1918, the Chilean ship *Baquedo* practiced in the Pacific Ocean and included a visit in Japan.[17] The Chilean chief of staff, General Pinto Concha, traveled to Japan on military business after making an initial courtesy stop in the United States. In early 1919, a Peruvian military mission made the same trip to Tokyo. Peruvian colonel E. F. Ballesteros headed a team of four lieutenant colonels to study the Japanese military on location.[18] The Japanese army brass knew how to create good feelings among soldiers and awarded the Peruvians high decorations.

Continuing pre–World War I traditions, the Japanese navy resumed its own trips across the Pacific, including South America. In 1920, the navy ships *Iwate* and *Asama* stopped in Callao while on a Pacific training mission.[19]

Finally, occasional military and navy contacts were made permanent by stationing Japanese military attachés in Chile, Peru, and Mexico. Soon thereafter these Latin American governments stationed their own military representatives in Tokyo. Japanese military relations had expanded beyond Mexico to the rest of Latin America.

Newly discovered intercepts of Mexican diplomatic cables prove a top secret dimension to Japanese outreach across the Pacific. They were efforts to establish more sophisticated options for anti-U.S. action, if that became necessary.

Ecuadorian islands in the South American Pacific had been part of imperialistic schemes before World War I. Already then, Tokyo had expressed interest in the Galapagos Islands, only to be discouraged by U.S. diplomatic intervention. Now, in 1920, as Chile sought weapons to deter a Peruvian attack, rumors reemerged that arms dealers close to the Japanese navy were trying to link arms deliveries with a lease of Chile's Easter Islands. A second interpretation suggests that Japan used the islands merely as a secluded harbor to transfer weapons from Japanese to Chilean ships. What happened in detail remains to be discovered in Chilean military archives. German sources confirm that, indeed, Japanese access to the Easter Islands had been part of Chilean–Japanese discussions in connection with arms purchases.

The onset of discrete, tailored Japanese diplomacy toward Argentina can be traced to the arrival of new ambassador Takashi Nakamura in December 1918. One telegram revealed that Tokyo offered Argentina backing in its claim for the Falkland Islands against Great Britain. This Japanese stance interjected itself in an Argentine territorial dispute against Japan's alliance partner.

More shocking developments unfolded as part of Japanese–Mexican friendship. Rumors about a secret Mexican–Japanese treaty had circulated already before the revolution. They became more detailed when Agent von der Goltz alleged that Jose Limantour, President Díaz's secretary of finance, had carried a draft Mexican–Japanese treaty to Paris before 1914. There he claimed to have stolen it and forwarded it to the U.S. Wilson administration.

In 1919, the rumor of a Mexican–Japanese treaty resurfaced when Arizona senator Albert B. Fall claimed to have seen a letter stating "that a high official of Mexico would communicate to another high official that the treaty with Japan is coming along" and that the writer was convinced that it would be an advantage to Mexico's national integrity.[20] Not surprisingly, an immediate Japanese denial was published in December 1918 in an *Osaka Mainichi* newspaper article.[21] Repeatedly, it looked as if rumors of a Japanese–Mexican treaty were, indeed, never more than racist anti-Japanese propaganda by the Arizona senator. Newly found intercepts, however, offer clarification of the issue.

Three Mexican diplomatic cables, intercepted by U.S. signal intelligence in Washington, D.C., proved that there was fire in the midst of this cloud of smoke. In October 1919, as the Carranza administration defended itself against U.S. interventionists and their aggressive machinations, Mexican undersecretary of state Medina wrote to his diplomat Eliseo Arredondo: "Japan and Spain are Mexico's only friends."[22] Telegrams from November 3 and November 5, 1919, prove that the Carranza administration was again trying to secure Japanese support against the United States. Undersecretary Medina cabled, "Japanese sympathy is counted on and an attempt is being made to obtain Japanese assistance."[23] Next, Medina provides a critical admission. In another telegram he admits: "Aguilar will advise you concerning the present status of the Treaty with Japan."[24] This proves that, indeed, Japanese–Mexican treaty negotiations were taking place on an informal and verbal level, initiated by the Carranza administration. It was a Mexican initiative, not a Japanese one.

Robert Guzmán, biographer of Mexican interim president de la Huerta, reports that thereafter, Japanese–Mexican treaty talk continued. According to Guzmán, after Carranza's death, the tables turned, and Japan became the driving force in the exchanges. In the second half of 1920, an unnamed secretary of the Japanese embassy in Mexico City visited Mexican interim president de la Huerta. He came to discuss the advantages of Japan and Mexico "moving closer together." The Japanese secretary suggested a formal agreement that would elevate the Japanese–Mexican relationship to the level of a secret alliance.[25] First, de la Huerta rejected the Japanese offer; however, he asked the secretary to continue his overtures after the inauguration of President-Elect Álvaro Obregón. If Guzmán is to be believed, Japanese diplomats did offer revolutionary Mexico an alliance that was neither just commercial nor diplomatic in nature. In 1921, it did include military cooperation. A Japanese diplomat visited newly installed president Obregón and made the following offer:

This time the proposal was neither vague nor veiled. In clear form, [he proposed] in the name of his government an offensive and defensive alliance between Japan and Mexico. It specified the point where to disembark military supplies and armed forces on our latitude in the Pacific Ocean, selected before hand, in case the situation presented itself; [he explained] the aid his country would offer us and, in his opinion, the advantages the suggested alliance meant for Mexico.[26]

What happened thereafter, at the top Mexican governmental level, remains obscure. Nevertheless, Japanese diplomats displayed a particular appreciation for Obregón at the end of his presidential term. Tokyo's diplomat took it upon himself to travel all the way from Mexico City to distant Sonora to award the Mexican leader an unspecified high Japanese honor. It is likely that he received it for continuing Japanese–Mexican cooperation. It remains open whether either side ever put the terms of cooperation into writing.[27] Perhaps, Mexico's Foreign Ministry archive has one *caja fuerte* that has not been made available to researchers. Or the agreement was so sensitive that it remained verbal and limited to exclusive discussion on the presidential level. What can be proved in detail is that talks about a Mexican–Japanese treaty that also addressed defense concerns had taken place. Their target was the United States and her national security interests in South America.

In summer 1918, Germany, Japan, Mexico, and Argentina all operated separate networks of agents in South America. In Argentina, Kinta Arai had taken over the job of interpreter at the Buenos Aires legation at Avenida de Mayo No. 560. He was the "low-level" Japanese secretary who in 1917, in Mexico, had discussed with Mexican foreign minister Aguilar the possibility of a German–Japanese–Mexican alliance during the Zimmerman Telegram episode. When Japan's official consul in Argentina left town, Kinta Arai also became acting consul. By October 1918, sources identify him as the leader of Japanese agents in the Río de la Plata region.[28]

One month after World War I, in December 1918, the Tokyo government dispatched Takashi Nakamura to Buenos Aires. Ambassador Nakamura arrived with new instructions.[29] Backed by the Yokohama Specie Bank, and with access to a functioning system of regional Japanese intelligence, a distinct Japanese policy toward Argentina and Chile could be tried.

From Chile, a German intelligence agent reported that the Japanese Foreign Ministry had instructed Nakamura to back an alleged Argentine–Chilean treaty. Officially no such treaty existed. But, at that time, Lima's foremost newspaper published a telegram repeating the allegation. Once again the Argentine legation in Lima publicly denied this newspaper claim. Then the president of Argentina's Senate replied with an extensive editorial in Argentina's *El Comercio*, offering further confirmation that, indeed, a special Argentine–Chilean understanding existed. A third confirmation came from a Mexican diplomat in Lima who insisted that an understanding existed and cabled Mexico City asking how to relate to this Chilean–Argentine entente.[30]

Short of a formal, written treaty, it might have been a verbal agreement between President Irigoyen and the Chilean president to maintain a distinctly South American political position that differed from Pan-American, U.S. policy wishes. Since the political future of the world seemed wide open and South American countries were not core members of the emerging League of Nations, it made sense to assert a separate, distinct South American stance in at least regional affairs. Special Chilean Ambassador Gonzalo Bulnes invited President Irigoyen to join Chile and Mexico to oppose any future European and

North American intervention in South American matters. Diplomats in Japan's Foreign Ministry instructed Nakamura to "adhere to" such a trend of South American differentiation.[31]

Secret Japanese policy also meant meeting with those factions inside the Argentine government interested in promoting anti-American projects. Even though publicly President Irigoyen moved strongly into the Allied camp, in 1919 there were individuals in his government who remained devoted to an anti-American bloc and a policy operating independently of the League of Nations.

For a second we need to interrupt the story. We need to cross the Atlantic from Latin America to Europe and follow how developments in the world's arms sector brought Japanese and German military planners closer. It is critical to realize that Japanese outreach in Latin America was part of a global effort. Across the world its army and navy feverishly worked to make it possible to engage in a Japanese–U.S. war.

The previous pages showed that the Japanese government had no interest in expanding its influence into ethnic Japanese communities by introducing a new political ideology. Japanese ethnic communities around the Pacific, from a political-cultural point of view, continued to live just as they had lived before World War I. In reality, however, such an interpretation is superficial.

Japanese mid-level bureaucrats were trying to find ways to make war with the United States possible. For that reason, first, Japanese navy representatives established unprecedented technological exchanges with the surviving German military industry even in the Weimar Republic.

Second, in Latin America, Tokyo expanded a permanent intelligence service into a blend of commercial infrastructure, select ethnic individuals, and military intelligence work against the United States. A quasi-pre-mobilization state was created during which it became harder to differentiate who was a peaceful civilian Japanese person, who was an ambitious commercial trader, and who was involved in military intelligence gathering. In Tokyo military planners desperately tried to make a war with the United States possible in the near future. Thus they made ethnic Japanese individuals and companies abroad part of military activity and strategy whether they liked it or not. Of course, Tokyo bureaucrats did not tell Japanese Americans that preparations for war were beginning to exploit community life and confusion about loyalty for espionage purposes.

The European component of this global approach had begun in 1919. The Japanese navy founded a new Kantoku branch in France. Headed by Utsunomiya Kanae, this fourth Kantoku branch abroad was to purchase ships, military goods, and war material. Officially diplomat Kanae worked as a member of the Japanese delegation to Versailles. Unofficially he and his French office gathered advanced European technical military information and coordinated investigations with the lead office in London.[32]

Already in March 1919, the Japanese navy had been given German ships as loot, promising direct access to the latest technology and hardware developed at the end of World War I. Navy engineers near the docks of Yokosuka, Kure, and Sasebo eagerly awaited seven submarines, five torpedo boats, and seventy-one airplanes of various types.[33] However, their hopes were not matched by reality. Germans had ripped out most of the advanced technology or made it useless. Still, the remaining technology was examined, taken apart, and studied in detail.[34] Perhaps even the first attempts at reverse engineering began.

The motivation behind this Japanese behavior was easy to understand. First, so far Japan had gained access to advanced technology mostly through the British navy. Now, as a victor of world war Japan could expand access to every German weapon technology. But Japan also faced uncertainty. What political

25. Parliamentarian delegation representing Japan at the International Labor Conference. Japanese policy became world policy after 1919, contested between sincere parliamentarians and militarists (Library of Congress, Washington, D.C.).

naval constellation would exist in 1921 after the expiration of British–Japanese alliance? In 1919, it made sense to collect submarines, airplanes, zeppelins, gas bombs, and other warfare technology in preparation for the likely end of the Japanese–British alliance. In addition, Japanese planners wanted technology for a potential war with the United States in the Pacific.

In public Japanese policy remained loyal to prewar political constellations. Debuchi Katsuiju, the Japanese chargé d'affaires in Berlin, urged Tokyo to keep policy in line with that of Great Britain.[35] But underneath members of Japan's navy nevertheless increased their contacts with key members of the defeated German navy.

Even more secret was the deepening Japanese intelligence cooperation with the recently created Polish state against Russia. On June 3, 1920, Captain Yonai Mitsumasa arrived in Germany and officially assumed his station in Berlin. From there it was not far to travel to Poland. The British historian J. W. M. Chapman has suggested that information from the Polish General Staff improved the Japanese military intelligence system on the other side of Eurasia against the Soviets.[36]

Then there was Vice Admiral Takeshita Isamy. Officially he worked as naval delegate at the League of Nations. He was joined by an army delegation, chaired by Inagaki Saburo. Experienced foreign diplomats quickly realized that Japan's delegations at the league were gathering intelligence more than they participated in diplomacy.[37] Already in one case this again included subversion. Japan was "not against supported interventionist policies in the Ukraine and the Caucasus, depending on how matters progressed."[38] Japan's secret war against Russia's southern flank was continuing.

There is need for cautious differentiation. Japan approaching the Germans did not yet mean Japanese–German intelligence cooperation in Europe. It meant the rise of a deep and complex technological exchange. According to Germany's former naval attaché to London, Widenmann, Japanese admiral Kato became the most important supporter of closer cooperation with Germany. Widenmann and Kato had both served as attachés in London during World War I. Widenmann wrote that in January 1919, Kato visited him in Berlin, expressing a particular interest in replacement fuels. And Kato, at that time, was supposed to have visited Admiral Tirpitz in full uniform.

In Japan, in February 1919, Naval Minister Kato discussed with a subcommittee of the Japanese diet whether Japan had the means to engage in a naval race with the United States. His answer was sobering: "Even if we tried to, it is a foregone conclusion that we are simply not up to it. . . . Whether or not the United States, with its unlimited wealth and resources, would continue its naval expansion, my policy is to build up an adequate defensive force within the limits of Japan's national power."[39] In early 1920, Kato gathered his vice minister and the heads of the Naval Affairs Bureau and the naval construction headquarters to interpret the nation's budget situation and its consequences for naval strategy. Once again he had to admit that "the national wealth has simply not increased in proportion to naval expenditure." Kato declared himself "at wits end."[40]

Experts in Tokyo's Finance Ministry backed his assessment. In contrast to the projected rising demands of Japan's ambitious naval strategy, finances were declining. The Naval Affairs Bureau estimated that in order to compete with U.S. naval strategy, that is, a planned 8–8 fleet, one-third of the imperial government budget would have to be devoted to naval affairs. In front of fifty naval officers Kato suggested that any solution depended entirely on the imperial navy and its war plans. Against the desire of most leading Japanese individuals, on March 14, 1920, Kato insisted that the great powers should find a suitable formula and impose naval limitations.[41] His insistence challenged Japan's core naval strategy as it had existed since 1907. Still, Tokyo's policy elite had to tolerate a postponement of war with the United States.

Underneath the public diplomatic stage, on the military bureaucratic midlevel, arms modernization short of war was accelerated. This was the reason why naval and military experts had traveled to Germany to acquire key World War I technology.

Several avenues of Japanese technology acquisition in Europe can be identified. First, there were official delegations staffed with members of the armed forces. For example, in early 1919, a naval inspection team, lead by Admiral Utusnamiy, organized the transfer of seven submarines.[42] Next, in summer of 1919, an army mission under General WatanYotaro arrived. Then there were Captain to the Sea Yokoi and Utsunomiya Kanae, two members of a group that cooperated with the diplomat Togo Shigenori. And finally, a navy group focused on replacement fuels. It consulted with the scientist Prof. Ando Kazuo from Kyushu University.[43]

Second, company representatives staffed the second-most prominent group of Japanese visitors. Already in 1919, the Furukawa group had approached Siemens and renewed its pre–World War I contact. They were interested in hiring private engineers who could work in electric machine construction, coal mining, and steel tube plant operation. After their eight-month stay in Germany, negotiations with Siemens concluded with the signing of a new cooperation agreement and the founding of a company called Fuji Denki.

In Japan, Gustav Amann worked as Siemens's leading representative. In 1920, he wrote to German minister Voretsch in Oslo assuring him that insiders were expecting a Japanese–American war on Chinese territory in the near future. Amann suggested that Siemens should sell technology to both sides. The contract included a renegotiation clause in case a war broke out.

The third Japanese strategy to obtain German war material was to purchase hardware through German middlemen. For example, in 1920, a Mr. Hack returned to Germany from World War I internment in Japan. His brother, Wilhelm Hack, had worked in the German fleet department of the navy commando office. More importantly, Hack's nephew was married to the niece of Wilhelm Canaris, Germany's future head of naval and military intelligence. For one year, Hack accompanied a group of Japanese industrialists exploring Germany.[44]

Another German to help the Japanese was Adolf Schinzinger, who before the war had worked as Krupp's representative in Japan. Now, the Deutsche Bank issued him a letter of recommendation, which opened doors to companies in Berlin eager to sell military goods to the Far East.[45] Right away the Japanese Foreign Ministry appointed Schinzinger Japanese consul in Berlin.

Finally, Hugo Stinnes Sr. also helped Japan. Stinnes was connected with the Mitsubishi company. In September 1920, he agreed to deliver additional steel to the Kawasaki naval yard. Stinnes's steel was to build twelve trade ships of 9,000 gross registered tons. The ships would sail under the Japanese flag but secretly remain Stinnes's property. One month later steel deliveries began that would add up to about 18,000,000 tons of steel during the next six years. The German historian Sander-Nagashima argues that these deliveries played an important role in Japan's ability to realize the construction of the Japanese fleet program. These were the ships that one day confronted the U.S. navy.[46]

Fourth, there was former naval attaché Wolfram von Knorr, now working as the founder of the Auslands GmbH in Berlin. He maintained contacts with the German naval leadership through a retired officer named Johann Bernhard Mann. Mann relayed his secret communications to the German commander in chief of navy. Only a handful of people realized that von Knorr, in a still unknown form, advised Japan during the upcoming 1921 Washington Naval Conference.[47]

The fifth Japanese practice was to send Japanese experts undercover to Germany. When military technology could not be bought openly it was acquired through disguised agents. For example, the owner of Nippon Kogahu was interested in military optics. Once he arrived in Europe he pretended to be Spanish and toured the Carl Zeiss optical company, Jena. Afterward, he hired eleven former company employees and sent them to Tokyo. Upon closer inspection they revealed themselves as specialists in the manufacture of periscopes and distance-measurement instruments. In this way the Japanese navy bought enough optical glasses to satisfy production for the next four years.[48]

A second case was Matsukata Kojiro. He was the president of Kawasaki Dock in Kobe. Officially, he relocated to Paris to focus on purchases for his collection of European paintings. In reality, he focused on obtaining blueprints of ships. A former German engineer and prisoner of war who had come to like Japan helped him. His top secret prints were smuggled to Switzerland in the diplomatic pouch of the Japanese embassy. This art collector was an industrial spy.[49]

In 1920 the Swiss company Fischer and Co., in Schaffhausen, manufactured submarine engine parts. Initially it delivered them to Germany to MAN, Deutz, and Daimler. But the German companies turned around and offered them, in violation of the Versailles Treaty, to Japan for submarine construction. In Bern, the Japanese legation explored other submarine equipment purchases from the Sulzer family in Winterthur.[50]

At least six individuals helped with the export of military parts from Germany to Japan. Most likely more people contributed to the clearing of goods.[51] In 1921 alone, twenty-three airplanes were shipped. In addition, 700 tons of diesel engines, 2,700 tons of steel plates, gunpowder, and machine guns arrived. Once in Japan they were redistributed to sites at Kure and Yokosuka.

Such increasing flow of German military technology to Japan did not go unnoticed by other Allied powers. Already in 1919, Great Britain protested. Then in November 1919, the U.S. attaché heard about secret deliveries of ammunition, one hangar for a zeppelin, and the potential employment of fifteen hundred German officers. Even though Allied powers complained, Japanese purchasers moved ahead through camouflaging and conspiratorial methods. A reduction of the flow of military goods was never considered.

Finally, the sixth and most fascinating way to obtain critical theoretical military knowledge was by financing German research in strategic military sectors. In 1920, Japanese yen funding, which, unlike the reichsmark, maintained a stable international exchange rate value, was offered to win German appreciation and goodwill in exchange for access to new breakthrough technology. German academies were suffering from national revolutionary disturbances and had little money to fund cutting-edge research in chemistry and physics.

Baron Hajime Hoshi offered to close the funding gap. He became the first Japanese aristocrat to donate research funds to Germany. Leading German chemists were most grateful, since the yen donations seemed to come without any strings attached, only realizing the submitted research proposals. Baron Hoshi's largesse provided scholarship gifts of 10,000 yen for general scientific research. A second donation gave 90,000 yen for development in the German chemical industry. For three years it provided critical money in monthly installments.[52]

Hoshi and other leading aristocrats knew that, in the words of German Nobel Prize in Physics winner Prof. Dr. Fritz Haber, "Japanese developments in the field of applied chemistry would be built on German theoretical achievements in the same field." The Hoshi Foundation kept alive a German capacity to advance research in theoretical chemistry and atom physics![53] Both fields promised most profound commercial and military applications.

How much German technology was appreciated in Tokyo becomes visible when we consider Japanese evaluations of the usefulness of German goods. Access to German know-how allowed Japan to make critical improvements to its military preparedness. A report delivered by Minister Kato on June 29, 1920, in front of the imperial family admitted,

The construction of artillery, ammunition, explosives, airplanes and airships, everything is of surprising precision; Lenses of reliable optical tools for photography and distance measure tools, or poisoned gas, the invention of fog machines, up to submarines are in an advanced state and results are outstanding, truly everything is of equal quality which has not been reached in all other countries.[54]

After introducing the Japanese–German technology component of Japan's military policy we can now return to the political and intelligence component in Latin America. Latin Americans could not offer technology to Japan that would help against the United States. However, they offered anti-American hostility and a few leaders eager to weaken the United States. At the very least Latin American territory offered a safe stage to prepare anti-U.S. action, as well as potential for economic warfare.

In 1919, in Mexico, President Carranza worked constantly to shore up Mexico's defensive capacity against a possible U.S. invasion. This made him a most interesting partner for Japan. Carranza continued to nurse a principled enmity against the United States. He had also gained extensive experience waging secret warfare. And, even better, he maintained excellent contacts in subversive circles in Central and South America. If Carranza was willing to cooperate, these three attributes would provide Japan with a dangerous ally next to U.S. territories. In return a reliable flow of Japanese weapons and a secret assistance treaty might enable

26. Venustiano Carranza's determination to fight the United States, not just resist her, continued in 1919 and remains underappreciated today (Library of Congress, Washington, D.C.).

Carranza to maintain guerrilla warfare along the U.S.–Mexican border, at least for a few months. Should a Japanese–U.S. war break out, Carranza's war experience, personal animosity, and Mexican nationalism promised a strong incentive to divert U.S. military power and resources away from a Japanese attacker.

No U.S. president had ever fought, at the same time, a war against Japan and a guerrilla war against Mexico. There was no guarantee that such simultaneous challenges could be defeated. It would be ideal for Japan to extract concessions in peace negotiations, as a U.S.–Mexican war could offer only a Pyrrhic victory. Thus it was in the obvious interest of Japanese war planners to strengthen revolutionary Mexico's military capacity and to fan its sweltering, reflexive anti-U.S. streak.

From Carranza's perspective, there was an obvious need to prepare for a U.S. invasion. North of the Rio Grande, anti-Mexican political groups, racist senators from border states, and hostile oil companies were joining resources. They advocated invasion, on a regular basis. Rightfully so, Mexican planners feared Senator Fall's constant clamor for intervention. Mexican diplomats reported from Washington, D.C.:

> We deduce that the desire for intervention in our country has for its object the taking possession of our sources of riches such as our petroleum beds, which have no rival in the world, as also our minerals are aspired for by some few ambitious men who are not hesitating to violate our right. They do wish to force us to surrender the same, and although part of the press is of this opinion our only resort has to be in expectation.[55]

Mexican undersecretary of foreign relations Hector Medina considered "probable" at least some type of U.S. invasion in 1919.[56]

Mexico would take all types of weapons to blunt a U.S. intervention to the point where it would be made to bleed by guerrilla warfare. Stockpiling weapons was a first step to enable Mexican soldiers to face this eventuality. A large quantity of new machine guns and abundant ammunition would allow Mexican officers to bloody the first wave of U.S. soldiers. Such a surprising fierce resistance would slow down U.S. forces. Or at least the infliction of heavy casualties might be enough of a shock to turn U.S. domestic opinion about the war against a Mexican invasion. Carranza prepared for a devastating welcome of U.S. forces.

Already in April 1919, Isidro Fabela, Carranza's newly appointed ambassador to Germany, had boasted to Spaniards in Cuba that his president was "ready to go to war against the United States."[57] He and his supporters were emboldened because they saw U.S. president Wilson struggling politically. Cándido Aguilar, Carranza's former secretary of state, reported in July 1919, "Wilson reveals himself every day more incompetent. If the failure in Europe was not enough, it should be apparent by the impertinent notes that we have received from Washington and which President Carranza has answered with the insolence that those Yankees merit."[58] At the same time, while President Wilson was bogged down in Europe trying to shape an ideal postwar world in Versailles, Mexican leaders saw an opportunity to arm, insisting that "there should be no excuse for us to be caught napping while the European situation is being arranged. They are unaware that they will not catch us unprepared and that if, unfortunately, the case should occur, they will pay dearly for their daring adventure."[59]

International armament markets were overflowing with unneeded weapons, since World War I had come to a stop. Japanese, Russian, German, Austrian, Hungarian, and French guns were no longer needed on European battlefields.

In addition, stealthy submarines no longer endangered weapon transports crossing the Atlantic. Overnight, Carranza, if he had the money, could achieve what had not been possible since 1917: to purchase an ample supply of weapons and to have them transported, without Allied opposition, from Europe to Veracruz or Acapulco. It was unthinkable that Wilson would launch an invasion of Mexico while negotiating in Versailles. Now was the time for revolutionary Mexico to buy weapons to increase the bloody price of any U.S. invasion.

In February 1919, European arms merchants offered Mexican buyers large quantities of guns, ammunition, airplanes, and even weapon-manufacturing plants, all at bargain prices.[60] It looked as if Spain would be the most obvious source. In September, one Mexican diplomat reported,

> The military industries of Spain are far ahead of the best organized of other countries. The machine gun is perfectly satisfactory and impossible to improve. It is necessary to obtain all available information that the greatest number possible may be obtained. Please sound the Ministry of War with the object of ascertaining how large an order could be filled. Do the same in regard to the powders, especially the smokeless, which are also perfectly satisfactory as powder for the rifles.[61]

Coincidentally, Spain owed weapons to Mexico. Before the revolution the Díaz government had purchased twenty thousand Spanish-model Mauser rifles. Their delivery had been disrupted, first, by the Madero Revolution and, thereafter, by General Huerta's counterrevolution. Then submarine warfare had postponed delivery a third time. In 1919, these weapons were still waiting in a warehouse in Bilbao, Spain.

Carranza made two efforts to learn whether Spanish military resources could help him. First, in July 1919, he dispatched General Trevino as new Mexican military attaché to Spain and minister to Belgium. After his arrival, he received an audience with King Alfonso XIII, where he asked for the delivery of the weapons.

A second attempt was spearheaded by Carranza's son-in-law, General Cándido Aguilar. In late May 1919, Carranza appointed him special envoy. He received diplomatic accreditations to the United States, France, Belgium, the Netherlands, and Switzerland.[62] Aguilar also received 5,000,000 gold pesos for a yet unidentified purpose. It would be safe to suggest that this money was earmarked for weapons or machinery to manufacture armaments. Aguilar revealed on June 20, 1919,

Whether the Americans will intervene in our country I do not know. There are many reasons that would lead one to believe that they will eventually do so. Their desire to intervene is unquestionable. If it should occur Mexico will be unable to obtain war supplies except in Spain. . . . We do not have war supply industries. We have succeeded after long and tedious negotiations in persuading Spain to deliver to us the rifles, which, before the war, she had obligated herself to manufacture for us. This will serve as an argument for our request to the Spanish government to furnish us the corresponding cartridges for the rifles . . . which are very satisfactory.[63]

Cándido Aguilar had great expectations in regard to expanding Spanish–Mexican business:

I urge upon you a complete study of the manufacture of guns, cartridges and gunpowder in Spain. Though we know that these industries are well established in Spain we are ignorant of their details. We know that she has gun factories in Trueba and Seville and factories for rifles and machines guns in Oviedo. But again, I emphasize the fact that it is necessary to know these details, that we may have specific data before making our request for 500 machine guns and ten million cartridges for the rifles already mentioned. Also inform yourself of the importance and operation of the centers at which torpedoes are prepared for the Spanish navy.[64]

Another telegram exclaimed, "The Spanish military industries [are] very progressive and Mexico does not wish to supply herself in the U.S."[65]

In late July General Aguilar took a steamboat from the United States to Cádiz, Spain. After reaching the Spanish port in the first week of August, he continued by railroad to Madrid. In the Spanish capital, cabinet ministers received him, and together they explored future cooperation in the arms sector. Right away, Aguilar asked for five hundred machine guns, gunpowder, discs for cartridges, bomb-dropping apparatus, and machine guns for airplanes.[66] Another report mentions interest in purchasing ten million rounds of rifle ammunition.[67]

But the Spaniards disappointed both Attaché Trevino and General Aguilar. In theory, the Spanish arms industry and stockpiles could help Mexico significantly. But in 1919, the larger international political context prohibited it, in the name of Spain's national interest. King Alfonso XIII hesitated to support Carranza openly, as he needed U.S. support in his continuing push to improve Spain's emerging stature in the League of Nations. Also, Alfonso XIII was scheduled to visit Great Britain in October 1919, and he needed British goodwill for Spanish aims in North Africa. Then there was France, which rivaled Spanish imperial expansion in Morocco. For Alfonso XIII and the Spanish government revolutionary Mexico was far less important than the United States and Europe. For the time being, Spain could serve as arms supplier to Mexico but not as regular military supplier for a U.S.–Mexican border conflict.

But Mexican negotiators did not give in easily. Next, Mexican buyers explored another path, hiring private Spanish intermediaries to buy weapons on the open market. They asked representatives of the Spanish banking house of Urquijo to approach the commission administering U.S. weapon stockpiles in France. Any Mexican use of weapons from this collection would offer its nationalist officers and soldiers the added satisfaction of killing U.S. soldiers with formerly U.S. weapons. However, this approach, too, failed. The Spanish bank backed the government's priority of Spanish colonial war in Morocco. Even then, yet another avenue was probed, to buy Winchester carbines from the Spanish Guardia Civil.[68]

In the end, how many weapons were purchased remains unknown. Only one purchase of one hundred machine guns in Spain can be documented, far too few to turn the tide against a U.S. intervention. Even though Mexico's efforts acquired some Spanish weapons from Spain for immediate use, they were not enough to equip a Mexican army against a U.S. invasion. Spain had revealed itself as a complicated friend whose European affairs remained more important than its often vehemently professed Hispanic linkages with Latin America.

Thereafter General Aguilar left Spain and tried his luck farther north in other European countries. Belgium was his first stop. Mexico's consul in France wired him another US$100,000 for unspecified purchases. Interestingly, Aguilar asked Carranza in Mexico to instruct him confidentially whether he should travel to the disintegrating Germany.

From Berlin, Mexican consul Leopoldo Ortiz joined in and pointed out a variety of interesting possibilities for Mexico. Already in January 1919, he had recommended hiring veteran German officers to participate in the buildup of a yet-to-be-created national Mexican army. One offer by former General Staff member Wilhelm Faupel stood out among the applications. In March, Ortiz reminded his superiors in Mexico City a second time of the potential value of German technicians, pointing at their military legacy in Chile.[69] Another German officer promised to develop in Mexico a school that would train Mexican storm troopers.[70]

Then, there were former officers wanting to buy land in Mexico and to start life over as agricultural colonists. For example, one syndicate financed by ex-naval officers promised Mexico an investment of 400,000 RM for a settlement.[71] Another, chaired by Colonel Hagelberg, wanted to relocate 150 families to Durango. None of these offers, however, helped Carranza to defeat a potential U.S. invasion.

Finishing his negotiations in Belgium, Aguilar awaited Carranza's instructions about Germany and crossed into the Netherlands. Finally, Carranza told him to complete his remaining tasks in all the other Western European countries before proceeding to Germany.[72]

All these negotiations yielded only three additional weapons deliveries for Mexico. In December 1919, the first shipment of arms left Antwerp, Belgium, and traveled to Mexico via Buenos Aires.[73] Mexican diplomat Padilla Nervo, attached to the Mexican legation in Buenos Aires, assisted Mexican lead secret agent Jacinto Díaz.[74] Once the weapons arrived in the Río de la Plata port they were reloaded as rail freight and crossed the Andes to Valparaiso. From there they continued, by ship, north to Mexico. This journey involved a carefully orchestrated chain of individuals from Germany, Argentina, Japan, Chile, Colombia, Great Britain, and Mexico. In January 1920, a load of airplane parts followed for Mexico.[75]

Carranza pursued a second track in postwar Europe. He was not content only with buying weapons. He also wanted machines that manufactured weapons and to operate them inside Mexico.[76] Now Mexico sought to break once and forever U.S., European, and Japanese arms manufacturing monopolies. Once up and running, a Mexican arms industry would guarantee an arms supply that could no longer be affected by U.S. arms embargos. Also, such an industry would provide the president with enough weapons to squash, once and forever, the remnants of movements of regional warlords Pancho Villa, Félix Díaz, and Manuel Pelayes. If Carranza could establish a reliable national weapons monopoly, he could consolidate the monopoly of violence inside the revolutionary state.

Already in 1916, Carranza's generals had acquired basic Japanese machinery to make cartridges. Now in 1920, his son-in-law used the trip to Europe to explore next who could provide more substantial building blocks for a Mexican industry.

After business in northern Europe, General Aguilar and his financial adviser, Fernandez Gonzalez Roa, traversed the Alps. They expected to visit one of Italy's most important arms manufacturers—the Ansaldo company. It was owned by the Perrone brothers, who had strong ties to Argentina. Pio Perrone, the more dynamic of the brothers, was eagerly waiting for Mexico's general. Now that World War I was over he needed new customers.

Once in Rome, the visitors were also received by Italy's Undersecretary Count Sforza and King Emmanuel, asking for a low profile. Requesting discretion, General Aguilar admitted to his hosts that he wanted to find "help for the establishment of a great national mechanical industry, a steel mill, airplane manufacturing and aviator school."[77] Then he toured the arms factories.

Afterward, Aguilar praised Ansaldo as a most versatile industrial conglomerate. Mexico could purchase from it "all types of war ships, from the fastest motor boats, which have proven themselves as ideal coast guard ships through their efficiency and economy, to the most powerful cruisers."[78] First, Ansaldo could help Mexico in acquiring a merchant marine. Its shipyards built all types of merchant marine ships. Second, it produced a wide variety of weapons, including airplanes. Third, Ansaldo manufactured locomotives and electrical machinery, all items needed for economic development. Certainly, arms manufacture in Italy appeared to be more reliable than production in the midst of the domestic turmoil of Germany or Austria. Ansaldo's forty different factories did not seem to slow down production, even though Italy was also experiencing political upheavals.

Pio Perrone assured General Aguilar that, unlike in Spain or Germany, Italian weapons were all for sale. Even better, his company, encouraged by the Italian government, was willing to accept as pay Mexican raw materials.[79] In theory, Mexican oil and ore could quickly purchase a plethora of weaponry and machinery. After pondering economic cooperation, it was only a small step to explore the possibilities of Italian–Mexican political-military cooperation. Aguilar reported from Italy that it seemed possible that the liberal, postwar Italian government was willing to expand purchase agreements into an Italian–Mexican "military economic treaty."

In 1920, Italy appeared to be a much more potent European supporter of Mexico than Spain. General Aguilar believed that ethnic affinity was the driving force behind Ansaldo's surprising friendliness toward Mexico:

> The House of Ansaldo, whose feelings of being Latin are well known in South America, and who already had given a fleet to the Argentine Republic (one of the members of the Ansaldo Mission which is currently in Mexico, is the son of the famous engineer Luiggi, builder of the famous military port Bahia Blanca, Argentina) offered something additional to Mexico: to construct a true strong alliance. Its value is incalculable because it presently offers Mexico the reasons for its well being . . . that

27. Carranza's son-
in-law, General
Cándido Aguilar,
identified Italy as
the country that
would furnish
Mexico with an
independent
national arms
industry after
1919 (Library
of Congress,
Washington, D.C.).

could allow Mexico military supply for Carranza's regime. That could be the solution to the North American Block and the never realized, specific business understandings with Germany.[80]

Now that Emperor Wilhelm II and the promises of his German monarchy had been wiped away by revolution and Spain had failed to back profuse invocations of Hispanic solidarity with weapon deliveries, Aguilar discovered Italy as a partner that revolutionary Mexico could count on. He probably knew that at the same time in Buenos Aires, Italian intelligence agents had approached a Japanese–Mexican–German spy network, wanting to join a campaign against U.S. interests in South America.

General Aguilar returned to Spain after his encouraging negotiations in Italy. He held one more audience with King Alfonso XIII. Once more he tried to impress the Spanish king by stating that revolutionary Mexico was planning to raise the status of its diplomatic representation from legation to embassy.[81] But to no avail. This visit concluded Aguilar's European explorations. Thereafter, he took a boat to start the long journey back to Veracruz and Mexico City. When he arrived in the Mexican capital he found the president making progress in the preparation of secret, now offensive, warfare against the Wilson administration.

Thus far Carranza had purchased weapons in Japan and Europe and negotiated the acquisition of workbenches for aerial bombs and machine guns. Next, he added clandestine revolutionary, political, and intelligence operations.

This was a policy Venustiano Carranza preferred to keep hidden. He pursued a revolutionary policy, preparing not only to defend Mexico against a possible invasion but also to attack the United States with small, offensive subversive actions. He was eager to use every available military, political, and propaganda tool to reduce future U.S. influence south of the Rio Grande.

His campaign consisted of three components. First, he backed radical labor and ethnic violence to revolutionize the social climate along the U.S.–Mexican border. Second, he nurtured anti-U.S. political organizations in Latin American countries, hoping to build a League of Latins that could oppose the United States, its Monroe Doctrine, Pan-Americanism, and the League of Nations. Third, Carranza ordered his intelligence service in South America to join with the networks of Chile, Argentina, Japan, Germany, and Italy, all of which were eager to fan regional South American rivalries and to destabilize South American international relations, making Pan-Americanism impossible.

Carranza's first policy sought to revive revolutionary strife along the U.S.–Mexican border, creating violence through labor strikes and the fanning of ethnic tension. Newly discovered telegrams of Mexican diplomats offer us the first Mexican descriptions of activities. Their bluntness is surprising. In October 1919, Mexican undersecretary Medina admitted confidentially to a colleague "that every effort is being made to foment trouble for the U.S."[82]

Creating trouble along the border meant that Carranza mobilized the familiar agitators whom he had employed selectively already during World War I. One effort was to disrupt the U.S. economy through strikes and labor violence, spearheaded by a few Mexican anarchists, syndicalists, and socialists. Even though the imperial powers had stopped their manipulations of Mexican labor violence, Mexican workers had never agreed to respect their armistice. From their perspective war against capitalist production had to continue on the grassroots level. They still saw a need to bring about a social and economic revolution north of Mexico. The revolutionary upheavals in former tsarist Russia had only energized independent Mexican socialists and anarchists further. Most of these activities were not accompanied by a detailed bureaucratic paper trail, thus it is easy to confuse an absence of sources with a nonexistence of events. But a few surviving documents indicate, at least, trends. One informer explained that there had been "white operatives recruited . . . from the ranks of the IWW and similar organizations. Their general objective was railroad and ocean steamship sabotage and they formulated very extensive plans for work of this kind along the Atlantic Coast and its immediate hinterland. Only the November, 1918 armistice had kept plans from being consummated." Importantly, the informer insisted that after 1918 these larger plans "were still available to be executed, if necessity should arise and opportunity permits."[83] To say it differently, even though German naval agents no longer enlisted U.S., Irish, and Mexican laborers to commit espionage or sabotage in the United States, now that World War I was over, President Carranza, by himself, continued to nurture the secret tool of targeted labor violence. And it could come in very handy in a Japanese war against the United States.

In Mexico City, on October 15, 1919, members of the International Workers of the World Lodge 23 met and pronounced that in November they would start a large strike among U.S. miners and metalworkers. Full of themselves, they claimed to have the blind following of three million adherents, enough to take over ports on the western and Atlantic U.S. coasts. Plus these men assumed that a large number of disgruntled U.S. soldiers would join the workers. This, of course, was a reference to African American soldiers returning from European battlefields once again having to chafe under the Jim Crow system. Hopefully, radical acts by strikers and black soldiers would succeed at occupying and isolating an area in the state of Colorado. Next they would proclaim a capital and, third, create "a reformed government of the U.S."[84] Labor organizers claimed that Carranza had promised them help as such a regional revolution gained strength. Obviously, these plans were full of hyperbole. Nevertheless, Carranza, once again, encouraged radical labor groups to advocate violence against the United States.

A second component of Carranza's "fomenting trouble policy" was the revival of the 1915 Plan of San Diego. U.S. historians Charles Harris and Ray Sadler discovered and analyzed Carranza's second-most cynical manipulation of racial and economic tensions along the border. His provocateurs were expected to cross into Texas, Arizona, and New Mexico in December 1919.[85] Previously, on June 14, 1919, Carranza had written to a Señor Berlanga that three principal provocateurs would cross into Texas to reintroduce a revised Plan of San Diego.[86] Once again Carranza manipulated factions in the Hispanic and African American community to create a race war along the U.S.–Mexican border.

A newly discovered aspect of this policy is an attempt made by Mexico to enlist France to file a claim for the return of the territories lost during the U.S.–Mexican war in 1848. A Mexican diplomat explored in Paris whether the French government could be manipulated into demanding a debate in the League of Nations about who owned the U.S.–Mexican border region. Perhaps European diplomats, unfamiliar with and far away from the border, might be convinced that it should come under international receivership, just like the contested German/French area Alsace-Lorraine and the Peruvian/Chilean region of Tacna-Arica. In the end, French diplomats rejected this Mexican "trial balloon." National ownership of the U.S.–Mexican border region never became a topic of discussion in Geneva.[87] In September 1919, the Mexican diplomat General Mondragon informed the Carranza administration that the French had "seemed to indicate that our international position will remain status quo for an indefinite period of time. Also, the French did not think that a U.S. invasion was imminent. In their opinion there is no fear of complications at present."[88] Nevertheless, it shows how Carranza's "trouble at the border" was connected with diplomatic manipulations in the emerging postwar Europe.

Finally, Carranza reinforced the initiative in France with pro-Mexican propaganda. Once again Spain functioned as a central base for his work. An appeal to ethnic solidarity between Spanish and Mexican people was used to measure support for Carranza's policies.

In August 1919, the Mexican Foreign Ministry sent a delegation to Madrid to participate in the Spanish Fiesta de la Raza celebrations. The press department of the Mexican legation, under the leadership of Luis G. Urbina, was enlarged with Antonio Mediz Bolio, Enrique Aragón, and Manuel Caballero. Mediz Bolio assumed the lead role and organized the Dia de la Raza festivities.[89] These men did not come to celebrate ethnic origin but, rather, to egg on Spaniards to challenge U.S. policy.

Quietly, they were supported by Isidro Fabela, Carranza's ambassador designate for Germany, still one of his confidants and most committed anti-U.S. diplomats. He attempted to increase financial support for propaganda work by coercing rich Spaniards with vulnerable assets in revolutionary Mexico. For example, Antonio Basagoiti, Julian Aragón, and Luis Ibañez owned important holdings in Mexico and had suffered during the revolution. Since they had connections with the Hispano American Bank Fabela approached them "asking" for 5,000,000 pesetas. The loan promised to buy them protection from further destruction or confiscation.[90] In essence it was a forced loan. Skillfully, the Spaniards played for time, asking Fabela to await the outcome of the 1920 presidential election. Luckily the stalling tactic worked. Carranza was assassinated and replaced by Álvaro Obregón. He removed Isidro Fabela from his ambassadorial post. The Spaniards had escaped this shake down effort.[91]

Mexican governmental propagandists in Spain also stayed in touch with Argentina's Hispanist Ugarte, who, still backed by German money, was working out of Barcelona as a Hispanic propagandist. His friend and banker Juan Echepare participated in the talks. Other wealthy men like Carl Pereyra and Manuel Llamoes were approached by Mexican diplomats hoping to enlist them in sponsoring pro-Mexican events.[92]

From Spain, the anti-U.S. press spread its propaganda to stations in South America. In March 1919, sensational articles published in a Brazilian paper reported an emerging political unification movement among groups in Mexico, Central America, and South America. The articles were written by Federico Cesar Calvo, a Colombian by birth and a citizen of Panama.

In 1913, Calvo had worked during Huerta's dictatorship as editor of the *Diario de Panama*. As Huerta experienced intensifying pressure to step down, he encouraged publications in Central and South America to publish appeals for the unification of all Latin American and Spanish anti-U.S. movements. Huerta's minister of state, Dr. Ignacio Alcocer, shortly thereafter named Calvo chief of Huerta's propaganda publications. In this capacity he toured Latin American capitals, financed by a large monthly salary, and used his expense account to agitate against Huerta's enemy Carranza. His conferences used the cover of the Associacion de Jovenes Cristianos and syndicalism, always invoking Spanish ethnicity as a shield against Yankee aggression. Once Huerta was forced into exile in Barcelona, Calvo was also expelled, and his work was suppressed. Now, in 1919, Calvo resurfaced, this time working on behalf of his former foe Carranza.[93]

Troublemaking along the U.S.–Mexican border, diplomatic trial balloons in Geneva's League of Nations, and Mexican anti-U.S. propaganda in Spain and South America were all part of Carranza's secret toolbox. These activities provide the background for additional secret political work, now in Central and South America.

In early 1919, from President Wilson's perspective, events in Versailles were developing according to plan. In January the Peace Commission agreed to create the Commission for the League of Nations.[94] A first draft of the Covenant of the League of Nations was presented by Wilson himself to the world in mid-February 1919.

Suddenly, by April his efforts experienced serious opposition at home. The Republican Party and its senators in the U.S. Congress insisted that the Monroe Doctrine should remain valid for the Western Hemisphere, regardless of the League of Nations treaty that diplomats in Versailles were crafting. If President Wilson wanted any favorable consideration of the emerging treaty in Congress, international league members needed to accept the Monroe Doctrine. On April 10, 1919, President Wilson presented this "poisonous pill" created by Republicans in Geneva. U.S. isolationists had begun to sabotage Wilson's internationalist and idealist outlook from the other side of the Atlantic.

On the same day, Japan insisted on introducing into the negotiations a racial equality clause.[95] In respect for Japan's rising global clout, diplomats agreed to discuss the demand for the equality clause and to schedule it for a vote. April 11, 1920, was devoted to a discussion about the relationship between the League of Nations and the Monroe Doctrine.

In the end, when it was time to vote, Wilson's demand for respect for the Monroe Doctrine prevailed, but the Japanese insistence on racial equality failed. The Australians vehemently opposed it. President Wilson himself manipulatively squashed it, exploiting a technicality.[96]

Seizing this opportunity, President Carranza established himself as a strong anti-U.S. nationalist who embodied the future of Latin American self-determination. But before Carranza's cooperation with other Latin American groups can be examined in detail, it is necessary to catch up with the evolution of Mexican intelligence operations in Argentina.

The official diplomatic face of revolutionary Mexico in Argentina was the Mexican legation located at Calle Peru 440. One of Carranza's most important secret agents in Argentina was Jacinto Díaz. He had to function in a complex service environment whereby Buenos Aires was appreciated as an intelligence base by a growing number of countries. Most often they worked separately. Sometimes, however, they cooperated if the project warranted it. Shared targets of these campaigns were the United States, Pan-Americanism, and the Monroe Doctrine.

Outside Mexico, Jacinto Díaz's power was unlimited, and he could act with impunity.[97] First, he was pivotal in organizing the flow of Mexican weapons from Europe across the Andes toward Mexico. Probably this also meant preparing weapon depots in Colombia for yet-to-be-identified rebel groups or future Mexican special operations teams against the Panama Canal.[98] Second, Díaz was the figurehead of a Mexican propaganda organization disseminating intense anti-U.S. propaganda into the Río de la Plata region. Third, he involved himself in supporting Chilean secret diplomacy against Peru and supporting Argentine groups that were active against U.S. interests.[99]

From Buenos Aires, Díaz also managed smaller cells in neighboring countries. There was a Mexican cell in Montevideo led by Agent Rothschild. Díaz communicated with a group in Santiago, Chile, and, on occasion, with Mexican envoy Siller. Finally, he helped a larger network of twenty-five agents in Rio de Janeiro, Brazil, supervised by Agent Ochoa.[100] Some of the agents were Brazilian, but some were Japanese.

Chilean military intelligence also operated in Argentina. In 1919 General Wilson Hurtado financed a secret office in Buenos Aires, headed by a Mr. Suzanna. The Argentine government knew that this office on occasion cooperated with Mexico's service and espionage projects against Peru. In addition they communicated with the Chilean Col. Luis Cabrera in charge of the Iquique region.

Already in November 1918, German reports had predicted the outbreak of a Chilean–Peruvian border war. They saw an opportunity for Chile, as Peru was considered too weak to repel a Chilean land grab. In this environment Gezir Remeny, Agent Leon Spikle, an Englishman with the last name Dixon, the Chilean Suzanna, and several unknown Mexican and Japanese agents operated against Peru.

German network leader zur Helle, alias J. C. Hall, had also made the acquaintance of Jacinto Díaz.[101] As the newly installed President Leguía began to attack the remaining German network operations in Peru, more and more German agents exchanged the Andean theater for a safer residence in Santiago. There regional head Riedel offered his services to Chilean intelligence chief Hurtado. Details of cooperation were worked out in a two-hour meeting among Riedel, Hurtado, and Chilean admiral Luis V. Lopez. Once again their target was the contested region between Chile and Peru. By September direct communication among agents in Peru, Chile, and Argentina was no longer possible. Even a secondary agent like the German Dr. Wagner was leaving the cover of his Drug Store Botica.[102]

Thereafter Japanese and German spying against Peru continued, only now it operated with renewed strength out of Argentina and Chile. For example, in November 1919, Chilean commander Navarette dispatched ethnic German Major Holz to conduct reconnaissance of Peruvian military installations and warfare capacities. He was to report back anything he could about Peruvian armament factories, magazines, explosives, the central army depot, armament warehouses, troops, aviation, and the raising of new units.[103]

The operations described above, however, were humbled by Japan's strengthening intelligence presence in Buenos Aires. The public face representing Japan was still the diplomat Nakamura, who had arrived in the Argentine capital in November 1918. By then undercover work had been taken over by Kinta Arai, who had relocated from Mexico City.

Japan's growing network established contacts with nationalist individuals on the highest government level. For example, Foreign Minister Pueyrredón was approached by diplomat Nakamura through Dr. Mane, his private secretary. Argentine Ambassador to Japan Alberto Pugnalin was engaged in civil Japanese–Argentine cooperation. Undersecretary Molinari could be reached through the diplomat Ricardo Aldoa, whose brother, Simon Aldoa, received from Arai a monthly stipend to operate a car and a small expense account.[104] Simon Aldoa also led Japan's network of street informers in Buenos Aires.

In addition, Kinta Arai had access to German agents who had become part of his payroll after November 1918. In March 1919, German and Japanese agents were getting used to working with each other. In South America one German agent wrote to another, "How are you getting along with the new Japanese agents? They give good returns, but one must know how to handle them."[105] German agents hoped that Japanese–German cooperation would also benefit future German goals. One of them stated, referring to Versailles, "The peace affair seems full of hitches and more than ever before have we now set our minds on the allied dogs, who only late will taste what Germany is."[106] Other German observers suggested in 1919 that Japan's "chief objective, for the time being, is South America and Mexico, but after that who knows."[107]

Into this environment Venustiano Carranza launched his attempt to derail Latin American participation in the League of Nations, perhaps even to prevent the League of Nations from becoming a reality. Ideally, "making all the trouble he could" was to lead to the creation of a League of Latins.

Already on April 23, 1919, Carranza had launched the public phase of this policy effort. That day, he rejected the Monroe Doctrine once again.[108] Next, Mexican embassies and legations across Latin America were ordered to communicate the Mexican protest to other Spanish American countries. In the United States, Secretary of State Polk received the protest on April 25. The Mexican press followed up with a publishing campaign and printed the diplomatic protest note two days later. Peru acknowledged the Mexican note on May 2, and Argentina received it shortly thereafter. Finally, Carranza concluded his publicity campaign with an address to U.S. citizens. On May 9, he gave an interview to left-wing writer Robert Murray, a correspondent of the pro–Democratic Party newspaper *New York World*. He explained to readers in the northeastern United States why the Monroe Doctrine was illegal, and he repeated his promise to fight it vehemently now and in the future. Skillfully, Carranza combined public diplomacy and political movements with his previously described hidden activities.[109]

It was a remarkable effort that brought together Mexican, German, Japanese, Italian, El Salvadorian, Colombian, Chilean, and Argentine factions to confront U.S. president Wilson. Toward Central America, Carranza dispatched a representative. In the summer of 1919, diplomat Gregorio Leal took the steamship *San Juan* from Mexico to Central America. His task was to ask the governments of Nicaragua, San Salvador, and Guatemala to resume efforts to form a Central American republic. Once this bloc was created it could align itself with a yet-to-be-created South American bloc.[110] Leal was to urge small government publications in Managua, San Salvador, and Tegucigalpa to join Mexico's protests against the Monroe Doctrine.

In Colombia, too, Carranza found vocal supporters in favor of Latin American departure from the League of Nations. Already in April 1919, Colombian diplomats had privately voiced their opposition to the league. In Madrid, Colombian minister Jose Urruttia sent to his minister to London, Dr. Gutierrez Ponce, a copy of a diplomatic note that the Spanish ambassador had presented to President Wilson in Paris, expressing support for the projected League of Nations. The Colombian diplomat talked about how detrimental this league would be to Colombia's interests. Instead, he preferred a preservation of Colombia's present "splendid isolation." Furthermore, he urged Colombian diplomats to reach out to Chilean and Argentine representatives. Together, they might be able to construct a united defense of South American interests. They thought it possible to bring pressure to bear at the Peace Conference, where no final signature agreeing to the peace treaty had yet been put on documents.[111]

But then support from Latin America for Mexico slowed down. Even worse for Carranza, in July enough great powers agreed with Wilson, and the covenant in Versailles launched the League of Nations.

Now Argentine policy split in two. One was a public, pro-U.S. stance. It presented itself as constructive support. The second one was secret and allowed Buenos Aires to be a location for opposition groups to coordinate against Wilson. Both policies were real, and the two camps did not seem to communicate with each other. Neither of them was pushed or troubled by the existence of the other.

In August, Argentina's government broke with Carranza's anti-U.S. public stance. First, there emerged a growing and surprising Argentine enthusiasm to play a leading role, at the side of the United States, once the League of Nations would meet.

Argentinean undersecretary of foreign affairs Molinari held a series of informal talks with the U.S. ambassador, where he gave the impression that President Wilson would find Argentina at his side, eager to act as Latin America's leader in the league. Especially surprising was Molinari's suggestion that his administration would be willing to counter Mexican president Venustiano Carranza's intensifying anti-league propaganda.

In May, Molinari told the U.S. ambassador that Argentina "should at once join the League of Nations" even though other Latin American elites voiced vehement outrage over the insistence of the U.S. Republican Party to make the Monroe Doctrine part of the league's legal framework. Clearly, Molinari seemed to promise an Argentina that would act as Wilson's advocate in South America.[112] Even better, soon words were followed by positive acts.

On the evening of July 16, 1919, Molinari sent to France an acceptance letter confirming that Argentina was joining the League of Nations. Two weeks later, President Irigoyen elaborated that Argentina "had remained out of the war and had not given the U.S. any assistance, [it] should be the first nation to support President Wilson and the U.S. in its advocacy of the League of Nations, which, he said, he and the President believed, if realized, would more than compensate for the sacrifices which humanity had made in the war."[113] Indeed, the Irigoyen government wanted Argentina to be the first Latin American country to adhere to the league. Its Foreign Ministry sent a cable to all Argentinean diplomats in South America "instructing them to notify their host governments that Argentina had joined the League of Nations without reservation of any kind. And it had suggested that Pan American cooperation in this question would be of the greatest moral support possible to the U.S. and its present policy."[114]

On August 4, Undersecretary Molinari informed the U.S. ambassador that the Argentine initiative pushing membership in the League of Nations was receiving a most favorable response. Chile had formally joined, and favorable replies had arrived from the governments of Colombia, Ecuador, and Uruguay.[115] Undersecretary Molinari told the U.S. ambassador one more time the "reasons for which he was in favor of the League of Nations and detailed the evidences of sympathy which the Argentine Government wished to prove to President Wilson in his effort to create the League." Much to the pleasure of the ambassador, he closed by expressing outrage over the ongoing attempts by the U.S.

Republican Party to torpedo President Wilson's League of Nations endeavor. He exclaimed, "Politicians are the pest of every country," and continued,

> The signing of the Treaty of Peace had brought home to the President and his administration the fact that the international policy of the Argentine Government must now definitely be determined for the future. And that the country could no longer be allowed to drift in apparently aimless fashion of the past, from one rapprochement with a European nation to rapprochement with another.[116]

Molinari promised the ambassador that President Irigoyen would "pursue a policy in accord with the international policy of the U.S." Seemingly appreciating the Monroe Doctrine, he reaffirmed his pro-U.S. stance by stating: "The continent must be surrounded so far as her sovereign interests are involved, with a high wall which will not permit interference from either Europe or Asia. He stated that this would be the policy of the Argentine government for at least the next three years and in all probability for the next nine years. In other words, Pan Americanism, not Latin Americanism."[117]

On August 18, 1919, the U.S. diplomat also learned about a more cautious Argentine position toward the League of Nations. As the U.S. ambassador talked with the editor in chief of *La Nacion*, conservative leaders emphasized skepticism about the advantages for Argentina of joining the League of Nations. The only benefit they could see was that it brought Argentina into line with the policy of the United States and, generally, strengthened Pan-Americanism. These men interpreted Argentina's entry merely as a tactical political move.[118] But the Argentine undersecretary tried to reassure the U.S. ambassador. The Irigoyen administration also demonstrated eagerness to participate constructively in the shaping of commercial tools to revive postwar trade.

Already in 1919, the Wilson administration had invited all Latin American governments to send experts to Washington, D.C., to negotiate the issues of currency convertibility and the creation of a gold clearance fund covering the entire hemisphere. Buenos Aires complied and sent a prominent delegation to the opening of the 2nd Pan-American Financial Conference on January 19, 1920.

Once in Washington, the Argentine delegation worked hard to bridge the distance between the Americas' two most prosperous economies. First, technocrats discussed railway transportation, uniformity of bills of lading, postal facilities, and cable, as well as telegraph and wireless communications. Second, they explored the establishment of relative equality in laws and regulations that would govern the organization and treatment of foreign corporations. Third, they established the uniformity of laws processing checks and the elimination of double taxation. Also, patents and copyright agreements were standardized.

Most importantly, in 1916, the Bolsa de Comercio of Buenos Aires and the Chamber of Buenos Aires had developed a model of arbitration for trademark disputes. Now, in 1920, this agreement was singled out as a model for other Latin American countries using U.S. patents.

Argentinean bankers also looked forward to profits from the first opening of Latin American bank branches in the United States. When the conference emphasized the need of exchanging commercial attachés, Argentinean delegates once again sided with the Wilson administration.[119] Based on Argentine behavior at this conference, a superficial observer could predict that Argentina's foreign policy was returning to the pro-Pan-American stance of pre-1916, strongly cooperating with the United States.

In Mexico, Carranza never changed his mind about the League of Nations. And he appreciated the continued presence of a most enthusiastic supporter for his undercover work in the former German head naval agent Kurt Jahnke. His old coconspirator, German Ambassador to Mexico von Eckardt, already had left Mexico for Spain on March 24, 1919.

When von Eckardt left the Mexican capital Carranza honored him by transporting him in his private train, including a cook and a servant. Also, a representative of the Ministry of Foreign Relations accompanied von Eckardt and his family. Additional protection came in the form of a strong military detachment as the train was traveling through uncertain territory. Carranza's sentimental honor guard accompanied the German to the U.S. border, where agents of the Bureau of Intelligence took over until von Eckardt disembarked at Pennsylvania Station. Two days later, he and his family took a taxi to the docks in order to board a Dutch steamer. Before the boat left the harbor, every single piece of von Eckardt's luggage was investigated; it lasted five hours. Once he reached Southampton, Great Britain, British military agents repeated the search for two hours.[120] From there he had traveled on to Berlin and assumed a position in the German Foreign Ministry.

Kurt Jahnke had stayed longer in Mexico City. On the one hand, superiors in Berlin had ordered him to stop all illegal activities, an order he received on May 14, 1919. Now new documents prove that Carranza had taken over Kurt Jahnke as his secret representative to the new emerging Weimar government.

One of Jahnke's sidekicks was a Mr. Geukel. He had been ordered out of Mexico and expected to travel to Tokyo to carry out a mission for von Eckardt. But suddenly he traveled south, via Panama and Lima across the Andes to Argentina. As soon as he arrived in Buenos Aires, in February 1919, he joined an intelligence environment that was using Argentine territory to pool resources and retool for a multinational confrontation with the United States, in disregard of the November 1918 armistice.[121] In Mexico, Jahnke offered to the Weimar Republic to continue to do secret work. He promised to use his contacts "with important labor leaders in the U.S. as well as Great Britain." Subsequently Jahnke held talks with Carranza. Then he decided to return to Europe to present their plans to superiors in Berlin.

He arrived in Madrid on September 18, 1919, hoping to gain access to a reliable signal transmitter. What he wrote in October was stunning.

Carranza had given him along a long shopping list. The Mexican president wanted to purchase from Germany immediately one factory manufacturing agricultural machines, one factory each producing cars and airplanes, one factory for ammunition and weapons, one steel plant, and one naval yard. As most

28. Agent Kurt Jahnke, after developing in 1918 the details for the largest prevented German sabotage campaign inside the United States, freelanced in 1919 as Carranza's emissary to the new Weimar Mueller cabinet. While Mueller angrily rejected "secret policies," his navy disregarded such conviction (Library of Congress, Washington, D.C.).

important purchase he singled out the construction of a cyanide factory, whose cyanide he wanted to use to process precious metals. It would end Mexican dependence on supplies from the United States. Once German investors built a factory inside Mexico, Carranza promised that it could export its products also to Central American and South America.

Next, the new democratic government in Berlin should finance the opening of a commercial department in Germany's embassy in Mexico City. It would coordinate such German industrial offensives in Mexico, only eleven months after the end of World War I. On a side note, Carranza also wanted to station a military and navy attaché. He wanted particular attention to be paid to wireless transmissions between Mexico City and Nauen, Germany's central transmitter station.[122]

The second part of the report was equally stunning. Jahnke cabled to Berlin that he had lined up a conspiracy that would bring together Carranza, Jahnke's contacts inside the United States, and representatives of the Republican Party. With Carranza's approval Jahnke had met a Mr. Keedy, a party representative, three times in Mexico City. The Republicans promised Carranza access to a loan of 1,000,000,000 pesos in exchange for conditions that remained to be specified.

Agent Jahnke wanted German politicians to act as mediators between Carranza and the Republicans. Such mediation was supposed to be advantageous to Germany in the future because German help now was supposed to translate into easier conditions as part of the German war reparations later. During the upcoming presidential elections, Jahnke suggested: "Germany has to help the Republicans in their fight against Wilson and Great Britain, by gaining an understanding with the Republicans, entering into a bond with them and by delivering Germany's backing which, in the future, provides it in the U.S. with the large pro-German element for the elections."[123] Via telegraph Jahnke assured Berlin that Carranza knew about these meetings and originated with him the proposed plans, through his emissary, Mario M. He implored his superiors to believe that Germany's influence on Mexican politics continued to exist. Measures should be taken immediately to exploit the current situation in favor of German interest.

Thereafter, the German naval attaché in Spain paid Jahnke 1,000 pesetas to continue to Barcelona, take a steamer to Hamburg, and hurry by train to Berlin to confer with the surviving members of Germany's naval intelligence system.[124] He arrived in Berlin in the middle of September.

In Berlin, Jahnke reunited with former minister to Mexico von Eckardt, who was eager to hear more about Carranza's and Jahnke's plans. Between October and December 1919 a group of men from the Foreign Ministry and naval intelligence worked on Jahnke's suggestion.[125] Together they planned to make serious contributions to a defeat of the Democratic Party in the upcoming U.S. presidential election.

For Germany the attraction of this secret anti-Wilson campaign was obvious. If the Republicans were to win the White House, U.S. acceptance of the League of Nations covenant would be unlikely. Then Allied postwar policy could seriously be disrupted.[126] Jahnke's proposal was taken seriously in the new Foreign Ministry. Talks involving Legationsrat v. Stohrer, Geheimrat Trautmann, and former ambassador von Eckardt lasted for one week. Then the proposal was accepted by Undersecretary von Haniel Haimhausen, who presented it for discussion to Foreign Secretary Mueller. But Mueller brushed it aside, exclaiming that his government would not engage in secret policies anymore.[127]

While Naval Agent Jahnke and Ambassador von Eckardt were conferring in Berlin, Buenos Aires naval agent zur Helle also traveled to Berlin in September 1919. The sources do not place him at a meeting with Jahnke. However, zur Helle returned to South America communicating a secret program that focused on influencing the outcome of U.S. presidential elections. Most likely the Weimar government refused to engage in secret policies; but the surviving components of the German navy pursued their own policy, regardless of what the foreign minister wanted. Mexicans and Germans found other unexpected coconspirators already present in the United States.

Now the Italian ambassadors wanted to work against the outgoing Wilson administration. As the Italian delegation in Versailles discussed the political future of South Tyrol, Trieste, Dalmatia, the Dodecanese Islands, and Fiume, Italian premier Vittorio Orlando and Foreign Minister Sidney Sonnino were skillfully using propaganda offices in the United States to reinforce diplomatic efforts with pseudo-public Italian American pressure.

This was also necessary because the Yugoslav National Council in January 1919 had established a Yugoslav Information Bureau in New York. It too used a determined public relations campaign in favor of the Kingdom of Serbs, Croats, and Slovenes and, correctly, painted Italian claims as imperialistic desires. Italy's Ambassador Count Macchi de Cellere convinced Rome to counter with an Italian information bureau in New York and Washington. Captain Pietro Tozzi then would lead a campaign that covered the U.S. public with Italian counterpropaganda.

Then, the Sons of Italy and Italia Irredenta Society mobilized Italian Americans to send petitions to the U.S. delegates in France.[128] Italian American newspapers printed petitions that readers simply had to clip, sign, and forward to the U.S. delegation in Europe. As President Wilson fought for his policy course, ethnic Italian organizations in the United States campaigned strongly against the Democratic Party and its president.

Next Italian premier Orlando withdrew the Italian delegation from Paris. Right away strong criticism of Wilson was published not only in Italy but also in U.S. cities where Italian Americans lived. By fall 1919, in Massachusetts, Italian American organizations bought advertisements in Italian-language newspapers supporting the presidential Republican candidacy of Calvin Coolidge. Ethnic press articles called for political revenge. They rejoiced, in the words of historian John B. Duff: "The Italian Americans taking up the challenge declared that they viewed the presidential contest as an opportunity to administer a final humiliation to Wilson and plunged energetically into the campaign to elect Warren G. Harding."[129]

At this point, Italian agents in South America joined the campaign. Their motivation was bitter disappointment over the treatment of Italy's interests in the Adriatic at the Versailles Peace Conference. The negative experience of Italian negotiators at the conference of Versailles in regard to future Italian colonial claims was taken personally. Italian politicians had not been treated as representing a major Allied power that had won World War I and could count on its territorial demands being satisfied. Instead, French, British, and U.S. negotiators treated Italians as representatives of a lesser Mediterranean country. In the last week of January 1920, the Italian count Solari reflected on the proceedings in Versailles and told the press,

We must frankly recognize that the Italian colonial program has entirely failed as a result of the Peace Conference. This is an injustice which Italy may correct with a broad program of economic expansion abroad, in close union with the Latin countries of Spain, Portugal, Rumania, and the nations of Central and South America. We trust in the enlightened assistance of our Latin brothers for the development of civilization and the progress and welfare of the Latin people.[130]

Curiously, in Argentina, Japan at the same time encouraged a more independent stance against the Allied powers. Japanese diplomats signaled in September to President Irigoyen that they would support Argentina's claim against Great Britain in the Falklands/Malvinas conflict. And Alberto Pugnalin, Argentina's minister to Japan, was returning to Argentina to lead new joint Argentine–Japanese projects.[131]

Then, in September 1919, as Agent zur Helle reported to Germany in Buenos Aires, regional agent Geukel assumed leadership of Mexican, German, and Japanese espionage networks. Suddenly, Italian secret agents probed Japanese and German efforts as to whether they could join. Italian services wanted to join existing efforts in Argentina.

Baron A. de Marchi had come to Argentina first in connection with Italy's aviation mission in July 1919. He had occasional contact with zur Helle before he crossed the Atlantic. Once back in Rome, de Marchi was asked to use his familiarity with South America to go to Argentina a second time and earn a living selling Italian government bonds. It did not take long for de Marchi to become acquainted with Geukel. He also worked with Agent No. 61, Alfredo Vitale. By early 1920, talks about a the possibility of Italians joining the Japanese–German–Mexican team progressed.[132]

In April 1920, the Italian government apparently instructed de Marchi to join the multinational anti-U.S. campaign. Orders for the Italian network would come from Air Attaché Julio Benigni.

In December 1919, a second Mexican publicity campaign was launched. This time the government of El Salvador took the lead. On December 14, 1919, the government published telegram No. 752 from the Palacio Nacional addressed to U.S. president Wilson. It asked him to define his understanding of the Monroe Doctrine.[133] Two days later, Carranza's Mexican Foreign Ministry joined and pushed the note to Venezuela, hoping to receive backing from Venezuela's Foreign Ministry.

Here, however, Carranza did not receive the desired reaction. Venezuelan leadership refused to be pulled into an open embarrassment of the United States.[134]

In Colombia, according to Mexico's Chapultepec Press from January 15, 1920, opposition groups advanced a resolution into full power that would allow the Colombian government to call for a congress of Spanish American countries. It would be the constituting meeting to initiate a study for a possible constitution for a League of Spanish American Nations:

> The proposed congress will not try to effect offensive alliances against any foreign country, but simply respect for the rights of the weak peoples of Latin America, in a permanent form which will insure the liberty of the peoples associated in the League. It is not known whether our government will take any account of the undertaking of the Congress of

Colombia, since according to official information up to until now, our government has received no invitation in regard to the matter.[135]

The congress was supposed to be convened in Buenos Aires in 1920. The idea was endorsed by Mexico, Chile, Argentina, Colombia, Venezuela, Spain, Paraguay, and perhaps Bolivia, Ecuador, and Italy: "The real purpose of the League is nothing more than a combination against the U.S. which when formed, will look upon Germany and Japan as its natural allies in any trouble between the countries and the U.S."[136] In the meantime in Geneva, Switzerland, on January 16, 1920, the League of Nations resumed its work.[137] Its enemies in Latin America did not wait for the opening session.

In January 1920, a Colombian government delegation headed by Jorge Ancizar traveled to Buenos Aires. Officially they came to discuss a trade increase between Argentina and Colombia. But intelligence information reported that Ancizar functioned only as the official head. The real purpose for the visit was discussion of the League of Latins Initiative by delegation member Guillermo Gutierrez. What happened in detail cannot be confirmed by the available sources. There were discussions with President Irigoyen and also Mexican special agent Jacinto Díaz. Ancizar's brother allegedly was a friend of Díaz. A confirmed meeting with Undersecretary Molinari took place on January 27, 1920.

Carranza's administration backed the initiative. Angel Laborde/Lagarde, also a former acquaintance of von Eckardt, was to travel to Chile and Argentina to advance the League of Latins idea. One source predicted that supporters of the initiative would come from Argentina, Paraguay, Chile, Ecuador, Colombia, San Salvador, Costa Rica, Mexico, and, indirectly, Venezuela, Spain, and Berlin.[138] Also, former Mexican general postmaster Cosmo Hinojoso told an acquaintance on February 17, 1920, that he was traveling to Buenos Aires to further an initiative designed to bring about an alliance of Central America and South America into a Union Latina Americana. This union would be to organize opposition to the Monroe Doctrine. The true leader of this effort remained President Carranza, along with support from the governments of El Salvador and some leaders in Colombia.[139]

On February 3, 1920, the delegation and Ancizar were given a prominent reception at the Ateneo Hispano Americano.[140] Commission head Ancizar gave a raging speech against the Wilson administration and proposed the unification of all Latin American countries. Five days later, another Ateneo meeting convened to raise funds for new leaflets and other propaganda material. Next new propaganda centers were supposed to be opened in Chile and Uruguay. Members were asked to affirm "that all Latin states should adhere to the League of Nations to get away from the Monroe Doctrine and, in addition, should form a League of Latins by which means the Monroe Doctrine would be destroyed."[141]

Finally, on March 18, 1920, the Colombian delegation reciprocated anti-U.S. Argentine hospitality with a banquet at Colombia's legation, located at Calle Maipu 1220. This time the invited guests were Mexico's Jacinto Díaz, a Mr. Blasquez, Mexico's chargé d'affaires to Argentina, and Gustavo Schlottermann, Venezuela's consul general in Buenos Aires. They were joined by the consuls general of San Salvador and Honduras, all of them fervent Latin American nationalists.[142]

Two days later a third Ateneo Hispano Americano event hosted Dr. Leon Suárez and a Chilean individual. A first straw poll predicted that groups from Mexico, Chile, Argentina, Colombia, Venezuela, Spain, Paraguay, possibly Bolivia, Ecuador, and perhaps even Italy would be willing to become Latin League members. El Salvador was expected to win over smaller Central American countries. Supporters were expected to devote much of 1921 to building an initial organization.[143] One intercepted telegram from April 20, 1920, provides a rare glimpse into who was cooperating and what issues were being discussed:

Respectable Friend: After my interview with DI [Jacinto Díaz] in the presence of Schlottman [Gustavo Schlottermann] I ought to declare to you that the file which was embarked in Aguila [U.S.], has arrived sound and safe in the hands of the designators, who will in turn in the next assembly of the C of CO [Chamber of Commerce–Ateneo Hispano Americano] make public all the details with respect to S Salv [San Salvador] uniting to the set those items which were sent to Ruiz [Gustav A. Ruiz]. Obliging to make the act in the presence of D.M olm next on behalf of LM GA and Suzana [Lieut. Susana] on behalf of Chile, for authority to assemble all the details of the BL LA [Bloc Latin Americano–League of Latins]. I await photos ordered in the course of this week as also information from Gavuzzi [Pedro Boselli] and Hanibal on behalf of L Italm [Liga Italiano–Latin League], Boselli [Piedro Boselli] embarks the wr R [SS., RE Vittorio Italian] the 24 Shall transfer himself to Berlin to procure purchase advised by H [Hall].

… Without Radio FHN, KA [Kinta Arai] asked me explanation regarding actual state of propaganda and expenses effected in special commission at the last minute before leaving from M del P [Mar del Plata], from where I await his return. One thousand pesos Banco A [Banco Aleman Transatlantico] dated 19th, Lima, signed Aldao.[144]

Finally, German conspirators were instructed of Berlin's preferences. In Brazil, zur Helle arrived on February 20, 1920, with his instructions from Germany. His ship docked in Brazil but was quarantined, preventing him from leaving. And yet he was able to communicate instructions to the network in Brazil. Local Brazilian police were happy to work as couriers and take directions to Agent Ochoa.

In Berlin, the plan for the Latin bloc had been endorsed. To advance its cause in Rio four propagandists would distribute anti–League of Nations

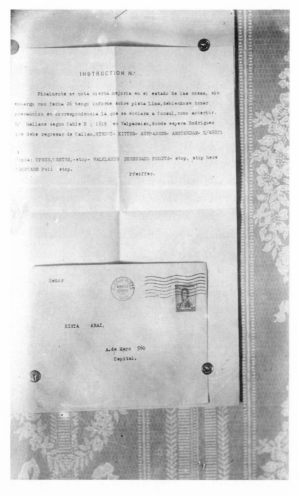

29. Recently discovered letters provide the first proof of German–Japanese intelligence cooperation in South America by 1919 (RG 45, National Archives of the United States, Washington, D.C.).

propaganda. In Lima and Callao, Peru, one agent each was to be positioned. In Valparaiso, two men would work, and four individuals would establish themselves in Santiago. Nevertheless, Buenos Aires would remain the headquarters of this anti-U.S. effort. Six agents would work on its behalf. All national cells would stay in regular contact with the help of two traveling agents. Funding for the Latin League support project came from combined German, Japanese, and Mexican funds. Zur Helle arrived with these instructions in Buenos Aires on March 2, 1920.[145]

First the Germans learned the extent of recently established Italian support. In Buenos Aires, the Italians had opened a propaganda office called Appia at Calle Cordoba 830. Its director was Innocenzo Cappa, an Italian lawyer and ex-member of Parliament who had been involved in the sale of Italian loans inside Argentina.

De Marchi and Cappa propagandized lower- and middle-class Italian immigrants who, already throughout the entire Argentine Republic, had been propagandized during World War I. Another important agent was Pietro Gavuzzi, the proprietor of the Plaza Hotel, Argentina's largest hotel. German espionage coordinator Geukel hired an Italian porter named Hanibal for 100 pesos per month. A third Italian agent was Austrian engineer J. Markovich, who also worked for the Germans.[146] De Marchi was helped by a fourth collaborator, J. Bianci, the director of the social review *Nosotros*. And there were two Italian agents who traveled into Argentina's provinces and neighboring countries. These men were Pascual Flanta and Pietro Boselli.

Even monarchic Spain now appeared more interested in revolutionary Mexico, as long as it drove Latin America away from the United States. On March 3, 1920, the marquis de Gonzalez became the new Spanish diplomat to revolutionary Mexico. He remarked that Spain could again be the force behind which all Latin American countries could unite in the future.[147] More importantly, King Alfonso XIII's son, Infante Don Fernando, was scheduled to visit South America to participate in the commemoration of the four hundredth anniversary of the discovery of the Strait of Magellan. There were rumors that eventually the king himself would make the first official visit of a Spanish king to Latin America.[148] Elite Spaniards explored increasing a Spanish presence in the rest of Spanish America as well.

Overnight, the most enthusiastic actor in the anti-U.S. alliance, Venustiano Carranza, was ripped off the stage of history. In April 1920, he was assassinated in response to imposing a hand-selected presidential successor. The multinational cooperation against the United States had experienced a strong jolt. And yet neither the network nor the cooperation collapsed.

Coincidentally, Lead Agent Kinta Arai had called for a major critical meeting in Buenos Aires on April 19, 1920. By then news about Carranza's assassination and renewed civil war in Mexico reached Buenos Aires. Present at the Japanese legation in Buenos Aires were Kinta Arai, Mexican head agent Jacinto Díaz, and the Japanese agents Wakabayashi and Matayoshi. Aria proposed to organize cooperation in a more systematic way and to accept an outlined but unknown Japanese plan.[149] The next day German net leader von Geukel learned about the meeting's results and reported them to Lead Agent zur Helle. Then, as

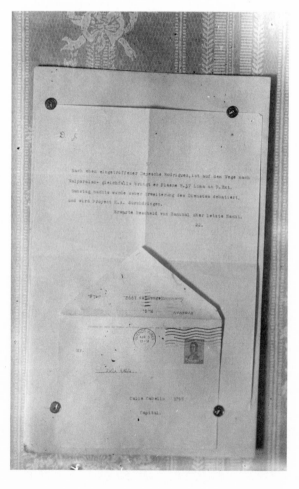

30. An agent's note from the Japanese–German–Mexican–Italian–Argentine–Spanish intelligence network aimed against the United States (RG 45, National Archives of the United States, Washington, D.C.).

Carranza's involvement stopped overnight, Japanese dominance and leadership became a simple, almost natural fact.

Thereafter, von Geukel worked as lead espionage coordinator. He wrote circular letters to agents in the field and reported to Kinta Arai every Saturday afternoon for tea in his residence at the Calle Jose Hernandez. The network's growth was not limited to the Argentine capital.

The next significant change occurred as domestic turmoil began to rearrange the foreign intelligence priorities of the Italian state. Also in April, the Italians informed Mexican general Aguilar that the previously negotiated order of weapons for Mexico needed to be shipped to another country first. Any direct Italian–Mexican delivery was no longer appropriate. He was asked to immediately dispatch a man of confidence from Spain to Rome to make a down payment, otherwise Mexico's order would be endangered.[150]

The Ansaldo company was itself coming under economic pressure due to the depression in international arms business after Versailles. Aguilar's supporter Perrone lost the leadership position in the company, and Mexico, therefore, lost its key contact. Next the Italian state broke the company into four independent units, and talks about becoming Mexico's pivotal supplier of armament technology faded. Then Mussolini came into office, and the Ansaldo company received some state funding to avoid complete collapse, but the Mexico business no longer had priority. The weak Italian state no longer had the ability to work on behalf of a League of Latins. As Italy's domestic crisis consumed more and more attention, Italian participation in the anti-U.S. net in the Río de la Plata region disappeared.[151] By October the net worked without Italy's agents or Carranza, though still with select Mexican agents.

Japan pushed on. In Mexico City, employees of the Japanese legation continued regardless of whether Carranza was dead or alive. Right away they approached his successor, Interim President de la Huerta. If we believe his biographer Guzmán, in the second half of 1920 the secretary of the embassy visited de la Huerta and explored the new possibilities of closer cooperation. The secretary insinuated Tokyo's desire to move again toward some kind of Japanese–Mexican agreement that, in essence, would be an alliance.[152]

At that point in time de la Huerta did not feel comfortable entering into such an agreement. He was only a temporary caretaker of the National Palace. Instead, he asked to wait until Álvaro Obregón was president. Once he had moved into the National Palace, Obregón continued much of what Carranza had inaugurated.

One Mexican general stated that President Obregón employed Japanese individuals in his intelligence service. However, unlike Carranza, Obregón did not employ them against targets in the United States.[153] But in Central America little change was registered in comparison to the time when Carranza was alive. Japan experienced a more dramatic breakthrough in Chile.

There Japanese navy requests for military cooperation fell increasingly on fruitful ground. A newly discovered source suggests that Chile's and Japan's navies reached an understanding that would allow Japan to use Chilean territory during a war against the United States. The Chilean naval attaché made the following sensational revelation to the head of the German navy in the mid-1920s: He admitted,

> The Japanese are our friends. In the last years the United States have made serious efforts to strengthen their influence in the other American nations and to bring them more and more into dependence to the United States.
>
> In Japan this has not gone unnoticed and has led to a certain understanding between Japan and Chile in the military sector. In Chile, nobody doubts that, over short or long, a military confrontation between Japan and the U.S. will take place. One expects that, in case of such a war, the Japanese fleet will need bases, not only in Central America, but also in South America. According to the words of the attaché there seems to exist firm agreements between the navies of both countries. A Chilean participation on the Japanese side does not seem to be intended. However, Chilean support will consist of the creation of one or several Japanese fleet bases in the channels of the Chilean coast, which are particularly appropriate for this. Quietly, they will be tolerated.[154]

Just as the Japanese government had entered into talks about an alliance with Mexico under General Carranza, it also had talked to this South American navy and established a firm agreement. Once again, Japanese work focused on making a sustained war against the United States possible.

By coincidence, at a different location in Washington, D.C., agents of the U.S. Office of Naval Intelligence discovered that factions of the Argentinean government sat still while Buenos Aires was evolving into the home of a Japanese, German, and Mexican conspiracy to torpedo greater Latin American participation in the League of Nations. Even more perplexing, Undersecretary of Foreign Relations Molinari, the same man who had so amiably presented a pro-U.S. position previously to the U.S. ambassador, also communicated with the enemies of Wilson. He, too, did nothing to stop their anti-U.S. activities. Even more astounding, the group focused on contributing to the electoral defeat of the Democratic Party during the upcoming 1920 U.S. presidential election.

In 1919, in Mexico, Lead Naval Agent Jahnke had received orders to stop subversive warfare. In Europe, the Tenerife branch of the naval supply intelligence service was ordered to shut down on March 31, 1920.[155] It looked as though there was no German intelligence service operating in the Western Hemisphere after 1919.

However, in Berlin a general meeting was held on October 14, 1920, to discuss the future of the supply intelligence service.[156] It is probably no coincidence that key agents Jahnke and zur Helle were in Berlin during that period.[157] At first in the deliberations, members at the meeting decided to move toward "wrapping up and to finish business affairs." And yet administrative work remained to be accomplished. For example, in New York, U.S. agents of the Bureau of Intelligence had missed many critical documents when they had arrested fourteen suspected German agents on April 8, 1917. Earlier, Military Attaché von Papen and Naval Attaché Boy-Ed had left the North American continent. Thereafter, Dr. Reimer, a naval staff paymaster, had kept administrative functions alive. Many important documents were not burned but, in fact, hidden in plain sight. A Mr. Gauerke rented an innocuous storage space in a warehouse in Brooklyn, New York. Gauerke was helped by A. E. Piorkowski as an informal contributor.[158] One source identified him as in charge of all German military reservists in the United States.[159] One of the men survived by holding down a job with the Guardian Life Insurance Company of New York.

In 1920, former naval attaché Boy-Ed reminded the men in Berlin that significant amounts of dollars remained to be recovered in New York. He estimated that several hundred thousand dollars could be collected and put to new use inside Germany.[160] Other items in storage were a wooden closet and a one-handle suitcase. Boy-Ed also reminded planners to get in touch with Robert Capelle, the head of the supply intelligence service on the U.S. West Coast.[161] Capelle had lived in Mill Valley, Marin County, at Coronet Avenue. He, however, is reported to have burned the war diary of his section.

From Chile, too, news reached Berlin that top secret documents from the ships *Dresden* and *Seeadler* remained hidden but in good shape. But the men in Berlin sat tight and waited until March 1922. Then a German-owned ship, whose cabin space could be 100 percent controlled, transported Admiral Staff Secretary Goetterman to South America to secretly retrieve the hot cargo and carry it back personally to Hamburg. He was also ordered to thank Reginald Westendorp, whose ethnic German company Foelsch had contributed so much to the survival of the incriminating material. In Callao, Mr. Krause, of the Kosmos Shipping

Agency Branch, had done Germany the same favor. There was no need to send somebody to Rio de Janeiro. Hans Stoltz, of the Stoltz Company, reportedly burned the incriminating records of the supply service in this Brazilian city.[162] In Havana, Cuba, the Uppman Company and a Mr. Tiedemann had done their utmost so that Allied investigators would never find incriminating records.[163]

However, the most interesting request came out of Buenos Aires. Former naval attaché Moeller still lived in Buenos Aires, at Calle Caseros 470. He had carefully compiled a list of individuals who had made a significant contribution to the fight against the Allies. Now, he wanted the navy leaders of the Weimar Republic to reward his fellow agents. His petition offers a first impression of the size and composition of his network during World War I. Moeller suggested eighty-eight individuals for decoration. Thirteen of them had been telegraph operators on land and on German ships. Seventy-five individuals had supported the operations in other ways.[164]

By then the new operation guided by Jahnke and Kinta Arai had begun. In the naval spy business there was never a 1919 armistice, despite the general order to cease actions.

At its core stood the idea that the secret and successful manipulation of the U.S. presidential election ending in a Republican victory promised to collapse the still very reluctant international support for the controversial League of Nations. Germans could not imagine that the league would function once Republicans refused full U.S. membership.[165] Even better, a league collapse would further burden the already strained unity between Great Britain and France. An end of Allied unity in 1921 would provide German navy and military leaders with a weak Great Britain and more regional political freedom, plus resources to resume the struggle for world power without having to defeat the Versailles Peace Treaty first. Officially the politicians of the Weimar Republic denied any such intent. Rightly so, because the vast majority of them were not privy to the secret machinations of surviving army and navy factions in Berlin. There existed several rival policies in the Weimar Republic in the early 1920s.

12   Argentina Imagines Arming Itself in the Midst of More Japanese Spying

---

Suddenly, Argentina's foreign minister contributed his share to weaken the League of Nations. Perhaps only President Irigoyen and his foreign minister were responsible for a 180-degree turn compared to before the summer of 1920. Regardless, Argentine foreign policy in the League of Nations suddenly dovetailed with the secret anti-U.S. work unfolding behind the scenes.

As soon as Argentina had attained membership in the League of Nations, Argentine Foreign Minister Pueyrredón abandoned the pro-U.S. stance his undersecretary had promised emphatically only months before. Instead of working within the emerging institutional parameters set by France, Great Britain, and the United States, Pueyrredón invoked Argentina's right to make alternative proposals. He demanded a categorical restructuring of the league. If other countries backed his policy, then the League of Nations structure, as it had been set up by the Allies, would be destroyed by the revolt of one Argentine diplomat. A report from Buenos Aires explained Argentina's new strategy "to adhere to the League of Nations they can utilize this as an open means of drawing away from the U.S. and the Monroe Doctrine. In official government circles in B.A. it is talked of openly, and it is stated that, now, that Argentina is a member of the League of Nations this country is free to do as the officials think best without any regard to the U.S."[1]

Thus, on October 8, 1920, Argentina's diplomatic delegation, headed by Foreign Minister Pueyrredón, left Buenos Aires on board the British ship *Avon*. In addition to the Argentinean delegation, representatives from Bolivia, Brazil, Chile, Colombia, Cuba, Guatemala, Haiti, Nicaragua, Panama, Paraguay, Peru,

Uruguay, Venezuela, and El Salvador started the journey to the first session of the league in Geneva, Switzerland.[2]

In the Swiss city, on November 17, 1920, Pueyrredón presented his dramatic call for an immediate, radical reorganization of the world body. First, he demanded an end to any political discrimination regarding who could join the league. It should be neither a "League of Interests" nor a "League of Winners" of World War I. Instead, all international countries should be eligible for membership. In other words, already in 1920, the defeated Germany should no longer be excluded from membership.

Second, Pueyrredón demanded the admission of revolutionary governments, such as Mexico, even though its Obregón administration had not been politically recognized by the international community.[3] The same demand also applied to revolutionary Russia.

Third, election to the League Council should take place by public, democratic vote, not by private agreement among World War I winners. This demand could help Alfonso XIII's Spain to become a permanent member of the council, if it was able to secure enough supportive Spanish American votes. A Spanish presence on the council was expected to counterbalance the United States' preferential treatment of Brazil in the league.[4]

Additional Argentine proposals demanded the creation of an international court of justice and a permanent organization of economic cooperation. On November 20, 1920, Pueyrredón insisted on complete acceptance of these drastic reforms, before the league could discuss other agenda items. Formerly neutral Argentina had confronted the Allied powers from inside the league. This move was either daring, antagonistic, or essentially Argentinean.

In the end, the Argentine push for dramatic change was elegantly deflected. In public session Foreign Minister Pueyrredón's proposals failed to win the required votes and were tabled for the next year. Five days later, the angry diplomat withdrew his delegation from Geneva and returned with indignation to Buenos Aires. Interestingly, Pueyrredón only suspended Argentina's presence in Geneva; Argentina was not thinking about resigning from the international body. The Buenos Aires government was keeping open the option to return to Europe with more diplomatic challenges to the global policies of the United States and European powers.

Right away Argentina's armed forces resumed their institutional growth and modernization agendas. Their push for new weapons took place regardless of alternative policies demanded by popular movements or diplomats who favored disarmament through League of Nations policies. To make matters more complex, other Latin American military purchases were encouraged by British, French, U.S., Spanish, and German arms manufacturers, while their diplomats urged disarmament. Latin American military leaders could not imagine disarming and refused to let go of their preference for an armed peace policy.

Military planners in Buenos Aires, Santiago, Rio de Janeiro, Lima, and La Paz had watched with incredulity how the governments of France, Great Britain, and the United States reconstructed European military affairs in the aftermath of World War I. Not for a second did they believe that the collapse of imperial Russia, Germany, and the Ottoman Empire and the arms limitations imposed upon Germans by the Treaty of Versailles should be followed by disarmament in Latin America. To the contrary, World War I had given birth to many new military strategies and technologies. The only pertinent question to be asked by Argentine generals should be how fast their armies could absorb the appropriate lessons and purchase the necessary hardware. Already in Mexico, new trench warfare strategy and the machine gun had helped the nationalist Venustiano Carranza to defeat the regional, populist revolutionary Pancho Villa. Would the lessons of World War I also change warfare in South America? And if so, what would that mean for ethnic immigrants living in such a changing environment?

World War I had merely interrupted decades-old cycles of South American arms modernization.[5] Most importantly, the stop of the supply of arms during the war had taught generals how much they continued to depend on European and U.S. arms manufacturers. For example, in the midst of global war chaos, Argentine generals were humiliated.

In April 1917, they faced an unbearable impotence when Argentina lacked the arms to make war. That month, President Irigoyen backed his generals and mobilized twenty thousand men. They were stationed at the Río de la Plata, opposite two hundred thousand recently mobilized Brazilian troops. As Irigoyen's soldiers reached Argentina's border they found themselves without a reliable supply of guns and ammunition to engage the Brazilians.

Here was a grotesque situation. In the midst of World War I, the Argentinean army could mobilize a myriad of soldiers, but these divisions could not sustain a single, long-term battle against Brazilian troops. Painfully, Argentineans were reminded that their capacity to wage war depended, to an intolerable degree, on suppliers from Europe, the United States, and imperial Japan. The lesson was that European military suppliers were blatantly slighting South American military needs.

Argentinean admirals experienced a similar embarrassment. In August 1918, news reached the United States that the Argentine navy was making new efforts to add battleships to its fleet. The goal was to expand Argentina's power, "which a large and efficient navy connotes and which it alone can guarantee."[6]

In military handbooks, charts listed huge Argentinean warships moored in Río de la Plata ports. A visit to the docks, however, revealed that key vessels were unable to join any battle. For example, the imposing dreadnought *Rivadivia* was badly pitted with rust. One of its propellers was twisted; it was hardly navigable. Even though the *Rivadivia* looked like an imposing battleship above the waterline, beneath it, it was nothing but a floating bowl of steel. It projected only shame, rather than Argentine might in the South Atlantic.[7] The weak state of Argentina's navy appeared in an even worse light when compared to developments in Brazil and Chile.

In Brazil, military attachés counted two dreadnought battleships, two cruisers, three light cruisers, destroyers, submarines, and additional auxiliary vessels.[8] The Brazilian naval attaché in Tokyo was the only Latin American representative that the Japanese navy allowed to inspect a German submarine that had arrived in Japan as part of war reparations.

Finally, German Ambassador to Argentina Count Luxburg's assertion that imperial Germany was desiring to take over southern Brazil during or after World War I had deeply frightened Rio's and São Paulo's elites. The possibility that Argentina might enlist German submarines or military help against Brazil or Uruguay convinced Brazilians to invite a permanent U.S. naval mission to Rio de Janeiro. If war were to be launched from Argentinean soil, they would also attack U.S. sailors and marines. Furthermore, a U.S. naval presence promised privileged access to U.S. weapons. As soon as World War I ended, Brazil invited a French military mission to modernize its armed forces. And France also promised to dispatch an air mission.

On the other side of the Andes, Chile owned five submarines. Four torpedo ships were scheduled for construction in 1920.

In comparison, Argentina owned no submarines at all. Not surprisingly, military and navy circles insisted on rapid force modernization. They were determined to exert painful pressure onto members of Argentina's Congress to finance a submarine wing and an air force. Already during World War I, generals had been powerful enough to convince President Irigoyen to keep the country neutral, even if that meant defying equally strong countervailing pressures in favor of entering the war on the side of the Allied powers presented by British company representatives and U.S. diplomats.

31. U.S. and British politicians attempted to force disarmament initiatives onto South American countries. The Argentine, Brazilian, and Chilean militaries evaded such initiatives (Library of Congress, Washington, D.C.).

Now, in 1920, neither U.S. president Wilson's appeal in Versailles to end all wars once and forever nor more moderate British and French arms limitation proposals could weaken the army's determination to modernize. Generals and admirals insisted that Argentina needed to have the option to win militarily against the forces of Brazil, Bolivia, Peru, Chile, or Paraguay. Now that there was peace in Europe, Argentines needed to hurry with military modernization.

Also for that purpose, military officers had founded the Logia General San Martin, a secret lodge. It enlisted three hundred men or one-fifth of all officers. The organization's demands were complex. They encompassed better political training and improved funding but also force modernization according to World War I lessons. Worst of all for the lodge members, disarmament was expected to mean the elimination of their institution of the armed forces, and that must never be allowed to happen.

Argentine armament purchases and troop retraining would have to take place in a most quixotic domestic policy environment. A single coherent, predictable Argentine policy that took the United States and Europe into equal consideration did not exist. Rather, there were different individuals and domestic groups pursuing their own institutional interests as they saw fit. This environment made the Argentine political arena unusually attractive for foreigners who might want to manipulate institutional rivalries or to encourage regional boundary tensions. Military modernization offered itself ideally for foreign power plays and covert manipulations. Peace was only a few months old, and its future was uncertain; the League of Nations met as an unprecedented experiment, and a future U.S.–Japanese war in the Pacific could not be ruled out.

The effort to create an Argentine military air force defies any description in simple, analytical terms. It was a blend of three processes. First, it was connected to the development of a general, civilian domestic market for the airplane, a technology many Argentineans were genuinely thrilled about. Second, it was an institutional initiative led by a few men with close ties to the military. These men blended military modernization with family and personal business profit. The navy leadership made its own distinct push for a small naval air force. Third, it was a surprising lesson in Allied airplane rivalry, revealing that a victory in World War I did not translate automatically into commercial victory during peace. Rather, airplane markets were developed and occupied because of the right fit between airplane product and user needs, but not military victory. It never dawned on French and British politicians that this reality might open the door for German competition, regardless of the prohibitions of Versailles.

The task of modernizing Argentina's military was executed in a most disturbed international arms market. There existed uncertainty about the future of German and Austrian-Hungarian armament needs. In Europe's east, smaller regional wars raged on, demanding supplies, and the superficial harmony of the British–Japanese naval alliance was to expire in two years. A 1922 Washington Naval Disarmament Conference and the elimination of an immediate Japanese–U.S. war threat had not yet even been conceived.

From the perspective of arms manufacturers, the unfamiliar "environment of peace" threatened drastically reduced sales and shrinking profits. Finally, an unprecedented amount of surplus weapons was beginning to pile up in European warehouses, depressing prices further.

In the midst of this highly unstable environment Argentina had to identify new weapon systems, select reliable manufacturers, and consider how to integrate new weapons into its distinct South American strategic context. The weapon systems Argentina should buy first were easily identified. The navy and army needed submarines and airplanes. Lower on the priority scale ranked trucks, chemical warfare units, and, if at all, tanks. These big purchases needed to be backed by the expansion of a small arms industry until it could spit out a reliable and sufficient amount of machine guns, cartridges, and black powder for the entire duration of one war. But before a single Argentine submarine could surface in the Río de la Plata, military planners had to address two important concerns.

The first was funding. In 1919, the Irigoyen government could not rely on a national budgeting process that would make long-term financing a predictable fact. In Argentina's Congress rival political factions often deadlocked over budget issues. In the presidential Casa Rosada, President Irigoyen approved and disapproved purchases based on personal and political likings. This uncoordinated behavior among policy elites promised only a weak base for building a credible Argentine threat posture.

The second concern was Brazil and its employment of French and U.S. military advisers. U.S. naval attachés and French military generals had begun to teach World War I lessons to Brazil and to Peru. Now, Argentineans could not possibly invite French and U.S. trainers and remain certain that their new mobilization plans would remain a secret in Paris, Annapolis, Lima, or Rio de Janeiro. Traditionally, the Argentinean military had solved this problem by openly employing German advisers. But the Treaty of Versailles was about to prohibit the hiring of Prussian military specialists by South American militaries. From which foreign war academy should Argentina hire its military modernizers? Nobody in Argentina had an easy answer to these two dilemmas.

The presence of submarines in Chilean and Brazilian ports made the creation of an Argentine submarine arm the most obvious naval purchase priority. In theory, Argentina could place orders for Holland-class submarines in the United States. In reality, the Japanese–U.S. naval competition in the Pacific was progressing, and it was uncertain whether U.S. companies could make Argentinean orders an immediate priority. In the past an alternative had been German submarine construction companies. But British, French, and U.S. attachés in Paris did everything possible to shut down, once and forever, any German capacity to build submarines. That left British Vickers subs and French and Dutch naval yards that manufactured ships according to foreign blueprints. Different factions inside Argentina's navy preferred different suppliers.

From Buenos Aires inquiries went to the U.S. Electric Boat Company. In Europe, the naval attaché at the Argentine embassy in London explored British offers and, more secretly, German promises to manufacture submarines, somehow in the near future, in shipyards in neutral countries.[9] While Argentine talks with Vickers and U.S. companies remain to be analyzed, new sources shed a first light on Argentine–German negotiations.

In Germany, submarine construction was connected to the Krupp Co. and to naval yards owned by Hugo Stinnes, Germany's Carnegie. In 1919, Stinnes had stated that he would be eager to help the disarming German navy to preserve a secret, small national capacity to construct submarines inside Germany.[10] It was public knowledge that he brokered German surplus naval ships. And he had just hired the Argentine Emilio Kinkelin, who, during the war, had worked as a propagandist in Stockholm, Sweden. Occasionally he had provided Germany with intelligence, happily abusing the privileges that Scandinavian neutrality had offered him. After the war, Stinnes hired Kinkelin first for his offices in Hamburg and Berlin. But then Kinkelin was reassigned to Copenhagen, Denmark, to help with Stinnes's future South American business expansion. Stinnes was a megalomaniac businessman and an industrial handmaiden to the emerging German Weimar Republic, constantly dissolving the boundaries among regular business, private speculation, and government work. Both Stinnes and Kinkelin were eager to circumvent the Treaty of Versailles from day one.

Hugo Stinnes, according to German Ambassador Pauli, was the one who introduced curious Argentine naval planners to German submarine builders. Desperate for employment possibilities, the leader of them was Captain Bartenbach.

During the war, Bartenbach had worked on submarine *U I*, accompanied by his second officer, Ulrich Blum. In 1918, he was transferred to land and led the submarine industry as one of Germany's most important submarine engineers. As the German monarchy collapsed, the submarine business faced uncompromising Allied orders to dismantle itself entirely.

In June 1919, Ulrich Blum had suggested they open a submarine construction office in Kiel, Germany, at Krupp's Germania naval yard. The office would collect the most current submarine technical knowledge, conduct new research, and employ engineers. Their insights producing new blueprints should be sold to neutral navies, helping them to acquire their own submarine fleets, even if the Allied powers opposed this strategy. The navies of Scandinavia, the Netherlands, Spain, and Japan were targeted as initial customers. But this proposal remained just an idea. In November 1919, Bartenbach retired from active duty and, for unknown reasons, relocated to Costa Rica.[11] He was now just another member of a group of former German naval officers, expropriated naval yard owners, and German politicians burning to throw off increasing Allied disarmament restrictions. But without any political strength to resist, all of them remained helpless. They watched powerlessly as the remnants of the imperial Germany navy were being sold off.

Captain Bartenbach, in late 1920, was in contact with a pro-German faction inside Argentina's navy. At the end of the year, this faction was gaining the upper hand and moved to secretly enlist Germans to design a new Argentine submarine wing. Captain Bartenbach presented himself as a natural leader of a submarine planning team consisting of Baurat Schuerer and a Mr. Krankenhagen, as well as chief engineer Heinrich Pagenberg.[12] By the end of 1920, these men relocated to Buenos Aires. The German ambassador described their first task: "A first goal of this small private navy mission was the introduction of a submarine weapon in Argentina. It was of greatest importance for the defense of the entry of the Río de la Plata. A submarine arm did not yet exist."[13] However, the Germans did not limit themselves to shipbuilding. They also served as a secret naval mission. Again, the German ambassador explained: "In addition, these representatives of our former naval might appeared, very discretely as civilian people, and developed, in writing, advice and plans for the strengthening and improvement of Argentina's defensive capacity on the oceans."[14] The Argentine navy had solved the dilemma of foreign technical naval expertise by hiring an illegal secret German naval mission.

In 1921, the army and navy finally proved strong enough to pressure the Argentine Congress to consider the finance of military modernization. National Deputy Albarracin published statistics that the army was lacking 2,275 cannons, 475,778 rifles, 586,346 carbines, 1,234 machine guns, and a large amount of artillery ammunition.[15] In addition, he introduced a bill financing the establishment of industries for the production of armament and war materials. German military expert Faupel identified the navy's budget as most promising. Shortly thereafter, in June 1921, the Argentine navy invited bids for submarines. A U.S. source learned about plans for six submarines. To the public, the navy's plans looked like a natural fit for boats of U.S. 509 Holland class, built by the U.S. Electric Boat Company.

To his dismay, the U.S. military attaché discovered that the bidding process did not unfold as easily as expected. President Irigoyen suddenly and inexplicably suspended negotiations with U.S. manufacturers. All of a sudden, an ex-German navy captain, Dietrich Niebuhr, appeared in Buenos Aires. He used the identity of a businessman as a cover to present an alternative submarine plan. Niebuhr promised Irigoyen the delivery of German submarine parts, manufactured in Sweden, to a naval yard somewhere in the Río de la Plata region.

There, he promised, they would be assembled into finished submarines. German vehicles, Niebuhr insisted, would be of better quality and better price and come with unmatched technological breakthroughs, among them the elimination of accumulators. Niebuhr urged Irigoyen to refrain from placing orders with the U.S. Electric Boat Co. and to explore his European offer in earnest. The president followed the German's advice and sent two officers to Sweden to investigate a yet-to-be-identified manufacturing site.

By fall 1921, the U.S. military attaché was protesting against this Argentine tactic, pointing at serious violations of the Versailles Treaty. But it made no difference. Irigoyen deflected the issue, arguing that he was suspending the search to await the outcome of the now scheduled Washington Naval Conference.[16] In reality, Argentineans never suspended German–Argentinean explorations.

Quietly Argentine–German secret talks progressed. In December 1921, Captain Bartenbach traveled with two Argentine officers to the Netherlands to investigate whether German technicians, working out of a camouflaged submarine development office in the Netherlands, could design the Argentine boats.[17] Once in The Hague they contacted Bartenbach's old friend Blum and engineer Techel.

On January 4, 1922, the U.S. navy attaché complained once again about these German violations, but they continued. Even better for Argentina, the Washington Naval Conference concluded in January 1922 without imposing any limit at all on submarines. Now Argentineans could resume their world explorations without affronting any new U.S. submarine disarmament policy. Bartenbach remained in the Netherlands until March 1922 and negotiated preliminary agreements with engineers Buschfeld and Stahl. By then everything was ready for a signature on the contract.[18]

While the submarine project moved along, a second Argentinean–Stinnes project surfaced. This time it involved a Hugo Stinnes company directly.

Argentina's minister of the navy wanted to buy amphibious airplanes for a naval air station at Bahía Blanca. Already in January 1921, a naval air station project existed in the planning phase. By September, airline manufacturers and Stinnes representatives discussed the Bahía Blanca station.[19] An Argentine signature would seal the deal, and this step would dovetail with important administrative decisions inside the Weimar Republic.

The Argentines could not know that secret German rearmament plans had moved to a more sophisticated level. Already on June 10, 1921, Otto Wiedenfeldt, a Krupp director, had promised German minister of finance Joseph Wirth that his company would guarantee until 1931 the survival of the know-how of German armament technology. Both men knew that 95,000,000 reichsmarks had been transferred to the Netherlands by the Bank of Mendelsohn and Co. Only 5,000,000 marks remained inside Germany.[20]

In early 1922, a meeting had taken place where the German navy leadership and Krupp representatives had explored the possible resurrection of a German submarine arm. A seed had been planted, and two weeks later, on March 21, 1922, Director Buschfeld outlined in a draft to the Vulkanwerft a possible cooperation agreement.

In the second week of April 1922, Krupp's Germaniawerft joined and agreed to combine its submarine operations with those of Weser and Vulkan naval yards.[21] Such a cooperative submarine design venture promised to consolidate all technical German U-boat experience, as well as to develop projects for its commercial exploitation. Captain Schuessler wanted "to keep together an efficient German submarine design office and by practical work for foreign nations keep it in continued practice and on top of technical development for the preservation and further development of German submarine U-boats. At least they could keep the technology alive."[22] Such an office would find immediate employment building six Argentine submarines.

Argentine–German talks, in the meantime, reached a new surprising impasse.[23] Every time the draft contract for six submarines was presented for signature, the signing was postponed. The only reasonable explanation that surfaced was that "Irigoyen disliked all costs related to armament."[24] The pro-German faction inside the navy was not strong enough to close the deal. All the group could do was preserve the relationship with their main supporter, Captain M. S. Fliess. They awarded him the medal of the Red Cross and began to hope that the next Argentine president would not only appear pro-German but also act pro-German. The secret German group was to expire in summer 1923, and so far not one submarine had been ordered.

Little by little, German planners realized that Argentineans would continue to take their time. It only made sense to shift their submarine efforts toward secret cooperation with revolutionary Russia and imperial Japan.

In the midst of these Argentine frustrations Stinnes's business with outfitting the Argentine navy with smaller boats came through. In February 1922, Argentineans bought a floating dock. It left Emden, Germany, in June 1922 and was expected to arrive on the River Plate in the early part of September.[25] Then Stinnes sold minesweepers *M79* and *M80* for 1,650,000 RM. *M79* was renamed *Melitta*, and *M80* became *Margot*. Thereafter they were deployed as mine hunters *M6* and *M7* against potential Brazilian or Chilean mine-laying submarines. Also in June, the Argentine cabinet authorized the purchase of eighteen auxiliary dispatch boats and eight smaller 185-ton ships for river use. Additional purchases were made for hydrographic services, lighthouses, and salvage vessels. Miraculously, each time the Hugo Stinnes Co. submitted the most attractive offer, and it received the bid.[26]

Argentine rearmament developed in unexpected ways. The history of Argentina as an intelligence territory followed in these footsteps.

Carranza's assassination, the political implosion of liberal Italy, and Argentina's diplomatic defeat in Geneva did not slow down the expansion of Japan's intelligence network in South America. After establishing Buenos Aires and Mexico as secure, permanent posts, Japan strengthened its intelligence operation in Panama. During peace the country was to serve as a critical relay point between Mexico and Argentina. Here Japan's agents worked closely with Chilean and Mexican intelligence supporters.

Panama mattered for the processing and distribution of intelligence. A secret mail service carried information by ship between Valparaiso, Chile; Panama; New York City; and Japanese ports. For example, from Valparaiso, Chilean steamers and boats of the Japanese Mitsui company transported mail northward until it reached Cristobal, Panama. There it was handed to the Chilean agent Puelma, who carried it safely into the Chilean consulate. A second mail carrier was the Mexican J. Rodriguez, who had worked before in Buenos Aires for the Kinta Aria group and Chilean military intelligence in South America.[27] Once inside the Chilean consulate, mail of special importance was translated into Japanese. Thereafter it was carried back to a ship and traveled to Mexico, San Francisco, or New York.

Panamanian, Mexican, and Japanese agents made a point of working together closely. An informant inside Panama's Japanese consulate admitted that Mexican president Obregón was employing Japanese individuals as agents.[28] Furthermore, Mexican general Kosterlitzky suggested that World War I operational practices were continuing in early 1921, although financed only with greatly diminished Mexican resources. German agents were no longer operating inside the United States, but agents with other nationalities continued to spy north of the Rio Grande.[29]

In the United States, cells worked, as a rule, through operatives that were recruited from the ranks of the International Workers of the World and other radical labor organizations.[30] During World War I their general objective had been sabotage of railroads and ocean steamships. Extensive plans for sabotage in ports along the U.S. Atlantic coast and its immediate hinterland continued to exist. These plans were understood as merely being postponed because of the November 1918 armistice.[31] As late as 1921 Kosterlitzky thought that the more ambitious plans could still be executed, if necessity should arise and opportunity permitted.

The head of the Panama organization was a native of Nakaidzumi, Iwata-Gun, Shizuoka-Ken, Japan. He had graduated in 1903 as a civil engineer from Tokyo Imperial University. Thereafter he had relocated to the United States, where his father, Foru Awoyama, and his brother, Koichi Awoyama, were living in Bellevue, Washington. After World War I he named Kisaku Ichikawa in an employment application as his closest relative. In August 1921, the same Kisaku Ichikawa was appointed consul of Japan to Panama, replacing Mitsuo Hamaguchi, a man who had not been very successful in espionage matters. Ichikawa brought his cousin Akira Awoyama along to Panama and appointed him head of the anti-U.S. secret organization in Panama. Awoyama focused on the destruction of the spillway of the canal. After he made the acquaintance of former German consul A. Hoelpke, the two men made a trip into the interior of the country to the Rio Sip Grande region.[32]

Mexican Consul to Panama F. Balasteros moved his office from the center of the business district at 11 Street and Central Avenue to directly across the street from the Japanese consulate. Both consulates, thereafter, shared a Mr. Serra as an agent. He had been in the Mexican navy or merchant marine.[33]

By October 14, 1921, U.S. intelligence felt it had gathered enough information to offer a suggestion about what Japan was up to in Panama: the organization's goal was to explore how the Panama Canal could be destroyed. The destruction of the Panama Canal would be achieved through either destroying the spillway, an armed attack with the aid of natives, or exploding ships to obstruct the canal.

U.S. observers believed that attacks by airplanes would be Japan's best option. One report stated that Japanese agents had begun to chart very small islands close to the Panama Canal on the west coast, which had never been charted before in detail. Recently, Japanese fishermen had measured the rise and fall of tides. Four different sources confirmed that Japanese agents had visited the islands to make soundings.

Kubei Kuboyama, alias Katalino Kuboyama, worked as head of the Japanese fishermen in Panama but also involved himself in explorations into finding places in Colombia to assemble planes, which would be flown from there to secret landing places before a massed attack against the canal. An air attack would focus on locks and other parts of the canal. The spillway would be detonated by sabotage. Here suddenly World War I saboteur Gezir Remeny was mentioned again.

A second strategy considered was an armed attack by Panamanians or Native Americans. As arms secretly traveled from Chile north, it was believed that they were set aside to be used in such a campaign. About a year ago the arms sent up from Argentina and Chile would have been stockpiled for such an event. But it turned out that the terrain was so impenetrable that an armed attack from land would prove difficult.

By November 1921, it was clear that these groups were making preparations to have networks in place in case a Japanese–U.S. war would break out. They did not seem to have plans to destroy the canal during times of peace. In the meantime Panama remained an important relay station between North and South America.[34]

Parallel to the preparations for war intelligence and the placing of sabotage teams to damage the United States, the Japanese elite maintained control over official Japanese policy. But 1921 was not yet the time to have an open military clash with the United States. The general public in the United States was presented with a kinder official Japanese face, that of a reasonable, restrained traditional warrior. Inside national elite politics Admiral Kato single-handedly made sure that factions that wanted to arm more aggressively for a confrontation with the United States remained controlled. In January 1921, he forced an end to the traditional 8:8 naval ratio.[35] The press published this change on January 18, 1921, as Vice Minister Ide Kenji told the *New York Tribune* that Japan might be open to naval reduction if other powers felt the same. Half a year later, a committee released a new study arguing that Japan's naval policy could function with a reduced ratio of 70 percent. In reality, the basic strategy of interception against the United States had not been abandoned. The question was only how it would be realized in a new way. Regardless, it would require excellent upfront intelligence.

Time and resources to figure out a new way to engage the U.S. fleet successfully were won when a naval holiday was negotiated at the Washington Naval Conference, which opened on December 12, 1921. The head of the Japanese delegation, Navy Minister Kato Tomosaburo, was prepared to accept a 60 percent ratio in capital ships out of respect for Japan's national budget limits. He preferred diplomacy adjustment and wanted to use his navy as a tool of deterrence but not war. However, Vice Admiral Kato Kanjii, his chief naval aide, clamored for at least a 70 percent ratio as a strategic imperative. This time he still lost to Kato the elder. At the conference, to Japan's surprise, the U.S. secretary of state offered a naval reduction to the ratio of 10:10:6. In addition, the United States, Britain, and Japan agreed to a ten-year naval holiday.[36] This agreement postponed the U.S.–Japanese naval race for one decade. It provided a reliable, contractual guarantee that a Japanese–U.S. Pacific war would not happen for years, short of an unforeseeable emergency. But on the military technological and intelligence level, the Washington agreements did not limit efforts to develop an effective military-industrial complex that would make the confrontation with the United States possible.

From the perspective of arms modernization the consequences of the Washington Treaty were different than expected. In theory, the elimination of so many capital ships should have freed up huge military budgets for civilian purposes. In Japan, however, the money was quickly mostly reallocated to sectors that were developing weapons that the conference had failed to prohibit. Japan's saving of 107,000,000 yen went to smaller naval yards to build smaller ships and to begin the construction of submarines at a newly founded Kawasaki naval yard in Kobe. Right away, planners concentrated on the submarine program, making new efforts to realize the construction of 120 boats.[37]

32. German World War I technology resurfaced in 1920 incorporated into Japanese armament designs in machine shops like these in Kobe (Library of Congress, Washington, D.C.).

This explains why an impressive amount of German technicians continued to travel to Japan for work. A small number of Germans inquired out of their own initiative about work in the Japanese military sector. Most of them moved directly from the interned German colony of Tsingtao. Three hundred eighty-one Germans decided to stay out of a total number of one thousand prisoners. Sixty-four of them found work with the Japanese navy, and forty-eight began work for the army.[38]

A 1921 approximation estimated that about sixty German engineers and technicians entered into the submarine construction business, ship construction, electric engineering, and signal intelligence. Others installed the main turbines of the planned dreadnoughts. In the submarine sector three additional engineers performed similar tasks. Two German experts focused on explosives. Eight additional electronics experts and chemical specialists arrived.[39] Krupp, in 1921, sent nine engineers to Japan. Eight of them had been hired for three years. One of them had an open contract with Tokyo Denki.

When the Japanese army and navy requested higher-level German military diplomatic representatives, the Allied powers objected. In February 1921, the U.S. naval attaché reported that Tokyo had asked for a German naval attaché or, at least, the dispatch of a delegation of naval experts.[40] This open exchange was denied in accordance with the Treaty of Versailles.[41] Quietly in August 1921, Colonel Renner was appointed minister of the German embassy in Tokyo. Before he left Germany he was briefed and ordered to observe military political developments in the Pacific. Navy Captain Gartzke explicitly initiated him into "the activity and objectives of the interests of Rear Admiral Kato who has supported a shift to the German system in the Japanese navy especially in weapons technology."[42]

German leaders also hoped that Latin American arms manufacturers could employ military experts until Versailles was turned over. The very minute World War I ended, an international competition was on to shape genuine civilian Argentinean enthusiasm for flight into a dominant market position. Right away, French and British companies sent former military pilots and military planes to Buenos Aires to win Argentine hearts. Already in 1919, the French Compania Franco-Argentina, the U.S. Curtiss Company, an Italian company, and an air service run by British major Shirley H. Kingsley operated airplanes in Argentina.[43] Next door, in Paraguay, the French pilot Pegoud flew French planes. Absent were only German pilots and German planes. A commercially viable Argentinean airplane manufacturer did not exist right after the war.

At first, British companies moved toward success. The Page Company, led by Major Hodgson, flew a Handley airplane. In August 1919, the British aviator

Kingsley founded the River Plate Aviation Company with fourteen planes. He transported passengers, mail, and general goods. Later he hoped to open a flight school. Thereafter a sales organization was supposed to sell planes to the rest of South America. Rumor had it that Kingsley, somehow, had secured a monopoly for the routes Buenos Aires–Montevideo and Buenos Aires–Rio de Janeiro.[44] Later it was revealed that Kingsley was backed by influential Argentine businessman Tornquist. In 1919, it looked as if the British would soon dominate South American airplane markets.

Argentineans at least dabbled in the virgin airline and airplane business. In June 1919, a Mr. von Bernard wrote from Buenos Aires to the Junkers company in Dessau, Germany, about purchasing a Junkers plane. Initially, Junkers replied with interest and considered cooperation. Bernhard was willing to buy a ship to transport the plane to Argentina.[45]

A second Argentinean interested was the son of famous general Uriburu. In fall 1919, the elder Uriburu hired a Mr. Breuler to travel to Germany. Breuler visited Junkers's Dessau plant and inquired about using Junkers airplanes for a potential airline. Their planes would challenge the weakening British railroad system.[46]

By then interest in German planes also grew in Argentina's Ministry of the Navy. Its head wanted to equip his future naval air station at Bahía Blanca with German planes. From April 1920 on, Hugo Junkers communicated with Señor Mr. Diana, the recently arriving military attaché in Berlin.[47] But again Junkers decided to wait. He insisted on manufacturing his planes, staffing them with his own pilots, and operating them abroad in some form of company-owned airline. Junkers did not just want to sell planes. He wanted to control planes, pilots, and airline operations. Argentines rejected such domineering. In 1919, German airplane manufacturers did not make it easy for Argentineans.

Germans had greater hopes to establish themselves first in the U.S. market. There were no devastations from the war, and huge distances remained to be covered, without having to compete with an efficient railroad system. Thus they brushed aside early Argentine requests. The Junkers company abandoned Mr. Bernard as too unimportant to entrust him with a Junkers representation in Argentina.

Junkers had just built the F 13, the first plane that could carry five passengers in a closed cabin. In June 1919, it took off for its first flight, and in September it won an international altitude record for an all-metal airplane, reaching 6,750 meters. This record suggested that it could cross many of the world's higher mountain ranges. Perhaps Junkers's former military plane manufacturer would make a successful transition into a major international civilian aircraft manufacturer. Large civilian U.S. orders were desperately needed, as the German air force was being dismantled and could no longer buy planes. Compared to large projected U.S. orders the anticipated order volume from Argentina promised to be small. Until fall 1919, for Germany, Argentina remained a place to refuel a plane before crossing the Andes, or, perhaps, flying north toward the United States, but not an important market in its own right.

After establishing Junkers in the U.S. market, company leaders wanted to connect domestic U.S. air operations with Europe. In May 1919, a meeting took place in Germany to discuss how "to fly to the U.S. with a small plane." A Lieutenant Becht of the navy infantry offered himself as pilot, nautical navigator, and future salesperson. It was decided to make the "America Flight" a reality.[48]

Professor Junkers, as airplane designer, dreamed about developing a larger plane that could carry heavier weights. He and his engineers envisioned economic gain, not military conquest. For Junkers joining the international civilian air race across the Atlantic meant "making propaganda and . . . establish[ing] economic relations with America. Also other purposes can be pursued (such as the collection of scientific data)."[49]

These America Flight plans were also discussed with famous U.S. journalist Wiegand. He assured Junkers director Major Seitz that Allied propaganda had created such a negative impression of Germany in the United States that a successful America Flight, a major technical achievement, would change popular U.S. impressions faster "than year long platonic negotiations and courting of U.S. affection and friendship."[50]

North and South American markets attracted Germans as a natural alternative to European markets. What set Junkers apart from French and British airline investors was the insight that it would take more than an excellent plane, an enthusiastic pilot, and a love of flying to conquer airplane markets in the Americas.

First, initial investment money needed to fund a hemispheric weather-observation system, the development of a navigation system, and an airplane that could handle the long trip halfway around the world. Second, replacement parts had to be positioned along the route, and fuel deposits had to be secured. Then there was a need for accurate maps. Finally, small airports had to be built where mechanics and food supplies could await the plane and its pilot.

Six weeks before a projected transatlantic experimental flight an advance team would have to leave Germany. An initial list of stops was Lisbon, the Canary Islands, the Cape Verde Islands, Tenerife, and Pernambuco and, before crossing the Andes, at the end Argentina. Slowly Argentina began to matter, at least as a stopover. For this plan, larger, upfront investments were required.

However, Junkers did not have such funds. He also needed larger amounts of foreign currency, a second component he lacked. In sum, outside investors were desperately required.[51]

The weak German Weimar government tried to help as much as it could. In order to begin pilot practice a group inside the navy located a used navy plane. The Reichsmarineamt offered additional airplane parts and identified former navy airports and a water storage facility that could serve as a temporary hangar. By the end of July, test flights were supposed to begin.[52]

Military insiders knew that a civilian all-metal plane could easily be converted into a military plane. For them the America Flight plan, indirectly, promised to produce a plane that could cover long distances and navigate over open oceans. Director Seitz hinted that German military and nationalist circles were following the America project. He remarked that the America Flight "was also undertaken in the interest of the fatherland and that certain high hearted people had been found who could be made enthusiastic for such a plan and contribute financially."[53] The Atlantic route remained the most promising space to realize this critical developmental goal, since secret cooperation agreements with the Soviet Union would not exist until 1922. Eventually it occurred to somebody to keep a lower profile. The name "America Flight" might invite misunderstandings. So the project was renamed the Long-Distance Flight Project.[54]

Reality slowly brought Professor Junkers's engineering dreams of a long-distance plane back to earth. The Reichsluftamt warned him that the French and British authorities might refuse to license a German plane that could cross the Atlantic. Their airline manufacturers, too, were trying to develop long-distance airplanes. And Allied prohibition could effectively weaken the highly qualified German competition.

Private signals from the United States looked encouraging. At first, in September 1919, a Mr. Larson, backed by a U.S. investor named Gardner, presented himself in Dessau. He claimed to be an expert and adviser of the U.S. government and inquired about licensing the F 13 for construction in the United States. The construction of one thousand airplanes seemed possible. Already he operated a U.S. mail service. Even better, he and his backers purchased a few F 13s in November 1919. Nevertheless, Junkers requested permission from the Allied Control Commission in September. Then, Junkers ploughed ahead and continued to disregard Argentina further.

But then all the dreams that Professor Junkers had for the Western Hemisphere came crashing down. On January 10, 1920, the Allied powers submitted a supplementary protocol to the peace treaty that prohibited the illegal export of planes from Germany.[55] In addition, Britain, France, and the United States began to pressure Germany's neighbors not to help in the sale of German airplanes. The limits of the peace treaty were now being enforced, even expanded.

In January 1920, the German government informed Junkers that the export of four planes to the United States had been prohibited. By coincidence, a series of equipment breakdowns and accidents damaged the enthusiastic support for Junkers planes inside the United States.[56] As bad news traveled the U.S. market no longer looked that promising or easy to access.

Under these circumstances Junkers began to pay more and renewed attention to Latin America. From Colombia came news that its military intended to buy enough planes to create three squadrons. Currently, the French were presenting their models in the Andean republics. Luckily for the Germans, the French airplane business also experienced technical and shipping difficulties. At least French accidents made the arguments of German Colombians to consider German planes as well more convincing.[57]

German individuals and associated companies now ranked potential airplane orders from Colombia above interests from Argentina. The ethnic German company Gieseke and Co. sought Junkers planes to perform aerial cartography of Colombia. They promised to create more precise maps and surveys. Gieseke's owners understood that these new data could provide a critical advantage over the land-based cartography used by U.S., British, and French scouts.[58] A Mr. Tietjen, a representative of Hugo Stinnes, wanted to locate new Colombian nickel mines. A Mr. Kaemmerer wanted to win the governor of Surinam for German airplane purchases. The joy of flying Junkers meant that they could discover a mine, secure a claim, and then, later, interest German multinationals in additional funding.

Once again individuals close to the German army pointed to the military advantages of keeping knowledge of such technology alive. Mr. Wagenfuehr was the German representative of the German Air Force Peace Commission in the German Ministry of Defense. He informed Junkers director Major Seitz about the army's interest in geodetic measurement from the air. On February 20, 1920, he endorsed its practice also in Argentina.[59]

In 1920, the representative of General Uriburu educated Junkers about a series of good reasons to do business in Argentina. First, civilian flight would encourage popular interest in flight in general and in economic applications in particular. Second, a Junkers air service in Argentina could provide employment for Germans from former German colonies with experience working in colonial areas. Later, they could be transferred to similar territorial and climactic conditions in other continents. Breuler teased Junkers by promising tacit support from President

Irigoyen. Third, planes could compete with British rail, which, increasingly, was in poor condition and of limited availability. Planes could transport, initially, high-value goods such as raw rubber, fur, and feathers. An interesting, additional suggestion emerged when a Mr. Koelitz suggested the use of Junkers planes to combat the annual plague of locusts. More honestly this meant spraying poison gas. But in South America it was supposed to kill locusts, not French soldiers.[60]

Finally, in December 1919, the goals of the Argentine military were also mentioned in a letter. Breuler and Uriburu promised Junkers to help with the acquisition of planes for the army. The engineer Dr. San Martin became a new, important military liaison. He knew President Irigoyen's first secretary personally and traveled to Berlin in spring 1920 to participate in a wireless conference. Records in the German Foreign Ministry show that he also picked up 250 Mercedes engines.[61] More importantly, on May 4, 1920, he and a Mr. Heckel traveled to Dessau's Junkers factory. Their visit ended with the selection of Erich Offermann as the first permanent communication channel between official Argentine and German interests. Not surprisingly, Offermann's brother worked as consul for the German embassy in Argentina.[62] Here a very discrete channel had been established that would remain out of public attention and diplomatic correspondence.

The option of an Argentine air force did not take off in 1920. In April 1920, Argentina's army hosted German military general Kretschmar, the commander of the 23rd Reichsregiment. He had taken a half year of leave to take care of personal business in Argentina. In Buenos Aires, his old Argentine friends and students celebrated him with a banquet. In front of invited guests, he explained German World War I experiences and their usefulness for the Argentine army. Higher officers asked him to write a manual about using troops on the ground to repress revolutionaries. His second lesson focused on troop tactics. After four weeks he left Buenos Aires without having placed any airplane orders.[63]

In December 1919, Mr. Breuler still focused on the possibility of creating an airline for General Uriburu's son.[64] An initial idea was to establish a regular flight connection with six to ten planes transporting high-value goods, where punctuality and reliability mattered less. Surprisingly German ethnicity in 1920 proved repeatedly not to be advantageous for companies in Germany.[65]

At the end of the year a new group of civilian Argentines wanted to dabble in the air business. First, Argentina's Aero Club was presided over by the head of the Martinez de Hoz family. His two sons also loved airplanes. More importantly, Martinez de Hoz was connected through marriage with former German

33. Former German
ambassador Hilmar
von dem Bussche-
Haddenhausen
remained a major
personality
influencing German
South American
policy and commercial
exchanges between
1900 and 1930
(Politisches Archiv
des Auswaertigen
Amts, Berlin).

ambassador von dem Bussche-Haddenhausen, who had served Emperor Wilhelm II. The Martinez de Hoz family also owned an airport terrain of 27 acres that could be offered to the Germans. In December 1920, de Hoz agreed to allow the use of the airport. He personally wanted only three-seaters and formally requested technical data about three-seaters.[66]

Second, there was the famous Meyer-Pelligrini family. One of the brothers of this prominent political and economic family was expected to travel to Bad Kissingen, Germany, to "take the waters." This visit could offer an opening to win him for Germany's airplane business.[67]

Third, the Argentine newspaper *La Nacion*, politically close to Germany, considered expanding its circulation by introducing airplane delivery. Perhaps

Junkers planes could realize this business plan. Finally, a fishing company in the South Georgia Islands wanted a Junkers plane, allowing it to operate quietly under local conditions. A successful operation inside Argentina might provide critical good news and dispel the negative rumors coming from the United States.

Finally, the Argentine army showed new interest. In April 1921, German nationalist organizations had decided to send Oberst Faupel on a speaking tour to South America. Part of his trip would include lectures about the use of Junkers planes.

Argentina's General Uriburu followed the example of Argentina's navy. Instead of hiring French military advisers Uriburu asked Faupel to stay and to work for him privately as chief adviser of military modernization. The Versailles Treaty made no stipulations about hiring a German general as a private consultant. Faupel, unlike Kretschmar the previous year, was eager to push Junkers planes inside the army.

In April 1911, he prepared himself for his work in South America by visiting the Junkers factory in Dessau. Accompanied by the investor Mr. v. Fremery and Mr. Offermann, he asked for brochures and, in particular, slides. Faupel wanted planes for air reconnaissance. Junkers was pleased and produced thirty-one expensive slides, plus brochures translated into Spanish. After his visit in Dessau, Oberst Faupel traveled to Hamburg and took a ship that arrived in Argentina in late summer 1921.[68] Once at the Río de la Plata he did as he had promised.

One stop of his propaganda tour included a visit to the Argentine military flight school, led by Oberst Mosconi. Previously he had been pro-German, but now he suddenly rejected Faupel's push to acquire Junkers planes. But Faupel was a pushy man and remained undeterred. He explained to Mosconi how to use the German plane during future wars. In particular, he emphasized the use of photography and the making of maps. He insisted that Junkers metal airplanes could offer advantages against other South American armies.

At the Buenos Aires War Academy he lectured in front of all commandeered officers. There too he presented Junkers planes and their military use. Suddenly a Junkers plane was no longer expected to carry people across the Río de la Plata to Uruguay. Instead, it was supposed to gather aerial intelligence over the Chaco region against Bolivia and Patagonia against Chile.[69] How quickly, already in 1921, a civilian plane could assume a moderate military function in South America.

In particular, Faupel focused on winning significant support from influential Argentinean personalities. Two of these were his former students Oberstleutnant Olachea and Major Crespo. The first one had remained pro-German, but the second one, Faupel learned, had doubts.

Suddenly the Argentine navy rushed ahead of the army. The navy planned to build an air station in Bahía Blanca. The size of the naval air station was alleged to be limited only by the budget. Either way, the plan was supposed to be kept secret from individuals close to the German embassy in Buenos Aires. Just as the German ambassador had no idea that a secret naval German naval mission was working in the same city, he was not involved in obtaining naval air armaments.

Secret trials for Argentina's naval air force were to be held in Copenhagen, where Stinnes's Landskrone estate offered a discrete naval yard, a flight station, and, most importantly, privacy.[70] At a September 8, 1921, meeting it was decided to convert a civilian Junkers plane, with a few small changes, into a naval reconnaissance plane.[71] Trials were scheduled for September 19 and 20.

Looking into the future, a purchase of five trainer planes and five reconnaissance planes was proposed. All would be retooled to reach the highest seaworthiness. One week later, Junkers offered water planes for US$13,000 a piece, including the installation of a wireless transmitter.[72] Then all two years of painstaking efforts to turn Argentine flight fever into German airplane market share came to a sudden end.

In June 1921, the Allied powers imposed a complete, open-ended prohibition of German airplane manufacture. French, British, and U.S. diplomats also prohibited the development of new large military and civilian airplanes. Finished or partly assembled machines had to be handed to Allied powers. Promising prototypes like the finished JG had to be destroyed, soon.

An open-ended absolute construction prohibition voided overnight all German expansion into Latin America. Junkers could not even manufacture orders from Argentina that might have been placed before. Two years of painful German lobbying had been for nothing. And after Allies shut down one of the world's leading airplane producers, the issue of international navy limitations appeared next on the agenda.

Not Acting as U.S., British, and French Political Idealists Had Hoped

(1922–24)

13   Latin American Diplomats Assert
a Policy of Armed Peace

The surprising success of the 1921 Naval Conference in Washington raised a troublesome possibility for South American military leaders. If Japanese, British, French, Italian, and U.S. admirals could put aside their historic rivalries and agree to an unprecedented ten-year naval holiday, then it could not be ruled out that their governments might also ask them to follow their disarmament example. And once naval armament was cut back, land force reduction might follow. From the perspectives of Latin American navy supporters, any diplomatic initiative that backed the expansion of the Washington Naval Conference agreements to smaller powers had to be defeated. In Rio, Buenos Aires, and Santiago civilian administrators shared this concern out of nationalist temperament. Latin American navy modernization must not be prevented by European and U.S. internationalism.

The fear was justified. Only half a year after the Washington conference, in July 1922, at the meeting of the Executive Council of the Pan-American Union in Washington, D.C., Chilean diplomats agreed that disarmament should be put on the organization's next meeting agenda. Nine months from then, in Santiago, Chile, the 5th Pan-American Conference was scheduled to open. U.S. diplomats wanted the Southern Hemisphere to move toward naval disarmament.

Also in Europe, circles close to the British navy used the League of Nations forum to impose naval holidays onto smaller, previously neutral countries. The navies of Argentina, Brazil, Chile, and Spain were prime candidates for such a policy initiative.

After gaining an appreciation for Argentina's quixotic foreign policy and arms purchasing efforts in the previous pages, next we need to gain an understanding of South American and Spanish diplomacy attacking U.S. and British disarmament initiatives. Suddenly, Spanish- and Portuguese-speaking diplomats from Europe and Latin America discovered an interest in defeating British and U.S. diplomatic initiatives.

U.S. diplomats, pushing disarmament, looked at Chile as the first South American government that potentially could be nudged to abandon its independent policy of armed peace and replace it with disarmament as modeled by the Washington Treaty. Before World War I, Chile had been influenced by German military advisers and German arms companies, just as Argentina had. But now the Treaty of Versailles prohibited German military advisers and arms imports.

Chile, unlike Argentina and Brazil, was also undergoing a most radical economic transition in the early 1920s. First, the discovery of how to manufacture artificial nitrates in Europe at the end of World War I had thrown Chile's natural nitrate economy—its government's financial rock—into disarray. Its economic base to finance immediate armament modernization had been profoundly weakened. Second, Peru had just hired a U.S. naval mission, creating the uncomfortable possibility that the Chilean navy could, at some time, face a U.S.-trained Peruvian navy. Third, Chile needed U.S. goodwill, as the Chilean–Peruvian struggle over the disputed Tacna–Arica border remained unresolved. More than ever before the solution to this politically highly symbolic problem depended on U.S. mediation. These three reasons alone provided enough incentives for newly elected Chilean president Alessandri to at least pretend to prefer U.S. disarmament policy over a traditional, nationalist Chilean armed peace approach.

Already in April 1922, Bertrand Mathieu, Chilean ambassador to the United States, had proposed to President Alessandri that replacing a policy of armed peace with one based on collective agreement would offer three advantages. First, it would generate a much needed reduction of government spending on military affairs. Second, a reduced defense budget would free up funds for accelerated debt payments. Third, a Chilean disarmament stance would challenge the general stereotype that Chileans were determined to remain the Prussians of South America.[1] All three points would earn U.S. goodwill. In the end they might even sway U.S. mediation with Peru toward a more pro-Chilean solution. President Alessandri followed his ambassador's counsel, and in July 1922, at the meeting of the Pan-American Union's Executive Council, Chile reinvented itself as South America's first champion of disarmament. Perhaps now Chilean civilian politicians might be willing to settle diplomatically what her generals had fought over for decades.[2]

Now that Germany was not even a modest counterweight, South American countries had to come to terms with the greater regional political weight of the United States in the Western Hemisphere. Otherwise, from whom would they buy weapons?

From the Moneda, Chile's presidential residence, diplomatic gestures dovetailed with diplomacy in the Pan-American Union. President Alessandri offered the resurrection of regional Pan-Americanism, as practiced until 1916, and to travel to Argentina and Brazil for talks. Central to his proposal was the revival of the still frozen pre–World War I draft treaty among Argentina, Brazil, and Chile. It would establish collective political dominance over the other smaller South American countries. If Chile's new approach took hold, South American navies and armies might find themselves confronted, in the not-too-distant future, with treaties that guaranteed peace and reduced budgets for armies.

For Latin American generals this was an irritating diplomatic trial balloon. If Alessandri found interest in Rio and Buenos Aires, he could showcase Chile's new fervor for disarmament at the upcoming 5th Pan-American Conference.[3]

In Europe factions of the British government pursued their own initiative. They, too, called for an international conference to extend the naval holiday to smaller neutral countries and those that did not yet have a navy. For the British the Geneva forum of the League of Nations served as the location to exert pressure. In September 1922, at the 3rd League Assembly, the first British presentation proposed an expansion of the Washington conference agreements into a wider initiative of global scope.

Right away the Brazilian representative at the league objected strongly. Brazilians refused the notion that a British government treaty with another government would be elevated to an internationally binding agreement. Besides, Brazil could not afford naval limitations because it had just begun to grow in economic and political importance. It had just initiated the construction of an adequate navy.[4] The Brazilian diplomat added that Brazil was speaking for many other countries.

The British delegation registered the Brazilian objection but proceeded as if no opposition had been voiced in Geneva. Next the league's naval armament commission selected Germany, the Soviet Union, Turkey, Hungary, Mexico, Ecuador, Hedjas, and Santo Domingo as members of the first group of small powers that should be invited to discuss naval armament limitations. In 1922, none of them owned a naval fleet worthwhile to speak of. In other words, it should be easy for their governments to agree to a naval holiday because they

34. Argentine president Alvear's commitment to policies that would create an Iberian Commonwealth were not trusted by Spanish diplomats (Library of Congress, Washington, D.C.).

possessed no navy to cut. Their sacrifice, in real terms, would be only symbolic. However, their agreement would establish a real weighty legal precedent that larger navies could follow later.

Back in Argentina, President Irigoyen looked at the Chilean offer and rejected it out of principle. He did not want any alternative to an armed peace policy. And he complained that the creation of a political disarmament bloc, consisting of Argentina, Brazil, and Chile, could be interpreted as an alliance working against smaller South American countries. Such a thinly disguised, imperial arrangement would be an affront to Latin American solidarity. Next, Irigoyen objected to President Alessandri's proposed trip across the Andes. Affirming Argentinean exceptionalism, he insisted that he and his government would do a better job providing leadership in South America than any Pan-American coalition scheme.

In September 1922, newly elected president Dr. Marcelo Torcuato de Alvear moved into Argentina's Casa Rosada. Previously, he had served as his country's ambassador to the League of Nations, and he was believed to be a man with pro-French leanings. His term was officially inaugurated on October 12, 1922. This festivity marked the most important 1922 political event in South American diplomatic circles.

Many diplomat groups considered anti–United States came to celebrate Alvear's inauguration. On September 30, 1922, José Vasconcelos, Mexico's most radical minister of education, arrived in Buenos Aires. From France, an aviation mission flew in. Previously it had participated in the Brazilian centenary, and soon it was expected to continue to Uruguay.[5] Even Japan dispatched a naval delegation.

Farther north of Argentina, politics as usual continued. Brazil, leaning toward the United States since 1917, could not appear openly to be anti-Pan-American. Thus, in November 1922, it forwarded an unexpected secret offer to Chile and Argentina. Rio proposed a quick, preliminary meeting to develop a distinct South American parameter that would define future naval disarmament. If it were up to Brazilian admirals, the deciding factor for how many ships a navy could operate would be the length of a country's coastline.[6] The proposal surfaced one week before the governing board of the 5th Pan-American Conference convened a meeting to establish the final program for the upcoming 1923 meeting.[7]

Right away, new president Alvear and Argentinean navy representatives repeated their principled rejection, which his predecessor, Irigoyen, had already thundered. First, Alvear insisted that there was not enough time left to negotiate before the Pan-American Conference. Second, the Argentine grandstanded that this Brazilian proposal reminded him of the arrogant behavior of the United States, Japan, and Great Britain. These three countries had set world policy in Washington and now pushed it onto the international community. Alvear was not willing to tell other Latin American countries how to arm or disarm. Instead, he proposed that they wait until March when the Santiago conference could provide a better public international forum for disarmament discussions.[8] Uruguay seconded President Alvear's objection on December 17.

Finally, the Alvear administration performed a spectacular piece of public theater that drove home Argentina's exceptionalist stance. Breaching diplomatic protocol, Buenos Aires published a confidential Chilean diplomatic note that had been sent previously. Thus Argentina publicly rejected the secret Chilean and Brazilian initiatives and now assumed a confrontational stance shortly before the conference started. Obviously, Argentina wanted to score public relations points with many Latin American nationalists. But most importantly, effective steps had been taken to weaken any informal, upfront steps in favor of disarmament.

After Alvear's inauguration, his military's push for modern weapons only accelerated. First, new cooperation with French naval yards offered itself. Already in 1918, Argentina had loaned France 100,000,000 gold pesos. In 1923, 18,500,000 gold pesos remained to be repaid. But now they might be used to finance navy ship construction in France.

Second, Alvear explored Japanese offers. By 1923, already eight Japanese engineers and mechanics were working in Argentine naval arsenals. Then, by the end of January 1923, Japan's military attaché to Santiago took the international train to Buenos Aires and assumed his new assignment on the other side of the Andes. He was Japan's first military expert stationed in the Río de la Plata region. In addition, the imperial navy announced the visit of Tatsuo Kobayashi from the Aeronautical Research Institute.[9]

Higher up, contacts moved beyond diplomatic pleasantries. In January 1923, the Japanese ambassador held a long meeting at Argentina's Ministry of Foreign Affairs. Some were shocked to learn that Emperor Hirohito's representative offered the sale of three modern cruisers for 2,000,000 yen, among them the *Awata*. In January, Argentina's administration neither accepted nor rejected the Japanese cruiser offer. The president asked to await the outcome of the Pan-American Conference and to see whether, later, Brazil would acquire the U.S. warships *Maryland* and *Nevada*.[10]

Also the battleship *Rivadavia* remained unrepaired in an Argentine port. As far as this dreadnought was concerned bureaucrats still explored repair and upgrades in the United States. Only the German naval mission seemed to lose clout all of a sudden. Suddenly, Kapitaen z. S. M. S. Fliess—Germany's submarine advocate—was reassigned to work as naval attaché in Washington.[11] Even worse, once he started his new job he refused, in an almost hurtful way, to resume his support for German submarine designs.[12] German mission head Bartenbach became so frustrated by his changing approach that he left for Europe. The German naval mission's contract would expire in summer 1923.

In Argentina's army, modernization continued with ever greater public pride and no restraint. On January 2, 1923, Argentina's Office of Inspector General of the Army was founded. It would act as the equivalent of the General of the Armies in the United States and depended directly on and answered immediately to Argentina's minister of war. Its name was just a different term for the office of commander in chief.

In addition, an office was created to conduct studies and proposals concerning the development of supplies and a weapons industry, which would be vital to national military success. Experts in seven subdivisions would research vital weapons questions and report exclusively to the armed forces.[13]

In January 1923, Argentina's minister of war, Colonel Justo, made at least a symbolic claim of leadership over South American military aviation. An aviation school for members of the Argentine Aero Club had been established. Already after January 1922, at San Isidro, pilot training had commenced on U.S. training planes under Curtiss Company leadership. Some pilots carried civilian mail, but the operation of the line remained firmly in the hands of the Army Aviation Service. Only budget problems prevented further intensification of Argentine military pilot training.[14]

At least Argentina wanted to lay a symbolic claim. Minister of War Justo announced that Argentina would rival efforts by U.S. and European airplane companies and finance an Argentine aviator to fly around the world. He introduced Major Pedro Zanni as the proud pilot-soldier to carry Argentina's flag across all continents. Zanni was to prove that, soon, Argentine aviation would have global relevance. Argentina's brand new air force should be noticed by those of other countries.[15]

As the March 1923 Pan-American Conference approached, Argentine bureaucrats believed that President Alvear would favor French ideas and cause the conference to fail. One informant predicted that every U.S. suggestion would be fought.

Argentina's delegation would be composed of Manuel Augusto Montes de Oca, Fernando Saguier, and Manuel Malbran. More noteworthy was that the Argentine delegation would represent excluded revolutionary Mexico's interests at the conference, of course in opposition to U.S. preferences. In general, Argentina was expected to speak in favor of Latin American sovereignty. Some predicted, probably even desired, a falling out with the United States.

The Pan-American Conference opened on March 25. Right away, Chile presented its armament limitation proposal. As before, a debate about parameters ensued. Brazil suggested a tonnage limit of 80,000 tons, and the Chilean delegation accepted it. When Argentina objected, 55,000 tons was proposed. Once again the Argentineans said no. Next, the Chilean Agustin Edwards proposed a limit on capital ships based on maximum tonnage. This time the Argentineans agreed but the Brazilians balked. Finally Argentina suggested a treaty limiting maximum tonnage for all types of ships.[16] Three weeks of discussion followed, and still nothing was resolved.

A British diplomat provided a personal impression of the mood of these weeks:.

The work of the Armaments Commission has been that which has kept most of the attention of the public and of the conference. No definite proposals were made in this commission for over a fortnight, because the office reporter Señor Antonio Huneous was anxious to hear the views of the Brazilian and Argentine delegations before summing up.

In the end he did not attempt to propose any plan for the reduction and limitation of armaments on a just and practical basis, but confined himself to generalities and a recommendation to adhere to the resolutions of the Disarmament Conference among the Great Power of Washington.[17]

In sum, the U.S. push for disarmament had been sandbagged.

There were discussions of other controversial proposals. One was to prohibit all foreign military missions to Latin America. A French observer suspected Germans behind its quick defeat, even though no evidence of German lobbying could be found.[18]

Now Argentine armament purchases could resume without concern. On May 15, Deputy Albarracin gave a speech in Argentina's Congress mixing pride and defiance with a subtle worry about the outlook for the future:

The Delegation to the 5th Pan-American Congress had upheld the Argentine traditions in international affairs and sustained the indisputable principle of pacifism which the Argentine Republic has always defended. . . . [P]eople have heard the echo of the conference as a warning sound. The difficulties encountered by the Argentine delegation and the disillusions suffered when they worked hard for the reduction of land and naval armament attempting to bring about concrete declarations and not just lonely diplomatic vagaries.

As a true and sad summary of the Chile Conference we find that the peoples of South America are to be left to their own efforts inasmuch as military preparedness is concerned.

What this really means is that armed peace in the states of the American continent is a fact. . . . Armed peace which has had such terrible consequences in Europe and which we did not wish under any circumstances in South America. Nevertheless, I do propose that Argentina should attend to her military preparedness. I propose that a special board for National Defense be constituted.

I suggest that the country prepare serenely and methodically the solution of these matters and not undertake a feverish purchasing of arms campaign at any price and of any quality.[19]

Publicly the Argentine delegation returned from Chile with pride. But inside the Alvear administration, key decision makers discovered new worries. German Ambassador Adolf Pauli in Buenos Aires registered worry about which country would now help Argentina to arm. Brazil, Peru, and perhaps even Chile could buy weapons from the United States, but who would supply Argentina? Argentina's admirals were most concerned.

Suddenly,

this insight caused the influence of private interests and jealousy on the lower level to pull back. A well meaning source reported that President Alvear might be looking at a renewal of the contract of German engineers. The adviser contract of German naval officers is being looked at with well meaning interest. It seems that the naval leadership, which broke off the relationship to German naval experts two months ago [January 1923], has interpreted the president's opinion wrongly and engaged itself too eagerly for French sympathies.[20]

On July 1, the contract with the German technicians would run out, unless Alvear and Minister of Navy Domeos García changed their minds. Captain Bartenbach remained outside the country and could be reached only through the Argentine naval attaché in Berlin.[21]

Surprisingly, Alvear proved to be a pragmatic man, rather than a loyal sympathizer of France. In May, the contract of the German submarine engineers was extended for another half year. Even better, Argentine interest returned to contracting submarines for construction in a Dutch naval yard. Of course it was the one secretly owned by the Krupp company.[22]

Perhaps Alvear's advisers should have worried less. Bids from other foreign arms sellers also poured into Argentina. In May, Franklin Herrera, a representative of one of the most important English shipbuilding firms, proposed the sale of several large cruisers. The French opened a direct radiotelegraphic service

35. German Ambassador
Adolf Pauli is
an example of a
diplomat from
Germany's Weimar
Republic who was
kept in the dark
about the German
navy's secret
rearmament design
cooperation with
Argentine navy
factions in 1922
(Politisches Archiv
des Auswaertigen
Amts, Berlin).

between Bordeaux and Argentina. A U.S. company bid for a radio company that before had been in British hands.[23]

In the end Alvear empowered the Argentine military not only through the creation of new military institutions and weaponry. Truly pathbreaking was his cleanup of the national budget. By creating the first planned national budget in the twentieth century, he opened up new predictable sources of income for military modernization.[24]

He also reformed the tax and custom system. The reform cut the national budget deficit to 35,000,000 paper pesos, a remarkable decline from 179,000,000 pesos in the previous year. It was hoped that it would also halt the decline of the Argentine peso, which had dropped 15 percent between December 1922 and July 1923.

In June 1923, the Chamber of Deputies passed a bill that pleased both navy and army. First, the navy received 9,500,000 gold pesos. The Ministry of Marine proposed acquiring six submarines similar to the U.S. S-40 types, six destroyers, and two light cruisers of the Richmond type. Second, the Ministry of War increased its appropriations by US$3,700,000.[25]

A Japanese observer from the Suzuki company in Argentina was outright jubilant about the potential for future armament sales. In his estimation,

> General conditions caused by the Santiago Conference have placed us in a much better situation than we could have hoped for. The breakup has taken from the U.S. what little prestige she still retained in Argentina, although today Chile seems to lean toward the North. Soon she will be isolated on account of her differences with Peru and Bolivia with both of whom she has controversies pending. Unofficially it is more than sure that there will be an early understanding between Argentina, Peru and Bolivia, followed by enmity for Chile which, it appears was working in combination with Brazil. This policy will produce unforeseen results for the continent.

North Americans have kept quiet and they would know that conference would be a failure. They discredited themselves with everybody. They thought they could sell canons and ships. Their calculations have fallen down badly. Also, for it is not possible for them to compete with our friends who hold, by contracts practically signed, firmly the Central and South American markets. For we have made the important sale in October 1922 of the St. Etienne, destined for Mexico, a cargo which despite the strict vigilance of those of the north has arrived at its destination.

The formation of Latin League [probably a mistake and meant to say Pan-American League] has also fallen down and if the U.S. is not opposed soon she will come to reap as is her custom. It is then necessary for us to display all of our activities and forces in order to transform Mexico into a strong and armed country and, at the same time, utilize the existing favorable current in Tokyo. Señor Torres Diaz, who is here incognito undertook an energetic campaign for Mexico, and also Fukuoka and Nagamine, both here on special mission for their government, have received orders to undertake a trip to Mexico in the interest of the International Association.

This is a step forward while waiting for the future plan of action. The plan was prepared by Newton in Tokyo and given to Backmann for execution. Backmann who has been working according to instructions he received directly, will be in Buenos Aires during the last of May or the first half of June. We have obtained valuable information from several people who are ready to do what we think most advantageous. Then there has been 1000 Pounds for C.W., C.P., CFJPW, B.V. all pertaining to the commission on armaments. Rec Ichikawa.

The Japanese Suzuki company had joined a private Japanese–French arms consortium with loose but manipulative contacts to government offices in Tokyo, Mexico, and Buenos Aires. Rejoicing about ongoing tensions, they were ready to arm all parties. In particular, the informer had singled out the Mexican Obregón administration, which he intended to arm and to encourage to take a hostile attitude toward the United States.[26]

Military attaché to Mexico City Yamada Kenzo also received the first Japanese naval visitors from the United States. For example, Naval Attaché Yamamoto, who later would be responsible for the attack on Pearl Harbor, toured Mexico's Tampico oil field region in 1923.[27]

On June 6, 1923, the Argentine army announced the completion of the General Plan of the Reorganization of the Army. It would reorganize the army into a modern organization based on the lessons learned during World War I. An independent cavalry brigade with trucks, as well as additional armament, and a new command would be created. Details of the project remained to be worked out.[28]

In August, the U.S. military attaché tried to find out whether funding was based on a loan, paper money, or gold pesos. One total amount that was floated was 150,000,000 gold pesos. In November 1923, the Argentinean Congress was rumored to increase the budget by 1,000,000 paper pesos. No doubt, Argentina was expanding militarily compared to smaller neighbors.[29]

In November 1923, after the introduction of the reform, Argentine government bonds earned the highest investment value of all South American bonds, even more than French investment bonds could earn. For 1924, Argentina would have enough money to purchase weapons that would allow it to remain neutral during the next major international war. Perhaps, for a while, Argentine troops might be able to resist even military pressure exerted by Great Britain, France, and the United States.[30]

By November 1923, the Permanent Technical Armament Commission had finalized the general plan of armaments and selected members for a purchasing commission to depart for Europe. The German diplomat predicted that the military rise of Argentina would have consequences: "So I believe that the political interplay in South America in the coming years is significantly more interesting than it has been in the past years."[31] How should the other Latin American countries react to such a determined Argentine rearmament effort?[32]

Chile responded by proposing a treaty of arbitration, solidarity, and mutual guarantees among Brazil, Argentina, and Uruguay. Not surprisingly, President Alvear again rejected the Chilean offer with familiar arguments. It was Alessandri's final, futile attempt to reach out politically to Argentina.[33]

Even though U.S. diplomatic disarmament efforts had been sandbagged in Santiago, British efforts, pursued inside the League of Nations, were still alive. Captain Segrave of the British navy spearheaded the push for his country's naval disarmament. Facing his proposals would be Admiral Penido from Brazil and Spain's Marquis de Magaz. The League of Nations' Permanent Advisory Commission for Military, Naval and Air Questions was scheduled to meet in Rome in 1924. It counted representatives from Britain, France, Japan, and Italy but also Spain and Brazil.

For the Brazilians and the Spaniards the Washington Treaty remained a treaty between nations. First, they used an important legal technicality to block the British initiative. Next, Brazilians and Spaniards decided to join Argentineans and Chileans and refused disarmament because of national security, geographical situation, and special circumstances. In the words of British historian Gerard Silverlock, an unprecedented "Hispano-Brazilian position" was solidifying. Together, this previously unlikely interest group stalled British and U.S. naval establishments.

The Rome conference took place in 1924 as planned. What would be the right legal justification? There Latin American diplomats deployed passive-aggressive behavior. The Brazilian representative simply refused to cooperate, and the Spanish representative argued that, even though he was present in Rome, he was only a private observer. He, too, could not speak for his administration in Madrid. Argentinean and Uruguayan observers agreed. Their governments, too, had instructed them not to participate in the discussions and to pretend to be observers only.[34]

In the end, in Rome, the British push for disarmament was also defeated. The Spanish representative affirmed categorically that Spain would not accept any limitations on its navy. Chile, Argentina, and Brazil refused to agree to a common denominator. One British observer kidded himself when he thought that there "had been a germ of an agreement between the three South American states."[35] Rear Admiral Aubrey Smith was more astute when he remarked that

South American admirals had failed to agree because of pride. All delegations went home across the Atlantic fully empowered to arm as their navies saw fit.

While Latin American and Spanish diplomats defeated U.S. and British disarmament initiatives, the ethnic context of their diplomacy had also begun to change. Manipulative ethnic community politics was resurfacing as a factor in international security relations. The following pages examine it within the context of Italian, German, Soviet Union, and Japanese policies.

14 Italian, German, and Japanese Governments and Soviet Communists Resume Manipulations of Ethnic Communities and Workers in the Americas (1923)

Italian Fascism asked the question of ethnic loyalty in the Americas in a new way. The first appearance of Hitler's National Socialist German Workers' Party (NSDAP) representative in Detroit in 1923 gave a disturbing hint at changes in German ethnic and racial political concepts. Not to be overlooked, the cousin of ethnic irredenta work—subversion through labor agitation—reasserted itself in the form of manipulating U.S. working-class groups in the Americas. Open communist legal political work and illegal intelligence in the United States were established. Japan quietly concluded the construction of its Western Hemisphere intelligence network, still in preparation of any future violent confrontation with the United States, as well as to keep open the possibility of encouraging Latin American rage against the United States. These new manipulations did not even try to influence the outcome of a war. Nevertheless, only four years after the 1919 World War I armistice, they again manipulated politics among Latin America, Japan, and Europe.

Italy's Fascism introduced two new dimensions into the relationship between Western Hemisphere immigrant communities and antidemocratic European political movements. Previously, members of ethnic groups had been asked to be loyal to an aristocratic dynasty, a monarch, Catholicism, or a labor movement trying to be internationalist. Now Italian fascists asked whether and how Italian

Americans should participate in a nationalistic, extreme right-wing political and social movement in their country of origin.[1] A first superficial answer was that Italian Fascism would merely be asking questions about ethnic loyalty in a new way. But two additional parts to this answer need to be considered. First, Fascism introduced a claim to exclusive control over Italian American ethnic communities in the name of a sovereign government that increasingly was controlled by a totalitarian party. Only the Soviet Union would do the same on the political Left.

Second, Italian Fascism developed contacts with foreign revolutionary organizations and exploited these linkages to further fascist Italian policy goals. Both aspects introduced radical innovations into relations between emigrant groups and Western Hemisphere notions.

Fascism was not just a social or political movement. It was also a charge by a politically organized group of individuals who encouraged the export of violent conflict, terrorism, and right-wing paramilitary groups. From the perspective of fascist Rome these tools promised an advantage. Policy and subversion, too, were parts of an Italian fascist policy already from 1920 on.

Today, historians of Latin America and the United States should consider with greater seriousness that Fascism, the Italian military, or the Italian government were poised to engage in subversion or ethnic disintegration in the Americas—*when the time was right* or an opportunity lent itself. Only the armed forces of the Allied powers made sure it never came to this. We need to keep in mind these true innovations to understand what model the German Nazi Party followed between 1933 and 1938.

In 1922, contemplating secret Italian fascist warfare in the Americas made no sense. First, a fascist organization had to be built, which only later might serve as a potential and reliable vehicle for disintegration work. To say it differently, 1920–24 signified a period of focused organization building while realizing short-term policy goals for Italy—but only in the Western Hemisphere.

In Europe Mussolini's contact with foreign terrorist organizations can be traced back to early 1920. He and fellow revolutionary Gabriele D'Annunzio were in contact with Irish revolutionary Michel Collins and the Irish Republican Army. These Irish revolutionaries had contacted the two Italians to buy weapons, hoping for guns and ammunition to kill British soldiers in their continued guerilla war for Irish independence. Soon thereafter, in April 1920, Irish–fascist Italian contacts stopped because of financial difficulties and because the British Secret Intelligence Service had discovered the blossoming contact between them.[2] Before Mussolini had joined any government that, later, could manipulate emigrant communities, he had contact with terrorists.

In 1921, many regional fascisms competed in Italy. Fascism was only just becoming a national phenomenon. And a growing number of sympathetic U.S. Italian Americans wanted to participate in this first fascist political bloom by founding in the United States their own local fascist cells. Right away the question emerged of how an Italian fascist abroad should relate to the Fascist Party and movement in Italy. Already in April 1921, Renzo Ferrata, a fascist organizer in Switzerland, had proposed the creation of one central bureaucratic party structure in Italy to take charge of fascist cells in the world.[3] However, since fascists were not yet part of the Italian government, at that time, the question remained unanswered.

In the meantime, another fascist revolutionary, Adolf Hitler, and the NSDAP sent the first confidant to Italy, even before Mussolini's March on Rome. The representative asked for an exchange of opinion with Mussolini.[4] But Hitler was also linked to the paramilitary organization Escherich, which horded thousands of weapons, under the control of Ernst Röhm, his later chief of SA. Mussolini, once again, was in communication with a paramilitary organization that sought to destroy a democratically elected republic, in this case Germany. From then on Mussolini's representative De Bosdari kept in contact with German fascists.

In fall 1922, in Italy, Mussolini finally was able to join an Italian coalition government. Right away he assumed the post of prime minister and foreign minister. His fellow fascist comrade Giuseppe Bottai suggested that branches of the Italian Fascist Party should operate outside the control of his Italian government. The Fascisti's revolutionary vanguard organizations had to remain under the exclusive control of Fascist Party leaders.

Mussolini and other regional party leaders now had to address the issue of the relationship between the Fascist Party and the Italian government. A remarkable debate resulted among Italian diplomats, foreign fascist activists, and a newly assembled Fascist Grand Council that met in Mussolini's private apartment in Rome.[5]

In October 1922, a Mr. Bonservizi moved the question from an idea to an outline on paper. He developed the first organizational blueprint detailing how a fascist-led organization should be organized internally. Each fascist branch was to be divided into a Welfare Office, a Press and Propaganda Office, and a Political Technical Office. Right away the more radical Italian fascist Mr. Bastianini went further. He demanded that Fascist Party bureaucrats should also act as Italian diplomats abroad, rivaling traditional diplomats from Italy's Foreign Ministry. The U.S. historian de Caprariis explains: "For the party leadership the Uffici, like the Gruppi di Competenza at home would be the nuclei of a new, modern and technocratic political structure. In the long run, a network of fascist experts would enable the Party to compete with and ultimately supplant the Ministry of Foreign Affairs."[6]

Now, Mussolini, speaking as foreign minister, added his personal interpretation. In November 1922, he agreed that party branches abroad should serve a distinct function in connection with a yet-to-be-developed fascist Italian state. He described to the journalist Roberto Cantalupo that, first, a massive wave of propaganda would be unleashed to nationalize emigrant communities abroad. Second, Italian youth abroad would receive special indoctrination. Finally, once they had internalized fascist ideals, "a dynamic expansion of the nation" would take place beyond its borders. Somehow fascist Italians abroad and their nationalized communities would play a role in bringing about a new fascist world. What this meant in detail he left unexplained.[7]

In the United States, Mussolini's newly appointed ambassador, Prince Gelasio Caetani di Sermoneta, remained excluded from the internal debates of the party leadership. Besides, he was a traditional career diplomat. When he arrived in the United States he did what traditional, nationalist Italian ambassadors had always done. He assumed he could extend the authority of his embassy and his role as Italy's ranking state diplomat also over Italian American communities.

His assumption of control also included the sprouting fascio branches along the U.S. East Coast. Ambassador Caetani's personalist-hierarchical policy demanded that his embassy would remain the exclusive governmental institution to centralize and to discipline all U.S. fascist branches, not just in New York or Washington but all future party branches in the entire United States. If it were up to Caetani, the Fasci in the United States would become merely an institutional shell, designed to suffocate independent fascism.[8] This diplomat was eager to neuter Fascist Party zeal.

Caetani believed his proposal to be well justified. He repeatedly emphasized that it was based on locally gained insights in the United States, not uninformed party dictates from Rome or simple personal loyalty. He correctly reported that party branches in the United States were burdened by class tensions and leaders with criminal backgrounds. None of them were remotely appropriate to represent Mussolini's Italian coalition government in the United States. All of them were harmful to Italy's policy priorities, involving desperately needed loans from the United States to strengthen financially Italy's ability to pursue an independent policy in Europe.

Ambassador Caetani brought into play all his social capital as he insisted that only a traditional Italian diplomat, living inside North and South America, could understand delicate local American contexts. Only he could know how to manipulate party cells within the context of greater Italian–U.S. relations. In contrast, he warned, Fascist Party leaders in Rome would be informed only by, at best, amateurish descriptions from distant party cell leaders without diplomacy experience.

Ambassador Caetani proposed "to guide" U.S. party groups from a central headquarters in New York. From there top-down supervision would shape party cells on the East Coast. Locally based fascist groups in the United States must not be allowed to act independently.

In the United States, on the ground, in New York, the reality inside Italian American communities defied the ambassador's descriptions. There was local New York Fascio head de Biasi, who insisted on acting as his own fascist leader. He refused to follow orders either from the diplomat or from the party in Rome. He, in turn, was challenged by rival fascist upstarts, rivaling him in his effort to develop his local vision of fascism in an Italian American community.

New fascio members sometimes defied de Biasi and acted out their personal fascist violence fantasies against leftist political organizations and unions. To make matters worse, socialist and communist Italian American groups in the United States pursued an every-bit-as-determined aggressive, violent struggle against U.S. Fascist Party cells. Political militancy remained a major issue in the Italian American community, regardless what diplomats in Rome or party leaders were decreeing.[9]

In Italy for the Fascist Party the first grab for real power came in February 1923. In Rome, on February 14, 1923, the Fascist Grand Council discussed the situation in the United States for three hours. Fascist activity in Latin America was discussed next. Suddenly, nationalist establishment diplomats of the Italian Foreign Ministry had to take into consideration what party leaders thought policy should be in North and South America.

At first, it looked as if council members would follow the arguments of the Italian diplomat in the United States. They established new guidelines for party cells. First, a fascio abroad must constitute itself from people who were beyond suspicion and unimpeachable from every point of view. Second, their actions were not to disturb Italian–U.S. relations and must not interfere in internal U.S. affairs. Third, they were to respect the laws and wishes of the host country. Bastianini, now as newly appointed Fascist Social Party political secretary, formulated that fasci abroad must not use militancy.[10]

And yet when it came to confirming institutionally that fascist cells abroad had to obey Italy's ambassadors and the Foreign Ministry, the Fascist Grand

Council and Mussolini refused to grant diplomats this explicit measure of control. When the Grand Council meeting ended fascio organizations abroad continued to be allowed to exist independently of governmental orders. Interestingly, their numbers were encouraged to expand. Perhaps the directives described above promised reasonable behavior to Italy's conservative establishment diplomats, but they also confirmed to fascio party heads that they could continue to exist and expand independently of Foreign Ministry control. They would act as members of an expanding organization outside traditional government control. Diplomats could not control them.[11] Italy's foreign service had just been told to arrange itself with the expansion of independent fascist cells abroad!

To add insult to injury to Italy's diplomats, the Fascist Grand Council supported Mussolini's selection of Giuseppe Bastianini, a twenty-three-year-old firebrand, as political secretary of the National Fascist Party. Bastianini held extreme right-wing revolutionary views and, already then, fervently rejected any control by Italy's Foreign Ministry and diplomats. If it were up to him, the fascio branches would come under his own personal and exclusive control. Also in the Americas they would bypass the Foreign Ministry or diplomats.[12]

In 1923, members of the very small Fascist Grand Council, indeed, continued to dream about building a new Italian society led by a fascist ruling class. According to the Australian historian Bosworth, this was also the time when Mussolini acquiesced to the creation of a secret party police under his personal command.[13]

While the Italian ambassador in the United States remained frustrated, desperate to sway Mussolini toward a more reasonable policy, in accordance with century-old rules of diplomacy, Mussolini made contact with a third terrorist organization in Europe. Already in November 1922, at the Conference of Lausanne, the future of Macedonia and Yugoslavia had been the central discussion topic. There Mussolini established opportunistic contacts with members of the Bulgarian officer corps who were anti-Yugoslavian.[14] In 1923, the Italian prime minister encouraged Macedonian rebels to increase pressure on the Yugoslav government. After exploiting the Irish–British and German–French conflict, he now skillfully encouraged subversion against the Yugoslavians.

In the United States and Latin America, Mussolini continued to refrain from subversion, though not from institutional growth. A new insult to Italy's diplomats in the Americas were special fascist envoys. They were sent with Mussolini's order to create and grow fascist parties. Personal emissaries began to drive party growth just as much as diplomats and local, passionate mini-Mussolinis.

In Argentina, Fascism entered into a tense environment. Already 412 nonfascist Italian emigrant organizations existed counting 146,000 members. Initially, "establishment" Italian Argentineans dealt with change in Rome in the way they thought was appropriate. In 1923, Arsenio Guidi Bufarini, the new head of the traditional *federazioni*, followed other fascist enthusiasts and traveled to Italy to pay respect to the new fascist Italian premier. Once in Rome he was received in Mussolini's increasingly fashionable office. There Bufarini assured that the Italo-Argentineans of the nationalist *federazione* stood 100 percent behind his new fascist movement. He promised to take back to Argentina Mussolini's grateful reception of greetings.[15]

But for Mussolini this was not enough. He also dispatched to Argentina his own organizer. His man was Ottavio Dinale, previously a revolutionary syndicalist. After arriving in Buenos Aires he was charged with penetrating the Italian Argentine community beyond the voluntarily efforts of traditional, nationalist Italians. One month later, Mussolini confirmed Dinale as South America's official delegate for the Partito Nazionale Fascista Italiano.[16]

Next he strengthened Dinale by sending a more pro-fascist Italian ambassador to Argentina. On July 20, 1923, Signor Luis Aldorrandi Marescotti Conde de Viano took office. Unlike in the United States, south of the equator, fascist diplomat and Mussolini's personal emissary confronted ethnic community division jointly.[17] Then there were still the many leftist Argentine Italian organizations to contend with.

In Brazil Mussolini also employed a personal emissary to create fascist cells. They too competed with 192 emigrant associations and their 22,503 members. Those, in turn, were part of 1,837,887 individuals with Italian ethnic background.[18] Mussolini's envoy founded forty new fascio branches.

As far as the United States was concerned, the Italian president asked Simone Semprevivo from Louisiana to organize new fasci in Alabama, Texas, Arkansas, Georgia, Florida, and North Carolina.[19] Traditionalist ambassador Caetani did his utmost to keep hidden the growing linkage between Rome and U.S. fascio organizations. On the one hand, future members were asked to "accept Italy's political and economic program, especially with regard to expanding Italian endeavors and national thought throughout the world."[20]

In May, Mussolini also sent a secret directive defining a short-term policy for the party. He instructed party members to limit activity to propaganda, immigrant existence, and culture. Party activity must not become an embarrassment to his government.

Plus the ambassador insisted that all fascio activities had to appear as a consequence of local U.S. political passions, not a directive from Rome or the Italian embassy. Ideally the fascio in the United States was to limit its energies to nonpolitical activities like sport and philanthropy. Fasci were not supposed to become activist political organizations.[21]

Finding a way that diplomats and fascists could live with proved demanding. Ambassador Caetani continued to lobby as top representative and general manager of the Italian community abroad. Finally both sides agreed to accept Dino Bigongiari, an unconventional Roman language professor from Columbia University, as the new establishment, more reputable face of fascist organizations in New York.

On a different stage, in Italy, the fascist political leaders advanced in their struggle against traditional, conservative diplomats and the Foreign Ministry. They targeted the less important consular system to place fascist leaders into ethnic communities abroad. It was the first breakthrough.

First, Mussolini allowed the National Fascist Party's Fascio all'Estero head Bastianini to charge a second time. He had never relented one minute in his push for ever increasing, exclusive control of party cells, including those in the United States. He began to selectively use the consular system to chip away at Foreign Ministry independence. It was a subtle but effective strategy, as there could be only one embassy in each American nation. However, a dozen consulates could be opened in major commercial and urban locations.

In early 1923, from Rome, the fascist war veteran Giuseppe Gangemi, in the Office of the General Secretary of Fasci all'Estero, identified appropriate Italian Americans who could chair a future U.S. fascio cell.[22] Then, in an aggressive salvo against Ambassador Caetani, Bastianini appointed Signore Gangemi consul general in New York. Promptly he was sent to the East Coast as Mussolini's first fascist consul in the United States to compete against Ambassador Caetani.[23]

In April 1923, Bastianini requested an office inside Italy's Ministry of Foreign Affairs, a symbolic penetration of the den of Italian traditionalists. The party radicals solicited Mussolini's support to confront diplomats inside their bureaucratic territory. That year, Mussolini brilliantly chose to deflect the issue. He cautiously refused the demand. But he did not rule it out in the future. Bastianini was comforted that the party, and thus, indirectly, his personal clout, would continue to grow abroad.

In essence, he confirmed the party as an institution that had the right to confront the diplomatic establishment. For the time being the party visionaries could sooth themselves in thinking that they were in a holding pattern of an organizational phase. One day it would be followed by the political phase and action beyond political meetings.

Once again Bastianini knew how to restrain himself. For the time being he cooperated grudgingly with the Foreign Ministry. But Bastianini was allowed to run party affairs in such a way that all embassies would be involved in the decision making. Bastianini had to tolerate this long-term approach toward power. At a later time, the party branches could take over a political function whether the ambassador wanted it or not.[24]

Even if the party refused to officially control ethnic communities directly, Mussolini could weaken rival traditionalist organizations. He dissolved two of Italy's most important emigrant organizations. In 1923, the Lega Italiana and the Società Umanitaria, old socialist organizations, lost their independence. It was a significant affront against the established ethnic Italian emigrant culture in North and South America. And it softened up the field for the fascists.

In Rome the Fascist Grand Council took another step in its slow bureaucratic development. It set up an Ufficio Centrale per i Fasci all'Estero inside its General Secretariat. Its task was to discipline and direct the Italian fascist movement worldwide. Right away Bastianini claimed future global jurisdiction by organizing this new office according to continents. Latin America and North America were united in one hemispheric section.

In essence Italian fascists were attempting to change the international diplomatic system as it had developed after the 1814 Congress of Vienna. Slowly they were constructing a parallel organization, misusing the diplomatic immunity of the office of consul. Official Italian government organizations could be, at the same time, a party tool and a government tool. How should traditional Western diplomats and governments deal with this evolution? How should they identify who was in charge and responsible?

Shortly thereafter Mussolini turned everything upside down again. He replaced the autonomous secretariat and began to supervise it as minister of foreign affairs and "Duce of Fascism."[25] Now he had three avenues to manipulate Italian American communities: the Ministry of Foreign Affairs, the Fascist Party channel, and himself, as primus inter pares, the foreign minister, and the Duce.

A second round of discussion about fascist policy in the United States took place in summer 1923. Once again Mussolini paid respect to Ambassador to the U.S. Caetani. He called him to Rome to report about the situation in the United

States. The Grand Council discussed it on July 26, 1923. Latin America was discussed on July 27.[26]

Transcripts of the detailed discussions have not survived. But officially after the meeting everything stayed the same. Sections abroad were simply "associations of citizens who have faith in the fascist government and favor Italian economic, commercial, industrial and intellectual expansion."[27] But this was not all. On July 31, a secret party circular was sent to the United States, once again asserting that the fasci remained de facto extensions of the party in Rome and previous assurances were merely a cover for public consumption. The fascist regime learned to distinguish between public pronouncements and party building.

Depending on personal context, in 1923, this outcome could be interpreted in several ways. All suited Mussolini well. On the one hand, Mussolini had asserted that the fasci must exist. Diplomats could draw reassurance from his statement that their activism must not create division in Italian American communities and should avoid any acts or gestures that made the work of diplomats more difficult.[28] Conservative nationalist ambassadors could feel appreciated and that they were still heard in person and that their expertise kept the Foreign Office involved in the establishment of discipline among fascio branches in the United States.

But at no point was the existence of the fascio cells put into question. Their bureaucratic validity was not questioned, regardless of what the membership was doing in the distant locales. At no time was Mussolini's confidant prohibited from ordaining new cells. It was a most cynical expansion of influence by the mere act of existence. And in the back the Duce always had the option to single out a party cell for special approval and bypassing of the diplomatic establishment. The U.S. historian de Caprariis suggests: "Between 1922 and 1925 Mussolini encouraged the establishment of the Fasci all'Estero and their transformation into one of the Party's major branches. Rome disavowed or restrained fascist activities abroad only when the party's tactless pressure threatened a major clash with other countries."[29]

America's Fascist Party cell growth was connected with a larger political Italian imperialist exploration toward Latin America. Already in November 1922, the possibility of a joint Italian–Spanish underwater cable to Latin America had been raised.[30] Also new and pro-fascist Italian Ambassador Signor Luis Aldorrandi Marescotti Conde de Viano tried to win President Alvear's sympathy for fascist Italy on July 20, 1923. Two days later Alvear's government responded with an official invitation to Italy's crown prince to visit Argentina. Nine days later, on May 24, the Italian legation in Buenos Aires was raised to the rank of an embassy.[31]

Out of sight a competition over "Latin" policy developed between Italy and Spain. In 1923, Spanish king Alfonso XIII and dictator Primo de Rivera visited Mussolini.

Part of their discussions covered the possibility of entering into an Italian–Spanish treaty. But Primo de Rivera declared himself unable to enter into an agreement on the spot. In reality he was not interested and preferred Spanish independent action. This was a skilled lie. In 1923, the ongoing war in Morocco, Spain's lobbying for a permanent seat at the League of Nations, and the relationship with France remained higher in priority than any uncharted approach between Spain and Italy. Nevertheless, news leaked out that a potential Spanish–Italian treaty proposal was tossed around containing an article specifying Mussolini's desire to engage in a collaborative policy in Central and South America.[32]

After king and dictator returned to Spain, in January 1924, Primo de Rivera asked the Italian ambassador to omit the issue of cooperation in Latin America. Only talks about a potentially benevolent neutrality in a future Mediterranean conflict continued.

Then Primo de Rivera performed a most elegant rejection of Italian activism. He suggested to the consternated Italians "that it could be possible to have an intimate and sincere union between the two countries without the necessity to sign a secret treaty."[33] At least Italy's diplomat interpreted these words as strong enough reason to end secret treaty explorations.

Still Mussolini backed the visit of Prince Humbert of Piedmont to Argentina in August 1924. In Buenos Aires he was received with great popular fanfare and enthusiasm.[34] In the end the crown prince's visit to Argentina failed to deepen Argentine–Italian bonds. The Spanish ambassador reported that a group of Argentines had wanted to bestow on him an honorable doctorate degree. But when university students objected, the plan was abandoned. Political elites were not even willing to make such a benign gesture. During the trip the crown prince, accompanied by Admiral Bonaldi, experienced mostly disrespect. The Spanish ambassador tried to identify some successes for Italy, but all he could come up with was: "The Prince [and his staff] had to content themselves to smile from the distance to gentlemen and lesser ladies."[35]

Regular diplomatic Italian–South American contacts deepened nevertheless. The Italian military attaché Colonel Domingo Siciliani was stationed in Argentina.[36] In April 1924, Argentina's army appointed one soldier to serve in an Italian Alpine specialty corps. For popular commercial interests Italy sent an exhibition ship accompanied by Ambassador Extraordinaire Signore Giurat.[37] One attempt was made to link emigration with weapons orders. U.S. naval attaché Howell wrote to Washington, D.C., that "the Italian Ambassador has visited the Minister of Marine three or four times recently and has informed the minister that Italy is prepared to treat very favorably with the Brazilian government on the subject of immigration and commerce should preference be given to the purchase of new submarines from Italy."[38]

Fascist Party cell growth, traditional diplomatic outreach, and arms sales began to interweave. Italian American emigrants looked at another event. In Rome the International Conference on Emigration and Immigration was held between May 15 and May 24, 1924. Before, meetings in Paris had failed to solve immigration issues, including the formulation of broad principles protecting labor markets. Fifty-nine nations attended the Rome conference hoping to find a way to break the anti-immigration stance crystallizing in U.S. Congress. At the least they hoped to counter it with a unified, well-balanced position. The effort failed.

Fascist destruction of Italian emigration organizations simply progressed. At the 1st Congress of the Fasci all'Estero in 1925, Orazio Pedrazzi called for all nonconsular functions among Italian American emigrants to be exercised only by the Fascist Party. Other private organizations should be shut down. Fascio head Bastianini made a second push to move from the organizational to the new aggressive political phase, once again trying to replace Italy's Foreign Ministry policy monopoly abroad.[39]

Mussolini's contacts with far right-wing military and political conspirators only deepened during this period. In early 1924, German right-wing leader Helferrich met Mussolini in Rome. In Germany Lieut. General von Cramon united some radical and traditionalist paramilitary organizations under his unofficial leadership. Both furthered contacts with Italian Fascism.

Now Mussolini sent political scouts to German fascist movements. From February to March 1924, General Luigi Capello, a famous Italian army commander of World War I, visited Germany as personal messenger. In Berlin and Munich he spoke to German nationalists, trying to find out the chances of a right-wing takeover. He explored how Italy might be able to support German rearmament.[40] Capello once again reported that the different groups were not yet ready to make a coup but wanted to await May 4 elections. He was certain that soon parliamentarism in Germany would be abolished.

Capello still paid attention to the chance that Germans could attack France in the nearer future. The Italian came home with a list of weapons that the right-wing paramilitary organizations needed to prepare for any upcoming attack of France. Indeed, Mussolini not only received the list but allowed weapons to be delivered.[41]

Also Capello met General Wilhelm Dommes, Crown Prince Wilhelm, Prince Oskar of Prussia, Hans von Kemnitz, Field Marshal August von Mackensen, and retired general Karl von Watter. All of them were interested in exploring Italian support for secret warfare.[42]

Mussolini supplied the men to keep French–German relations disturbed, which translated into relief of French pressure against Italy. Historian Raffael Schreck reports that he also leaked some information to the British.[43]

Finally, German military intelligence chief von Boetticher traveled to Rome and talked to Mussolini on May 26, 1924. Here Mussolini proposed that in the future Italy and Germany should jointly confront France. Yet in 1924, Mussolini deemed the Ebert administration as too weak to warrant open Italian support and Italy as militarily too unprepared to wage a war with France.[44] But he expected a better time would come. In June Mussolini invited Boetticher for a second talk.

In sum, by 1924, Mussolini played all sides. The absence of fascist subversion in the Americas until 1925 was a policy choice, not proof of innocence of fascist vituperance on the other side of the Atlantic. It could have been used anytime the Duce so decided.

National conservative and proto-fascist manipulations in the Americas were executed not only by Italians. Germans also revived them in 1923. Before German activity after 1920 can be understood, a short excursion before that year is necessary.

Germans, as individuals, organized ethnicists according to rivaling concepts. They did not need a functioning national government party to revel in ethnic self-gratification. Hundreds of regional ethnic organizations all over Germany rivaled for importance and dominance.

Already in 1916, in Hamburg, Germany, a Mr. Schaedel, a merchant, had founded out of his own initiative the Ibero-American Society. Also he served as honorary representative of the America Institute.[45] This institute was not just another indulgence in the exoticisms of American cultures. At its center stood the idea to reeducate Berlin aristocrats before they began work as German diplomats in Latin America.

It was the time when submarine warfare threatened the commercial lifelines of ethnic Germans in Argentina. As World War I began to go wrong, Hamburg importers remembered how their fathers had acted autonomously from the emperor or from Germany before the founding of the second German Reich in 1871.

Among themselves, German Hanseatics enjoyed German ethnicity as a private, regional cultural affair. Their values were closer to Anglo-Saxon trading culture, appreciating society and culture woven around economic liberalism. These merchants from Argentina complained about how aristocratic German Ambassador Luxburg was using and abusing their presence for imperial priorities that did not respect their economic needs. Here was the tender first non-aristocratic attempt to develop an alternative autonomous ethnic Germanness that was activist and still chauvinistic at heart, but it did not serve as a cover for state-sponsored ethnic subversion or colonial expansion.

So far the diplomats that Germany was dispatching were picked not because of their country experience but because of their personal connections or because they were rich enough to carry the entertainment costs and represent German aristocracy better than a professional bureaucrat with a small government income could. Most of the aristocrats brought to Rio de Janeiro, Santiago de Chile, or Lima a healthy portion of upper-class arrogance. In contrast, their knowledge of trade and finance was often nil. For them representing Germany in North and South America meant representing the imperial monarchy first. Business interests were treated as a secondary appendix. Compared to princes, dukes, and counts, the merchants of Hamburg and Bremen represented lower-ranked "new money."

In 1917, unrestricted submarine warfare changed the power relationship between merchant and diplomat. The supremacy of warfare was destroying profitable trade relations that had been built painstakingly for conditions of peace over the last decades. In the all or nothing of a world war the boundaries between civil society and military society also in ethnic communities were contested. Economic success was now less and less a matter of personal business skill or area expertise.[46] Agricultural raw material could be exported to Europe only if the government assigned its import priority and a daring captain and his ship made it through the Allied blockades. It was not a situation to flourish economically.

The 1917 British publication of the discussions between Ambassador Luxburg in Buenos Aires and the Foreign Office in Berlin illustrated how ruthless aristocrats were gambling with the reputations of their entire ethnic community. Ever more to save the empire, but not their business, merchants were asked to endorse Wilhelm II's and the German aristocrats' war policies—even if that meant sacrificing their entire wealth.

By November 1917, North Germans confronted the imperial government. Walter Dauch, owner of Schlubach and Co., and establishment merchants in

Hamburg accused Berlin politicians of incompetence. Looking into the future, they argued that the ethnic German community in Argentina would be protected not by imperialism but only by "courage and entrepreneurship." Only those attributes would guarantee a postwar Germany the supply of raw materials and the sale of domestic export products. Dauch demanded that imperial war needed to step back again, behind imperial trade policy.[47]

The confrontation was formalized in a hard-hitting memorandum to Berlin signed by the members of the chambers of commerce in Hamburg, Bremen, and Lübeck. The Hanseatic memo circulated in Berlin with the signatures of one hundred names of the who's who of overseas trade.[48]

One remedy pointed at was a complete reform of the German consular system. In the future professional consuls who knew trade were to replace honorary consuls. After World War I, the German consulate was supposed to be an economic information center, not a cover for espionage and secret navy supply activity. Consuls were supposed to work for pay, not just social recognition or upward mobility.[49]

The British consular system was suggested as an example. First, consuls should acquire country expertise. Second, representatives should speak the local language and know a country's peculiarities. Merit, not wealth, should be the decisive factor for their employment.

In the midst of this debate the imperial government in Berlin announced the creation of Germany's first Ministry of Economy. Right away, Hamburg merchants argued that the consular system, because it was supposed to focus on business, should be moved from the Foreign Ministry to this new Ministry of Economy. Also a Foreign Trade Office and an Economic Information Service were to be created.

Juxtaposed against the notion of ethnic Germandom, rooted in a culture of independent transatlantic traders, Prussians revived the classic eighteenth-century romantic notion that individual Germans were merely single expressions of one larger mysterious, quasi-biological political organism. Still during the 1918 November Revolution the government-supported ethnic Association for German Cultural Foreign Relations (VDA) organization had proposed that all ethnic Germans, regardless of where they lived, needed to unite into one "Living Cultural Community."

This notion rejected the class- or region-based stratification of the German monarchy but also socialists and anarchists. Most importantly, its care was entrusted to the German state. This vision elevated ethnicity above lower-, middle-, or aristocratic class stratifications. And this community concept also included individuals living outside Germany. In 1920, the new categories of Germans living abroad (*Auslandsdeutsche*), Germans living in border zones (*Grenzdeutsche*), and Germans living inside the political state boundaries (*Reichsdeutsche*) were created. Each category, however, represented one organic piece of a unified ethnicity that could never be limited to state boundaries.

And there was a third understanding of ethnicity, this one based on folk culture. In the Kingdom of Württemberg, when the German Empire still existed, ethnic identity depended on descending from poor Swabian farmers or day laborers in southern Germany. Southern regional ethnicity refused to join neatly with national German ethnicity. Whereas northern Germans demanded state-sponsored ethnicity built around the centuries-old traditions of trade, in Württemberg, Baden, and the city of Stuttgart, the rural folk culture of Swabian emigrants was the pivot.

This rural folk focus received an institutional anchor. In 1917, a regional coalition founded the Institute of Germans Abroad (DAI) in Stuttgart. It became a showcase for the path of emigration of Swabians into southeastern Europe and Latin America.

Ethnic Swabians' pride demanded staying connected with emigrants from Swabia. As the German monarchy weakened and then collapsed, and the national future of Germany became uncertain, it made sense to reaffirm regional southern German ethnicity.

Swabian ethnic planners realized that people liked to touch and to see folk artifacts that expressed identity, rather than just read about them in complicated, abstract, or even worse, academic works. In Stuttgart staying in touch with ethnic Germandom meant building a museum with a collection of artifacts proving the global relevance of Swabian ethnicity. The Stuttgart institute hired curators who systematically collected everyday furnishings, toys, and dishes.

The Stuttgart institute rivaled the illusionary ethnicity propagated by the national VDA organization in Berlin.[50] Germany did not resolve these issues effectively by 1918. Its monarchy collapsed. Hundreds of local ethnic associations were left without one national focus.

Finally, if they did not want to gather in favor of regional ethnic identity, Germans could also create identity by organizing against an ethnic group. A thoroughly anti-Semitic group had been founded by the All-German Association on February 18, 1919. This "Deutscher Schutz and Trutz Bund" united anti-Semitic organizations from before and during World War I.[51] It mushroomed into one of the largest anti-Semitic national political organizations. By 1922, it counted nationwide about two hundred thousand members and was organized into nineteen administrative units and 530 city chapters.

It was far stronger than National Socialism that year. Leading National Socialists of later years often gained their first agitation experiences as speakers of this Schutz- und Trutzbund. It became a training ground for many ethnic activists of all later years.

The German army leadership still practiced subversive ethnic politics in Poland. By coincidence, on August 14, 1920, the Polish defeated the Russians in "the miracle at the Weichsel." All dreams of a communist Poland came to an end. As the League of Nations backed this weak Polish state, Germans hurried to sustain subversive ethnic agitation against Poland.[52] One year after World War I Germans lacked the ability to use open violence in Poland. Right away they deployed the hidden tool of ethnic separatism.

Later a German consul admitted that the Foreign Ministry did back it. Its anti-Polish policy was handed to a seemingly autonomous private Krahmer-Möllenberg Stiftung. Nobody could argue convincingly that it represented the Weimar government:[53] "The total effort served the goal of ethnic Germans, who now owned a Polish citizenship, to strengthen them in being ethnically German and to maintain the ethnic Germans as a distinct cultural factor."[54]

German ethnic fanatics, without national or regional government order, also conducted ethnic subversion along the new German–French border, in the Alsace-Lorraine region. There the German Schutz- und Trutzbund created an Alsace-Lorraine press organization and conducted aggressive propaganda against the French takeover of this region. Specialists exploited inflationary surges and the falling values of ethnic publishing businesses to systematically purchase German-speaking newspapers under the cover of the Konkordia Literary Agency LLC.[55] Eventually it separated from the Schutz- und Trutzbund and reemerged as a semiprivate foundation. Ethnic disintegration began with anti-French book donations and light journalistic support for pro-German journalists.

Government ministries of the Weimar Republic understood the continued need to centralize these competing large and small, regional and national organizations, all of them claiming to speak for Germany and representing true German ethnicity. The official Germany was blamed for all of it. One observer complained: "There is official work and private work: official work carried out by numerous departments of the Reich and of the lands, private work carried out by a string of organizations, partly in cooperation with the authorities, partly without such cooperation and even against the authorities, in short a turbulent variety of goings on."[56]

The Foreign Office called a meeting for February 14, 1922, hoping to gather at one table key government departments and the major private and ethnic agitation organizations. Diplomats demanded a monopoly over political ethnic affairs at home and abroad. Its "Organisationsplan für die Zusammenfassung der Deutschtumspflege" even proposed the creation of a Parliament for Ethnic Germandom. It would initiate the creation of a streamlined process that would allow the ministry to hold or deploy ethnic fervor, depending on elite policy choices.

But fighting among Weimar's ministries prevented the imposition of a state monopoly over ethnic activities. The Ministry of Interior in particular opposed the claim of the Ministry of Foreign Relations. In March 1923, it backed a *Zweckverband* of "Free Ethnic Germandom Clubs." This organization dominated mostly private organizations of a rightist political nature. Outside, it remained, according to a 1922 Foreign Ministry survey, a mere 10 percent of the German Auslandsdeutsche movement.

In the end the Weimar Foreign Ministry gained some assurance that the *Zweckverband* would be prevented from exercising unwanted interference at least in Poland. At least demarcations between ministries over ethnic policy in Europe had been agreed upon.[57]

In this context the VDA was pushed forward to specialize in cultural activities that looked nonpolitical. Now was not the time to use ethnic issues offensively on behalf of boundary adjustments against Versailles.

Official work was limited to nonpolitical cultural events. For this purpose the VDA was ideal. It focused mainly on contested zones in Europe. The German historian Michael Fahlbusch discovered that "here the goal of association work consisted of founding school clubs and the education of leading cadres of Irredenta. The goal was to stop the emigration of Germans from contested border zones." Fahlbusch categorizes this policy as "defensive." It aimed at winning support among middle-class parties and strengthening affinities for future imperial positions.[58]

In Stuttgart, at the same time, small bureaucrats paid little attention to developments in Berlin. They simply continued gathering data about German Americans and their organizations in the United States. The DAI dutifully tried to establish a better collection of names and addresses of ethnic German organizations. Here was the beginning of a list of global reach that the Nazis would inherit in 1933 and use for increasingly illegal purposes. But in 1922 this was not yet so.

Two employees maintained this archive. Sometimes, when the financial situation allowed, the department could afford to hire interns or supervised volunteers without any prior experience in library work. They were dedicated ethnic enthusiasts profoundly lacking in geography skills. In their hands data about ethnic Germans abroad remained not much more than a collection of names, addresses, and clubs.

A look at the collection of German clubs and groups in Cincinnati offers an example of the quality of the archive in its earliest years. The first entries were made in 1922, registering thirty-one German clubs in the Midwestern city. Over the years fifty-nine other organizations were added to the file. Seventy percent of their names were copied from a newspaper article, a letter, or some form of printed matter. Forty percent of the club names came without a contact person or a club officer. In the 1920s, Stuttgart attempted to engage in some form of written exchange with 60 percent of them. Forty percent of the entries were little more than a name. No mailing address existed for them, nor were they in contact with German institutions. Whenever the DAI mailed a brochure it did so hoping that it would receive back a letter with a correct or corrected address.

Finally, Hitler and the weak NSDAP sent their first representative to the United States. He and others introduced in 1923 a new motive for propagandists from the Weimar Republic to contact German Americans: money for campaigns. In Austria, in December 1923, after the failed Hitler–Ludendorff coup, Kurt G. W. Luedecke was appointed the first Nazi delegate to the United States. He was supposed to do fund-raising. Ideally he would raise enough money to pay for a foreign political office of the Nazi Party inside the United States. During a second trip he traveled to Detroit to meet with Henry Ford, asking for his financial support for the Nazi Party. But the automaker declined.[59] Thereafter Luedecke traveled through ethnic German communities in Pittsburgh, Cleveland, and Chicago, without ever finding enough supporters to leave a lasting trace. Even outreach to the KKK proved disappointing.[60]

Taking notice of the arrival of Hitler's first representative in the United States merely serves the purpose of marking the beginning point for later German fascist activity. In 1924, Teutonia, the first pro-Nazi U.S. organization, was founded in Chicago.

Truly significant in 1923 was the return of conservative German propaganda speakers to support irredenta work in the contested ethnic territories in Europe. Outside Germany, the first European governments already fought back against German secret machinations. In 1923, the new Polish state reacted to German ethnic troublemaking by prohibiting German ethnic affiliations inside Poland. From then on inside the German ethnic community in Poland no central organization existed to run the ethnic propaganda minority work.[61]

One of its leaders had been a Dr. Robert Treut. Now he was asked to leave Poland. Previously he had founded and run a pro-German school support organization. He had agitated as a fierce propaganda fighter in the cultural ethnic war against the new Polish state, in particular during the vote over the contested Upper Silesia region.

From Poland he traveled to Germany first. But then he continued on across the Atlantic to the United States. There Dr. Treut propagandized on behalf of ethnic Germans in the regions of Posen, West Prussia, and Upper Silesia and the Deutsche Verband Nord-Schleswig; German Verband, Southern Tyrolia; and Deutscher Kulturverband, Czechoslovakia. He was also supported by the Wohlfahrt und Kulturamt der Deutschen Vereine Gross Rumania and the Saarverein.[62] He traveled through key U.S. cities to raise funds on behalf of the ethnic groups in the lost territories. He spoke as representative of the groups mentioned above, not as part of a conspiracy inside the United States. And yet his work was backed from Germany at least by the semigovernmental ethnic umbrella organization VDA. A VDA list gave him the names and addresses of six thousand ethnic Germans in the United States. They received a special invitation to his lecture appearances.

Immediately his efforts showed success. To draw new crowds he employed film, a new attraction then. It projected romantic images of the contested regions and appealed effectively to spectators through emotions.

In March 1924, in Baltimore, Treut drew three thousand people. Around Easter he gave a presentation in Minneapolis at the Germanistic Society of Minnesota. During the summer he stayed in Minnesota and Wisconsin. His days were spent preparing for a new 1925 tour of the U.S. East Coast.

His second task was to create committees that would continue to propagandize on behalf of these ethnic Germans and stay in touch with Dr. Treut for future fund-raising activities. He proved to be a skilled organizer and left behind activist support circles in Chicago; Milwaukee; Detroit; Cleveland; Youngstown; Pittsburgh; Buffalo; Springfield, Illinois; and Boston.

Suddenly German diplomats in the United States, unfamiliar with Dr. Treut's task, were visited by him, requesting a bit more direct government financial backing. Diplomats of the new Weimar Germany wanted to appear disconnected from such manipulations, which were once again associated with an irredenta activity.

A second truly influential German touring the Americas was the retired head of the German navy, Admiral Behnke. Admiral Behnke toured South America for the German navy beginning a year later than Dr. Treut. The records in the German archive reveal a determined and profound personal effort to pursue two tasks. First, he explored with military and navy advisers whether German arms manufacturers, the Rheinmetall company in particular, could obtain South American armament orders. Second, Behnke toured regions with ethnic German residents in order to gauge for the navy how much their economic activity could be linked more consciously and effectively to the strengthening of industry inside Germany. Assuming a bird's-eye view he evaluated the capacity of ethnic German communities across the world to trade as part of an economic German resurgence to fund secret rearmament.

His reports have been preserved. After the trip he addressed attentive industry members inside Germany. In front of industrialists and merchants he fiercely advocated for trade intensification with ethnic German settlement regions so that they would become an economic factor in Germany's resurgence.[63] Behnke showed a deep understanding of the connection between political and military economies in Germany and Latin America.

Ethnic Germans who participated on their own behalf in Latin American revolts were a more puzzling challenge. This was a new public relations nightmare for diplomats of the Weimar Republic.

In São Paulo, Brazil, in July 1924, a major military revolt took place. Unemployed ethnic Germans, out of their own initiative, joined the revolt. Before they had lived in the Immigrant Home of São Paulo, waiting for a land grant. Now they established a "German Battalion." Its members joined factions regardless of whether they still held German passports or whether they were descendants of immigrants. Most eluded government capture. One year later in 1925, some of them again joined the uprising of the Brazilian lieutenants.[64]

Diplomats of the Weimar Republic were horrified how easily individual participation was misinterpreted as a revival of sinister governmental plots. Soon a press campaign began to educate the Brazilian people about the facts. But the damage had been done. Fears about Germans in southern Brazil reenergized, for once without justification.

As far as Mexico was concerned, another old German ghost reemerged. In 1924, during the de la Huerta rebellion, Carranza's attaché Arnoldo Krum-Heller joined the rebellion against President Obregón. Another ethnic German, Kurt Selzer, even publicly presented himself as a spokesman of a provisional Mexican government.[65] This time there was no world war making the manipulation of the domestic conflict rewarding for naval intelligence in Berlin.

In Venezuela, dictator Gómez used fear about Germans to scare U.S. rivals into concessions. The well-known Stinnes company emerged connected to a Venezuelan coup faction.[66] In June 1923, a company called CVP opened an office in New York.

Suddenly the president of Venezuela began to use oil concessions as a political bargaining chip. Stinnes representatives Guillermo Sturrup and Wilhelm Waltking were strongly encouraged to travel from Germany to Venezuela to negotiate with Roberto Ramirez. Soon it seemed that the German company would purchase a land option for over 200,000 hectares and other federal lands. In the words of the British historian B. McBeth, this move appeared like "the creation of a strong monopoly with official backing." McBeth speculates that Venezuelan interest in Germany might have intended to scare U.S. companies to jump into action and to develop Venezuela's oil sector faster and more extensively. Then hyperinflation in Germany and Stinnes's death made it impossible for the Stinnes group to realize the Venezuelan option.[67]

In Chile, the most fascinating episode of ethnic German private expansion occurred. German general and military adviser Kiesling, in early 1924, returned to Santiago. This time he did not come as a soldier and advisor as he had done before World War I. Instead he wished to build a German colony in Chile's Patagonia. He had left Germany after the failed 1923 Hitler coup. He explained, "There were thousands of square miles of West Patagonia that are not inhabited and are just waiting for creative hands to open it up." He intended to unify transatlantic trade with ethnic emigration and private colonial development. Only a single street needed to be built to benefit trade flow from the mouth of the Yelcho to Yelcho Lake, up the Futalefu to the already settled areas of Argentine Patagonia. Along the road, ranchos would be developed. This effort would be followed by the construction of German farmhouses and churches. Then cattle raising would begin, and wood milling would follow and develop into a manufacturing industry with Bavarians as lumberjacks. Kiesling remembered: "I held the conviction that it would be possible to count on the creation of a small Germany."[68] He wanted to repeat a piece of Bavarian history:

Just as 2000 years ago the Bavarian tribes had settled upper Bavarian and Tyrolian lakes, . . . I imagined the same way the colonization of the Yelcho area could take place.

We imagined predominantly a settlement of second born Bavarian sons, which, according to Bavarian law, had no inheritance right to operate the father's farm. However they had the right of receiving payment of a certain sum of money by the heir. They could bring this money into Chile where they could become independent farmers.[69]

Next to the settlement a grand economic organization was supposed to be built. A cooperative would build streets, traffic organizations, distribute land claims, support settlers, and process the raw products of the community. A large amount of the profit would be reinvested in settlement expansion. Finally, they also planned the creation of a port at the Bay of Palpidad, which would connect with international ocean traffic: "Rarely had there been a colonization project so well thought through and well justified. With a start capital of 20000 engl Pounds the enterprise would be put on a sound footing. German influence on one of the largest trade enterprises in South America would have been guaranteed."[70]

In the end investors from Girozentrale Munich stepped back from the Yelcho Project. No other financier could be found. And yet Kiesling continued to beat the drum for his project in Bavaria. He negotiated with the largest wood exporter, Forstrat Escherich. Of course Escherich was also head of Bavaria's largest proto-fascist organization and head of the right-wing terror organization Orgesch. Another interested party was Herzog Adolph Friedrich von Mecklenburg. In desperation, Kiesling offered the colonial settlement to Dutch people. He even traveled to Rotterdam to meet with potential Dutch investors.

In the end von Kiesling's plans were destroyed because of a lack of finances and hyperinflation. He had no other choice but to travel back through the Panama Canal to Chile and resume work as a military adviser.[71]

This segment needs to end with a look at the revival of official German intelligence activity in North and South America. Fragments of the German naval intelligence system in the Americas lingered on. Remnants simply rested until leaders in Germany decided what to do next. In New York, there remained a Mr. Sauerbeck. In Buenos Aires remnants were administered by the former naval attaché. In Rio de Janeiro Mr. Stoltz waited. He also administered two subsections in Bahia and Pernambuco. In Bahia, Capt. Liet. Buente helped him. In Valparaiso, Chile, a Mr. Westendarp had saved whatever could be saved. In the Atlantic there was still the station in Las Palmas, under Captain Loewenhard.

In the Pacific, the Manila station also remained mothballed.[72] And a low-level minimal naval supply reporting system limped along between 1920 and 1925. Later analysts would say that incoming reports were of poor quality, but in the 1925 documents no complaints are stated.[73]

Some already played with fire in public. Surprisingly the former head of Department IIIb, Nicolai, still linked to illegal German rearmament in the Soviet Union, wrote a propagandistic book about Allied intelligence services. Interestingly the book closed with the following paragraph, reviving the fears of World War I race wars in the United States:

As never before this time has been made for the intelligence services. In particular this is true for Great Britain and the U.S. The construction of the British World Empire and Immigrant and Racial question in North America are a tempting challenge [*reizen gerade zu*] to try out the art of intelligence. In the future the secret power of intelligence service will be far greater than in the past and the present.[74]

By June 1924, a trickle of activities began when German shipping agencies quietly made available a few spaces for army officers. Their trips across the Atlantic were organized with the knowledge and appreciation of Intelligence Chief Major von Boetticher and Director Beusch of the Gutehoffnungshütte company.[75]

Already, in October 1923, the German navy had asked for an update of its knowledge of U.S. signal intelligence. On October 24, 1923, the first officer was to be sent to Central America. One of his tasks would be to collect signal intelligence data. The very first German military officers, camouflaged as sailors, were attempting to train again on a global scale.[76]

They were supposed to gather information about the reliability of U.S. signal intelligence traffic along the East Coast, count the frequency of the U.S. use of direction finders, and estimate the strength of direction finders on British and U.S. merchant ships. And finally they were supposed to find out how many British and U.S. tankers had access to wireless telephone and telegram transmitters.[77]

A Captain Herrmann was supposed to travel to Cuba in spring 1925. Another trip from May to June 1925 would introduce a German officer to the port facilities of Baltimore, Philadelphia, and Norfolk. A frigate captain, Groos, toured Nicaraguan ports in the same year.[78]

Also the signal intelligence office of the German Foreign Ministry did its best to train some code breakers to attack diplomatic cables. Reliable statistics from early 1925 reveal that this small decoding office devoted 1,405 working days to decode about 2,800 telegrams. These intercepts included the U.S. code ABC. Once decoded the content proved so irrelevant and boring that analysts complained about the work. From there Germans moved to breaking the diplomatic codes of Mexico, Ecuador, Chile, Brazil, and Argentina. Also Spanish diplomatic codes were not spared.[79]

In March 1925, Consul Fricke pushed a German government office to open a transmitter station for Spaniards in Cartagena. Its parts had been delivered for assembly. A Mr. Bruno Richter was supposed to travel as additional telegrapher to the Spanish east coast.[80] Of course he would read Spanish traffic. In August 1925 the navy held a meeting to discuss whether signal intelligence operators should be stationed on German steamers just like during World War I.[81]

In 1925, the foreign ministries needed to make preparations if the upcoming disarmament conference still trumped the intelligence needs of the navy. Immediate navy expansion was again postponed, just to be safe.[82]

Only volunteer, individual correspondents sent reports from North and South America. In November 1925, a Mr. Junkermann sent reports from Bermuda. These letters worried the navy enough to call a meeting to discuss overenthusiastic freelancers.[83]

A second discussion explored whether the naval supply system and its informal reporter system should be revitalized in a more systematic fashion in 1925. Because there was no immediate need, a systematic revival was postponed. Navy leaders knew that they would have to approach the Foreign Ministry eventually and ask for help. But right now was not the time, and Germans did not have enough ships circulating the globe that needed protection.

In November 1925, a meeting concluded that currently a new organization did not need to be built. The time still had not yet come.[84] The meeting ended with a commitment only to maintain a small reporting system to gain information from abroad. It enlisted again the use of existing German merchant companies to forward mail for what little spying still took place. This way informal reporters abroad would not come into direct contact with captains of ships.[85] The navy felt strongly that the existence of this reporting system should be hidden from the German Foreign Ministry and ambassadors. This meeting document proves that the low-level naval reporting system had never been wrapped up entirely.

To the outside correspondents were not supposed to appear as helping Germany. Intelligence Chief Stahmer himself ordered secrecy vis-à-vis diplomats abroad on November 23, 1925. The documents do not show that this news organization's service was of poor quality or that the professionals were not happy about it, as later books about the 1920s and 1930s would argue.[86]

A deeper understanding of the 1923 intelligence expansion must include communist activities. By 1923, not just German fascists and navy officers were active again. Antidemocratic and anticapitalist movements in the West, across the entire ideological spectrum, resumed network building and attempted initial covert activities in the Americas. Italians were caught up in struggles between Fascist Party representatives and traditional diplomats over how to use Italian Americans. Germans just reintroduced propaganda speakers, and naval agents resumed touring through select American ports. In anticipation of transoceanic economic warfare against Poland and France, a few ethnic Germans contributed voluntarily to the German naval intelligence network.

Besides the Japanese, only Moscow's communists selected the U.S. army as a target so early after World War I. A more comprehensive anti-U.S. intelligence approach would have to wait until 1928. They nevertheless established the first stage of a professional intelligence system inside the United States and Latin America.

In 1924, its organizational roots were cemented as part of Zinoniev's struggle to replace the deceased Lenin. Today he is forgotten. But he attacked the peripheries of French and British colonial empires, which included some Latin American workers. Zinoniev's experiments with national liberation movements and worker internationalism predated the opening of Stalin's Comintern office in Buenos Aires.

After the failed 1923 Ruhr communist revolt, the Soviet army took the best men of the German Communist Party and bundled them into its first intelligence service. It included a tiny section that gathered information about the U.S. army and served for the Red Army.[87] Espionage activities outside Russia between 1921 and 1929 were headed by Mikhail Trilliser.[88]

From Europe communist instructions for intelligence and military espionage were sent to New York. Unidentified communist agents were ordered to collect all available published information on any subject before a penetration of the United States had been achieved. A British internal report explained: "Many handbooks and catalogues were obtained, including those with restricted circulation.... Little information is available on the activity of the agents except that they do not always appear to have produced satisfactory reports. Evidently there were several groups working under the one resident."[89]

What were the network's priorities?

> The work now developing on the U.S. must have as its first task the dispatch of much more important military, military technical and political-economic literature. On a part with this is the study of the latest achievements in all classes of military technology, especially in the field of chemical warfare, of the air force and of war industries. It is also essential to devote special attention to U.S. foreign policy in Europe.

What mattered were

> its order of battle, its strength and organization, its weapons system, training and communications systems and equipment. Some particularly detailed questionnaires were also sent on the navy and on chemical warfare. At the time the British Admiralty commented that the naval and gas sections of the questionnaire were very thorough and undoubtedly originated from technical experts and that the greater number of questions would have involved espionage.

Financing for these operations was dispensed, sometimes, through the Moness Chemical Company, located in New York at 426 Broome Street.[90] Mr. J. Moness's private address was 787 Crotons Park North, the Bronx.[91] Records show a first business payment from the Hammer Company to the Moness Company in 1923. From then on, a significant amount of money continued to flow to the company, and US$33,500 was dispersed probably through Julius Heiman, alias Heymann Lachowsky. Soon he was suspected to be the principle financial channel between Moscow's Comintern and the American Communist Party. Later he would be connected to the notorious spy Arthur Alexandrovich Adams.[92] The U.S. historian Harvey Klehr suggests that in 1923 $25,000 funded illegal activities of the party.[93] It remains to be seen if this money also financed military espionage growth.

Moness offered the use of his company as an espionage and military intelligence front. The Soviets had dispatched a yet-to-be-identified resident to the United States to manage the collection of material for questionnaires and directives from inside the country.

This resident received instructions from an agent located at an intermediate controlling station in Western Europe. Documentable instructions to the United States began in 1924. An analyst of the British Secret Intelligence Service detailed the development:

The Moness Documents reveal in the first place that the Soviet Network in America was an intelligence organization in the widest sense. The directives in the Moness documents were not sent from Moscow but from a controlling station outside America almost certainly Europe. It is quite certain that the controlling station was not in Berlin, London or Moscow, but most likely Paris.[94]

Intelligence work was sandwiched between domestic and foreign political tasks. Inside the United States there was regular political party work. The Latvian Karlis Ernestovich Janson, using the pseudonym Charles Edward Scott, and Sen Katayama and Louis C. Fraina established themselves as the Comintern's official 1922 American Agency. The first task of these three men was to break the independence of U.S. communists. Second, they were to bolshevize the party. Third, they were to establish pro-Moscow communist parties in Canada and Mexico. Fraina was rumored to have an additional task in South America. But soon thereafter he dropped out and left the Communist International.[95]

Julius Heiman funded party work by converting jewels, sent in 1920 and 1921, into cash. A 1923 budget estimated $50,000 to travel through a Berlin front organization that worked for workers famine relief.[96]

Already in 1923, some communists explored entering into alliances with other U.S. populist political groups. For example, in 1923, Comintern agent John Pepper targeted the Farmer Labor Party. He founded front organizations that fielded "independent" delegates who were really representatives of the Communist Party. One year later some communists experimented with support for the U.S. presidential campaign of Robert La Follette. Such cross-party cooperation in the United States, however, remained limited. Fighting between rivaling factions from Chicago and New York kept them stifled. But also from distant Moscow Leon Trotsky argued against this strategy.[97]

Most importantly, Latin America was already in the view of party leader insiders. Independent Latin American communists and the influence of Spanish anarchism remained a constant irritant for those who wanted the Comintern to be the one to lead world communist affairs. Exchanges and cooperation between independent communists from Buenos Aires and Havana, Cuba, were to be shut down. Echoes of Argentina's university reform movement in Córdoba reverberated north into Cuba as the First National Student Congress was held in Havana in 1923. Also, the rector of the University of Buenos Aires, Dr. Jose R. C. Cyrus, traveled to Cuba on December 4, 1922, and lectured. The congress planned an anti-U.S. week of protest against the U.S. Platt Amendment. By themselves students experimented with cross-class alliances with Havana workers and demanded diplomatic recognition of the Soviet Union.

By then a few leaders in Moscow also explored Spanish revolutionary potential. Trotsky was especially interested in Spain. For him the Iberian Peninsula would be the revolutionary stepping-stone to Latin America, not the United States. Closest to Trotsky was Joaquin Maurin. He had met the Russian revolutionary in 1921 and continued to correspond with him thereafter.

In August 1923, a general strike was attempted to bring the Spanish political system to collapse. However, it was answered with massive repression.[98]

Against this background communist leaders also tried to diagnose the evolving revolutionary potential of Latin America. The U.S. All-Russian Communist Party faction sent a Mr. Abramson to report about South America. He arrived in Lima on January 10, 1924. From there he traveled on to Santiago. After crossing the Andes he stayed for several weeks in Buenos Aires before concluding his inspection in Montevideo, Uruguay. In the Uruguayan capital he received an order from Comrade Rudan in Madrid to report what he had seen.

On the one hand, he evaluated the revolutionary situation in South American republics as favorable. Economic crises were persisting, and in Argentina, immigrants were arriving "fully class conscious." They joined the ranks of a militant proletariat where wages remained punishingly low. But such encouraging facts were also neutralized by negative factors.

On the down side, many workers still lacked class consciousness and were unorganized. Abramson believed that Argentina's "perverse atmosphere of political life was killing every germ of class consciousness." There

Italians were far from willing to be organized; Spaniards were drenched with desire for bloody retaliation. Newly arriving Germans affiliated with them but only to slip into a savagery of disposition, the decline into a primitive stage of culture, hatred for one another, and complete passive dependence on capital. These are universal impoverishing demons . . . the moral condition of the population is so primitive that it can only be compared with that of the Negroes.[99]

At the very least Abramson had located bandits in southern Argentina willing to start an insurrection in exchange for pay. Still, if Zinoniev wanted to organize the workers of Argentina's industrial proletariat, a "considerable amount of

European leaders would have to be sent to organize the principal centers. Smaller urban centers where workers lived were entirely unfit for this."[100]

Abramson acquainted himself with the work of Argentine labor organizations and even directed one for several weeks. He attested that, undoubtedly, the possibility of creating a revolutionary movement existed. If an efficient organization of the centers by party workers could be established, communists would be able to dominate the situation. By themselves "local labor organizations did not possess the necessary financial means. Europeans or U.S. communists would have to furnish money regularly and systematically. In 1924, subsidies transmitted by Comrade Martins, were of enormous importance in strengthening our authority, but they did not lead to results in the organization of the work."[101]

In the end, Abramson counseled that the question of a communist revolution significant enough to hurt European capitalists was only thinkable in Buenos Aires. Paraguay and Uruguay presented no independent value. To the contrary, these developments would be controlled by events in Argentina. Chile remained a potential second revolutionary setting.[102]

Progress was made first in Mexico. The Soviet Union seemed to increase its chance to receive diplomatic recognition, which would grant diplomatic immunity and a safe outpost for a communist connection close to the U.S. border. Suddenly Mexican negotiations with the Soviets were interrupted by the de la Huerta rebellion. But in Moscow, in October, the two sides moved closer again. At the founding of the communist peasant organization Krestintern the Mexican peasant leagues affiliated Mexican members. Also at Moscow's first international Agricultural Exhibit Úrsulo Galván from Mexico participated.[103] But the legal establishment of a Soviet presence in Mexico would have to wait until summer 1924.

On other continents, in 1923, communist subversion proved similarly difficult. First, the Comintern had to accept a peace treaty between the USSR and Turkey. Then, in Iran the revolutionary movement suffered defeat.[104] In Peshawar, India, nine communists trained at Tashkent's Indian Communist Party were sentenced.[105]

Only from China could a modest breakthrough be reported. On October 6, 1923, Comintern delegate Borodin was able to convince revolutionary leader Sun Yat-sen to reorganize the Kuomintang and to accept communist members. In exchange the Communist Party would send military trainers to train Chinese soldiers. Revolutionary generals, among them Chiang Kai-shek, were sent to Moscow for initial military training. After June 1924, systematic professional communist military training began outside Russia with the inauguration of the Whampoa Military Academy in China. Its soldiers would attack British, French, or U.S. interests in the Far East.[106]

A most important change was Lenin's death on January 21, 1924. It opened a new phase in the internal Bolshevik fight over future political direction. Trotsky wanted to push European revolution. Stalin wanted revolution in one country.

But Zinoniev took charge of the Comintern. First, he reorganized its propaganda system and put himself at its top.[107] Second, Zinoniev started a new attempt to attack Great Britain by revolutionizing its colonies. In April 1924, as long as British–Soviet trade negotiations were taking place, communist activism was limited to exerting pressure in favor of the Soviet delegation and the signing of the British–Soviet agreement.[108] But in the British colonies organizations prepared to move toward a subversive war footing.

The British historian Andrew cites an intelligence report from January 14, 1924, instructing the Soviet representative in Kabul to work for the establishment of a united Empire of Muslim India and Afghanistan. Its promise would be to liberate millions of Indians from under the foreign yoke. Afghanistan was supposed to be penetrated through Turkistan. In January 1925, disintegration work against India ranked higher than subversion work against Persia and Turkey.[109]

Leadership for the fight in the British colonies was entrusted to the British Communist Party. Its colonial department in Britain sent the first agents to organize a communist party in India. Emissary Percy Glading arrived in February 1925. A year later Donald Campbell came to work in the trade union movement. To develop the left wing of the party Spratt was sent as the third agent in 1925. He also opened a labor publishing house. Very small party sections operated in Bombay and Calcutta.[110]

Quickly advice came to acquiesce for the time being to nationalist Indian opposition as potential leaders of the initial confrontation against Great Britain. A 1924 secret document ordered them to play down the "Communist note" in propaganda, where it was likely to offend the native populations, and to concentrate instead on exploiting Indian nationalism as an unconscious means of furthering communist aims. In June and July 1924 at the Comintern Congress Zinoniev "showed himself wildly optimistic about the prospects for a British revolution."[111]

With the exception of Great Britain, it became clear that Europe would be less of a target for Soviet revolution and that "in the future it would be necessary to devote far more attention than hitherto to work in the East." British imperialism in India and Afghanistan had priority.[112]

Zinoniev, president of the Executive Committee of the Comintern (ECCI), and Heller, president of the Special Commission attached to the ECCI for Eastern Affairs, agreed to the establishment of a "United Front of Eastern States." It was to extend from the Pacific to the Black Sea.[113]

Into this situation Moscow received the news that it could open an embassy in Mexico next to the United States. This would be the closest location to the most important emerging capitalist country of the world. It would offer extraterritorial security, the absolute secrecy of a diplomatic pouch, and immunity for Soviet diplomats, as long as no Soviet embassy existed inside the United States. Mexican territory adjacent to the United States gained in importance.

Mexican–Soviet diplomatic relations were established in July 1924.[114] Soviet Ambassador Pestkovsky took until the end of the year to present his credentials in Mexico City on November 7, 1924.

In Mexico, there existed no army, navy, or air force that would be important for the Soviet Union to spy on. Thus attacking independent Mexican leftist politics resumed.

Inside the Soviet legation Labor Attaché Grigori Lapikian and Press Secretary Viktor Volinsky propagandized alternative leftist discourses. It was a provocation in the midst of adverse territory, where Luis N. Morones and his Regional Confederation of Mexican Workers (CROM) labor organization dominated labor agitation for the Sonoran dynasty.[115]

Mexico's small Communist Party funded the newspaper *El Machete*, hoping to disseminate pro-Soviet labor policy ideas among the elites of Mexico's labor movement who could read. In addition it provided money to publish *El Libertador*, a publication of the Anti-imperialist League.

Certainly Moscow's foreign minister understood the potential of the site. In May 1925, in a speech at a meeting of the Executive Committee in Tbilisi, Georgia, Chicherin stated, "We have succeeded in re-establishing diplomatic relations with a neighbor of the U.S., Mexico, and this gives us a political base in the New World."[116] Even though the words were spoken in Russia's Asian area, they did reach the United States and Mexico. Quickly they became a political liability.

Also behavior by local communists in Mexico did not help the Soviet presence inside Mexico. In April 1925, the Mexican Communist Party had its third annual meeting. Moscow's envoy Charles Philipp was present and talked about continuing experiments in Mexico to harness the anger of mass pressure.

Soviet Ambassador Pestkovsky focused on building an organization that could bring Moscow's message to Latin American literate workers. And he maintained relations with workers and peasant organizations. He described the Soviet presence in Mexico "as an opportunity to emancipate an entire continent from here." He urged the dispatch of money and additional secret funds. At least he wanted to spread the Soviet party line by publishing *El Libertador* and disseminate it south with a press fund of $300.[117] The negative consequences of such a proposal would be far worse than those of the Zimmerman Telegram in 1918. Increasingly the CROM leadership discretely signaled their disfavor with Soviet propaganda. Calles's messenger de Negri signaled the caudillo's displeasure.

Bertram Wolfe at that time taught communist classes to railroad workers. On one level, this was merely political consciousness-raising. On a deeper level, operators of railroads were strategic professionals who drove army reinforcements to Mexican uprisings and kept traffic and commerce between the U.S. border and Mexico City alive. If Mexico's railroad were to stop running due to strike or sabotage, the Mexican border economy would be impacted. A simple soap in the boiler of a Mexican steam engine railroad could accomplish effective industrial sabotage.[118] Soviet organizing of the railroad workers involved an economic sector whose strategic value went beyond profit. What if communist engine operators were willing to transport Japanese agents in Mexico toward the United States?

Pestkovsky's presence in Mexico, while not a direct danger, helped to bring to light the fact that the Japanese ambassador in Mexico City had translated to the Western Hemisphere the traditional Japanese and German policy of funding socialists and communists if they promised to hurt their present and future enemies. Confirming Japan's systematic duplicitous behavior in the Western Hemisphere, Pestkovsky reported: "Already before I had received information from communist circles that the Japanese ambassador proposed to different left-wing personalities (among them D.N.) their help in fight against U.S."[119] Pestkovsky, out of his own initiative, visited the Japanese diplomat to explore this temptation. Officially the Japanese ambassador did not commit himself to anything. The signing of a Japanese–Mexican friendship treaty was under way, and he wanted to keep the appearance of a purely commercial Japanese–Mexican bond in the Western Hemisphere. If U.S. intelligence were to get wind of any Japanese–Soviet understanding about paying leftist groups to act against the United States, this could be exaggerated into a Japanese–Russian conspiracy in the Americas.[120]

Obregón's and Calles's security forces did not wait any longer and weakened the communist presence on the U.S.–Mexican border. In the summer of 1925, Wolfe was expelled from the country.

Soviet activity in the Western Hemisphere was always part of a global strategy. The first part was to drive a more effective communications structure into the areas that supplied the United States, Great Britain, and France with raw materials. Zinoniev, in Moscow, doubled his revolutionary push. By now he fought as much against Stalin as against Britain and France. His position was becoming shaky. He needed success and therefore pushed for a December 1, 1924, revolution in Reval. He sent orders to prepare for a new international revolutionary situation. On January 6, 1925, he sent additional instructions further stressing the importance of coordinating the movements in Algeria and Tripoli with the movements in India. The organization in this connection was to be entrusted to the French communists Doriot and Ferrand.[121] Next, in early 1925, the Comintern focused on Egypt. The ECCI met on March 30, 1925, to discuss the "program tasks of the Egyptian communist party." Russian leaders, in spite of the struggle over leadership, stopped revolutionizing Europe and turned to colonial areas and not just Asia.

In this context South America also figured more prominently. In the summer of 1925, Zinoniev established in Buenos Aires the Communist International Secretariat for South America. It was supposed to function as the central Comintern office for South America.[122] By the end of the year, Zinoniev directed Marcel Cachin, the French Communist Party leader, to foster an armed revolt in North Africa. The order came with an offer of 1,400,000 francs to finance the subversion.[123]

Zinoniev's position within the communist leadership became more shaky. He needed to show success. On October 8, 1925, Zinoniev secured the adoption of resolutions for placing the British, French, and German parties "on a military footing."[124] Soon Zinoniev would fall out of leadership. Stalin would pursue a different policy.

The development of the Japanese intelligence system in Latin America occurred parallel to the Italian, German, and Soviet activities explored on previous pages. The only difference is that Japanese political and military elites were strong enough to exercise complete discipline over it and to have it idle in neutral. Imperial Japan between 1923 and 1925 had no interest in moving from Latin American territory against the United States or other imperial rivals. Japanese policy, then, focused inward at system building, training, and information gathering. Once built the organization could be used at another time, during the next imperial clash in the Pacific.

Building a functioning Japanese network in Latin America was only one of three processes being realized by Japanese navy leaders. The second one was the settlement of territories in the Pacific given to Japan as a mandate by the League of Nations. Third, while Japanese and German spies cooperated in Latin America, in Europe an expanding Japanese and German technology exchange began, strengthening Japan militarily for a war over the Pacific against the United States or Great Britain.

As innocent Japanese emigrants relocated across the Pacific and Japanese traders shipped raw materials, ethnic Japanese spies and select Mexican supporters hid among them and targeted U.S. installations. Their spy organization evolved parallel to Japanese emigration and trade.

In Honolulu, Hawaii, a small spy network led by a Mr. Kinishita observed U.S. military installations. The group counted eight men, one agent for each Hawaiian island. The organization's main focus was the island of Oahu and its U.S. naval base.

Their first task was to evaluate the readiness of the U.S. navy in Hawaii. They reported nine thousand troops that were equipped with provisions, fuel, and equipment that was in a very bad state. They assessed it as "almost useless."

Second, the network identified potential targets for Japanese and other ethnic saboteurs. Ammunition and food depots seemed easy to set on fire. If superiors in Japan wanted to sponsor a revolt among Hawaiian islanders, agents assured them that U.S. forces would not be able to respond appropriately against such an uprising. Native Hawaiians held sentiments toward the United States that were " unfavorable in every way."

In contrast, ethnic Japanese communities were evaluated as "very strong." Two agents reported that they felt fervent enough to die for Japan, if the Tokyo government would order such sacrifice. An outside agent, a Mexican individual, evaluated the quality of this Hawaiian group as "valuable." Their conduct was ranked "good." In conclusion one report stated that Honolulu and the army base would be "very fertile soil for the purpose of the C/S/S/A."[125]

Japan also developed a second network on the islands that ran minor informers. Both networks communicated through couriers with still unknown superiors in South America.[126]

A third account evaluated the psychological state of U.S. troops. One report described sailors as weak. Among troops, the consumption and sale of narcotics was "more important than in any other zone." Not surprisingly, Japanese agents stated that drugs were one of two ways to gather intelligible information.

Japanese suppliers also sent drugs to other places in South America. The purpose was always to loosen the tongues of U.S. sailors.[127] In Santiago, another location of Japan's growing spy network, an order was given on May 13 to move drugs to Punta Arenas. An individual on board the US *Cincinnati* would receive them.

A Mr. Shidahara, living at 633 Corrientes Street, was mentioned as central agent manipulating individuals with drugs.[128] Another message reported the handing over of "2400 vials of Co. and Mor." Here, too, Shidahara and a Mr. Mendoza were involved.[129]

In Buenos Aires the Japanese intelligence leaders maintained apartments where U.S. sailors could take drugs, party, and spill their information. At 1315 Rocha Street, sailors disembarking from American ships could buy cocaine, opium, and other drugs. At parties here the naive or already "high" sailors were manipulated by female agents Spencer, Aida Lamas, and Castro. Sometimes former U.S. enlisted personnel helped them.

Ex-navy officer J. Jacob was supplied by a Mr. Sakati, who was still an officer and was employed on the *Cleveland*. He had also been in Panama.[130] Another former sailor from the U.S. *Delaware* supplied sailors on shore. One letter revealed them as occasional informants: " In the Coo. S. we have now one of the sailors of the *Delaware* expelled in Nov 1922, who has been in these parts for sometime and was a waiter in the Washington Hotel. With good results to 23 who knows him very well and know how much he is really worth."[131]

Exploiting ethnic anti-U.S. sentiments was a second commonly used Japanese tool. In Colón, Panama, during winter maneuvers of the U.S. fleet from January 18 to January 22, 1924, numerous Filipino sailors, who were U.S. navy chief petty officers, visited a Japanese barber with the name K. Ogane. At his barbershop at Calle Bolivar 110–119 in Colón, they stopped in not for a haircut but for a long undisclosed conversation. It continued even though the shop was full.[132]

But rank-and-file sailors of the U.S. navy were not the only target of Japanese spying. In Buenos Aires informers worked on enticing the U.S. vice consul. Elsewhere, in December 1923, the intelligence target was Mr. M, another unidentified new U.S. consul. The spy was instructed "to get full information regarding financial standing new Aguila Consul Mr. M and people close to him, spec women. With much prudence." Latin America's upper class was a third target. One agent announced: "I hope to establish a net in the country club as it is near to the administration and Ancon H."[133] The country club was also located close to a U.S. military installation.

In addition to soliciting information from U.S. service personnel, Japanese agents continued to sell weapons to areas of great tension in South America.

One agent was ecstatic that the failure of the Pan-American Conference had weakened future prospects for disarmament.

In 1922, one secret arms shipment from France had been brought to Mexico. Perhaps arms were shipped also to Central American countries. The order had been handled by a Mr. Poodt of the Lloyd Royal Belgium Line. In Valparaiso the firm of Kennedy and Hunter helped.[134] The intent of this arms sale group to encourage a Mexican arms buildup against the United States was discussed previously. In the words of one participant: "It is then necessary for us to display all of our activities and forces in order to transform Mexico into a strong and armed country and, at the same time, utilize the existing favorable current in Tokyo."[135]

These cases also describe the emergence of a French–Japanese arms sales organization in South America. The French–Japanese group provided military factions across Latin America access to weapons for their next uprising, coup, or cross-border attack. Japanese managers knew about this profoundly destabilizing effect. Still this group was eager to keep regional rivalries alive and violent.

The Japanese network also maintained contact with rebel groups. Revolutionary groups in Hawaii, the Philippines, and China seem to have been the preferred targets for Japanese agents. Here select Mexican individuals played a prominent role as couriers, as mediators, or, perhaps, even as advisers. One group was in contact with individuals who presented themselves as an aspiring revolutionary group named "The Committee Pro Liberty." Its members requested help from a Mexican agent named Mr. Lanz. He was expected to be in Honolulu to make contact with sympathizers at a Chinese/American bank.

Japanese agent Mr. Kinoshita told Mexican co-agent Rueda that he would be posted "definitely in some point of the Hawaii Islands": "But as yet the question has not been declared official, . . . if it should be you, you will have a brilliant opportunity shortly to be the chief of a very special organization, in peace as well as in a perhaps future war." And

> the news which is had from Central is quite delicate, as in these moments the people, the sovereign people, demand reparations from their mortal enemies, and a ministerial crisis and perhaps a governmental one is very sure. Then the secret sects will enter into action and if an internal revolution does not arise, a war will break out of a complication with the Chinese Government. It will be the grand moment for all our men and friends. I don't want to go into too many details, but I have already said much and during your stay I have occasion to converse with you.[136]

In another letter, Mexican agent Rueda was promised that he would receive details about the Japanese organization in Hawaii. He was asked to limit his correspondence to the prescribed channels to avoid disagreeable and dangerous consequences.[137] Reports of agents traveled from Peru all the way to China.

We do not know anything else about these groups. Still, the sources prove that Japanese intelligence was using South American sites to stay in touch with rebel groups in Hawaii, the Philippines, and China in 1924. The Western Hemisphere was not free of Japanese support for secret warfare targeting U.S. interests. All assertions to the contrary are wrong.

A distinct feature of the evolving Japanese intelligence system was its close cooperation with major Japanese trading houses. The records prove that at least the Suzuki company and the Mitsubishi company allowed spies to operate under commercial cover for their trips in South America. Most prominent was the Suzuki company. Japanese intelligence workers piggybacked on the commercial activities of some Japanese zaibatsus.

The supervisor in South America who processed news about the Hawaiian network was the Mexican individual Rueda. He resided in Buenos Aires and was close to the branch of the Suzuki corporation. He picked up his mail and instructions at Post Box No. 664 at the Suzuki office.

The Argentine heads of the Suzuki branch were Mr. Yamashi and his deputy, a Mr. Shigeshi Moto.[138] In May 1923, they relocated to a new office in San Martin, Buenos Aires. The new building had a watchman. And just like at the old location, a U.S. officer bribed the night watchman to make it possible to snoop into their correspondence. These notes provide a first impression of the joint evolution of Japanese trade and espionage cells.

At the end of May 1923, a letter proved that Mr. Moto worked not just as branch deputy of Argentine Suzuki but also as higher-ranking lead agent in cross-Pacific intelligence work. For example, one letter from the Cristobal Canal Zone, in Panama, informed him about the arrival of a new agent who was currently evading U.S. intelligence observation:

I am not yet in complete security but have arrived well and my pursuers have abandoned the chase. Under an assumed name I have resided for eight days in this hotel, which is, as you know, the property of the U.S. government. As always I had to use my good passport prepared for me sometime ago when I was working for Germany. I have conversed much with our friends in Panama and below I am giving you a list of friends intimately connected with the subject that is of such vital interests to us. They are Ali Sahik Anhar, J. A. Arango, Juan Tinker, Gerald Typaldos, very important, Marcial Torrente, Tucc Wo Hing Lung, for drug purveyor, and Gonzalez of the "The National."

The situation is very good and I will soon be able to count upon very valuable information for us with the assistance of Akawa and Ichikawa. There is little organization and much less a corps of agents and Morrow, who is not well, has gone away. I have paid much for them and the Chinese Chong who got them from a Captain at Fort Randolp who received 2,000,000.

I will continue within a week to Peru and Chile and will attend the conferences in order to be able to appreciate its real value.[139]

At the end of November 1923, a French spy wrote about Moto to Agent Gourley:

We acknowledge. According to what Moto tells us it will be very convenient to find friends among the Yanks and your system looks good to us. From Rio we are advised that the Franco-B. J. affair is in good hands. The principal work in it has fallen to Miss Mary Green, who has distinguished herself in first order. And who will shortly leave for the U.S., near the State Department, where is found her royal and very old friend Mr. St. H.K., who is pleased with our offer and still more so with the return of his ex-mistress. Addressed to Gourley.[140]

Moto's agents traveled up and down the western Pacific coast. Already in the first week of January 1923, one spy had left San Francisco for Colón. He was accompanied by Agents Matsubara and Kato. Together they were traveling on a Japanese cargo ship, hoping not to attract the attention of U.S. counterintelligence. The Japanese agents evaluated the skill of U.S. agents to catch them as very inadequate.

A second individual was traveling agent Mr. Takashita. He was traveling from Buenos Aires to Rio. Later he was planning to proceed to Chile and from there on to the United States, via Panama. Taking a break in Buenos Aires he visited the apartment of social spy Aida Lamas at Alsoma Street.

The Suzuki company branch was also in touch with Agent Fujisaki, who met people at 1268 Lavalle. These men also socialized with the French military attaché at the Confitería del Aguila.[141] Several Japanese arrived on the *Southern*

Cross. Standing out among them was Kiozo Okonoga. He employed two secretaries and, shortly, was going to Chile and Peru. They were also visited by the German Luedeke. Luedeke had an office at 729 Moreno and visited Suzuki's place at 459 Sarmiento.[142]

From Panama communication traveled farther north either toward Mexico or to San Francisco, with Japan as final destination. A second route went north to Suzuki's East Coast New York branch. In New York, the Suzuki branch was led by Mr. Kashiwa. A report about one of his 1924 trips opens a wider window on the organization.

He left New York on April 28 and spent one day in Washington, D.C. Then he proceeded to New Orleans in May and resided at the Grunewald Hotel. In the humid delta city, he visited the Antoine Hotel to converse with a Mr. Chandler. As he began to drink, the alcohol loosened his tongue. This gave voice to rare insights into how the noncommercial side of Suzuki Co. functioned.

Kashiwa knew a Mr. Tomematsu Hinata in New Orleans. He had arrived in the United States in 1904. He was forty-six years old and had three children. Officially he earned his living selling items from his store at 203 Royale. But he also ran a private courier and mail service from his third-floor apartment. His private post office received letters and forwarded them to a variety of people. These were not just private letters but also letters that in 1924 relayed commercial and other messages to intelligence agents in Mexico, Central America, and South America.[143]

The second major Japanese zaibatsu cooperating with espionage agents involved some branches of the Mitsubishi company. One intercepted letter revealed:

Certified and sealed in the same mail, I send these documents. They should be sent to Newberry to Tokyo. Other news and order will be transmitted by Mr. G. T. Kazama, who travels under No. E. J 219, and as representative of the Mitsubishi Shoyi Kaisha Ltd. . . . to Tokyo who should arrive there next month.

I will remain here some two months and then I will make the voyage of instruction, arriving in Santiago. A visit to Buenos Aires is not probable. Have heard from old friend Gourley who is in the Argentine after being an ace in Brazil for our machinations and surely his work will bring very good fruits.[144]

The previous pages provided an impression of the growing complexity of secret Japanese activities along South America's Pacific Ocean. After opening bases in most nations touching the Pacific Ocean, lead agents moved to improve the system's efficiency.

In Chile the network needed improvement. Once again Mexican agent Rueda was sent across the Andes to fix the problem. Rueda was to take charge of, at least, three tasks. First, attention needed to be paid to propaganda pertaining to Mexico. Second, some "revision" of the base in Panama had to be undertaken. And third, "the more important affairs of the islands of Hawaii" had to be paid attention to.

Rueda was expected to stay in Chile for fifteen days and was promised the help of additional agents. From there he might be asked to continue on to a side trip to Lima.

Rueda did as told. On May 24, a Saturday, he took the train to Mendoza and crossed into Chile.[145] By June Rueda and Lorel worked from the Pacific side. Rueda concluded the reorganization of the Chilean network successfully. Later he boasted, "In Chile all marches on tracks. We are totally aided by the government, whom we make believe that we are working against Peru etc. but you may imagine."[146] Rueda's superior was an unidentified Superior Council, chaired by a Captain Ikeda. All that is known about Ikeda is that he was a traveling lead agent and planned to arrive in an unknown South American city on April 19, 1924.

In the same year even old familiar German agents reemerge in the sources. There was zur Helle, once again working for the Japanese, this time living at 37 Reconquista.[147] And World War I saboteur Gezir Remeny was frequenting the social circle of Aida Lamas.[148] Perhaps he combined explosives with sex.

In early 1924, news suggested that a Japanese–Mexican intelligence system in times of peace could deteriorate fast. Peace enticed network members to lose focus. For example, members of the social espionage network failed to obtain good intelligence: "Most of our people are diverting themselves in Montevideo and Mar del Plata. Without worrying much about their affairs. Which all run by themselves and especially now that we have those shipments for F with all good luck." In Montevideo, Agent Rueda remained in contact with a Mr. Gourley, who was playing his usual game. But he had also become quite friendly with influential persons. Ms. Lamas's social intelligence work was going well "in the circle which belongs to her."[149] But others were not.

A Mr. Mella was taking a vacation but offered his son as an agent in the meantime. A Mr. or Mrs. Long returned in the beginning of March with results about some trip. A Mr. Spencer revealed himself as "a bigger fool than thought." Rueda thought he was not worth a payment of 5,000 reals.[150]

Maria Bustamente remained the central agent for social and amorous espionage. She maintained her own set of women for the solicitation of classified information. In reality, however, the women and their targets of inquiry increasingly enjoyed partying more than spying. Some seemed to fall in love with each other and looked forward to another bacchanalia paid for by Tokyo. By April 1924, Rueda admonished Bustamente:

You must proceed with the recommended type in a more concrete form, in order to obtain something more important on the part of the girls in relations with these officers. We have spent over the limit and we must justify our procedures. These women that you have with you may be very beautiful but perhaps they are not sufficiently smart for your activities. It has been decided to continue providing that in the future you work with more energy.

Then he ordered the prostitutes to relocate: "Two or three must be sent to San Francisco one to Chicago and one very good one to Honolulu under the orders of Iwakami. An important agent will arrive shortly in New York and will visit you together with No 89."[151]

Japanese–French intelligence cooperation thrived. In 1924, Office of Naval Intelligence agents had become certain that Japanese intelligence and France's Bureau International de Renseignements also cooperated in South America. The Buenos Aires office was connected with branches in Paris, Brussels, Tokyo, San Francisco, and Shanghai. In Buenos Aires, a Mr. Ishy served as major Japanese correspondent. Officially he worked was the embassy's trade specialist.

In May 1924, Viscount Delatot, using the cover of general manager of the Havas agency, was identified as key lead French agent. He had just left San Francisco on board the steamer *Lutetia* and planned to stay in South America. The French were covering their own tracks using Polish individuals to run communication trips. One was P. De Hochbaum, also called Delia Kolschinsky. A second was Adela Damranovich. Sometimes they were used to travel into the United States to communicate with arms merchants and spies named Backmann and Lorel.[152]

This spy work unfolded in the midst of a new cycle of Japanese emigration to Latin America. Japanese elites could impose neither military, commercial, nor administrative rights in Latin America. Still, government ministries had learned from the time before World War I and, now, began to improve the flow and quality of emigration.

In 1920, the Ministry of Interior allocated about $10,000 and $5,000 to hold predeparture orientation programs for prospective emigrants. The next year the ministry significantly raised funds and provided $100,000 and $49,850 to promote emigration. Tokyo was determined to provide better protection for emigrants.[153]

Brazil emerged as Japan's preferred country of emigration. The movement of people was improved by monopolizing it in the hands of a so-called Overseas Development Corporation. Only this state-sanctioned company was allowed to recruit and transport emigrants to Brazil.

The 1923 Kanto earthquake was a major disaster not only for the Japanese navy but also for Japan's general population. The destruction was so great that social pressures once again increased and, therefore, heightened the need for places to emigrate to. From then on the Ministry of Interior offered financial encouragement to emigrants. At first, the costs of a individual's train trip from hometown to port of departure were subsidized by cutting it in half. Soon thereafter the ministry paid a bonus to individuals who were willing to recruit emigrants for Brazil. One year later the government took over the entire cost of a sea trip from Japan to Brazil. Emigrants could travel for free.[154] Upon their arrival, individual emigrants had to register with the Japanese consulate or embassy in their new region of settlement.

Regional Japanese governments joined the efforts of the national government. In 1923, the Nagano Prefecture Shinano Overseas Association purchased 2,200 acres of land in Brazil. Other prefectures interested in land were Kumamoto, Tottori, and Toyama. Not many of these projects lived on successfully, but government links between Japan and South America steadily increased. Even though these projects failed because of divisiveness and deadlock, Japanese ethnic settlement increasingly developed according to government-directed settlement patterns.

Then the principled, racist clamor in U.S. state legislatures against all ethnic Japanese Americans in the United States further complicated emigration to the Americas. Even in Brazil, a Senator Fidelis introduced in congress the first anti-Japanese bill.[155] Still, 3,689 individuals decided to make Brazil their new Japanese home abroad.

By then, in the United States, the nativist movement had reached a fever pitch and radical antiforeigner legislation was passed and enacted in May 1924. Once the U.S. Congress passed the exclusion bill, Japan reacted by holding an Imperial Conference launching a new policy approach called prosperous coexistence.

None of these emigrants knew about the spy networks. Also emigrants were rapidly joined by businessmen who conducted business with no consideration for their poorer countrymen and -women.

Japan's commercial expansion continued more than ever before. They invested in raw material extraction, communication projects, or land purchases in geographical zones that carried a strategic value. Already in 1922, a Japanese commercial mission had toured Latin American markets.[156]

One year later, in Mexico, a Japanese investment group presented a proposal to the Mexican government to construct a railroad from Acapulco, Mexico's most important and strategic Pacific port, to the Mexican capital. Of course, there it would connect to Mexico's already existing railroads going north. Such a network could carry goods but also troops all the way to the U.S. border. This railroad had a military and a civilian function, depending on the situation.

The proposal was presented by a high-level member of the Japanese embassy to the Obregón administration. The extensive dossier was well researched, correctly identifying every Mexican landowner along the projected track.[157]

At the same time a high-level Japanese official visited Mexico for at least four weeks. During the trip the possibility of an alliance was mentioned at least once. Obregón and the Mexican army rejected both the strategic railroad proposal and exploration of an open alliance.

Nevertheless, Japan's government did not feel rejected. It decorated President Álvaro Obregón with the same medal that France's World War I winner, General Foch, had received. More importantly, the Japanese minister to Mexico did not hesitate to travel all the way from the capital to Sonora to pin this medal of honor on the parting president's lapel. Imperial Japan knew how to charm Mexican politicians. Obregón declined neither the visit nor the medal.

In Chile, Iko Magsaki explored mines in the name of an unknown Japanese syndicate. Soon thereafter, he proposed investment in strategic Chilean mines offering copper and nitrates.[158]

By 1925, Japanese policy refocused strongly on trade, since war would be out of the question until the 1930s. In October 1924, a Japanese trade mission had left for the United States and South America. The chief of the mission was Dr. Uchi Yama, only recently made a secretary at Japan's Foreign Ministry. He had also worked as the private secretary of the Japanese minister to Rio de Janeiro, Mr. Tatsuke. He was accompanied by Dr. Koshida, currently a secretary at the Japanese legation in Mexico City. Most important among them was

Dr. Muroki, a mining engineer specialist and an employee of the Ministry of Industries. Finally, there was the chancellor of the Japanese legation to Buenos Aires. Initially, the group traveled to the United States. Then they continued to Mexico and Central America. In Colombia, they visited Bogotá and a salt mine. The next planned stay was Venezuela. A visit to all other South American countries would follow. The principal object of the mission was to study the commercial political and social conditions of the countries.[159]

Thus Mexican conspirators, now supported by President Álvaro Obregón, refocused their efforts on subverting rival Latin American regimes without Japanese help. For example, Mexican agents doubled their efforts against Venezuelan dictator Juan V. Gómez.[160]

Much farther in the west, across the Pacific, Japanese navy representatives eliminated any remaining German presence in the strategically important islands of Micronesia. In this geographical zone closer to Hawaii, the Japanese navy attended not only to military affairs but also to civil territorial administration.

Already in 1914, the navy had quickly occupied Micronesia in the name of the English–Japanese naval alliance. For the next seven years the navy administered the islands, until the Treaty of Versailles made the German removal permanent and converted the Japanese occupation into a permanent mandate. Previously Germans had governed the island group with twenty-five administrators. When it passed from Japanese navy hands to civilian administrators, Tokyo appointed six hundred administrators to execute a more systematic, permanent settlement policy. One year later, in 1923, the Japanese government subsidized the first tours to the Japanese homeland.[161]

The claiming of these Pacific islands by the Japanese through emigrants as well as the extension of the reach of the Japanese navy had begun. By 1925, 7,340 ethnic Japanese would be settled there. Even if later the League of Nations administration were to end the Japanese mandate, the strong Japanese civil administrative influence over the islands would be difficult to uproot. Its segregated, nonassimilation tone effectively turned the space into something dominated by Japanese tools of power on several levels.

Japanese governance was strengthened through a new type of civilian administration called the Nanyo Cho or South Seas Government. Now the Japanese navy, private commercial money, and ethnic Japanese settlers worked side by side. Private financiers invested in a so-called South Seas Development Company (Nanyo Kohatsu company) and a South Seas Trading Company (Nanyo Boeki company). The companies took control of the islands' industries and communications system. The Japanese government itself focused on strategic phosphate deposits and financed a mining company. Settling Micronesia was easy because Japan had been given not only settlement rights but also direct political control.

And yet the Japanese–German relationship seemed unaffected by Japanese occupation of a formerly German colony. To the contrary, Admiral Behnke, the head of the Weimar navy, reimagined Japanese–German technological connections from simple military sales and technological exchange capabilities to a deliberate, grand strategy. He hoped to deflect British and U.S. pressure on European naval affairs by strengthening Japan's military technological rise in the Far East.

The 1923 French and Belgian occupation of the Ruhr area provided a sobering realization of Germany's complete lack of capacity in naval and army affairs. Moreover, the Ruhr crisis emphasized submarines as important for future mobilization plans. They would have to fight French naval units and attack military convoys in the North Sea and the Mediterranean.[162] But Germany had no submarines and could not take over immediate service. It would take time to develop and to build them.

In 1922, negotiations failed to secretly contract German submarines for the Russian navy. In late 1923, Admiral Behnke received 10,500,000 gold RM.[163] He instructed Captain Lohmann to supplement his mobilization preparations.

Part of this effort was to find sites to construct submarines. Suddenly the Japanese naval yard in Kobe gained new importance for Germany. Sometime between January 1923 and May 1924, a secret Japanese–German treaty was reached, which contracted the construction of three cruisers according to German design. According to the British historian Chapman, the most important agreements were made orally, between Kapitaenleutnant Steffan and Japanese navy negotiators.[164]

The first of the cruisers was expected to be finished in 1925. By the end of 1926, the other two would be finished. In addition the Japanese built three minelaying boats based on improved plans from Blohm and Voss.

Already the next year one cruiser submarine was assembled from parts wholly supplied by Germany.[165] German blueprints, materials, and personnel, supervised by Brauetigam, now built a Japanese submarine wing. Later it would be able to deliver painful strikes against the U.S. fleet.[166]

In early 1922, Kawasaki created its own submarine construction department. Blueprints from German submarines *U-125* and *U-142* provided important technological know-how.[167]

The Kawasaki company hired former submarine technicians and one submarine commander. The construction office of the Germaniawerft and AG Weser in Bremen provided technicians. Submarine commander Brauetigam was selected, and he brought with him the technicians Sandner, Strehlow, Heise, Vogler, and Ilse. Officially these individuals simply went on vacation to Southeast Asia. But they crossed Europe, India, and Asia to work as submarine constructors in Japan.[168]

From there it was only logical to place small airplanes on Japanese submarines. Here the Heinkel company made available its catapult planes, happy to find one more international customer. The U.S. navy was also interested.

Japanese navy officer Kaga visited with Ingeni Yonezawa of the Japanese company Aichi, Tokei, Denki KK. They wanted airplanes that could be used as torpedo planes based on land and sea warfare. The Japanese promised to warn the Germans if international controls came and investigated.[169]

Already in 1922, two delegations, consisting of twenty people, traveled to German airline companies and stayed for one year. One group of Japanese navy engineers studied the use of metals in airplane construction at the Rohrbach company. The Mitsubishi company, in particular, wanted to use their techniques and added an engineer to the team. A second group visited the Duerener Metallwerke to learn about aluminum manufacturing.[170] The Sumitomo company also participated.

Purchasing existing airplane licenses was the second leg of the Japanese strategy. In 1923, Dornier and Kawasaki signed a ten-year licensing agreement for the construction of nine types of airplanes. The Dornier company was eager to stay in business and delivered airplanes but also technical personnel. Dr. Richardt Vogt, plus five engineers and pilots, traveled to Japan. In Japan, Dornier employees not only assembled existing parts but became the key technical advisers to help Japan make the transition from wood construction and cloth covers to Japanese planes built out of aluminum.[171]

A third Japanese team visited Friedrichshafen, Germany, and learned about zeppelins. This group purchased engines, disassembled them, and shipped them to Japan for reassembly.

In 1923, the Kanto earthquake changed Japanese naval policy. It destroyed so much property that customary government spending patterns were interrupted and rededicated toward domestic reconstruction. The consequences of the earthquake called into question the idea of allocating large amounts of money to the building of a navy that could fight those of the United States and Great Britain. But the death of the esteemed Admiral Kato in 1923 removed from imperial leadership the key national naval leader, who had unquestionably restrained the more radical factions and their desire to engage the U.S. fleet.

In 1924, this story comes full circle in a most fascinating way. In 1919, Japanese technicians had traveled to Germany to investigate the benefit of German technology for their armament. Five years later, in 1924, it was German captain Wilhelm Canaris who traveled from Germany to Japan to evaluate the benefit of Japanese factories for German rearmament. His task was to gain a personal impression of German–Japanese cooperation in the submarine and naval sector and to predict the potential of German–Japanese technological exchange.

Previously, in World War I, Wilhelm Canaris had served on the SMS *Dresden* until it had scuttled itself in South America. In 1914, Canaris was interned in South America, but he managed to escape with the help of ethnic German merchants. Once back in Germany, he resumed his life as an officer of the navy and served as an intelligence officer and submarine commander in the Mediterranean.

In 1924, Admiral Behnke selected Canaris as point man for cooperation with the Japanese to continue under Behnke's successor, Admiral Zenker.[172] Canaris was to contact leading members of the Japanese navy and to offer German support to the navy's leadership. At the same time he was to identify the state of the submarine construction based on German designs at the Kawasaki yard in Kobe. Wilhelm Canaris embarked on June 17, 1924, on the steamer *Rhine*, disguised as a cosmopolitan German tourist.[173] It took the ship until July to reach Kobe.

On July 23, 1924, Canaris visited the Kawasaki naval yard and its submarine cruisers. Three types were under construction. He also saw three mine-laying boats based on improved Blohm and Voss plans, designed in Germany.[174]

At the Nagasaki yard, Canaris talked with German engineers Vogel, Strehlow, and Rogge. They expressed great satisfaction about the state of the work. Next, at the Mitsubishi yard, Canaris saw ships and was honored with a tea ceremony.[175]

After visiting naval yards Canaris talked naval policy. On July 25, he and Attaché Arakis traveled to Tokyo to visit Japan's Navy Ministry. A high-level reception committee received him, and three days of discussions with select experts at the ministry followed. The talks proved to Canaris that they were interested in continued serious technology cooperation.[176]

Canaris met key high-ranking Japanese partners. One of them was Admiral Ide Kenji. Then there was Counter Admiral Ide Mitsuteru, who headed the 6th Section of the 3rd Group of the Admiral Staff. In 1924, he was in charge of Japanese navy intelligence dealing with Europe. A third was Vice Admiral

Yoshikawa Yasuhira, the head of Japan's armament department. Finally, Canaris was introduced to Captain Ide Koki, the head of the 5th and 6th sections, a bureaucrat who digested intelligence from Europe and America, as well as analyzed war historical themes.[177] According to the German historian Sander-Nagashima, these men were some of the highest-qualified officers of the Navy Ministry at that time. In particular, they were experts in charge of what Sander-Nagashima refers to as "Navy Foreign Policy."[178]

Canaris's visit ended on August 10. Thereafter, he took a boat back to Shanghai, where the *Rhineland* was waiting to take him back to Germany.

How did Canaris evaluate his insights gained in Japan? He had not revealed much new to his Japanese counterparts. Nevertheless, he informed them about the top secret measures that the Reichsmarine had taken to preserve forbidden expertise about U-boat construction.

In truth, Canaris returned frustrated. He had not discovered any common interest between the Japanese navy and the Reichsmarine. He attributed this to the Japanese notion that Germany lacked essential weight to be a serious coalition partner. He explained to his superiors, "The navy is not driven by any feeling of sympathy or common interest with Germany. . . . In Japanese eyes Germany lacks the necessary precondition for a community of interest: the ability to enter into an alliance."[179]

What did he suggest should be future German policy? Canaris recommended, first, that the Japanese, in individual cases, should receive minor concessions. Right away, however, these concessions should be neutralized. Second, Germans should insist on "true reciprocal measures" in the form of financial compensation. This could allow German industry to develop expertise in particular areas and then to make insights available to the Japanese navy. This continued effort to divert the focus of the entente powers from Europe to the Far East would require, however, total secrecy. Even diplomats were not allowed to know about these understandings between the German and Japanese navies.[180] Canaris's suggestions circulated in German navy offices from November 1924 to May 1925.

His new boss, Admiral Zenker, decided to move German attention from Japan to Spain. Also, expanding German–Japanese technological cooperation might endanger German chancellor Stresemann's ability to receive loans in the United States.[181]

In Berlin, Canaris remained assigned to Flottenabteilung AII, under Arno Spindler. From then on his task was to play the invisible hand of the navy to force competing German design offices and companies into one secret, unified armament movement. It needed to become strong enough to prepare for the construction of a new German navy, violating the restrictions imposed by the official limits of the Treaty of Versailles. For that goal Canaris had to align the organizational machine of the navy and finances with private German U-boat development efforts. To say it differently, Canaris was laying the foundation for the first, illegal German submarine wing since World War I.

Spain fast emerged as a preferred place over Japan or Argentina. To prepare the shift from Japan to Spain, Canaris traveled to the Iberian country and stayed between January 28 and February 17, 1925.

In Spain he impressed upon German companies the need to work together. He criticized their tendency to compete, instead of working together for Germany. Canaris began to identify and analyze selfish German company behavior in Primo de Rivera's Spain.[182] German secret naval rearmament was once again located in Europe and significantly closer to Latin America.

Secret naval armament moved in step with secret air force development. First, this meant to make sure that French policy would not prohibit a direct German air route into Latin America and from there on north toward the United States. Second, this meant developing and executing a singular German air policy. So far several rival German factions and companies realized only their particular vision of air policy, even if that meant the nation had to come second.

Initial policy efforts between 1920 and 1922 consisted simply of conquering market share for aircraft manufacturers. The companies Dornier and Junkers experimented with establishing a sales outlet in South America. But then the Allied powers prohibited airplane export to the Western Hemisphere.

A second time, policy was made by three German and Austrian individuals. On May 5, 1921, Mr. Schlubach and the Austrians Fritz Hammer and Bauer founded Aero Lloyd. Bauer proposed the founding of a study syndicate that would explore the use of new technology in an economic struggle against U.S. competitors. A technical system was to locate raw material deposits by plane in South America, before U.S. explorers reached them on foot or by truck. For that the SCADTA Colombian airline company was to be expanded into a raw materials exploration company. Dr. Hammer, as chief pilot, wanted to operate five Junkers planes. Hammer wrote to Professor Junkers, "I would like to hope that you, highly esteemed Professor, will duly take into consideration our activity and position as pioneers of reconstruction of our overseas interests, which have experienced such serious damage."[183]

Bauer quickly learned that being German and having a passionate economic vision were not enough to overcome the key obstacle of many strategies: the lack of foreign investment capital. U.S. companies did not have better ideas than Germans, but at least they had access to foreign exchange that could become venture capital. Thus a new push began, a search for Latin American investors who would be willing to devote precious savings to German dreams of economic expansion in Latin America. One assumed that businesspeople and the German government would be natural supporters for this strategy.

Three years later, on May 5, 1924, a new study group was created to explore the operation of German airplanes under the weather conditions of the Caribbean Sea. Coastal and sea conditions data would be collected systematically. Airplane instruments would be tested, and airports would be asked whether they wanted to train personnel, pilots, and mechanics. All sides agreed on secrecy as the plan became reality. Public ignorance was supposed to guarantee a German advantage over British, French, and U.S. companies that were also trying to jump the Atlantic by plane and to establish a reliable commercial air service. The men also understood how national air laws influenced future commercial routes. They were determined to influence national Latin American policy makers to pass air laws favorable to German goals. Once passed, they would help the creation of airlines, which in turn was expected to be followed by orders for German airplanes.

36. A plane of the German Condor Syndicate traveling near São Sebastião (Ibero Amerikanisches Institut, Stiftung Preussischer Kulturbesitz, Bildarchiv, Berlin).

In Brazil another group had finally successfully founded Aero Lloyd backed by German Brazilian trade houses and banks. Here too a committee was supposed to study the operation of an airline along the Brazilian coastline. They knew of and attempted to connect with the larger Junkers Central America project, expected to take place in 1926 or 1927. But Brazilian Germans were particularly interested in Dornier Wal airplanes and wanted to explore the Wal under tropical conditions.[184]

Much of their political clout came for their connections with the Brazilian secretary of transportation, Victor Conger. Two-thirds of their capital was Brazilian. However, Brazilian investors were more interested in creating a national airplane, not necessarily an air network.

A third group founded in Bolivia on September 15, 1925, South America's second commercial airline, the Lloyd Boliviana. Its founder was Guillermo Tillman from Cochabamba. He began operations with one Junkers plane. It was a joint gift from the German community and Bolivia. His business outlook improved

37. King Alfonso XIII interested himself in airplanes already before World War I (Library of Congress, Washington, D.C.).

as the Bolivian government recognized the company officially in November 1925. Later the company would buy three more Junkers F 15s.[185]

In sum, the struggle for German air routes resembled a shoving match among ethnic investors, airplane manufacturers, military air strategists, and government civilian planners. From the outside they were all assumed to think and act as nationalist Germans. In reality they were competing wrestlers sharing the same mat. This was not a good setup to defeat French or U.S. air pioneers.

Spaniards were aware of German experimentations and rivalries in the air sector. They themselves had selected Dornier planes for Spain's air force. But Spaniards wanted more. Like the Latin American countries, they wanted their own national military-industrial complex.

The end of this chapter returns to the Spanish-speaking world. It is not Argentina, however, that moves back into focus. It is the Spain of Alfonso XIII and General Primo de Rivera.

King and dictator were eager to add the most modern technology to the second-rate machines that Great Britain and France were willing to give Spain. In this context German military technical experts, among them Wilhelm Canaris, were of the highest interest.

15   Spain's Elites Lay the Foundations for a Global Iberian Commonwealth

S uddenly a new player entered the scene, the Spanish monarch Alfonso XIII and Spanish aristocratic investors and banks. In Madrid, Spanish aristocrats, entrepreneurs, and the monarch himself began to use Spanish–Argentine ties to realize more immediate political goals in Europe. Spain prepared to strengthen its political standing as a postwar European power by enlisting Latin American endorsements in favor of a distinct Iberian bloc inside a future League of Nations. Spanish American votes were to translate into a permanent seat for the Spaniards on the League Council. Spanish diplomats hoped that Argentina would play a leadership role, lobbying the Spanish American republics in favor of the previously rejected motherland.

Also, Argentina could become a natural distribution center for a major Spanish world trade expansion. From the Río de la Plata, merchandize could be forwarded across the Andes or up north to the Rio Paraná. Such a reliable, fast, ship/rail infrastructure combination would make renewed European imperial economic penetration of South America much easier. And Spain, once again, might be the country of origin for a second European commercial conquest of the Western Hemisphere.

Transport via this line was expected to be cheaper than transport by boat from the United States to Buenos Aires. This possibility was not just a mere pipe dream. Already on February 25, 1918, the Spanish Ministry of War had resumed discussions about the project.

King Alfonso XIII also issued a Royal Order to find a point west of Tarifa to drill a tunnel to the Moroccan Coast by 1923. The Spaniards were eager to secure for themselves one of the great transport conduits of the world. Until now Great Britain had put up insurmountable opposition. But now movement seemed possible. In June 1918, the *New York Times* confirmed renewed interest among Spanish investors in the project. One month after the World War I armistice, a Spanish technical commission, led by Pedro Javencis, arrived in Algeciras. He continued where engineer Don Moriani Rubio y Bellue had stopped in 1916. Now engineers and geologists examined the nature of the soil and the depth of the channel. This would yield critical technical data to develop a business plan for the historical transportation tunnel. By June 1919, a study commission under the leadership of Don Romuli Bosch y Alsina had been founded.[1]

Alfonso XIII and Primo de Rivera were eager to modernize their armed forces. The irony was, for both men, that Spanish society and its key social, religious, and political institutions did not share their zeal for modernization. Since 1923 the question was, how should Alfonso XIII and Primo de Rivera transform Spain into a late-rising significant economic European power, if lower-class Spaniards preferred the eternal conflict of ethnic identity politics? German captain Canaris,

38. Dictator Primo de Rivera pushed Spain's military to modernize with the help of secret arms developments involving the Weimar navy (Library of Congress, Washington, D.C.).

after he arrived in Spain in 1925, realized the great fissures of Spanish society. Spain needed to acquire key industrial sectors and infrastructure, just as Great Britain, France, and Germany had done in the nineteenth century. This was the Spanish context into which secret armament expert Wilhelm Canaris traveled.

The Spain that Canaris encountered was difficult to understand for a European from north of the Pyrenees. At its political core rested stubbornly regional identities, the Spanish Catholic Church, the army, aristocrats, King Alfonso XIII, and, after 1923, recently installed dictator General Primo de Rivera. Both men acted out of the deepest personal love for their dynasty and their nation. Both understood, and had shared with each other, that the Spanish monarchy and its nation needed to modernize as fast as possible.

Once Alfonso XIII and Primo de Rivera negotiated with Canaris it became apparent that the German need for secrecy about illegal rearmament could provide Spain with breakthrough technology, potentially offering real advantages over British, Italian, and French navies. Even better, with Canaris they seemed to have to deal with only one German decision maker. And Canaris's technology offer could be accepted without having to destroy the British and French military supply relationship that the Spanish army would continue to need for years. Perhaps Spanish generals and admirals could cherry-pick from both suppliers for a while.

If secret German–Spanish cooperation would weaken the military standing of France, Italy, and Great Britain, the king and his dictator did not object. Their elites and armament industries had oppressed Spanish naval development long enough.

Alfonso XIII was a Spanish imperialist, with designs not just toward Africa but also toward South America. Only he did not display his imperial passion for Spanish America in public. Alfonso XIII's mentoring of neo-imperial Hispanistic forces went as far back as 1900, when a Congress of Spanish America had been held with the intent to reenergize Spanish ties with Spanish America following Spain's 1898 loss in the Spanish–American War.[2]

In April 1914, when a Hispanic Congress for History and Geography convened, Alfonso XIII had already been king for ten years. At the conclusion of the meeting historians and geographers agreed to meet again in 1916. Several months later, however, the outbreak of World War I forced a suspension of such cultural fraternity for the next five years.

A new call for the congress was issued in June 1919. But now it was connected with a long-planned but also unrealized national exhibition at Seville, Spain. Alfonso XIII connected these separate events into one broader, government-

39. Alfonso XIII
as a young man
shooting clay pots
(Fondo Cultura,
F 1078–01–001,
Archivo General de
la Administración,
Alcalá de Henares).

coordinated Hispanic program. Most importantly, these cultural events would be merely the visible top layer of systematic Spanish economic and political outreach toward Spanish America. The goal was to reconnect with Spanish American governments in such a way that they would begin to share social, economic, and legal practices and concepts. In the end it was hoped that the community of shared practices would turn into a global political Iberian Commonwealth. It should include the Philippines and Portugal.

Alfonso XIII wanted to use historians and geographers as a core group of individuals who could be counted on to attract other groups to come to an all-encompassing congress at Seville. Ideally the Iberian exposition at Seville would be the king's symbolic convention of a new Spanish-led commonwealth. Of course, there were immediate political concerns.

Spanish policy also meant exploiting opportunities in Latin America. In 1919, news reached Spanish aristocrats that excellent oil fields might be available in Mexico. Here might be a fantastic opportunity to make Spain an owner of a concession and to guarantee a supply of raw petroleum in Latin America. Carranza wanted only a 10 percent royalty of the field near Tuxpan. Suddenly the Spanish Ambassador to Mexico Duke de Amalfi urged decision makers in Madrid to send money. By July 1919, a deposit of US$25,000 was asked. Soon thereafter $625,000 would be required. Leading Spanish aristocrats became excited, among them the Marqués de Urquijo. The director of the Bank of Vizcaya received the task of exploring the offer.[3]

Also in 1919, a Spanish stock company had been founded to prepare for the future exploitation of any major Spanish–Argentine commerce. This Sociedad Comercial Hispano-Argentina was incorporated by Don Francisco Moreno Zuleta, also known as the Conde de los Andes. To keep high aristocratic ownership hidden he positioned Enrique González da Careaga as front straw man. He, in turn, accepted investments from four other investors who functioned officially as members of the board. In reality none of the four had the riches to match the 25,000,000 pesetas investment capital that the Conde de los Andes had placed inside the company.[4]

For Spain's elites this was only one of several key strategic acquisitions. A more significant one was pulled off by Spanish bankers. Already in 1919, unnoticed by average Spaniards, a group of Spanish banks led by Count Urquijo had accepted ownership of German investments in the electrical and public transportation companies of South America. Made a few months after the end of World War I, this deal was clearly an attempt to hide assets from British, American, and French confiscation. Still such interpretation does not go far enough. The Spanish economic takeover also represented a successful power grab by Spaniards of major South American public utilities. Future research needs to examine how much money the previous German owners received from the Spaniards. But there is no indication that the Spaniards intended to return the property. It did not hurt that the Germans thought of Spanish ownership as a favor to Spain.

In the meantime Spain hoped to position itself in the emerging League of

Nations as exclusive advocate for all things Spanish American. Leading Spanish diplomat Quinones right away portrayed himself and his country as Protector of Hispanidad. In that spirit in the eighth session of the league nineteen Spanish-speaking nations backed an official resolution to elevate Spanish to official league language, next to French and English.[5]

Spanish diplomats also made special efforts to nominate Latin American diplomats to league committees. Social contacts were deepened with the help of a lavish annual banquet in honor of Hispanidad. Over and over again, Spanish diplomats in Geneva emphasized that they were spokesmen for all Spanish-speaking countries.[6]

Alfonso XIII backed his diplomats' efforts. Already in 1920, when Argentine foreign minister Pueyrredón traveled to the league, the king asked him to make a detour and visit Madrid. The proud Argentine refused, but the two men still met in Paris on November 8, 1920, at the Hotel Maurice.[7] And in Paris too the Spanish king advertised his alleged special affection for Argentina.

Next, at the end of 1920, Spain's Infante Don Fernando visited the Pacific coast of South America. He participated in the Chilean commemoration of the four hundredth anniversary of the discovery of the Strait of Magellan. The journey was rumored to be a feeler for a potential later visit by Alfonso XIII himself.[8] It would be the first time a Spanish king would set a foot onto Latin American soil.

Chileans politely returned such Spanish courtesy and affirmed October 12 as an annual national holiday for the celebration of the Dia de la Raza. Then Don Fernando proceeded to Venezuela, where he arrived in May 1921. The British ambassador to Caracas declared his visit as the most important and spectacular event in Venezuelan politics in 1921.[9]

Conservative Spanish politicians went further. They increasingly said aloud that improved relations with South America might provide Spain with an attractive alternative to playing second fiddle to French and British policies in Europe. Spanish university professors, businessmen and civic societies, the monarch and the royal court all increasingly indulged in such hope.[10] At the most extreme end stood Spaniards like Jeronimo Becker. He urged the Spanish government to defend La Raza in the Western Hemisphere against North American and European encroachment. If it were up to him, Spain's new postwar political task would be to liberate Latin America from the chains of dependence of British commerce, French literature, and U.S. politics.[11]

If Alfonso XIII was motivated by imperial *grandezza*, other aristocrats and elites speculated that the king's policy might be good for their financial well-being as well. It was culturally normal for an aristocrat to make national policy and to profit from it. But unlike Alfonso XIII, many dukes were driven primarily by money and far less love for a cantankerous nation whose inhabitants refused to be won over.

The Iberian Commonwealth idea was both an expression of yearning of political royal imperialism and the economic outreach of aristocrats and elites who felt entitled to exploit the economic plums of a possible commonwealth. Profiting from Iberian bonds was the birthright of a political class that could not imagine that history would soon, after 1930, attempt to sideline them and turn them into mere rentiers in Parisian exile.

Then there was Spanish naval aviation interest in German air technology. Already in 1921, Spanish supporters of innovative air service had pushed for zeppelin construction inside Spain. The goal was obvious: The successful construction of a zeppelin would allow the operation of an airline that would connect Spain with the Western Hemisphere. The Madrid government granted a German zeppelin company a contract worth 1,000,000 pesetas, based on the

40. Already in 1920, Spanish investors hoped to turn into reality the notion of a Spanish–Argentine zeppelin connection with German technology (Ibero Amerikanisches Institut, Stiftung Preussischer Kulturbesitz, Bildarchiv, Berlin).

understanding that it would eventually would open a zeppelin factory in the country. Then a regular air service between Spain and Argentina would follow.

But then the Allied powers, in June 1921, imposed a complete, open-ended prohibition of all German aircraft manufacture. After the following destruction of prototypes for a future transatlantic flight, German aircraft manufacturers had an additional motive to seek a secret site to resume plane construction. It did not take long for Junkers to send a director to Spain to explore manufacturing possibilities. This feeler remained unsuccessful because the leaders of Spain's meek air force remained beholden to French and British aircraft constructors. And the head of the Spanish navy preferred Dornier over Junkers planes. Interestingly, Dornier could still build its planes under license in Italy. Other secret airplane manufacturing was relocated to the Soviet Union.

A fourth Spanish interest was telegraph communication. Here the first approaches had been made by Argentina. In 1919, President Irigoyen had entered into a wireless agreement with the Siemens-Schuckert company of Germany. Now that it was peacetime, this telegraph connection could help business contacts communicate more effectively between Spain and Argentina and, thus, compete with British and U.S. companies.[12]

Most history books do not mention the areas of interconnection among Spain, Germany, and Latin America listed above. The few that hint at them argue that Spain's disastrous military defeat at the 1921 Battle of Annual shelved these initiatives. New sources show that the victory by North African forces was not powerful enough to end these cooperations. And Annual also did not slow down Spanish preparations for an Iberian Commonwealth.

To the contrary, the Annual defeat added one critical, decidedly anticommercial Spanish–German connection. It laid the groundwork for later military connections between Spain–Latin America and Germany.

Already in 1921, when French gas bomb deliveries to Spain proved disappointing, Spanish buyers turned to the United States, hoping to purchase 105 tons of poisoned gas.[13] But U.S. Congress denied the request. And yet Spanish generals, the Foreign Ministry, and Alfonso XIII remained desperate to acquire one effective weapon to defeat the successful rebels in North Africa and their leader, Abd el-Krim.

The victory of tribal North Africans raised too many troubling questions about race, national identity, and the health of the remaining Spanish Empire. Spanish generals, diplomats, and aristocrats did not think it possible to accept defeat and a further reduction of Spain's remaining colonial possessions in

North Africa—if the current elite wanted to remain at the top of Spain's very brittle political system.

The Spanish army, a European army after all, must not be defeated by tribally organized fighters from "racially inferior" North Africans. Within this mind-set it became acceptable among Spanish leaders to secretly drop poison gas on the tribesmen. It would preserve the public impression of the might of the Spanish, and it would buy valuable time to force a most distasteful "but necessary" victory, in order to lift domestic political morale. Spain's population had not stomached easily the defeat at Annual. Even worse, French military observers, on the other side of the Pyrenees, also looked at how Spain was reacting. Perhaps France might soon expand further and be sole dominator of northern Africa.

Genocidal gas warfare required, at the very least, a reliable supply of gas and gas bombs. Suddenly, German technicians with expertise in building a gas-production factory were of high interest. Their expertise might free Spain from foreign purchases in the gas bomb sector. After summer 1921, the Spanish military, the Spanish Foreign Ministry, and King Alfonso XIII were at least willing to ponder what advantages Spain could achieve if they secretly hired German technicians from the prohibited gas sector and allowed them to manufacture in Spain.[14]

On August 16, 1921, Spain's Council of Ministers passed a royal decree that allowed the hiring of Germans to build a poison gas factory. Years down the road it would make Spain independent from foreign gas imports. The Spanish historian Jose Maria Manrique discovered that the government pooled 14,000,000 pesetas to finance the construction. In addition, Spaniards purchased hand grenades and gas masks from Germany. The first significant break away from exclusive deals with British and French arms manufacturers had taken place.[15]

The best German gas expert to hire was Hugo Stolzenberg. Initial feelers toward Germany were established through Spanish German banker Julio Kocherthaler.[16] In 1921, he was advising German professor Fritz Haber, the inventor of German World War I gas warfare and also a Nobel Prize in Chemistry winner. As Kocherthaler advised him about Spanish patent issues, he also forwarded the Spanish request to explore what German technicians could offer to the Spanish army. Professor Haber, who comfortably combined the zeal of a neutral researcher with the friendship of poison gas specialists in the German army, introduced Hugo Stolzenberg to the Spaniards.

Officially, Stolzenberg and his company in Hamburg were in charge of the destruction of the remnants of World War I German gas warfare. Unofficially, Stolzenberg did everything to hide as much raw material and functioning equipment as possible from Allied inspectors to keep a basic German gas warfare capacity alive. He only disposed of old, irrelevant bomb stocks. And he desperately sought new, secret locations, resources, and technology to resume his gas manufacture experiments. He and Haber stayed in contact with the German army, where generals continued to appreciate their cooperation, loyalty, and knowledge.

For a German gas warfare specialist Spain was of particular importance. Seen within the wider context of illegal rearmament, Spain was a country that potentially could provide German army planners with off-limits locations for the most innovative research. For example, Professor Haber himself explored with the Russian military gas expert Vladimir Nikolayevich Ipatiev whether the vast open spaces in the Soviet Union could provide cover for German gas factories. In communist Russia but also in formerly neutral Spain, British, U.S., and French inspectors would be prohibited from snooping into the state of experiments. For the German army the Soviet Union emerged as the preferred location. But for Stolzenberg, Alfonso XIII's Spain was, nevertheless, an important secondary country. He traveled to Spain to see for himself in November 1921.[17]

First, Stolzenberg hoped that the Spanish need for a national gas bomb factory would allow him to build a technologically up-to-date factory site to refine his one-step production process for the highly poisonous LOST gas. Second, Stolzenberg wanted to experiment with improving the delivery of preprocessed poison gas, in particular Oxol. Third, he hoped to advance the separation of chemical bomb components. This would allow the storage of separate components closer to the front and assembly shortly before attack close to the battlefield. In Spain, far from public view and Allied inspectors, such experiments could take place. Currently, in Germany, gas bombs could be deployed only against agricultural pests. Right away, the potential Spanish–German military cooperation in the gas sector looked like a win-win situation for the Spanish army, the Germany army, their gas experts, and Hugo Stolzenberg himself. No wonder Stolzenberg returned to Spain for a second trip on June 10, 1922.

When the negotiations concluded Stolzenberg carried an agreement in his pocket, detailing Spanish financing for the construction and use of a poison gas factory. The initial goals of daily production were 1.5 tons of phosgene, 1.2 tons of ethyldichloroarsine, and 1 ton of yperite.[18] The factory would be called La Marañosa or Fábrica Nacional de Productos Químicos del Jarama. The contract was signed on August 31, 1922. Historian Manrique discovered that Spain paid German manufacturers 4,000,000 pesetas.[19]

A second contract detailed the construction of a bomb filling station and the employment of technical advisers who would teach Spaniards their

German know-how. Furthermore, Spain bought a gas mask factory through the Auergesellschaft. Spanish generals, even before the Primo de Rivera dictatorship, diversified their dealings with foreign military supplies.

As prohibited bomb raw materials, technology, and filling stations were purchased from Germany, it was only natural to explore whether Germans could also offer airplanes, which could drop those bombs onto tribesmen. In a separate event in Madrid, already on September 15, 1921, the representative of the Steffen Heymann company had telegraphed to the Junkers airplane company in Dessau, Germany, that the Spanish government wished to purchase metal airplanes.[20] This request coincided with interest by Junkers to circumvent the recently imposed Allied prohibition to develop or to produce any airplane inside Germany. In the airplane sector, too, Germans came to recognize Spain as a possible protected site where airplane manufacture factories could be relocated. Perhaps their airplane manufacturing know-how and skills could be kept alive, until the limitations of Versailles were thrown off and production could be relocated back to Germany.

Future airplane production inside Spain could offer company profit and the penetration of the Spanish military and civilian airplane market, but hopefully also sales to South American military commissions. Only three years after World War I Spanish–German connections had been established in commerce, utilities, transportation, zeppelin construction, telegraph communication, gas warfare, and airplanes.

Alfonso XIII, in 1922, resumed efforts to move toward the Iberian American Commonwealth by deepening commerce between small and mid-size companies on both sides of the Atlantic. An economic congress was announced for 1923. On July 30, 1922, a royal decree delineated the specifics.

The plan suggested that in 1923 Spanish American business owners and Spanish manufacturers meet at three different locations in Spain, each time realizing a distinct but interconnected task to further the integration of Spanish and Latin American economies. First, Barcelona would host a gathering from March 21 until March 27, 1923. In Spain's most important commercial and industrial city economists and merchants would gather to exchange data that identified the deeper structures of Spanish–American trade exchanges. Their gathering would take place at the same time as the Fourth International Barcelona Fair of Samples. Spanish American conference delegates could walk to the exhibit and see with their own eyes which products Spanish and Spanish American factories were manufacturing and adopt them for export. The potential for commerce was obvious. Exhibitors from Spain and visitors from Latin America would plant seeds of Hispanic transatlantic commerce.

A second meeting would take place in the Spanish capital, Madrid. From April 1 to April 8, 1923, delegates would reorganize and integrate the system of Spanish chambers of commerce. A modernized chamber system could nurture exports between the two continents and serve as institutional bridges between Spanish and Spanish American markets.[21]

The secretary-general of the commission for reform of the Spanish chambers of commerce was Dr. Rafael Vehils y Grau. Officially he was in charge of representing the campaign in Latin America. He also worked as director of the Casa the America, chaired the official Committee of the Book, and was the head of the Institute of Commerce and Industry.[22] Vehils was a close associate of Mr. Cambo. This meant both men were friends and supporters of the bank house of Urquijo. The same group of men who managed much of South American electricity and transport now embarked on organizing Spanish American merchants in a complementary way to the utility business.

Finally, delegates would travel to Seville for a third meeting from April 10 to April 16, 1923. There they would visit the International Exposition of Electrical and General Spanish Industry and be introduced to the city.[23] It was the same location were the planned Exposition of Seville would open its doors. In Seville transatlantic commercial and cultural integration would unfold in parallel and synergistic ways.

The Spanish government developed additional measures. A traveling exhibit of Spanish artisan industry was dispatched to South America. It demonstrated Spanish products to Spanish American buyers who did not have the money to travel across the Atlantic.[24]

Most importantly for this book, the Spanish Foreign Ministry assigned to Spanish emigrant communities in Latin America a vital part in the creation of the foundations of Spanish neo-imperialism. Already in May 1921, a government decree had established a census of all Spanish people living abroad.[25] In August 1922, the Spanish Foreign Ministry explained to its ambassador,

> The number of established Spaniards in America is the most valuable development that Spain can count on to maintain and increase interests of all order and to stay connected to those countries. And one can also talk about the possibility of creating relations with the Philippines. . . .
> The results of this new policy would lay the basis for, a yet unspecified, base that would yield greater dividends in the future.[26]

The Madrid Foreign Ministry was to reach out systematically to Spanish American countries so that as many delegations as possible from across Latin America would participate. Their presence would validate the king's claim that Spanish Americans were reaching back toward Spain.

In December 1922, Spanish ambassadors were asked to reintroduce the Exposition in Seville to Argentineans, Uruguayans, Chileans, and Paraguayans. In addition they should form committees for the History and Geography Conference.

Argentina received special attention. Since Argentina was the richest and one of the most important South American countries, an improvement of Argentinean–Spanish ties might also translate into closer ties with Argentina's South American friends.[27] Spanish diplomats were replacing a two-decade-old, backward-looking Hispanismo with a forward-looking policy built around forming a Hispanic bloc.

The Spanish king made a special point to meet Argentine president-elect Marcelo de Alvear, interrupting his trip from Paris home to Buenos Aires as he was about to assume the presidency.[28] In Santander, Spain, Alfonso XIII and Alvear met on a cruiser in the first week of August 1922. Of course, an unconscious assertion of Spanish principled arrogance toward Latin America almost discolored the meeting. The king's speech writer suggested that Alfonso XIII should express hope that Argentina "would honor and love with the affection of sons the glorious Spanish mother." An alternative was "to the glorious Spanish mother that was blessed in a thousand ways." But Alfonso displayed enough sensibility to erase these lines in the manuscript, avoiding a patronizing affront. Hispanistic reactions to the meeting reached Spain all the way from Cuba. From distant Havana, the president of the Spanish Casino praised the meeting between the Spanish king and the Argentine president-elect as one that "initiated an era of indestructible mutual interconnection [*compenetración*] of the peoples."[29]

The Spanish ambassador in Argentina was to find out if Argentina would be willing to commit money early to the construction of the pavilion in Seville. He was to solicit specific amounts in order to advance the budgetary process in Spain. And rather than focusing on cultural exhibits, the ambassador was instructed to recruit representatives from agriculture, livestock, and agricultural machinery companies. Also industrial manufacturing, commerce, and primary material manufacturing companies were supposed to be invited. Hispanic cultural concepts were to be industrialized and moved away from the beaux arts.

The old notion of Hispanismo woven around culture was rapidly falling out of favor in Primo de Rivera's Spain of 1923.[30] The Foreign Ministry's interest in artistic representations was only at a distant fifth place.

The projected opening for the Seville conference was October 1925. It would last until June 1926. It would confront and certainly compete with the Paris Olympics of 1924.[31] Such was the ideal conception.

Then came the Spanish American response. In March 1923, the Argentine government responded only with a request for patience. A government decree was required before official committees could be formed. The Argentine press had simply ignored all projects.[32] Then there was the issue of disseminating the news about the planned conference beyond Argentina's capital into the provinces. Spanish pamphlets were distributed in the provinces until the end of 1922.[33]

President Alvear simply handed the initiative to Minister of Agriculture Le Breton. He in turn was interested in national government issues and the upcoming Pan-American Conference, but a Spanish exposition at Seville received low priority. Argentina's incoming President Alvear, too, did not reciprocate King Alfonso XIII's passion for a joint Iberian exposition.[34] This would have to change in the near future.

In 1919, a group of Spanish banks took ownership of German investments in South America electrical and public transportation businesses. After the transfer of stocks in 1919, it was the Spanish bankers who called the shots in the electrical and public transportation sectors of Chile, Argentina, and other Latin American capitals. The transfer of stocks from Berlin to Madrid was also a transfer of power.

Next the national Council of Spanish Overseas Commerce selected two special delegates who were to travel to South America to explain to Spanish ambassadors and consuls, Spanish ethnic organizations, and Spanish American companies the deeper meaning of this new Spanish initiative. Previously Emilio Boix y Ferrer had worked as economic expert for the Spanish Publication Center of Economic Information. In 1923, he was to focus on Argentina, Uruguay, Bolivia, and Peru. He was paid 8,000 pesetas a month to achieve three goals. First, he was to visit Spanish American businessmen and community leaders and explain policy details. Second, he was to motivate every Spanish chamber of commerce in South America to back the Spanish policy. Third, he was to recruit at least one hundred delegates to travel from South America to Spain. Ideally, each Spanish American chamber of commerce would dispatch at least ten delegates. In addition, each Spanish mutual aid association would dispatch ten delegates.

A second person was selected to engage northern Spanish America and Central America. Don Cayetano Rosich was to cover Chile, Peru, Ecuador, and Panama. And he would establish the first Spanish chamber of commerce branches in Lima, Guayaquil, and La Paz, Bolivia.

Spanish political vision and Spanish American reception did not naturally come together. Around the Río de La Plata states Don Boix y Ferrer diagnosed a disheartening reluctance, even indifference, to become united. For example, instead of ten delegates, the Spanish Buenos Aires business community promised to send only three. Montevideo financed two delegates, and Paraguay followed its example. In general, Boix reported a friendly reception but a persistent hesitation to commit.[35] Even state-subsidized ship tickets did not immediately increase the number of travelers to the Iberian Peninsula.

Lack of success in Argentina did not keep the Barcelona meeting from taking place as the First Congress of Overseas Spanish Commerce. In Catalan's capital the Spaniards presented themselves as self-assured economic actors. Even though the Spanish army had just been defeated at Annual, calling into question Spanish imperialism even in northern Africa, bureaucrats from the Foreign Ministry, the Ministry of Labor, and Spanish banks engaged Spanish Americans and even Philippine merchants. They insisted that their future business activity would be part of an expanding transnational Spanish American market; even Philippine markets should be connected to Spain's industry. Hopefully participants would return to Spain in 1926, when a Second Congress of Overseas Spanish Commerce should update the commonwealth effort.

Somehow the Spanish continued to try to usher in this new era of trade exchanges between Spain and South America.[36] After the conference, economic departments in the Foreign Ministry simply pushed on, asking bureaucrats to generate concrete economic data, rather than just ethnic solidarity or Hispanismo rhetoric.

Still in 1923, Spanish embassies in South America were to send back available data about Spanish societies in Argentina and Paraguay. Then Decree No. 801, from November 20, 1923, established a census registry of Spanish commercial firms overseas. A questionnaire was mailed to all Spanish embassies in South American capitals and Manila, the Philippines. After it was distributed in the community, each economic secretary in each embassy was supposed to see to it that it was filled out and results were returned to Madrid.[37]

On October 3, 1923, a second call went out to register all Spaniards living abroad.[38] Finally, economic expert Boix was to conduct specific research to measure how Spanish American communities could help Spanish trade expansion and the move toward a Spanish Commonwealth.[39]

Economic diplomat Boix proved himself as a one-man research engine to propagate Spanish trade policy toward South America. On November 1, he helped the Spanish embassy in Argentina to publish an article in the newspaper *El Diario Español* to explain his work.[40] Once again Boix cabled from Buenos Aires that Spanish American societies continued to fail to see the value of helping him gather data about Spanish American communities and their economic and social importance. The distributed questionnaires often remained unanswered or, at best, were returned late.

King Alfonso XIII knew Boix personally, and his royal secretary kept him modestly appraised on the economic development work. In early 1924, Boix's task was described to General Muslera simply as "increasing Spanish exports to South America."[41] But in a letter to the High Council of the Chamber of Commerce his task was defined as "to create and grow the exchange of products and to disseminate ideas, effective conventions and inspire treaties into reciprocal agreements."[42]

In the years to come Boix researched and analyzed eight hundred economic topics. His insights were summarized and regularly presented to Primo de Rivera's National Economic Council. The amount his work and its quality easily surpassed that of German and U.S. economists working at the same time.[43] Boix's work remains truly remarkable until today.

Mussolini's Italy is underappreciated as a rival of Spain's renewed outreach to Latin America. The details of Italian policy toward Latin America in 1923 remain to be investigated. But the Spanish administration identified Italy's changing government as a worrisome presence in Spanish America. The list of potential competitors also included an overwhelming U.S. economic presence, financially intimidating British strength, and minor French economic activity.

King Alfonso and Primo de Rivera visited Mussolini in Italy in 1923. They discussed the possibility of entering into an Italian–Spanish treaty, but the ongoing war in Morocco, Spain's seat at the League of Nations, and the relationship with France were higher priority. Besides, Primo de Rivera preferred a Spain that could continue to act independently. Nevertheless, news leaked out about Mussolini's desire to engage in a collaborative Spanish–Italian policy in Central and South America.[44]

After the king and dictator returned to Spain in January 1924, Primo de Rivera asked the Italian ambassador to leave out the issue of cooperation in

Latin America and consider only a mutual benevolent neutrality in any future Mediterranean conflict. Still, any secret Spanish–Italian treaty would be quite a provocation against the French and the British. Primo switched to communicating exclusively through a special envoy and excluded regular diplomats from treaty discussions.[45]

In talks Primo de Rivera evaluated Spain's ability to achieve measurable results with its current navy and military in 1923 as absolutely nonexistent. In his words, "Spain was a cadaver," in contrast to the "living body" of Mussolini's Italy.

Then Primo de Rivera elegantly put an end to the discussion. He declared that it was possible for Spain to have a close union with Italy without the necessity of signing a formal, secret treaty. Italy's diplomat interpreted this as reason enough to stop further talks.

If the Italian king Emmanuel reciprocated Alfonso XIII's visit to Italy in the near future, only vague pleasantries should be released to the Italian public, but not updates on some sort of more formal tie. When King Emmanuel traveled to Spain in June 1924, this is exactly what happened. In 1923, some kind of very definite bond had been created, but toward the public the government insisted on the impossibility of more extended cooperation.[46] And ultimately, Primo was still genuinely interested in working within the framework of the League of Nations.

Nobody controlled Spanish politicians; nor could anybody manipulate them easily. At the most, Spanish and British aristocrats and their economic and social ties to banks and trading houses could sway national policies to a noticeable degree. Independent of these truly upper-class men, only a few Spanish nationalists existed inside the army and the navy, eager to realize national armament development, free from foreign priorities. These men would always be determined to lessen Spanish dependence on British, German, or French armament designs. Their biggest obstacle in the domestic realm remained Spain's constipated and self-paralyzing national political process. In the foreign realm it was British and French determination to keep Spain politically weak and to stop Spain from developing a strong and independent military. For politicians in London and Paris, Spain was never to become a premier European power.

Already in 1915, initial Spanish military modernization had been spelled out in the Miranda law. Spain would project naval might into the Mediterranean and Atlantic Ocean by constructing two large battle cruisers and two light cruisers, plus several other smaller ships. After 1918, the lessons of World War I had created the additional need to acquire submarines, airplanes, and zeppelins. By the early 1920s, Spain's navy had purchased six U.S. submarines of 105 F Holland design. But Spanish engineers did not own the blueprints that would allow them to build their own ships according to their own parameters.

In Spain, the only space to build warships remained Cartagena. There, the Sociedad Española de Construcción Naval, also called La Naval, built predominantly foreign ship designs. Unfortunately, as before World War I, the company's majority ownership was tightly held in the hands of the British Vickers armament factory.

Some admirals were infuriated by how Vickers remained able to influence their navy's program. First, Vickers dominated the importation of raw materials into Spain for the manufacturing of ship parts. Vickers imported 80 percent of the parts and raw materials used in Spanish shipbuilding and charged Spain a bill that amounted to a debt of 25,000,000 pesetas by 1933.[47] It was a significant chunk of the military budget that builders from other nations could never compete for. Vickers investors treated La Naval as a subsidiary, not as a Spanish naval yard that should be allowed to pursue independent Spanish objectives.[48]

Spanish leaders too preferred to think that La Naval was a Spanish company run by the highly influential banker Marqués de Urquijo. But insiders knew that its day-to-day business was run by subdirectors José María Cervera and Alejandro Calonje. And Calonje enforced British policy preferences.

Alejandro Calonje was influential elsewhere as well. He sat on Spain's Council of Naval Administration and served as Vickers's confidential connection with the Empresa Plasencia de las Armas, its second Spanish subsidiary.[49] Calonje also created and presided over the Empresa Experiencias Industriales, S.A. de Aranjuez (EISA).[50] De facto, Calonje acted as Britain's armament development supervisor in Spain. And Naval Minister Marqués de Cortina backed dependency on Britain.

In contrast there was Juan Antonia Suanzes, a nationalistic military engineer who, in 1922, was decommissioned as an active soldier and took over the technical leadership of La Naval. From the very beginning, he was more determined to limit the exclusive import of supplies from Vickers.[51] But his fervor to reach independence remained the determination of a lone man. More had to happen to break open the military establishment's mind-set and financial ties to consider radical alternative options. It would take until 1924.

German success in gaining access to Spain's military gas sector did not mean a similarly warm welcome for other German experts in the Spanish army, air force, and navy. Spanish leaders decided whether German help was desired. Spanish generals and admirals decided what Germany could secretly build inside Spain. And both groups refused German alternatives to French and British military hardware.

This left one possibility: bribes and deception. This lesson was driven home by events in the airline sector. On May 3, 1922, a Mr. Rolland, Germany's key naval intelligence agent in Barcelona before 1918, once again surfaced in Berlin. Even though he lived in Spain Rolland had maintained business relations with Kommerzienrat Polysius and Direktor Schleissing. He understood the potential of using bribes to break into the Spanish air sector. So far, Rolland had negotiated with the German Albatros airplane company about representation. Now, German administrator Polysius wondered if Junkers was willing to receive Rolland to explore the manufacture of planes inside Spain.

Rolland told the German administrators that he had access to leading personalities inside Spain's ministries. The correct connection in aristocratic circles might allow the opening of a factory or, allegedly, access to 20,000,000 pesetas for future Spanish airplane purchases. In the words of Rolland, in 1922, Spain remained a unique opportunity for German airplane companies. Then he added the critical ingredient for success. It would take more than a good product and a skilled sales team to be successful. What was required was propaganda "and to bribe the appropriate number of parliamentarians and ministers, then everything would go by itself."[52]

The Junkers airline factory leadership in Dessau was at least willing to listen to Rolland. He was invited to repeat his sales pitch at the factory in Dessau. Rolland explained that access to the Spanish market could be bought with bribes. The Junkers director became curious and asked Rolland how many pesetas were necessary to be effective. The former agent's answer was veiled: "Well it depended on what you want to achieve." First, Junkers should define its objectives and share with him how much bribe money was available. Then Rolland would propose the type of enterprise that was appropriate to design around it. Once Junkers was ready to offer money, he could be reached through Señor Don Antonio Pi y Rabassco in Barcelona. He lived at Cortes 646.[53]

In the end Junkers took Rolland's advice and modified their strategy but picked another man to work with. Agent Rolland was considered lacking when it came to representing Junkers in Spain.[54] Airline managers offered him only basic propaganda brochures.

Instead, Junkers threw its support behind Frank Savamay, a man who promised excellent contacts to leading members of the Spanish cabinet and parliament. A former Austrian pilot, Savamay was related to Spanish senator Palomo. The senator, in turn, was a relative of Prime Minister Maura.

Beginning in 1923, Junkers director Schmuckler explored the possibility of using an existing business relationship with a Spanish company to build a manufacturing plant inside Spain. By then Junkers was interested as much in the civilian as in the military market. There were rumors that leading Spanish army members were thinking of acquiring forty planes per year, until a Spanish air force was assembled that would demand respect from the French and Italian air forces.

Schmuckler contacted the company Linke and Hoffman, which owned a potential manufacturing site at Forjas de Alcala. Initial talks were held in May 1923, at Berlin's Hotel Esplanade.[55] One strategy was a step approach. First Junkers would open only a repair shop. Later it could be expanded into an assembly site, perhaps even a factory. A second potential contact was the Factoria company, owned by Spanish general de la Puente. The general was of interest because he held a government concession that would allow the operation of Junkers planes as vehicles for a domestic airline. Finally, in June 1923, Junkers director Hans Sachsenberg went to Spain to see for himself.[56]

None of these efforts worked out. Because Spanish airplane orders continued to be controlled by French and British manufacturers, it remained uncertain whether Junkers could capture enough of a future market segment to justify massive upfront investment to construct and operate a factory on Spanish soil. Besides, Professor Junkers was talking to two other not-yet-identified Mediterranean countries, where possibilities were more promising than the difficult Spanish market.[57] Not to be overlooked, Junkers faced competition in Spain from German manufacturers Dornier and Fokker. Particularly Spanish navy pilots liked Dornier's Wal airplane. The Spanish military remained loyal to the Breguet 14, France's World War I workhorse.

The only lasting result out of the 1923 explorations for Junkers was the decision on Seville as the key future base for a variety of airplane and airline options, once profitability could be achieved. An airport already existed there, and it was well positioned to serve water as well as land airplanes.

Then, in fall 1923, Spain's political order collapsed. The only temporarily viable compromise to maintain the monarchy was the confirmation of General Primo de Rivera as Spain's military dictator. The establishment of an authoritarian Spanish state motivated those military factions that wanted to speed up modernization against the old traditionalists.

And Primo de Rivera's unique power brought the first results. In October 1923, the Spanish army administration passed a decree detailing the reorganization of airlines in Spain.

It was only bad news for German airplane manufacturers because it stipulated that Spanish airlines must exclusively use airplanes built in Spain. Even worse, Primo de Rivera suggested the creation of a consortium owned entirely by Spaniards that would bring Spain closer toward gaining independence in the airplane and airline sector.[58] Primo's authoritarian clout had decreed a budget of 10,500,000 pesetas for airplanes and 7,500,000 pesetas for engines.

No doubt the Spanish market for civilian and military planes would remain closed in the near future. Certainly Germans would dominate neither the Spanish military air force nor the civilian air sector. Perhaps Naval Agent Rolland's insistence, in 1922, on using juicy bribes had been correct. Perhaps it also offered the only path to circumvent Spanish law, and the Junkers company had rejected Rolland's offer too fast.

Indeed, without government support or huge bribes, in 1924, breaking into the Spanish air sector remained a punishing undertaking. In the end Junkers used deceit to establish at least the proverbial foot in Spain's air sector. Nationalist laws were circumvented by building a civilian airline company that looked Spanish from the outside. But inside, it was dependent on Junkers money and Junkers airplanes. Its name was the Unión Aérea Española (UAE).

As UAE's official president Junkers selected Moreno Caracciolo, who taught at Madrid's Technical University. A Dr. Rodriguez served as legal adviser, and Junkers was able to gain the support of a certain Dr. Yanguas, who later would become Spain's foreign minister. But in 1924, Yanguas was only an unimportant legal adviser of the Foreign Ministry.

Then there existed a second tier of Spanish investors, suggesting publicly that UAE was a Spanish company. For example, a Prof. Janques invested 60,000 pesetas. Prof. Moreno Caracciolo provided 50,000 pesetas. Marqués de Rubí, a sailor and officer of alleged influence at Alfonso XIII's court, placed 50,000 pesetas. A Captain Alonso deposited 10,000 pesetas. Finally there was Ramón Franco, the brother of Spain's future caudillo Francisco Franco. He invested 10,000 pesetas. Later, he would break with UAE and, once again, support Dornier. Then his shares were taken over by a Captain Ansaldo.

These Spanish investors provided only one-third of UAE's stock capital. The remaining two-thirds of the investment capital came from Junkers in Dessau. UAE was a German company operating a company airline in Spain. It was a subsidiary of Junkers.

UAE's true executive director was Junkers director Patze. He did his best to realize the Junkers sales concept. Unlike the German Dornier company, which contented itself just with airplane sales, Junkers wanted to create a vertically integrated company that controlled everything, from airplane production to operation of the airline. This approach was the antithesis of the Spanish Law of Nationalization.[59]

After the first year of operation, this cover-up had failed to make any respectable inroads. Director Patze and Herr Savamay operated only two F 13s for operations in Spain. All they could do was engage in the most basic flight operation. That meant inviting paying customers to enjoy short demonstration flights over Seville. At the same time, they tried feverishly to identify any Spanish government agency or ministry wanting to buy Junkers planes and to operate them permanently. All they could come up with was the Spanish Red Cross. Still, in 1924, UAE's investment capital was raised to 1,000,000 pesetas.[60]

Efforts to break into Spain's naval air force market proved even more frustrating. In March 1924, an A 20 water plane was dispatched to Barcelona. It was the first time that the Spanish navy was even willing to look at a Junkers plane for purchase.[61] By the end of March, Savamay had also demonstrated the F 13 in Madrid and, right away, took up negotiations with General Cardona of the navy air service.

The navy put Junkers planes through punishing test flights. One afternoon, the F 13 was loaded with 450 kilograms and tested over the open sea. The plane started and landed twice. Next, different types of propellers were installed and different heights were reached. Once a flight was interrupted at 13,500 feet, and observers were impressed that the machine could have climbed even higher. Another test consisted of a five-hour-long flight with a 1-ton load, including the pilot and one assemblyman. A third flight reached the Canary Islands carrying 1 ton of freight, plus 1.2 tons of fuel and oil.

At first, the Spaniards liked the engines they tested.[62] Then it was time to commit to an order. Suddenly Admiral Cardona experienced unexpected "feelings of reservations." Unlike during the airplane's trials, he voiced hesitations, pointing at the British Admiralty, which also still rejected land-based airplanes and preferred seaplanes. Also, he wanted to explore Italian Macchi machines before making a final decision. In essence, despite very impressive tests, Cardona, and therefore the navy, remained against purchasing Junkers all-metal planes. After months of painstaking lobbying, all that Junkers representative Savamay could report to Dessau was that they had to wait until the British switched to all-metal planes. Then the Spaniards could be expected to follow suit.

In the Spanish army, General Soriano proved friendlier than his navy colleague toward metal airplanes. Still, he objected to buying any metal plane that was not constructed in Spain. Even though the army was scheduled to purchase about one hundred planes in the near future, he refused to place any order with Junkers until a factory had been built and opened inside Spain.

Only the city of Seville seemed mildly interested in helping Junkers. The City Council identified some terrain in Tablada as a location for a possible twenty-year lease for a future factory site. Aeronautica Militar in Seville offered half a hangar, depending on the final word from General Soriano.

There was also a new government subsidy for workers and assemblymen willing to go abroad to learn airplane manufacturing. Nine applicants had been selected to learn the construction of metal airplanes, later to return to Spain to apply their knowledge for the benefit of the entire nation.

But these events were not even a consolation prize for Junkers. By the end of 1924, neither branch of the Spanish armed forces had placed an order for military planes with Junkers. All that German airline companies could do was maintain representation in Spain and keep their hopes alive for some unforeseen break.

Unexpectedly, Argentines showed more serious interest in Junkers than Spaniards. The Argentine military did not have to be pushed to consider a Junkers airplane. Argentine consul Diana visited Junkers in Dessau on April 24, 1924. He was accompanied by Argentine military attaché Oberst Brette, German military adviser Oberst a.D. Faupel, and Mr. Schubert of Staudt and Co. Their visit had been prepared by Military Adviser Faupel himself. He intended "to raise the interest for Junkers' factory. Hopefully, this would translate into influencing the Argentine Commission that currently was present at Brussels."[63]

Prof. Junkers personally welcomed the Argentines at 10:00 a.m. The meeting began with his lecture about the advantages of metal construction, and he showed postbattle photographs and other material that reinforced his sales pitch. Thereafter the group walked to the manufacturing halls and observed the construction of individual pieces, experimental constructions, assembly, engine construction, and the propeller factory. A pleasant lunch followed.

Then the visitors drove to Junkers's airport to witness flight demonstrations of the J 16, J 20 Land, J 13, and J 22. The visitors were impressed that a Junkers all-metal plane could stay outside even though there was no hanger available for protection—the typical situation in South America.[64] The men left with an excellent impression and were open to Junkers planes.

Now all the Germans involved could see common ground and agreed on a sales representative for Argentina. Junkers civil and military planes were both to be offered exclusively through a newly founded Compañía Argentina de Comercio (Coarico) company, which was supervised by the Staudt company.[65]

Coarico received the exclusive rights to sell civilian planes, military engines, and replacement parts until 1927. The contract would extend automatically unless cancelled half a year before it was scheduled to expire. Coarico would earn 6 percent commission and receive 6 percent for costs. The basic calculation for a plane was 15,000 pesetas. And Junkers agreed to send an expedition with airplanes to Argentina to introduce models of Junkers civilian, sport, and military airplanes.

As hoped, Argentina's military commission did follow the recommendation of the first group of visitors and also visited Dessau. On June 26, 1924, Oberstleutnant Albornez and Major Marquez, accompanied by a Mr. von Virchow, arrived by car from the train station in Bitterfeld, Germany. The men stayed at the Hotel Golden Pouch. After settling in, they traveled to Leopoldshafen, where Junkers showed them airplane type F, which soon was to fly to Sweden. This was just another way of saying that this was a civilian airplane that was about to be converted into a military machine.

Neither the Junkers directors nor the Argentines realized that, soon, the process of airplane procurement would change radically and all individuals would become involved in a Spanish-led initiative still unimaginable in 1923. Change was coming in the person of Oberst Max Bauer and his education of King Alfonso XIII about transatlantic flight. There could hardly be a more complex individual to enter the historical picture.

Bauer was a former World War I member of the German General Staff responsible for military relations with German industry. In 1920, he had also participated as major conspirator in the failed German Kapp Putsch. Thereafter, he served as key liaison to Austrian-Hungarian conspirators, hoping to bring the Austrian royal house back into power in Vienna.

Bauer did not go to Spain to work in any official capacity for the armed forces of the Weimar Republic. Instead, he had been recommended by Ferdinand of Bavaria, Alfonso XIII's cousin. The German was to advise the king and Primo de Rivera about military modernization. This was a different term for breaking through the resistance of most of the traditionalists in the army.

But Bauer also came as a private businessman, representing investors who hoped to profit from modernization of the Spanish armed forces through Bauer's advice. Bauer was a business partner in at least thirteen planned projects. A list from 1925 detailed a settlement project called Mira Sierra, the construction of wood houses for Trubia, a machine factory, a spiral drill factory, and a real estate business in Berlin. Even Frank Savamay was his partner in the possible construction of future airplane hangars and signal towers in Spain. Then there were potential weapon deliveries for Mexico. Finally, he was also connected to the EISA gas bomb project of Mr. Stolzenberg.[66]

Not surprisingly, Bauer had also received a small stipend to help with Junkers's planes. He, a Mr. Mariodas, E. Wilhelm, and Piegl would share the potential profit in case Junkers airplanes were sold in Spain. There were also hopes for a machine factory for Argentina and Mexico.[67] In other words, military advising promised to generate private financial benefit as well.

Bauer interwove private business, transnational armament support, the modernization of the Spanish armed forces, and Primo de Rivera's larger strategic goals, all of them attempting to overcome resistance by reluctant Spanish mid-level military officers who just wanted to preserve the status quo. If all of this turned out to be successful, Bauer also hoped to be reinstated as a major German military person of highest military honor, rather than somebody who had to be outside Germany after the failed coups and earn a living advising foreigners.

Bauer and his administrator, Piegl, had connected with the Spanish royal house in spring 1924. Spain, as a possible location for military-industrial business, is mentioned in Piegl's surviving diary for the first time on March 10, 1924. Negotiations stretched until September 1924, when Piegl was asked to come to the Spanish embassy in Vienna to sign the contract for himself and Bauer. Of course their appointment would be a provocation to pro-French groups inside the Spanish army.[68]

Bauer arrived in Spain on October 14, 1924. Piegl picked up the military adviser-entrepreneur from the main Spanish train station. Both men took a taxi to a residence and office at Avenida Plaza de Toros 20, owned by Señora Weitzel.[69]

Right away, Bauer was received by King Alfonso XIII. In a special audience, the two men talked about the reorganization of the Spanish army. From then on Bauer began to pull Alfonso into an increasing amount of projects. His first priority would remain heavy weapons.[70] But Bauer also pushed gas bombs and airplanes.

During the remainder of 1924 Bauer and Piegl tried to get a feeling for the Spanish market. Stolzenberg's gas factory was visited on October 23, 1924, where the men talked with Director Zimmermann and his *prokurist*, Herr Albert. On November 6, they visited the company Empresencias Industriales. Also in November, Bauer and Piegl met with Savamay and Emil Killinger, the head of Junkers in Spain.[71]

From their Spanish office Bauer and Piegl also pursued business opportunities in other countries. They were in touch with a Mr. Reiss, who was interested in projects involving Russian petroleum, anthracite coal, and cork. But in December, the Russian deal collapsed. Somebody had offered lower prices.[72]

Military modernization in Spain happened because Primo de Rivera insisted on it and King Alfonso XIII backed him. Oberst Bauer's first task would be to make new designs for EISA, the national tool and machinery factory. Most likely this referred to bomb designs. Spanish sources from these meetings remain to be located. The German historian Vogt suggests that Bauer also wrote memoranda for Alfonso XIII about military strategy and reorganization.

The surviving diary of Bauer's team shows a remarkable absence of meetings between Bauer and other Spanish generals. Bauer's presence was very much focused on the king. He was not there to engage with the Spanish military establishment.

By the end of 1924, select Spanish navy leaders also were becoming open to considering naval advice. Even though British naval technology might be superior in Europe, British treatment of Spaniards was driving them into German hands. Enrique Fricke, a naval intelligence informant and the German consul to Cartagena, reported that Spanish captains were increasingly interested in German naval technology.

In December 1924, Fricke urged the Weimar navy leadership to pay attention to the increasing Spanish desires to reconsider the use of German navy technology. In a letter to Berlin he wrote: "I've gained the impression that things are back up here and if I can help, even in a modest way, I ask you to make use of me without any limitation."[73]

The British naval presence in Spain was strong. At least ten large warships of Britain's Atlantic Fleet were about to journey to the Spanish east coast. Fricke advised German navy leaders to also send ships. The advice was followed, and the dispatch of three smaller German cruisers to Spanish harbors to show the German flag was endorsed. Then Consul Fricke explained why "things are pointing up, once again": "One is increasingly sick of being presented with tin boxes manufactured by Vickers [*Torpedoboats*], and to receive submarines that are useless. Spanish commanders were protesting that Great Britain was not allowing modern equipped boats to dock in Gibraltar. Now they are hoping that Krupp and Blohm and Voss could deliver alternatives."[74]

By coincidence, a Spanish naval commission was visiting Berlin. The Spaniards were shown a new compass. Right away, the enthusiastic visitors ordered three complete sets. Patriotic Spanish navy leaders knew that the British and French were treating them as second-class admirals.

This was the institutional context for an opening toward secret German naval rearmament inside the Spanish navy. Since neither La Naval nor French military hardware yards could be weakened in Spain because of broad establishment backing and investment in them, Primo de Rivera and the king favored an alternative path. A third shipyard industry should be built inside Spain based on German technology. In essence, British, French, and German manufacturers would each have their Spanish partners. And Spanish naval armament would benefit from all three.

The strongest suitor for managing cooperation with the Germans was the company of the Basque industrialist Horacio Echevarrieta. He operated naval yards in Cádiz and El Ferrol. He was also eager to build ships that were more powerful than the British or French models. If they would benefit the Spanish state, why not? How much he was driven by nationalism and how much by profit and personal ego was difficult to discern in 1924. He fit into the typical upper-class behavior, where making money for one's family and helping the nation could go hand in hand without public shame.

Also Mateo García de los Reyes, the commander of the Spanish naval yard, needed no convincing that German technology and prototype designs would be better than those offered by Great Britain and the United States. Combined Spanish feelings of Allied discrimination and German intent for secret naval rearmament against France and Poland created a win-win situation on Spanish soil. For both sides it certainly made sense to explore what and how many benefits secret cooperation could bring.

In Berlin Admiral Hans Zenker had been able to obtain a significant budget increase from 104,000,000 RM to 155,000,000 RM. German strategy for the North and Baltic seas required torpedoes against France and Poland.[75] Since their design and production were prohibited inside Germany, Wilhelm Canaris, after his disappointing trip to Japan, suggested Spain as a place for future work.

In Berlin, Canaris was charged with playing the role of the invisible hand of government and with forcing competing German design offices and construction companies into one unified process, strong and coordinated enough to lay the groundwork for the technological retooling of the entire future German navy—of course, in violation of the official limits of the Treaty of Versailles. Then he would connect the eventually unified German technological expertise with the navy's illegal funds. Thus Canaris became the key liaison between the German navy and Spain.[76]

Canaris next visited Spain to explore the situation on location during January 1925. He came home convinced that only the navy supreme command would be strong enough to exercise a supervisory role over German companies and also force them to work toward one officially imposed rearmament goal.[77]

Canaris hoped that German–Spanish cooperation in the torpedo field would make a first deep inroad into the Spanish navy and challenge pro-British and pro-French navy leaders. Finally, successful cooperation with Spain would also convince opponents in the German Foreign Ministry to look more kindly on an expansion of deepening German–Spanish cooperation.

Canaris proposed the creation of an experimental torpedo installation in Cádiz. After solving design issues, the plant was expected to produce one thousand torpedoes. The company received support from the accumulator engine factory of Hagen, Siemens-Schuckert, and the associate Ingenieurskantoor voor Scheepsbouw. German efforts were backed by support from Alfonso XIII and Primo de Rivera, rated as high priority.[78]

In 1924, there followed a reform of Spain's emigration law. Impressed by the changes in the United States but also the results of the 1924 Congress of Emigration, the administration, at the end of 1924, produced a comprehensive new emigration law. Inside the Ministry of Labor, Commerce and Industry, a Dirección General de Emigracion was opened as well.

In Madrid, a central junta was established, plus smaller juntas in each Spanish port city. On the other side of the Atlantic, government offices were opened in principal cities and were expected to help Spanish consuls in their work. But the centers also networked with Spanish community organizations in South America and the Spanish chambers of commerce.

The historian Frederick B. Pike suggests that the centers lacked the necessary funds for noticeable outreach work. Still, the Spanish Foreign Ministry increased its representation in the former colonies to a total of seventy-five diplomats and consuls.[79]

The concentrated presence of reciprocal trade treaties in one geographical region could eventually be translated into a distinctly ethnic Spanish–American trade zone. A Spanish Commonwealth might become a reality and follow the British world model. Spain, therefore, in Latin America might be able to pull ahead in the second half of the 1920s.

If goods could be carried faster from Europe to Latin America and Alfonso's Spain could monopolize the traffic aspect of this commercial interchange, then Spanish neo-imperialism could be financed by the wealth from such a traffic monopoly. King Alfonso XIII understood this strategy. He had a deep understanding of transportation issues and how they connected with Latin America. He was well informed about discussions about zeppelins.

The diary of German military adviser Bauer records that he and the king discussed the potential of transoceanic air traffic in fall 1924. Moreover, Bauer presented himself as a burning lobbyist for the German Junkers airplane factory. This company, to say not the Weimar state, advertised itself as eager to receive the king's blessing to establish an exclusive transoceanic airline. Bauer records the king's enthusiastic agreement.

Bauer wanted to misunderstand the king and mistook enthusiasm for agreement. Nevertheless, his words establish the king as aware and supportive of the transoceanic air strategy. During 1925 Alfonso was educated on how to make a Spanish air monopoly possible.

Establishing Spanish supremacy in the air sector would first require the destruction of the international air agreement established as part of the 1919 peace treaty. Already in 1918, France's General Duval had created a commission that attempted to lay claim to how future airlines would receive overflight rights across the world! Overflight rights were distributed by a top tier of five states: France, Great Britain, the United States, Italy, and Japan. Article 5 of the treaty allowed a privileged regimen for the great powers. Allied powers imposed international air law on smaller countries.

In 1919, Spain was too weak to challenge the fact that France would also determine how future Latin American airlines would operate in the Western Hemisphere. The decision-making structure CENA was accepted on September 27, 1919. But reality quickly proved to be different than the law imagined. Only four Latin American countries joined the European and U.S. initiative. Then, in 1924, Bolivia revoked its signature and became less and less enthusiastic about the 1919 structure. It was not absurd to probe whether the twenty Latin American governments might be willing to join a new international body that administered airline licenses out of Madrid. Spain would still not control Latin American air traffic, but it could coordinate reciprocal trade treaties with potential transoceanic airline monopolies, a powerful duo.

V

Forging Military Connections for the Transnational Fascism of the 1930s (1925–28)

16   Now That We Can Arm Freely

O n the international, elite political level, 1925 appears as a year that moved European nations closer to real peace. In early summer, the Allies finally handed Germany conditions for the evacuation of the Rhineland. And on June 16 France accepted the German proposal for a security pact. The British government, too, relieved pressure on German territory and, in July, withdrew seven thousand troops, ending a seven-year presence. Even though the U.S. Congress rejected once again joining a future Western guarantee pact, negotiations concluded with a draft treaty on October 16, 1925, in Locarno, Switzerland.

In the Locarno Treaty, Germany and France promised to end war against each other. In case either power broke the pact, Great Britain and Italy agreed to come to the aid of the attacked country. Germany was finally dealt with as an equal partner in top-level international negotiations. Members of the German Reichstag backed the sentiment of leading diplomats and ratified the Locarno Treaty on November 26. A few days later seven other nations ratified their draft agreement, pledging peace in Europe. Insiders knew that now Germany could be officially invited to join the League of Nations.

The next major international struggle would not be war but diplomacy. Germany competed with Poland, Brazil, and Spain over a permanent seat in the League of Nations. At the end of 1925, all political struggles north of Spain promised to be guaranteed peaceful for years to come.

In Spain Primo de Rivera's authoritarian government also seemed stronger. On May 17, 1925, Spanish king Alfonso XIII was able to lift the state of siege that had been in force since the 1923 coup of General Primo de Rivera. Next the king traveled to Paris to pay his respect to the complicated neighbor in the north.[1]

On June 22, France and Spain agreed to combine their military strength and to attack Abd el-Krim. French marshal Pétain began his campaign in Morocco on July 17. In September, a major attack was launched with the successful Spanish surprise landing at Al Hoceima.

This French–Spanish cooperation in North Africa required a moratorium of further rapid German–Spanish cooperation in naval and air force technology.[2] Regardless of developments in North Africa, the majority of Spanish military leaders remained unwilling to follow the lead of king and dictator. Modernization, it was feared, would not only bring new weapons but also imply a reorganization of the military as a social organization.

Neither were military priorities for the coming years agreed upon. On the one hand, complete agreement existed that Spain's expansion in northern Africa should remain the army's main task in the years to come. But beyond that only a few generals and admirals could imagine modernization for the purpose of engaging in an open clash with Italy and France. War with Great Britain was out of the question. At the most, the institutional mind-set allowed for an intensification of the hidden maritime rivalry over influence in the western Mediterranean. During the next five years the Spanish military was not expected to fight a war on the European continent.[3] Regardless, Primo de Rivera already had begun to look for diplomatic alternatives to Spanish–French relations and alternative military technological cooperation with Germany, which promised Spain benevolent neutrality in case of a war in the Mediterranean.[4]

German navy representatives were not interested in any Spanish war against its neighbor. Navy leader Admiral Zehnker and Wilhelm Canaris had a second goal in mind. After the failure of the 1924 Rome Naval Armament Limitation Conference, 1925 promised to be a year when major government orders would be placed to buy ships and air forces. The orders would bring unprecedented amounts of foreign currency untouched by high German inflation. Such large resources could fund German design expansion and employee training of skilled military construction workers.

Furthermore, Germany should try to prevent its rival France from earning such large amounts of stable foreign currency. As French currency was suffering, any funds that could be taken from Germany's archrival would keep it from strengthening militarily. And the expansion of German military construction capability might even advance efforts to build nationalist Latin American militaries that could resist U.S. armed forces in the future.

41. After the surrender of the Moroccan Abd el-Krim, Spanish efforts to build an Iberian Commonwealth were pursued with unprecedented fervor (Library of Congress, Washington, D.C.).

On May 2, 1925, in Berlin, the German Mexican Chamber of Commerce announced that a steamer would carry a delegation of German merchants and industrial experts to Mexico. The trip would be sponsored by the Mexican government and would last 2.5 months.

The men would spend one month in Mexico City. There German manufacturers would receive the opportunity to display their regular industrial wares for interested Mexican customers. Also Mexican president Calles was expected to receive the Germans.

Nobody knew that one sales representative of the group, Mr. Morath, was really a navy representative who planned to use the trip as a cover to renew German–Mexican naval contacts. Behind Morath stood the unified secret navy engineer office Ingenieurskantoor voor Scheepsbouw (IvS), still idling with a few specific projects in Holland.

In detail, "renewing contacts" meant that Morath was to go to Mexico to find a way to build up Mexico's military-industrial structure. In particular, he was to sell navy ship designs. Previously, Germans had knocked on the doors of Turkey, Japan, and Spain.

In Mexico, President Calles was delighted to welcome the Germans. He welcomed in particular navy representative Morath. Right away he introduced him to Julio Villaseñor, a former student of his when he was still a schoolteacher in Sonora. Villaseñor was also the brother-in-law of General Fausto Topete, a friend of General Serrano.

The Mexican leaders told Morath that their navy was in bad shape. Its leadership had made the mistake of rising up against President Obregón during the 1924 de la Huerta rebellion. As a result Obregón and Calles had fired all officers. Now it was a profoundly emaciated institution, run by young engineers. In the Ministry of War Commodore Varela headed the Department of the Navy and supervised the sailors.

Mexican interest remained limited to domestic military goals. First, specialists desired to operate in coastal waters to support the maintenance of domestic order. This meant acquiring troop transport ships and coast guard ships. Second, they desired a limited ability to confront private Japanese and U.S. fishing boats that operated along California's coast in blatant disregard of Mexico's sovereignty. American and Japanese fishing boats served themselves without restraint from the rich fisheries off Mexico's coast. Finally, the navy wanted to build a national fishing fleet that could harvest the rich schools living off its national shorelines.

German navy construction specialist Morath was told that the Mexican Ministry of War, in theory, had budgeted 182,000,000 pesos, about 370,000,000 gold RM, a princely sum. However, in 1926, of that amount, 122,000,000 pesos had already been spent to fight civil war. Thus Germans learned not to expect the beginning of any naval construction of Mexican ships until 1927. Initially, the Mexican navy department had asked for bids from fifteen to twenty European and U.S. navy construction companies. But only a smaller number of companies had cared to respond. Offers had come from two Italian naval yards, one British yard, one Swedish yard, and one private German yard; and now the German navy's IvS engineering agency in Holland was invited to make a bid.

It looked as if Germans had a good chance to be successful in Mexico. One Italian offer was rejected because its representative was still expecting money from a previous Mexican order. A second Italian offer was too expensive. The British navy, probably through Vickers, was insisting on opening a subsidiary in Mexico that would supervise the entire Mexican naval construction program. No wonder, Mexican bureaucrats were eager to hear whether the German navy

42. German representative Hans Morath revived secret German–Mexican naval armament talks with President Plutarco Calles (Politisches Archiv des Auswaertigen Amts, Berlin).

representative could offer less invasive alternatives. The negotiations proceeded in a fascinating way.

Morath was introduced to Mexico's preferred liaison, Mr. Evers. He was a small man with glasses and suffered from a heart murmur. His wife was German, and the two had one child. The Prussian major Evers had come to Mexico as part of the colonial settlement society. After losing money as a land surveyor he took a prominent position in Mexico's Agricultural Ministry. He maintained both citizenships. Already he was involved in another secret project, the founding of a Mexican iron ore industry. German advisers planned the iron industry as the first step for a cluster of factories that later could manufacture steel for Mexican weapons and free it from purchases from the Allied powers.

Still in Mexico, Morath sketched the creation of an iron ore–processing capacity.[5] He counseled against a parallel realization of machine gun factories, ammunition factories, and naval yards. He insisted that Mexico first needed to focus on winning raw materials. This would create orders for German furnaces and smelters. Once constructed a factory could make steel nails and beams. This first factory would finance itself through sales to Mexican railroads, the Mexican government, and private companies. Its profits in turn would finance the transition to an armament factory. At that stage this steel mill would manufacture finer products such as arms cartridges and steel plates for ships. Morath and his advisers stated that the transition from manufacturing site to a war industry would take several steps and cost between 1,000,000 and 2,000,000 pesos.

Morath emphasized to the Mexicans that such an industry should remain entirely in state hands. He promised that if Mexico remained interested, he would entrust an engineer in Berlin to develop detailed projects. He urged President Calles, General Amaro, and General Serrano to make Mexico independent of Allied arms deliveries.[6] After Morath's return, discussions with Mexico about this project continued.

In December 1925, submarine expert Blum and Dr. Tegel presented a bid for six Mexican ships to Mexico's legation in Berlin. The diplomat also offered a letter of introduction to General Amaro, who wanted to discuss further the advancement of Mexico's iron industry.[7]

Next Morath received an impression of the factories Mexico owned six years after the end of World War I. On one visit he toured the ammunition factory in Chapultepec accompanied by President Calles and Minister Amaro. Later Morath was introduced to a Mexican commodore. He could read German and was asked to translate the German proposal for the Mexican navy. Negotiations for the offer would be handled personally by General of War Amaro. Morath was also introduced to General González.

He was most fascinated by General Amaro. He remarked that Mexico's minister of war was called "the small Indian" and belonged to "a special Indian tribe and still three years ago he wore earrings. He was a young, slim full-blooded Indian of good military features and wore a flawless fitting general's uniform of English design." Amaro was identified as the true brain of the Ministry of War, including the navy.

Thereafter Morath treated the Mexicans with a Prussian-inspired military presentation. He regaled listeners with military lectures from World War I and Spanish-language slides. He showed drafts of battle scenes and reported about his experience as a submarine commander. He repeated the same lecture on March 3 in front of the Association of the Military College. These presentations were a smashing success. As a result Mexican officers stopped seeing Morath as a businessman and began to relate to him as a soldier.

Morath had expected to negotiate prices and funding for his navy proposal with navy representatives. Instead, the discussions were held by Calles's confidant Villaseñor. Also, the number of 10 percent was floated, which might have referred to a bribe.

At the end of the trip Morath left Mexico with the impression that the Calles administration was serious about German bids. However, Calles could make only a down payment of 30 percent. Subsequent payments would be made in installments from a first-rate bank in New York.

In 1926, it all seemed to pay off. On March 19, 1926, Mexico informed Germany that the IvS engineering office would receive the bid for the entire fleet-building program. This meant orders for one training ship, two transport ships of 7.2 tons, two troop transport ships of 5.5 tons, two canon boots, two coast guard ships, one tanker, and ten patrol boats: in total, 28.2 tons of ships with an estimated value of 40,000,000 gold RM. The orders would be spread over three years. Here was a significant inflow of money into German accounts and the renewal of military contacts, so cherished in World War I.

Argentina remained a second, potentially most promising Latin American country, ready to place major orders. For example, already in 1924, the Direction of Navigation and Ports had finalized plans for the construction of a naval base at Mar del Plata. This project included depots, workshops, and ship anchoring places. The Marine Department was budgeting the estimated costs at about 4,000,000 pesos. The proposal had been sent to President Alvear, who issued a decree that moved efforts from planning to construction.[8] The naval base would house cruisers, submarines, and dreadnoughts.

How to get access to the Argentine orders remained a major challenge. The Weimar Republic did not send a trade delegation with a naval administrator. In this case it was one individual, Oberst Max Bauer, who renewed efforts from previous years.

Already in 1924, while still in Spain Max Bauer had approached Wilhelm Canaris, writing to him that, as he was relocating to Argentina, he would also represent IvS navy engineering and Junkers airplanes. He would advocate for German submarine designs, hoping to use the king's cousin's reference letters to impress people and to gain access to high-level decision makers.[9]

The Argentina Bauer came to in October 1925 performed its war games, as it did every year. This year it encompassed an area of 80 by 40 kilometers. Every Argentine soldier who could be spared had been mobilized.

A group of spectators witnessed the war game with great interest. The military attachés from France, Spain, Japan, Brazil, Chile, and the United States, plus the air attachés of Great Britain and Italy, were joined by General Ruprecht of the Uruguayan army and Brigadier General Schenoni of the Paraguayan army.

At Argentine commander in chief General Uriburu's headquarters the military attachés observed five German ex-officers. Some of them had previously worked as instructors in the Superior School of War in Buenos Aires. They were not dressed as Argentine soldiers but wore all the same civilian khaki riding suits and tropical helmets. During the game they consulted frequently with Argentine staff officers. Also they assisted in the criticism after Argentine leaders had made their evaluations.[10] Observers from Europe, Japan, the United States, and Latin America recognized that the advice and training of Wilhelm Faupel had created an Argentine army based on German war tactics that could engage selectively in modernized warfare. This was no longer the incompetent, ill-supplied Argentine army that had been forced to withdraw from confrontation with the Brazilian army in 1918.

Faupel had made contact with the recently arrived Bauer.[11] He backed Bauer's intent to write a report about the armament and organization of the Argentine army. It would emphasize the interconnection of economic and military sectors. Also it confirmed Faupel's approach, pointing out that trench warfare and massive war fronts would be passé in the future. The future depended on fast, movable, and light infantry, in particular machine gun detachments.

Most importantly, Bauer stated that Argentina, too, should develop its own armament industry and equip its forces with modern machine guns, light cannons, and fighter planes. As he had done in Spain, he offered the military in Buenos Aires contracts with illegal German armament companies.[12]

Colombia also approached German contractors. In October the Colombian government asked the Colombian representative to Germany, Dr. Miguel Jimenez Lopez, to ask if the German Weimar government could build a war fleet for the Colombians. It was argued that if Germany was willing to help Mexico, then it could also help Columbia. Dr. Morath was asked to meet with Colombians, whose newly elected president seemed particularly pro-German.[13]

In 1925, even Venezuela came to German attention. In November, Lohmann, head of one the secret naval rearmament departments, asked to find out everything about coffee and German trade with Venezuela.[14]

Finally, German admiral a.D. Behnke worked as Rheinmetall company representative. After entering retirement he planned a world tour. He would cross the Atlantic to South and North America and later continue on to Japan, China, Korea, Indonesia, and Russia. This was not just a tourist trip, as he was accompanied by Korvettenkapitaen Goetting, the aide of the German minister of war. The German historian Sander-Nagashimi states that this trip had military political aims. Behnke was close to Rheinmetall company in particular.[15]

But the most serious German attention was paid to Spain. In late 1925 the Spanish government finally felt strong enough to resume building its Iberian Commonwealth. Efforts in late 1925 concentrated on reestablishing one permanent base to further the creation of a Spanish Commonwealth in Spanish America.

Three Spanish factions participated in this project: first, there was King Alfonso XIII himself; second, diplomatic professionals under the lead of new foreign minister Yanguas; and third, select members of Spain's air force. The last group promised timid politicians that airplanes would create a new, tangible connection between Spain and South America.

In order to succeed, Hispanismo would have to be modernized and retooled. A new generation of Spanish explorers and conquistadores would appear not as uneducated soldiers from poor areas of Spain but as educated urban advocates, whose weapons would be commercial treaties, air laws, and the technology of flying. They expected to be transported by transoceanic airplanes, built with technology from Germany but exclusively controlled by fierce Spanish nationalists. King Alfonso XIII mentored them quietly, with remarkable determination and sustained by an impressive long-term historical vision.

The king found in the young Spanish air force general Alfredo Kindelan a skilled and effective institutional partner. He replaced Soriano Escudero as director general of the Aeronautica Militar.[16] Kindelan was inspired as much by the physical sense of freedom that came with flying as by the possibilities that came with long-distance flight and its technological foundations. The feeling of openness and forward looking that came with flying inspired Spaniards to reach into geographic areas that could be reached more easily by pilots than by army officers in trucks. Now military aviators claimed to be national pioneers. Alfonso XIII hoped they would make possible a faster, and eventually more profitable, physical connection with a sphere of influence Spain hoped to reclaim.

Diplomats and lawyers made up the second group of professionals helping Alfonso XIII. In Madrid it was decided to confront French domination of international air law. Experts in the Spanish Foreign Ministry and the Ministry of Transport aimed at weakening the French-dominated 1919 International Air Law Convention. Their challenge would come in the form of a 1926 Spanish

Air Congress. It was supposed to establish a separatist Iberian Air Law for Latin America, Portugal, and Spain. Then the French would no longer dominate Spanish and Spanish American air space.

To win Spanish American support for the Iberian initiative important alternative political procedures were offered to Latin American governments. If their governments would join the Spanish convention, they would do so as equal members. No longer would Latin American air planners be dominated and be treated as second class compared to Allied powers. Together Spaniards, Portuguese, Spanish Americans, and Brazilians would create the Ibero-American Commission for Air Navigation (CIANA).

An expert explained to King Alfonso XIII how CIANA would be advantageous: "The creation of this Ibero-American Union is of great importance and legal order in the political, technical and industrial law because it establishes the exchange of primary materials and the fabrication of airplanes."[17] It was an elegant attempt to build on bilateral trade treaties and ethnic group policies by linking them with international transport policy and air law. From 1926 on, ethnic Spanish businesses, Spanish trade treaties, and a new Iberian air law would together become Spanish cannonballs that would shoot a first gap into the commercial and legal world as France, but also Great Britain and the United States, had created it in 1919.

In 1925, Spain's macropolitical context also looked encouraging. The military campaign in Morocco appeared increasingly successful. This symbolic military Spanish issue of previous decades promised to dissolve in the not-too-distant future, even if it would take regional cooperation with the French military. Thereafter energy and resources would be freed up to move toward at least informal Spanish outreach in Latin America.

Also encouraging were France's ongoing national financial calamities. Already in April 1925, a government crisis had forced the French Herriot cabinet to resign. The mounting World War I debt problem also burdened the next cabinet. Then French finance minister Caillaux traveled to Washington, D.C., to negotiate a reliable repayment plan. But during the remainder of September 1925, French and U.S. negotiators failed to reach an easy agreement. In the end only a relatively weak five-year plan could be agreed upon that promised an annual payment of US$40,000,000 per year.

Then French premier Aristide Briand achieved a major international diplomatic victory with the Locarno Pact. Still, his first cabinet also collapsed on March 6, 1926, and France's monetary crisis continued. France lacked a solid financial backbone to penetrate Latin America with a French neo-imperial strategy in 1925. At best, France would be present culturally among Latin American elites. Spain's major rival looked internally weakened and distracted. It was a good time to act.

In December 1925, General Primo de Rivera accepted Jose Yanguas as the next foreign minister. Right away he displayed unusual personal zeal. From the very beginning he articulated a systematic and more thought-out outreach plan for Spanish America. He pushed the modernization of Hispanidad.

Unlike the Hispanidad of 1898 and its all-too-familiar rhetoric of cultural romanticism, Yanguas's Hispanidad transcended cultural romanticism and was anchored in shared legal and commercial practices. It was not a broad imperial approach but, rather, a selection of a few effective priorities.

Modernizing Spain's claim to a unique, powerful link with Spanish America required more than angry postcolonial yearning. Yanguas had been warned that if the rhetoric of Hispanismo were summoned, "all this Ibero-American solidarity would dissolve into soapy foam when it was time to get serious and demonstrate its existence."[18] Yanguas attempted to strengthen Spanish policy by combining the efforts of traders and airline operators with those of cultural elites and diplomats.

Probably in December 1925, representatives of the royal court, the Madrid executive, the Foreign Ministry, and the air force met to combine their efforts into one interconnected thrust demonstrating renewed Spanish zeal to become again a leading player in Latin America. Until today no single document exists that could detail a coordinated action plan. But, perhaps, the creation of one written plan might not have been necessary during this year. Spanish interest groups, looking toward Latin America, had internalized longings and expectations so that verbal exchanges sufficed until first success. Making an Iberian Commonwealth a reality was the goal, and there were many obvious ways to contribute to this policy. What was new at the end of 1925 was that all factions promised to work well. And they did.

On January 22, 1926, aviator Ramón Franco, his copilot, and a navigator boarded a Dornier Wal plane in Palos de Maguer. In contrast to Junkers pilots and their company, described in the previous chapter, Franco could not rely on even a semicommercial network of Dornier supporters on the ground. As he climbed into the German-designed airplane to attempt a Spanish Atlantic crossing, he would either succeed through insane luck or vanish into the clouds and crash into the Atlantic.[19]

If he became scared early enough, he might be able to achieve a landing at the coast and return alive. Ramón Franco was not fazed by such doubt and proceeded.

Already limited planning was taking place among the king's palace, the Foreign Ministry, and the air force. On January 10, 1926, twelve days before take-off, the Spanish navy had ordered the Spanish ambassador in Buenos Aires to do everything possible to help the pilots but to wait until they crossed the ocean and arrived in Latin America.[20] In Buenos Aires, too, the leadership of the Spanish collectivity was informed and asked to design a historic public welcome. A dramatic ten-point welcome program was being developed.

On the day Franco took off, Foreign Ministry diplomats resumed the construction of cultural propaganda. Layer upon layer of Spanish–Argentine interactions would be started to build up a strong bond until it became a bridgehead for future expansion into the Spanish American interior. First, on January 22, 1926, the Foreign Ministry requested new, detailed data about Spanish ethnic populations in Argentina.[21] Second, the ministry announced that, in October 1926, Spain would hold its First Air Congress of Ibero-American Aeronautics. On the same day King Alfonso XIII endorsed Madrid as the convention's gathering site.[22]

Here was a government-coordinated, multilevel Spanish policy. It attempted to connect common people, politicians who could dream, traders who wanted to profit from export, and military aviators who wanted to become as revered and powerful as generals of the army. A modernized Hispanismo was formed. In a few years these policies would bring together groups from all Ibero-American countries at the Ibero-American Exposition at Seville. Luck helped the aviators, politicians, and king.

Ramón Franco and his crew flew exactly between two Atlantic low fronts that otherwise would have tossed his Plus Ultra into the ocean. Air specialists knew that his success was unique. It would never be a safe and predictable example for later regular commercial, transatlantic crossings. Nevertheless, Franco delivered a critical public relations stunt, which, for the first time, attracted commoners on both sides of the Atlantic.

The flight triggered tremendous popular pride. Spaniards had realized what French, U.S., British, and German aviators were only dreaming about. Charles Lindberg was still only an airmail pilot flying inside the United States. The physical crossing symbolized the new special Spanish claim to the air space between Spain and Latin America. There had not been a similar, positive Spanish cause that everybody could celebrate. Ramón Franco arrived in Rio de Janeiro on February 3, 1926.

Now previous planning paid off. The very next day the Spanish army approved the dispatch of Spanish soldiers, coincidentally present in Argentina, to guard

43. The Plus Ultra shortly after arrival in Pernambuco, Brazil (Fondo Cultura, F 698–08–003, Archivo General de la Administración, Alcalá de Henares).

44. The Plus Ultra and its aircrew shortly after their arrival in Pernambuco (Fondo Cultura, F 698–08–05, Archivo General de la Administración, Alcalá de Henares).

Franco's Plus Ultra. Subtly, their presence visually laid claim to the leading role of Spain's armed forces, continuing the competition among Spain's elites.

On the same day the Spanish collectivity in Buenos Aires presented its plan for a celebration to the Spanish embassy. Four main events had been planned. First, a luncheon would be held in the Pavilion of the Roses. Second, at the Theatro de Cervantes a patriotic celebration would take place. Third, the mechanic of the crew, not just the pilots, would be honored with a special day. Fourth, the Plus Ultra crew would be driven through Buenos Aires to visit all major companies owned by ethnic Spanish individuals or important to the Spanish collectivity.

Next, the planners suggested twelve additional ways to express Spanish joy about the accomplishment. A special holiday should be declared. The light-rail of Buenos Aires would be decorated with Spanish flags, and the Hispanic-American Electric Light Co. would construct an arch out of light bulbs. Then it was time to create souvenirs people could take home and share with enthusiasts outside the capital. A special printed photo album would be available, a film

45. Recife, Pernambuco, Brazil, as the first European pilots saw it after crossing the Atlantic (Ibero Amerikanisches Institut, Stiftung Preussischer Kulturbesitz, Bildarchiv, Berlin).

would be made, a stamp would be designed, and a book would be published. Cars in Buenos Aires could be decorated with a special sticker. Finally, a street in Buenos Aires should be renamed and a monument should be erected in honor of the Plus Ultra crew. And just to make sure that popular expressions of jubilation would take place beyond Buenos Aires, Spanish community organizations were asked to mail printed greetings from their distant celebrations to the Spanish embassy in Buenos Aires.[23]

The luck of these aviators and their plane was bringing to life what no king, foreign minister, diplomat, or dictator could decree. Alfonso XIII paid less attention to them. Instead he conducted high diplomacy. True to his policy of Iberian assumptions, he bestowed the Medal of the Order of the Great Cross of Isabel the Catholic to the Argentine ambassador plus the minister of Brazil in Madrid. This aristocratic pampering was part of the Hispanic charm offensive. How flattering, the Spanish motherland expressed esteem for the leaders of the former Iberian colonies!

For a few weeks, the flight bridged otherwise divisive Spanish regionalisms, classes, and political institutions. The plane and three pilots suggested the possibility of one unified, modern Spanish American spirit establishing a true connection with all Latin Americans. There was a sense of Spanish distinction. This feeling would build while the crew rested for a few days in Brazil and explode across Buenos Aires once they arrived.

Even Franco's return was becoming a symbolic act. This hero could not just simply fly home. His return, too, would have to be staged as a dramatic celebration. One suggestion was to return the Spaniards on an ocean liner. Plus they should go directly to Spain without stopping first in Brazil or Africa.

Finally, the Argentine government joined in and responded with a policy of grand gestures of its own. President Alvear announced that he would do everything possible to celebrate the Spanish aircrew. He agreed to keep an open calendar for them and to welcome them at the Casa Rosada on any day.[24] In addition, he offered the Argentine cruiser *Buenos Aires* to transport the pilots home to Spain. On February 27, 1926, the Spanish government accepted the offer of the Argentine government that Ramón Franco should return on the cruiser at Buenos Aires.

Suddenly Franco was compared to Columbus. In 1492, Spanish ships had carried the Italian to the Caribbean. Now airplanes had carried a Spaniard on divine air to the bulge of Brazil and down to the Río de la Plata.[25]

Keeping discipline in this celebration proved difficult for the pilots. By February 5, discussions emerged that Franco and his crew might continue to fly on to Chile.

46. Enthusiastic Spaniards following flight announcements at Las Ramblas in Barcelona, Spain (Fondo Cultura, F 698–08–07, Archivo General de la Administración, Alcalá de Henares).

After resting in Brazil Franco piloted the Plus Ultra down the Brazilian coast to Montevideo, Uruguay. There he created much public excitement before continuing on to Buenos Aires, where he arrived on February 10, 1926, at 12:20.

Far away in Madrid, but not ignorant of events in Buenos Aires, the Spanish king was visited by German Oberst Bauer as he returned from his half-year-long work in Argentina. By coincidence, he arrived in Spain on the same day that Ramón Franco touched down in Buenos Aires.

Bauer proceeded to Madrid to talk with Spanish decision makers about gas warfare production and transoceanic traffic. Already in November 1925, still in Argentina, Bauer had written to his office in Madrid that "of greatest interest should be airplane connection over the ocean."[26] Bauer, partly motivated by a modest 500 RM payoff from the Junkers airplane factory, had begun to attack the nationalistic, closed Spanish airplane culture, dominated by British and French companies.

First, Bauer's tactic was to use the untested influence of Prince Ferdinand of Bavaria over his cousin King Alfonso XIII. Never plagued by doubt, Bauer seemed to know how to proceed: "What is needed is a push from Spain to Argentina. It would be best if King Alfonso or Don Fernando cabled the Argentine Ambassador expressing their personal interest in the matter."[27]

Second, Bauer suggested that Junkers airline Unión Aérea Española (UAE) should send an official letter from Madrid to Buenos Aires to express its desire to open transoceanic business. Bauer thought that one of UAE's board members, Rodriguez, should enlist influential friends in Buenos Aires. Such a letter was supposed to create the impression in Argentina that Spaniards, out of their own initiative, were pushing transoceanic airline business.

Finally, Bauer's administrator in Madrid, Piegl, was to enlist Prince Ferdinand in an approach to the Argentine ambassador in Madrid. But the prince refused to act as an official representative of the royal house.[28]

Suddenly unforeseen obstacles emerged. One Spanish UAE board member told the king that talk about a Junkers transatlantic project was only just that and not more than talk. Still no engine existed that was strong enough to carry a plane across the Atlantic in one stretch. This was ironic news because it surfaced in the same weeks when Ramón Franco's Dornier Wal plane suggested the opposite.

The industrious Bauer proceeded undeterred. After his return to Madrid he would propose to the king the creation of a Spanish–Argentine company that would finance the design and manufacture of planes and operate a transatlantic airline.

Bauer had to admit that Junkers lacked the funds to pay for such airplane prototype development. Bauer single-handedly wanted to change this. His instructions, still coming from Argentina, beamed with confidence: "the matter is ready to go [*spruchreif*] so it can be treated seriously."[29]

Four days after returning from Argentina, Bauer was received by Alfonso XIII in a private audience. Bauer displayed fierceness in the meeting. First, he told the king that pure luck, but not skill, had carried Ramón Franco across the ocean. Next, he disparaged the Dornier plane. Then, he compared the Dornier Plus Ultra with the recently completed Junkers three-engine plane. Finally, Bauer invited the king to invest in a yet-to-be-created company that would make reliable commercial transoceanic flight a reality.[30] Bauer proposed to anchor the business around an Argentine personality of high social standing. He demanded Alfonso's support as an investor, hoping that he would raise enough money to finance the construction of at least one Junkers prototype strong enough to cross the Atlantic risk free in 1926. He closed demanding an initial investment of 50,000,000 pesetas.

Bauer's surviving letters reveal additional intriguing aspects. He mentioned Argentine president Alvear as being interested in the proposal. This suggests that Bauer had met him informally at least once to discuss the "Transoceanic Flight" initiative as a confidential project.

Alfonso's answer demonstrated his awareness that such giants would carry raw materials and valuable commercial goods between two parts of the future Iberian Commonwealth. And he was comfortable hearing about his total cost package of 40,000,000 RM. Bauer had interested him in the development of three types of planes. Initially, a 15-ton prototype plane should be built. Next, the size should be increased to 30 tons, and then a 40-ton construction would be attempted. The realization of all construction plans would take years. When the audience ended Alfonso considered making a onetime 600,000 RM investment for the first small prototype.

Afterward Bauer reported an almost ideal business outlook. The king would not ask that the plane be finished at a particular month. His investment would come from a secret fund (*fonds perdu*). In other words Junkers could look forward to almost luxurious freedom to design his first transoceanic carrier with an initial Spanish royal down payment.[31]

The surviving sources do not share the king's version of this meeting, but Bauer had raised the king's interest. He was awaiting a more formal and more technical and commercial proposal. An inspired Bauer traveled on February 17, 1926, to Barcelona to catch the boat to Germany.[32] By early March he had contacted Junkers in Dessau and requested the hurried assembly of a broader written proposal for Alfonso XIII.

Bauer did not believe that the king grasped the essence of what he had suggested. He asked Junkers for a light presentation that would focus on certainty, rather than on unresolved difficulties of the project, and "in particular the mental state of Southlanders needs to be taken into consideration." Bauer wanted to show off technical innovations such as Junkers's heavy oil engines and free-standing pistons. Such specifics should compare favorably to those of Dornier and Curtiss planes. And Bauer wanted Professor Junkers to travel to Madrid, so that the famous airplane engineer could make the next pitch personally in front of the Spanish royal. The king would trust only Professor Junkers, he insisted.[33]

In Germany the first meeting of transoceanic enthusiasts took place on March 17, 1926. There Professor Junkers emerged as reluctant to devote everything to the South American route. He could not forget the initial 1919 America Flight project and still preferred the connection between Europe and New York over Spain and Brazil. On the one hand, he stated: "The pushing of lines across the ocean is not dictated by political and strategic points of views. On the ocean the only rules are the competition of transportation enterprises which work based on trade principles. Here, therefore, is a challenge that consists exclusively of economic importance, free from all political influences." He preferred the Junkers planes to benefit the entire world, in developing an airplane that would generate higher economic value compared to existing means of traffic.[34] For him Alfonso XIII appeared more as a romantic investor whose money and naïveté could be taken advantage of for the higher purposes of the German airplane designer. That the Spanish king was an utterly political individual working on his commonwealth project and adept at playing the world's political arenas was not recognized in Dessau.[35]

In Argentina, as the Plus Ultra celebrations took off, the Spanish Foreign Ministry intensified cultural politics. It announced the dispatch of an official mission to South America to study the state of cultural relations between Spain and Latin America. It would be led by the writer Don Manuel Linares Rios.[36]

Foreign Minister Yanguas published an order detailing the future importance of the Spanish book. A good Spanish book should focus on topics spanning from Visigoth Spain until 1926. Also, a Hispanic American children's book contest was launched. Not surprisingly, on April 10, 1926, Madrid called for an intensification of all propaganda pushing the Ibero-American Exposition at Seville.[37]

By now even Spanish diplomats fell for their own propaganda. From Buenos Aires, 1st Chargé d'Affaires Danvila telegraphed Alfonso XIII congratulating him personally on the energy that the Plus Ultra interjected into the political realm.[38] At the inauguration of the Chilean president Figueroa Larraín another Spanish diplomat confirmed that Argentina was the ideal place to anchor revived Spanish outreach into Spanish America. He emphasized that in Buenos Aires the political influence of the United States was nonexistent. There it seemed possible to establish a unique commercial linkage between the Río de la Plata and Spain. Slowly this single link could give birth to alternative Ibero-American commercial relations, strong enough to rival those among the United States, Great Britain, and Latin America.[39]

The Office of the Spanish Commercial Attaché in Buenos Aires also adjusted its work: The attaché, too, was fighting the dispersion of the moral and economic forces of the Spanish collectivity in the Argentine Republic. Community building and trade were now connected "to principally renovate the energies for progress and to increase the influence of the Spanish collectivity that it deserved based on its number and rank."[40] The largest multilayered diplomatic Spanish offensive toward Latin America since 1900 was taking off.

47. Arrival of the Plus Ultra in Buenos Aires, Argentina (Fondo Cultura,
     F 698–08–001, Archivo General de la Administración, Alcalá de Henares).

For a moment pilot Ramón Franco threatened the coherent and systematic execution of policy. He and the crew of the Plus Ultra refused to fly home
and, rather, wanted to continue their trip to other South American countries.
If it were up to Franco, he would continue and conduct a very personal airplane
diplomacy in North and South America.

His grandstanding was difficult to contain. He cabled to the Ministry of
Aviation that the success of his flight had heightened the feelings of Spaniards
of South America.

Whereas Spanish diplomats in Buenos Aires continued to debate how he and
his plane could return home by boat—not tempting fate a second time—Franco
proposed to cross Patagonia to reach Valparaiso, Chile. From there he would
reach north to Colombia, refuel, and surprise Havana in the first week of April.
There an engine change would have to be accomplished before he could travel
on to a, hopefully, triumphal arrival in New York. After inspiring Spaniards and
New Yorkers alike, he promised to turn around and fly to Newfoundland. Then

a second Atlantic crossing would lead him to the Azores Islands. From there he would fly home, not to Madrid, but to Galicia.[41]

These suggestions were not just dreams. The Spanish archive in Alcalá de Henares preserves fuel orders for Peru, Chile, Colombia, Panama, and Ecuador.[42] It seems that for a while the Plus Ultra's continuation was a possibility. But then Foreign Minister Yanguas prevailed. Whereas in 1492 the island of Hispaniola, in the Caribbean, had served as a launching pad of the Spanish advance into the Americas, in 1926, only Argentina was to serve a similar function for Primo de Rivera's Spain.

On March 3, Yanguas cabled new policy definitions and instructions to Argentina. He began by admitting that the efforts of previous years had not created the desired success. But now, partly as a result of Ramón Franco's flight, he diagnosed in Spain and America "a vehement desire for approximation. One could almost say fraternization ... which expresses itself in the behavior of individuals."

What should approximation mean in everyday life? Yanguas assured, with vehemence, that approximation did not mean Spanish reconquest. He insisted that the Spanish government had never wanted to intervene in the interior affairs of the peoples in Latin America. Also in 1926, no insinuation should be made suggesting event faint future interference into domestic affairs. Spanish policy agreed that Spanish American countries were to remain perfectly and completely independent from Spain.

Yanguas insisted that his policy did not mean intervention. Claims to the contrary "by the most fearful, exaggerated elements in Spanish-America were wrong." All that the Primo de Rivera administration wanted to do in 1926 was to act "as a brother country to Spanish American nations."

And yet Yanguas's assurances remained, at heart, ambivalent. He also insisted, "It is impossible for Spain, and also impossible for nations who originated from Iberia, to escape the strong power of blood. Today races, in particular ours so energetic and strong, maintain their common characters and ways over time and infinite space. This is true for the countries on this side and that side of the Atlantic." He regretted that

often a phraseology, even though well meant, has ridiculed deep feelings, such as profound sympathy, common thoughts and instinctive and unconscious urge of these peoples toward Spain. Nevertheless they exist in reality, and even though conveniently reduced and pushed into the spiritual realm, they can produce a closeness so intimate and sincere that mother Iberia and its sons will profit.

Yanguas hoped that such words would reassure Latin Americans "but also other nations eager to disturb the union between Spain and the nations of Iberian origin." Hinting at U.S. fears, he wrote, "This is how I would phrase the terms of this problem to keep away the fears of a nation that is not of Iberian origin, that one could experiment with a nation of the new world." Then came specific instructions for the work of the next few months:

The first manifestation of this South American political project that the current government was undertaking has to show fruits in the assistance of this republic [Argentina] at the Ibero-American Exposition at Seville. And during the reunion at that time, the support for a conference of private international law. . . . [T]hese two questions are the first that need to be faced concretely for favorable resolution.[43]

Yanguas's order was revolutionary in nature. The creation "of a private Spanish international law" meant the restructuring of Spanish American societies based on ethnic legal concepts. Here Yanguas hinted at a new social cornerstone that would dovetail the economic commonwealth, air law, and cultural celebrations. At least according to Yanguas, one day there could exist an exclusive geographic Iberian realm with a civil law as socially distinct as Anglo-Saxon law or the Code Napoleon. Spanish commerce, culture, and law would work hand in hand, creating a historical movement toward a distinct community of shared Hispanic values: "They would be a giant step for this necessary intimate and loyal union that will exist in the future between Spain and the Ibero-American nations that unite themselves in a racial solidarity, the only union that will last."[44]

After changes in Buenos Aires in Spanish diplomats' code of conduct, Madrid's Foreign Ministry should be changed to help the rebirth of the Iberian realm. Yanguas's office typeset a six-page-long instruction manual detailing how the ministry should communicate with Spanish American diplomats.

First, from the very first seconds of any encounter they should be made to feel special. No longer must they be received in a dry formal way. Instead, Spanish American, Portuguese American, and Portuguese diplomats should be received in an effusive and intimate style.

Second, Spanish answers should move the diplomats, by stressing connections of blood and soul, but also a living history that was again uniting all the people represented by them. Meetings at the Spanish Foreign Ministry should become "acts that celebrate familiar facts that ennoble and inspire all involved."[45]

On June 23, 1926, Yanguas tried to make final helpful changes. He introduced a new classification system for embassies and legations reporting from the Americas.

From then on report writing by diplomats had to be done in a systematic fashion. Records had to be precise and report all important information. The new classification system was sent to Buenos Aires in July. The ambassador was reminded that diplomatic report writing was not a onetime event. Yanguas expected follow-up reports exploring key issues on a continuing basis.[46] They had to capture better political, social, and economic aspects of the American republics.

In June Yanguas finalized preparations for the upcoming Iberian Air Congress. It would open on October 24 and last six days. The charge against French global air law had begun.

The final program specified four immediate goals. First, conference participants would develop, discuss, and adopt a common Spanish terminology dealing with air traffic. Second, they would begin developing a distinctly Ibero-American legal code dealing with airplane matters. Third, they would begin collecting and displaying technical data and air statistics of Latin America. Fourth, the conference would bring together civilian and military air representatives.

If everything went as planned, Madrid would become the primary collection place of Spanish, Spanish American, and Portuguese technical airplane data. Spain's capital would house the best knowledge about the manufacture of planes and make possible the exchange of knowledge and teachers in the field of aviation in Spain and Latin America. Yanguas ordered his diplomat in Buenos Aires to collect as much data upfront as possible and to ship it to Madrid before the congress.[47]

On June 2, the conference program was officially handed to Argentine president Alvear.[48] A Dr. Ricardo C. Aldoa advertised the upcoming conference at the Buenos Aires Aero Club. Still it took ten weeks, until August 23, until the first Argentine delegate to the conference was officially identified. The Argentine ambassador to Madrid joined him.[49] Paraguayans waited until September 3 to select their delegation. On the same day the Spanish diplomat Danvila had to ask the Alvear administration again to ask for urgent consideration of the upcoming Ibero-American Air Navigation Act.[50] Unlike Spanish enthusiasm, Spanish American enthusiasm was hard to discover weeks before the conference in Argentina.

In June an in-house memorandum helped identify the dangers that "were threatening sincerely" Spanish spiritual patrimony in the Americas. First was the form of the economic invasion by the United States in the internal life of the Hispanic American nations, and politics, its natural by-product. The second was a spiritual influence that was becoming more penetrating day by day. It was exercised foremost by France and to a lesser degree by Italy.

First, as far as the influence of the United States was concerned, the memo author, the Spanish diplomat Yanguas, did not know how to persevere against a rival so difficult to restrain. The United States and its people, with gigantic possibilities and powerful organizations, had launched an army of engineers, bankers, and businessmen toward South America to conquer markets and the constitutions of business houses, factories, and societies. He feared that their goal was to monopolize the exportation of natural riches. He promised that the Spanish government would soon counter U.S. efforts in some republics with a series of projects.

Second, Yanguas discussed French policy as a challenge. Even though French culture was appreciated with profound admiration and sympathy, the Spanish administrator appealed to his colleague to believe that the affinity that came from Spanish–American connections constituted an alternative higher reality. The intellectual tradition of France could not match Iberian splendor. As far as Italian cultural policy was concerned, it was classified as weaker because it had less time to spread in Latin America.

The Foreign Ministry diplomat instructed the Spanish ambassador to record the projects, points of view, campaigns, and aspirations of French and Italian representatives in the Spanish American republics. Also, he should follow Latin American press coverage. It was imperative to replace the term *Latin America* with *Spanish America*.

In this fight against France, Italy, and the United States, Iberian Spain had to deploy itself with force of notable valor. It would be helped by the magnificent instruments of the Spanish language and the community that came from joint origin, race, civilization, law, religion, and mentality. These factors would always be abundant and sufficient in the struggle against French spirituality, as well as Italian offerings. The task of Spanish diplomats was to reduce French and Italian strength to a normal and tolerable level. Foreign Minister Yanguas concluded, "In principle, we have to conserve in America our vast spiritual empire that one day we will proclaim to the world. The glory of all past and, at the same time, prepare the grandness of our future."[51]

In the League of Nations developments unfolded less favorably for Spain. Primo de Rivera's determination to obtain a permanent seat in the League of Nations floundered. Already in March 1926, he had stated that he was willing to relent on the question of Spain's place in the League of Nations if the league would cede Tangier to Spain. Primo was losing hope that the league, eventually, would be Spain's path toward becoming a permanent, major European power.

Painfully, Germany emerged as winner in the race for the permanent seat in the League of Nations. On June 6, 1926, a report surfaced that Spain "will not oppose the accession of Germany but has planned not to be represented at the September Council and Assembly." Spain would cooperate with the league only as a permanent member of the council.[52] Six days later Brazil went further and resigned from the league in protest. Finally, on June 17, the Spanish government stated that eventually it would follow the Brazilian example.

Still, after the joint Spanish–French victory in Morocco, King Alfonso XIII had traveled to Paris. But the France he visited was in political turmoil because of financial weakness resulting from war debt financing. On July 17, 1926, Premier Briand was thrown out of office for the third time. But even though France was in domestic turmoil, its politicians never became more sensitive toward Spanish hopes for a political rise in the League of Nations.[53] These developments were another important context for reviving secret Spanish–German armament discussions.

On September 8, 1926, German delegates left Berlin overjoyed to claim the permanent League of Nations seat only eight years after the end of the German monarchy and the German loss of World War I. From a European point of view, France and Britain made the right move in lifting the esteem of constructive German political forces, pulling them away from those armed forces members that were eager to temporarily align themselves with the Red Army against the West, in perverse anticipation of an Armageddon wiping out modernity and capitalism.

For Spain the development was still insulting, even though it was wise. Spain had never caused a world war and had engaged in constructive, supportive courting in the League of Nations. Now the Spanish government recalled the Spanish delegate from Geneva, insisting that the recall demonstrated an "Attitude of Dignified Abstention."[54]

In Madrid the Spanish Cabinet Council met, chaired by Alfonso XIII. The group decided that Spain should resign from the League of Nations. The politicians declared that the league had insulted Spain as a European country as well as her prestige, traditions, and importance as the mother country of twenty Spanish-speaking nations.[55] Now Primo de Rivera uttered toward Italian visitors that the league should be replaced by "something more just, founded on the cross."[56]

In North Africa events were more fortuitous. On May 3, 1926, the French captured the Moroccan Rif's capital. Twenty-three days later, on May 26, Abd el-Krim surrendered. This most bloody victory through genocide by French and the Spanish armed forces promised a new space of action in the near future.

Primo de Rivera also faced Italian colonial ambitions. Mussolini nudged himself into North Africa, personally reminding Europe's politicians that Italy, too, wanted to be a North African colonial power. In April he crossed the Mediterranean and advocated in favor of Italy's colonial expansion. On May 19, 1926, he went further and declared democracy as deceased. Fascism would be its replacement. Disturbing echoes of the End of Democracy theme also came from Poland, where General Piłsudski made himself dictator on June 1. Three days earlier, in Portugal, Gomes de Costa was replaced by António Óscar de Fragoso Carmona. At the end of July, once again, Mussolini proclaimed that Italy "must expand or explode." Two months later, he abolished all organized political opposition in Italy. The Fascist Party was now the party of the state.

Against this background he again reached out to Primo de Rivera, insisting that Spain should move closer to fascist Italy. To begin with he proposed a public exchange of congratulatory telegrams between Italy's king Emmanuel and Primo de Rivera's Council de Consejo.[57]

But, once again, Primo de Rivera kept perspective vis-à-vis his Mediterranean competitors. The pro-Italian fascist invitation was politely rejected. Spain could not join Italy openly and oppose parliamentary systems, he explained, because the Spanish nation was still weak and not yet formed.

Nevertheless, behind the scenes, the Mussolini administration was comforted that Primo de Rivera's Spain "was emotionally connected with Italy and Mussolini." Unfortunately Spain had to recognize its limits with respect to other powers, especially France: "Spain could not demonstrate publicly itself as sister in weaponhood of Italy." The Italian minister in Spain became frustrated and interpreted this answer as a "painful admission of impotence." Still, in fall 1926, Primo de Rivera entered with Italy into a Treaty of Friendship, Conciliation, and Judicial Settlement.[58]

17 Primo de Rivera and Alfonso XIII Exploit Germany's Secret Rearmament

⇥≡⊙ ──

A most important breakthrough came in the naval sector. Spanish–German secret naval cooperation resumed, moving Spain toward obtaining the best weapon technology in submarines and torpedoes. While Junkers advocate Bauer was still waiting in Berlin for the completion of his transatlantic airplane prospectus, in Madrid Primo de Rivera and Alfonso XIII blessed an unprecedented and illegal secret joining of resources with the Weimar navy.

And in Buenos Aires in May 1926, Argentine naval armament was moving closer toward funding. Whereas in 1922 only submarine purchases and a naval air force had been talked about, now an entire navy fleet program was approved.

First the parliament appropriated US$32,000,000 for ship construction. Confusion existed about the nature of funding. Was it gold pesos, paper pesos, or credits accumulated from World War I war damage and credits? Some reports circulated the sum of 100,000,000 gold pesos. Others said the money would be released in chunks year by year.[1] Either way Argentina was expected to spend three times its 1919 armament budget in 1927. Argentine military leaders had been able to force parliament to devote 23.1 percent of the national budget to arms purchases.[2]

Spain's Primo de Rivera and Foreign Minister Yanguas, in the midst of their Iberian Commonwealth outreach, expected to benefit from Argentina's armament orders. But they were shocked to learn that Argentine admirals did not easily share their belief in Hispanist solidarity and considered ship purchases outside of Spain. Argentina's purchase commission wanted only the very best ships and would tour all leading European warship manufacturers. But Spain was not known for naval constructions. Spanish diplomat Danvila reported that Argentina's Ministry of War and Navy did not even consider sending its purchase commission to Spain.

An additional mystery was the Argentine decision-making process. Who decided what ships would be built? Did the military purchase commission or the ministry in Buenos Aires decide? Until specifics could be known, capturing a share of this Argentine budget bonanza would remain difficult for Spain.[3] Spanish commercial Hispanismo was not automatically reciprocated by Argentina's armed forces.[4] And Spanish hopes were not the only ones hurt.

U.S. observers also feared that the Argentines would not place orders with U.S. ship construction companies. U.S. naval attaché Samuel Hickey wrote to his superiors in Annapolis that Argentina would not buy weapons from the United States because some U.S. merchants had slandered one Argentine contractor: "If the American businessman felt that it was worth 32,000,000 gold dollars to call a man a 'whop' then I am afraid it is a rather expensive expression."[5]

On the other side of the Atlantic, in Madrid, Foreign Minister Yanguas did more than sulk. He insisted that the new Hispanismo should translate into definite orders for Spain, at least helping Spain with a difficult employment situation. He insisted that Spanish naval yards could compete with ship manufacturers of the United States, Great Britain, France, and Italy.[6] He instructed the embassy in Argentina to find out how to enter a bid into the competition.[7]

Then corruption raised its familiar, ugly head. In August, in Paris, the Argentine businessman Miguel de Sautu visited a diplomat at the German embassy. He explained that in Argentina he was a great industrialist with access to large financial means. In the near future he wanted to travel to Germany to import articles for pneumatic machines. But he also knew that the Argentine government was intending to create a massive naval yard to construct and repair warships. A lease for this factory was to be given to a foreign company and would last ninety-nine years.

The Argentine government was expected to give significant help. The factory could import goods free of customs for the manufacturing of quality arms. Santu considered the volume of future business to be worth 50,000,000 Argentine pesos. Currently the Argentine government was in contact with British manufacturers and France's Schneider-Creuset military foundry. Now, Señor de Sautu claimed that Argentina was also interested in German companies.

He wanted to educate the Germans that they could expect only to be admitted to the bidding process if one Argentine personality with great financial and political influence would represent them. Señor de Sautu wanted to play that role for Germany. He insisted that his initiative work would have the greatest impact if the Argentine legation in Berlin were kept out of the deal and he was granted a monopoly to lead the effort from the very beginning.[8]

Then the placing of specific Argentine orders was moved to 1927. The matter would become a central diplomatic issue six months down the road.

In Germany, Oberst Bauer knew that his transatlantic airplane proposal was overdue. May had passed without a finished presentation. June came, and Bauer decided to warn Junkers that further delays must not take place if they wanted to place orders in Madrid.

In the meantime Bauer also introduced his transoceanic project to other key German military individuals, including army leader General Seeckt. Slowly, Bauer realized that the struggle over establishing German airlines in Spain and South America was changing in a way that he could no longer understand. It became clear that any plan of the Junkers company would differ from the preferences of the Weimar government.

As before Junkers still wanted to work only with existing Junkers airlines, to establish a global airline and business project. But individuals in the German Ministry of Transportation increasingly thought in national terms, without regard for the financial benefit of the Junkers company. The government bureaucrats were insisting on the fusion of all private companies into one national Lufthansa company. It would control overseas flight. In this rival plan, Bauer would not earn any commission. He was confronting a new military air business culture that rejected the, by now, outmoded military advisers of World War I for national projects.

Bauer drew the wrong conclusions. He decided to dig in and oppose the Weimar administrators and their new preference.[9] Bauer would fight Lufthansa, its associated bank leaders, and the Weimar government to win the transatlantic route for himself and Junkers.

Old navy air force point man Laas joined Bauer, hoping to reverse the imposition of Lufthansa as the dominant future force in the German air business. In May 1926, he urged secret navy armament Section Chief Lohmann to keep navy air force developments exclusively attached to the navy and always away from the Lufthansa. And he supported efforts to keep the Transoceanic Flight project exclusively in the hands of Junkers.[10] Lufthansa must not have any influence over it.

But the opposition of the two men made no lasting impact. The Foreign Ministry, the Ministry of Navy, and the Ministry of Transportation saw Lufthansa as the exclusive transport enterprise of the German Reich. They were willing to support Junkers only as an airplane manufacturer. As soon as Junkers involved itself in running airlines, any support would be removed. To the contrary, in this case the ministries promised to fight Junkers.

To everybody's surprise Spanish industrialist and naval yard owner Echevarrieta jumped into the airline business. After moving into the German camp of ship constructors he next eyed a Spanish–German air agreement. Canaris, a second time, played a pivotal role.

Success, however, was handed to the German Ministry of Transportation and the German navy. While Bauer courted the king to sign on with Junkers, Canaris won Echevarrieta to also carry the flag in the airline sector. Canaris introduced Junkers representative Killinger to Echevarrieta, while Canaris negotiated the torpedo and submarine naval yards.

Later they traveled to Germany accompanied by Canaris's point man for Spain, Kapitaen Lieut. Meyerhofer. Echevarrieta was interested in Junkers's raw oil engine. He was expected to come to Junkers in 1926. Suddenly, Echevarrieta appeared as an unexpected, more promising way through the door into the Spanish air force for Junkers.

In October 1926, Echevarrieta was back in Berlin accompanied by three people. Now the German Ministry of Transport was interested in creating an airline in Spain. In the end Canaris's involvement guaranteed that Echevarrieta also received a bid in the airline sector. Afterward Echevarrieta, Raffael Ferrer, and Captain Daniel de Araoz were expected to travel from Bremen to Hamburg. There they would stay at the Hotel Atlantic on October 19. Later they would leave for Cuxhaven, where they would take the steamer *Reliance*.[11] Echevarrieta and his team were received in Berlin like kings. The Ministry of Communication and the Foreign Ministry sent representatives. It was perceived as a victory for Lufthansa, not one for Junkers.

Within months a basic agreement was reached among the German government, the Lufthansa faction, and Echevarrieta. An agreement was signed on October 11.[12] The Weimar ministry right away appropriated 1,200,000 marks support.

Even though Bauer hoped that the king's cousin would be able to make an end run around the Spanish air force and Transportation Ministry, this proved wrong. By April, it was clear that also the transoceanic project would have to be discussed by Primo de Rivera's Council of Ministers. By May 6, word came: "We will need time as usual in Spain." Still, Spain remained the "first stopover for the flight overseas."[13]

Bauer had explored in April and May 1926 Argentine–German military support for Argentine–German cooperation in gas warfare. After arriving from Madrid he traveled to Potsdam to talk to members of the German army.

Bauer envisioned that Stolzenberg's poison gas factory in Spain could produce bombs for a variety of armies. Among them were Mexico's, Argentina's, and Turkey's.

Argentine minister of war Justo was aware of his idea and, according to Bauer, had written in support to the Argentine military purchase commission in Brussels. In Madrid, Bauer's key liaison became Argentine military attaché Estrada. The Spanish factory Empresa Experiencas Industriales, SA de Aranjuez (EISA), would manufacture experimental bomb designs for the Argentine army.[14]

Initially six bombs would be designed. Then the Argentines would be invited to a live demonstration of fog and gas bombs. Bauer also wanted to demonstrate poisonous liquids that could be poured from planes. Once again the EISA should manufacture the technology for the Argentines.[15] The EISA had access to the patents of Carbonit, a former German bomb manufacturer.[16]

There existed other interesting military contacts between Spanish and German gas factories. In the Fábrica Nacional de Productos Químicos Alfonso XIII a German engineer, Mr. Wachsmann, worked in gas development. Whenever he learned about gas war developments from Britain or France he passed the knowledge to Germany, including scientists at the Kaiser Wilhelm Institute Department for Chemical Studies. It reported to the German army.

For the Spanish EISA company this was simply a business exchange, not some sinister plot to bring gas to Argentina. Its capacity was not used very much, and contracts, including from foreigners, were welcome. An Argentine order might increase capacity use.[17]

By April 20, Argentines had agreed to participate in a test firing of gas and fog bombs on Spanish soil. On May 14, Bauer presented a proposal to Spain. Even though by May 24 all sides agreed, the process slowed down again. Suddenly Bauer had difficulties obtaining the necessary spraying apparatus from Junkers.[18]

In the midst of this effort, Primo de Rivera announced a massive Spanish air force production program. Spain would rival Argentina in the air sector. Primo de Rivera's vision for the military sector was dramatic. He unveiled an astonishing investment in the Spanish air force. In July 1926, the government appropriated 160,000,000 pesetas to be spent between 1927 and 1937. This budget was broken down into 120,000,000 pesetas for airplanes, 23,000,000 pesetas for airports, 7,000,000 pesetas for reserve machines, 7,000,000 pesetas for engines, 2,000,000 pesetas for armaments, and 1,000,000 pesetas for radio telegraphy.

In addition the air force would be backed up by a strengthened naval air force. It would receive 15,000,000 pesetas for permanent installations and 20,000,000 pesetas for a naval flight school in Barcelona. In addition Spanish factories for aeronautic services would be built, and a new military air administrative guide was published.[19] This was a most remarkable display of budget prowess, more than anything a Latin American air force could demonstrate at that time. If all of this money was spent as planned, Spain could project real air power into North Africa, the Mediterranean, and even the western Atlantic. General Kindelan and his young air force did their best to connect air force growth with symbolic displays of rising Spanish power.

The Plus Ultra flight to Buenos Aires had been only one symbolic flight example. Three other spectacular stunts were in the planning. First, a Spanish pilot took off to reach the Philippines. But on April 5, 1926, a Patrulla Elcano by three Breguet XIXs had to turn around. In the same months another long-distance practice flight began, officially to reach India. In reality a symbolic flight was supposed to fly west until it reached Cuba. In May, the *Jesús del Gran Poder* project began.[20]

All of this was enhanced with public diplomacy. On August 11, in a special supplement of the *London Times*, Primo de Rivera confirmed Spain's new transatlantic outreach: "It is Spain's aspiration to hold the rank of a great power rooted in Hispanic civilization, which, without detriment to the absolute sovereignty and independence of the Hispano-American nations, she believes she can maintain."

Right away the advertising for the Ibero-American Exhibition at Seville intensified. Exhibitors planning to participate at Seville were offered reduced ticket prices for family members to accompany them to the Spanish peninsula. Also, a 100-cubic-foot space was offered free to ship goods from all Spanish American countries to the exhibition in Spain.[21] Most important, on September 23, 1926, the new official date for the opening of the Seville Exposition was fixed at October 12, 1928, Columbus Day two years from then.[22]

In Madrid Primo de Rivera and King Alfonso welcomed Wilhelm Canaris in 1926 as a critical supporter of navy modernization. Here was a highly skilled, Spanish-speaking German individual who promised them access to the best submarine technology available. No longer would Spanish captains have to accept Great Britain's second-best technologies.

Canaris offered the manufacture of torpedoes as the first area of German–Spanish technological development cooperation. He offered to create an experimental torpedo factory in Cádiz. First, design advancements would have to

48. Historical float entitled "Discovery" at the Parade of the Hispanic-American Race at the 1928 Ibero-American Exhibition (Fondo Cultura, F 968–02–003, Archivo General de la Administración, Alcalá de Henares).

be made. Then the plant would produce one thousand torpedoes annually. The secret project would employ engineers from the accumulator engine factory of Hagen, Siemens-Schuckert, and the Unión Naval de Levante associate Ingenieurskantoor voor Scheepsbouw (IvS). Alfonso XIII and Primo de Rivera treated this project as high priority.[23] Eventually it would give birth to the German torpedo prototype G7a and e, which U.S. experts later rated as perfect.

For Spain the torpedoes promised an edge over Italian naval expansion in the Mediterranean, but also against French ships, should competition in the Mediterranean ever become openly violent. For Germany, torpedoes stood at the core of a strategy for sinking Polish, Danish, and French ships.

Interestingly Canaris had to win over not only Spanish leaders. As important were policy makers in the German Foreign Ministry and Ministry of Economics who looked at secret rearmament with great concern in regard to Germany's admission to the League of Nations.[24]

Canaris's Spanish counterpart, the industrialist Echevarrieta, conducted business very egotistically, burning to demonstrate his unique personal power through willfulness, erratically changing demands, and toleration of bribes to middlemen. As Canaris tried to succeed at submarine and torpedo construction in Spain, he had to learn to swallow his disgust at the Basque's business methods.

Echevarrieta did everything possible to exploit German vulnerability and to extract maximum gain.[25] While Argentines celebrated Ramón Franco's flight and Foreign Secretary Yanguas pushed aspects of Spain's commonwealth policy, German administrators from various ministries gathered at the Berlin Ministry of Economy to discuss a large state credit guarantee for Echevarrieta's naval yard and torpedo company. The records of this most uncommon meeting offered civilian administrators a rare glimpse at the deeper aspects of secret German rearmament.

On April 13, 1926, economists, diplomats, and navy advisers debated the need for a government guarantee of 5,000,000 RM. Most likely the Basque was requesting German government money because the other major Spanish banks remained tied to British and French manufacturers.

In exchange Echevarrieta promised the Germans pie in the sky. He envisioned building three shipyards and factories, one each in Cádiz, Cartagena, and a third location. He would staff them with Spanish workers, supervised by German engineers. Together they would build ships based on German blueprints. The navy leadership argued strongly in favor of the proposal.

Canaris explained to the German civilian administrators Echevarrieta's intimidating demands. He explained how Germany's new designs for torpedoes and submarines for the first time could be translated into prototypes. Then they could be tested on the high seas. Technical evaluations would provide initial, much needed data for improvement. Proven ship designs would be ready for the day when the Treaty of Versailles collapsed. Then France and Poland could be confronted by superior ships. The chance for victory was good.

Canaris also described a darker scenario if bureaucrats were to refuse financing. Then France and Poland would keep superiority on the North Atlantic and Baltic Sea.

German Foreign Ministry diplomats raised valid objections. They insisted on priority for negotiations that redefined international legal terms, specifying which machinery Germany could own and operate and whether it could manufacture weapons inside the country. Most certainly, if the secret Spanish–German cooperation were discovered, French, British, and U.S. diplomats would exact drastic punishment. And deeper inspections of all German military affairs would be renewed. Besides, diplomats pointed out, lately Germany had moved politically closer to the British. A tacit British–German understanding was developing that, in theory, offered Germany more independence from French strictures. The previous year Weimar Germany had put on the public mask of peace and signed the Locarno Treaty. The diplomats needed British support against France and feared that making Spain independent from British weapons now would hurt their efforts in the league.[26]

Seven days later Canaris was back in Spain. On May 20, 1926, he and the navy forged ahead regardless of objections. Alfonso XIII met with Canaris. While Bauer was still steaming in Berlin, burning to obtain his transoceanic airplane proposal, Canaris received not just an open royal welcome but the king's approval for collaboration in the submarine field. Canaris was impressed that Alfonso wanted Spain to operate a purely national arms industry. Even though Spain's minister of the navy still favored Great Britain, the king wanted to add the finest German technology and an independent naval yard.[27]

Canaris made the first breakthroughs in the torpedo factory project. The German navy was able to send 240,000 British pounds to the Banco Alemán Transatlántico in Madrid to fund its initial construction stage. In return,

49. Dictator Primo de Rivera discussing affairs with King Alfonso XIII (Fondo Cultura, F 1090 18–001, Archivo General de la Administración, Alcalá de Henares).

Echevarrieta agreed to order in Germany all construction material for the factory and, later, for the manufacture of the torpedoes. Also German engineers would run the factory for the next ten years.

The torpedo factory would be directed by former German ambassador to Mexico and Peking Admiral a.D. Hintze. He would supervise three Germans as deputy directors. The torpedo would be built according to German plans on machine benches ordered in Germany. The guidance system would be purchased through a Siemens and Halske subsidiary. The submarine to fire the torpedo would be designed by IvS.

Spain could expect to own this factory in 1936. It would produce one thousand torpedoes per year.[28]

By then the first Spanish Air Congress was coming up in Madrid from October 3 until October 10. A few days before the congress, Alfonso XIII allowed Oberst Bauer to travel to Spain and to finally present Junkers's transatlantic proposal. Bauer arrived with a transatlantic project proposal on September 23, 1926. After stopping first at the residence of the king's cousin, Don Fernando, Bauer went next to meet Alfonso XIII in his apartments. On October 9, 1926, at 2:30 p.m., both men visited the king.

Bauer described Alfonso's welcome as particularly warm. He appreciated Bauer's greetings from Prof. Junkers, who apologized that this presentation had not taken place as promised in May. Now Alfonso and Ferdinand were interested to hear what Junkers would propose.

First, Bauer lectured about the transoceanic project, presenting key points:

His Majesty was entirely in agreement that one should pursue a developmental path leading from the 15 t to the 40 t and, then, on to a 60 t plane. In particular he was impressed by the wide range of action that enables already the 15 t airplane with heavy oil engine to realize a transatlantic flight with noteworthy payload. Already fast transport of important documents of banks might suffice to assure a sufficient income. He agreed that the transocean project would be financially rewarding. Besides the faster transport of mail and documents, etc but especially passengers, trade and change would enliven things in unimaginable ways.[29]

Then Bauer attacked Junkers's new rival Lufthansa, Zeppelin, and Dornier. Bauer tried to say very little about the potential of zeppelins crossing to South America.

But Alfonso XIII insisted on comparing the airplane option against the zeppelins. Bauer repeated that the zeppelin would be not useful. Pending plans to cross the Atlantic to Argentina, he predicted, would soon run out of steam.

Second, he disparaged the preferred Lufthansa approach of German government bureaucrats. He vehemently urged His Majesty to keep the Transoceanic Flight in exclusive Spanish hands. Bauer portrayed Lufthansa as a private German enterprise, exclusively dedicated to earning money. Even though Lufthansa was working with a Spanish industrialist, the basic character of the project remained a for-profit enterprise. It needed to be a nationalist Spanish enterprise.

Bauer urged Alfonso XIII to accept that Spain should have an interest in keeping the transoceanic question entirely in Spanish hands. This way Spain would determine the role it wanted to play. Cross-ocean traffic and the development of air service would push Spain more and more into an exposed position, which could have political consequences. And those who carried the responsibility should absolutely remain master of the issue. Alfonso XIII agreed entirely. At the end the king asked how much a 15-ton plane would cost. Bauer could not provide a precise answer and promised to organize additional documents soon.

Bauer emphasized how important it was that Spain, finally, would take a decisive step forward and open a major national airline service. As long as Spain only granted concessions but did not operate the airline, a positive development of Spain's airline system could not to be expected.

Then Bauer made an important point. The large machines and engines of the Junkers G 23 and 24 constituted the first base for a large Spanish warplane squadron. The men discussed air service not only from a civilian and trade standpoint but also from a military perspective. All involved knew that their plan had always included the conversion of transoceanic airplanes into long-distance troop and material transporters, perhaps even bombers. Bauer assured Alfonso XIII

that each civilian airplane could be used as a military plane in times of war. Particular in this regard the Junkers plane had an advantage: the cabin for peacetime operations could be exchanged, in shortest time, for a cabin serving purposes of war. Therefore the Junkers was also a warplane. Bauer admitted that from the point of view of pilots a fast one seat attack fighter was preferable. But he believed, more and more a large plane would be accepted as decisive factor in battle. It was slower than the attack fighter but it was quasi impossible to attack, because it could be hurt less through machine gun fire.[30]

In regard to the bombing equipment Bauer pointed out that EISA and Guernica in Spain, by all means, would be able to deliver quality explosive bombs to drop from the planes. Besides, Spain had the great advantage that it could take a leading role in warfare using gas and fog.

Next Bauer lectured extensively about Junkers's staff of experienced pilots and artillery and bomb specialists who could handle the development of warplanes for Spain. Then he suggested an order of one fully equipped Junkers warplane (R 42). Alfonso was strongly in favor of his proposition.

At the end of the talk Bauer teased Alfonso with an offer of an airplane factory. Alfonso was open to it but wanted any construction to take place in Seville. The development of transoceanic planes would require swimming planes and therefore one had to be near water. Junkers should open a central repair station in Seville. Once a 15-ton plane had been developed and parts were ordered in Dessau, they would be transported to Seville for final assembly.

Of course later this "repair station" would have to be expanded significantly to accommodate the 40- to 60-ton planes. Bauer told Alfonso that Prof. Junkers was willing to make available his patents and licenses, as well as special personnel who would work at the repair station.

Alfonso liked Junkers's offer to construct at the factory in Seville. After 1.5 hours of discussions Alfonso thanked Bauer and "expressed his hope that he should experience to fly with Prof. Junkers together in a flight across the ocean in a 60 t machine."[31]

Afterward Bauer took his tasks seriously. He reported that his main work was only beginning. The task remaining "was to influence the many—and there are many—offices, which want to speak along in this question."[32]

He wrote and distributed memoranda to all the bureaucrats in the byzantine Spanish administration that might play a role in making decisions about plane purchases.[33] Little by little, this German talked himself into being a contender for major Spanish air force orders.

Then the Madrid Air Congress concluded, and it too ended with a draft treaty that Latin American delegations agreed to take back across the Atlantic and have their political elites or congresses enact as law. In 1926 one could argue that Spain had successfully established a draft Convention of Ibero-American Aeronautics. All the Latin American delegates had to do was to ratify it. Spanish foreign minister Yanguas urged prompt ratification.[34]

During the air congress a very small Junkers aircrew was present in Madrid. It invited the conference's interministerial commission to free demonstration flights, hoping this would increase goodwill for Junkers after the congress not only in Spain but also in South America.[35]

Oberst Bauer's fall visit with Alfonso had convinced Spanish air force members to also include German companies in their visits to manufacturers: "Thanks to the support of Oberst Bauer, he succeeded to interest his majesty to a high degree for our war planes. We were asked to send to all ministries extensive reports to those who matter . . . work of Junkers of far reaching importance." One Spanish general who had been pro-Germany now headed a ministry that unified civilian and army air forces. Two commissions were formed to visit countries producing large-scale fighter planes.

One "unimportant" commission would be sent to France, Belgium, and Italy, staffed by Capt. Alvarrez Buylla and Commander Arias. The second "important" one would go to England, Denmark, and Germany. Both commissions were headed and controlled by General Kindelan, as well as Prince Infante Alfonso de Orleans.

As planned the Spaniards traveled to Great Britain first. Thereafter they went to Denmark, where Rohrbach was manufacturing, and then Linham, Sweden, Junkers's military aircraft manufacturing site. Finally they headed to Dessau, Germany.

Bauer prepared a presentation that would make British warplanes look second rate. Spanish–German airplane relations were now advancing in both civilian aircraft and military aircraft. As suggested Bauer showed the K 30 and R 53 equipped as warplanes.[36] The Spanish visitors were also received by Oberst von Merkatz, who was in charge of armament for Junkers planes.[37]

If it were up to Bauer, Spanish purchases should serve an offensive Spanish purpose. Bauer explained,

Also the development of air traffic and the possession of the Canary Islands seems to be more valuable, but also the rising value must provoke certain people to take the position from Spain. Now that Spain wants to arm itself against such endeavor it does not need to do anything different than to develop the appropriate air fleet. Our idea, which is critical is that civilian airplanes, at any time, can be converted into warplanes. In the future, 15 t, 40 t and 60 t airplanes will become war machines which can clear up fast an enemy fleet. Thus we have arrived at the military application, and we need to underline this, in particular when we relate to Primo de Rivera, Kindelan, and Saro.[38]

The transoceanic project still remained difficult. Insiders doubted that the Primo de Rivera administration would purchase 15-ton transoceanic airplanes without a single existing prototype.[39] And in December, Dornier also scored points when a Spanish flight, called the Patrulla Atlántica, flew from Melilla to Guinea using a Dornier Wal. The military contract continued to be contested, but now Junkers seemed to be in the race.

In Germany, the Weimar government, rather than letting Lufthansa and Junkers clash in Spain in one final decisive confrontation, pressured all sides to discover common ground and to merge efforts for one German policy toward the Iberian Peninsula and, implicitly, Latin America. Junkers head Killinger began to reform Unión Aérea Española (UAE) statutes but also cooperate with the German navy rearmament point man Lohmann.[40] Lohmann had just purchased the Casper Aircraft Company to obtain facilities for the testing of commercial aircraft types that closely resembled the fighter, bomber, and reconnaissance planes being built abroad by such firms as Boeing, Vickers, and Douglass.[41]

In January, in the civilian sector, talks were under way to merge UAE and Iberia into one company. UAE was supposed to let go of its independence as a company. First and foremost this meant cashing out current investors who might not want to merge UAE with Iberia. Either the German bank would supply the funds, or administrators would try to find a Spanish bank that was willing to put up funds.[42] In the end President Moreno proved a loyal actor on behalf of the company in favor of the bigger project. It was he who had suggested to Junkers to exploit Primo de Rivera's growing frustration with the advances of France in South America.

The signing of the Latécoère treaties had provided the Junkers initiative with a breakthrough where before they had encountered indifference and resistance. As the French pushed in Latin America, the Spaniards awarded UAE the concession servicing Madrid–Lisbon–Seville. Sometime after April a Spanish navy commission was scheduled to visit Berlin. On April 29, a Junkers airplane was baptized with the name *Seville*, and the air service Seville–Lisbon–Madrid was opened. But winning the contract did not mean making money as imagined.

In January Killinger still needed Rodriguez to improve the accounting of the UAE books. There remained very little money to buy planes in preparation of merging into Iberia.

After the visit of the Spanish commission members were convinced that Junkers was building the best airplane. But the key issue remained the price. Also, Echevarrieta entered into the conflict with Dornier and refused to partner with Rohrbach, because he was undercapitalized. Echevarrieta tried to use Mr. Messerschmidt as mediator, and through Araoz, Barón de Sacro Lirio, he tried to push the risk and the organization of capital into the hands of his German partners.

Killinger focused on not angering Echevarrieta. The Germans suggested that Echevarrieta get more money from the Spanish state and make a better profit but not to lower German prices. Canaris has just arrived at the end of January. He pretended to be a friend of Junkers.

Lufthansa's Mr. Hirschfeld was rapidly falling out of favor. The contract with Echevarrieta remained unsigned. Araoz stated that it made no sense to join an airline that did not make a profit. Rumors stated that Echevarrieta went around Hirschfeld and negotiated directly with Lufthansa. Hirschfeld's financial position remained poor. Killinger, exploiting Hirschfeld's weakness, offered to find a basis for cooperation if Lufthansa wanted to.

In Madrid Spanish foreign minister Yanguas intensified Spanish cultural policy offers toward Latin America. Already an invitation had been extended for the International Geological Congress in Madrid. The last one had met in 1922 in Brussels. Argentina promised to send a participant.[43] When the second Pan-American Postal Congress took place, Madrid applied as a potential candidate for the third congress.[44]

Spanish efforts to ram the foundations for a new Iberian bridgehead into the Argentine realm remained puzzling work for Spaniards. King Alfonso looked forward to new guidance from one of his most experienced diplomats who, at the end of 1926, was being reassigned to lead the Spanish charge inside Argentina. The duke of Amalfi had served Alfonso XIII already during the Mexican Revolution. Personally, the duke was disappointed to return to Latin America, because he had had great hopes to receive the ambassadorship in Brussels, Belgium. Still, he followed the order of Primo de Rivera and Yanguas and relocated to Buenos Aires on November 30, 1926. Six days later President Alvear received Ambassador Amalfi and offered the Spaniard his personal dedication to collaboration and his "affection for his Majesty and Spain."[45]

In the first weeks the ambassador wrote private letters to the foreign minister and the king, offering his private thoughts about the state of Spanish and Argentine relations and the state of the Spanish ethnic community in Buenos Aires. As far as the Spanish community was concerned, Amalfi described it as lacking unity. Its buildings did not radiate Spanish might into Argentina, and the community remained torn apart by ethnic regionalism. The Center of Catalonia was 130,000 pesos in debt. When the Spanish community met it would fly at least two flags, one of Spain and the other of Catalonia. Duke Amalfi criticized the Spanish love for regional separatism and the consequences of the lack of national unity in at least three speeches.[46]

Outside Buenos Aires, Spanish separatism was even stronger. In February, in Mendoza, a nucleus of Catalonians basked in their non-Spanishness. Their newspaper even received disparaging articles about Spain from a Catalan based in Paris. The ambassador suspected French intent to sabotage the economic rise of Spain and Argentina.[47] Even Capuchin monks spread separatist propaganda.[48]

Some of Argentina's elite appreciated kickbacks when it came to Spanish affairs. For example, even though Spain had difficulty raising funds for the construction of a more suitable Spanish embassy, various Argentine circles demanded 1,000,000 pesos in order to issue construction permits.[49] The duke even suspected Argentines of working quietly against Alfonso XIII's commonwealth offensive, probably encouraged by German and British residents.[50] Finally, there was also simple, practical frustration. The Spanish embassy did not maintain a car for official presentations. Only the Spanish military attaché drove an automobile, which he had bought for 7,000 pesos from the Italian ambassador, Count Martin Franklin.[51]

Duke Amalfi evaluated the Spanish community as unable to act as a player in Spanish diplomacy. Not surprisingly, he stated that one of his main jobs was "to combat energetically and relentlessly, but with indispensable tact, the profound division of the Spanish community, thanks to the unqualified impunity of expressions that the Argentine law allows."[52] Also Buenos Aires and Argentines appeared to him as an arrogant city and people who only looked down on Spain: "They think that Spain is a village and Buenos Aires a metropolis. They confuse liberty with being without discipline. They are anti-Semites and they confuse grossness with greatness." He explained to Primo de Rivera and the king that Argentines had a "moral character that constantly protests beautiful words about the love for Spain but they were inconsistent with government decisions. Behind it was implacable hatred of Spain." He thought it was important to Argentines to appear friendly to Spain. But underneath "they have the envy of the petulant, who prefers to recognize his inferiority in different cultural aspects and continue to cover up their eyes from somebody foreign. It would have required them to implicitly confess their state of mind to the great and generous nation to whom they owe their existence."[53]

After settling in, Amalfi reported that no Argentine government ministry was willing to help Spain develop its Iberian bridgehead on location. The

Argentine government proved continuously indifferent toward Spanish priorities. For example, on November 17, Foreign Minister Yanguas had asked the Spanish embassy to push for immediate ratification of the draft agreement reached at the Madrid Air Congress in October 1926. On December 29, Duke Amalfi "observed in these last days perfect unfamiliarity with the issue."[54] Argentine policy makers seemed to be unaware of the new Spanish air convention.

Only Argentine foreign minister Gallardo vaguely assured Amalfi that his country wanted to be the first to sign the Madrid air convention. However, Amalfi could not name one act that the Argentine government was doing to overcome political lethargy in its congress. He diagnosed a lack of willpower by the Argentine president as a second obstacle for the development of Spanish policy. Amalfi perceived Alvear as a pro-French politician. He was not expected to work in favor of Spanish policy that would eliminate French oversight of Spanish–American airline policy.

Duke Amalfi, however, did not just complain. He did make efforts to improve Spain's standing. First, he suggested that vanity might help Alfonso XIII and Primo de Rivera. He suggested that the Argentine president should receive the medal of Charles III attached to a collar. Because the medal was tied to the name of a king it might quietly offer royal status, something the French Republic could never offer. Sometimes simple symbols promised to overcome complicated obstacles.[55]

Suddenly two political earthquakes shook up the situation. First, on January 31, 1927, Amalfi discovered that Argentina was about to grant the French company Latécoère the monopoly for flight in Argentina. Argentina's general director of mail wanted to award the monopoly for the transport of mail from Brazil, Africa, and Europe to Spain's rival. All that was missing on the contract offer was President Alvear's signature.

So far Latécoère had been able to establish air service only from France to Africa. Now the next step was about to be taken, and an airline would cross from France to Cape Verde, to Fernando Noronha, Brazil, and on to Buenos Aires. French plans were based on land airplanes, not Dornier Wal planes, which needed coasts or rivers to start and land. Already the French were building airports along the projected route and performed propaganda and practice flights.

All the French were missing was the successful construction of a French plane, strong and large enough to cross the Atlantic safely, predictably, and profitably. For a short while the French would have to use dispatch boats, called *avisos*, to carry passengers from Senegal to Brazil. A monopoly contract from Africa to Argentina would mean that the airlines of all other nations would be excluded from crossing from the Atlantic to the Pacific side of South America.

50. The tiny island of Fernando de Noronha, north of Brazil, remained critical for the refueling of German planes crossing the Atlantic Ocean (Ibero Amerikanisches Institut, Stiftung Preussischer Kulturbesitz, Bildarchiv, Berlin).

Any Spanish hope to operate a viable and independent air connection between Spain and Argentina would be doomed. Of course, the German transatlantic initiative would also end.

On February 5, 1927, the Spanish government ordered Amalfi to run determined and intelligent interference against the French. The contract with Latécoère needed to be reversed.[56] A strong objection was submitted in writing. Eight days later, Amalfi was able to explain it personally to Foreign Minister Gallardo.

This meeting offered the first silver lining. The talks revealed that the minister of mail was not at all opposed to signing a second treaty with a Spanish company that used zeppelins. The words *contract* and *monopoly* did not necessarily mean "contract" and "monopoly" in the Argentine political culture.[57]

Amalfi's intervention bought time. In Madrid bureaucrats used it. Deciding to use zeppelins, in greatest haste they converted the promising Colón Investment Company into the Línea Aérea Seville–Buenos Aires.

On February 12, 1927, a royal decree gave this zeppelin company the right to service a future route between Seville and Buenos Aires. The forty-year concession obliged the company to build a complete airport in Seville within four years. The airship was to carry at least forty passengers and a certain amount of commercial tonnage. In a little bit more than ten days the Sociedad Colón Transportes Aéreos Españoles had been created.[58] Highly unusual, the king himself entered the discussions.

On March 6, 1927, Alfonso XIII communicated through his secretary Torres to Amalfi in Argentina that keeping open possibilities for a zeppelin route was not enough: "Spain needs to be able to aspire to the creation of an airline as well and for some time now has projected to do so."[59] Spanish diplomacy insisted on a future right to operate an airplane between Seville and Argentina. Suddenly the Argentine–French postal air agreement was reopened for discussion. By March 18 the Argentine administration was relenting. It promised to study the Spanish protest and react "in prudent time."[60]

In the midst of this initiative, on February 21, 1927, Spain lost her foreign minister. Minister Yanguas resigned in a huff because he had been excluded from diplomatic negotiations between Spain and France. From then on Primo

51. The view out of the zeppelin also offered tactical and strategic reconnaissance opportunities. Military professionals were aware of this fact (Ibero Amerikanisches Institut, Stiftung Preussischer Kulturbesitz, Bildarchiv, Berlin).

de Rivera served as his own foreign minister.[61] The crisis in the leadership of the Madrid Foreign Ministry, however, did not impact relations with Buenos Aires.

Suddenly Italian competition emerged. From Italy pilot De Pinedo flew to Buenos Aires. There he gave speeches about Mussolini and fascism to which Ambassador Amalfi was invited. While he had to torpedo the French–Argentine air connection, he had to celebrate an Italian pilot.

Then the Spanish aviator Ramón Franco intervened unexpectedly and issued his own personal protest against the emerging Argentine–French agreement. Franco wrote a memorandum to Alfonso XIII revealing a far-reaching business plan. First, he was preparing for a second transoceanic crossing with a Dornier airplane. Second, he and a group of Spanish investors were planning to manufacture in Spain at La Naval, with Spanish workers, Dornier Wal airplanes, under a license agreement with Germany. The planes were to fly across the Atlantic on a regular schedule.

Ramón Franco and Julio Ruiz de Alda pushed a project entitled "new flight to create the postal union with South America in the *Dornier* airplane." What set this project apart was that all its aspects were realized under exclusive Spanish control. The plane would be manufactured in Spain, the crew would be Spanish, and the contract was with the Spanish company CASA. It was exactly what the Spanish nationalization policy in the air sector was demanding. All that was missing was an investment of 625,000 pesetas.

Before then Franco planned to fly first from Seville to Buenos Aires. From there he and his copilot would cross the Andes and continue into Chile and then Peru, Ecuador, Colombia, Panama, and Cuba. Then the men would turn north, on to New York, and start the third Atlantic crossing until they reached the Azores.[62] The Spanish Foreign Ministry was annoyed that this air force member was trying to conduct his own commercial air policy.[63]

Then the second political earthquake hit. Amalfi learned that the Argentine navy refused to spend any part of its budget in Spanish naval yards. Already at the end of September and early October 1926, in a number of secret sessions, both chambers of Argentina's Congress had passed the law to modernize the Argentine navy. They appropriated 75,000,000 gold pesos, spread over a period of ten years! Immediately the executive was allowed to float an internal or external loan.[64]

By October, experts had learned how this money would be spent. Admirals wanted "cruisers, three submarines, two destroyers." And if it were up to the admirals, all bids would be placed in Great Britain, France, and Italy. Spain and the United States would receive nothing. Germany was not even mentioned. By early

1927, Argentina would order three cruisers of 7,000 tons each, six destroyers of 1,200 tons, 1,800 tons for a smaller flotilla, and a still uncertain number of submarines.[65]

Right away a delicate diplomatic battle royal began. Toward the British, Argentine general Uriburu assuaged potential worries that Vickers might be excluded. He explained to the British ambassador that "Great Britain was Argentina's best customer and that it was wise to buy from those who bought from you."[66] Uriburu estimated that probably half of the naval program would be given to British companies. Naturally, the British ambassador was delighted.

This begged the question how much money would be spent at U.S. yards. One source learned that the bidding had already been held up for two months so that the Bethlehem Steel Company could join the competition. Another U.S. observer feared that the orders for cruisers would go to Italy, the destroyers to England, and the submarines to France. Italian offers were 40 percent cheaper than Bethlehem Steel bids. Higher U.S. costs of labor seemed to exclude U.S. companies.

In March it became obvious that the Argentine naval budget was being used for political purposes.[67] Major financial incentives could sway orders as well. A major loan could mean an order for a national shipyard.

Argentina might play it safe and split its orders among three countries. Great Britain would receive the orders for destroyers, France would build submarines, and Italy would build the cruisers. If contracts would be awarded based on price only, all offers would go to fascist Italy.

Italy clearly was the favorite of Admiral Galindez, the chief of the Argentine naval mission. Perhaps it was his Italian-born wife that encouraged this choice. Then Argentine generals added insult to injury. On March 24, 1927, it became known that France would also receive the bid for Argentine artillery cannons.[68]

Spain's Primo de Rivera was simply outraged.[69] On March 25, 1927, the Spanish Foreign Ministry ordered Ambassador Amalfi to demand a visit with President Alvear. He was to point out how much Spain had helped Argentina economically in the last months. For example, it had opened its market almost exclusively to Argentine corn and frozen beef. Then it had granted a concession to Radio Argentina.

From Madrid's royal palace Alfonso XIII joined in and communicated to Amalfi how much Spanish efforts toward Argentina were, indeed, royal policy priority. The king's secretary implored Amalfi to understand his role in the Spanish policy offensive:

> The King, whom you know well, gives such special importance to you during these circumstances, your literary personality, your oratory skills

and sensibility, but also your loyalty to the king and your love of Spain. They have contributed to the implementation of this policy which is more necessary than ever for us. It was a policy of attraction that was resisted by the indigenous and Spanish groups.[70]

This time Spanish opinion would not be delivered in the spirit of effusive, warm, Hispanic solidarity. Primo de Rivera ordered Amalfi to demand ship construction orders. If Alvear refused to place ship orders, Argentine generals should at least buy Spanish cannons.[71]

Amalfi asked for a presidential audience on March 27. When the men met, the meeting demonstrated little Hispanic, brotherly warmth. Instead, Ambassador Amalfi straightforwardly complained. First, he raised the issue of an insulting verse in an Argentine hymn. Second, he explained how preferentially the Spanish Trade Ministry had treated Argentine beef. Third, he promised that Argentine corn would also receive preferred attention.[72]

President Alvear answered evasively. He replied that Spanish olive oil commerce had done much damage to Argentine olive oil exports. Plus the president had little influence in the military sector. Orders for land weapons had already been placed. And naval orders depended entirely on technical specifications, not on nationality.[73]

Ambassador Amalfi wrote to Madrid that his pessimistic fears were fast becoming reality. He implored Alfonso XIII and Primo de Rivera not to trust the Argentines. In his words, the members of the Argentine military purchasing commission were all traitors and ungrateful to Spain.[74]

First, overnight, the Spanish administration offered Argentina a 100,000,000-peseta loan. Second, it asked whether Argentina, since it did not order the construction of ships, would instead buy two almost finished ships from Spanish naval yards at a cost of $3,000,000.[75] No other country extended itself financially in such a dramatic fashion. The loan offer received warm public approval from President Alvear.

Surprisingly, Amalfi's protest produced positive results. Complaints and the offer of a tremendously large Spanish loan—even though Argentina had no apparent need for it, nor had the government asked for it—changed somebody's mind, most likely that of Alvear. Suddenly he was willing to talk to Admiral Galindez.

On April 12, key Argentine politicians finally reacted more warmly to Spain's modernized Hispanismo approach. Amalfi reported a second visit with President Alvear. Now the tone of the visit was cordial and friendly. At least an atmosphere of friendship appeared between Spain and Argentina.[76]

Unexpectedly, Alfonso XIII and Primo de Rivera received help from unwitting members of U.S. Congress. U.S. enforcement of agricultural disease standards was perceived by Argentine weapons commission leaders as a personal insult to them and their country's pride. Suddenly ominous clouds gathered above Argentine–U.S. relations. On April 5, 1927, the Buenos Aires Stock Exchange declined the invitation to send a delegate to the Commercial Pan-American Conference in May in Washington, D.C. They protested the prohibitive measures against Argentine fruit, meat, and seeds.[77]

The second shoe fell a few days later. The U.S. military attaché learned that the Argentinean purchasing commission in the United States was about to be recalled. Worse, money set aside for orders for U.S. armament producers would also be removed. Unofficially U.S. observers were told that this was an expression of the frustration of high-level Argentine circles against U.S. sanitary measures.[78]

The Alvear administration was planning to raise a $15,000,000 loan on the British and U.S. financial markets to cover the expenses of the current program.[79] It had been customary that contracts would be given to the country where the money was being raised. For example, the Baring Brothers loan company required that two-thirds of the construction would take place in British naval yards. Also the money should be deposited in British banks for a period of at least six months. The Argentine government objected to these requirements on April 22, 1927.

In Spanish–Argentine relations a new possibility emerged on April 19. The Argentine minister of navy asked if the Spanish government was willing to sell two destroyers that were already under construction in Spanish naval yards. Previously Italy had also sold two unidentified ships to Argentina in such a fashion. President Alvear wanted to close the deal before his term expired. He suddenly felt an urgent desire to accomplish some form of Argentine purchase before the end of his presidency the next year.[80] A U.S. observer suggested that the upcoming local Argentine elections might be a motivating factor.

Right away Primo de Rivera knew how to exploit the Argentine opening. On April 28, Spanish Royal Order No. 7 was cabled to Buenos Aires. Amalfi was supposed to push for immediate Argentine acceptance of the proposed Spanish Air Law Pact. Alvear was asked to contradict the numerous Argentine voices who counseled against a separate Iberian Air Law.[81]

In Spain the *Noticiera Gaditiano* had summarized arguments in favor of it. The pact should be interpreted as a move toward a customs union. Later Spain would manufacture raw materials into products, selling them to Spanish American trusts. A "commercial customs union of racial equals" on both sides of the Atlantic could become a reality. These ideas were endorsed by Vincente de Urrutia y Gomez, a professor of trade.

Unexpectedly, the Spaniards took their time providing an official answer about the destroyers. Amalfi inquired again on May 3, 1927, whether the Spanish Foreign Ministry had an answer for the Argentine Navy Ministry. On May 4, the Spanish government agreed to sell two ships.[82] By May 5, the news became official.[83] On May 25, 1927, a royal decree confirmed the sale of the destroyers *Churruca* and *Alcalá Galiano* to Buenos Aires.

Spain had helped with its most profound loan policy in the twentieth century. The loan was not a Spanish government loan but a private loan. It was organized by members of the Spanish "Consejo Superior Bancario," among them the pro-British and pro-French Banco Hispano-Americano, the Banco Español de Crédito, and the Banco Urquijo.[84] A U.S. observer declared:

> The political character of this loan is clearly indicated by the declarations of the Spanish and Argentine authorities. The Spanish ambassador in Buenos Aires, in a statement to *La Nacion* refers to the far reaching political and moral importance of this economic agreement which discloses the error of those who consider that the friendly relations between the branches of the Spanish American family are impractical dreams. Mr. Molina and Mr. Gallardo, Argentine Minister of Finance and Foreign Affairs, expressed themselves in similar terms. The latter stating that Spanish–American brotherhood has left the period of after dinner phrase making and has entered upon the ground of concrete facts. . . .
>
> It is evident that the Spanish authorities are using this opportunity to increase the popularity and influence of Spain in the most progressive and influential of the Latin American republics. President Alvear in Argentina approved the transaction with Spain in order to strengthen the political position of his party with the important Spanish colony, and thus obtain its support during the coming elections. The same may be said with respect to the awarding of the contract for the construction of two cruisers to the Orlando shipbuilding company Leghorn.[85]

Now Alvear engaged in profound public political theatrics. For example, a Te Deum Mass was read with Argentina's vice-president present. The Spanish ambassador made a formal presentation at the monument given to Argentina in 1910 in commemoration of the Centenary of Independence. Its completion had been delayed due to World War I.[86]

Then Italy also made a loan offer.[87] On May 25, Italy offered money to build two cruisers for which contracts had been signed. Once again Alvear repeated his symbolic politics. On May 22, he assisted at the presentation to the Italian Colony in Buenos Aires of an elaborate monumental flagstaff in commemoration of the visit of the Italian prince to Buenos Aires in 1924.[88]

Once Argentine admiral Don Manuel Domecq Garcia was informed of the Spanish approval, the government ordered Admiral Galindez, the head of the Argentine navy purchase commission to Europe, to change his travel plans and to hurry to Madrid. The details of the Argentine–Spanish purchase would be finalized in person in the capital of the former colonial motherland.[89]

The Argentine turn toward Italy and Spain had been encouraged by odd historical forces. The U.S. beef quarantine provisions and the upcoming Argentine presidential elections had convinced Argentine politicians and military to enter into a deeper relationship with Spain. It was not Hispanic affinity or acceptance of the Iberian Commonwealth idea.

Fall 1927 witnessed an unprecedented coming together of German and Spanish interests. In August 1927, the Consejo de Defensa gave industrialist Echevarrieta the approval to move ahead in the submarine selection and begin construction.

Echevarrieta, quietly coordinating himself with Spanish head Captain Mateo, was named an owner and selected the illegally created German design from camouflaged firm IvS. Once sub construction was finished, Echevarrieta would sell it to the Spanish government. This way the Spanish navy did not appear to help secret German interests. It looked like a legal private deal, instead of illegal Spanish–German rearmament cooperation.

The submarine would be built in Cádiz. Its main advantage was that it was lighter. For example, a new 600-ton submarine would achieve the same speed as a 1,000-ton boat. German navy technicians would provide all the technology necessary. It would be powered by an entirely new MAN engine.

If this cooperation was successful, the Spanish navy planned to order six additional subs through Echevarrieta.[90] In August an additional order was given to build one cruiser based on a new illegal German design. It too would involve Echevarrieta's construction company and a Siemens and Halske company.[91]

Then negotiations about the construction of new tankers began. Echevarrieta and the technicians from the Weserwerft design office wanted two tankers built in Cádiz according to new German plans.[92] The ships would weigh 10,500 tons each and have a regular speed of 12 sea miles per hour. But they also had a hidden second engine that could increase speed to 17 sm. Contract negotiations began, and a down payment would follow. Once completed, these ships would serve in the Spanish fleet.

Furthermore, the construction of eight Spanish speedboats at the Neesen company in Travemünde was discussed. Echevarrieta ordered the delivery of one finished speedboat plus options for seven boats and additional plans and the cooperation in Cádiz.[93] Engines would come from Maybach.

In addition, the construction and operation of fishing fleets was negotiated with Sirius High Sea Fishing Co. They expected to run a joint venture with the Spaniards out of Bremerhaven.

Finally, the Siemens and Halske company received the contract to expand and improve Spanish air defenses. An artillery specialist was to study the air defense questions. The results would be presented in a proposal to Alfonso XIII and Primo de Rivera. Once again Echevarrieta would be involved in the development of the air defense system.[94] Approval would mean the construction of an AAA factory at Seville, based on Siemens designs. The cannon factory Rheinmetall and Siemens had also been informed.[95]

Once in a while these exchanges could yield solid military espionage gains. For example, in December the German navy had expressed interest in obtaining a British torpedo that recently had been delivered to Spain. The Germans were asked to wait until the torpedo was transported from Cádiz to Cartagena. There Wilhelm Canaris could take it apart and photograph it.[96]

Next, August 1927 saw the beginnings of German efforts to reclaim property in Spanish Morocco. The Mannesmann claim in Spanish Morocco was to be revisited, and a small German–Spanish project was also explored in Ifnis, south of Agadir, North Africa. Primo de Rivera was asked to negotiate through General Jordana, once again involving Echevarrieta. The Basque claimed to have close connections to the tribes of the Sus area. Echevarrieta made sure he remained at the center of these projects and promised to inform diplomats about further developments.[97]

In Spanish Guinea, Echevarrieta had already found a German partner. The Mercator Orloff Co. talked about joining the exploitation of a 10,000-hectare colony in Río Muni.[98] Concessions had been granted. It would create a Spanish society with a decisive German influence.[99]

Also the Bremer Colonial Gesellschaft and a German company specializing in sales of African woods had entered into agreements. The plantation and wood production society would be managed by a Mr. Schmidt. Already he was on his way to Africa by August 3, 1927. Additional representatives would follow, and soon Echevarrieta would submit a petition to the Spanish government asking for a large expansion.[100]

Finally, the German navy explored whether Echevarrieta could also help in acquiring fuel. In the first week of August a German visit dealt with the issue of petroleum. The establishment of a Spanish oil monopoly was expected to strengthen the hand of Echeveriatta inside Spain.

Already Primo's administration had asked for bids for a monopoly petroleum company and had asked Echevarrieta to submit one. Germans feared that British and American companies would be strong enough to establish a petroleum boycott against Spain. On the other hand, Echevarrieta might enter into an agreement with the German tank shipping agency Atlantic Tank Reederei. It guaranteed Spain access to German ships, regardless of British or U.S. oil companies' feelings.[101] Spain would be strengthened by Germany.

In the air sector, too, fall 1927 was a watershed. All sides came together in a first venture. Echevarrieta formed a Spanish airline in connection with Lufthansa serving the line Barcelona–Madrid, Madrid–Seville, and Seville–Vigo. The line was inaugurated by King Alfonso. Additional talks took place between Echevarrieta and Lufthansa to define the basic parameters of an expansion of this company into overseas traffic to South America.[102]

This Iberia contract became known on September 17, 1927. Echevarrieta had signed for 70 percent of its shares, and Lufthansa had signed for 30 percent.[103] Later Echevarrieta sold his shares to Lufthansa. Germans had manipulated themselves into complete ownership of a Spanish air line.

Iberia would focus on foreign service, and the UAE would focus on domestic service. Alfonso XIII was aware of these developments.[104]

The icing on the top of Spanish–German air cooperation, however, was the top secret Spanish–German Air Treaty. Signed in fall 1927, it gave German overflight rights over Spain, guaranteeing it, indirectly, the use of the Spanish islands off the coast in the near future to jump to Latin America.[105] In December 1927, diplomat Zechlin in Berlin confirmed to the German ambassador in Madrid: "The German interest consists of creating a South America line. The German government does not desire German participation at domestic Spanish air service. Only to create the ability to travel to South America through cooperation of Germany, Spain, Portugal and South America. We thought to achieve this by participating in Iberia."[106] German–French air rivalry over Latin America could continue.

The last cooperation breakthrough came in the intelligence field. According to the German historian Heinz Hoehne, Germany entered into the first intelligence exchange agreement with Spain. On February 17, 1928, the Canaris–Bazan agreement established mutual exchange relations between German and Spanish police authorities. General Bazan agreed to investigate the "planning of insurrections and sedition campaigns, in both countries and to assist one another in the surveillance and pursuit of politically suspect persons." To Spanish and German cooperation in poison gas and naval construction now had been added select counterintelligence work, against the Soviets, Poles, French, and Italians.[107]

Such a sudden broad scope of Spanish–German cooperation in navy, air, gas, and intelligence cooperation was unprecedented in the history of the two countries. It was a cooperation to circumvent Allied arms production prohibitions as they had emerged after 1919.

In Place of an End

A Sketch of the New Round of Secret Activities

A t the same time as Spain and Germany were solidifying ties, in 1928 in Italy, shipyards were making progress building the Argentine submarines *Salta, Santa Fe,* and *Santiago del Estero.* Already in January the Supermarine Aviation Company, Southampton, had been contracted to build six flying boats for the Argentine navy. Bids from Italian, French, and German competition had been rejected.[1] Also the French government received Argentine orders. At the end of November Argentina accepted the proposal of the French government to liquidate a 1918 loan that France owed Argentina amounting to 18,000,000 gold pesos. The generals and admirals in Buenos Aires wanted to dissolve it by purchasing war material. Top secret negotiations began about covered seaplanes for the navy and artillery for the army.[2] Real ships, planes, and cannons would gather soon on Argentine soil. Indeed on February 11, 1928, Argentine president Alvear inaugurated a 600-meter-long mole near Buenos Aires. The newly inaugurated shipyard would house the submarines, scout ships, torpedo destroyers, and mine layers.[3]

In November 1927, Primo de Rivera had withdrawn the duke of Amalfi from Buenos Aires within forty-eight hours.[4] By January 1928, a new Spanish ambassador, Ramiro de Maeztu, had replaced him. After his arrival the new ambassador gave a rousing speech declaring that "Spain desires today as never before, to grow its connections with South American countries." His arrival coincided with a three-day carnival.[5] Now additional celebrations welcomed the Hispanist Maeztu to the Río de la Plata. A banquet was given by members of the Argentine National Assembly to honor Spain. Other celebratory voices heard were the Argentine Press Association, the Ateneo de Madrid, the colony Alavesa, and the Ibero-American Union. Even the Pan-American Union welcomed him.[6]

Maeztu's arrival in Buenos Aires coincided with the delivery of the two recently purchased Spanish destroyers. After their docking at the newly opened naval pier, right away Argentine president Alvear paid an official visit to the ships. Argentina's and Spain's leading political classes were enchanted by this gesture.[7] Finally definite proof of real cooperation became visible. Transatlantic Hispanic cooperation was gaining a face. In February the destroyers were put through speed trials. In March the Argentine minister of the navy trained on board the ship *Garay*.[8] Suddenly, the British tried to please this ornery Argentina a bit. The British legation in Buenos Aires was raised to the rank of embassy.[9]

In Berlin and Wilhelmshaven, German navy armament experts followed the Spanish–Argentine approach with great interest. They decided that it was time to make another attempt to break into the Argentine arms modernization market. The second time the initiative would be led by the man who had established illegal armament cooperation in Spain, Wilhelm Canaris.

Canaris traveled to Argentina, leaving Mr. Suadicani as his successor to work with Echevarrieta in Spain. Canaris was also encouraged that in April 1928 the Irigoyen political faction defeated President Alvear's group in the presidential elections 57.4 percent to 29.3 percent. It was predicted that French influence would be less in the future. By no means did this signify an Argentine switch to pro-German policy, but at the very least it might suggest a more welcoming arms-purchasing environment for German companies.

The British already benefited, as their Avro Model had been selected to become Argentina's military airplane. As Argentine admirals appreciated the Spanish ships, British advisers helped the Argentine air force convert the Instituto Aerotécnico into the Fábrica Nacional de Aeroplanes to manufacture the Avro Gosport. The factory would be inaugurated on October 10, 1928, two days before President Alvear would hand his office to Irigoyen for his second presidential term.

Once he arrived in Buenos Aires, Canaris contacted Oberst Jagwitz, the head of the newly created Compañía Argentina de Comercio, a German arms sales organization for Argentina. It would serve as a conduit to deepen German and Argentine military-industrial cooperation. They tried to win a greater share of Argentine naval armament funds.

Already there was a modest opening. Admirals in Buenos Aires had ordered German guidance systems for three Argentine torpedo boats, two small cruisers, and three subs.[10] Just because the ships had been ordered in Italy, France, or Great Britain, it did not mean that German technology would be excluded completely.

Farther north in Peru, Wilhelm Faupel had established himself as the new military modernizer and potential armament purchaser.[11] He inspected and evaluated the Peruvian artillery regiments. Next he introduced a dress code, rules of attendance, and skills tests to decide promotion. Soon thereafter Faupel recruited active officers from Argentina to help his work in Peru.

His important contributor was fighter pilot von Döhring.[12] Already in May 1927, Faupel had wanted the German army to accept von Döhring as lead adviser of a future Peruvian air force. Faupel asked German commander Wilberg and ministerial director Brandenburg to court the Peruvian military attaché in Berlin until he approved Döhring as a leading trainer for an air force mission to Peru.[13]

It should not surprise that the head of the Weimar army, General Heye, paid an official visit to Chile in 1928. In the year before General Kiesling had prepared important contacts.[14] Also the new Chilean president intended to outfit the Chilean army with everything necessary to defend the nation. The number of Germans teaching in the Chilean army rose to twelve.[15] Their potentially excellent quality was known.

The visits of Canaris, Heye, and Faupel took place at a time when the world's international stock markets were at an all-time high. Nobody could imagine that barely a year later Black Monday would crash onto the scene, and all international financial, trade, and manufacturing relations would be disrupted in a most profound way. Transnational military cooperation would also pause, until Nazi Germany invented new financial and trade tools to resume armament exports to Latin America and Spain in even greater numbers.

Before the crash in early 1929, armament cooperation led to the first fascist ideological cross-pollenization from Italy to Argentina. The 1929 handover of Argentine ships in Italy was attended by high members of the Italian government, the Fascist Party, and the royal militia. Among those present were Admiral Galindez of the Argentine navy and Signor Costanzo Ciano from the Ministry of Communications at Rome. Others were Admiral Adrianni, undersecretary of the Italian navy; General Veruzzi, chief of staff of the Fascist Militia; Signor Murati, general secretary of the Fascist Party; and members of Italian Parliament.

Ceremonies unfolded during the course of the day, and several speeches eulogized Italian labor and technicians. A casual observer might have concluded that this day had been set aside as a fascist holiday. No opportunities were overlooked to emphasize the institution of Fascism; all local flags were flown; and all available wall space had been embellished with conspicuous posters proclaiming,

"Long live Il Duce," "Long Live Turati," and "Long Live Fascism." One of the ceremonies featured a fascist military review in connection with the distribution of sheath knives to a battalion of "Blackshirt" volunteers. The day closed with a fancy reception at the Palace Hotel.[16]

In Buenos Aires, Canaris made progress. Canaris proposed that Argentina contract still unknown orders in Spain. Of course, they would be manufactured according to German blueprints. Canaris suggested a broad agreement starting a triangular German–Spanish–Argentine synergetic military cooperation. Argentina was expected to buy weapons; Spain would make available its workers and factories; and Germany would provide the technological know-how. German Fascism had not yet come to power to send fascist speakers to accompany the delivery of ships and planes. After 1933, this would not be a problem anymore.

As if to remind everybody of the role Spain would play in this triangular military cooperation, in 1929, a Spanish crew flew from Seville to Bahia, Brazil, spanning 6,880 kilometers.[17] Also, Alfonso XIII's Ibero-American Exhibit in Seville opened, finally, on May 9, 1929. The largest international fair since the 1915 San Francisco World's Fair, it began to demonstrate to the world the ongoing rise of Spain as a resurging partner of Latin America. Spain's total trade, exports, and imports with its eight principal Spanish American trading partners would add up to 534,000,000 pesetas.

Then history treated Alfonso XIII and his Spanish Commonwealth policy with cruelty. Black Monday on the New York Stock Exchange exploded onto the scene in October 1929. In the months thereafter, first, the financial systems of the West and Japan collapsed. Right away protectionist members of U.S. Congress instituted severe tariff barriers under the leadership of Senators Smoot and Hawley. Thereafter currency devaluations across the board followed. By 1930, France and Great Britain had reaffirmed their colonial markets as a preferred exclusionary trading zone. The United States used the North American continent as an exclusive trade zone to attempt domestic recovery of its collapsing economy.

Spanish efforts had not advanced far enough to assert immediately an exclusive Spanish–American trade zone. The consequences of Black Monday wiped out all the gains Spain had made toward motivating Spanish Americans, Portuguese Americans, and Portuguese to join one Iberian Commonwealth against British, French, and U.S. rival commonwealths. It did not take long until dramatic economic news caused the most profound political contraction of all trade between Spain and Latin America.

52. Alfonso XIII and his children arrive at a pavilion of the exhibit (Fondo Cultura, F968–02–013, Archivo General de la Administración, Alcalá de Henares).

53. The door frame of the Mexican Pavilion exclaimed: "Mother Spain: Now my fields and my heart are bearing fruit, because the sun of your culture lit on my fields and, in my soul, the candle of devotion of your spirit" (Fondo Cultura, F 968–02–005, Archivo General de la Administración, Alcalá de Henares).

On January 28, 1930, General Primo de Rivera, the most conscientious pursuer of the Iberian Commonwealth option, stepped down from office. From then on Alfonso XIII had to focus exclusively on the survival of Spanish domestic industry and his monarchy. Facing the protectionist measures invoked by economic experts across the world's major economies, there was not the slightest possibility of resuming the Spanish outreach toward South America.

Finally, as Spanish factional domestic wrangling put too much stress on Spain's already very weak political system, the monarchy of Alfonso XIII collapsed on April 14, 1931. The king went into exile and left behind his dream of reviving a Spanish world power. It would be five years until General Francisco Franco would attempt a new version of this old idea. Then Adolf Hitler and Minister of Air Force Hermann Göring would again look eagerly at Spain, still the preferred German springboard to Latin America.

Now in 1929, select ethnic Germans overseas came back to the attention of the German navy. As economies and trade collapsed, the world's powers seemed to rush closer to conflict. In 1929, it was time to breathe new life and funds into the German naval intelligence organization abroad that had worked so well between 1914 and 1918. This time, too, the work would consist of data procurement and ship supply support.[18]

The resumption of using Germans and select ethnic Germans abroad began by instructing visiting German navy ship commanders to keep their eyes open and recruit potential spies in preselected ports around the world. For example, in May 1930, Capt. Lieut. Meisel and, probably, Mr. Frisius, the representative of the Ministry of Defense, reached an agreement. Wherever the cruiser *Karlsruhe* moored in the world, its captain "should find appropriate personalities, who would be useful for a still to be created supply service and overseas intelligence system."

The agreement stated explicitly that only individuals who possessed a German passport should be considered for recruitment. Future spies should have excellent personal connections, be well off economically, and, first and foremost, be reliable and able to keep things confidential under all circumstances. When the cruiser *Karlsruhe* came to visit, German ethnic community members in Rio de Janeiro, Panama, and Havana did not know that the friendly German captain would scan their community for ex-patriots who would work as recruits. In preparation the ministry handed the cruiser captain a list of German citizens it had military contacts with prior to 1929.[19]

A memo indicated individuals who stood out for their potential success. For

54. King Alfonso XIII saved the Spain–Argentina zeppelin air route but was no longer in office when the first German zeppelin appeared over South America in the early 1930s (Ibero Amerikanisches Institut, Stiftung Preussischer Kulturbesitz, Bildarchiv, Berlin).

example, the captain should consider Dr. Otto Bromberg in Rio. He was the brother of the owner of the Hamburg–South American Export House. Then there was the head of the German Ethnic Club in Rio de Janeiro, Mr. Henninger. He was the owner of the local Mercedes-Benz dealership. In Rio Grande lived Fernador Bromberg, the brother of the potential recruit in Rio. Carlos Fraeb, who served as German consul, should not be forgotten. Also the files of Stuttgart's German Foreign Institute were consulted to narrow down the list of potential recruits.[20]

The memo also reevaluated agents used before. In Brazil there was Walter Hillefeld of the company Stoltz and Co., a key representative of North German Lloyd. He was considered in addition to Richard Voss from Wille and Co. Voss had provided information since 1926.

The captain was also asked to reward existing contributors. In Callao, Lima, Mr. Heinz Junge had contributed for years. He needed to be recognized and appreciated. Eventually, Junge was expected to leave Lima, and Ernst Wehner was supposed to be considered as his possible replacement.[21]

Finally, the recruiter was also warned to stay away from some ethnic Germans. In Rio Blanca the publisher of the ethnic newspaper *Heimatgruss* was supposed to be avoided. He was a seemingly good academic but not appropriate as an informer or upper-level agent.[22] In Havana the shipping agent Mr. Clasing should be evaluated. If the impression was favorable, he should be enlisted a second time. If not, perhaps another suitable person could be found "since the recruitment of a man of connection in Havana was very much desired." Other cities where the captain was to find new agents were Veracruz, Mexico; La Quiero, Prince Rupert Bay, Colón, Panama; the British Bermudas; and Galveston, Texas.[23] A few documents in the records also mention Houston, Texas, and Mexico, where individuals who worked at the firm of Beick, Felix and Co. might be candidates.[24]

Following the initial selection of a naval supply apprentice the navy recruiter was supposed to send his name immediately to Germany. Before the ship moved to the next port, the captain would mail this letter to Germany, allowing Berlin to contact the new recruit already before the recruiter had returned to Germany.[25]

Potential agent training was a slow, careful process. At first they should be employed as port correspondents. In exchange for 30 RM per month they should submit a monthly typewritten two-page report.[26] These report writing exercises would indicate who was useful for future, more serious intelligence work. After half a year of report writing the ministry would make the final selection from the pool of certified agents on the short list.[27]

Select German consuls already worked as agents without the knowledge of the Foreign Ministry. As in World War I, select honorary consuls in ethnic communities were interesting because their private job afforded them good cover. One year before Hitler came to power a 1932 document stated that the German Foreign Ministry had also become more comfortable providing cover for intelligence work: "Steps have been initiated with the Foreign Ministry, in order to make the far reaching organization of the Foreign Ministry abroad useful, as long as it does not impact the required secrecy."[28]

Then there was Captain Mensing, who worked for North German Lloyd. During World War I he and his wife had served as a back channel for peace negotiation feelers. By 1918, both had been asked to stop working as agents. Now they would reemerge as influential contacts in New York.[29]

This increased usage of port visits by German cruisers achieved the desired revival of the naval intelligence system. One document stated that the cruiser *Karlsruhe* had *"significantly supported the expansion of the supply service overseas."* Agents had been evaluated and received training with equipment and new codes. Reliable contacts had been established in Lima, Buenos Aires, and Pernambuco. New German recruits had been identified for Galveston, Houston, New York,

Montevideo, Puebla, Veracruz, Panama, Colón, and Havana.[30] Already then select individuals had received wireless transmitters.

The revival of the service began with a 1931 focus on Africa. And select Latin American and U.S. port cities were part of a global courier route.[31] A systematic expansion into Latin America would come after 1934.[32]

Now the Nazis appear in the records targeting ethnic Germans, once again for fund-raising purposes. On June 26, 1930, Heinrich Himmler, head of the SS, wrote to the town of Oruro in Bolivia. There Hauptmann Ernst Röhm worked as military commander of the 1st Division. Röhm had written to him in March. Himmler was frank to Röhm: "You have such an organizational talent, would you please organize all the people of the German ethnic community in Oruro as supporting members of the SS."[33]

The future model of a Nazi branch in Latin America was being developed in Chile by one loyal Nazi Party member out of his own ideological enthusiasm. Willi Koehn attempted to establish a network of branches throughout Chile and, more importantly, aimed to weave them into one nationally disciplined party system. Once Hitler came to power and selected Ernst Bohle as head of the Nazi branches outside Germany, Koehn's work would become the poster child of foreign party branches in Latin America.

Koehn followed organizational blueprints from Germany. At the top resided one country leader, followed by one deputy leader, a treasurer, and one propaganda and library leader, as well as a security chief. If possible and affordable, a party branch employed a Spanish-speaking specialist for Chilean newspapers. Also a leader for the women's organization was employed.

Successful party organization also meant the raising of voluntary funds inside the community to maintain a permanent meeting place. This building could house a legal department and a social services department that might provide tangible help to ethnic Germans during this economic world depression. This could mean finding new jobs inside the ethnic community but also communicating with government agencies inside Germany that helped former emigrants and interested returnees. Eventually, it was hoped, party social service work would translate into support of its political-ideological tenets. A larger meeting house, possibly with an attic, could also become a place to practice "physical education" very much in the spirit of pre-militaristic education, something that was common to parties of the political extremes on the Left and Right during the late 1920s.[34] Koehn in Chile proved better at fund-raising than Heinrich Himmler's colleague Ernst Röhm in Bolivia.

Another reason for Koehn's excellent reputation in Hamburg headquarters was his successful maintenance of a separate party newspaper.[35] Already in 1931, Koehn had begun propaganda efforts by placing select articles in existing Chilean community newspapers.[36] He published the first party newsletter, the *Mitteilungsblatt der NSDAP—Landesgruppe Chile*, on November 15, 1932. As publisher, Koehn regularly used press material supplied from the party press office in Munich. This propaganda work was deemed important to forge a deeper emotional bond with National Socialism, as books for indoctrination from Germany proved prohibitively expensive to mail from Germany. The party newsletter was the only tool to provide information about Fascism, but it also encouraged, in print, a separate fascist identity for ethnic Germans inside Chile who felt threatened by the rise of Socialism and communist strikes as the depression continued.[37]

Most troubling for traditional ethnic Germans in Chile, Koehn's publication articulated one multilayered, focused message with a systematic, distinct racial ideology. National Socialism, as it was being presented by Koehn, was to maintain and to nurture a distinct ethnic community among German Chileans based on blood but not national origin! One day it might no longer be enough to be of German ethnic origin: Aryanness would be demanded. But what was that? Koehn insisted that as soon as "German blood" was flowing in one's veins a political duty existed for this person to support the German state in Europe. As Germany was far away, the German Chileans at least had the obligation, he demanded, to care about and support German culture inside Chile. This was not presented as an exercise in fuzzy diversity but, rather, as an aggressive communal defense against ideas and cultures that were deemed hostile to a distinct "pure" German self-identity. Koehn's writings insisted on a universal, quasi-biological connection between Germans in Europe and the Western Hemisphere. A tiny number of ethnic Germans abroad might be screened for intelligence work, but all of them would be confronted with the demand that ethnic conscience and blood were signs of a global fascist ethnic German community.

Finally, in 1932, in Brazil there was a Professor Dr. P. Vogeler, who prepared a project that promised to offer Hitler a German colony in Paraná, if he would say yes in the first months after coming to office. The head of the next German government still had to be convinced to resume large-scale German emigration to southern Brazil just like in 1898.

Already before January 1933, Vogeler had been negotiating with the Paraná government and regional caudillos about creating a German colony in Paraná. He formed a study commission and concluded a draft proposal by late summer 1933. On September 18, 1933, Dr. Vogeler and his commission submitted their plan to Hitler's government.

Vogeler's plan, he stated, was backed by the German embassy in Brazil and important local investors. The German Ministry of Economy also knew about his designs and certainly did not discourage him from proceeding. Perhaps it even committed a small part of the exploratory funding.

Vogeler wanted the Hitler administration to resume right away government-sponsored emigration to southern Brazil so that unemployed people would get off the streets and the German government would not have the financial burden of paying for their social services. He advocated ethnic settlements abroad under the supervision and management of the Hitler government.

This would also bring "fresh German blood" to southern Brazil and the already existing concentrations of ethnic Germans. From Brazil he wrote, "Germans living abroad are burning to refresh themselves with new German blood."[38] As important was the economic aspect. Vogeler described how Brazil was moving toward greater economic independence. The presence of ethnic German colonies would guarantee that they would buy German goods in the future.

Regardless, the Ministry of Foreign Affairs or the Ministry of Economy had to agree by October 31, 1933. This was an opportunity "that would never return, an irrevocably final opportunity for Germany, to secure for itself the dominating economic and national political influence in Southern Brazil, where already more than one million people of German ethnicity were living."[39] Vogeler's plan would hand Hitler and his administration an informal colony in South America in the first year of its government, without any prior effort or Nazi manipulations.

Indeed, Vogeler's proposal was put on Hitler's desk, who read it on October 24, 1933. From there the proposal went to Hitler's economic point man, Keppler.[40] It was rejected as inopportune. Hitler wanted a different use of ethnic Germans in South America.

Nazi Party development in the United States had made great improvements. In 1932, National Socialist German Workers' Party deputy Rudolf Hess had appointed Ludwig Luedecke representative in the United States for a second time, once again to increase donations for Hitler's fight inside Germany.

Once Hitler became head of the German government, the Nazi politics in the United States turned competitive. First, the variety of German pro-fascist groups in the United States had to be unified and instructed with new policy guidelines from Nazi Germany. Before it was appropriate to have support organizations; now all of them would have to be unified under one leader of national, and in this case continental, scope.

Heinz Spanknoebel was the person who showed, in these uncertain times, the most creative initiative. He thought that traveling to Nazi Germany would hopefully create an opportunity to meet Hitler and Hess and receive their personal backing for him in a national position. Months before the Nazi leadership had settled the power struggle over ethnic German policy among itself, Spanknoebel left New York for Hamburg on a transatlantic cruiser on April 26, 1933. He left with the expectation to receive the nod as the exclusive German ethnic leader in America, just like the Italian fascist leader in 1922. He arrived in early May.

Spanknoebel's political negotiations with party representatives in Berlin, Munich, and Hamburg lasted several weeks. At the end of May, Spanknoebel wrote to his supporters in the United States that Rudolf Hess, but not Hitler, had bestowed on him the exclusive right to build an organization with the name Friends of New Germany (FONG), in addition to running the U.S. branch of the German Nazi Party.

The FONG was to function as the exclusive organization for all individuals in North America who wanted to be connected politically with the evolving National Socialist state, regardless of their citizenship. Most importantly, Hess gave Spanknoebel the exclusive right to collect membership fees from FONG members and party members.

The Nazi Party inside the United States was also restructured. The newly established party office dealing with Nazis outside Germany—the Auslands-Organisation—created a new administrative unit, Gau U.S.A., that combined the United States and Canada. By June 1933, negotiations finished, Spanknoebel prepared to return to the United States as officially anointed exclusive head of the Nazi Party.[41] At that time Hitler had not yet appointed one official person in charge of ethnic issues.

Upon his return to New York there was still no clear chain of command dealing with ethnic Germans and party members. Improvisation and competition, it seemed, would continue. Quickly Spanknoebel convened a national conference of all major German American organizations between July 28 and July 30, 1933. There he presented the official sanctioned organizational blueprint from Germany that all were expected to join. Surprisingly, the conference ended with agreement and a noticeable reduction of fighting between rival Nazi factions. Now, one national structure had to be created, and relationships were redefined among clubs, social organizations, and this newly codified party structure.[42]

Only two years later, in 1935, German navy leaders in Berlin would discuss under what conditions a German agent could commit sabotage, even in the United States, as part of his or her work during the next world war. The result is revealed on the first page of this book. History had come full circle.

Notes

Introduction

1. Ali to AIz, "Regards: Supply Service Job Instruction," Secret, 31 October 1935, File Page Nos. 232–33, RM 20/1862, Bundesarchiv, Freiburg.

Chapter 1

1. Walter Nugent, *Crossings: The Great Transatlantic Migrations, 1870–1914* (Bloomington: Indiana University Press, 1992), 63–83.

2. Egmont Zechlin, *Friedensbestrebungen und Revolutionierungsversuche* (Bonn: Aus Politik und Zeitgeschichte, 1963), B 24, 14 June 1916, cited in Donald M. McKale, *The Swastika outside Germany* (Kent: Kent State University Press, 1977), 235n17.

3. Donald M. McKale, *War by Revolution: Germany and Great Britain in the Middle East in the Era of World War I* (Kent: Kent State University Press, 1989), 6.

4. One German government document admitted that this method had been employed with great success. See Denkschrift, Landesplaner Liedecke, "Ueber die Schaffung einer volksnahen und gestaltungsfaehigen Organisation des laendlichen Siedlungswesens," Adlerhorst, 2 April 1943, T-175, Reel 194, Fr. 2739560-2732967, National Archives of the United States, Washington, D.C.

5. Holger H. Herwig, *German's Vision of Empire in Venezuela 1871–1914* (Princeton: Princeton University Press, 1986), 143. In 1874 the Venezuelan president, Antonio Guzman Blanco, offered to German officer von der Goltz a coaling station in Venezuela.

6. Juergen Hell, "Die Politik des Deutschen Reiches zur Umwandlung Suedbrasiliens in ein Ueberseeisches Neudeutschland (1890–1914)" (Ph.D. diss., University of Rostock, 1966), 58.

7. Gerhard Wiechmann, *Die Preussisch–Deutsche Marine in Lateinamerika (1866–1914)* (Bremen: Verlag H. M. Hausschild Gmbh, 2002), 30–31.

8. Cord Ebersspaecher and Gerhard Wiechmann, "Admiral Eduard von Knorr (1840–1920). Eine Karriere in der neuen Elite der Seeoffiziere in Preussen-Deutschland," in *Eliten im Wandel: Gesellschaftliche Fuehrungsschichten im 19. und 20. Jahrhundert*, ed. Karl Christian Fuehrer, Karen Hagemann, and Birthe Kundrus (Münster: Westfaelisches Dampfboot, 2004), 248.

9. Paul Schmalenbach, *German Raiders: A History of Auxiliary Cruisers of the German Navy 1895–1945* (Cambridge: Patrick Stephens, 1979), 11.

10. Wiechmann, *Die Preussisch–Deutsche Marine in Lateinamerika*, 30–31.

11. Iyo Iimura Kunimoto, "Japan and Mexico, 1886–1917" (Ph.D. diss., University of Texas, 1975), introduction.

12. "A History of Japanese Americans in California: Immigration," http://www.nps.gov/history/history/online_books/5views/5views4a.htm.

13. C. Harvey Gardiner, *The Japanese and Peru 1873–1973* (Albuquerque: University of New Mexico Press, 1975), 4–5.

14. Wieland Wagner, *Japan's Aussenpolitik in der Frühen Meiji-Zeit (1868–1894)* (Stuttgart: Franz Steiner Verlag, 1990), 237–38.

15. Alan Takeo Moriyama, *Imingaisha: Japanese Emigration Companies and Hawaii, 1894–1908* (Honolulu: University of Hawaii Press, 1985), 32.

16. Patricia E. Roy and J. L. Granatstein, *Mutual Hostages: Canadians and Japanese during the Second World War* (Toronto: University of Toronto Press, 1990), 1, 246.

17. Wagner, *Japan's Aussenpolitik in der Frühen Meiji-Zeit*, 236.

18. Ibid., 240.

19. Ibid., 238.

20. Henry P. Frei, *Japan's Southward Advance and Australia: From the Sixteenth Century to World War II* (Honolulu: University of Hawaii Press, 1991), 39.

21. John J. Stephan, *Hawaii under the Rising Sun: Japan's Plans for Conquest after Pearl Harbor* (Honolulu: University of Hawaii Press, 1984), 17.

22. Ibid., 248.

23. Wagner, *Japan's Aussenpolitik in der Frühen Meiji-Zeit*, 246n77, based on Josepha Saniel, *Japan and the Philippines* (New York: Russell and Russell, 1973), 90–95.

24. Stephan, *Hawaii under the Rising Sun*, 17.

25. Moriyama, *Imingaisha*, 30.

26. Todd A. Henry, Web posting, Sophia University, 2006.

27. Daniel M. Masterson, with Sayaka Funada-Classen, *The Japanese in Latin America* (Urbana: University of Illinois Press, 2004), 27.

28. Kunimoto, "Japan and Mexico."

29. Wagner, *Japan's Aussenpolitik in der Frühen Meiji-Zeit*, 240, citing Saniel, *Japan and the Philippines*, 155–60.

30. Ibid., 248n87, Kida, Nagokki.

31. Masterson, *The Japanese in Latin America*, 16.

32. Nihonjin Mekishiko Ijushi Hensankai, ed., *Nihonjin Mekishiko I Jushi (History of Japanese Emigration and Colonization in Mexico)* (Tokyo: Mekishiko Ijushi Hensan Iinkai, 1971), 231–33.

33. Kunimoto, "Japan and Mexico," 58.

34. Frei, *Japan's Southward Advance and Australia*, 39.

35. Moriyama, *Imingaisha*, 32.

36. Torajie Irie and Meiji Nanshin Ko, *A Study of Emigration Trends toward the South in the Meiji Period* (Tokyo: Ida Shoten, 1943); and Frei, *Japan's Southward Advance and Australia*, 39.

37. Saniel, *Japan and the Philippines*, 226.

38. Ibid., 255.

39. Ibid., 226. Saniel emphasizes a differentiation between military *shishi* and civilian *shishi*. Military observers were Lieutenant Colonel Kususe Kiyohiko, General Fujimaro, Lieut. Nakano, Lieut. Col. Akashi, Captain Kamimura, Capt. Hara Tei, and Capt. Tokizawa. Sakamoto Shiro wrote about his activities in his autobiography (written with Ozaki Takyua). He had gathered experience and military contact in Korea. Governor General of Taiwan Nogi gave the blessing to Shiro to travel to the Philippines (see ibid., 229).

40. Ibid., 229.

41. Ibid., 232.

42. Ibid., 255.

43. Ibid., 254.

44. Ibid., 243–44. Rebel delegates learned that Agent Tokizawa might return to the archipelago. His task would be the training of rebels with the blessing of the Tokyo General Staff Office.

Chapter 2

1. Elizalde, Espana, cited in Sebastian Balfour, *The End of the Spanish Empire 1898–1923* (Oxford: Clarendon Press, 1997), 30.

2. Gerhard Brunn, *Deutschland und Brasilien, 1889–1914* (Cologne: Boehlau Verlag, 1971), 130.

3. Balfour, *The End of the Spanish Empire*, 99.

4. Caroline Shaw, "Rothshild and Brazil," *Latin American Research Review* 40, no. 1 (February 2005): 175.

5. Holger H. Herwig, *Luxury Fleet: The Imperial German Navy 1880–1918* (London: Allen and Unwin, 1980), 139.

6. Abschrift Sitzung des Koeniglichen Staatsrats, 8 June 1898, R901/30825, Bundesarchiv, Berlin-Lichterfelde.

7. Brunn, *Deutschland und Brasilien*, 148.

8. Rolf Peter Tschapek, *Bausteine eines zukuenftigen deutschen Mittelafrika: Deutscher Imperialismus und die portugiesischen Kolonien. Deutsches Interesse an den Suedafrikanischen Kolonien Portugals vom ausgehenden 19. Jahrhundert bis zum ersten Weltkrieg* (Stuttgart: Franz Steiner, 2000), 169.

9. Akira Iriye, *After Imperialism: The Search for a New Order in the Far East 1921–1931* (Cambridge: Harvard University Press, 1965), 5.

10. Brunn, *Deutschland und Brasilien*, 179.

11. Ibid., 178.

12. Ibid., 127, citing Paul Rohrbach, *Deutschland unter den Weltvoelkern* (Berlin, 1911), 394 ff. in 591–92.

13. Ibid., 126.

14. Nancy Mitchell, *The Danger of Dreams* (Chapel Hill: University of North Carolina Press, 1999), 24.

15. Brunn, *Deutschland und Brasilien*, 149.

16. Prince von Buelow, *Memoirs 1897–1903* (London: Putnam, 1931), 328.

17. Brunn, *Deutschland und Brasilien*, 148.

18. Ibid.

19. Ibid., 127.

20. Holger H. Herwig, *Germany's Vision of Empire in Venezuela 1871–1914* (Princeton: Princeton University Press, 1986), 224–25.

21. Ibid., 230–31.

22. Ibid., 234.

23. Brunn, *Deutschland und Brasilien*, 153.

24. Baldur Kaulisch, "Zur Ueberseeischen Stuetzpunktpolitik der Kaiserlichen Deutschen Marinefuehrung am Ende des 19 Jahrhunderts und im Ersten Weltkrieg," *East Berlin*, 1965: 585.

25. Gerhard Wiechmann, *Die Preussisch–Deutsche Marine in Lateinamerika (1866–1914)* (Bremen: Verlag H. M. Hausschild Gmbh, 2002), 175.
26. Kaulisch, "Zur Ueberseeischen Stuetzpunktpolitik der Kaiserlichen Deutschen Marinefuehrung," 588.
27. Ibid., 587.
28. Herwig, *Luxury Fleet*, 101. For unknown reasons Emperor Wilhelm objected.
29. William Roger Louis, *Great Britain and Germany's Lost Colonies, 1914–1919* (Oxford: Clarendon Press, 1967), 27.
30. Herwig, *Germany's Vision of Empire in Venezuela*, 102–3.
31. Ibid., 142–43.
32. Ibid., 160.
33. Ibid., 158n48.
34. Mitchell, *The Danger of Dreams*, 47.
35. Friedrich Katz, *The Secret War in Mexico* (Chicago: University of Chicago Press, 1981), 63.
36. Phil H. C. E. Raeder, *Der Kreuzerkrieg in den Auslaendischen Gewässern: Das Kreuzergeschwader*, 2nd improved ed. (Berlin: Mittler and Son, 1927), 19.
37. Michael L. Hadley and Roger Sarty, *Tin-Pots and Pirate Ships: Canadian Naval Forces and German Sea Raiders* (Montreal: McGill-Queens University Press, 1991), 47.
38. No. A 90, Unsigned letter to the German chancellor, 9 November 1907, Japanese–American relations and Mexico, Embassy in Mexico City, Vol. 28, Political Archive of the German Foreign Ministry, Berlin.
39. Hadley and Sarty, *Tin-Pots and Pirate Ships*, 49.
40. Raeder, *Der Kreuzerkrieg in den Auslaendischen Gewässern*, 19.
41. Ibid., 21.
42. Ibid., 22.
43. Ibid., 28: "Grundlagen fuer den Kreuzerkrieg im Auslande in einem deutsch-englischen Krieg."
44. Ibid., 29. They were fast enough to evade counterattacks.
45. Ibid., 3.
46. Doc. No. a IAD 6623, Abschrift zu B 5476/15, Nachlass von Knorr, The Supply Service Activity in the United States of America, Ist part, Top Secret, 137, Service Report, Bundesarchiv, Freiburg.
47. Ibid., 135–37. He misinterpreted this as a sign that the Japanese had prepared warlike acts against the Californian coast. No further details or proof were presented.
48. Reinhard Doerries, ed., *Diplomaten und Agenten: Nachrichtendienste in der Geschichte der Deutsche–Amerikanischen Beziehungen* (Heidelberg: C. Winter, 2001), "Die Taetigkeit deutscher Agenten in den USA," 12.
49. Joseph Pilsudski hoped that Japanese support would counter the tsarist policy of Russification; see Ian Nish, "Japanese Intelligence and the Approach of the Russo-Japanese War," in Christopher Andrew and David Dilks, *The Missing Dimension* (Urbana: University of Illinois Press, 1984), 24.
50. Konrad Zilliacus lived from 1855 to 1914. He stayed in Japan for two years during the Sino-Japanese war. His approach was Leninist, asking for support wherever it looked promising. He funneled his requests through the Japanese embassy in Stockholm (see ibid.).
51. Akashi Motojiro, *Rakka Ryūsui: Colonel Akashi's Report on His Secret Cooperation with the Russian Revolutionary Parties during the Russo-Japanese War*, selected chapters trans.

Inaba Chiharu and ed. Olavi K. Fält and Antti Kujala, Studia Historica 31 (Helsinki: SHS, Finnish Historical Society, 1988).

52. Nish, "Japanese Intelligence and the Approach of the Russo-Japanese War," 26.

53. Nish cites this quote from Kobane Shigeru, Akashi's biographer (ibid., 25).

54. Akashi, *Rakka Ryūsui*, 128.

55. Ibid., 72, 161.

56. Shumpei Okamoto, *The Japanese Oligarchy and the Russo Japanese War* (New York: Columbia University Press, 1970).

57. Nish, "Japanese Intelligence and the Approach of the Russo-Japanese War," 24–25.

58. Akashi, *Rakka Ryūsui*, 161. See also Michael H. Futrell, *Colonel Akashi and Japanese Contacts with Russian Revolutionaries in 1904–1905* (Oxford: Oxford University Press, 1967), 18–19. Information provided by Inaba in Akashi, *Rakka Ryūsui*, n. 233.

59. Andrew and Dilks's *The Missing Dimension* is an exception.

60. Peter Duus, *The Abacus and the Sword: The Japanese Penetration of Korea 1895–1910* (Berkeley: University of California Press, 1995), 302.

61. Yoshihisa Tak Matsusaka, *The Making of Japanese Manchuria 1904–1932* (Cambridge: Harvard University Asia Center, distributed by Harvard University Press, 2001), 81.

62. Ibid., 77.

63. Ibid., 80.

64. Iyo Iimura Kunimoto, "Japan and Mexico, 1886–1917" (Ph.D. diss., University of Texas, 1975), n23, Sugimur to Komura.

65. Ibid. The Inca Rubber Company initiated talks with the Mejii Emigration Company to contract five hundred laborers for the zone of Tambopata.

66. Nobuya Tsuchida, "The Japanese in Brazil" (Ph.D. diss., University of California at Los Angeles, 1978), 79.

67. BAMA RM5/V 5408, cited in Ferenc Fischer, *El Modelo Militar Prusiano y la Fuerzas Armadas de Chile: 1885–1945* (Pécs: Hungary University Press, 1999), 84.

68. Alan Takeo Moriyama, *Imingaisha: Japanese Emigration Companies and Hawaii, 1894–1908* (Honolulu: University of Hawaii Press, 1985), 151–55. This figure is for 1908.

69. Kunimoto, "Japan and Mexico," 68. In 1907, a further 3,945 applications were filed.

70. Ibid., 73.

71. Patricia E. Roy and J. L. Granatstein, *Mutual Hostages: Canadians and Japanese during the Second World War* (Toronto: University of Toronto Press, 1990), 10–13.

72. Roger Daniels, *The Politics of Prejudice: The Anti-Japanese Movement in California and the Struggle for Japanese Exclusion* (Berkeley: University of California Press, 1962), 20–21.

73. Moriyama, *Imingaisha*, 154.

74. Stephen Howarth, *The Fighting Ships of the Rising Sun: The Drama of the Japanese Navy 1895–1945* (New York: Athenemun, 1983), 104.

75. Tsuchida, "The Japanese in Brazil," 121.

Chapter 3

1. John J. Williams, *The Isthmus of Tehuantepec: Being the Result of a Survey for a Railroad to connect the Atlantic and Pacific Oceans, made by the scientific commission under the direction of Major J. G. Barnard, US. Engineer* (New York: D. Appleton and Co., 1852).

2. Doc. No. 25, Unsigned letter to Buelow, German legation Mexico, 5 April 1907, Japanese–American Relations and Mexico, Embassy in Mexico City, Vol. 28, Politisches Archiv des Auswaertigen Amts, Berlin (hereafter cited as PAAA).

3. No. 8036, Unsigned letter to the German chancellor, German observer, signed W. or H., to the German Foreign Ministry, Mexico City, 26 July 1907, Japanese–American Relations and Mexico, Embassy in Mexico City, Vol. 28, PAAA.

4. Friedrich Katz, *The Secret War in Mexico* (Chicago: University of Chicago Press, 1981), 69.

5. No. 822, Unsigned letter to the German chancellor, German Royal legation Mexico to the German chancellor, 7 March 1907, Embassy in Mexico City, Vol. 28, PAAA.

6. Katz, *The Secret War in Mexico*, 69.

7. Ibid., 68.

8. No. 822, Unsigned letter to the German chancellor, 7 March 1907, on the tension between the United States and Japan and its consequences in Mexico, Vol. 28, PAAA.

9. No. A22 and No. 822, letter to the German chancellor, 7 March 1907, Vol. 28, PAAA.

10. No. A83, Letter to the German chancellor, 26 October 1907, Embassy in Mexico City, Vol. 28, PAAA.

11. No. A55, Letter to the German chancellor, 15 July 1907, and No. A22, 7 March 1907, Embassy in Mexico City, Vol. 28, PAAA.

12. Katz, *The Secret War in Mexico*, 69n93. Katz reports and cites the following underhanded provocation: "Japan is apparently already preoccupied with the question of a military base in Mexico and an attack from Canada also has not been ruled out. Wouldn't support from German troops be of considerable value to Americans?"

13. No. A61, Unsigned letter to the German chancellor, 3 August 1907, Embassy in Mexico City, Vol. 28, PAAA.

14. "Diaz Unloads Freight," *New York Times*, 26 January 1907, 5.

15. Geheim, no signature, Mexico City, 8 April 1907, German–American Relations and Mexico, Embassy in Mexico City, Vol. 28, PAAA.

16. Roger Daniels, *The Politics of Prejudice: The Anti-Japanese Movement in California and the Struggle for Japanese Exclusion* (Berkeley: University of California Press, 1962), 30.

17. No. 38 A, Mum, Tokyo, to Count Buelow, 12 March 1908, Foreign policy of Japan, Embassy in Mexico City, Vol. 28, PAAA.

18. Doc. No. A76, Confidential, 6 May 1908, and "Japanese immigration to Mexico," signed Mumm, Tokyo, 3 April 1908, Embassy in Mexico City, Vol. 28, PAAA.

19. Iyo Iimura Kunimoto, "Japan and Mexico, 1886–1917" (Ph.D. diss., University of Texas, 1975), 71.

20. Nobuya Tsuchida, "The Japanese in Brazil" (Ph.D. diss., University of California at Los Angeles, 1978), 121.

21. No. A 85, letter to the German chancellor, 28 October 1907, "Report to Reich's chancellor: The Japanese diplomat Mr. Ari, about Japanese–American relations," Embassy in Mexico City, Vol. 28, PAAA.

22. Nbaotaro Kobayashi, Mehishiko Koku taiheuyo engangyogyo choshokuku, 28 July 1910, Japanese Foreign Ministry Archive, MT 385.131/31-5-, National Archives of the United States, Washington, D.C. (hereafter cited as NAUS). The talks led to the signing of a treaty with the Mexican government on October 17, 1911. It was signed by Lic. Rafael L. Hernandes, the Mexican government representative, and Naotaro Baayashi.

23. Eiichi Shibusawa, Soichiro Asana, and other to Horiguchi to Uchida, Mexico City, 16 February 1912, Japanese Foreign Ministry Archive, MT 358.131/263–65, NAUS. On

July 4, 1912, the Bokkoku Gyogyo Chosakia was reorganized at a general meeting and formed into the Bokkoku Guoguo Tshi Kumiai, Syndicate of Fishing Investment in Mexico (MT 358.131/661). Thereafter, the license was sold to a Tokyo company that also operated in mainland China.

24. Patricia E. Roy and J. L. Granatstein, *Mutual Hostages: Canadians and Japanese during the Second World War* (Toronto: University of Toronto Press, 1990), 9.

25. Tsuchida, "The Japanese in Brazil," 79.

26. Ibid., 84.

27. Kunimoto, "Japan and Mexico," 79.

28. Letter to the German chancellor, Abschrift II.E. 351, Uebersetzung aus *Nichi Nichi Shimbun*, 20 November 1907, Embassy in Mexico City, Vol. 28, PAAA.

29. Freire Gilberto, *Herrenhaus und Sklavenhütte: Ein Bild der brasilianischen Gesellschaft*, trans. Ludwig Graf von Schönfeldt (Berlin: Kiepenheur und Witsch, 1965).

30. Ibid., 126.

31. The sources do not state whether his appointment was a coincidence or whether he was chosen purposely because of his economic expertise.

32. Tsuchida, "The Japanese in Brazil," 109.

33. Gilberto, *Herrenhaus und Sklavenhütte*, 128.

34. Tsuchida, "The Japanese in Brazil," 113. One main rival was the French company Chargeurs Reunis. It had formed an alliance with Lloyd Brazileiro and was working hard for Brazilian government subsidies to go to the European enterprise.

35. Kunimoto, "Japan and Mexico," 126.

Chapter 4

1. In 1914 Bolivian plenipotentiary J. Cupertino Arteaga signed a Treaty of Commerce with Japan's Eki Hioki Jushu.

2. Iyo Iimura Kunimoto, "Japan and Mexico, 1886–1917" (Ph.D. diss., University of Texas, 1975), 101.

3. Japan also established first connections with South Africa, and the explorer Nobu Choku Shirase tried to explore the Antarctic. It took a second attempt one year later for a Japanese explorer to baptize bays in the area of the Bahia de las Ballenas.

4. Letter No. 9793-60, author's signature unreadable, Major, General Staff, to Leland Harrison, 1 March 1917, "Reports and Japanese activities in Mexico," RG 59, Department of State, Office of Counselor, National Archives of the United States, Washington, D.C. (hereafter cited as NAUS).

5. William Schell Jr., *Integral Outsiders: The American Colony in Mexico City 1876–1911* (Wilmington, Del.: Scholarly Resources, 2001), 173.

6. Ibid.

7. Doc. No. 27, 25 April 1911, and Doc. No. A5988, Montgelas, Tokyo to Berlin, 23 March 1911, Embassy in Mexico City, Vol. 28, Political Archive of the German Foreign Ministry, Berlin (hereafter cited as PAAA). I believe that von der Goltz's statement, published in 1917, that he stole a Japanese–Mexican treaty out of Limantour's possession was war propaganda or just sensationalism to earn money. He published this statement after having been arrested by the British. During his extensive interrogation by the British he never mentioned such a treaty. There is a difference in the credibility of Goltz's words before and after his arrest by the British in 1914. See the von der Goltz interrogation under KV 2 in the National Archives of the United Kingdom, London.

8. Schell, *Integral Outsiders*, 189.

9. Rosendo Suárez Suárez, *Breve Historia del Ejército Mexicano* (Mexico City: Impr. y Editorial Militar "Anahuac," 1938).
10. Kunimoto, "Japan and Mexico," 167.
11. Ibid., 213, Fr. 35 and 218.
12. Ibid., 168, citing Hachirojiro Mitsui to Makina, Tokyo, 23 October 1913, NGM, 1913, pt. 1, 391–92.
13. Ibid., 167.
14. Ibid., 154.
15. Ibid., 183, citing Adachi to Makino, Mexico City, 25 February 1914, NGM, 1914, pt. 1, 806–9.
16. Ibid., 78.
17. Ibid., 167–68, citing Hachirojiro Mitsui to Makina, 23 October 1913; Friedrich Katz, *The Secret War in Mexico* (Chicago: University of Chicago Press, 1981), 214.
18. Investigative case files, 1908 to 1922, Mexican Files: 1909–1921, Case No. 232-3910, Bureau of Intelligence, Washington, D.C., "Japanese Corporations Securing Concession to Colonize Certain Parts of Lower California," M-1085, NAUS.
19. Ibid.
20. "Japan Mexico and the Union," *Berliner Tageblatt*, dispatch filed in Yokohama by correspondent, August 18, 1913, Embassy in Mexico City, Vol. 28, PAAA.
21. Kunimoto, "Japan and Mexico," 177.
22. Ibid.
23. Doc. No. A 1355, Falkenhausen, Tokyo, 4 January 1914, Embassy in Mexico City, Vol. 28, PAAA.
24. Kunimoto, "Japan and Mexico," 153. At first, Huerta tried to kill two political birds with one stone, asking his political rival Félix Díaz, Porfirio Díaz's nephew, to lead the delegation.
25. William Schell Jr. ("Integral Outsiders: Mexico City's American Colony 1876–1911: Society and Political Economy in Porfirian Mexico" [Ph.D. diss., University of North Carolina at Chapel Hill, 1992]) cites File No. 41-25-42, Ayuda del Japon al Gobierno de Huerta sobre diversas informaciones. Supuesta ayuda con armas y municioince a cambo de permitir el establecimineto de una base naval en la citada bahio Magdalena, AREM.
26. Kunimoto, "Japan and Mexico," 164. He met with Count Shibusawa, Mitsui, Iwasaki, and others, based on *Tokyo Nichi Nichi*.
27. Ibid., 165.
28. Only one lone voice of the recently founded opposition party Chusaikai opposed the public rapprochement between Japan and Mexico. He accused the government of "playing with a Mexican card."
29. Doc. No. 8916, Tokyo, 29 December 1913, Mexican Special Mission to Japan, Embassy in Mexico City, Vol. 28, PAAA.
30. Kunimoto, "Japan and Mexico," 168.
31. Ibid., 182. The Foreign Ministry counseled against the action.
32. Ibid., 193. His advice to Tokyo remains unknown. But it was clear that he wanted Huerta to survive.
33. Ibid., 194, citing Adachi to Kato, telegram, Mexico City, 21 April 1914, NGM, 1914, pt. 1, 855–56.
34. Later this scheme emerged as part of British oil magnate Lord Cowdray's effort to secure himself Mexico's oil. For that purpose he was trying to breathe air into Huerta's administration. He was backed by Ambassador Carden, who tried to make Japan a party to the

effort in order to prevent a U.S. intervention that might eliminate British influence over Mexican oil. Japan's ambassador did not object vehemently in public.

35. Kunimoto, "Japan and Mexico," 192n125, citing Adachi to Makino, Mexico City, 18 March 1914.

36. Ibid., 184n105, citing Chinda to Makino, telegram, Washington, D.C., 29 January 1914, NGM, 1914, pt. I, 799.

37. Ibid., 194n121, citing Kato to Adachi, telegram, 22 April 1914, and 196.

38. Doc No. 16616, Rex to Bethmann Hollweg, 28 July 1913, "Japan and Mexico," Embassy in Mexico City, Vol. 28, PAAA. The chancellor read this dispatch on September 11.

39. No. 9793-60, Chief of Staff to Leland Harrison, Office of Counselor, Department of State, cover letter, 1 March 1917, War College Division, War Department, NAUS. The following is based on a report written by an intelligence officer at El Paso, Texas: Report No. WCD 8532-52, 6 March 1917, RG 59, Office of Counselor, NAUS.

40. Doc. No. 9410, Tokyo, 27 April 1914, "Japan and the situation in Mexico," Embassy in Mexico City, Vol. 28, PAAA.

41. Doc. No. 9722, 25 May 1914; Rex, 4 May 1914; and Doc. No. 13788, 16 July 1914, "Japan and the question of California"—all in Embassy in Mexico City, Vol. 28, PAAA.

42. Nachlass Hintze, 78, Bundesarchiv, Freiburg.

Chapter 5

1. The best published study remains Johannes Reiling, *Deutschland Safe for Democracy? Deutschamerikanische Beziehungen aus dem Tätigkeitsbereich, Heinrich F. Alberts, Kaiserlicher Geheimrat in Amerika* (Stuttgart: F. Steiner, 1997), 84.

2. Ibid., 84–85.

3. Werner Schiefel, *Bernhard Dernburg, (1865–1937), Kolonialpolitiker und Bankier im Wilhelminischen Deutschland* (Zurich: Atlantis, 1977).

4. Ron Chernow, *The House of Morgan: An American Dynasty and the Rise of Modern Finance* (New York: New Atlantic Monthly Press, 1990), 196.

5. Reiling, *Deutschland Safe for Democracy?* 94.

6. Fritz Fischer, *Griff nach der Weltmacht: Die Kriegszielpolitik des kaiserlichen Deutschland 1914/1918* (Düsseldorf: Droste, 1961), 147, 150.

7. Ibid., 150–51.

8. Ibid., 153.

9. Ibid., 146, 156.

10. Ibid., 169.

11. Ibid., 159.

12. Ibid., 144.

13. T-136, Reel 30, National Archives of the United States, Washington, D.C. (hereafter cited as NAUS): see the ongoing flow of telegrams inquiring about the success and failure of railroad destruction in Siberia in S.A./Wk No. 11h.

14. C. F. Petersdorff, Old German Files, 8000-6133, Bureau of Intelligence, Washington, D.C. (hereafter cited as BI). The authorities questioned the right man. But he kept his composure during the interrogation. The link between access to dynamite as a mining engineer and sabotage work for von Papen is obvious. Von Papen admitted von Petersdorff's recruitment in T-136, Reel 30, NAUS.

15. Baerensprung is also mentioned by Petersdorff. See Old German Files, 8000-6133, BI.

16. Nachlass Knorr, Supply Service Report, Bundesarchiv, Freiburg (hereafter cited as BA-Freiburg).

17. Case File C. C. Crowley, Old German Files, 8000-383, BI.
18. Reiling, *Deutschland Safe for Democracy?* 158n423.
19. File von Papen, Secret, KV2/520, Public Records Office, National Archives of the United Kingdom, London (hereafter cited as PRO).
20. Von Papen, Protocoll Zeugenaussage von Papen, Barch KO, R 43I/90:308, in Reiling, *Deutschland Safe for Democracy?* 156; Reinhard R. Doerries, *Imperial Challenge: Ambassador Count Bernstorff and German–American Relations, 1908–1917*, trans. Christa D. Shannon (Chapel Hill: University of North Carolina Press, 1989), 179; Papen to Deputy general staff, 11 February 1915, and Nadolny to AA., 11 March 1915, AA WK 11h. Secr. Bd. 1, Politisches Archiv des Auswaertigen Amts, Berlin (hereafter cited as PAAA).
21. File Page Nos. 130–32, von Papen, J. No. 338/15, New York, 11 February 1915, "Military Report Canada," T-136, Reel 30, NAUS.
22. File von Papen, Secret, KV2/520, PRO.
23. Fischer, *Griff nach der Weltmacht*, 100: "Die Stimmung Amerikas ist Deutschland freundlich berichtete Moltke, vielleicht lassen sich die Vereinigten Staaten, zu einer Flottenaktion gegen England veranlassen, fuer die ihnen als Siegespreis Kanada winkt."
24. Horst von der Goltz, *My Adventures as a German Secret Agent* (New York: R. M. McGride, 1917), 157–58.
25. File von der Goltz confession, Secret, KV2/519, PRO.
26. Reinhard R. Doerries, "Die Taetigkeit deutscher Agenten in den USA," in *Diplomaten und Agenten: Nachrichtendienste in der Geschichte der Deutsche–Amerikanischen Beziehungen*, ed. Reinhard R. Doerries (Heidelberg: C. Winter, 2001), 23.
27. Doerries, *Imperial Challenge*, 337n244.
28. Ibid., 338n249.
29. Doerries, "Die Taetigkeit deutscher Agenten in den USA," 25, citing Rudolf Nadolny, Abt. IIIb, Stellvertretender Generalstab, to AA, Bericht von Oberleutnant a.d. D. Boehm weitergebend, Berlin, 2 March 1915, Geheim und Anlage I, PA, AA, Weltkrieg 11k Secr., Bd. 6, PAAA; Rudolf Nadolny, *Mein Beitrag: Erinnerungen eines Botschafters des deutschen Reiches* (Cologne: DME Verlag, 1985). Nadolny omits mentioning his leading role in German sabotage affairs across the world in his memoirs. In 1937 German Ambassador Dieckhoff cited testimony by Agent Olshausen "that one must not write or cable to Nadolny about Herman [a lead saboteur in the field in the United States]. Officially only (garbled) and telegrams no written material must be exchanged and officials of the embassy must not put together records or memos about Hermann and his affair" (No. 291, Dieckhoff, Washington, D.C., 4 November 1937, T-120, Reel 2967, Fr. E 478236, NAUS).
30. Thereafter Boehm was supposed to leave the United States again in the first week of February 1915.
31. File von Papen, Secret, KV2/520, PRO.
32. The following is based on *Argentina and Chile, Suggested Disclosure of German Intrigues*, Secret, "Projected Collection, Arming and Despatch of a German Expedition from South America to German West Africa," Classified Case Files, Box 4, Folder 99, RG 59, Office of Counselor (OoC), NAUS. How this material traveled from Great Britain to the United States is explained in Report No. 461, Beil to Leland Harrison, Most Secret, 4 September 1918.
33. *Argentina and Chile*, Appendix A, 6.
34. No. 432, Santiago telegram, Washington, D.C., to Berlin, 10 November 1914, in ibid.

35. No. 26, telegram, Washington, D.C., to Berlin, in ibid., Appendix A, 6.
36. No. 432, Santiago telegram.
37. *Argentina and Chile*, Appendix A, Appendix A, 7.
38. Ibid., Appendix A, 8.
39. No. 262, Berlin to Washington, D.C., in ibid; No. 27, Santiago, 16 November 1914, in ibid., 6.
40. *Argentina and Chile*, Appendix A continued, 7.
41. Purchase of Argentine Government Munitions and Equipment by German legation, Buenos Aires, Appendix B, 9; No. 31, For Imperial legation, Santiago; No. 346, Washington, D.C., to Berlin, 5 December 1914, Appendix A, 8; Nos. 34 and 54, Minister at Santiago telegraphs, Washington, D.C., to Berlin, 15 December 1914—all in ibid.
42. No. 34, Minister at Santiago telegraph, 15 December 1914, , 54.
43. Purchase of Argentine Government Munitions and Equipment by German legation, Buenos Aires, 9.
44. *Argentina and Chile*, 5.
45. Ibid.
46. Goltz, *My Adventures as a German Secret Agent*, 159. Since this plan was published in a 1917 book, after von der Goltz had turned British double agent, the story needs to be treated with reservation. No assembly of a subversion team in Jamaica can be found in sources. Still it is likely that von Papen used the United States to hurt British interests where they presented themselves.
47. Letter Otto, Abschrift, 9 November 1914, Old German Files, 8000-2752, BI.
48. Chernow, *The House of Morgan*, 188.
49. Heinrich Julius von Eckardt, Unpublished Memoir, Erinnerungen, Manuscript Collection, 255, PAAA.
50. Department for Import and Export, document pertaining to No. 3486/17, Top Secret, 28 December 1917, RM 5/2178, 1–7, Film 1, File 25–26, BA-Freiburg.
51. Reiling, *Deutschland Safe for Democracy?* n128. Carl Schmidlapp was a member of a German American banking family in Cincinnati, headed by Jakob Schmidlapp.
52. Ibid., citing a BI assessment in Albert, NS, Box 35, 0425, RG 65, NAUS.
53. Ibid., citing SF Box 7, "Calendar log of appointments, 1914–1915," n. 448, 163–64. Albert had not met Boy-Ed until January 3, 1915.
54. Ibid., 133n284, citing Barch KO, R 43 I/90: 278.
55. Von Rintelen, excerpts in De Woody to Allen, Personal and Confidential, 27 February 1919, Old German Files, Case No. 8000-174, BI.
56. Von Rintelen, excerpts in Mr Offley, Personal and Confidential, 4 March 1919, Old German Files, Case No. 8000-174, BI.
57. Reiling, *Deutschland Safe for Democracy?* 101.
58. Ibid., 133n284, citing Barch KO, R 43 I/90: 278.
59. Ibid., 144–45.
60. Special mission of Captain Lieutenant von Rintelen, IV 4 a 1Sonderaufgabe des Kapitaenleutnants v. Rintelen, 12–26, RM 5/2176, BA-Freiburg.
61. Ibid., File Page 12.
62. Special mission of Captain Lieutenant von Rintelen, IV 4 a 1Sonderaufgabe des Kapitaenleutnants v. Rintelen, 12. At one time Agent von Rintelen was almost discovered by a reporter. But, according to his testimony, he convinced the journalist that he was only in charge of organizing exports through neutral ports.
63. Frederick Stallforth, Old German Files, Case No. 8000-3089, BI.

64. Memorandum to Mr. Warren, 28 May 1917, Old German Files, 8000-2752, BI. Rudolf Otto the former German consul from Jamaica received $2,000 per month from Albert to forward to Hans Liebau.

65. Reiling, *Deutschland Safe for Democracy?* 147.

66. Ausl. No. 938, Washington, D.C., to Germany, Abschrift T-77, 12 October 1916, Reel 1386, Fr. 0166–67; and Ausl. No. 938, An KM, KA Berlin von Papen an AA, 29 December 1916, Fr. 77–1386—both in W-I, Wi/Ivb99, Zusammenstellung aus verschiedenen Akten, NAUS.

67. Reiling, *Deutschland Safe for Democracy?* 148.

68. Emmet Larkin, *James Larkin: Irish Labor Leader, 1876–1947* (Cambridge: MIT Press, 1965), 204–7.

69. Reiling, *Deutschland Safe for Democracy?* citing SF Box 7, "Calendar log of appointments, 1914–1915," n. 448, 163–64.

70. Larkin, *James Larkin.*

71. Reiling, *Deutschland Safe for Democracy?* 161.

72. Franz von Rintelen, *The Dark Invader: Reminiscences of a German Naval Intelligence Officer* (New York: Macmillan Co., 1933), 175, cited in Doerries, *Imperial Challenge*, 340.

73. Larkin, *James Larkin.*

74. Reiling, *Deutschland Safe for Democracy?* citing Bernstorff to Bethmann, 3 November 1915, Amerika 16, R 17357, 161, PAAA.

75. Ibid., citing Diary Albert, 24 May 1915, n. 437.

76. Ibid., 161: according to Reiling, press attention in *The World* stopped the strike.

77. See Doerries, *Imperial Challenge*, 183; and Reiling, *Deutschland Safe for Democracy?* 158.

78. Stallforth, Memorandum: "When von Rintelen Left," no date, and Stallforth Statement after Second Arrest 1918, Old German Files, Case File 8000-3089, BI.

79. Note 25, Box 8, Exhibit 761, 11 April 1930, RG 76, NAUS, in Mark Wheelis, "Biological Sabotage in World War I," in *Biological and Toxin Weapons: Research, Development and Use from the Middle Ages to 1945*, ed. Erhard Geissler and John Ellis van Courtland Moon, Sipri Chemical and Biological Warfare Studies, no. 18 (Oxford: Oxford University Press, 1999), 35–62.

80. Goltz, *My Adventures as a German Secret Agent*, 161.

81. Franz von Papen, *Der Wahrheit eine Gasse* (Munich: P. List, 1952), 47.

82. Suspect name Krumm-Heller, Old Mexican Files 1909 to 1921, Case No. 531, BI.

83. Ibid.

84. See Papen's Report about His Trip to the West Coast, including work against the Panama Canal, S.A./Wk No. 11h., T-136, Reel 30, NAUS.

85. Friedrich Katz, *The Secret War in Mexico* (Chicago: University of Chicago Press, 1981), 342–43.

86. Also see Reiling, *Deutschland Safe for Democracy?* on Sommerfeld and purchasing weapons as a diversion.

87. Testimony of Major Edwin Hume, Senate Doc. 62, III, 2166–67, cited in James A. Sandos, "German Involvement in Northern Mexico," *Hispanic American Historical Review* 50, no. 1 (February 1970): 84.

88. Ibid.

89. In Re: Felix A. Sommerfeld, Confidential, Report Agent Skadden, BSF, 9-16-12-5305-0, BI.

90. Doc. No. AS 2183, no author, no signature, 10 May 1915, T-149, Reel 377, Fr. 737–39, NAUS.
91. Doerries, *Imperial Challenge*, 171.
92. Von Rintelen, "Precis of the Rintelen and Meloy Case," Old German Files, Case No. 8000-174, BI. This document appears to be a British summary mailed to the Bureau of Intelligence. See also File 9140-645.
93. Michael Meyer, *Huerta: A Political Portrait* (Lincoln: University of Nebraska Press, 1972); and Charles H. Harris and Louis R. Sadler, *The Secret War in El Paso* (Albuquerque: University of New Mexico Press, 2009).
94. Franz von Rintelen, *The Dark Invader* (reprint; London: L. Dickson, Ltd., 1990), 212–13. The actual detailed specifics of how Huerta communicated with the Germans and prepared his return remain to be identified. For example, see how von Rintelen denied everything in his interrogations in von Rintelen, Old German Files, Case File 8000-174, BI.
95. Von Rintelen, *The Dark Invader* (1990), 179.
96. Reiling, *Deutschland Safe for Democracy?* 202, 204n14.
97. Barbara Tuchman, *The Zimmerman Telegram* (New York: Macmillan, 1966), 77.
98. Reiling, *Deutschland Safe for Democracy?* 218.
99. Reinhard R. Doerries, *Prelude to Easter Rising: Sir Roger Casement in Germany* (London: Frank Cass, 2000), 43, citing Eoin Mac Neill to Sir Roger Casement, 7 July 1914.
100. Ibid., 44, citing Source No. 3.
101. Juergen Kloosterhuis, *Friedliche Imperialisten: Deutsche Auslandsvereine und auswaertige Kulturpolitik, 1906–1918* (Frankfurt: Peter Lang Verlag, 1994), vol. 2, 817.
102. "German-Americans Meet," *New York Times*, 7 October 1911, 32.
103. Doerries, *Prelude to Easter Rising*, citing Bernstorff to AA via German legation in Stockholm, Washington, D.C., 15 October 1914, Doc. 11, p. 51, WK 11k Sect., vol. 1 (R 21153), PAAA.
104. Ibid., 46, citing Doc. 4.
105. Ibid., citing Doc. 10, Bernstorff to Bethmann Hollweg, Secret, A No. 184.
106. Report No. 19, Albert, 10 October 1914, Ministry of Interior, Secret Collection, Fr. 187, R 1501/B9156, Bundesarchiv, Berlin-Lichterfelde.
107. Reiling, *Deutschland Safe for Democracy?* 168.
108. Doerries, *Prelude to Easter Rising*, 51n2, citing Dep. IIIb. Nadolny took over the Irish case after November 5, 1914.
109. Ibid., 69–71.
110. Ibid., 59, citing Doc. 16, Sir Roger Casement to Joseph Mc Garrity, Berlin, 11 November 1914; and Doerries, "Die Taetigkeit deutscher Agenten in den USA," 15.
111. Charles H. Harris and Louis R. Sadler, *The Archaeologist Was a Spy: Sylvanus G. Morley and the Office of Naval Intelligence* (Albuquerque: University of New Mexico Press, 2003).
112. The Japanese labor migration agent Terasawa retooled from recruiting laborers to recruiting fellow countrymen as mercenaries. Terasawa was acquainted with the commander of railways in Monterrey, who was connected with Carranzista generals Gonzalez and Nafarrete. Iyo Iimura Kunimoto ("Japan and Mexico, 1886–1917" [Ph.D. diss., University of Texas, 1975], 201–2) cites an offer to Carranza of eight hundred Japanese soldiers.
113. David Piñera Ramírez, coord., *Vision Historica de la Frontera Norte de Mexico* (Mexicali: Instituto Autonoma de Baja California, 1994), 131–45.

114. They in turn employed De la Rosa, a major figure in the Plan of San Diego. James A. Sandos, *Rebellion in the Borderlands: Anarchism and the Plan of San Diego, 1904–1923* (Norman: University of Oklahoma Press, 1992), 143, 202.

115. Von Rintelen, Copy AA No. 105 from 17 July 1914, in Offly to Allen, Personal and Confidential, Old German Files, Case File 8000-174, BI.

116. Roger Daniels, *The Politics of Prejudice: The Anti-Japanese Movement in California and the Struggle for Japanese Exclusion* (Berkeley: University of California Press, 1962), 75.

117. Ibid.

118. Ibid.

119. Viereck to Bernhard Dernburg, 14 May 1915, U.S. Congress, Senate, Brewing and Liquor Interests and German and Bolshevik Propaganda, 66th Cong., 1st sess., Washington, D.C., 1919, Doc. 62, vol. 2, 1426.

120. Ibid., Bielaski Exhibit 41, Viereck 110.

121. Doc. No. 12, von Eckardt to Reichskanzler Herrn Grafen von Hertling, 7 August 1918, Tgb. No. 2947/18, 11–12, Paket 26, Embassy in Mexico City, PAAA; and von Eckardt, Unpublished Memoir, 254.

122. Reiling, *Deutschland Safe for Democracy?* 175. DANA collected until January 31, 1915, and gave $233,000 to Bernstorff and $67,000 to Dumba.

123. S. D. Lovell, *The Presidential Election of 1916* (Carbondale: Southern Illinois University Press, 1980), 181.

124. Richard Bartholdt, *From Steerage to Congress: Reminiscences and Reflections* (Philadelphia: Dorrance and Co., 1930).

125. Ohlinger Testimony, 16 January 1918, U.S. Congress, Senate Judiciary Committee, 65th Cong., Washington, D.C., S 3529, 67.

126. Meeting, 11 November 1914, Box 27, 00179:5, cited in Reiling, *Deutschland Safe for Democracy?* 174.

127. Albert, Aufzeichnungen, quoted in ibid., 177.

128. Ohlinger Testimony, 16 January 1918, 67.

129. See the correspondence of the German consul general in New York to the German Foreign Ministry, 1915–16, PAAA.

130. Ohlinger Testimony, 16 January 1918, 69.

131. "To Offer Peace Plan Again," *New York Times*, 2 July 1915, 13.

132. "Americans Smile at Weissman Slures," *New York Times*, 2 July 1915, 22.

133. "German Society for Peace," *New York Times*, 11 July 1915, 5.

134. Report No. 19, Albert, 10 October 1914.

135. *New York Times*, 6 August 1915, 9.

136. "German Day at the Fair," *New York Times*, 6 August 1915, 9; and *New York Times*, 2 August 1915, 2.

137. "Appeal by Dr. Hexamer," *New York Times*, 16 September 1915, 3.

138. Rensselaer Country Historical Society, Online Exhibition, "Gruess Gott in Rensselaer County, Exhibitions, the 20th century" (http://www.rchsonline.org/grus_gott.htm).

139. "German Votes to Go to Anti-Wilson Men," *New York Times*, 24 April 1916, 1.

140. "German Alliance to Enter Politics," *New York Times*, 8 March 1916, 1, 3. Emphasis was laid on the necessity for secrecy, and it was suggested that not more than twenty men should be "in the know" and that the money to carry on the campaign should be raised from the smallest possible number of contributors. It was provided that all officers of the proposed organization should be men whose names were not Teutonic, Hungarian, or Irish and that the movement should be organized "politically throughout the country

for the purpose of influencing Presidents, Senators and members of Congress now and of electing those friendly to us during the next election."

141. Ibid., 1.
142. Ibid., 3.
143. Ridder's newspaper also began to experience financial difficulties. Thus he was a propaganda conduit for the imperial government, a passionate individual speaking out in favor of German policy, and a businessman partially subsidized by U.S. brewers George Ehrst and Jacob Ruppert's heirs, for whom the global propaganda game was rapidly getting over their heads. See testimony Norbert Kantor, 30 October 1918, Old German Files, 8000-17683, BI.
144. "German Votes to Go to Anti-Wilson Men," 1.
145. Ibid.
146. "German Alliance to Enter Politics," 1, 3.
147. "German American Alliance Also Against Roosevelt . . . ," *New York Times*, 2 April 1916, 20.
148. "Germans Go into Politics," *New York Times*, 3 April 1916, 2.
149. "Germans Sympathise with Irish," *New York Times*, 29 May 1916, 2.
150. Ohlinger Testimony, 16 January 1918, 65.
151. Ibid., 66.
152. Ibid., 63.
153. Ibid., 34; on Official Bulletin October 1915, see ibid., 63.
154. Ibid., 64, on Official Bulletin October 1915.
155. "Teutonic Sons for Hughes," *New York Times*, June 14, 1916.
156. "Germans Claim Credit, Secretary of Illinois Alliance Talks of Campaign for Hughes," *New York Times*, 11 June 1916, 3.
157. Testimony of Henry H. Campbell, assistant editor of the *Milwaukee Journal*, Wisc., U.S. Congress, Senate Judiciary Committee, 65th Cong., Washington, D.C., S 3529, 97.
158. "German Alliance Head Criticizes President," *New York Times*, 3 July 1916, 5.
159. "Germans Overrate Political Strength," *New York Times*, 8 October 1916, 4.
160. "Germans in Ohio Secede," *New York Times*, 31 October 1916, 5.
161. Copy of the letter printed in Mr. Campbell, Testimony of Henry H. Campbell, 98.
162. Lovell, *The Presidential Election of 1916*, 171, 174.
163. Ibid., 174.
164. A defense of German Americans, blaming exclusively British smear propaganda and without access to key documents, is Clifton James Child, *The German American in Politics 1914–1917* (Madison: University of Wisconsin Press, 1940).
165. In Re: Hexamer, Old German Files, 8000-553, BI.
166. John Price Jones and Paul Merrick Hollister, *The German Secret Service in America, 1914–1918* (Boston: Small, Maynard and Co., 1919), 264.
167. Earl E. Sperry, Professor of History, Syracuse University, and Willis M. West, former head of the History Department in the University of Maryland, "'Germany's Effort to Incite Revolution in India': German Plots and Intrigues in the United States during the Period of Our Neutrality," Red, White and Blue Series, No. 10 (Washington, D.C.: Committee on Public Information, July 1918).
168. Ibid., 252.
169. Donald M. McKale, *War by Revolution: Germany and Great Britain in the Middle East in the Era of World War I* (Kent: Kent State University Press, 1989), 120; and Jones and Hollister, *The German Secret Service in America*, 255.

170. Jones and Hollister, *The German Secret Service in America*, 252. The U.S. author Hollister, closely involved in the uncovering of Hindu plots, argues that the Indians had also established contacts with the U.S. Irish pro-independence group Clan na Gael.

171. S.A./WK No. IIh, I, T-136, Reel 30, NAUS. A German telegram states that von Brinken volunteered his services; however, he wanted them to count for his military service (A 2803, No. 92, 23 January 1915 [originally No. 123, Consulate San Francisco, Bernstorff to Lucius to Berlin]).

172. McKale, *War by Revolution*, 123.

173. Military Attaché von Papen (*Memoirs* [New York: E. P. Dutton and Co., Inc., 1953], 40) admitted to purchasing arms in the United States and shipping them to Asia, using a German shipping agency and the agent Carlos Heynen in Mexico. The plan eventually failed.

174. Ruth Price, *The Lives of Agnes Smedley* (Oxford: Oxford University Press, 2005), 60.

175. Telegram, 4 February 1916, Classified Case Files, Bell, Nos. 86–112, Box 4, RG 59, OoC, NAUS.

176. Telegram, 28 May 1916, and Letter No. 305, Chandra to Eisenhut, Copenhagen, Classified Case Files, Bell, Nos. 86–112, Box 4, RG 59, OoC, NAUS.

177. No. 274, Chandra to ZNG Officers, Sloterdyck, Amsterdam, Washington, D.C., to Berlin, 25 August 1916, Classified Case Files, Bell, Nos. 86–112, Box 4, RG 59, OoC, NAUS.

178. It is also possible that the party was called Gorgoles.

179. No. 274, Chandra to ZNG Officers, 25 August 1916.

180. Ibid.

181. Washington, D.C., to Eisenhut, Copenhagen, 17 October 1916, Bell, Nos. 86–112, Box 4, RG 59, OoC, NAUS.

182. Jones and Hollister, *The German Secret Service in America*, 263.

183. Purport book, RG 59, NAUS.

184. S.A./Wk No.IIm, secr. 2, A 4544, zu Ab 4768, Huelsen to embassy Washington, D.C., Top Secret, Berlin, 4 January 1917, T-136, Reel 30, NAUS.

185. S.A./WK No, IIm Secr. 2, T-136, Reel 30, Fr. 2211, NAUS.

186. T-136, Reel 30, NAUS; also sent in Telegram No. 40, Berlin to Kristiana, Lithuania, 27 January 1917.

187. No. 18, Huelsen to Washington, D.C., 2 January 1917, T-136, Reel 30, NAUS.

188. No. 37, Mexico to Berlin, 27 August 1917, Classified Case Files, Bell, Nos. 113–28, Box 5, RG 59, OoC, NAUS.

189. No. 2363, T-149, Reel 400, Fr. 75, NAUS. This pertains to Agent Gehrmann, 7 October 1917: "Regierungsrat Dr. Gehrmann dem es gelang bei Kriegsausbruch nach Batavia zu entkommen."

190. Department of State of unreadable to Command, Edward Mc Cauly, J., Personal and Confidential, 12 November 1917, Confidential Correspondence, 1913–1924, Box 21, Office of Naval Intelligence (ONI), NAUS.

191. Samaren Roy, *The Twice-Born Heretic: M. N. Roy and Comintern* (Calcutta: Firma KLM Private Ltd., 1986), 51–52.

192. Old German Files, Various No. 8000-147377, BI.

193. No. 1558, Fr. 436–37; No. 3662, Abschrift Madrid, Military Attaché, 7 October 1917; and No. 7, Entzifferung, telegram to General Stab Politik, probably Kalle, 28 October 1917, Fr. 443—all in T-149, Reel 378, NAUS.

194. Telegram No. 37, Mexico to Berlin, 27 August 1917, Box 5, RG 59, OoC, NAUS.

195. Dispatched as No. 707, Ratibor, Madrid, 29 October 1917, T-149, Reel 378, NAUS.

196. Ibid.

197. Unternehmungen und Aufwiegelungen in Spanien, April–September 1915, Der Weltkrieg, No. 11, Secr. Bd. 1, No. 806, Ratibor to AA, 31 May 1915, T-149, Reel 402, NAUS.

198. 17 June and 29 June 1915, T-149, Reel 402, NAUS.

199. Michael Toy Campbell, "Triumph of the Word: The German Struggle to Maintain Spanish Neutrality during the First World War" (Ph.D. diss., University of Wisconsin, 1989), 288.

200. No. 7761, 402, Nadolny, 29 May 1916, T-145, NAUS.

201. No. 72, 9 June 1916, and Telegram No. 7929, 8 June 1916, T-145, NAUS.

202. No. 99, Kalle, 23 June 1916, and No. 9001, 8 August 1916, T-145, NAUS.

203. Wheelis, "Biological Sabotage in World War I," 39–46: "The German Biological Sabotage Programme in the USA."

204. No. 128, 6 July 1916, T-145, NAUS.

205. No. 8497, Nadolny, 20 July 1916, and No. Pol. 8980, 3 August 1916, T-145, NAUS.

206. Patrick Beesly, *Room 40: British Naval Intelligence 1914–1918* (San Diego: Harcourt, Brace, Jovanovich, 1982), 200.

207. "Held as U-Boat Agent, Says He's American," *New York Times*, 23 February 1917, 1.

208. 28 February 1917, T-149, Reel 402, NAUS.

209. 3 March 1917, T-149, Reel 402, NAUS.

210. 28 February 1917, T-149, Reel 402, NAUS.

211. Deutsch Suedamerikanische Bank to Mr. Hardt, Strictly Confidential, Berlin, 12 March 1917, T-149, Reel 402, Fr. 378–11, Fr. 310, NAUS.

212. Ibid., 3.

213. "On Secret Service in Mexico," *Chicago Daily Tribune*, 14 November 1919, 17.

214. No. 1031, Washington, D.C., to Operations Naval Attaché Madrid, "Spanish Steamers between Argentina and Spain," 8 November 1918, Subject File, Box 806, RG 45, ONI, WP, NAUS. Also see the *Infanta Isabel* use throughout 1918.

215. Ibid.

216. Ibid.

217. Ibid., 7. Engineers could double their pay with an occasional service.

218. No. 8, Bell to Leland Harrison, 28 January 1918, Box 1, RG 59, OoC, NAUS.

219. 17 March 1917, T-149, Reel 402, NAUS.

220. U.S. Naval Attaché to W. E. Gonzales, 3 August 1918, Box 8, RG 59, OoC, NAUS.

221. Bode Alias Wilson, Confidential Suspects General Correspondence, Box 1, File 20956-6-B, RG 38, ONI, NAUS.

222. Ibid., 2.

Chapter 6

1. Donald H. Estes, "Asama Gunkan: The Reappraisal of a War Scare," *Journal of San Diego* 24, no. 3 (Summer 1978): 7.

2. Ibid., 11. Admiral Moriyama and Admiral Baron Dewa Shigoto, scheduled to arrive in San Francisco in early March, represented the Japanese emperor at the opening of the Panama Canal.

3. E. Joseph Cronon, ed., *Josephus Daniels: The Cabinet Diaries of Josephus Daniels* (Lincoln: University of Nebraska Press, 1963).

4. Sadao Asada, "Japan and the United States" (Ph.D. diss., Yale University, 1962), 15.

5. Mark R. Peattie, *Nan' yo: The Rise and Fall of the Japanese in Micronesia* (Honolulu: University of Hawaii Press, 1988), 42.

6. Ibid., 45.

7. Ibid., 47.

8. Ibid., 324, quoting Kato Takaaki in *Kieda* 2 (1967): 28–29, in n. 6.

9. Krautinger to Erzberger, 26 April 1915, T-149, Reel 381, Fr. 193, National Archives of the United States, Washington, D.C. (hereafter cited as NAUS).

10. Purport list, U.S. Department of State, RG 59, NAUS.

11. William Schell Jr., *Integral Outsiders: The American Colony in Mexico City 1876–1911* (Wilmington, Del.: Scholarly Resources, 2001), 188.

12. All figures cited by Edgar Turlington, *Mexico and Her Foreign Creditors* (New York: Columbia University Press, 1930), 263, based on Law of Payments, 24 December 1917, Article 10, *Diario Official*, 29 December 1917.

13. Ibid., 265.

14. Madeleine Chi, "Bureaucratic Capitalists in Operation: Ts'ao Ju-lin and His New Communications Clique, 1916–1919," *Journal of Asian Studies* 34, no. 3 (May 1975): 675–88.

15. Friedrich Katz, *The Secret War in Mexico* (Chicago: University of Chicago Press, 1981), 346.

16. The embassy in Mexico City wrote back that Terasawa had been critical in organizing the visit of the Mexican armament-purchasing commission to Japan.

17. Jun Morikawa, *Japan and Africa: Big Business and Diplomacy* (Trenton, N.J.: Africa World Press, 1997), 33.

18. Nobuya Tsuchida, "The Japanese in Brazil" (Ph.D. diss., University of California at Los Angeles, 1978), 191.

19. Michael A. Barnhart, *Japan Prepares for Total War: The Search for Economic Security 1919–1941* (Ithaca: Cornell University Press, 1987), 23.

20. Terauchi Masatake knakei monjo 208–11, Nishihara to Terauchi, 2 October 1916, in TNS, 1:101/102, cited in Frederick R. Dickinson, *War and National Reinvention: Japan in the Great War, 1914–1919* (Cambridge: Harvard University Asia Center, 1999), 163, see n. 34.

21. Iyo Iimura Kunimoto, "Japan and Mexico, 1886–1917" (Ph.D. diss., University of Texas, 1975), 220.

22. Ibid., 221.

23. Author signature unreadable to Mr. Leland Harrison, 19 March 1917, and Extract from the *Pacific Commercial Advertiser*, Honolulu, 7 March 1917, RG 59, Office of Counselor, Box 14, NAUS; No. 143, Stockholm, 15 March 1917, T-149, Reel 378, Fr. 287, NAUS.

24. Mitsui, 1916, Confidential Correspondence, 1913–1924, Box 26, File 20963-1720, RG 45, Office of Naval Intelligence (ONI), NAUS. At that time the Japanese legation of Chile also covered diplomatic representations with Argentina. Mr. Amari was secretary at Santiago.

25. No. 2579, Ratibor to AA, Madrid, 23 November 1917, T-149, Reel 377, Fr. 425, NAUS.

26. To Secretary of State, Tokyo, 12 December 1921, M-1389, Reel 1, Fr. 102–5, 794.00/16, NAUS. It became operational in March 1919.

27. To Secretary of State on 17 November 1919, Tokyo, 12 December 1921, M-1389, Reel 1, Fr. 102–5, 794.00/16, NAUS. It became operative in August 1921.

28. David Matthew Khazanov, "The Diplomacy of Control: U.S.–Argentine Relations, 1910–1928" (Ph.D. diss., University of Connecticut, 1989), 33.
29. Tsuchida, "The Japanese in Brazil," 173, 191.
30. See "A History of Japanese Americans in California: Patterns of Settlement and Occupational Characteristics," http://www.nps.gov/history/history/online_books/5views/5views4b .htm; and Major General to Leland Harrison, 1 March 1917, War College Division 9793-60, RG 59, Office of Counselor, Box 14, NAUS.
31. Asada, "Japan and the United States," 24.
32. Anschluss an No. 4571, No. 4577, Military Attaché Madrid to Pol. 21970, 9 December 1917; and Unterstaatssekretaer to von Eckardt, 13 January 1918, Fr. 460—both in T-149, Reel 378, NAUS.
33. James William Morely, *The Japanese Thrust into Siberia, 1918* (New York: Columbia University Press, 1957), 68n19. He cites as source Rikugunsho Kiroku, "Mitsu Dai Nikki," 490, 7 December 1917; JRK, MDN, 1918 II; MJ494, 10 December 1917.
34. Ibid., 68.
35. Ibid.
36. Ibid., 68n18, based on Japan, Rikugunsho Kiroku, "Mitsu Dai Nikki."
37. A. P. Niblack, Statement of former Semionoff Representative, Received 20 February 1920, Washington, D.C., 4 March 1920, Navy Department, ONI, File 64-262, NAUS.
38. Chae-Jui Lee, *Zhou En Lai: The Early Years* (Stanford: Stanford University Press, 1994).
39. Asada, "Japan and the United States," 54.
40. Saito, 4, RG 45, ONI, WP, NAUS.
41. Kinta Arai, 3, RG 45, ONI, WP, NAUS.
42. Hall, 8, and Letter No. 2, Riedle to Hall, Callao, 15 July 1918, Summary Correspondence, 3, RG 45, ONI, WP, NAUS.
43. Saito, 3–4.
44. Saito, Riedel to Hall, Callao, 23 October 1918, Summary 4/5, RG 45, ONI, WP, NAUS.
45. Hall, 8.
46. Saito, 5.
47. Mid Letter of 2 March 1919, 4, J. C. Hall Papers, and Letter No. 5, Riedel to Hall, Callao, December 1918, RG 45, ONI, WP, NAUS.

Chapter 7

1. Roberto Guzmán Esparza, *Memorias de don Adolfo de la Huerta según su propio dictado* (Mexico City: Ediciones Guzmán, 1957), 99–100.
2. Charles H. Harris and Louis R. Sadler describe the constant flurry of ethnic rumors before World War I in *The Texas Rangers and the Mexican Revolution* (Albuquerque: University of New Mexico Press, 2004).
3. Ibid., 215.
4. Ibid., 212.
5. Ibid., 211–12.
6. Ibid., 217.
7. Ibid., 219. See also the more passionate but far less documented interpretation that stretches history until it serves the desired political purpose in Benjamin Heber Johnson, *Revolution in Texas* (New Haven: Yale University Press, 2005).

8. Harris and Sadler, *The Texas Rangers and the Mexican Revolution*, 221.

9. Ibid.

10. Iyo Iimura Kunimoto, "Japan and Mexico, 1886–1917" (Ph.D. diss., University of Texas, 1975), 171–74, 213n35, 218.

11. Friedrich Katz, *Pancho Villa* (Stanford: Stanford University Press, 1998), 545ff.

12. Harris and Sadler, *The Texas Rangers and the Mexican Revolution*, 297.

13. Kunimoto, "Japan and Mexico," 171–74.

14. Michael C. Smith, "Carrancista Propaganda and the Print Media in the United States: An Overview of Institutions," *The Americas* 52, no. 2 (October 1995): 155–74; and Michael C. Smith, "The Mexican Secret Service in the U.S. 1910–1920," *The Americas* 59, no. 1 (July 2002): 65–87.

15. Pablo Yankelevich, "Las Campanas Solidaria, Manuel Ugarte," in *La Revolucion Mexicana en America Latina: Intereses politicas e itinerarios intelectuales* (Mexico City: Instituto Mora, 1996), 25.

16. Manuel Ugarte, *The Destiny of a Continent* (reprint; New York: AMS Press, 1970); and Yankelevich, "Las Campanas Solidaria," 25.

17. Yankelevich, "Las Campanas Solidaria," 25.

18. Ibid., 32–34.

19. Ibid., 36–38.

20. Juergen Buchenau, *In the Shadow of the Giant: The Making of Mexico's Central America Policy, 1876–1930* (Tuscaloosa: University of Alabama Press, 1996), 123–24.

21. "Vision lationamericanista del General Mugica," *Desdeldiez*, Boletin del Centro de Estudios de la Revolucion Mexicana "Lazaro Cardenas," Michoacan, A.C., July 1985: 69–89, also see 75, 79.

22. No. 498, Washington, D.C., 1 November 1915, T-149, Reel 378, Fr. 130, National Archives of the United States, Washington, D.C. (hereafter cited as NAUS).

23. Buchenau, *In the Shadow of the Giant*.

24. 12 May 1917, RG 59, Office of Counselor (OoC), Box 11, NAUS.

25. FTB, New York, to R. V. Oulahan, Washington, D.C., 22 April 1917, Newspaper Special Report, RG 59, OoC, Box 8, NAUS.

26. Pablo Yankelevich, "Centroamerica: Armas y Propaganda," in *La Revolucion Mexicana en America Latina: Intereses politicas e itinerarios intelectuales* (Mexico City: Instituto Mora, 1996), 119–20.

27. Buchenau, *In the Shadow of the Giant*, 127.

28. Rotting to Mr. Stabler, Division of Latin American Affairs, Memorandum, 29 December 1916, Classified Case Files 1915–1926, RG 59, OoC, NAUS.

29. FTB to R. V. Oulahan, 22 April 1917.

30. Revolutionary Movement in Guatemala, based on WINO, 29 July 1916, and WINO, 31 July 1916, RG 59, OoC, Box 8, NAUS.

31. For different background on the Tinoco story, see Alfredo Gonzalez, *El Petroleo y la Politica en Costa Rica* (San José: Imprenta y Libreria Trejas, Hermanos, 1920).

32. Enrile, Carothers to Canova, 18 February 1917, OoC, Box 11, NAUS.

33. 17 February 1916, T-141, Reel 20, Fr. 436, NAUS.

34. Doc No. 168, Fr. 439, and Abschrift A 7681, Wesel, Top Secret, 17 March 1916, Fr. 458, T-141, Reel 20, NAUS. Mongelas advised against sending money to Mexico. Among other reasons, "the U.S. had more of it and available through 'endlessly more channels.' It would be something different if one could channel to Villa and his band weapons and

ammunition (best if of U.S. origin). Currently this is more difficult since the connection to the North of Mexico via Vera Cruz is made more difficult."

35. No. 15 of 5 April 1917, von Eckhart to AA, 7 April 1916, T-141, Reel 20, Fr. 388, NAUS.
36. Karlsruhe, 29 April 1916, Stellvertretendes Generalkommando Nachrichtenabteilung 5267, T-141, Reel 20, Fr. 483, NAUS.
37. Handwritten Note bottom of page, 28 April 1916, T-141, Reel 20, Fr. 481, NAUS.
38. A 11153 Secret War read on May 3, T-141, Reel 20, Fr. 483, NAUS.
39. Carothers to Canova, New York, 18 February 1917, Department of State, OoC, Box 11, NAUS; and T-141, Reel 20, Fr. 496, NAUS.
40. No. 9364, Karlsruhe Manteuffel, 5 May 1916, T-141, Reel 20, Fr. 490, NAUS.
41. No. 172, Madrid, 24 July 1916, T-141, Reel 20, Fr. 649, NAUS.
42. T-141, Reel 20, Fr. 476, NAUS.
43. Heinrich Julius von Eckardt, Unpublished Memoir, Erinnerungen, Manuscript Collection, 243, , Politisches Archiv des Auswaertigen Amts, Berlin. For the best interpretation according to this paradigm, see John Mason Hart, *Empire and Revolution: The Americans in Mexico since the Civil War* (Berkeley: University of California Press, 2002).
44. Von Eckardt, Unpublished Memoir.
45. Washington Bernstorff to AA, 4 May 1916, and No. 255, Based on Mexico, 3 May 1916, T-141, Reel 20, Fr. 560, NAUS.
46. Report No. 30, von Eckardt to Germany, Mission of Mexican Oberst Krumm-Heller to Berlin, 11 June 1916; Fr. 564, 5 May 1916; and Letter to Reichschancellor, Fr. 563–65—all in T-141, Reel 20, NAUS.
47. No. 1552, Stockholm, to Foreign Ministry, 9 June 1916, T-141, Reel 20, Fr. 565, NAUS.
48. Department of State, Memorandum to Polk, 19 July 1916; No. 924, Einsiedel, Bern, to AA, Secret, 5 September 1916, T-141, Reel 20, Fr. 710; to Bethmann Hollweg, Secret, 15 September 1916, Fr. 723; and Krumm-Heller to an unknown friend, 20 July 1917, T-149, Reel 378, Fr. 413—all in RG 59, OoC, Box 11, NAUS.
49. Von Eckardt, Unpublished Memoir, 243.
50. Harris and Sadler, *The Texas Rangers and the Mexican Revolution*, 301–4.
51. Whether the visit actually took place remains unclear (Kunimoto, "Japan and Mexico," 209). This trip might have been an effort to remove a potential political rival.
52. Ibid., 209, 213n35, 218.
53. Ibid., 211.
54. Acting Chief to Ira Patchin, Secretary to the Counselor, Department of Justice, RG 59, OoC, NAUS.
55. In Re: Francisco Villa, Neutrality Matter, receipt 29 March 1916, 4th copy, 25 March 1916, RG 59, OoC, NAUS; District No. 24 to Frank L. Polk, Treasury, 2 June 1916, Department, El Paso, Texas, and OoC, Classified Case Files 1915–1926, Box 11, RG 59, OoC, NAUS. Medina told another person that he went to Japan to purchase weapons. Later Medina denied that he made weapon inquiries and claimed that he went for pleasure only (Letter to Jonathan Arnell, Japanese Secretary American Embassy, Tokyo, 8 June 1916).
56. No. 37, von Eckardt to AA, 4 October 1916, T-141, Reel 20, Fr. 728, NAUS.
57. U.S. versus Baumgartner, 17 August 1916, RG 59, OoC, Box 4, NAUS. The record is from March 29, 1917.
58. Douglas W. Richmond, *Venustiano Carranza's Nationalist Struggle* (Lincoln: University of Nebraska Press, 1983), 210.

59. Harris and Sadler, *The Texas Rangers and the Mexican Revolution*, 302–4.
60. Kunimoto, "Japan and Mexico," chronicles the following events between 212 and 218.
61. No. 1158, von Eckardt, Mexico City, 7 October 1916 (originally No. 37, 4 October 1916), T-141, Reel 20, Fr. 727, NAUS.
62. Kunimoto, "Japan and Mexico," 220; Friedrich Katz, *The Secret War in Mexico* (Chicago: University of Chicago Press, 1981), 419.
63. Katz, *The Secret War in Mexico*. Katz found the memorandum in Potsdam, AA, II, No. 4462, 349.
64. Martin Nassua, *Gemeinsame Kriegsführung, Gemeinsamer Friedensschluss: Das Zimmermann Telegram vom 13 Januar 1917 und der Eintritt der USA in den Ersten Weltkrieg* (Frankfurt am Main: Peter Lang, 1992), 20.
65. Katz, *The Secret War in Mexico*, 349–50.
66. Nassua, *Gemeinsame Kriegsführung, Gemeinsamer Friedensschluss*, 20.
67. Yankelevich, "Centroamerica," 115.
68. Ibid., 117.
69. Ibid., 119–20.
70. *New York Times*, March 1917.
71. "German Plot Bared in Central America: Teutons and Carranzistas Conspired to Start Revolts in Five Republics," *New York Times*, 24 April 1917, 3.
72. President Cabrera was supposed to be removed by a joint uprising along the Mexican and Nicaraguan border. The insurrectionists would link themselves with a disgruntled Guatemalan group. This plot was joined by the Costa Rican minister of war, one Cuban revolutionist, and a Salvadorian politician. El Salvador would become the base. Carranza was to invade Guatemala from the north. Colombia was promised the return of Panama.

Chapter 8

1. Admiral Georg Alexander von Mueller, Diary, 10 June 1916, in Walter Goerlitz, *Regierte der Kaiser: Kriegstagebücher, Aufzeichnungen und Briefe des Chefs des Marine Kabinetts Admiral Georg Alexander von Mueller 1914–1918* (Berlin: Musterschmidt-Verlag, 1959), 190–91.
2. Ibid., 194.
3. Michael L. Hadley and Roger Sarty, *Tin-Pots and Pirate Ships: Canadian Naval Forces and German Sea Raiders* (Montreal: McGill-Queens University Press, 1991), 141.
4. Ibid., 144.
5. Ibid., 149, 163.
6. Division Operation Navy Department, Officer in Charge, Decoded German Telegram, Confidential, 11 October 1916, Office of Counselor, Box 7, National Archives of the United States, Washington, D.C. (hereafter cited as NAUS).
7. Reinhard R. Doerries, *Imperial Challenge: Ambassador Count Bernstorff and German–American Relations, 1908–1917*, trans. Christa D. Shannon (Chapel Hill: University of North Carolina Press, 1989), 173.
8. Addison papers, Bodleian Library, Diary, May 8, cited in Kathleen Burk, *Britain, America and the Sinews of War, 1914–1918* (Boston: G. Allen and Unwin, 1985), 78.
9. Burk, *Britain, America and the Sinews of War*, 81.
10. Ibid., 85.
11. Ibid., 79–91.

12. Robert Lansing, *War Memoirs of Robert Lansing* (Indianapolis: Bobbs-Merrill Co., 1935).

13. U.S. Department of State, *Papers Relating to the Foreign Relations of the United States. The Lansing Papers 1914–1920*, 2 vols. (Washington, D.C.: Government Printing Office, 1940), 184.

14. RG 59, Office of Counselor, Box 11, NAUS. The Felicistas and Legalistas on the U.S. side were alleged to have considered such an offer. Pancho Villa was alleged to have supported the offer but then was talked out of it by Raoul Madero.

15. Martin Nassua, *Gemeinsame Kriegsführung, Gemeinsamer Friedensschluss: Das Zimmermann Telegram vom 13 Januar 1917 und der Eintritt der USA in den Ersten Weltkrieg* (Frankfurt am Main: Peter Lang, 1992), 20–21.

16. U.S. Department of State, *Papers Relating to the Foreign Relations of the United States*; von Mueller, Diary, 20 November 1916, and 10 June 1916, in Goerlitz, *Regierte der Kaiser*, 241.

17. Von Mueller, Diary, 24 December 1916, in Goerlitz, *Regierte der Kaiser.*

18. David F. Trask, *Captains and Cabinets: Anglo-American Naval Relations, 1917–1918* (Columbia: University of Missouri Press, 1972), 35.

19. Ibid., 31.

Chapter 9

1. Michael C. Smith, "The Mexican Secret Service in the U.S. 1910–1920," *The Americas* 59, no. 1 (July 2002): 71.

2. The cable is contained in No. 7195, Bell to Harrison, Confidential, 18 September 1917, Classified Case Files, Bell, Nos. 113–28, RG 59, Office of Counselor (OoC), Box 5, National Archives of the United States, Washington, D.C. (hereafter cited as NAUS).

3. Telegram No. 15, Zimmerman to von Eckardt, Classified Case Files, Bell, Nos. 113–28, RG 59, OoC, Box 5, NAUS.

4. G.H.C., Oberleutnant Freiherr v. Berckheim of the Foreign Department, Main Headquarters, 3 December 1917, KV2/520 v.2, Public Records Office, National Archives of the United Kingdom, London (hereafter cited as PRO); emphasis added.

5. Telegram No. 22, von Eckardt, Mexico, to Berlin, 2 May 1917, Classified Case Files, Bell, Nos. 113–28, RG 59, OoC, Box 5, NAUS.

6. Baldur Kaulisch, "Zur Ueberseeischen Stuetzpunktpolitik der Kaiserlichen Deutschen Marinefuehrung am Ende des 19 Jahrhunderts und im Ersten Weltkrieg," *East Berlin*, 1965: 589.

7. Sekt. Pol. Berlin Generalstab, Pol. 13918, Citissime, 20 February 1917, T-149, Reel 378, Fr. 249, NAUS. The German army asked the Oberste Heeresleitung to make a decision within hours. See No. 230, Beziehungen Mexico to German, February–30 September 1917, Mexico, No. 16, Bd. 1, OoC, NAUS. A total of $2,000 per month was to fund press propaganda.

8. In his diary, he noted that experts stated outrage over this proposition: Heinrich Julius von Eckardt, Unpublished Memoir, Erinnerungen, Manuscript Collection, 248, Politisches Archiv des Auswaertigen Amts, Berlin (hereafter cited as PAAA).

9. Ibid.

10. Ibid., 247.

11. Friedrich Katz, *The Secret War in Mexico* (Chicago: University of Chicago Press, 1981), 420.

12. No. 22, paraphrase of telegram, Fletcher to Secretary of State, 13 March 1917, Special Agent Human Espionage Activity, RG 59, OoC, Box 15, NAUS. The British thought that no apparatus in Mexico was capable of communicating with Europe.

13. Confidential, 15 January 1917, Special Agent Human Espionage Activity, 2491999-U, War Department Washington, D.C., 862.20212/54, War College Correspondence, RG 59, OoC, Box 14, NAUS.

14. No. 632, 12 April, Mexico, for Hauptman Magea or Nadolny, sent through Stockholm, 16 April 1917, T-149, Reel 378, NAUS.

15. Knabenshue, Special Border Report, "German Activities: Reported Plot to Raid Pacific Coast in Event of War," Nogales, Arizona, 13 February 1917, Special Agent Human Espionage Activity, Box 14, WCD 8536-160, RG 59, OoC, NAUS. Their gathering was not a planned presence for an organized plot.

16. Von Eckardt, Unpublished Memoir, 256.

17. Extract from the *Pacific Commercial Advertiser*, Honolulu, 7 March 1917, and Major, General Staff unreadable to Mr. Leland Harrison, 19 March 1917, RG 59, OoC, Box 14, NAUS; No. 143, Stockholm, 15 March 1917, T-149, Reel 378, Fr. 287, NAUS.

18. Telegram No. 22, von Eckardt, Mexico, to Berlin, 2 May 1917.

19. Knabenhue F.G., Special Border Report, "Military: Munition Landing at Manzanillo," 26 March 1917, Department of Justice, Bureau of Intelligence, Washington, D.C. (hereafter cited as BI); Bielaski to Leland Harrison, 16 April 1917, AHP-JOC, Classified Case Files, 1915–1926, Box 10, RG 59, OoC, NAUS. *La Prensa* in San Antonio published corroborating information. See also Telegram No. 22, von Eckardt, Mexico, to Berlin, 2 May 1917.

20. U.S. Department of the State, *Foreign Relations of the United States, 1917* (Washington, D.C.: Government Printing Office, 1940; hereafter cited as FRUS), not printed but cited in 23 February 1917, 763.72119/507, 241.

21. Von Eckardt wrote that he had not been involved in the preparation of this diplomatic initiative (see Unpublished Memoir, 246).

22. Secretary of State Lansing to Minister in Honduras Ewing, 1917, FRUS, 763.72/3233, 225.

23. Minister in Panama Price to the Secretary of State, 8 February 1917, FRUS, 763.72/3262, 225. The arrested crews were readied to be sent to the United States so that they could not injure the canal through sabotage. The same conference also decided not to arrest all ethnic Germans in Panama as a general precaution measure (Minister in Panama Price to Secretary of State, Telegram, 4 February 1917, FRUS, 763.72/8203, 221).

24. Raimundo Siepe, *Yrigoyen, la Primera Guerra Mundial y las relaciones económicas* (Buenos Aires: Centro Editor de América Latina, 1992), 41.

25. Ambassador in Argentina (Stimson) to Secretary of State, Buenos Aires, 8 February 1917, FRUS, 763.72/3274, 225.

26. Richard V. Salisbury, *Anti-Imperialism and International Competition in Central America, 1920–1929* (Wilmington, Del.: Scholarly Resources, 1989).

27. Juergen Buchenau, *In the Shadow of the Giant: The Making of Mexico's Central America Policy, 1876–1930* (Tuscaloosa: University of Alabama Press, 1996), 127.

28. Ibid., 126, 133–34.

29. Ibid., 127. Buchenau argues that Carranza did not further the goals of the Mexican Revolution in Latin America, and he interprets the Alomia mission only as an example of hard-nosed pragmatism. He argues that Mexico could not subvert the sovereignty of another country and stay true to the Carranza doctrine.

30. Jefferson to Secretary, Managua, Secret, 16 February 1917, FRUS, 817.00/2565, 242; and Salisbury, *Anti-Imperialism and International Competition in Central America*, 70–71. The evidence for this purported plotting, however, remains inconclusive. No indication of any contact between Martinez Alomia and Irias exists in Mexican archives. See FRUS, notes on 125–27 and 241n69; Aguilar to Nicaragua Foreign Secretary Queretaro, 12 February 1917, enclosed in Jefferson to Secretary, 16 February 1917, 242n84.

31. Leavell to Secretary, Guatemala, 31 August 1917, Department of State, 813.00/863, NAUS. The union of five countries had shrunk to two (Buchenau, *In the Shadow of the Giant*, 243n100).

32. Minister in Paraguay Mooney to the Secretary of State, Asunción, 15 February 1917, FRUS, 763.72/3337, 232.

33. Ecuadorian Minister Eliyalde to the Secretary of State, 19 February 1917, FRUS, 763.72/3358, II, 233.

34. Venezuelan Minister Dominici to Secretary of State, 7 March 1917, FRUS, 763.72/3491, 239.

35. Ambassador in Chile Shea to Secretary of State, 15 March 1917, FRUS, 763.72119/504, 241.

36. Minister in Peru McMillan to Secretary of State, Lima, 24 March 1917, FRUS, 763.72119/525, 242.

37. Ambassador in Mexico Fletcher to Secretary of State, 3 April 1917, FRUS, 763.72119/534, 243.

38. Pablo Yankelevich, *La Revolucion Mexicana en America Latina: Intereses politicos e itineraries intelectuales* (Mexico City: Instituto Mora, 1996) 40.

39. No. 1298, Kienkelin to AA, T-149, Reel 378, Fr. 417, NAUS. Kienkelin also handled the transfer of new intelligence recruits from Argentina to Europe.

40. Yankelevich, *La Revolucion Mexicana en America Latina*, 41.

41. Kathleen Burk, *Britain, America and the Sinews of War, 1914–1918* (Boston: G. Allen and Unwin, 1985), 243n105. This included a smaller amount of gold from France and Russia. The British exported almost 1.5 billion dollars of gold to the United States until the second half of 1917.

42. Ibid., 94.

43. B. J. C. McKercher, *Transition to Power: Britain's Loss of Global Pre-eminence to the United States, 1930–1945* (Cambridge, Mass.: Cambridge University Press, 1999), 5. Nevertheless, the London money market continued as a viable, influential presence in New York.

44. Cited in Katz, *The Secret War in Mexico*, 363n132.

45. See the records of the Office of Naval Intelligence and the Military Intelligence Name File in M-1194, NAUS, Entry Arai, K.

46. Katz, *The Secret War in Mexico*, 353.

47. Telegram No. 352, Stockholm, 1 March 1917, T-149, Reel 378, Fr. 255, NAUS.

48. Ernest R. May, *The World War and American Isolation 1914–1917* (Cambridge: Harvard University Press, 1959), 423.

49. Ibid., 416.

50. Ibid., 423; and William Gibs McAdoo, *Crowded Years. The Reminiscences of William G. McAdoo* (Boston: Houghton Mifflin, 1931), 367.

51. Nos. 14244 and 7012, Sek. Pol., Doc. 14244, Abschrift, 28 March 1917, Fr. 489, and No. 22935, Generalstab des Feldheeres, Secret, T-149, Reel 378, Fr. 271, NAUS.

52. May, *The World War and American Isolation*, 427.

53. Ibid., 427–32.
54. Note and Vermerk Magnus, Paket 28, Embassy in Mexico City, PAAA.
55. No. 18376, Ludendorff, Secret, Fr. 305, and No. 7774, Chief of Admiralty, Top Secret, 8 March 1917, Fr. 271, T-149, Reel 378, NAUS.
56. 19 April 1917, T-149, Reel 378, Fr. 326, NAUS.
57. No. 18 from 14 April, von Eckardt to AA, 19 April 1917, Stockholm, T-149, Reel 378, Fr. 326, NAUS.
58. Von Eckardt, Stockholm, 19 April 1917, T-149, Reel 378, Fr. 331, NAUS.
59. A No. 13, von Eckardt report, 7 August 1918, T-149, Reel 378, Fr. 709, NAUS.
60. Von Eckardt, Unpublished Memoir, 257.
61. German Activities in Mexican Oil Fields, 16 April 1917, File 2831, BI.
62. Telegram No. 867, Stockholm, 22 May 1917, Fr. 369, and No. 732, Stockholm, Fr. 351, T-149, Reel 378, NAUS. Von Eckardt suggested this from Mexico.
63. Von Eckardt, Unpublished Memoir, 257.
64. Ibid., 258.
65. Ibid.
66. A heartfelt thank-you goes to the late Marvin D. Bernstein for entrusting me with his draft of an unpublished financial history of Mexico during the revolution.
67. Robert Freeman Smith, *The United States and Revolutionary Nationalism in Mexico 1916–1932* (Chicago: University of Chicago Press, 1972), 111.
68. Mc Affee to Bielaski, Chief of B.I., Personal and Confidential, 26 March 1917, Classified Case Files, 1915–1926, Box 4, WMO, RG 59, OoC, NAUS.
69. No. 693, von Eckardt to Lucius to AA, 25 April 1917, Fr. 804, and Aus Mexico No. 20, 21 April 1917, T-149, Reel 377, NAUS.
70. Anderson Diary, 18 June 1917, Anderson MSS, cited in Smith, *The United States and Revolutionary Nationalism in Mexico*, 113n69.
71. Federico Stallforth, 1917, p. 200, #8000-3089, BI.
72. A 13622 zu 23/5.16, Report A. No. 7, von Eckardt to Berlin J, 24 January 1916, R 16914, PAAA.
73. No. 496, von Eckardt, Stockholm, 23 March 1917, R 16914, PAAA.
74. Ibid.
75. Report No. A No. 24, Magnus to Berlin, Abschrift to III, a 20604, 10 August 1915, R 16914, PAAA.
76. Doc. No. 12, von Eckardt to Reichskanzler Herrn Grafen von Hertling, Tgb. No. 2947/18, 7 August 1918, Paket 26, Embassy in Mexico City, PAAA.
77. No. 1051, Cable sent through Stockholm, 19 June 1917, T-149, Reel 378, Fr. 383, NAUS.
78. Report A. No. 25, to Berlin, 28 August 1917, R 16914, PAAA.
79. Classified Case Files, Bell, Nos. 113–28, Box 5, RG 59, OoC, NAUS.
80. Berlin to Mexico, following to be deciphered personally, 8 June 1917, Classified Case Files, Bell, Nos. 43, 113, and 128, RG 59, OoC, NAUS.
81. Handwritten telegraph draft, Untersecretary of State to Stockholm, T-149, Reel 378, Fr. 378, NAUS.
82. Telegram No. Pol 17225, Geheim to AA, R 16914, PAAA.
83. Nieto, David Retana, Caturegli, BI.
84. Lorenzo Meyer, *Su Majestad Britannica contra la Revolucion Mexicana: El fin de un imperio informal* (Mexico City: El Colegio de Mexico, 1991), 252; Katz, *The Secret War in Mexico*, 399.

85. No. 28 from 17 June, Lucius to AA, Stockholm, 19 June 1917, T-149, Reel 378, Fr. 383, NAUS. The original cable says 200,000,000 pesos; it was corrected the next day to 100,000,000 pesos.

86. Secretary of State, 26 October 1917, T-149, Reel 378, Fr. 440, NAUS.

87. Smith, *The United States and Revolutionary Nationalism in Mexico*, 114.

88. Tel. 21970, Anlage 2, Vorschlaege des AA, die Dr. Delmar von hier aus mitgenommen hat, Berlin, 11 April 1917, T-149, Reel 378, Fr. 463, NAUS.

89. Dilger sent agents to Peláez at that time and individuals to make overtures to the Zapatistas and Villistas.

90. No. 4548, Telegram, Military Attaché Madrid, 8 December 1917, T-149, Reel 378, Fr. 455, NAUS.

91. Foreign Office, Secret, 25 December 1917, Classified Case Files, Bell, Nos. 113–28, Box 3, RG 59, OoC, NAUS.

92. Postal Censorship, Committee Office of Naval Intelligence; and see Fany Anitua's article in *La Nacion* (Santiago de Chile), 10 October 1918, File No. 116710-4058, RG 59, OoC, NAUS.

93. Bernardo Altendorf, "Secret Agent in Mexico," *Chicago Daily Tribune*, Art. 4, 5 November 1919, 17.

94. Barnes report, 1 July 1916, Old Mexican Files, 232–462, BI; also see File No. 8000-1037 Varios.

95. "Secret Service in Mexico," *Chicago Daily Tribune*, Art. 4, 6 November 1919, 15.

96. Altendorf, "Secret Agent in Mexico," 5 November 1919, 17.

97. Max Rudolph Ulbrich, Old German Files, Case File 54263, BI.

98. Bernardo Altendorf, "Secret Agent in Mexico," *Chicago Daily Tribune*, 6 November 1919, 15.

99. Consulat San Francisco, Paket 28, PAAA.

100. "The Lothar Witzke Affair," in Charles H. Harris and Louis R. Sadler, *Trouble at the Border* (Silver City, N.M.: High Lonesome Books, 1988), 113–29.

101. *Chicago Daily Tribune*, 16 November 1919, 27. The German consul Rademacher was also involved.

102. See Negroe Subversion, Military Intelligence, File No. 10218-32, NAUS.

103. *Chicago Daily Tribune*, 16 November 1919, 27.

104. No. 8790, American Embassy to Department of State, Secret, 24 February 1918, answer to M8066 from December 26, Card File, 10541-120-1NAUS, Classified Case Files, Bell, No. 113A, 800M/50, OoC, NAUS.

105. No. 460, 13 January 1918, T-149, Fr. 378, NAUS.

106. No. 8790, American Embassy to Department of State, 24 February 1918, and Harrison to Leland, Classified Case Files, Bell, No. 113A, 800M/50, OoC, NAUS.

107. No. 8790, American Embassy to Department of State, 24 February 1918.

108. File 1013, February 1918, and No. 8947, American Embassy to Department of State, 7 March 1918, Classified Case Files, Bell, No. 113A, 800M/57, RG 59, OoC, NAUS. The Bleichschroeders would earn half a percent commission.

109. Nos. 1223 and 1224, Telegram of Military Attaché, Madrid, 5 April 1918, T-149, Reel 378, Fr. 509, NAUS.

110. To Military Attaché, 11 March 1918, Box 2869, File 10130-83, NAUS.

111. No. 195, 12 and 22 April 1918, Box 2869, File 10130-83, NAUS.

112. Treasury to Bielaski, 18 April 1918, Box 2869, File 10130, 8510, NAUS; Doc. No. 12, . Treasury to Bielaski, 19 April 1918, Paket 26, Embassy in Mexico City, PAAA; and Doc. No. 12, von Eckardt to Reichskanzler Herrn Grafen von Hertling, 7 August 1918.

113. No. 7429, Bell to Harrison, 25 April 1918, RG 59, 800M/195, NAUS; "The following information cannot be used owing to its source," Most Secret, written 6 April 1918, sent 27 May 1918, Classified Case Files, Bell, No. 113A, Box 5, RG 59, OoC, and T-149, Reel 378, Fr. 729, NAUS.

114. No. 1786, Telegram, Military Attaché Madrid, Secret, 13 May 1918, T-149, Reel 387, Fr. 533 and 588, NAUS. He was told that they could not pick him up. It was too dangerous. See also Sec. Memo, 800/435, 16 December 1918, OoC, Box 3, NAUS.

115. Doc. No. 12, von Eckardt to Reichskanzler Herrn Grafen von Hertling, 7 August 1918.

116. Smith, *The United States and Revolutionary Nationalism in Mexico*, 120.

117. Lansing to Fletcher, 26 June 1918, SD 711.12/103, in ibid., 123.

118. Smith, *The United States and Revolutionary Nationalism in Mexico*, 128.

119. No. 1750/A, Confidential Italian Source, 13 June 1918,, File 10130-83-43; Bell to Harrison, Secret, 7 July 1918, 800M/248; and No. 11, Paris, Harrison to Leland, Secret, London, 1 January 1919—all in Classified Case Files, Bell, No. 113A, Box 5, RG 59, OoC, NAUS.

120. Bell to Harrison, Secret, 18 August 1918, 800M/305; Bell to Harrison, Secret, 21 October 1918, 800M/305, 800 M/353; No. 2751, Bell to Harrison, Secret, 12 November 1918, 800M/403; Harrison to Bell, Confidential, 24 December 1918, 800M/448; and 24 December 1918, Card File, 10541-815-44—all in Classified Case Files, Bell, No. 113A, RG 59, OoC, NAUS.

Chapter 10

1. Thomas A. Bailey, *The Policy of the United States toward the Neutrals, 1917–1918* (Gloucester, Mass.: Peter Smith, 1942), 306.

2. No. 59, Luxburg to Berlin, 9 July 1917, *Naval Proceedings*, 1917, Diplomatic Notes, 2437, based on U.S. intercept, National Archives of the United States, Washington, D.C. (hereafter cited as NAUS).

3. Nelson Page to Secretary of State, 18 June 1917, M-1276, Reel 3, Fr. 350, 710.11/327, NAUS. On June 18, the U.S. ambassador in Rome reported that imperial Spain was "earnestly for a Pan Spanish union. Also hear Argentine supporting idea."

4. No. 1018, von Eckardt to Berlin, Stockholm, 12 June 1917, originally mailed as based on No. 27 from 9 June 1917, T-149, Reel 378, Fr. 380, NAUS.

5. A 17062, 25 May 1917, T-149, Reel 215, Fr. 64, NAUS.

6. A 17130, 26 May 1917, Fr. 66, and A 17062, No. 63, Luxburg via Stockholm, 7 July 1917, Fr. 65, T-149, Reel 215, NAUS. The messages were handled through an Austrian-Hungarian diplomat.

7. A 19207, Fr. 67; No. 1006, Luxburg to AA, Stockholm, 13 June 1917; and A 19207, No. 1005, Luxburg, 12 June 1917, Fr. 67—all in T-149, Reel 215, NAUS.

8. No. 62, Bell to Harrison, Luxburg, Secret, 10 September 1917, RG 59, Office of Counselor (OoC), NAUS. Ambassador Luxburg characterized Irigoyen's foreign minister as "a notorious ass and an Anglophile."

9. No. 67, 10 July 1917, and No. 71, 15 July 1917, Bell, Nos. 113–28, RG 59, OoC, Box 5, NAUS, on how to assuage the enraged Argentine public over the sinking of the *Toro* and the possibility that Argentine ships in the future would stay clear of the blockade zone in the Atlantic.

10. U.S. Ambassador London to Secretary of State, Secret, 31 October 1917, Sheet 4, 7570, Bell, Nos. 113–28, RG 59, OoC, NAUS; and No. 172, Berlin to Buenos Aires, 25 August 1917, NAUS, in "Lansing Exposes South American Plot by Luxburg," *New York Times*, 21 December 1917, 1–2.

11. No. 89, Telegram, Luxburg to Berlin, 4 August 1917, in Bell to Harrison, Secret, 11 September 1917, Classified Case Files, RG 59, OoC, NAUS; and "Bare Berlin Plot to Rule in Brazil," *New York Times*, 31 October 1917, 1–3.

12. No. 85, Telegram, 1 August 1917, Classified Case Files, RG 59, OoC, NAUS.

13. No. 98, Telegram, 17 August 1917, Classified Case Files, RG 59, OoC, NAUS.

14. No. 77, Telegram, 21 July 1917, Classified Case Files, RG 59, OoC, NAUS.

15. No. 64, Telegram, Luxburg, Buenos Aires to Santiago, Chile, 19 July 1917, Classified Case Files, RG 59, OoC, NAUS, in "Lansing Exposes South American Plot by Luxburg," 1–2.

16. U.S. Ambassador London to Secretary of State, 31 October 1917.

17. Rio de Janeiro Morgan to Secretary of State, Confidential, 18 September 1917, M-1276, Reel 3, Fr. 440, 710.11/342, NAUS.

18. Lansing to Rio, 21 September 1917, M-1276, Reel 3, Fr. 441, 710.11/342, NAUS.

19. Bailey, *The Policy of the United States toward the Neutrals*, 306.

20. No. 4577, no name, from Military Attaché, Madrid, to Pol. 21970, 9 December 1917, Anschluss an No. 4571, T-149, Reel 378, NAUS.

21. Diego Ramos, 29 December 1917, Old Mexican Files, 1909 to 1921, Case No. 945, Bureau of Intelligence, Washington, D.C.

22. No. 327/18, Imperial German Consulate to Berlin, Buenos Aires, 8 February 1918, T-149, Reel 375, Fr. 21–22, NAUS. A single gold peso was worth 4.05 RM.

23. U.S. Department of the State, *Foreign Relations of the United States, 1917* (Washington, D.C.: Government Printing Office, 1940), 763.72/8563, Suppl. I, 662, and Suppl. I, 9 February 1918, 665.

24. Stimson to Secretary of State, 5 February 1918, in ibid., 763.72119/1239, Suppl. I, 665.

Chapter 11

1. "Japan Buys 800,000 Acres to Start Colony in Peru," *New York Times*, 28 July 1919.

2. No. 313, to State Department, 7 November 1918, Japanese, English, Mexican Espionage, Confidential Correspondence, 1913–1924, File 20961-3164, RG 45, Office of Naval Intelligence (ONI), Box 21, National Archives of the United States, Washington, D.C. (hereafter cited as NAUS).

3. No. 25, German legation Chile to AA, 23 May 1919, T-149, Reel 377, Fr. 608–9, NAUS.

4. American Embassy, Secret, 14 May 1918, File 800B3, RG 59, Office of Counselor (OoC), Box 1, NAUS; American Embassy to London, Harrison to Bell, Confidential, Secret, 31 July 1918, File 800B3, RG 59, OoC, Box 1, NAUS; "Bolivian–Japanese Treaty Signed," *New York Times*, 15 February 1913, 6.

5. Tokyo to Secretary of State, 12 December 1919, M-1389, Reel 1, Fr. 102–5, 794.00/16, NAUS. This document contains information about all three previously mentioned treaties. The treaty with Paraguay became operative in August 1921.

6. No. 25, German legation Chile to AA, 23 May 1919.

7. Yasuo Wakatsuki and Iyo Kunimoto, *La Immigracion Japonesa en Bolivia* (Tokyo: Chuo University, 1985), 15; "Japanese in Bolivia," *New York Times*, 14 December 1919, 8.

8. Nobuya Tsuchida, "The Japanese in Brazil" (Ph.D. diss., University of California at Los Angeles, 1978), 177.

9. Daniela Carvalho, "Japan's Second World War Victory: An Analysis of the Reaction of the Japanese Immigrants in Brazil to Japanese Defeat," *Dialogos* 3 (December 2003): 2, available at http://www.dhi.uem.br/publicacoesdhi/dialogos/volume01/vol03_atg2. htm (accessed fall 2008).

10. Daniel M. Masterson, with Sayaka Funada-Classen, *The Japanese in Latin America* (Urbana: University of Illinois Press, 2004), 104.

11. Ibid., 90.

12. Ibid., 94.

13. Chief Naval, Chester Wells, Naval Attaché Madrid, 24 November 1919, and Box 586, Commander 15 Naval District, to Director of Navy Intelligence Bilbao, report written by G. T. Hew, Confidential, 3 January 1920, RG 38, Box 1392, NAUS.

14. File 10987-636-39, 17 July 1920, RG, Box 3829, NAUS; Secret memo, based on a statement of a prominent Japanese business man, 6 April 1920, Memorandum on Evidence of Japan's Preparation for War, M-1389, Reel 1, Fr. 128ff. and 161, NAUS.

15. Secret memo, based on a statement of a prominent Japanese business man, 6 April 1920.

16. Arms and Ammunition, An Comba 2586, Combat Munitions 65, 6 April 1920, RG 38, Box 586, NAUS.

17. C. Harvey Gardiner, *The Japanese and Peru 1873–1973* (Albuquerque: University of New Mexico Press, 1975), 45.

18. Colonel E. F. Ballesteros was the team's president. The team also included Lieutenant Colonels Lionel Lison and Hector Martinez and Majors Leonides Gonzales and Antonion L. Santisteban. Secret No. 840, London, 7 February 1919, Classified Case Files, Bell, Nos. 73D–85, and Bell to Lanier, Secret File 823.00/24a, Peru Political Folder 80, RG 59, Box 3, OoC, NAUS.

19. Gardiner, *The Japanese and Peru*, 45.

20. Carranza to Lic. Manuel Aguirre Berlanga, cited in U.S. Congress, Investigation of Mexican Affairs, Partial and Interim Report, Report of Senator Albert B. Fall to the Subcommittee of the Committee on Foreign Relations, Examination into Mexican Affairs, 66th Cong., 2nd sess., Washington, D.C., 9 December 1919, 8.

21. No. 493, in File C-10-j, 21 December 1919, Japanese Mexican Relations, File No. 12574, RG 38, Entry 98, Box 590, NAUS.

22. Report Van Natta, Madrid, renumbered as No. 244, 26 November 1919, RG 38, Entry 98, Box 1392, NAUS.

23. No. 250, Van Natta, War Department Office of the Chief of Staff, Military Intelligence Division (MID), Washington, D.C., Madrid, Telegram, 9 December 1919, Based on Letters signed by H. Medina, 3 and 5 November 1919, RG 38, Entry 98, Box 20, NAUS.

24. Ibid.

25. Roberto Guzmán Esparza, *Memorias de don Adolfo de la Huerta según su propio dictado* (Mexico City: Ediciones Guzmán, 1957), 178.

26. Ibid.

27. E. Kosterlitzky, Re: Mex Japn German Cooperative Secret Service, Cont., 29 June 1921, Confidential Correspondence, 1913–1924, File 20961-316A, Japanese English Mexican Espionage Ring, RG 38, Box 21, ONI, NAUS.

28. Kinta Arai, 2, J. C. Hall Papers, RG 45, NAUS.

29. Ibid., 6.

30. Am Mex to Secretary of State, Special green, for your secret information, Confidential, 4 December 1918, M-1276, Reel 3, Fr. 859–60, 710.11/7380, NAUS.

31. Letter No. 5, Riedel to Hall, Callao, December 1918, J. C. Hall Papers, RG 45, NAUS.

32. Berthold J. Sander-Nagashima, "Die Deutsch–Japanischen Marinebeziehungen 1919 bis 1942" (Ph.D. diss., Universitaet Hamburg, 1998), 144–45.

33. Ibid., 51.

34. Erich Pauer, "German Engineers in Japan: Japanese Engineers in Germany in the Interwar Period," in *Deutschland–Japan in der Zwischenkriegszeit*, ed. Josef Kreiner and Regine Mathias (Bonn: Bouvier Verlag, 1990), 295–96.

35. John W. M. Chapman, *Japan, Germany and International Political Economy of Intelligence* (Bonn: Bouvier Verlag, 1990), 39.

36. Ibid.; Sander-Nagashima, "Die Deutsch–Japanischen Marinebeziehungen," 63.

37. Sander-Nagashima, "Die Deutsch–Japanischen Marinebeziehungen," 68–69.

38. John W. M. Chapman, "Japan in German Aviation Policies of the Weimar Period," in *Japan und die Mittelmächte im Ersten Weltkrieg und in den Zwanziger Jahren*, ed. Josef Kreiner (Bonn: Bouvier Verlag Herbert Grundmann, 1986), 155–58.

39. Sadao Asada, "Japanese Admirals and the Politics of Naval Limitation: Kato Tomosaburo vs. Kato Kanji," in *Naval Warfare in the Twentieth Century 1900–1945: Essays in Honor of Arthur Marder*, ed. Gerald Jordan (New York: Crane Russak, 1977), 146.

40. Ibid., 147.

41. Ibid.

42. John W. M. Chapman cites No. 9, Memo or a conversation with Grand Admiral von Tirpitz, 8 November 1923, 170, MGFA, Freiburg, in "The Transfer of German Underwater Weapons Technology to Japan, 1919–1976," in *European Studies on Japan*, ed. Ian Nish and Charles Dunn (Kent: Paul Norbury Publications, 1979), 165–72.

43. U.S. Naval Attaché, Tokyo 1766-L-5, "Prof. Ando En route to Germany on behalf of Japan," RG 165, Box 548, NAUS, in Sander-Nagashima, "Die Deutsch–Japanischen Marinebeziehungen," 54n115; Pauer, "German Engineers in Japan," 296–306.

44. Sander-Nagashima, "Die Deutsch–Japanischen Marinebeziehungen," 58.

45. Ibid., 104.

46. Ibid., 68, 125.

47. Berthold J. Sander-Nagashima, "Naval Relations between Japan and Germany from the Late Nineteenth-Century until the End of World War II," in *Japanese–German Relations, 1895–1945: War, Diplomacy and Public Opinion*, ed. Christian W. Spang and Rolf-Harald Wippich (Abingdon, U.K.: Routledge, 2006), 40–59n10.

48. Sander-Nagashima, "Die Deutsch–Japanischen Marinebeziehungen," 62.

49. Pauer, "German Engineers in Japan," 296.

50. Sander-Nagashima, "Die Deutsch–Japanischen Marinebeziehungen," 60, 122.

51. Ibid., 55n116, citing Report No. 1766-L-3(2), Military Attaché U.S., 4 November 1919, Aktennotiz German and Japanese collusion regarding the delivery of arms and ammunition, RG 165, Box 548, NAUS.

52. Sander-Nagashima, "Die Deutsch–Japanischen Marinebeziehungen," 103.

53. Acknowledgments, in *Deutsche Wissenschaftliche Untersuchungen auf dem Gebiete der Chemie, Ausgeführt mit Unterstützung von Hajime Hoshi* (Leipzig: Verlag Chemie Leipzig und Berlin, 1924), v–vii.

54. Cited in Berthold J. Sander-Nagashima, "Tahira, Daihon' ei kaigunbu, Rengo Kantai, Kaisen made" (Ph.D. diss.), 333.

55. Ministry of Foreign Affairs, Mexico, Intercepted Letter, L. Bernaldez, 23 August 1919, RG 38, NAUS.
56. Van Natta to Washington, War Department, MID, 26 November 1919, RG 38, NAUS.
57. Memo to Bielaski, 19 April 1919, Treadway, 10130-83-10, RG 38, Box 2869, NAUS.
58. Aguilar to Arredondo, "Activities of the Mexican Government in Spain," 15 December 1919, RG 38, NAUS: the excerpt is from Aguilar to Arredondo, 7 July 1919.
59. L. Bernandez, 3 September 1919, RG 38, Entry 98, Box 1392, NAUS; Ministry of Foreign Affairs, Mexico, Intercepted Letter, L. Bernaldez, 23 August 1919.
60. No. 1948/103, Leopoldo Ortiz to SRE, 12 March 1918, 25 February 1919, RG 38, NAUS.
61. Chief Naval, L. Bernandez, 6 September 1919, RG 38, Entry 98, Box 1392, NAUS.
62. Ricardo Corzo Ramirez and Jose G. Gonzalez Sierra, *Nunca un Desleal: Candido Aguilar 1889–1960* (Mexico City: El Colegio de Mexico, Gobierno del Estado de Veracruz, 1986), 231–32.
63. Aguilar to Arredondo, "Activities of the Mexican Government in Spain," 15 December 1919: the excerpt is from Aguilar to Arredondo, 20 June 1919.
64. Ibid.: the excerpt is from Aguilar to Arredondo, 25 June 1919.
65. Enclosure, Letter 19-16B, Translation, Please telegraph Captain Wells the following, RG 38, Entry 98, NAUS.
66. Though he was officially representing Mexico at the Paris Peace Conference, Aguilar's real mission was to procure munitions for Mexico from Spain. An unconfirmed report stated that Aguilar's real mission was to block a papal envoy to offer $10,000,000 to Félix Díaz. It was alleged to be raised in the United States under the direction of Cardinal Gibbons. No sources could be found to corroborate this allegation. See Chief Navy, RG 38, Entry 98, Box 1392, NAUS.
67. Ministry of Foreign Affairs, Mexico, Intercepted Letter, L. Bernaldez to Arredondo, 5 September 1919, RG 38, Entry 98, NAUS.
68. No. 19-164-4, Chester Wells, Chief Naval 1392, Naval Attaché U.S. Embassy Madrid to Director of ONI, Washington, D.C., 8 October 1919, RG 38, NAUS; and No. 250, Van Natta, Madrid, Code Milstaff, Washington, D.C., 9 December 1919, Transmit to State and Navy Departments, 4, RG 38, NAUS. Military Attaché Trevino continued talks with Spain's minister of war but also ordinance officers of the Spanish army and private ammunition manufacturers. Also, Aguilar assigned an aide to focus on more procurement efforts.
69. Report No. 2020/103, 28 March 1919, RG 59, OoC, 812.00/54, NAUS.
70. 5 February 1919, RG 59, OoC, NAUS.
71. No. 1934/103, Information from Agent, Secret File, Letter from Agent, 21 February 1919, and Krumm-Heller to SRE, 12 April 1918, RG 59, OoC, 812.00/37, NAUS.
72. See the many arms deals at R 33399, Politisches Archiv des Auswaertigen Amts, Berlin (hereafter cited as PAAA). It also became fashionable in 1919 to use Mexico as an official destination even though the weapons went elsewhere.
73. Jacinto Díaz, 10–11, J. C. Hall Papers, RG 45, WP, NAUS.
74. Mexico shipment of arms via S.A., 21 February 1920, RG 38, Box 586, NAUS.
75. Ibid. The airplane and parts were shipped to Mexico and forwarded by Agent Abraham Lewisohn, 5 Ferdinand St., January 26–February, 1920. Papers from the Mexican legation Buenos Aires, Calle Peru 440, Copenhagen, No. 671, Washington, D.C., 17 January 1920, RG 38, ONI, Box 586, NAUS.
76. Mexico, AGN RP Oc. 104 A-A-73, exp. 2–6, cited in Ramirez and Gonzalez, *Nunca un Desleal*, 236.

77. Ramirez and Gonzalez, *Nunca un Desleal*, 236; and Mexico, AGN RP Oc. 104 A-A-73, exp. 2–6, in ibid.

78. Ramirez and Gonzalez, *Nunca un Desleal*, 237.

79. Ibid., 236.

80. Ibid., 238: "Esta podia ser la solucion al bloqueo Norte americano ya los nunca concretizados tratos con Alemania" was written by the authors, not Aguilar. And see AGN RP Oc. 104 A-A-73, exp. 2–6, in ibid., 236.

81. Ramirez and Gonzalez, *Nunca un Desleal*, 238; and No. 19-164-4, Chester Wells, Chief Naval 1392, Naval Attaché U.S. Embassy Madrid to Director of ONI, 8 October 1919.

82. Van Natta to Washington, 26 November 1919.

83. War Department Office of Chief of Staff to Captain Mc Namee, Cowles, 10 October 1921, File 10687-103, MI 4F, RG 165, MID, NAUS.

84. Carranza to Lic. Manuel Aguirre Berlanga, cited in U.S. Congress, Investigation of Mexican Affairs, Partial and Interim Report, Report of Senator Albert B. Fall to the Subcommittee of the Committee on Foreign Relations, Examination into Mexican Affairs, 66th Cong., 2nd sess., Washington, D.C., 9 December 1919, 7.

85. Charles H. Harris and Louis R. Sadler, *Texas Rangers and the Mexican Revolution* (Albuquerque: University of New Mexico Press, 2007), 482.

86. Carranza to Lic. Manuel Aguirre Berlanga, cited in U.S. Congress, Investigation of Mexican Affairs, Partial and Interim Report, Report of Senator Albert B. Fall to the Subcommittee of the Committee on Foreign Relations, Examination into Mexican Affairs, 66th Cong., 2nd sess., Washington, D.C., 9 December 1919, 7–8.

87. No. 250, Van Natta, Code Milstaff, 9 December 1919.

88. Chief, Van Natta, L. Bernandez, 3 September 1919, RG 38, Box 1392, NAUS.

89. Memorandum, Lt. Valentini, MID, 15 January 1920, Correspondence 1917–1941, File No. 10987-604, RG 165, Box 3829, NAUS. Urbina celebrated his Native American ancestry and took a provocative stance in Spain, where being white was paramount for public social standing. And see Report PN 1233, Military Attaché Madrid to Director of Military Intelligence, Washington, D.C., Secret, 5 April 1920, "Mexican Propaganda," Correspondence 1917–1941, File No. 10987-662, 10987-604-675, RG 165, Box 3829, MID, NAUS.

90. RG 165, Card File, and Chief Naval Gr, 12 December 1919, RG 38, Entry 98, Box 1392, NAUS.

91. Mid., 10987-665, Military Attaché Madrid to Van Deman, Secret, 19 April 1920, RG 165, Box 3829, NAUS. They were Don Antonio Basagoiti Artete, Julian Aragón y Aragón, Don Luis Ibañez, Don Santiago Sainz de la Calleja, and Don Oncin y Aragón. And see No. 250, Van Natta, Code Milstaff, 9 December 1919. Another source mentioned the unlikely sum of 750,000,000 pesetas to be raised in Spain.

92. Report No. 1233, Military Attaché Madrid to Director of Military Intelligence, 5 April 1920.

93. 22 March 1920, File 10987-604-675, and PN-1224, Military Attaché to Director of Military Intelligence, Federico Cesar Calvo, 22 March 1920, Correspondence, File 10987-660, RG 165, Box 3829, MID, NAUS.

94. Thomas Wesley Burkman, "Japan, the League of Nations and the New World Order" (Ph.D. diss., University of Michigan, 1975).

95. Ibid., 319.

96. Ibid., 321.

97. C. Díaz, 10, J. C. Hall Papers, RG 45, WP, NAUS; Mex Shipment of arms in B.A., 21 February 1920, RG 38, Box 586, NAUS.

98. J. C. Hall, 32, J. C. Hall Papers, RG 45, WP, NAUS.

99. Jacinto Díaz, 4–6.

100. Ibid., 4; and Ochoa, J. C. Hall Papers, RG 45, WP, NAUS.

101. The Bureau of Intelligence had also stumbled on zur Helle earlier. See C. C. Crowley, Old German Files, 8000-383, Bureau of Intelligence, Washington, D.C. (hereafter cited as BI).

102. Other People, Dr. Wagner, J. C. Hall Papers, RG 45, WP, NAUS.

103. Am Mex to Secretary of State, Special green, for your secret information, 4 December 1918; and Hurtado, 7–9, J. C. Hall Papers, RG 45, WP, NAUS.

104. Hall, 21; Simon Aldoa, Details of other men, 11, J. C. Hall Papers, RG 45, WP, NAUS; Kinta Arai, 8.

105. Letter No. 6, Riedel to Hall, Santiago, 1 March 1919, J. C. Hall Papers, RG 45, WP, NAUS.

106. Letter No. 3, Riedel to Hall, Chile, 11–13, 3 April 1919, J. C. Hall Papers, RG 45, WP, NAUS.

107. Letter No. 6, Riedel to Hall, 1 March 1919.

108. Summerlin to Mexico City to Secretary of State, 23 April 1919, M-514, Reel 3, Fr. 1043, NAUS; U.S. Mex to Secretary of State, M-1276, Reel 3, Fr. 1044, NAUS. In Mexico City, the next day, a small group went to the U.S. embassy and expressed their opposition to Carranza's stance.

109. No. 1065, McMillan to Secretary of State, 29 April 1919, 710.11/396; McMillan to Secretary of State, Lima, 2 May 1919, Fr. 1067, 710.11/398; 9 May 1919, Fr. 1079, 710.11/402; and Fr. 1052, 710.11/7394—all in M-1276, Reel 3, NAUS. Ramirez and Gonzalez, *Nunca un Desleal*, 234. His son-in-law, Cándido Aguilar, repeated the same message to the readers of the *New York Times* on August 7, 1919.

110. 19 June 1919, M-1276, Reel 3, Fr. 1079, 710.11/410, NAUS; M-1276, Reel 3, Fr. 1121–22, NAUS. Also Mexican general Máximo Rosales traveled on the same boat and departed in San Salvador.

111. No. 2073/103, Information from Agent, Secret File, 25 April 1919, American embassy London, Peace Conference League of Nations, Classified Case Files, Bell, Nos. 59–73c, Box 2, RG 59, OoC, 821.00/10, NAUS.

112. Diary, Hallet Johnson to Assistant Chief of Latin American Division, Personal and Strictly Confidential, 16 May 1919, M-514, Reel 3, Fr. 521, NAUS.

113. Ibid., Fr. 521, 562, 579–80.

114. Ibid., Fr. 579–80.

115. Ibid., 4 and 22 August 1919, M-1276, Fr. 586.

116. Ibid., M-514.

117. Ibid., Fr. 598–99.

118. Ibid., 18 August, Fr. 600.

119. John Bassett Moore, "The Pan American Financial Conferences and the Inter-American High Commission," *American Journal of International Law* 14, no. 3 (July 1920): 343–55.

120. Heinrich Julius von Eckardt, Unpublished Memoir, Erinnerungen, Manuscript Collection, 258, PAAA.

121. Von Geukel, 3, J. C. Hall Papers, RG 45, WP, NAUS.

122. Rep. 218, No. 853, unsigned, but because of detailed specific statements in the report obviously written by Jahnke, Hauptbericht, June/July 1918–19, October 1919, 1, Nachlass Kapp, Dahlem, Hauptarchiv Abt VI., Geheimes Preussisches Staatsarchiv, Berlin.

123. Ibid., 6.

124. No. 526, Madrid Basewitz to AA, Secret Encoding, 7 September 1919, T-149, Reel 377, Fr. 871, NAUS.

125. No. 7, "Akten betreffend Beziehung Mexicos to Nordamerika," PAAA, in Hsi-Huey Liang, *The Sino-German Connection: Alexander von Falkenhausen between China and Germany, 1900–1941* (Assen: Van Gorcum, 1978), 116n5.

126. Reinhard R. Doerries, ed., *Diplomaten und Agenten: Nachrichtendienste in der Geschichte der Deutsche–Amerikanischen Beziehungen* (Heidelberg: C. Winter, 2001), 42–43.

127. Rep. 218, No. 853, unsigned [Jahnke], June/July 1918–19, October 1919, 12.

128. John B. Duff, "The Italians," in *The Immigrant Influence on Wilson's Peace Policies*, ed. Joseph P. O'Grady (Lexington: University of Kentucky Press, 1967), 119–21.

129. Ibid., 135.

130. J. C. Hall Papers, RG 45, WP, NAUS; "Advocates Latin Ties," *New York Times*, 24 January 1920, 10.

131. Hall, 21.

132. Jacinto Díaz, 12.

133. No. 752, Palacio Nacional to President Wilson, 14 December 1919, M-1276, Reel 4, Fr. 85, NAUS.

134. No. 1881, Goodwin Confidential to SS, 14 January 1920, M-1276, Reel 4, Fr. 50, 710.117/426, NAUS; and Tel. No. 2720, 31 December 1919, M-1276, Reel 4, 710.11/422, NAUS.

135. RTU U 47, Chapultepec Press, Mexico, 15 January 1920, Correspondence 1917–1941, radio messages, File 1098-604, RG 165, Box 3829, MID, NAUS.

136. Form League of Latin, File 10987-640-60, RG 165, MID, NAUS.

137. No. 1149, 20 April 1920, M-514, Reel 3, Fr. 657, 835.00/201, NAUS.

138. Subject League of Nations, 18 February 1920, Correspondence, File 10987-649, RG 165, Box 3829, MID, NAUS; War Department telegram to Military Attaché Embassy Rome, Italy, 7 February 1920, File 10987-640-14, RG 165, Box 3829, MID, NAUS.

139. No. 2, HQ Southern Department Fort Sam Houston, Woodruff to Mexican Affairs, 20 February 1920, File 10987-640-8, RG 165, Box 3829, NAUS.

140. A leading figure there was Dr. Jose Leon Suárez. See Leg. 393, Letter Boix, AGA 54/4181, located at Rivadivia 1906, UT 6894, Archivo General de la Administración, Alcalá de Henares.

141. League of Latins, 4, J. C. Hall Papers, RG 45, WP, NAUS.

142. Ibid., 6. Then Jorge Ancizar was appointed consul general to Colombia on February 25, 1920, with the backing of Foreign Minister Pueyrredón and President Irigoyen. By February 1920 the Ateneo Hispano Americano received an invitation to help the Venezuelan organization. In December 1919 in Caracas, Venezuela, the Union Libertadora Venezoalana was organized.

143. Ibid., 9.

144. Ibid., 10–11.

145. Hall, 24–25.

146. J. C. Hall Papers, RG 45, WP, NAUS. Hall wrote in April 1920 that Markovich had been invited to a conference of anti-U.S. espionage agents. Atilio Brambilla also worked for

Robert von Geukel. Alfredo Vitale remained de Marchi's principle agent. He had been born in Triest, Italy, and was thirty-eight years old.

147. 3 March 1920, M-1276, Fr. 61, NAUS.
148. No. 1887, Report of an Observer, From Spain, 29 August 1921, Hispano American relations, Correspondence 1917–1941, File 10987-640, RG 165, Box 3829, MID, NAUS.
149. Von Geukel, 206; and Hall, 33.
150. Ramirez and Gonzalez, *Nunca un Desleal*, 242.
151. Richard Lewinsohn (Morus), *Die Umschichtung der Europäischen Vermögen* (Berlin: S. Fischer, 1926), 333–36; and J Engl, Mex, Agent 256, to ONI, New Orleans, 29 October 1921, Confidential Correspondence, 1913–1924, File 20961-3164, RG 165, ONI, Box 21, NAUS.
152. Guzmán writes, "Era casi un convenio que no llevaria a una allianza" (*Memorias de Don Adolfo de la Huerta*), 178.
153. E. Kosterlitzky, Re: Mex Japn German Cooperation Secret Service, Cont., 29 June 1921.
154. RM 20/1635, Folder Page 310, AII G Stbs No. 584/36, gez. AIIc, 6 August 1926, Bundesarchiv, Freiburg (hereafter cited as BA-Freiburg).
155. Order to Jahnke, May 1919, T-120, NAUS; and RM 6/483 and PG 75148, File Page 16, Abwicklung Etappe, Las Palmas, Teneriffa, BA-Freiburg.
156. RM6/475, Etappenangelegenheit, Allgemein, zu B 1307 III, Aag., 16 October 1920, BA-Freiburg.
157. See zur Helle's File at RM5/2208, Fiche 8, BA-Freiburg.
158. Piorkowski had been recognized by the Bureau of Intelligence, but his importance had been missed. Report, H. W. Grunewald, 9 September 1918, Old German Files, 8000-23113, BI.
159. RM 6/477 and PG 75143, File Page 5, Abwicklung der Etappen New York und San Francisco, BA-Freiburg.
160. Boyd-Ed, Hamburg, File Page 29, to Admiral Staff, Berlin W10, 20 September 1920, BA-Freiburg.
161. Ibid., IIb 5A03/15, File Page 20. His cover had been his work as general Pacific coast agent, including San Francisco, for the North German Lloyd.
162. RM 6/485, File Pages 14–15, 6 March 1922; RM 6/485, File Pages 15–16; and RM 6/481, 1922—all in BA-Freiburg.
163. RM 6/479, PG 75144, Letter No. G315, File Page 5, Abwicklung Etappe Havanna, BA-Freiburg.
164. RM 6/480, PG 75145, File Page 56, Etappe, Buenos Aires, Abwicklung, BA-Freiburg. Moeller also confirmed the existence of zur Helle in the file.
165. Doerries, *Diplomaten und Agenten*, 42–43.

Chapter 12

1. League of Latins, 10–15, J. C. Hall Papers, RG 45, WP, National Archives of the United States, Washington, D.C. (NAUS).
2. Daniel Antokoletz, *La Liga de las Naciones y la Primera Asamblea de Ginebra* (Buenos Aires: n.p., 1921), 69–86.
3. Ibid., 85–86.
4. Ibid., 93.

5. See, for example, Jürgen Schaefer, *Deutsche Militärhilfe in Suedamerika. Militaer- und Rüstungsinteressen in Argentinien, Bolivien und Chile vor 1914* (Düsseldorf: Bertelsmann Universitaetsverlag, 1974).

6. No. 1359, Embassy to Secretary of State, Rio de Janeiro, M-514, Fr. 59, 835.34/361, NAUS.

7. Stimson to Secretary of State, 3 May 1918, M-514, Fr. 45, 835.34/356, NAUS.

8. The British observed that it constituted "a small, but already rather outdated navy" (British, 100, Doc. 67, in *British Documents on Foreign Affairs: Reports and Papers from the Foreign Office Confidential Print. Part II, Series D: Latin America 1914–1939, vol. 3: 1920–1924,* ed. George Philip [Bethesda, Md.: University Publications of America, 1989–92], see 13–14).

9. Betrifft: Argentinien-Stinnes, Aufzeichnung Offermann, 12 September 1922, 0902, T3, Firmen Archiv Junkers (FAJ), Deutsches Museum, Munich (hereafter cited as DMM).

10. Manuscript Collection N 173/12, Bundesarchiv, Freiburg (hereafter cited as BA-Freiburg).

11. Bjoern Forsen and Anette Forsen, "German Secret Submarine Efforts, 1919–1935," in *Girding for Battle: The Arms Trade in Global Perspective, 1815–1940,* ed. Donald Stoker Jr. and Jonathan A. Grant (Westport, Conn.: Praeger, 2003), 114–15.

12. Ibid.

13. No. 13, Telegram No. 107, Vertraulich A. Pauli. An das Auswaertige Amt., 16 March 1923, R 33400, Buenos Aires, Politisches Archiv des Auswaertigen Amts, Berlin (hereafter cited as PAAA).

14. Letter Kretschmar, Confidential, 16 December 1929, RH 2/2947, 43, BA-Freiburg.

15. 3 December 1923, M-514, Reel 3, Fr. 309, 3238, NAUS.

16. Letter to Secretary of State, 15 February 1922, M-514, Reel 18, 835.34/368, NAUS.

17. Forsen and Forsen, "German Secret Submarine Efforts."

18. Letter Kretschmar, 16 December 1929: "war bis zum Abschluss vorbereitet."

19. Ferdinand Ferber and Adolf Rohrbach, *Pioniere der Luftfahrt Hugo Junkers,* Deutsche Luft und Raumfahrt Mitteilung No. 74-15 (Cologne: Deusche Gesellschaft fuer Luft und Raumfahrt, 1974), 22–23.

20. Abschrift letter, Wiedenfeldt to Wirth, repeated in Wirth to Bohlen und Halbach, Lucerne, 10 June 1921, T-120, Reel 317, Fr. 479597, NAUS.

21. Allison Winthrop Saville, "The Development of the German U-Boat Arm, 1919–1935" (Ph.D. diss., University of Washington, 1963), 61.

22. Ibid., 62.

23. Ibid., 61.

24. Saville, "The Development of the German U-Boat Arm," 61.

25. No. 2732, B.A. to Secretary of State, 13 June 1922, M-514, Reel 18, Fr. 494, 835.3453, NAUS.

26. No. 2579, Executive Decree Authorizing Purchase of Auxiliary Vessels in Germany, U.S. Consul to Secretary of State, 17 February 1922, M-514, Reel 18, Fr. 101–2, 835.34/369, NAUS. The ships were renamed *Meta, Margarita,* and *Mecha.* They protected Argentine ports as mine hunters M_5, M_9, and M_{10}. In 1925, the M_{10} was converted into President Alvear's presidential yacht. For 1923 the purchase of German minesweepers M_{74}, M_{101}, and M_{105} was planned.

27. Subject ARG, Confidential Activity of Jacinto Díaz, RG 38, Ser. No. 129, File No. 10987-677, NAUS.

28. Smith to Admiral Lowrey, WD Office Chief of Staff, 21 July, File No. C 12574, C-10-J, Mexican Japanese Cooperation, File 10687-103, MI 4F, RG 38, Box 590, NAUS.

29. E. Kosterlitzky, 29 June 1921, Confidential Correspondence, 1913–1924, RG 38, Office of Naval Intelligence (ONI), NAUS. In June, Mexican general Kosterlitzky agreed that, most likely, President Obregón was not shying away from using Japanese agents. Also Mexican brigadier general Salvador J. Yokohama arrived in the United States on September 18, 1921. Three days later he was interviewed about Japanese–Mexican cooperation. He was the third source to admit that Mexican civilian and military intelligence services were both employing Japanese individuals as agents. He evaluated the performance of Japanese agents as slow but reliable.

30. War Department Office of Chief of Staff, to Captain Mc Namee, Cowles, 10 October 1921, and letter, 27 April 1921, File 10687-103, MI 4F, RG 165, Military Intelligence Division, NAUS.

31. Matthew Smith to Rear Admiral Long, Director of Naval Intelligence, 27 April 1921, RG 38, NAUS.

32. Agent 266, Naval Intelligence Anti-American Activities in Panama, 14 October 1921, Confidential Correspondence, 1913–1924, File 20961-3164, Japanese English, Mexican Espionage, New Orleans, Box 21, RG 38, ONI, NAUS.

33. Agent 256 to Director of Naval Intelligence, Anti-American activities in Panama plus exhibits, October 1921, Confidential Correspondence, 1913–1924, File 20961-316 A, Japanese English, Mexican Espionage, New Orleans, Box 21, RG 38, ONI, NAUS.

34. INO. Mc Namee to Mr. Means, Op 16-b, 7 November 1921, Confidential Correspondence, Box 21, and Mc Namee &, November 1921, File 20961-316, Box 21, RG 38, ONI, NAUS.

35. Sadao Asada, "Japanese Admirals and the Politics of Naval Limitation: Kato Tomosaburo vs. Kato Kanji," in *Naval Warfare in the Twentieth Century, 1900–1945: Essays in Honor of Arthur Marder*, ed. Gerald Jordan (New York: Crane Russak, 1977), 147.

36. Berthold J. Sander-Nagashima, "Naval Relations between Japan and Germany from the Late Nineteenth-Century until the End of World War II," in *Japanese–German Relations, 1895–1945: War, Diplomacy and Public Opinion*, ed. Christian W. Spang and Rolf-Harald Wippich (Abingdon, U.K.: Routledge, 2006), 40–59n10.

37. Berthold J. Sander-Nagashima, "Die Deutsch–Japanischen Marinebeziehungen 1919 bis 1942" (Ph.D. diss., Universitaet Hamburg, 1998), 120.

38. Ibid., 65.

39. Ibid., 79.

40. Report of U.S. Military Attaché, Tokyo, 1766-L-23 (1), 1 February 1921, RG 165, Box 548, NAUS, cited in Sander-Nagashima, "Naval Relations between Japan and Germany from the Late Nineteenth-Century until the End of World War II," 59n9.

41. Sander-Nagashima, "Die Deutsch–Japanischen Marinebeziehungen 1919 bis 1942," 79.

42. Ibid., 170, based on Marineleitung AII 9000, 27 August 1921, BA-Freiburg.

43. Brief an FA Junkers Flugzeugwerk, Dessau, 20 June 1920, 0902, T02, FAJ, DMM; and R. E. G. Davies, *Airlines of Latin America since 1919* (Washington, D.C.: Smithsonian Institute Press, 1984), 543. Auszug Zeitschrift *Flugsport*, No. 4, 18 February 1920, 0902, T02, FAJ, DMM.

44. Brief an FA Junkers Flugzeugwerk, 20 June 1920.

45. Unverbindliche Besprechung ueber das Projekt Argentinien am Januar 17, 1920, 0902, T02, FAJ, DMM.

46. "Besprechung am 15 December, 1919," 19 December 1919, Dessau, 0902, T01, FAJ, DMM.

47. Betrifft Argentinien-Meckel, 21 April 1920, 0902, T02, FAJ, DMM.

48. Brief, 6 May 1919, 0401, T03, FAJ, DMM.

49. Betrifft Fernflug, 12 May 1919, 0401, T13, FAJ, DMM.

50. Se/Kle, Protokoll, 6 May 1919, 0401, T13, FAJ, DMM.

51. Betrifft Fernflug, 12 May 1919, 0401, T13, FAJ, DMM.

52. Protokoll Betrifft Fernflug, 17 May 1919, 0401, T13, FAJ, DMM.

53. Memo, 6 May 1919, 0401, T13, FAJ, DMM.

54. Mie-W, Betrifft Fernflug, Dessau, 12 May 1919, 0401, T13, FAJ, DMM.

55. Jürgen Heideking, *Aeropag der Diplomaten: Die Pariser Botschafterkonferenz der alliierten Hauptmächte und die Probleme der europäischen Politik 1920–1931* (Husum, Germany: Historische Studien Matthiesen Verlag, 1979).

56. There were engine failures, and the manufacturing of the airplane hardware was shoddy.

57. Fritz Hammer to Director, 14 August 1920, Online Collection F 13, http://www.juf13.de/land/esa/esaD15.html (accessed 2006).

58. Ibid.

59. One year later, Wagenfuehr quit government work and began to work for Stinnes. Aktennotiz von Seitz, Betrifft Argentinien 1920, 20 February 1920, 0902, T2, FAJ, DMM.

60. Seitz to Junkers, 20 January 1920, 0902, T2, FAJ, DMM.

61. "Besprechung am 15. Dezember, 1919," 19 December 1919; and Marine, 27 April 1920, R 33400, II F M Militaer, PAAA.

62. Betrifft Argentinien-Meckel, 21 April 1920, ; Brief an Erich Offermann, 4 May 1920, Buenos Aires, 0902, T2, FAJ, DMM.

63. Allgemeiner Bericht ueber Verhaeltnis in Argentinien, 20 October 1920, 0902, T2, FAJ, DMM.

64. No. 50281, Vertrieb Argentinien, Besuch Herrn Breuler, 15 December 1919, 0902, T2, FAJ, DMM.

65. Auszuege aus einem Privatschreiben des Herrn Karl Hoffman, 6 March 1920, 0902, T1, FAJ, DMM.

66. Brief to Geheimrat Offermann, 16 November 1920, 0902, T2, FAJ, DMM; and Vertraulich "Nur fuer persoenlichen Gebrauch," Schwebende Absatzmoeglichkeiten fuer Flugzeuge in Argentinien und hierzu beachtende Punkte. Junkerswerke Hauptbuero Dessau, Aus dem Herrn Stahl mitgegebenen Unterlagen, 18 April 1923 (original date of writing 1 November 1922), 0902, T4, FAJ, DMM. The latter was written before the expedition took off.

67. Brief C. Offermann an Dessau, 19 June 1920, 0902, T2, FAJ, DMM.

68. Niederschrift, 26 April 1921, 0902, T2, FAJ, DMM. Faupel defined his task: "Meine Hauptaufgabe war dort den franzoesischen Einfluss einzuschwaechen und die deutsche Ideologie zu kraeftigen."

69. Vortragsunterlagen, und kurze Angaben zu den Diapositiven fuer Vortragsreise, Oberst Faupel, Dessau, 3 May 1921, 0902, T3, FAJ, DMM.

70. Firma Junkers Flugzeugwerk, Betrifft, Argentinische Marine Besprechung mit Direktor Hormel aus Warnemuende am 19. und 20. 9. 1921, 0902, T3, FAJ, DMM.

71. Ferber and Rohrbach, *Pioniere der Luftfahrt Hugo Junkers*, 22–23.

72. Brief Schleising an Hugo Stinnes AG fuer Seeschiffahrt and Ueberseehandel, 26 September 1921, 0902, T3, FAJ, DMM.

Chapter 13

1. Cited in "Los Intentos Chiles por reflotar la politica de ABC en la Decada de 1920," in *Historia General de las Relaciones Exteriores de la República Argentina*, University of CEMA, available at http://www.cema.edu.ar (accessed May 20, 2006).

2. Ibid.

3. 8 March and 16 April 1923, Reel 3, National Archives of the United States, Washington, D.C. (hereafter cited as NAUS). However, until Argentina and Brazil agreed to join the Chilean disarmament proposal, Chile would maintain a silent but powerful insistent push for armed forces growth. A comparison of South American navy budgets revealed that Chile's remained larger than those of Brazil and Argentina.

4. Notes on the work of the third committee (reduction of armaments) at the third assembly of the League of Nations, 21 October 1922, FO 371/8319, Great Britain, cited in Gerard Silverlock, "British Disarmament Policy and the Rome Naval Conference, 1924," *War in History* 10, no. 2 (2003): 191.

5. Argentina, Embassy Despatch No. 130, 11 October 1922, and *La Prensa*, Buenos Aires, 1 October 1922, M-514, Reel 3, NAUS.

6. A 152, 57/51, Doc. 48, 12 December 1922, in *British Documents on Foreign Affairs: Reports and Papers from the Foreign Office Confidential Print. Part II, Series D: Latin America 1914–1939, vol. 3: 1920–1924*, ed. George Philip (Bethesda, Md.: University Publications of America, 1989–92; hereafter cited as *British Docs*).

7. A 172/172/57, Doc. 49, 6 December 1922, *British Docs*.

8. A 152, 57/51, Doc. 48, 12 December 1922.

9. Memo for Commander 3rd Naval District, Confidential, 12 May 1923, RG 38, Entry 82, Box 20, Op. 16-B, NAUS. There were also tender Japanese–Argentine military contacts. A Mr. T. Vanna and H. Yoko had connections in Argentine government offices and were visited by Argentine military men.

10. No. 25, Memo for Commander 3rd Naval District, Anti-American Activities, Ingersoll, Attaché Report, L-34 Information Extracts from latest reports, Confidential, 27 February 1923, RG 38, Entry 82, Box 20, NAUS.

11. Another spelling is Fleiss.

12. No. G 13, No. 107, A. Pauli to AA, 16 March 1923, R 33400; and Durchdruck to AA, Confidential, Buenos Aires, 16 March 1923—both in Politisches Archiv des Auswaertigen Amts, Berlin (hereafter cited as PAAA).

13. Collin Webster, *Argentine Mauser Rifles* (Atglen, Pa.: Schiffer: Military History, 2003), 210.

14. M-514, Reel 3, Fr. 337, NAUS.

15. Report no. unreadable, 19 January 1923, M-514, Reel 3, NAUS.

16. Report by A. C. Grant-Duff, 19 April 1923, A 3041/172/51, Doc. 74, *British Docs*.

17. Ibid.

18. Thomas Schoonover, *The French in Central America: Culture and Commerce, 1820–1930* (Wilmington, Del.: Scholarly Resources, 2000), 172.

19. No. 3159, Argentina, For Information Digest, 24 May 1923, M-514, Reel 3, Fr. 199–200, NAUS.

20. German Ambassador Pauli to AA, Vertraulich, Buenos Aires, 23 May 1923, R 33400, J No. 6804, K.N. 191, PAAA.

21. Ibid.; No. G 13, No. 107, A. Pauli to AA, 16 March 1923; Durchdruck to AA, 16 March 1923.

22. Buenos Aires to Berlin, 23 May 1923, R 33400, II F 1671/23, J No. 6804, PAAA.

23. Espionage Ring 1923, RG 38, NAUS; B.A. MA reports 2755, 5 May 1922, M-514, Reel 3, NAUS; Argentina, Private Letter to Dieckhoff, Valparaiso, 30 August 1923, T-120, German Foreign Archive, Washington Embassy Collection, NAUS.

24. No. 2026/26, "Die Finanzlage Argentiniens," Freiherr von Reisvitz to AA, 27 October 1926, T-290, Reel 5, Fr. 121–38, NAUS.

25. No. 845, Letter to John W. Riddle, U.S. Ambassador Buenos Aires, and Report 3176, 1 July 1923, M-514, Reel 3, Fr. 156, 835.34/383a, NAUS.

26. No. 12, "Argentina, Letters Intercepted and Late Reports on A. Gerchunoff, Kazama, Terunobo Tamaki, Massagora Yamada, Martin Brito, T. Gourley," 11 January 1924, RG 38, Entry 82, Box 20, NAUS.

27. Hiroyuki Agawa, *The Reluctant Admiral: Yamamoto and the Imperial Navy* (Tokyo: Kodansha International Ltd., 1979), 73.

28. Proposed Reorganization of the Argentine Army, 6 June and 9 May 1923, M-514, Reel 3, Fr. 192–94, NAUS.

29. Webster, *Argentine Mauser Rifles*, 210.

30. No. 2026/26, "Die Finanzlage Argentiniens," Freiherr von Reisvitz to AA, 27 October 1926.

31. Argentina, Private Letter to Dieckhoff, 30 August 1923.

32. Unfortunately, excellent studies by Stanley Hilton are largely forgotten. See Stanley H. Hilton, "The Armed Forces and Industrialists in Modern Brazil: The Drive for Military Autonomy (1889–1954)," *Hispanic American Historical Review* 62, no. 4 (November 1982): 629–73.

33. "Los Intentos Chiles por reflotar la politica de ABC en la Decada de 1920."

34. Silverlock, "British Disarmament Policy and the Rome Naval Conference," 188–89.

35. Roskil, "An Appreciation of the Rome Naval Meeting," NBKR 4X/68, cited in ibid., 205.

Chapter 14

1. A significant portion of the following pages is based on the excellent research in Luca de Caprariis, "Fascism for Export? The Rise and Eclipse of the Fasci Italiani all'Estero," *Journal of Contemporary History* 35, no. 2 (April 2000): 151–83; and Philip V. Cannistraro, *Blackshirts in Little Italy: Italian Americans and Fascism 1921–1929* (West Lafayette, Ind.: Bordighera Press, 1999). There was no time or funds to travel to Italy and begin to work through the archives. I acknowledge my intellectual debt to their groundbreaking work.

2. John F. Murphy Jr., "Michael Collins and the Craft of Intelligence," *International Journal of Intelligence and Counterintelligence* 17, no. 2 (2004): 347. Unfortunately Murphy cites no specific source.

3. De Caprariis, "Fascism for Export?" 153.

4. Klaus-Peter Hoepke, *Die Deutsche Rechte und der Italienische Faschismus* (Düsseldorf: Droste, 1968), 267.

5. R. J. B. Bosworth, *Mussolini* (Oxford: Oxford University Press, 2002), 181.

6. De Caprariis, "Fascism for Export?" 155.

7. Bosworth, *Mussolini*, 181.

8. De Caprariis, "Fascism for Export?" 166.

9. Cannistraro, *Blackshirts in Little Italy*, 37.

10. De Caprariis, "Fascism for Export?" 165.

11. Bosworth, *Mussolini*, 181–82.

12. De Caprariis, "Fascism for Export?" 166.

13. Bosworth, *Mussolini*, 191–99.

14. Stefan Troebst, *Mussolini, Makedonien und die Mächte, 1922–1930* (Cologne: Böhlau, 1987), 144.

15. Ronald C. Newton, "Ducini, Prominenti, Antifascisti: Italian Fascism and the Italo-Argentine Collectivity, 1922–1945," *The Americas* 51, no. 1 (July 1994): 49.

16. E. Gentile, "L'emigracione italiana in Argentina nella politica d'espansione del naziolnalismo e del fascism," *Storia Contemporane* 17 (June 1986): 355–96, at 389–93, in de Caprariis, "Fascism for Export?" 158; and Newton, "Ducini, Prominenti, Antifascisti," 46.

17. *La Prensa* (Buenos Aires), 26 July 1924.

18. Based on *L'emigracione Italiana negli anni 1924–1925* (Rome: Commissariato Generale all'Emigrazione, 1926), 265.

19. Cannistraro, *Blackshirts in Little Italy*, 40.

20. Ibid., 30.

21. Ibid., 29.

22. Ibid., 32.

23. Ibid., 35.

24. Ibid., 23.

25. De Caprariis, "Fascism for Export?" 155.

26. Cannistraro, *Blackshirts in Little Italy*, 42.

27. Official communiqué by the PNF Il Gran Consiglio nei primi dieci anni dell era fascista, in de Caprariis, "Fascism for Export?" 166.

28. Cannistraro, *Blackshirts in Little Italy*, 43–44.

29. De Caprariis, "Fascism for Export?" 156.

30. No. 33, Politica, 9 February 1923, 54/9179, Archivo General de la Administración, Alcalá de Henares.

31. Ibid.; *La Prensa*, 17 May, 18 May, 21 June, and 26 July 1924.

32. Javier Tussell and Ismael Saz, "Primo de Rivera and Mussolini," *Boletín de la Real Academia de la Historia* 179, no. 3 (September–December 1982): 429.

33. Ibid., 431.

34. *La Prensa*, 10 May 1924.

35. Ibid., 15 May 1924.

36. Jeffery M. Dorwart, *Conflict of Duty: The U.S. Navy's Intelligence Dilemma, 1919–1945* (Annapolis: U.S. Navy Institute, 1983), 103n10; *La Prensa*, 10 May 1924.

37. *La Prensa*, 15 May 1924.

38. Dorwart, *Conflict of Duty*, 103n10.

39. De Caprariis, "Fascism for Export?" 165.

40. Raffael Schreck, "Politics of Illusion: Tirpitz and Right Wing Putschism, 1922–1924," *German Studies Review* 18, no. 1 (February 1995): 29–49.

41. Ibid., 38.

42. Ibid., 47.

43. Ibid., 38.

44. Schreck cites von Boetticher recalling the meeting in his unpublished memoirs "So War Es" located in the Military Archive, 183–85, Bundesarchiv, Freiburg (hereafter cited as BA-Freiburg).

45. Kurt Doss, *Das Deutsche Auswaertige Amt im Uebergang vom Kaiserreich zur Weimarer Republik: Die Schuelersche Reform* (Düsseldorf: Droste Verlag, 1977), 96–97.

46. See Juergen Buchenau, *Tools of Progress: A German Merchant Family in Mexico* (Albuquerque: University of New Mexico Press, 2004).

47. Doss, *Das Deutsche Auswaertige Amt im Uebergang vom Kaiserreich zur Weimarer Republik*, 94.

48. Ibid., 96. The owner of Germany's leading shipping company Ballin himself complained that unrestricted submarine warfare did not pay attention to merchant needs. In his case the Berlin government reimbursed him for ships lost due to submarine warfare.

49. Ibid., 108

50. Juergen Kloosterhuis, *Friedliche Imperialisten Deutsche Auslandsvereine und auswaertige Kulturpolitik, 1906–1918* (Frankfurt: Peter Lang Verlag, 1994), 212–13.

51. Stadt Stuttgart, *Stuttgart im Dritten Reich: Voelkische Radikale in Stuttgart. Zur Vorgeschichte und Fruehphase der NSDAP 1890–1925* (Stuttgart: Stadt Stuttgart, 1982), 45.

52. The Political Archive of the German Foreign Ministry just published a superb new guide about German political ethnic affairs documents that will shed new light on many events across the world.

53. Norbert Krekeler, *Revisionsanspruch und Geheime Ostpolitik der Weimarer Republik. Die Subventionierung der deutschen Minderheiten in Polen* (Stuttgart: DVA, 1973), 18–19.

54. Ibid., 21.

55. Ibid., 23; and Entwicklung und Stand der Elsass-Lothringischen Heimatbewegung, T-120, Reel 2277, Fr. E 134055-66, National Archives of the United States, Washington, D.C. (hereafter cited as NAUS).

56. Krekeler, *Revisionsanspruch und Geheime Ostpolitik der Weimarer Republik*, 34.

57. H. Grothe, "Schicksal und Entwicklung des Auslandsdeutschtums im letzten Jahrzehnt, insbesonderer seit dem Weltkrieg," in *Jahrbuch des VDA*, 1/1922 (Berlin: VDA, 1921). Grothe argued that the goal was the creation of a greater Germany and the creation of a bloc of unity in middle Europe.

58. Michael Fahlbusch, *Wo der Deutsche . . . . . . ist, ist Deutschland: Die Stiftung fuer Deutsche Volks und Kulturbodenforschung in Leipzig, 1920–1933* (Bochum: Universitaetsverlag Dr. N. Brockmeyer, 1994), 187.

59. Kurt G. W. Luedecke, *I Knew Hitler* (New York: Charles Scribner, 1937), 190, 194–97.

60. Ibid., 205.

61. Krekeler, *Revisionsanspruch und Geheime Ostpolitik der Weimarer Republik*, 71.

62. Kulturpropaganda Abt, Deutschtum, Dr. Treut, Zu VI A 1015, 1 July 1922, gez Pollow, Politisches Archiv des Auswaertigen Amts, Berlin.

63. Report, N 173/14, BA-Freiburg. Behnke was accompanied by an aide-de-camp of Minister of Defense Gessler. The visit remains unexplored in detail. Chapman mentions that the purpose of the trip was signing contracts with companies manufacturing for the German navy. Rahn mentions this trip only in regard to Behnke's talk with Soviet foreign minister Chicherin and talks with the Chinese government. Another alleged task was to explore whether the German cruiser *Hamburg* could stop in Shanghai on its future world tour. In Japan Behnke must have visited the same facilities and individuals as Canaris in 1924.

64. Stefan Rinke, *"Der letzte freie Kontinent": Deutsche Lateinamerikapolitik im Zeichen transnationaler Beziehungen, 1918–1933*, Historamericana Bd. 1 (Stuttgart: Heinz Verlag, 1996), 189–90.

65. Ibid., 191.

66. B. McBeth, *Juan Vincente Gómez and the Oil Companies in Venezuela, 1908–1935* (Cambridge: Cambridge University Press, 1983). This is based on the documents

Department of State 831.6363/195, 21 February 1924, and Chad to the Secretary of State, 6 May 1924 (ibid., 101).

67. Ibid., 100.
68. Hans von Kiesling, *Soldat in drei Weltteilen* (Leipzig: Grethlein und Co., 1935), 20.
69. Ibid., 420–21.
70. Ibid., 421.
71. Ibid., 435.
72. Letter No. 1307 III. Ang., RM 6/487, BA-Freiburg.
73. Abschrift, VA WA II n 5280 II, Berlin, 23 November 1925, RM 20/1635, BA-Freiburg.
74. Oberst W. Nicolai, *Geheime Maechte: Internationale Spionage und ihre Bekaempfung im Weltkrieg und Heute* (Leipzig: R. F. Koehler, 1923), 184.
75. Letter, Office Chief, be 28, Berlin, 17 June 1924, Folder Page Nos. 94–96, RM 21/164, BA-Freiburg.
76. Uber Amtschef B bei A I, from B.S., 17 June 1924, File Page Nos. 94–96, RM 21/164, BA-Freiburg.
77. Zu A.I.c. 6197, Abschrift, and Letter from AIIh, 5 October 1923, File Page Nos. 84–85, RM 20/988, BA-Freiburg.
78. Doc. No. 64, Office of Navy Leadership, Leipzig, to Captain Lieutenant Mewis, Navy Leadership of the Sea Department in Berlin, Secret, 17 April 1925, Folder Page Nos. 151–50; letter to Mr. Seiffert, Berlin, 28 August 1925, Folder Page No. 127; and Doc. No. 262, letter to Gayer, 29 April 1925, Folder Page No. 112—all in RM 21/186, BA-Freiburg.
79. No. 30/206G KD OS, Top Secret, Reports for October, November, December 1925, RW 5/V7 00, BA-Freiburg.
80. No. 146, Letter to Richter, no signature, 10 March 1925, Folder Page No. 42, RM 21/183, BA-Freiburg.
81. RM 21/187, BA-Freiburg.
82. NL zu AII Gstb No. 575/25IV, Folder Page No. 444, RM 20/1635, BA-Freiburg.
83. 10 November 1925, Folder Page No. 229, RM 20/1635, BA-Freiburg.
84. Anlage zu AII Gstb No. 575/25IV, Folder Page No. 444, RM 20/1635, BA-Freiburg.
85. 10 November 1925, Folder Page No. 229.
86. Abschrift, VA WA II n 5280 II, Aktenvermerk Vortrag Chef Marineleitung about Questions of BE VM System, Berlin, 23 November 1925, Folder Page No. 221, RM 20/1635, BA-Freiburg.
87. F. N. Krivitsky, *I Was Stalin's Agent* (New York: Right Book Club, 1940), 47. From the very beginning it housed a disintegration component. Werner Rakos, alias Felix Wolf, headed the Intelligence Department of the Central Committee and its military apparatus until being relieved in 1924.
88. Harvey Klehr, *The Secret World of American Communism* (New Haven: Yale University Press, 1995), 20.
89. The following pieces of the documents are all in "Targets, Sources," KV2/982, 1, Public Records Office, National Archives of the United Kingdom, London (hereafter cited as PRO).
90. Soviet Intelligence Cooperation before 1927, KV2/501, PRO.
91. Appendix A, KV2/982, 1, PRO.
92. Hammer's Allied American corporation established close liaison with Arcos in the UK and in New York, KV2, Finance, 2, PRO.
93. Klehr, *The Secret World of American Communism*, 25.
94. "Targets, Sources," KV2/982, 1, PRO.

95. Reiner Tosstorff, *Profintern: Die Rote Gewerkschaftsinternationale 1920–1937* (Paderborn, Germany: Ferdinand Schoeningh, 2005), 291.
96. Klehr, *The Secret World of American Communism*, 26–27.
97. James G. Ryan, *Earl Browder: The Failure of American Communism* (Tuscaloosa: University of Alabama Press, 1997), 25–27; Philip Jay Jaffe, *The Rise and Fall of American Communism* (New York: Horizon Press, 1975), 193.
98. Geoffrey Payne, *The Spanish Civil War, the Soviet Union and Communism* (New Haven: Yale University Press, 1925), 14–15.
99. No. A 832, Doc. No. 3, Bolshevism in Argentina, Chile and Other S.A. Countries, Confidential, Various 1919, File C-10-j 12588, RG 38, Entry 98, Box 590, NAUS.
100. Ibid.
101. Ibid. Probably the name Martins should be spelled Martens.
102. No. A 832, Doc. No. 3, Report of Abramson, member of the Central Executive Committee of the All-Russian Communist Party, sent by the representatives of the Russian Socialist Federated Soviet Republics in the U.S. to the republics of S.America, Bolshevism in Argentina, Chile and Other S.A. Countries, Confidential, Various 1919, File C-10-j 12588, RG 38, Entry 98, Box 590, NAUS.
103. George D. Jackson Jr., *Comintern and Peasant in Eastern Europe 1919–1930* (New York: Columbia University Press, 1966), 70.
104. Solmaz Rustamova-Tohidi, "First Congress of the Peoples of the East: Aims, Tasks, Results," in *Centre and Periphery: The History of the Comintern in the Light of New Documents*, ed. M. Narinsky and J. Rojahn (Amsterdam: International Institute of Social History, 1996), 74–80.
105. Samaren Roy, *The Twice-Born Heretic: M. N. Roy and the Comintern* (Calcutta: Firma KLM Private Ltd., 1986), 240, appendix 3.
106. Ibid., 241, appendix 3.
107. Zinoniev, cited as FO/S. 1288, 24 March 1924, KV2/501, PRO.
108. Christopher M. Andrew, *Her Majesty's Secret Service* (London: Viking, 1985), 302.
109. Ibid., 304.
110. Ibid., 324.
111. Cited as SZ/1251 CX 2750, 10 September 1924, KV2/501, PRO.
112. Roy, *The Twice-Born Heretic*, 241, appendix 3.
113. Zinoniev, cited as SZ/1434, 25 March 1924, KV2/501, PRO.
114. Daniela Spenser, *El Triángulo Imposible: México, Rusia Sovietica y Estado Unidos en los años Veinte* (Mexico City: CIESAS, 1998), 70; and Barry Carr, *Marxism and Communism in 20th Century Mexico* (Norman: University of Nebraska Press, 1992).
115. Spenser, *El Triángulo Imposible*, 100.
116. Ibid., 102.
117. Ibid., 101.
118. Ibid., 104.
119. Ibid., 101.
120. Ibid.
121. Cited as CX 3969, KV2/501, PRO.
122. Vadim A. Staklo, "Harnessing Revolution: The Communist International in Central America, 1929–1935" (Ph.D. diss., University of Pittsburgh, 2001), 35; and SZ 1251 CX 3969, 30 September 1925, KV2/501, PRO.
123. Cited as SZ 4380, 10 February 1925, KV2/501, PRO. It was published in the *Daily Telegraph* on February 10, 1925, as part of an article about the Soviet Union and Egypt.

124. Cited as SZ 1251, 20 October 1925, KV2/501, PRO.
125. Translation of Confidential Letter, Valparaiso, Branch 8994, RG 38, NAUS.
126. MFR. to Sakoda, the Pacific Trade Co., Translation, Valparaiso, 2 May 1924, RG 38, Box 20, Entry 82, NAUS.
127. Translation of C. Rueda to K. Sakada, Buenos Aires, 18 April 1924, RG 38, Box 20, Entry 82, NAUS.
128. Translation of G, to MFR, by Shibahara, 13 May 1924, RG 38, Box 20, Entry 82, NAUS.
129. Translation Enclosure F, Agents PT Co. Inf., Manuel Fernandez Rueda, 31 July 1924, Serial No. 366, Report to L-34, RG 38, Box 20, Entry 82, NAUS.
130. Memo for Justice Mr. Burn Subject Espionage Activities, Ingersoll, 15 June 1923, RG 38, Entry 92, Box 20, Op. 16-B, NAUS.
131. No. 12, "Argentina, Letters Intercepted and Late Reports on Alberto Gerchunoff, Kazama, Terunobo Tamaki, Massagora Yamada, Martin Brito, Thomas Gourley," 11 January 1924, RG 38, Entry 82, Box 20, NAUS.
132. WGP-JRB "Japanese Activities," 1 February 1924, RG 38, Entry 82, Box 20, NAUS.
133. No. 12, "Argentina, Letters Intercepted and Late Reports on Alberto Gerchunoff, Kazama, Terunobo Tamaki, Massagora Yamada, Martin Brito, Thomas Gourley," 11 January 1924.
134. No. 25, Memo for Commander 3rd Naval District, Anti-American Activities, Ingersoll, Attaché Report, L-34 Information Extracts from Latest Report, Confidential, 27 February 1923, RG 38, Entry 82, Box 20, NAUS.
135. Valparaiso Branch 8984, Pacific Trading Co. Very esteemed agents (special or P. Agent No. MFR), 18 April 1924, RG 38, Entry 19, Box 20, NAUS.
136. Ibid.
137. Ibid.
138. No. 25, Memo for Commander 3rd Naval District, 27 February 1923.
139. No. 100, Argentina, Report of L-34, Confidential, 23 May 1923, RG 38, Entry 82, Box 20, NAUS.
140. No. 12, "Argentina, Letters intercepted and late reports on Alberto Gerchunoff, Kazama, Terunobo Tamaki, Massagora Yamada, Martin Brito, Thomas Gourley," 11 January 1924.
141. No. 25, Memo for Commander 3rd Naval District, , 27 February 1923.
142. Resume of latest reports submitted by L-34, Confidential, 27 February 1923, Serial No. 42, RG 38, Entry 82, Box 20, NAUS.
143. Memo for Justice Report on trip of A. M. Kashiwa, 11 May 1923, RG 38, Entry 82, Box 20, Op. 16-B, NAUS.
144. No. 12, "Argentina, Letters intercepted and late reports on Alberto Gerchunoff, Kazama, Terunobo Tamaki, Massagora Yamada, Martin Brito, Thomas Gourley," 11 January 1924.
145. Translation of J, Important, 28 May 1924, RG 38, Entry 82, Box 20, NAUS.
146. Translation of D, to Mr. Shidahara from Rueda, 26 August 1924, RG 38, Entry 82, Box 20, NAUS.
147. Translation of J, Important, 28 May 1924.
148. Report by Agent No. 65, Translation B, Confidential, 19 April 1924, RG 38, Entry 82, Box 20, NAUS.
149. Buenos Aires Report, 2 February 1924, RG 38, Entry 82, Box 20, NAUS.
150. Ibid.

151. Translation of B., Buenos Aires, Rueda to Bustamente, Hotel Le Marquis, New York, 16 April 1924, RG 38, Entry 82, Box 20, NAUS.

152. Reports L-34, 21 October 1924, Serial No. 396, RG 38, Box 20, Entry 82, NAUS.

153. Nobuya Tsuchida, "The Japanese in Brazil" (Ph.D. diss., University of California at Los Angeles, 1978), 177.

154. Ibid.

155. It would take until 1927 to become enacted.

156. C. Harvey Gardiner, *The Japanese and Peru 1873–1973* (Albuquerque: University of New Mexico Press, 1975), 45.

157. Roberto Guzmán Esparza, *Memorias de don Adolfo de la Huerta según su propio dictado* (Mexico City: Ediciones Guzmán, 1957), 179.

158. Mc Namee to Memo Commander 3rd Naval District, L-34 reports on return from Panama, Confidential, Buenos Aires, 3 January 1923, RG 38, Box 20, Op. 16-yb, NAUS.

159. Translation–DG, interview with the chief of the Japanese mission which arrived last night, will Mitsui, Confidential Correspondence, 1913–24, File 20963-1806, RG 38, Office of Naval Intelligence, NAUS.

160. Brian S. McBeth, "Foreign Support for Venezuelan Political Exiles during the Regime of Juan V. Gómez: The Case of México, 1923–33," *The Historian* 69, no. 2 (Summer 2007): 275–304.

161. Grant K. Goodman and Felix Moos, *The U.S. and Japan in the Western Pacific: Micronesia and Papua New Guinea* (Boulder: Westview Press, 1981).

162. Allison Winthrop Saville, "The Development of the German U-Boat Arm, 1919–1935" (Ph.D. diss., University of Washington, 1963), 83.

163. Ibid., 84.

164. Based on Canarisbericht, Folder 540, BA-Freiburg; Berthold J. Sander-Nagashima, "Die Deutsch–Japanischen Marinebeziehungen 1919 bis 1942" (Ph.D. diss., Universitaet Hamburg, 1998), 106n229. Due to the delicacy of the matter, important parts of the agreement were not put down in written form but kept orally. They are, however, mentioned in Bericht des Korvettenkapitaen Canaris ueber die Reise nach Japan, Vom 17.5 bis 30.9.1924, undated, B. No. A II 500/24 Geheim, Stabssache, RM 20/1635, BA-Freiburg, cited in Berthold J. Sander-Nagashima, "Naval Relations between Japan and Germany from the Late Nineteenth-Century until the End of World War II," in *Japanese–German Relations, 1895–1945: War, Diplomacy and Public Opinion*, ed. Christian W. Spang and Rolf-Harald Wippich (Abingdon, U.K.: Routledge, 2006), 59n11.

165. John W. M. Chapman, "The Transfer of German Underwater Weapons Technology to Japan, 1919–1976," in *European Studies on Japan*, ed. Ian Nish and Charles Dunn (Kent: Paul Norbury Publications, 1979), 169.

166. Schinzinger and Hack to Marineleitung, KL Steffan, 13 June, J No. 1369, H/Z, RM 20/1638, Folder 7, BA-Freiburg.

167. Erich Pauer, "German Engineers in Japan: Japanese Engineers in Germany in the Interwar Period," in *Deutschland–Japan in der Zwischenkriegszeit*, ed. Josef Kreiner and Regine Mathias (Bonn: Bouvier Verlag, 1990), 296.

168. Ibid., 296n19, based on the 1957 manuscript from Yamanaka Saburo, in the Kawasaki Jukogyo KK archive in Kobe.

169. Sander-Nagashima, "Die Deutsch–Japanischen Marinebeziehungen 1919 bis 1942," 144–45.

170. Pauer, "German Engineers in Japan," 299–300.

171. Ibid., 301.

172. Chapman, "The Transfer of German Underwater Weapons Technology to Japan," 171.
173. Sander-Nagashima, "Die Deutsch–Japanischen Marinebeziehungen 1919 bis 1942," 46.
174. Ibid., 157.
175. Ibid., 156.
176. Ibid., 149.
177. Ibid., 151–53.
178. Ibid., 155. Canaris's last week in Japan was spent at other yards visiting ships at the navy station Yokosuka. Also there were meetings the former naval attaché Knorr.
179. Ibid., 162.
180. Ibid., 163.
181. Chapman, "The Transfer of German Underwater Weapons Technology to Japan," 171.
182. Saville, "The Development of the German U-Boat Arm," 103.
183. Dr. Peter von Bauer to Junkers, Vertraulich, 2 January 1921, 0907, T2, Firmen Archiv Junkers, Deutsches Museum, Munich.
184. Rinke, "Der letzte freie Kontinent," 689.
185. R. E. G. Davies, History of the World's Airlines (Oxford: Oxford University Press, 1983), 320.

Chapter 15

1. Spanish Foreign Ministry to Spanish Embassy in Argentina, 25 February 1918, Colleción Embassy Argentina, and M. G. Hontoria to Sen Presidente del Consejo de Ministros, 26 June 1919, Paquete 2826, Archivo Histórico de la Secretaria de la Relaciones Exteriores, Madrid; New York Times, 19 June 1918 and 22 December 1918, 3.
2. Aclaraciones Al Estuto del Congreso, 54/9178, Leg. 379, Archivo General de la Administración, Alcalá de Henares (hereafter cited as AGA).
3. Alfonso XIII, Caja 12.424, Exp. 20 1919, Patrimonio Nacional, Archivo de los Reyes, Madrid (hereafter cited PNRA).
4. No. 8, Leg. 1166, 1919, Madrid, No. 45, PNRA.
5. Gerie B. Bledsoe, "Spanish Foreign Policy, 1898–1936," in Spain in the 20th Century, Essays on Spanish Diplomacy, 1898–1978, ed. James W. Cortada (Westport, Conn.: Greenwood Press, 1980).
6. Ibid., 194. Nevertheless, primary Spanish concern remained the question of Morocco and the International Zone of Tangier. Hispano-Americanismo remained in third place.
7. Luis C. Alén Lascano, Pueyrredón, el Mensajero de un Destino (Buenos Aires: n.p., 1951), 84.
8. Hispano American relations, Report of an Observer, From Spain No. 1887, 29 August 1921, Correspondence 1917–1941, File 10987-640, RG 165, Military Intelligence Division, Box 3829, National Archives of the United States, Washington, D.C.
9. Annual Report Venezuela, 38, Annual Report Chile, 1921, in British Documents on Foreign Affairs: Reports and Papers from the Foreign Office Confidential Print. Part II, Series D: Latin America 1914–1939, vol. 3: 1920–1924, ed. George Philip (Bethesda, Md.: University Publications of America, 1989–92).
10. Bledsoe, "Spanish Foreign Policy," 189.
11. Ibid., 189–91.
12. Daniel R. Headrick, The Invisible Weapon: Telecommunications and International Politics, 1851–1945 (Oxford: Oxford University Press, 1991), 187; and the telegrams in

London, Piscator to Admirals, My 1854, 25 July 1918, ADM 223/758, Public Records Office, National Archives of the United Kingdom, London.

13. U.S. Congress, Hearing, Doc. Arms Delivery to Mexico, 1924.

14. Ibid., 66.

15. Jose Maria de Manrique and Lucas Molina Franco, *Antes que Sadam: Las armas de destrucción masiva y la protección civil en España, 1924–2000* (Valladolid: Edición Propia, 2003). I am grateful to Señor Manrique for his kind support.

16. Margit Szöellöesi-Janze, *Fritz Haber, 1868–1934: Eine Biographie* (Munich: Verlag C. H. Beck, 1998).

17. Ibid., 66.

18. Manrique and Molina, *Antes que Sadam*.

19. In 2006 Euros.

20. Besprechung mit Major Steffen, Signature unreadable, Vertraulich, Dessau, 15 September 1921, Deutsches Museum, Munich (hereafter cited as DMM).

21. *La Nación* (Buenos Aires), 12 November 1922, 54/9178, Leg. 379, AGA.

22. No. C-2, Ministerio de Estado, 25 February 1924, 54/9181, Leg. 398, AGA.

23. Memo and Royal decree Junta Nacional del Comercio Español en Ultramar, 30 July 1922, 54/9178, Leg. 379, AGA.

24. Circular No. 783, 5 July 1923, 54/9178, Leg. 379, AGA.

25. La Población Española en Buenos Aires, 16 May 1921, end 3 October 1923, 54/9196, Leg. 454, AGA.

26. Ministro de Estado, Commerce section, telegram No. 14 to ambassador in Argentina, 22 August 1922, 54/9178, Leg. 379, AGA.

27. Bledsoe, "Spanish Foreign Policy," 196.

28. Linea Aerea Sevilla–Buenos Aires, 1922, letter to Torres, no author, 20 July 1922, Caja 15589, Exp. No. 4, PNRA.

29. Viaje del Presidente electo de 1 Re. Argentina Sr. Alvear a Santander, August 1922, Caja 12440, Exp. O, PNRA.

30. Chief of Diplomatic Cabinet to Amposta, 2 and 5 December 1922, 54/9233, AGA.

31. Chief diplomatic cabinet to Amposta, 3 February 1923, 54/9233, AGA.

32. No. 155, 15 June 1922, 54/9178, Leg. 379, AGA.

33. Spanish Embassy in Buenos Aires to Madrid, 22 December 1922, 54/9178, Leg. 379, AGA.

34. Ibero-American exposition, Seville, 54/9178, Leg. 379, AGA.

35. Boix to Ambassador Amposta, 3 February 1923, 54/9178, Leg. No. 379, AGA.

36. Mr. Emilio Boix, General instructions to the delegates of the organizing committee of the first national Congress of Spanish overseas commerce, 54/9178, Leg. No. 379, AGA.

37. Commerce section, national Council of Spanish overseas commerce, 16 January 1924, 54/1924, Leg. 398, AGA.

38. La Población Española en Buenos Aires, 16 May 1921, end 3 October 1923.

39. No. 3, Political department, Undersecretary to Ambassador, 21 May 1923, 54/9179, Leg. 383, AGA.

40. Ibid.

41. Request Boix to Muslera, 22 January 1918, Primo de Rivera, No. 10, Ministerio de Marina, Relacion de Commissiones Para El Extranjero, Fondo CC, Archivo Histórico Nacional, Madrid (hereafter cited as AHN).

42. Letter Consejo Superior de Camaras de Comercio Industria y Navigacion, Primo de Rivera, No. 10, Ministerio de Marina, Relacion de Commissiones Para El Extranjero, Fo.CC., AHN.

43. Comercio, 54/9192, Leg. 438, AGA.

44. Javier Tussell and Ismael Saz, "Primo de Rivera and Mussolini," *Boletín de la Real Academia de la Historia* 179, no. 3 (September–December 1982): 429.

45. Ibid., 429–30.

46. Ibid., 431–34.

47. Alfonso Ballestero, *Juan Antonio Suanzes, 1891–1977: La Política Industrial de la Postguerra* (León, Spain: LID Editorial Empresarial, 1993), 49. By 1933, this amount would be reduced to 3 percent.

48. Ibid., 48.

49. Ibid., 34.

50. Ibid., 49.

51. Ibid., 39.

52. Report about Rolland Visit Dessau, 1922, DMM.

53. Bericht ueber die Besprechung mit Herrn Baron v. Rolland, on 3 to 5 May 1922, 0621, T1, Firmen Archiv Junkers (FAJ), DMM.

54. Junkers Werke Hauptbuero to Junkers Direktion Sachsenberg, "Betr. Rolland," 17 May 1922, 0621, T1, FAJ, DMM. Rolland also introduced a fifty-year-old Irishman named Bellingham. He seemed interested in an Irish–German air service but left the impression of a lack of trust.

55. Niederschrift eber die am 8 Mai 1923, abends zu Berlin im Hotel Esplanade stattgefundene discussion about fabrication in Spain, 8 May 1923, 0621, T1, FAJ, DMM.

56. Reisebericht, Direktor Sachsenberg eber Reise nach Spanien in der Zeit vom 15 Juni bis 1 Juli 1923, 0621, T1, FAJ, DMM.

57. Niederschrift einer Besprechung ueber Spanien bei der Firma Breest und Co., Berlin, 4 May 1923, 0621, T1, FAJ, DMM.

58. Bericht ueber den Stand der Verhandlungen Savamay Madrid ueber Fabrikationsaufnahme in Spanien, Dessau, Ziebig, 25 January 1924, 0621, T1, FAJ, DMM.

59. No. 10, B2/W Vertriebsbericht, Betriebssystem Spanien, 22 October 1925, Ju 0621-T1, FAJ, DMM.

60. Auszug Vertriebsbericht No. 10, Eingang 23.10, Hauptbuero Dr. Kr. Betrifft Spanien, 0621, T1, FAJ, DMM; No. 10, B2/W Vertriebsbericht, Betriebssystem Spanien, 22 October 1925.

61. No. 10, B2/W Vertriebsbericht, Betriebssystem Spanien, 22 October 1925, 3.

62. Betr. Abnahme J 20, 22 March 1924, 0621, T1, FAJ, DMM.

63. Niederschrift, Besuch des ARG Konsuls Herrn Diana, Dessau, 24 April 1924, 0902, T4, FAJ, DMM.

64. Ibid.

65. An die Direktion der Junkers Flugwerkzeuge, Betrifft Argentinien, 23 April 1924, 0902, T4, FAJ, DMM.

66. Fol. 1-724, File 1, Fr. 45, 16 August 1925, 5, NL 22/36, Bundesarchiv, Koblenz (hereafter cited as BA-Koblenz).

67. 61, NL 22/36, BA-Koblenz.

68. Piegl, Fiche one 2, NL 22/36, BA-Koblenz.

69. Folder 724, Fiche f1, Fr. 33, NL 22/36, BA-Koblenz.

70. Adolf Vogt, *Oberst Max Bauer: Generalstabsoffizier im Zwielicht, 1869–1929* (Osnabrück: Biblio Verlag, 1974), 408. The book treats the topic selectively and superficially.

71. Fiche 1, 2 Piegl, NL 22/36, BA-Koblenz.

72. Piegl to Bauer, September 1925, Fr. 55, and Fr. 142, NL 22/36, BA-Koblenz.

73. Enrique Fricke to Lohmann, 11 January 1925, Folder Page 196, RM 21/183, Bundesarchiv, Freiburg.

74. Cartagena Fricke to Lohmann, 11 January 1925, File Page No. 196, RM 21/183; and Fricke to Lohmann, 11 January 1925, O.S. 196, RM 21/164—both in Bundesarchiv, Freiburg.

75. Allison Winthrop Saville, "The Development of the German U-Boat Arm, 1919–1935" (Ph.D. diss., University of Washington, 1963), 114–15.

76. Ibid., 102.

77. Ibid., 114.

78. Ibid., 124.

79. Frederick B. Pike, *Hispanismo, 1898–1936: Spanish Conservatives and Liberals and Their Relations with Spanish America* (Notre Dame: University of Notre Dame Press, 1971), 248.

Chapter 16

1. Javier Tussell and Ismael Saz, "Primo de Rivera and Mussolini," *Boletín de la Real Academia de la Historia* 179, no. 3 (September–December 1982): 443.

2. Allison Winthrop Saville, "The Development of the German U-Boat Arm, 1919–1935" (Ph.D. diss., University of Washington, 1963), 123.

3. Chief diplomatic cabinet to Amposta, 3 February 1923, 54/9233, Archivo General de la Administración, Alcalá de Henares (hereafter cited as AGA).

4. Tussell and Saz, "Primo de Rivera and Mussolini," 442.

5. Morath to Canaris, Mexico, 19 March 1926, File Page No. 7184, RM 21/190, Bundesarchiv, Freiburg (hereafter cited as BA-Freiburg).

6. Morath to Loesche, 19 March 1926, File Page No. 89, RM 21/190, BA-Freiburg. In Mexico one company was Lever and Lassman, which represented Krupp. It employed an engineer who previously had worked in Monterrey. Morath suggested that Mexico should invite Director Loesche to travel to Mexico.

7. Morath to Lohmann, 15 December 1925, File Page Nos. 219–21, RM 21/189, BA-Freiburg.

8. No. 48, U.S. Embassy, Buenos Aires, 14 January 1925, and No. 681, to Secretary of State, 20 April 1925, M-514, Reel 18, Fr. 497, 835.345/5, National Archives of the United States, Washington, D.C. (hereafter cited as NAUS). In April 1925, the Argentine navy also purchased eight airplanes from the U.S. Ruff Daland Company. The planes were expected to be finished in five months.

9. Manuscript Collection Bauer, Abschrift, P. 3, Fiche 1, 4 June 1925, NL 22/36, Bundesarchiv, Koblenz (hereafter cited as BA-Koblenz).

10. No. 3553, Military Attaché Dusenbury, Report on Current Event, 19 November 1925, M-514, Reel 1, Fr. 318–19, NAUS.

11. Adolf Vogt, *Oberst Max Bauer: Generalstabsoffizier im Zwielicht, 1869–1929* (Osnabrück: Biblio Verlag, 1974), 414.

12. Ibid., 415. He would enlist in particular the help of factories in Oerlikon, Switzerland, and Nordhausen, Germany.

13. AII Gkdo., 785/26, Aufzeichung Unterredung Geheimrat Bosnick, of AA, mit Korv. Kapitaen Reiner, 5 October 1926, File Page No. 351, RM 20/1635, BA-Freiburg.
14. Letter No. 922, Lohmann to Gayer, 1 November 1926, Page No. 229, RM 21/191, BA-Freiburg.
15. Berthold J. Sander-Nagashima, "Die Deutsch–Japanischen Marinebeziehungen 1919 bis 1942" (Ph.D. diss., Universitaet Hamburg, 1998), 177n379. See letter Reimer in Auftrag Zenkers to Saalwaechter, 19 April 1926, Fol. 288, RM 20/1635, BA-Freiburg.
16. Carlos Sáiz Cidoncha, *Aviación Republicana: Historia de las Fuerzas Aereas de la Republica Española 1931–1939* (Madrid: Almena Edicones, 2006), 35.
17. Premier Ibero-American Congress Aeronautico, 1925, Sec. Part., Caja 15.672, Exp. 25, Patrimonio Nacional, Archivo de los Reyes, Madrid.
18. Yanguas to Ambassador, 26 February 1926, 54/9191, AGA.
19. 16 January 1926, 54/9191, Leg. 432, AGA. Mr. Wiest, a Dornier representative, was also in Buenos Aires. Chief engineer Mr. Hauser was also present at Belgrano.
20. Letter to Danvila, 22 January 1926, 54/9191, Leg. 432, AGA.
21. 22 January 1926, 54/9196, Leg. 454, AGA.
22. Royal Order No. 30, 7 January 1926, 54/9196, AGA.
23. Letter Spanish Popular Commission to embassy, 3 February 1926, 54/9191, Leg. 432, AGA.
24. Telegrams, 3 to 12 February 1926, 54/9193, Leg. 439, AGA.
25. Correspondencia particular, 1926, 54/9191, Leg. 432, AGA.
26. Fiche 2, Fr. 109, NL 22/36, BA-Koblenz.
27. Ibid.
28. Fiche 2, Fr. 142, NL 22/36, BA-Koblenz. Don Ferdinand wanted to know if Argentina was able to create weapons or war gas. Bauer said its capacity was currently nonexistent.
29. Fiche 2, Fr. 155–57, NL 22/36, BA-Koblenz. Bauer also revealed how difficult it was to establish Junkers's airline business inside Spain. He complained that it had taken 1.5 years to establish good connections in Spain. He again asked Piegl to court General Vigon and Marquez.
30. Fiche 2, Fr. 168, NL 22/36, BA-Koblenz.
31. Aktennotiz Besprechung zwischen Dr. Bauer und Dr. Buescher, Dienstag, 16 March 1926, 0621, T2, Firmen Archiv Junkers (FAJ), Deutsches Museum, Munich (hereafter cited as DMM).
32. Fiche 2, Fr. 167, NL 22/36, BA-Koblenz.
33. Aktennotiz Besprechung zwischen Dr. Bauer und Dr. Buescher, 16 March 1926.
34. Denkschrift ueber Transatlantik-Luftverkehr, Ausfuehrungen zu A, Ausfuehrungen zu B, 0401, T13, FAJ, DMM.
35. Aktennotiz Besprechung zwischen Dr. Bauer und Dr. Buescher, 16 March 1926.
36. Ministry of State to Spanish Ambassador, 24 February 1926, 54/9190, Leg. 427, AGA.
37. Booklet, Madrid, 10 April 1926, 54/9233, AGA.
38. Telegram to Chief of Palace, 11 March 1926, 54/9193, Leg. 439, AGA.
39. Letter No. 40, Embassy Buenos Aires to Madrid, 24 March 1926, 54/9190, Leg. 427, AGA.
40. Letter No. 235, Boix to Ministry of State, 22 December 1926, 54/9192, Leg. 438, AGA.
41. Telegramas Salidas, 24 February 1926, 54/9193, Leg. 439, AGA.
42. March 1926, 54/9191, Leg. 432, AGA.
43. Doc. No. 53, Ministry of State, America, Muy Reservado, Yanguas to Ambassador, 3 March 1926, 54/193, Leg. 439, AGA.

44. Ibid.

45. "Recepción Hispanoamericana en el Ministerio de Estado," Exp. 54/9190, AGA.

46. Ministry of State, section 2, American politics and Spanish cultural relations, reserved Report No. 11, Edmund Matteo to the Spanish ambassador in Buenos Aires, 2 July 1926, 54/9193, Leg. 439, AGA.

47. Telegram, Yanguas to Embassy Buenos Aires, 14 June 1926, 54/9190, Leg. 427, AGA.

48. Telegram No. 12, 21 June 1926, 54/9188, Leg. 468, AGA.

49. Telegrams, 22 June, 23 August, 21 September, and 6 October 1926, 54/9188, Leg. 468, AGA.

50. Telegram No. 84, 3 September 1926, 54/9198, Leg. 468, AGA.

51. Letter No. C-A.7, Edmund Matteo to Spanish Ambassador in Buenos Aires, Ministry of State, American Politics and Cultural Relations, 23 June 1926, 54/9198, AGA.

52. "Rumor that Spain Will Not Attend," *New York Times*, 7 June 1926, 4.

53. Tussell and Saz, "Primo de Rivera and Mussolini," 443.

54. "Germany's Entry Assured," *New York Times*, 5 September 1926, 1.

55. "Spanish Cabinet Decides to Resign from the League," *New York Times*, 8 September 1926, 1.

56. Tussell and Saz, "Primo de Rivera and Mussolini," 440.

57. Ibid., 443.

58. Ibid., 441–45. The first exploration of a deeper Spanish–Italian relationship had taken place on the ministerial level. In spring 1926 Spain's Minister of Work Eduardo Aunos traveled to Italy to study fascist social legislation. Later Mussolini would argue that this visit made Primo de Rivera's Spain the first nation to recognize the fascist revolution. The Duce talked the linkage up, mentioning Italy, Spain, Hungary, Bulgaria, and Greece abandoning authoritarian parliamentary systems.

Chapter 17

1. G2 report combat efficiency and value, 13 March 1925, M-514, Reel 3, Fr. 492, National Archives of the United States, Washington, D.C. (hereafter cited as NAUS).

2. Collin Webster, *Argentine Mauser Rifles* (Atglen, Pa.: Schiffer: Military History, 2003), 210.

3. No. 87, Danvila to Foreign Ministry, 28 May 1926, Embajada Buenos Aires, Paquete 1358, Archivo Histórico de la Secretaria de la Relaciones Exteriores, Madrid (hereafter cited as SRE).

4. Tel. No. 43, 5 March 1926, 54/9193, Leg. 439, Archivo General de la Administración, Alcalá de Henares (hereafter cited as AGA).

5. Jeffery M. Dorwart, *Conflict of Duty: The U.S. Navy's Intelligence Dilemma, 1919–1945* (Annapolis: U.S. Navy Institute, 1983), 104, based on ONIGC, Box 230, 101n12.

6. Tel. No. 53, Yanguas to Buenos Aires, 25 May 1926, 54/9233, a G-8, SRE.

7. Tel. No. 53, Foreign Ministry to Embassy Buenos Aires, Yanguas to Davila, Embajada Buenos Aires, Paquete 1358, SRE; IIG8, 27 February 1926, R 33400, Politisches Archiv des Auswaertigen Amts, Berlin (hereafter cited as PAAA). Efforts intensified further, as the Brazilians had also sent a purchasing commission to Paris under the leadership of General Leite De Castro.

8. A No. 4939 No. 1562, German Embassy Paris, Secret to the Foreign Ministry Rolland, GSM 33/4716, Fr. L 478049–52, Public Records Office, National Archives of the United Kingdom, London.

9. Bauer to Piegl, Diary, pp. 383–94, 16 July 1926, NL 22/36, Bundesarchiv, Koblenz (hereafter cited as BA-Koblenz).

10. Telefongespraech zwischen Prof. Js und Sago am 12. Mai .vormittags. Stand des Marine Projektes. Diktat Js., 13 May 1926, 0401, T14, Firmen Archiv Junkers (FAJ), Deutsches Museum, Munich (hereafter cited as DMM).

11. Doc. No. 861, Lohmann to Atlantic Hotel, RM 21/191, Bundesarchiv, Freiburg.

12. Doc. No. 864, Lohmann to Brandenburg, Strictly Confidential, 12 October 1926, RM 21/191, Bundesarchiv, Freiburg.

13. Bauer to Piegl, Potsdam, Fr. 235, NL 22/36, BA-Koblenz.

14. Fr. 27, NL 22/36, BA-Koblenz. EISA's director was Oberst Tortosa. His laboratory's head was Major Planell. He employed two Germans who would translate Bauer's designs into bombs. Fr. 295and Fr. 201, NL 22/36, BA-Koblenz.

15. 19 March 1923, Fr. 219–20, NL 22/26, BA-Koblenz.

16. Fr. 319, NL 22/36, BA-Koblenz. The Deutsches Museum, Munich, archive holds the Carbonit Archive, awaiting a detailed, skilled examination.

17. Piegl to Bauer from Madrid, 24 March 1926, Fr. 226–29, NL 22/36, BA-Koblenz.

18. Fr. 261, 289, 291, NL 22/36, BA-Koblenz. The Argentine commission also invited Bauer to travel to Brussels for talks, but he stayed in Berlin working on the airplane demonstration for the king. He expected planning for the next big presentation to the king to take place in June.

19. Ausserordentlicher Kostenvorschlag fuer Militaerfliegerei, Spanien, Kostenvorschlag Militaerfliegeri, 1926, 0621, T2, FAJ, DMM; Carlos Sáiz Cidoncha, *Aviación Republicana: Historia de las Fuerzas Aereas de la Republica Española 1931–1939* (Madrid: Almena Edicones, 2006), 35.

20. Sáiz Cidoncha, *Aviación Republicana*, 35.

21. No. 146, State Department to Embassy, 4 September 1926, 54/9233, AGA.

22. Arg to Danvila, 23 September 1926, 54/9233, AGA.

23. Allison Winthrop Saville, "The Development of the German U-Boat Arm, 1919–1935" (Ph.D. diss., University of Washington, 1963), 124.

24. Ibid., 102.

25. An Botschaft Madrid, T-120, Reel 3899, Fr. E 458928–29, NAUS.

26. Aufzeichung, Nord, 6 April 1926, T-120, Reel 3899, Fr. E 458920–22, NAUS.

27. Saville, "The Development of the German U-Boat Arm," 202–3.

28. Merkblatt, Fuer die Kabinettbesprechung (about 12 January 1931), T-120, Reel 3899, Fr. E 459095–97, NAUS. If Echevarrieta and the state did not achieve the contract, the German bank could step back. In 1931 it did not have the money and might now seek to get close to the French. Echevarrieta won from Primo de Rivera's government the funds to finish the factory and to pay off the building costs during the coming years.

29. Madrid, Vortrag bei S.M. dem Koenig von Spanien am 9 October 1926, 2:30 nachmittags, original Bauer, nach Abaenderung fuer Dr. Kaumann, 11 October 1926, 0621, T2, FAJ, DMM.

30. Ibid. At first the king interested himself in the 2-cm canon of Oerlikon, and he explained its significant achievements. Alfonso was especially interested in this gun and wanted specific data about it (but also about its use for the so-called heavy infantry machine gun on the ground). These data were to be sent from Germany as soon as possible.

31. Ibid.

32. Letter to Kurt Weil, Weil Technischer Aussendienst Junkers, Confidential, 20 October 1926, 0621, T2, FAJ, DMM.

33. Ibid.
34. Yanguas to Embassy Buenos Aires, 17 November 1926, 54/9198, Leg. 468, AGA.
35. Killinger, Madrid, to Junkers Flugzeugwerk, Lagebericht, 3 November 1926, 0621, T2, FAJ, DMM
36. M. A. Wagner to G. Kaumann, Berlin, 26 January 1927, 0621, T3, FAJ, DMM.
37. Killinger, Madrid, to Junkers Flugzeugwerk, Lagebericht, 13 November 1926, 0621, T2, FAJ, DMM.
38. Piegl to Bauer, 17 October 1927, F 7, Fr. 573–79, NL 22/36, BA-Koblenz.
39. Bauer to Piegl, 5 December 1926, F 5, Fr. 673–78, NL 22/36, BA-Koblenz.
40. Killinger to Bobby, 17 February 1927, 0621, T3, FAJ, DMM.
41. CIA Historical Review Program, "The Lohmann Affair," September 22, 1993, available at https://www.cia.gov/library/center-for-the-study-of-intelligence/kent-csi/vol4no2/html/v04i2a08p_0001.htm (accessed May 28, 2006).
42. Killinger to Gotthard, 22 January 1927, 0621, T3, FAJ, DMM.
43. 13 April 1926, 54/9190, Leg. 427, AGA.
44. No. 137, Yanguas to Boix, Comercio, 16 October 1926, 54/9192, Leg. 438, AGA.
45. Doc. No. 98, the Foreign Minister was Angel Gallardo, 6 December 1926, Paquete 1358, SRE.
46. Caja 15.441, Exp. 3, Patrimonio Nacional, Archivo de los Reyes, Madrid (hereafter cited as PNRA). First, at the Spanish club of Buenos Aires; second, at the celebration of the pilgrimage to the sanctuary of the Virgin of Pilar; and third, at a luncheon at the House of Galicea.
47. No. 4, Amalfi to Torres, 3 February 1927, PNRA.
48. Sent 31 December 1926, Caja 15.438, Exp. 4, PNRA.
49. No. 3, Amalfi to Torres, 25 January 1927, Exp. 5, PNRA.
50. No. 5, Amalfi to Torres, 20 February and 2 April 1927, Exp. 5, PNRA. So far no proof of this allegation can be backed up with sources from the archives.
51. Amalfi to AAE, 29 December 1926, Caja 15.438, Exp. 4, PNRA.
52. Caja 15.441, Exp. 3, PNRA.
53. Telegram 154, Reservado, 12 April 1927, 54/9233, AGA.
54. Amalfi to Yanguas, 29 December 1926, Caja 15.438, Exp. 4, PNRA.
55. Ibid.
56. Yanguas to Amalfi, 5 February 1927, 54/9196, Leg. 456, AGA.
57. Amalfi to Gallardo, 1 February 1927, 54/9196, Leg. 456, AGA.
58. Telegram No. 16, Yanguas to Amalfi, 16 February 1927, 54/9196, Leg. 456, AGA.
59. Colleccion Alfonso XIII, 6 March 1927, PNRA.
60. 12 March 1927, 54/9196, Leg. 456, AGA.
61. 21 February 1927, SRE.
62. Letter, unsigned, undated [25 April 1927], Caja 15.589, Exp. 4, PNRA.
63. Letter No. 5, Amalfi to Torres, 20 February 1927, Exp. 3, PNRA.
64. No. 168, 6 October 1926, M-514, Fr. 245–46, 835.34/414, NAUS.
65. Secretary of State Kellog to Embassy B.A., 18 October 1926, M-514, Fr. 234, 835.34/409, NAUS; Telegram to Madrid, 3 November 1926, Embajada Buenos Aires, Paquete 1358, SRE; No. 2026/26, "Die Finanzlage Argentiniens," Freiherr von Reisvitz to AA, 27 October 1926, T-290, Reel 5, Fr. 121–38, NAUS; annexed to Dispatch No. 57, from *La Prensa*, 17 February 1927, Paquete 1358, SRE; and Telegram No. 57, Amalfi to Yanguas, Reservado, 17 February 1927, 54/9233, AGA.

66. Chamberlain to Mallet, 17 February 1927, FO 420/273, A1027/78/2, File Page No. 62, Public Records Office, National Archives of the United Kingdom, London.

67. Contracts for the construction of warships for the Arg. Gov. 268–69, Conversation, Secretary of State, the Undersecretary, 28 February 1927, M-514, 835.34/421, NAUS.

68. No. 38, Reservado, 24 March 1927, 54/9233, AGA.

69. No. 57, Reserved, Political America, Argentine Ambassador to Spain Amalfi, sent 17 February 1927, Paquete 1358, SRE.

70. Torres to Amalfi, 1 April 1927, PNRA.

71. Telegram No. 27, Minister of Spain to Ambassador Buenos Aires, Urgent, 25 March 1927, Paquete 1358, SRE.

72. Telegram No. 23, Estella to Amalfi, 5 April 1927, Paquete 1358, SRE.

73. CN, 27 March 1927, 54/9233, AGA. Official Mayor to Amalfi, 30 March 1927; Telegram No. 23, Estella to Amalfi, 5 April 1927; No. 39, 1 April 1927; and No. 42, 6 April 1927—all in Paquete 1358, SRE.

74. Tel. No. 44, Amalfi to Madrid, Confidential, 9 April 1927, Paquete 1358, SRE; Letter No. 12, Amalfi to Torres, 12 April 1927, PNRA; Telegram No. 44, 8 April 1927, 54/923, AGA.

75. No. 3798, Military Attaché Report, 31 March 1927, Military Intelligence Division, Argentina 1919–30, Folder 2048-183, M-514, NAUS.

76. Telegram 154, 12 April 1927.

77. No. A-42, Military Intelligence Report, Argentina, File 2048-182, Current Events for the Month of March, to A.C. of S. G-2, Confidential, 5 April 1927, M-514, Reel 1, Fr. 330–32, NAUS.

78. Ibid.; Telegram No. 73, 28 February 1927, Package 1358, SRE; Secretary of State, Buenos Aires, Department of State, 1 March 1927, M-514, 835.34/421, NAUS.

79. Buenos Aires to Secretary of State, 15 April 1927, M-514, Reel 18, Fr. 291–92, 835.34/426, NAUS.

80. No. 40, Amalfi to Estado, 12 April 1927, 54/9233, AGA; No. 46, Amalfi to Foreign Ministry, 19 April 1927, Paquete 1358, SRE; Fr. 286, M-514, NAUS; Telegram No. 73, Fairbury 281927, Paquete 1358, SRE; Secretary of State, Buenos Aires, Department of State, 1 March 1927.

81. Dispatch 153, 11 April 1927, 54/9198, Leg. 468, AGA.

82. Telegram No. 57, 4 May 1927, Paquete 1358, SRE; Telegram 154, 12 April 1927.

83. Telegram No. 34, answer to 55, 5 May 1927, Paquete 1358, SRE; Secretary of State, U.S. Ambassador, Confidential, 24 May 1927, M-514, Reel 18, 835.34/433, NAUS; Cable to Secretary of State, 14 May 1927, M-514, Reel 18, 835.34/431, NAUS.

84. La Prensa, 27 May 1927, Paquete 1358, SRE.

85. Cable to Secretary of State, 31 May 1927, M-514, Reel 18, 835.34/441, NAUS.

86. Telegram No. 226, 3 June 1927, Paquete 1358, SRE; Report No. 3798, Argentina, Military Intelligence Reports, File 2048-182, B.A. Military Attaché Office, 31 May 1927, M-514, Reel 8, Fr. 336–39, NAUS.

87. Report No. 3798, Argentina, Military Intelligence Reports, File 2048-182, B.A. Military Attaché Office, 31 May 1927.

88. Ibid.

89. Tel. 54, 3 May 1927; Tel. 58, Buenos Aires to Madrid, 54/9233, AGA.

90. Abschrift, Reise to Spain, from 8–19 and 21 November 1927, T-120, Reel 3899, Fr. E 459008–11, NAUS.

91. Pertains to Spanish Affairs, 4 August 1927, T-120, Reel 3899, Fr. E 458961–65, NAUS.

92. Aufzeichung, 9 August 1937, T-120, Reel 3899, Fr. E 458959–60, NAUS.

93. Pertains to Spanish Affairs, 4 August 1927, Fr. E 458961–65.

94. Ibid.

95. No. 3931/27, Top Secret, 25 December 1927, T-120, Reel 3988, Fr. E 459016, NAUS; No. 984, Confidential, 25 August 1927, T-120, Reel 3899, Fr. E 458976–78, NAUS.

96. No. 931/27, 25 December 1927, T-120, Reel 3988, Fr. E 459020, NAUS.

97. No. 3931/27, 25 December 1927.

98. Aufzeichung, 9 August 1937.

99. No. 3931/27, 25 December 1927.

100. Pertains to Spanish Affairs, 4 August 1927, Fr. E 458961–65.

101. Ibid., Fr. E 458962–66.

102. Ibid., Fr. E 458961–65.

103. Sáiz Cidoncha, *Aviación Republicana*, 37.

104. 29 August 1926, 451–53, BA-Koblenz.

105. For example, Dr. G. von Hirschfeld to Count Welczeck, 25 August 1927, Embassy in Madrid, PAAA. Already on February 17, 1927, a German subsidiary had received the right to fly from Madrid to Petrópolis, Brazil, using British airplanes. 17 February 1927, 54/9196, Leg. 456, AGA.

106. Zechlin to Ambassador, Eyes Only, 30 December 1927, J. No. 3973/27, Embassy in Madrid, PAAA.

107. Heinz Hoehne, *Canaris: Patriot im Zwielicht* (Munich: Bertelsmann, 1976), 105.

Part VI

1. Cross Referencing Note, 19 September 1928, M-514, Reel 18, 835.34/476, National Archives of the United States, Washington, D.C. (hereafter cited as NAUS).

2. No. 85.410–11, 30 November 1927, M-514, Reel 18, 835.34/468, NAUS. This refers to la Nos. 11266 and 11378.

3. Cross Referenced, 835.00 Pol. Reports/4, M-514, Reel 18, Fr. 499, 835.345/6, NAUS.

4. The Recall of the Spanish Ambassador, 2 November 1927, RG 38, Chief of Naval Office, File Nos. 110–200, NAUS.

5. Telegram No. 42, Maeztu to Madrid, 20 February 1928, and *La Razon* (Buenos Aires), 18 February 1928, Paquete 1358, Archivo Histórico de la Secretaria de la Relaciones Exteriores, Madrid (hereafter cited as SRE).

6. 10 January 1928, Paquete 1358, SRE.

7. Telegram No. 14, 31 January 1928, Paquete 1358, SRE.

8. No. 5, 2 March 1928, Paquete 1358, SRE.

9. Political Telegram No. 5, Confidential Home, 2 March 1928, Paquete 1358, SRE.

10. Letter to Kretschmar 2 and 7, Confidential, 16 December 1929, RH2/2947, Bundesarchiv, Freiburg (hereafter cited as BA-Freiburg).

11. Friedrich E. Schuler, "Vom Kulturinstitut zum SS-Institut? Das Ibero-Amerikanische Institut im Dritten Reich," in *Ein Institut und sein General*, ed. Reinhard Liehr, Guenther Maihold, and Guenter Vollmer (Frankfurt: Verfuehrt Verlag, 2003), 359.

12. RH2/2953, 10, BA-Freiburg.

13. Otto Moyer to Reichwehrministerium, 20 May 1927, 12. and Dezernat A II, AII, n 1908027-6 to Abwehrgruppe Heeresleitung, Stammer, 14 and 15, RH2/2953, BA-Freiburg. By October 1927 Chileans began to complain about Faupel's presence in Peru. They complained to Hindenburg.

14. Hans von Kiesling, *Soldat in drei Weltteilen* (Leipzig: Grethlein und Co., 1935), 460–61.

15. Ibid., 498; Fr. 7, RH2/1860, BA-Freiburg.

16. M-514, Reel 18, NAUS; David H. Buffun, *American Vice Consul in Charge*, 431–33; Allison Winthrop Saville, "The Development of the German U-Boat Arm, 1919–1935" (Ph.D. diss., University of Washington, 1963), 302.

17. Breguet XIX, EADS Web site, http://www.eads.com/eads/int/en.html.

18. Final guidelines were defined in Verfuegung A II from 19 August 1930, in T-1022, Reel 3342, PG 31083, NAUS.

19. Kommandeur des Kreuzers *Karlsruhe*, Abwehrabteilung 90/unreadable, Top Secret, 19 May 1930, T-1022, Reel 3342, PG 31083, NAUS.

20. Ibid., 4.

21. Kommando *Karlsruhe*, T-1022, Reel 3342, V/172/31ghK, NAUS.

22. Anlage 2 Geh. Kom. Namen derjenigen Persoenlichkeiten mit denen das Reichsministerium seiner Zeit in Verbindung stand (in den Haefen die von *Karlsruhe* angelaufen werden, Anlage zwei), T-1022, Reel 3342, NAUS.

23. An Kreuzer *Karlsruhe*, 24 November 1931, T-1022, Reel 3342, Abw 172/31/Vb g kds, NAUS.

24. Zusammenstellung ueber die in den einzelnen anzulaufenden Haefen geschaffenen bezw. noch zu schaffenden Verbindungen, T-1022, Reel 3342, Gh Kd, 172/31/VB, NAUS.

25. Vortragsnotiz Ergebnis der Auslandsreisen des Kreuzers *Karlsruhe* fuer den Etappendienst, Secret, 30 January 1933, T-1022, Reel 3342, NAUS.

26. Ibid.

27. Dischler to Frisius, unreadable signature probably Stammer, 28 February 1931, T-1022, Reel 3342, NAUS; Frisius to Dischler, report to letter from 28 February 1931, 3 March 1931, T-1022, Reel 3342, NAUS.

28. Stamp on Document Kommando *Karlsruhe*, Etappendienst, T-1022, Reel 3342, V/42/33 gh Kom, NAUS.

29. Botschaft Bern, File No. 766, Mensing, Politisches Archiv des Auswaertigen Amts, Berlin.

30. Vortragsnotiz Ergebnis der Auslandsreisen des Kreuzers *Karlsruhe* fuer den Etappendienst, 30 January 1933.

31. Zusammenstellung uber die in den einzelnen anzulaufenden Haefen geschaffenen bezw. noch zu schaffenden Verbindungen.

32. Der Etappendienst in Übersee, to Abw 71/33V/gkd, Exemplar Anlage 3, T-1022, Reel 3367, PF 31068, NAUS.

33. Typed reproduction of Röhm to Himmler, front page missing, no date [28 March 1930], T-175, Reel 199, Fr. 7739864, 2739868, NAUS.

34. Juergen Mueller, *Nationalsozialismus in Lateinamerika: Die Auslandsorganisation der NSDAP in Argentinien, Brasilien, Chile und Mexico, 1931–1945* (Stuttgart: Verlag Hans Dieter Heinz, 1997), 100, Mitteilungsblatt, Rio, April bis November 1932.

35. Ibid., 103.

36. Christel K. Converse, "The Rise and Fall of Nazi Influence among the German-Chileans" (Ph.D. diss., Georgetown University, 1990), 131–33.

37. Ibid., 149.

38. São Paulo Dr. Vogeler to Hitler, 18 September 1933, T-120, Reel 550, C001491, NAUS.

39. Ibid.

40. Ibid. Keppler was supposed to talk about this with Herrn Stieve (RK 12403, Bundesarchiv, Berlin-Lichterfelde).

41. Cornelia Wilhelm, *Bewegung oder Verein? Nationalsozialistische Volkstumspolitik in den USA* (Stuttgart: Franz Steiner, 1998), 49.

42. There was a national executive leader, Fritz Gissibl; a national press leader, Walter Knappe; a national treasurer, Engelbert Roell; the Mediation Division; and the position of head of propaganda, which Spanknoebel himself insisted on controlling.

Bibliography

1. Primary Sources

GERMANY
Bundesarchiv, Berlin-Lichterfelde
Bundesarchiv, Freiburg
Bundesarchiv, Koblenz
Firmen Archiv Junkers, Deutsches Museum, Munich
Politisches Archiv des Auswaertigen Amts, Bonn and Berlin

SPAIN
Archivo General de la Administración, Alcalá de Henares
Archivo Histórico de la Secretaria de la Relaciones Exteriores, Madrid
Archivo Histórico Nacional, Madrid
Patrimonio Nacional, Archivo de los Reyes, Madrid

UNITED KINGDOM
British Documents on Foreign Affairs: Reports and Papers from the Foreign Office Confidential Print. Part II, Series D: Latin America 1914–1939, vol. 3: 1920–1924. Ed. George Philip. Bethesda, Md.: University Publications of America, 1989–92.
Public Records Office, National Archives of the United Kingdom, London. Call No. KV/2 and ADM.

UNITED STATES
Center for Research Libraries, University of Chicago, Chicago
FDR Presidential Library, Poughkeepsie, New York
Library of Congress, Washington, D.C.
National Archives of the United States, Washington, D.C.

M-514, Microform Collection Argentina
RG 38, Office of the Chief of Naval Operation
RG 45, Naval Records Collection
RG 59, Department of State
RG 84, Embassy File Records, Mexico City, Madrid, Buenos Aires
RG 165, Records of War Department General and Special Staff
T-120, Captured Records of the German Foreign Ministry

Yale Historical Archive, Sir Wiseman Collection

542

Secondary Sources

1. PH.D. DISSERTATIONS

Asada, Sadao. "Japan and the United States." Ph.D. diss., Yale University, 1962.

Berton, Peter Alexander. "The Secret Russo-Japanese Alliance of 1916." Ph.D. diss., Columbia University, 1956.

Burkman, Thomas Wesley. "Japan, the League of Nations and the New World Order." Ph.D. diss., University of Michigan, 1975.

Campbell, Michael Toy. "Triumph of the Word: The German Struggle to Maintain Spanish Neutrality during the First World War." Ph.D. diss., University of Wisconsin, 1989.

Converse, Christel K. "The Rise and Fall of Nazi Influence among the German-Chileans." Ph.D. diss., Georgetown University, 1990.

Hell, Juergen. "Die Politik des Deutschen Reiches zur Umwandlung Suedbrasiliens in ein Ueberseeisches Neudeutschland (1890–1914)." Ph.D. diss., University of Rostock, 1966.

Khazanov, David Matthew. "The Diplomacy of Control: U.S.–Argentine Relations, 1910–1928." PhD diss., University of Connecticut, 1989.

Kunimoto, Iyo Iimura. "Japan and Mexico, 1886–1917." Ph.D. diss., University of Texas, 1975.

Sander-Nagashima, Berthold J. "Die Deutsch–Japanischen Marinebeziehungen 1919 bis 1942." Ph.D. diss., Universitaet Hamburg, 1998.

Saville, Allison Winthrop. "The Development of the German U-Boat Arm, 1919–1935." Ph.D. diss., University of Washington, 1963.

Schell, William, Jr. "Integral Outsiders: Mexico City's American Colony 1876–1911: Society and Political Economy in Porfirian Mexico." Ph.D. diss., University of North Carolina at Chapel Hill, 1992.

Seidel, Robert Neal. "Progressive Pan Americanism: Development and United States Policy toward South America, 1906–1931." Ph.D. diss., Cornell University, 1973.

Staklo, Vadim A. "Harnessing Revolution: The Communist International in Central America, 1929–1935." Ph.D. diss., University of Pittsburgh, 2001.

Tsuchida, Nobuya. "The Japanese in Brazil." Ph.D. diss., University of California at Los Angeles, 1978.

2. ARTICLES AND BOOK CHAPTERS

Bledsoe, Gerie B. "Spanish Foreign Policy, 1898–1936." In *Spain in the 20th Century, Essays on Spanish Diplomacy, 1898–1978*, ed. James W. Cortada, 3–41. Westport, Conn.: Greenwood Press, 1980.

Chi, Madeleine. "Bureaucratic Capitalists in Operation: Ts'ao Ju-lin and His New Communications Clique, 1916–1919." *Journal of Asian Studies* 34, no. 3 (May 1975): 675–88.

de Caprariis, Luca. "Fascism for Export? The Rise and Eclipse of the Fasci Italiani all'Estero." *Journal of Contemporary History* 35, no. 2 (April 2000): 151–83.

Ebersspaecher, Cord, and Gerhard Wiechmann. "Admiral Eduard von Knorr (1840–1920). Eine Karriere in der neuen Elite der Seeoffiziere in Preussen-Deutschland." In *Eliten im Wandel: Gesellschaftliche Fuehrungsschichten im 19. und 20. Jahrhundert*, ed. Karl Christian Fuehrer, Karen Hagemann, and Birthe Kundrus, 239–58. Münster: Westfaelisches Dampfboot, 2004.

Estes, Donald H. "Asama Gunkan: The Reappraisal of a War Scare." *Journal of San Diego* 24 no. 3 (1978): 1–34.

Fischer, Ferenc. "Noruega via Chile?" In *Iberoamericana 2, Quinqueecclesiensis*, 15–33. Budapest: Universidad de Pecs, Centro Iberoamericana, 2004.

Forsen, Bjoern, and Anette Forsen. "German Secret Submarine Efforts, 1919–1935." In *Girding for Battle: The Arms Trade in Global Perspective, 1815–1940*, ed. Donald Stoker Jr. and Jonathan A. Grant, 113–34. Westport, Conn.: Praeger, 2003.

Gentile, E. "L'emigracione italiana in Argentina nella politica d'espansione del naziolnalismo e del fascism." *Storia Contemporane* 17 (June 1986): 355–96.

Hilton, Stanley H. "The Armed Forces and Industrialists in Modern Brazil: The Drive for Military Autonomy (1889–1954)." *Hispanic American Historical Review* 62, no. 4 (November 1982): 629–73.

Ipsen, Carl. "The Organization of Demographic Totalitarianism: Early Population Policy in Fascist Italy." *Social Science History* 17, no. 1 (Spring 1993): 71–108.

Kaulisch, Baldur. "Zur Ueberseeischen Stuetzpunktpolitik der Kaiserlichen Deutschen Marinefuehrung am Ende des 19 Jahrhunderts und im Ersten Weltkrieg." *East Berlin*, 1965: 585–98.

Krueger, Gerd. "Ich bitte darueber nichts sagen zu duerfen. Halbstaatliche und Private Politische Nachrichtensdienste in der Weimarer Republik." *Zeitgeschichte*, 27 February 2000: 87–107.

"Los Intentos Chiles por reflotar la politica de ABC en la Decada de 1920." In *Historia General de las Relaciones Exteriores de la República Argentine*. University of CEMA, available at http://www.cema.edu.ar (accessed May 20, 2006).

McBeth, Brian S. "Foreign Support for Venezuelan Political Exiles during the Regime of Juan V. Gómez: The Case of México, 1923–33." *The Historian* 69, no. 2 (Summer 2007): 275–304.

Moore, John Bassett. "The Pan American Financial Conferences and the Inter-American High Commission." *American Journal of International Law* 14, no. 3 (July 1920): 343–55.

Murphy, John F., Jr. "Michael Collins and the Craft of Intelligence." *International Journal of Intelligence and Counterintelligence* 17, no. 2 (2004): 333–57.

Newton, Ronald C. "Ducini, Prominenti, Antifascisti: Italian Fascism and the Italo-Argentine Collectivity, 1922–1945." *The Americas* 51, no. 1 (July 1994): 41–66.

Nouailhait, Yves Henri. "Francais, Anglai e Americains face au probleme de la reorganisation du commerce international (1914–1918)." *Relations Internationales* 10 (1977): 95–114.

Rustamova-Tohidi, Solmaz. "First Congress of the Peoples of the East: Aims, Tasks, Results." In *Centre and Periphery: The History of the Comintern in the Light of New Documents*, ed. M. Narinsky and J. Rojahn, 74–80. Amsterdam: International Institute of Social History, 1996.

Sandos, James A. "German Involvement in Northern Mexico." *Hispanic American Historical Review* 50, no. 1 (February 1970): 70–88.

Schreck, Raffael. "Politics of Illusion: Tirpitz and Right Wing Putschism, 1922–1924." *German Studies Review* 18, no. 1 (February 1995): 29–49.

Schuler, Friedrich E. "Latin America and Nazi Economic Policy." In *Germany and the Americas: Culture Politics and History*, ed. Thomas Adam, 647–51. Santa Barbara: ABC-CLIO, 2005a.

———. "Latin America, Nazi Party." In *Germany and the Americas: Culture Politics and History*, ed. Thomas Adam, 643–46. Santa Barbara: ABC-CLIO, 2005b.

———. "Nachwirkende Vorkommnisse. Argentinien als Taetigkeitsfeld fuer Geheimdienst und verdeckte Kriegsaktivitaeten 1915–1922." In *Argentinien und das Dritte Reich: Mediale und reale Praesenz, Ideologietransfer, Folgewirkungen*, ed. Holger M. Meding and Georg Ismar, 75–101. Berlin: Wissenschaftlicher Verlag, 2008.

———. "Vom Kulturinstitut zum SS-Institut? Das Ibero-Amerikanische Institut im Dritten Reich." In *Ein Institut und sein General*, ed. Reinhard Liehr, Guenther Maihold, and Guenter Vollmer, 351–409. Frankfurt: Verfuehrt Verlag, 2003.

Shaw, Caroline. "Rothshild and Brazil." *Latin American Research Review* 40, no. 1 (February 2005): 165–85.

Silverlock, Gerard. "British Disarmament Policy and the Rome Naval Conference, 1924." *War in History* 10, no. 2 (2003): 184–205.

Smith, Michael C. "Carrancista Propaganda and the Print Media in the United States: An Overview of Institutions." *The Americas* 52, no. 2 (October 1995): 155–74.

———. "The Mexican Secret Service in the U.S. 1910–1920." *The Americas* 59, no. 1 (July 2002): 65–87.

Spence, Richard B. "K. A. Jahnke and the German Sabotage Campaign in the United States and Mexico, 1914–1918." *The Historian* 59 (1996): 89–112.

Tussell, Javier, and Ismael Saz. "Primo de Rivera and Mussolini." *Boletín de la Real Academia de la Historia* 179, no. 3 (September–December 1982).

Wheelis, Mark. "Biological Sabotage in World War I." In *Biological and Toxin Weapons: Research, Development and Use from the Middle Ages to 1945*, ed. Erhard Geissler and John Ellis van Courtland Moon, 35–62. Sipri Chemical and Biological Warfare Studies, no. 18. Oxford: Oxford University Press, 1999.

3. BOOKS

Agawa, Hiroyuki. *The Reluctant Admiral: Yamamoto and the Imperial Navy.* Tokyo: Kodansha International Ltd., 1979.

Alén Lascano, Luis C. *Pueyrredón, el Mensajero de un Destino.* Buenos Aires: n.p., 1951.

Andrew, Christopher M. *Her Majesty's Secret Service.* London: Viking, 1985.

Andrew, Christopher, and David Dilks, eds. *The Missing Dimension.* Urbana: University of Illinois Press, 1984.

Antokoletz, Daniel. *La Liga de las Naciones y la Primera Asamblea de Ginebra.* Buenos Aires: n.p., 1921.

Bailey, Thomas A. *The Policy of the United States toward the Neutrals, 1917–1918.* Gloucester, Mass.: Peter Smith, 1942.

Balfour, Sebastian. *The End of the Spanish Empire 1898–1923.* Oxford: Clarendon Press, 1997.

Ballestero, Alfonso. *Juan Antonio Suanzes, 1891–1977: La Política Industrial de la Postguerra.* León, Spain: LID Editorial Empresarial, 1993.

Barnhart, Michael A. *Japan Prepares for Total War: The Search for Economic Security 1919–1941.* Ithaca: Cornell University Press, 1987.

Barrientos, Daniel Rivadulla. *La "Amistad Irrenconciliable": España y Argentine, 1900–1914.* Madrid: Editorial Mapfre, 1992.

Bartholdt, Richard. *From Steerage to Congress: Reminiscences and Reflections.* Philadelphia: Dorrance and Co., 1930.

Becker, Josef, ed. *Bismarcks Spanische Diversion 1870 und der Preussisch–Deutsche Reichsgruendungskrieg. Band I, Der Weg zum spanischen Thronangebot, Spaetjahr 1866–4. April 1870.* Paderborn, Germany: Ferdinand Schoeningh Verlag, 2002.

Becú, Carlos A. *El A.B.C. y Su Concepto Político y Jurídico.* Buenos Aires: Libreria La Facultad de Juan Roldan, 1915.

Beesly, Patrick. *Room 40: British Naval Intelligence 1914–1918*. San Diego: Harcourt, Brace, Jovanovich, 1982.

Bosworth, R. J. B. *Mussolini*. Oxford: Oxford University Press, 2002.

Brahm Garcia, Enrique. *Preparados Para La Guerra: Pensamiento Militar Chileno Bajo Influencia Alemana*. Santiago: Edicion Universidad Catholica, 2003.

Brunn, Gerhard. *Deutschland und Brasilien, 1889–1914*. Cologne: Boehlau Verlag, 1971.

Buchenau, Juergen. *In the Shadow of the Giant: The Making of Mexico's Central America Policy, 1876–1930*. Tuscaloosa : University of Alabama Press, 1996.

———. *Plutarco Elias Calles: Calles and the Mexican Revolution*. Lanham, Md.: Rowman and Littlefield, 2007.

———. *Tools of Progress: A German Merchant Family in Mexico*. Albuquerque: University of New Mexico Press, 2004.

Buelow, Prince von. *Memoirs 1897–1903*. London: Putnam, 1931.

Burgwyn, James H. *Italian Foreign Policy in the Interwar Period, 1918–1940*. London: Praeger, 1997.

Burk, Kathleen. *Britain, America and the Sinews of War, 1914–1918*. Boston: G. Allen and Unwin, 1985.

Cannistraro, Philip V. *Blackshirts in Little Italy: Italian Americans and Fascism 1921–1929*. West Lafayette, Ind.: Bordighera Press, 1999.

Carr, Barry. *Marxism and Communism in 20th Century Mexico*. Norman: University of Nebraska Press, 1992.

Carvalho, Daniela. "Japan's Second World War Victory: An Analysis of the Reaction of the Japanese Immigrants in Brazil to Japanese Defeat." *Dialogos* 3 (December 2003). Available at http://www.dhi.uem.br/publicacoesdhi/dialogos/volume01/vol03_atg2.htm (accessed fall 2008).

Chapman, John W. M. *Japan, Germany and International Political Economy of Intelligence*. Bonn: Bouvier Verlag, 1990.

Chernow, Ron. *The House of Morgan: An American Dynasty and the Rise of Modern Finance*. New York: New Atlantic Monthly Press, 1990.

Child, Clifton James. *The German American in Politics 1914–1917*. Madison: University of Wisconsin Press, 1940.

Corzo Ramirez, Ricardo, and Jose G. Gonzalez Sierra. *Nunca un Desleal: Candido Aguilar 1889–1960*. Mexico City: El Colegio de Mexico, Gobierno del Estado de Veracruz, 1986.

Cronon, E. Joseph., ed. *Josephus Daniels: The Cabinet Diaries of Josephus Daniels*. Lincoln: University of Nebraska Press, 1963.

Daniels, Roger. *The Politics of Prejudice: The Anti-Japanese Movement in California and the Struggle for Japanese Exclusion*. Berkeley: University of California Press, 1962.

Davies, R. E. G. *Airlines of Latin America since 1919*. Washington, D.C.: Smithsonian Institute Press, 1984.

———. *History of the World's Airlines*. Oxford: Oxford University Press, 1983.

Deutsche Wissenschaftliche Untersuchungen auf dem Gebiete der Chemie, Ausgeführt mit Unterstützung von Hajime Hoshi. Leipzig: Verlag Chemie Leipzig und Berlin, 1924.

Diaz Hernandez, Onesimo. *Los Marqueses de Urquijo: El Apogeo de una saga ponderosa y los inicios del Banco Urquijo, 1870–1931*. Pamplona: Ediciones Universidad de Navarra, 1963.

Dickinson, Frederick R. *War and National Reinvention: Japan in the Great War, 1914–1919*. Cambridge: Harvard University Asia Center, 1999.

Dirks, Carl, and Karl Heinz Janssen. *Der Krieg der Generaele*. Propylaen, 2001.

Doerries, Reinhard R. *Imperial Challenge: Ambassador Count Bernstorff and German–American Relations, 1908–1917*. Trans. Christa D. Shannon. Chapel Hill: University of North Carolina Press, 1989.

———. *Prelude to Easter Rising: Sir Roger Casement in Germany*. London: Frank Cass, 2000.

———, ed. *Diplomaten und Agenten: Nachrichtendienste in der Geschichte der Deutsche–Amerikanischen Beziehungen*. Heidelberg: C. Winter, 2001.

Dorwart, Jeffrey M. *Conflict of Duty: The U.S. Navy's Intelligence Dilemma, 1919–1945*. Annapolis: U.S. Navy Institute, 1983.

Doss, Kurt. *Das Deutsche Auswaertige Amt im Uebergang vom Kaiserreich zur Weimarer Republik: Die Schuelersche Reform*. Düsseldorf: Droste Verlag, 1977.

Duus, Peter. *The Abacus and the Sword: The Japanese Penetration of Korea 1895–1910*. Berkeley: University of California Press, 1995.

Fabela, Isidro. *La Politica Interior y Exterior de Carranza*. Mexico City: Editorial Jus, S.A., 1979.

Fahlbusch, Michael. *Wo der Deutsche . . . ist, ist Deutschland: Die Stiftung fuer Deutsche Volks und Kulturbodenforschung in Leipzig, 1920–1933*. Bochum: Universitaetsverlag Dr. N. Brockmeyer, 1994.

Ferber, Ferdinand, and Adolf Rohrbach. *Pioniere der Luftfahrt Hugo Junkers*. Deutsche Luft und Raumfahrt Mitteilung No. 74-15. Cologne: Deusche Gesellschaft fuer Luft und Raumfahrt, 1974.

Fiebig von Hase, Ragnhild. *Lateinamerika als Konfliktherd Der Deutsch–Amerikanischen Beziehungen: 1890–1903: Vom Beginn Der Panamerikapolitik Bis zur Venezuelakrise von 1902/1903*. Göttingen: Vandenhoeck und Ruprecht, 1986.

Fischer, Ferenc. *El Modelo Militar Prusiano y la Fuerzas Armadas de Chile: 1885–1945*. Pécs: Hungary University Press, 1999.

Fischer, Fritz. *Griff nach der Weltmacht: Die Kriegszielpolitik des kaiserlichen Deutschland 1914/1918*. Düsseldorf: Droste, 1961.

Frei, Henry P. *Japan's Southward Advance and Australia: From the Sixteenth Century to World War II*. Honolulu: University of Hawaii Press, 1991.

Froeschle, Hartmut, ed. *Die Deutschen in Lateinamerika*. Tübingen: Horst Erdmann, 1979.

Futrell, Michael H. *Colonel Akashi and Japanese Contacts with Russian Revolutionaries in 1904–1905*. Oxford: Oxford University Press, 1967.

Gardiner, C. Harvey. *The Japanese and Peru 1873–1973*. Albuquerque: University of New Mexico Press, 1975.

Gilberto, Freire. *Herrenhaus und Sklavenhütte: Ein Bild der brasilianischen Gesellschaft*. Trans. Ludwig Graf von Schönfeldt. Berlin: Kiepenheur und Witsch, 1965.

Goerlitz, Walter. *Regierte der Kaiser: Kriefstagebücher, Aufzeichnungen und Briefe des Chefs des Marine Kabinetts Admiral Georg Alexander von Müller 1914–1918*. Berlin: Musterschmidt-Verlag, 1959.

Goltz, Horst von der. *My Adventures as a German Secret Agent*. New York: R. M. McGride, 1917.

Gonzalez, Alfredo. *El Petroleo y la Politica en Costa Rica*. San José: Imprenta y Libreria Trejas, Hermanos, 1920.

Goodman, Grant K., and Felix Moos. *The U.S. and Japan in the Western Pacific: Micronesia and Papua New Guinea*. Boulder: Westview Press, 1981.

Guzmán Esparza, Roberto. *Memorias de don Adolfo de la Huerta según su propio dictado*. Mexico City: Ediciones Guzmán, 1957.

Hadley, Michael L., and Roger Sarty. *Tin-Pots and Pirate Ships: Canadian Naval Forces and German Sea Raiders*. Montreal: McGill-Queens University Press, 1991.

Harris, Charles H., and Louis R. Sadler. *The Archaeologist Was a Spy: Sylvanus G. Morley and the Office of Naval Intelligence*. Albuquerque: University of New Mexico Press, 2003.

———. *The Secret War in El Paso*. Albuquerque: University of New Mexico Press, 2009.

———. *The Texas Rangers and the Mexican Revolution*. Albuquerque: University of New Mexico Press, 2004.

———. *Trouble at the Border*. Silver City, N.M.: High Lonesome Books, 1988.

Hart, John Mason. *Empire and Revolution: The Americans in Mexico since the Civil War*. Berkeley: University of California Press, 2002.

Haywood, Harry. *Black Bolshevik: Autobiography of an Afro-American Communist*. Chicago: Liberator Press, 1978.

Headrick, Daniel R. *The Invisible Weapon: Telecommunications and International Politics, 1851–1945*. Oxford: Oxford University Press, 1991.

Heideking, Jürgen. *Aeropag der Diplomaten: Die Pariser Botschafterkonferenz der allierten Hauptmächte und die Probleme der europäischen Politik 1920–1931*. Husum, Germany: Historische Studien Matthiesen Verlag, 1979.

Herwig, Holger H. *Germany's Vision of Empire in Venezuela 1871–1914*. Princeton: Princeton University Press, 1986.

———. *Luxury Fleet: The Imperial German Navy 1880–1918*. London: Allen and Unwin, 1980.

Hoehne, Heinz. *Canaris: Patriot im Zwielicht*. Munich: Bertelsmann, 1976.

Hoepke, Klaus-Peter. *Die Deutsche Rechte und der Italienische Faschismus*. Düsseldorf: Droste, 1968.

Howarth, Stephen. *The Fighting Ships of the Rising Sun: The Drama of the Japanese Navy 1895–1945*. New York: Athenemun, 1983.

Hürter, Juergen. *Paul von Hintze. Marineoffizier, Diplomat, Staatssekretär. Dokumente einer Karriere zwischen Militär und Politik, 1903–1918*. R. Lahme, 1998.

Ibero-amerikanisches Institut Preussischer Kulturbesitz and the Museum für Völkerkunde Staatliche Museen zu Berlin, eds. *Neue Welten–neue Wirklichkeiten 1492–1992. Essays*. Brunswick, Germany: Ibero-amerikanisches Institut Preussischer Kulturbesitz and the Museum für Völkerkunde Staatliche Museen zu Berlin, 1992.

Ipsen, Carl. *Dictating Demography: The Problem of Population in Fascist Italy*. Cambridge: Cambridge University Press, 1991.

Iriye, Akira. *After Imperialism: The Search for a New Order in the Far East 1921–1931*. Cambridge: Harvard University Press, 1965.

Jackson, George D., Jr. *Comintern and Peasant in Eastern Europe 1919–1930*. New York: Columbia University Press, 1966.

Jacobs, Dan N. *Borodin: Stalin's Man in China*. Cambridge: Harvard University Press, 1981.

Jaffee, Philip Jay. *The Rise and Fall of American Communism*. New York: Horizon Press, 1975.

Johnson, Benjamin Heber. *Revolution in Texas*. New Haven: Yale University Press, 2005.

Jones, John Price, and Paul Merrick Hollister. *The German Secret Service in America, 1914–1918*. Boston: Small, Maynard and Co., 1919.

Jordan, Gerald, ed. *Naval Warfare in the Twentieth Century, 1900–1945: Essays in Honor of Arthur Marder*. New York: Crane Russak, 1977.

Katz, Friedrich. *Pancho Villa*. Stanford: Stanford University Press, 1998.

———. *The Secret War in Mexico*. Chicago: University of Chicago Press, 1981.

Kiesling, Hans von. *Soldat in drei Weltteilen*. Leipzig: Grethlein und Co., 1935.

Klaiber, Jeffrey L. *The Catholic Church in Peru: A Social History*. Washington, D.C.: Catholic University of America Press, 1992.

Klehr, Harvey. *The Secret World of American Communism*. New Haven: Yale University Press, 1995.

Kloosterhuis, Juergen. *Friedliche Imperialisten: Deutsche Auslandsvereine und auswaertige Kulturpolitik, 1906–1918*. Frankfurt: Peter Lang Verlag, 1994.

Kreiner, Josef, ed. *Japan und die Mittelmächte im Ersten Weltkrieg und in den Zwanziger Jahren*. Bonn: Bouvier Verlag Herbert Grundmann, 1986.

Kreiner, Josef, and Regine Mathias, eds. *Deutschland–Japan in der Zwischenkriegszeit*. Bonn: Bouvier Verlag, 1990.

Krekeler, Norbert. *Revisionsanspruch und Geheime Ostpolitik der Weimarer Republik. Die Subventionierung der deutschen Minderheiten in Polen*. Stuttgart: DVA, 1973.

Krivitsky, F. N. *I Was Stalin's Agent*. New York: Right Book Club, 1940.

Krug, Hans Joachim, Hirama Sander-Nagashima, and Axel Niestle. *Reluctant Allies: German Japanese Naval Relations in World War II*. Annapolis: Naval Institute Press, 2001.

Lansing, Robert. *War Memoirs of Robert Lansing*. Indianapolis: Bobbs-Merrill Co., 1935.

Larkin, Emmet. *James Larkin: Irish Labor Leader, 1876–1947*. Cambridge: MIT Press, 1965.

Lee, Chae-Jui. *Zhou En Lai: The Early Years*. Stanford: Stanford University Press, 1994.

L'emigracione Italiana negli anni 1924–1925. Rome: Commissariato Generale all'Emigrazione, 1926.

Lewinsohn, Richard (Morus). *Die Umschichtung der Europäischen Vermögen*. Berlin: S. Fischer, 1926.

Liang, Hsi-Huey. *The Sino-German Connection: Alexander von Falkenhausen between China and Germany, 1900–1941*. Assen: Van Gorcum, 1978.

Louis, William Roger. *Great Britain and Germany's Lost Colonies, 1914–1919*. Oxford: Clarendon Press, 1967.

Lovell, S. D. *The Presidential Election of 1916*. Carbondale: Southern Illinois University Press, 1980.

Luedecke, Kurt G. W. *I Knew Hitler*. New York: Charles Scribner, 1937.

Manchester, William. *The Arms of Krupp, 1587–1968*. New York: Bantam, 1970.

Manrique Garcia, Jose Maria de, and Lucas Molina Franco. *Antes que Sadam: Las Armas de destruccion masiva y la proteccion civil en España, 1924–2000*. Valladolid: Edicion Propia, 2003.

Masterson, Daniel M., with Sayaka Funada-Classen. *The Japanese in Latin America*. Urbana: University of Illinois Press, 2004.

Matsusaka, Yoshihisa Tak. *The Making of Japanese Manchuria 1904–1932*. Cambridge: Harvard University Asia Center, distributed by Harvard University Press, 2001.

May, Ernest R. *The World War and American Isolation 1914–1917*. Cambridge: Harvard University Press, 1959.

Mc Adoo, William Gibs. *Crowded Years. The Reminiscences of William G. Mc Adoo*. Boston: Houghton Mifflin, 1931.

McBeth, B. *Juan Vincente Gómez and the Oil Companies in Venezuela, 1908–1935*. Cambridge: Cambridge University Press, 1983.

McKale, Donald M. *Curt Pruefer, German Diplomat from the Kaiser to Hitler*. Kent: Kent State University, 1987.

———. *The Swastika outside Germany.* Kent: Kent State University Press, 1977.

———. *War by Revolution: Germany and Great Britain in the Middle East in the Era of World War I.* Kent: Kent State University Press, 1998.

McKercher, B. J. C. *Transition to Power: Britain's Loss of Global Pre-eminence to the United States, 1930–1945.* Cambridge, Mass.: Cambridge University Press, 1999.

Meyer, Henry Cord. *Mitteleuropa in German Thought and Action 1815–1945.* The Hague: Martinus Nijhoff, 1955.

Meyer, Lorenzo. *Su Majestad Britannica contra la Revolucion Mexicana: El fin de un imperio informal.* Mexico City: El Colegio de Mexico, 1991.

Meyer, Michael. *Huerta: A Political Portrait.* Lincoln: University of Nebraska Press, 1972.

Mitchell, Nancy. *The Danger of Dreams.* Chapel Hill: University of North Carolina Press, 1999.

Morely, James William. *The Japanese Thrust into Siberia, 1918.* New York: Columbia University Press, 1957.

Morikawa, Hidesama. *Zaibatsu: The Rise and Fall of Family Enterprise Groups in Japan.* Tokyo: University of Tokyo Press, 1992.

Morikawa, Jun. *Japan and Africa: Big Business and Diplomacy.* Trenton, N.J.: Africa World Press, 1997.

Moriyama, Alan Takeo. *Imingaisha: Japanese Emigration Companies and Hawaii, 1894–1908.* Honolulu: University of Hawaii Press, 1985.

Motojiiro, Akashi. *Rakka Ryūsui: Colonel Akashi's Report on His Secret Cooperation with the Russian Revolutionary Parties during the Russo-Japanese War.* Selected chapters trans. Inaba Chiharu and ed. Olavi K. Fält and Antti Kujala. Studia Historica 31. Helsinki: SHS, Finnish Historical Society, 1988.

Mueller, Juergen. *Nationalsozialismus in Lateinamerika: Die Auslandsorganisation der NSDAP in Argentinien, Brasilien, Chile und Mexico, 1931–1945.* Stuttgart: Verlag Hans Dieter Heinz, 1997.

Nadolny, Rudolf. *Mein Beitrag: Errinerungen eines Botschafters des deutschen Reiches.* Cologne: DME Verlag, 1985.

Nagel, Silke. *Auslaender in Mexico: Die Kolonien der Deutschen und U.S. Amerikanischen Einwanderer in der Mexikanischen Hauptstadt 1890–1942.* Frankfurt: Vervuert, 2005.

Nassua, Martin. *Gemeinsame Kriegsführung, Gemeinsamer Friedensschluss: Das Zimmermann Telegramm vom 13 Januar 1917 und der Eintritt der USA in den Ersten Weltkrieg.* Frankfurt am Main: Peter Lang, 1992.

Naumann, Friedrich. *Mitteleuropa.* Berlin: G. Reimer, 1915.

Nicolai, Oberst W. *Geheime Maecht: Internationale Spionage und ihre Bekaempfung im Weltkrieg und Heute.* Leipzig: R. F. Koehler, 1923.

Nihonjin Mekishiko Ijushi Hensankai, ed. *Nihonjin Mekishiko I Jushi (History of Japanese Emigration and Colonization in Mexico).* Tokyo: Mekishiko Ijushi Hensan Iinkai, 1971.

Nish, Ian, and Charles Dunn, eds. *European Studies on Japan.* Kent: Paul Norbury Publications, 1979. Nugent, Walter. *Crossings: The Great Transatlantic Migrations, 1870–1914.* Bloomington: Indiana University Press, 1992.

O'Grady, Joseph P., ed. *The Immigrant Influence on Wilson's Peace Policies.* Lexington: University of Kentucky Press, 1967.

Okamoto, Shumpei. *The Japanese Oligarchy and the Russo Japanese War.* New York: Columbia University Press, 1970.

Papen, Franz von. *Der Wahrheit eine Gasse.* Munich: P. List, 1952.

———. *Memoirs.* New York: E. P. Dutton and Co., Inc., 1953.

Payne, Geoffrey. *The Spanish Civil War, the Soviet Union and Communism*. New Haven: Yale University Press, 1925.

Peattie, Mark R. *Nan'yo: The Rise and Fall of the Japanese in Micronesia*. Honolulu: University of Hawaii Press, 1988.

Pike, Frederick B. *Chile and the United States, 1880–1962*. Notre Dame: University of Notre Dame Press, 1963.

———. *Hispanismo, 1898–1936: Spanish Conservatives and Liberals and Their Relations with Spanish America*. Notre Dame: University of Notre Dame Press, 1971.

———. *The Politics of the Miraculous in Peru*. Lincoln: University of Nebraska Press, 1986.

Price, Ruth. *The Lives of Agnes Smedley*. Oxford: Oxford University Press, 2005.

Quirk, Robert E. *The Mexican Revolution and the Catholic Church*. Bloomington: University of Indiana Press, 1973.

Raeder, Phil H. C. E. *Der Kreuzerkrieg in den Auslaendischen Gewässern: Das Kreuzergeschwader*. 2nd improved ed. Berlin: Mittler and Son, 1927.

Ramírez, David Piñera, coord. *Vision Historica de la Frontera Norte de Mexico*. Mexicali: Instituto Autonoma de Baja California, 1994.

Reiling, Johannes. *Deutschland Safe for Democracy? Deutschamerikanische Beziehungen aus dem Tätigkeitsbereich, Heinrich F. Alberts, Kaiserlicher Geheimrat in Amerika*. Stuttgart: F. Steiner, 1997.

Reyes, Alfonso. *Mision Diplomatica*. Mexico City: SRE Fondo de Economico, 2001.

Richmond, Douglas W. *Venustiano Carranza's Nationalist Struggle*. Lincoln: University of Nebraska Press, 1983.

Rinke, Stefan. *"Der letzte freie Kontinent": Deutsche Lateinamerikapolitik im Zeichen transnationaler Beziehungen, 1918–1933*. Historamericana Bd. 1–2. Stuttgart: Heinz Verlag, 1996.

Roy, Patricia E., and J. L. Granatstein. *Mutual Hostages: Canadians and Japanese during the Second World War*. Toronto: University of Toronto Press, 1990.

Roy, Samaren. *The Twice-Born Heretic: M. N. Roy and Comintern*. Calcutta: Firma KLM Private Ltd., 1986.

Ryan, James G. *Earl Browder: The Failure of American Communism*. Tuscaloosa: University of Alabama Press, 1997.

Sáiz Cidoncha, Carlos. *Aviación Republicana: Historia de las Fuerzas Aereas de la Republica Española 1931–1939*. Madrid: Almena Edicones, 2006.

Salisbury, Richard V. *Anti-Imperialism and International Competition in Central America, 1920–1929*. Wilmington, Del.: Scholarly Resources, 1989.

Sandos, James A. *Rebellion in the Borderlands: Anarchism and the Plan of San Diego, 1904–1923*. Norman: University of Oklahoma Press, 1992.

Saniel, Josepha. *Japan and the Philippines*. New York: Russell and Russell, 1973.

Schaefer, Jürgen. *Deutsche Militärhilfe in Südamerika. Militaer- und Rüstungsinteressen in Argentinien, Bolivien und Chile vor 1914*. Düsseldorf: Bertelsmann Universitaetsverlag, 1974.

Schell, William, Jr. *Integral Outsiders: The American Colony in Mexico City 1876–1911*. Wilmington, Del.: Scholarly Resources, 2001.

Schiefel, Werner. *Bernhard Dernburg, (1865–1937), Kolonialpolitiker und Bankier im Wilhelminischen Deutschland*. Zurich: Atlantis, 1977.

Schmalenbach, Paul. *German Raiders: A History of Auxiliary Cruisers of the German Navy 1895–1945*. Cambridge: Patrick Stephens, 1979.

Schoonover, Thomas. *The French in Central America: Culture and Commerce, 1820–1930*. Wilmington, Del.: Scholarly Resources, 2000.

Schult, Volker. *Rebellion und Revolution in den Philippinen: Die Rolle des Deutschen Reiches*. Passau, Germany: Lehrstuhl fuer Suedostasienkunde, 2000.

Siepe, Raimundo. *Yrigoyen, la Primera Guerra Mundial y las relaciones económicas*. Buenos Aires: Centro Editor de América Latina, 1992.

Smith, Robert Freeman. *The United States and Revolutionary Nationalism in Mexico 1916–1932*. Chicago: University of Chicago Press, 1972.

Soloman, Mark. *The Cry Was Unity: Communists and African Americans, 1917–1936*. Jackson: University Press of Mississippi, 1998.

Spang, Christian W., and Rolf-Harald Wippich, eds. *Japanese–German Relations, 1895–1945: War, Diplomacy and Public Opinion*. Abingdon, U.K.: Routledge, 2006.

Spenser, Daniela. *El Triángulo Imposible: México, Rusia Sovietica y Estado Unidos en los años Veinte*. Mexico City: CIESAS, 1998.

Stadt Stuttgart. *Stuttgart im Dritten Reich: Voelkische Radikale in Stuttgart. Zur Vorgeschichte und Fruehphase der NSDAP 1890–1925*. Stuttgart: Stadt Stuttgart, 1982.

Stephan, John J. *Hawaii under the Rising Sun: Japan's Plans for Conquest after Pearl Harbor*. Honolulu: University of Hawaii Press, 1984.

Stoker, Donald, Jr. *Girding for Battle: The Arms Trade in Global Perspective, 1815–1940*. Westport, Conn.: Praeger, 2003.

Suárez Suárez, Rosendo. *Breve Historia del Ejército Mexicano*. Mexico City: Impr. y Editorial Militar "Anahuac," 1938.

Szöellöesi-Janze, Margit. *Fritz Haber, 1868–1934: Eine Biographie*. Munich: Verlag C. H. Beck, 1998.

Tamames, Ramon. *Ni Mussolini ni Franco: La dictatura de Primo de Rivera y su trabajo*. Barcelona: Planeta, 2008.

Torajie Irie and Meiji Nanshin Ko. *A Study of Emigration Trends toward the South in the Meiji Period*. Tokyo: Ida Shoten, 1943.

Tosstorff, Reiner. *Profintern: Die Rote Gewerkschaftsinternationale 1920–1937*. Paderborn, Germany: Ferdinand Schoeningh, 2005.

Trask, David F. *Captains and Cabinets: Anglo-American Naval Relations, 1917–1918*. Columbia: University of Missouri Press, 1972.

Troebst, Stefan. *Mussolini, Makedonien und die Mächte, 1922–1930*. Cologne: Böhlau, 1987.

Tschapek, Rolf P. *Bausteine eines kuenftigen deutschen Mittelafrika. Deutscher Imperialismus und die portugiesische Kolonien. Deutsches Interesse an den Suedafrikanischen Kolonien Portugals vom ausgehenden 19. Jahrhundert bis zum ersten Weltkrieg*. Stuttgart: Franz Steiner, 2000.

Tuchman, Barbara. *The Zimmerman Telegram*. New York: Macmillan, 1966.

Turlington, Edgar. *Mexico and Her Foreign Creditors*. New York: Columbia University Press, 1930.

Ugarte, Manuel. *The Destiny of a Continent*. Reprint. New York: AMS Press, 1970.

U.S. Department of State. *Papers Relating to the Foreign Relations of the United States. The Lansing Papers 1914–1920*. 2 vols. Washington, D.C.: Government Printing Office, 1940.

Vogt, Adolf. *Oberst Max Bauer: Generalstabsoffizier im Zwielicht, 1869–1929*. Osnabrück: Biblio Verlag, 1974.

von Rintelen, Franz. *The Dark Invader*. Reprint. London: L. Dickson, Ltd., 1990.

Wagner, Wieland. *Japan's Aussenpolitik in der Frühen Meiji-Zeit (1868–1894)*. Stuttgart: Franz Steiner Verlag, 1990.

Wakatsuki, Yasuo, and Iyo Kunimoto. *La Immigracion Japonesa en Bolivia*. Tokyo: Chuo University, 1985.

Webster, Collin. *Argentine Mauser Rifles*. Atglen, Pa.: Schiffer: Military History, 2003.

Weinberg, Gerhard. *Hitlers Zweites Buch, Ein Dokument aus dem Jahr 1928*. Ed. and intro. by Gerhard L. Weinberg, with a foreword by Hans Rothfels. Quellen und Darstellungen zur Zeitgeschichte, Band 7. Stuttgart: DVA, 1961.

Wiechmann, Gerhard. *Die Preussisch–Deutsche Marine in Lateinamerika (1866–1914)*. Bremen: Verlag H. M. Hausschild Gmbh, 2002.

Wilhelm, Cornelia. *Bewegung oder Verein? Nationalsozialistische Volkstumspolitik in den USA*. Stuttgart: Franz Steiner, 1998.

Williams, John J. *The Isthmus of Tehuantepec: Being the Result of a Survey for a Railroad to connect the Atlantic and Pacific Oceans, made by the scientific commission under the direction of Major J. G. Barnard, US. Engineer*. New York: D. Appleton and Co., 1852.

Yankelevich, Pablo. *La Diplomacia Imaginaria, Argentina y la revolucion Mexicana 1910–1916*. Mexico City: SRE, 1996.

———. *La Revolucion Mexicana en America Latina: Intereses politicos e itineraries intelectuales*. Mexico City: Instituto Mora, 1996.

Yardley, Herbert O. *The American Black Chamber*. New York: Putnam, 1931.

Zechlin, Egmont. *Friedensbestrebungen und Revolutionierungsversuche*. Bonn: Aus Politik und Zeitgeschichte, 1963.

California and India: separatist recruitment in, 135–36

California and Japan: alleged wireless transmitters, 45, beaching of *Asama*, 149; fishing boats off coast, 163, 170, 200, 219,416; Japanese Exclusion League, 60–61

Calles, Plutarco Elias, 223, 361; German delegation visit (1925), 415–19

Canada, 15, 52, 54, 61, 63, 153; allied troop shipments across, 89–90

Canada and Comintern, 356

Canada and Germany: navy surveillance of coast, 42, 222; NSDAP branch in, 480; poisoning of U.S.–Canadian relations, 107–8; propaganda campaign against, 45; reservist invasion of, 91, 93, 98; secret warfare in, 84, 92

Canada and Japan: anti-Japanese policy, 64; immigration, 62

Canaris, Wilhelm, 253, 338, 414; Alfonso XIII, 383, 444, 447; Argentine arms orders, 470; Bauer, Max, 419; Echevarrieta, 446, 453; German Foreign Ministry, 445; German-Spanish air agreement, 442; German-Spanish intelligence agreement (1928), 465; obtaining naval intelligence in Spain, 464; torpedo construction in Spain, 409; visit to Argentina (1928), 471–72; visit to Japan, 376–78; Weimar Republic secret rearmament, 408

Capello Luigi, 340–41

Cappelle, Robert, 287

Carranza, Venustiano, 111, 138, 150, 160, 173, 192, 207, 229, 239, 291; arms supply after 1919, 263; Central American support, 175–76, 186–88, 203–4; death of, 283–84, 300; race war against U.S., 119, 168–70, 180–82, 256, 264; sabotage oil fields, 212; use of subversion, 171; using labor unions to fight U.S., 265

Carranza and Argentina, 205–6, 234–35, 272

Carranza and Germany, 177–81, 193–99, 201–14, 221–28, 230, 260, 279; early Weimar Republic, 275; financial secret policy, 153–54, 213–20; intelligence support for, 181; Jahnke, Kurt, 276; Krummheller, 108, 179, 349; Zimmerman telegram, 208

Carranza and Italy: post–WWI arms supplier, 285

Carranza and Japan: arms purchases in, 139, 159, 200; support for, 155, 164, 184, 197; Mexican-Japanese alliance, 246–47; Mitsui, 172

Carranza and League of Nations, 259, 266, 270–74

Carranza and South America: agents in, 268; attack of U.S., 183–85, 213

Carranza and Spain, 267, 386

Carranza and U.S., 222; U.S.–Mexican war, 225–26, 255–61

Carrizal, battle of, 183

CENA, 410

Central America, 34, 42, 53, 59, 62–67, 85–89, 97, 118, 132, 133, 136–37, 142, 145, 152–54, 174–79, 186–88, 202–5, 220, 229, 241–42, 255, 266–71, 276, 278, 280, 281, 286, 317, 325, 331–39, 352, 362–73, 380, 396–97, 409, 441, 450

Chakravarty, Phani, 136–38

Chile, 51, 78, 82, 149, 184, 205, 260, 261, 271, 293, 311, 358; Chilean intelligence, 264, 269, 300

Chile and Argentina, 232, 292, 420; arms traveling through, 302

Chile and Germany: ethnic community in, 142; Gen. Kiesling's Patagonia project, 350–53; Mexican agent in, 369; NSDAP branch in, 477; policy toward, 233, 342, 471; selection Carranza as Mexican president, 150, 171; spies in, 165–67; supply service in, 287; WWI illegal use of territory, 95–96

Chile and Japan: Chilean-Japanese verbal naval treaty, 60, 286; relations between, 59, 161–62, 240–48, 372; spies in, 367–68

Chile and League of Nations: disarmament initiative after 1920, 272, 280, 289, 315, 316–27

Chile and Mexico: Carranza, 186, 204, 235

Chile and Peru: enmity between, 52, 67, 244, 246, 266

Chile and Spain, 387, 394–96, 420, 431; *Plus Ultra*, 431–58, 202; submarines in, 295, 299

Chile and United States of America: anti-U.S. Chileans, 281

CIANA, Ibero American Commission for Air Navigation, 422

COARICA, 404, 405

Coibita islands, 152

Colombia, 39; Argentina, 234, 281; as transit place for airplane parts transports, 261

Carranza, 205, 271; inquiry to purchase German airplanes, 308; inquiry to purchase German ships, 420; Japanese interest in, 373; League of Nations, 272, 280, 289; League of Spanish American Nations, 279; potential secret weapons depot in, 268

Comintern, 354–62, 498

communists: India, activity in, 359

communists and Japan: manipulation of Mexican labor, 164

communists and Mexico, 358, 360

communists and South America: secretariat in and scouting for revolutionary potential (1924), 357

Manuel Gonzalez Cosio: speech to Japanese navy delegation, 68

Marchi, de, 279; Italian agents in South America, 283

Mariscal, Ignacio, 57

Maru Kotohira, 159, 184, 244

Mauser machine gun, 96, 109, 188, 183, 258

Medina, Juan: Pancho Villa and Japan, 181

Medina, Mexican Undersecretary of State, 246–47, 257, 264

Merkatz, von: Junker's military conversion program, 451

Mexico: agents in South America, 248; *Asama*, 149; Baja California purchase proposal, 40; as a battleground for U.S.–Japanese war, 57; creation of a U.S.-Mexican war, 112; exploring race war option, 169–71; fear of Japanese naval landing, 56; intelligence couriers, 147; Niagara Falls conference, 153, 171, 173; plot with U.S. Republican Party, 275–76; poison gas for, 443; politics of central bank creation, 154, 217, 220, 225; preparation of submarine base near, 185, 193–94; preparing for war against the U.S. (1920), 256–59, 264–66, 365; as racial brethren, 74; sabotage in, 200, 212; wireless stations in, 185

Mexico and Argentina, 205, 234, 268; Ugarte, 206

Mexico and Central America, 204

Mexico and Comintern, 356–58

Mexico and France: WWI anti-French propaganda, 123

Mexico and Germany: considering Japanese plans for Mexico, 59; establishing agents in, 476; financing secret war in, 213, 216; Japanese outreach to Germany in Mexico, 164; secret military industrial complex proposal (1925), 415, 419; Zimmerman telegram, 198, 207–11

Mexico and individuals: Denzo, Mori, 76, 78; Heynen, Carlos, 113, 136; Huerta, Victoriano, 113, 144; Nakao, agent, 139; Roy, M. N., 139; Sommerfield, Felix, 109; Ugarte, Manuel, 206; Vasconcelos, José, in Chile, 321; Villa, Pancho, 108; Wilhelm II, 202

Mexico and Italy: as post-WWI arms supplier, 62

Mexico and Japan: arms for, 159, 184, 244; Compania Japonesa Mexicana, Comercio y Colonización, de la Bara in Japan, 77; ending Japanese immigration to, 62–64; exploration for colonization, 16–17; hosting navy delegation of, 68; *Izumo* visit, 71; investment in, 372; loan offer to, 155; Mitsui, 67, 71; navy ships off coast, 148; outreach to Germany in Mexico, 164;

Nishihara plan, 158; treaty with Japan, 246–48

Mexico and League of Nation: policy against, 279–81

Mexico and Pan American Conference, 321

Mexico and Soviet Union: embassy in, 360

Mexico and Spain: as arms supplier, 260, 283

Mexico and United States of America: defeating U.S. Democrats in presidential election, 275–76

Mexican plots: Enrile plot, 110; Meloy plot, 111; Witzke affair (Jahnke), 224; Zimmermann telegram, 207

Miguel de Sautu, 310

Mitsubishi Co., 253, 366–68, 375–76

Mitsui Co., 67, 245, 300; arms for Mexico, 71, 74–79, 154, 170–72

Molinari, Diego Luis, Argentine foreign relations, 270, 272–73, 280, 286

Moness Chemical Company, N.Y., funding for communist subversion, 355–56

Monroe Doctrine, 39, 59, 70, 232, 245, 264, 268, 270–73, 279–81, 289

Montgelas, Max, 69

Montt, Jorge Alvarez: Japan and Chile, 52, 59, 95

Morath, Hans: Mexico's navy and secret armament industry proposal, 415–20

Moreno Zuleta, Don Francisco, 386

Morin, José M.: ethnic warfare recruitment, 180

Morioka Emigration Company, 51, 242

Moriyama, Keizaburo, 68, 79, 183

Morones, Luis N., 360

Moto Shigeshi: Argentine branch of Suzuki, 312; French-Japanese intelligence cooperation, 366–67

Mújica, Francisco: Guatemalan revolutionaries, 174

Mussolini, Benito, 3, 285, 330–34; Argentina and, 335, 458, 336–37; secret proposal for Latin America, 339–41, 397–98, 438

Nakamura, Takashi, 246, 248, 249, 276

Nakao, Hideo, 138

Nationalsocialism, 345; German-Chilean community, 478

Native Americans. *See* Canada and Germany

Niagara Falls Conference (1914), 153, 171, 173

Nicolai, Walter, vi, 352

Nieto, Rafael, 214

North Africa, 36, 87, 141, 260, 362, 384, 389, 390, 396, 414, 438, 444, 464

Ochoa, Mexican agent, 269, 282

oil companies, 91; sabotage of Mexican oil fields, 108, 114, 194, 200, 212, 386

Okuma, Shigenobu, 79; rejecting Zimmermann telegram proposal, 137, 181

Onedera, Toshio: Mitsui Mexico, 71, 154, 170

Orlando Vittorio: Italian irridenta work, 277
Ortíz, Leopold, 228, 260
Osaka, Invest. Corp.: Mexican west coast fishing rights, 18, 52, 59, 61, 74, 157, 162, 241, 246
Overseas Development Corporation, 163, 371

Pabst Brewery, 134
Panama, 38, 56, 128, 136, 146, 161–62, 175
Panama Canal: agent von Petersdorff, 109, 476; attack against 268, 302; German sabotage of, 89, 109; Japan, 152–53; Japanese spies near, 167, 300–331, 366–69; League of Nations, 289; potential role in U.S.–Japanese war, 58–59, 68; Spain, 396; strategic significance of, 39, 41, 57; submarine operation near, 112
Pan American Conference, 205, 273, 315–22, 365, 395, 461; Japan as potential mediator in Latin America, 183
Papen, Franz von, 88; activities in Africa, 94; the Caribbean, 97; Mexico, 106, 114, 176; the U.S., 89–93, 98–100, 111, 113, 117–18, 124–26, 135, 196–97, 287
Paraguay, 10, 162, 205, 241, 280, 281, 289, 293, 304, 358, 394, 396, 420, 435
Patrulla Atlántica, 444
Pauli, Adolf, 296, 323
Pershing, John J., 178, 180–83
Peru: Argentina, 205, 232; Faupel, Wilhelm, 471; first Japanese traders, 11; fishery off Ancon, 52; foreign military missions, 295, 316, 323; Italian–Japanese–Mexican–German–Argentine initiative against the U.S., 283; Japanese agents, 366–68; Japanese arms offers, 51, 67, 244, 325; Japanese colonies in; 244; Japanese contract labor, 15; Japanese merchants, 240–41; League of Nations, 289; Lima spies, 158, 165, 166, 205, 248, 275, 282, 283, 291, 295; Nishihara proposal, 158; offer to hire German agents by Japanese, 165; Peruvian delegation visits Tokyo, 245; *Plus Ultra*, 433, 458; Saito, Japanese consul to Lima, 165; Spain, 395–96; Tacna-Arica, 260, 269, 369; World War I, 234
Piedmont, Humberto, Prince: Argentina visit, 339
Pio Perrone, 261–62, 285. *See also* Ansaldo Company
Plan of San Diego, 170, 265
Plus Ultra, 424–33, 444
Polish revolutionaries, 46–47, 118, 251
Primo de Rivera, Miguel y Orbaneja, 339; Spanish arms modernization, 383–84, 392, 397–409, 413–14, 423, 437–42, 443–74. *See also* Alfonso XIII; Spain
Pueyrrodón, Honorio, 185, 231–33, 270–89, 290, 387

Quinoñes, de León, José Maria, 387

race war, 169; along the U.S.–Mexican border, 170, 182, 265. *See also* Plan of San Diego
racial equality clause: League of Nations and Japan, 268
Raeder, Erich, 42, 43, 45
Ratibor, Max von, 141, 143, 176, 226
Reimer, Dr., 287
Remeny, Gezir: German sabotage in South America, 269, 301, 369
Republican Party (U.S.): secret contacts with Mexican rebels, 276–78, 288
Riedel: German agent in Peru, 165, 166, 269
Rincon Gallardo: ethnic uprisings in Zacatecas, 82
Rodriguez: Mexican agent, 300, 402, 429, 452
Rolland, Ino von, 400, 402
Root, Elihu, 61
Rosa, Luís de la: recruiting for ethnic warfare, 180–82, 221
Roy, M. N., 139
Rueda: Mexican agent, 365, 366, 369, 370
Russia, 17; Japanese subversion against, 45–48, 54–57, 64, 68, 70, 73, 76, 79, 82–90, 98, 104, 111, 119, 137, 142, 149, 161–66, 188, 192, 207–9, 219, 221

sabotage: against U.S. factories, 2, 481; Black Tom, 222; Boy-Ed, 105; Canada, 91, 94, 98; Canadian Railway, 90; Jahnke, Kurt, 275; Japan, 302; League of Nations, 268; Mexican railroad, 361; movement of goods, 107; ocean steamships, 265, 300–301; poisoning of wheat in Argentina, 144, 147; reconnaissance, 93; sabotage orders, 399; Siberian railroad, 89; Spanish industry, 143, 145, 454; Tampico, 101–200, 212; zink and lead mines, 138
Saito, Consul, first Japanese-German intelligence cooperation in Latin America, 165–66
São Paulo Military revolt (1924), 44; ethnic German soldiers in, 155–58, 292, 349
Scadta Colombian Airline Company, 378
Schlubach & Co., 342, 378
Schwiertz, Ricardo, 222; recruitment German-Americans along U.S.–Mexican border, 223
Semprevivo, Simone, 335
Seville, Ibero American Exposition, 259, 384, 386, 393–95, 401–4, 424, 431, 434, 444, 450, 452, 456–58, 464–65, 472. *See also* Alfonso XIII; Spain
Shugijama, Ambassador, 75
Siemens-Schuckert Company, 389, 409, 445
Socialists, 51, 98, 172, 185, 264–65, 345; Conferences of Paris 1904 and Geneva